Aquinas on the
Twofold Human Good

Aquinas on the Twofold Human Good

Reason and Human Happiness in
Aquinas's Moral Science

Denis J. M. Bradley

The Catholic University of America Press
Washington, D.C.

The Hellenica font used to print the Greek in this work is available from
Linguist's Software, Inc., PO Box 580, Edmonds, WA 98020–0580;
Telephone: (425) 775–1130.

The paper used in this publication meets the minimum requirements of
American National Standards for Information Science—Permanence
of Paper for Printed Library materials, ANSI z39.48–1984.

∞

LIBRARY OF CONGRESS CATALOGING-IN-PUBLICATION DATA

Bradley, Denis J. M., 1943–
    Aquinas on the twofold human good : reason and human happiness
in Aquinas's moral science / Denis J. M. Bradley.
        p.   cm.
    Includes bibliographical references and index.
    1. Thomas, Aquinas, Saint, 1225?–1274–Ethics. 2. Christian ethics–
History–Middle Ages, 600–1500. 3. Ethics, Medieval. 4. Man (Christian
Theology)—History of doctrines—Middle Ages, 600–1500. 5. Man. 6.
Aristotle. Nicomachean ethics. I. Title.
    BJ1278.5.T48B73 1996
    171'.2'092—dc20
    96–8286
    ISBN 0–8132–0861–0
    ISBN 0–8132–0952–8 (pbk.)

For

Robert Paul Holman

and

Robert James Rokusek

"Ecce quam bonum et quam iucundum
habitare fratres in unum."

Contents

Preface

This book begins by considering a non-controversial fact: Aquinas's moral science is replete with rational principles and arguments. The evident rationality of Thomistic "moral theory" prompts many philosophers to think that a philosophical ethics can be extracted from Aquinas's theological writings. Here, though, I pause and ponder: there has been a long history, rooted in the late medieval and early modern disjunction of faith and reason, of misconstruing the integrally theological character of Aquinas's rational argumentation. This history of misinterpreting Aquinas is implicated in the charged but sometimes jejune twentieth-century debates about the alleged self-contradiction in the notion of "Christian philosophy." Still, the old issues are often the best ones. If one does grant—perhaps in the present-day spirit of ecumenical philosophical pluralism—the conceptual possibility and coherence of "Christian philosophy," why not also grant that one can construct an autonomous Thomistic philosophical ethics? This is the question that motivates the present study.

My answer to this question, however, is not evident but controversial, inasmuch as it rejects a foundation stone of that famously longstanding but still quite alive "Aristotelian-Thomist" tradition. I reject, in short, the conceptual possibility and coherence of an autonomous or, equivalently, systematic Thomistic moral philosophy. Doubtless my answer will seem to many excellent scholars and philosophers a deeply wrong-headed and perhaps perilous conclusion about Aquinas in particular and Christian moral philosophy in general.

Of course, Aquinas's moral science incorporates rational doctrines, congruent with but not logically dependent upon revealed beliefs. But it does so, I shall insist, without thereby becoming moral philosophy or—more controversially—licensing Thomist epigones to extract a systematic Thomistic moral philosophy from its native theological setting. Aquinas's conception of a unified "scientific theology," consistently focused on its own proper subject matter, the *"revelabilia,"* is the key to understanding the integrally theological and rational character of Thomistic moral science. But this key should not be turned too quickly. In order to understand adequately the contrast between Aquinas's rational theological ethics and a strictly philosophical ethics, we need to know how Aquinas read Aristotle.

Aquinas, while skirting eisegesis, nonetheless read the *Nicomachean Ethics* with his own theological beliefs and metaphysical tenets in mind, especially the Thomistic metaphysical doctrine of "participation." For Aquinas, practical reason is both logically autonomous and metaphysically theonomous: the first precepts of practical reason (grasped by the intellectual habit of *"synderesis")* are logically immediate or indemonstrable natural principles. But when viewed metaphysically, these same natural law precepts reflect the nature of the human mind as created by God; in other words, they "participate" in the eternal law, which is the exemplar of creation in the mind of God.

This theological conception of *synderesis* is the basis upon which Aquinas attempts to stabilize the foundations of Aristotelian practical wisdom *(phronesis).* Aristotelian theoretical sciences are grounded (through the cognitive activity of *nous)* in immediate or indemonstrable principles. In practical reasoning, however, Aristotle confines the function of *nous* to the quasi-sensible intuition of the fluctuating moral character of contingent, singular actions. Aquinas, in contrast, claims that through practical *intellectus* we do grasp a number of indemonstrable universal (exceptionless) precepts that "self-evidently" enjoin certain basic and indemonstrable ends. Since Thomistic natural law theory is often presented in truncated fashion, I go into considerable detail explaining how Aquinas's multifaceted psychological doctrine about the interaction of intellect and will is the only adequate background for interpreting his theory of moral prescription. But these details are only prolegomena to a bigger question.

How does Aquinas's conception of prescription fit into the larger context of his (theological) moral teleology? Put succinctly, Aquinas transforms the Aristotelian notion of *eudaimonia* by introducing the theological distinction between "imperfect" and "perfect" happiness. Upon the later distinction rests the Thomistic claim that immortality is a necessary if not sufficient condition for perfect human happiness. Perfect human happiness is found after death, *"in patria,"* but only if men are granted the immediate vision of the divine essence. "Seeing God" alone satisfies human nature's desire for a perfect intelligible and a perfect good.

Aquinas's rational argument for the possibility of seeing God, which appeals to the ineluctable natural desire for *beatitudo,* terminates in a philosophical paradox because human nature, contrary to the Aristotelian conception of nature, desires an end that it cannot naturally achieve. The strenuous efforts of three major classical Thomist commentators (Cajetan, Ferrariensis, and Báñez) to explain away the paradox are, in my judgment, not consonant with Aquinas's own doctrine. Since the seventeenth century, modern theological controversies about the "state of pure nature" have further obscured the

Thomistic conception of man's natural endlessness. These controversies have generated numerous, allegedly Thomistic philosophical ethics based on the concept of *the* natural end of man. But this Thomist notion, it seems to me, cannot be correctly attributed to Aquinas. To keep a long book from becoming even longer, I principally examine and criticize only two of the most distinguished twentieth-century Thomists, Jacques Maritain and Santiago Ramírez, O.P. They are the contemporary giants upon whose shoulders we lesser students of Aquinas can—or think we can—see things more clearly.

From my point of view, their efforts to extract a systematic philosophical ethics from Aquinas's theological moral science produced instead (1) a moral theology mistakenly calling itself a moral philosophy (Maritain); (2) a quasi-Aristotelian philosophical ethics misguidedly presenting itself as a Thomistic philosophical ethics (Ramírez). Against these learned Thomists, I argue that the thrust of Aquinas's authentic doctrine, the natural endlessness of human nature, leads to an *aporia:* any moral philosophy inspired by Aquinas cannot legitimately return to a quasi-Aristotelian form of eudaimonism; but neither can it, as philosophy, go forward to a theological affirmation of man's ultimate supernatural end. Aquinas's moral science thus opens to the postmodern debate about the historical contingency of all human projects. But I make what I hope is a cautious connection with this fashionable debate. It is a connection, to be sure, that someone needs to develop more fully.

To write in the field of Thomistic studies is to add, usually, one more small voice to bigger voices in an almost innumerable chorus that spans many centuries. Certainly, things can still be said about Aquinas that are topical and even culturally pressing, but can anything be said that is originatively insightful and, in that tolerable sense, "new"? Rather than tarry over so personally awkward a question, I take refuge in thanking those many scholars, whose names animate the footnotes of this book, from whom I have learned *multum et multa*. Most of all, of course, one learns from the incomparable saint himself. He will, I am confident, pardon what is mistaken in this book.

In Quadragesima 1997   D.J.M.B.
Georgetown University
Washington, D.C.

Acknowledgments

For carefully reading earlier versions of this book in typescript, I thank the Reverend Joseph Koterski, S.J., of Fordham University; the Reverend Professor Joseph Owens, C.Ss.R., of the Pontifical Institute of Mediaeval Studies; and Professor Doctor Wolfgang Kluxen, of the University of Bonn. I gratefully acknowledge that the latter two eminent scholars have magnanimously recommended a book that is sometimes at variance with their own respective interpretations and standpoints.

Many colleagues at Georgetown University and elsewhere have fostered my teaching and writing. But here I can only single out, for their special support, Professors Henry B. Veatch, Roger A. Hornsby, Thomas McTighe, Wilfried Ver Eecke, John Glavin, and Wayne Davis. Differently but no less helpful were the Georgetown University academic administrators who provided a generous subvention for the publication of this book: the Reverend Patrick A. Heelan, S.J., the Reverend Robert B. Lawton, S.J., and Dean Richard B. Schwartz.

Distinguished librarians have abetted my research: at the Woodstock Library, the Reverend Henry Berthells, S.J., the Reverend William Sheehan, C.S.B., the Reverend Eugene Rooney, S.J., and Mr. Paul Osmanski; at the Pontifical Institute of Mediaeval Studies Library, the Reverend Donald Finlay, C.S.B.

Out of supererogatory virtue, the Reverend Leo F. Stelten, of the Pontifical College Josephinum, checked the Greek and Latin texts. Ms. Melody McKinney kindly and expertly prepared the typescript for printing.

Mr. Edward A. Reno, who secreted in our ninth-grade study hall Maritain's *Introduction to Philosophy,* introduced me to philosophy. But, properly, *gratias pietatis causa ago* for my undergraduate teachers from whom I learned to read and revere the writings of Saint Thomas Aquinas: at Assumption University of Windsor, the Reverend D. Gordon MacDonald, C.S.B., and Professor John Deck. No better instruction could have been asked for. Among my graduate teachers at the University of Toronto, the Reverend Professor Joseph Owens, C.Ss.R., and Professor Anton Pegis set, and in their works embody, the canon for philosophical "intelligence in the service of Christ the King." My indebtedness to them is evident.

Finally, Professor John Catan, *philos maieutikos,* has ever encouraged me when encouragement was sorely needed. His manifold assistance, above all, has enabled me to finish, with whatever defects that remain, a project too long gestating.

Aquinas on the
Twofold Human Good

I

Aquinas's Theological Ethics

1. Philosophy, Theology, and "Moral Theory"

The part of St.Thomas Aquinas's *Summa theologiae* that deals with morality, the *Secunda pars*, which as its principal topics treats man's ultimate end, the criteria for assessing the morality of human actions, the natural law, and the virtues and the vices, has been praised as "the unsurpassed tribute to Thomas's genius."[1] That genius or at least industry is patent, even to the casual reader, in the intricate web of strictly rational arguments that Aquinas so effortlessly spins. An academic reader, one impressed by the architectonic strength and coherence of these arguments, might regard them as constituting a *"Thomistic moral theory."*[2] Yet to apply this contemporary label to a segment of Aquinas's theology is misleading. Aquinas, following Aristotle, numbers ethics among the practical and not the theoretical sciences.[3]

Aristotle, it is true, once uses *(APo.,* I, 33, 89b9) the term "moral theory" (τὰ δὲ ἠθικῆς θεωρίας) to designate ethics as a particular branch of study (θεωρία). But, in this instance, the designation does not mean that, for Aristotle, ethics is a theoretical science. The end of ethics is practical; it is action guided by knowledge. Ethics treats the virtues and vices not just to know what they are but to use that knowledge to

1. James A. Weisheipl, O.P., "The Meaning of *Sacra Doctrina* in *Summa Theologiae,* I, q. 1," *Thomist* 38 (1974): 54.
2. See William K. Frankena, "Love and Principles in Christian Ethics," in *Perspectives on Morality,* ed. Kenneth E. Goodpaster (Notre Dame, Ind.: University of Notre Dame Press, 1976), 87.
3. See *SLE,* II, 2, 1103b26, 15–38 *(In Ethic.,* II, lect. 2 [Spiazzi, n. 256, pp. 73–74]). Cf. *Metaph.,* VI, 2, 1026a18; *EN,* I, 3, 1095a5–6; II, 1, 1103b26–27.

foster morally good actions. Consequently, in order not to obscure the practical end of moral science,[4] as that is consistently maintained in the Aristotelian tradition, I shall refrain from using the phrase *"Thomistic moral theory"* and refer instead to *"Aquinas's moral science"* or to *"Thomistic ethics"* throughout this book.[5] But neither of the latter two phrases perfectly resonates with Aquinas's own terminology or with his conception of the unity of theology. Aquinas reserves *"moralis philosophia,"* that is, that part of "moral philosophy" that focuses on the activities of one man *(monastica)*, to what Aristotle does in the *Nicomachean Ethics*.[6] *"Thomistic ethics,"* that is, what Aquinas does in the *Secunda pars* of the *Summa theologiae*, must be understood to be a shortened form of *"Thomistic theological ethics."*[7] However, what is the status of this theological ethics? Is it an independent or distinct theological science as the phrase suggests?

According to Aquinas, and the other great medieval theologians prior to the middle of the sixteenth century, the science of theology cannot be subdivided into distinct parts. Because of its subject matter, whatever is "divinely revealable" *(divinitus revelabilis)*, theology has a unity that is superior to any philosophical science. It embraces, within the unity of the supernatural faith that sustains it, numerous things

4. Georgios Anagnostopoulos, *Aristotle on the Goals and Exactness of Ethics* (Berkeley and Los Angeles: University of California Press, 1994), 87, alleges that Aristotle often underestimates and overlooks the "cognitive objectives" of the practical sciences. Anagnostopoulos contends that, by analogy with medicine, the immediate or "proper end" (as distinguished from the practical "ultimate end") of ethics is "like the other cognitive [i.e., theoretical] disciplines . . . understanding or explaining a certain domain" (73). While one cannot gainsay that ethics aims at truth and is a form of knowledge *(EN, VI, 2, 1139b12)*, it must be stressed that, for Aristotle, ethics is *not* (at some immediate stage) a form of disinterested theoretical knowledge; rather, it is from the beginning and always *practical thinking* (διάνοια πρακτική), i.e., thinking that aims at an action-guiding conception of some end (λόγος ὁ ἕνεκά τινος): see *EN*, VI, 2, 1139a26–36.

5. Although Aquinas allows for a speculative or theoretical consideration of human action, he does so only by separating *"secundum intellectum"* features of action that are not able to be separated from each other *"secundum esse"*: see *De ver.*, q. 3, a. 3 (Spiazzi, 68). But attaining this kind of speculative knowledge of human action is not the proper end of an ethics designed to promote morally good actions: ". . . finis huius scientiae [moralis] non est manifestatio veritatis, sed bonum operis" *(SLE, II, 9, 1108a9, 103–4; In Ethic., II, lect. 9 [Spiazzi, n. 351, p. 100])*.

6. See *SLE, I, 1, ante 1094a1, 99–110 (In Ethic., I, lect. 1 [Spiazzi, nn. 6–7, p. 4])*.

7. Since the *"Thomist"* constructions of Aquinas's commentators and disciples must be distinguished from Aquinas's own theology, no matter how profoundly the latter inspired the former, I shall attempt to mark the distinction between master and followers by applying *"Thomistic"* only to Aquinas's own doctrines in their original contexts.

that pertain to diverse philosophical sciences.[8] It bridges, for example, the division of the theoretical and practical sciences. "Revealed theology" or the theology based on *sacred doctrine*, since it is primarily about God, is more speculative than practical, but it includes in its purview the morality of human actions by which men are led to or away from God. Theology, therefore, has a practical as well as a speculative *function*.

Inasmuch as Thomistic theology is not a genus that can be divided into specifically distinct theological sciences, there can be, strictly speaking, no distinct "Thomistic theological ethics." In speaking so, we cut up what Aquinas, given the subject matter of theology, leaves whole.[9] Accordingly, "Thomistic moral science" as well as "Thomistic ethics" must be understood to be but an application of the unitary habit of theological science to one of its main objects, namely, human actions.

Nonetheless, let us allow for the moment that the contemporary term "moral theory" can be taken in a neutral sense so that we can apply it to the ethical writings of Aquinas without contradicting the Aristotelian distinction between the theoretical and practical sciences. Suppose, then, we query our academic reader of Aquinas: Is Thomistic ethics a *philosophical* or a *theological* "moral theory"? As we shall soon see, the question put in these terms suggests its own answer due to the strong philosophical connotations of "moral theory." Still, present-day academic usage remains rather loose: a *"theological* moral theory" is not regarded as a blatant oxymoron.[10]

Aquinas himself variously distinguishes moral philosophy from theological moral science.[11] Among other differences, he notes that the

8. See *I Sent.*, prologus, q. 1., aa. 2–3; *III Sent.*, d. 23, q. 2, a. 4, sol. 2, ad 3; *ST*, I, q. 1, aa. 3–4.

9. See *I Sent.*, d. 35, q. 1, a. 2, ad 4 (Mandonnet, 815): ". . . unde si plura scita reducuntur in unum medium, secundum numerorum illorum omnium non erit nisi scientia una in numero. . . ."

10. For example, James M. Gustafson, *Ethics from a Theocentric Perspective*, Vol. 1: *Theology and Ethics* (Chicago: University of Chicago Press, 1981), is prepared to argue contra moral philosophers that "proper moral theory must be theocentric" (81), i.e., theological. Gustafson attributes (118) a "moral theory" to Thomas Aquinas but it is not clear whether he classifies Thomistic moral theory as consistently philosophical or theological: cf. 78, 92, 118, 152, 313.

11. For a survey of these differences, see William A. Wallace, O.P., *The Role of Demonstration in Moral Theology: A Study of Methodology in St. Thomas Aquinas* (Washington, D.C.: Thomist Press, 1962), 152–62. Wallace stresses that moral philosophy has a different *subject* and *principle* than moral theology: the *subject* of moral philosophy is man's rational and volitional activity in the order of nature; the *principle* of moral philosophy is human reason alone.

two types of moral science rely on different principles or starting points, a difference which, in the venerable Augustinian tradition,[12] corresponds to the superior and inferior use of reason.[13] Although, materially, the same human act can be investigated by either type of reason,[14] superior and inferior reason appeal to different criteria in making moral judgments. Speaking generally, inferior reason appeals to what we would call *philosophical* criteria—the concepts of the "useful" and the "good"; superior reason appeals to exclusively *theological* criteria—the divinely revealed law.

Inferior reason advises about making choices starting from the concepts of temporal things, whether something is too much or too little, useful or good in itself, and, similarly, about the other conditions that the moral philosopher treats. Superior reason takes advice from eternal and divine concepts—that something is contrary to the law of God, or brings about an offense against it, or something of this sort. *(II Sent.*, d. 24, q. 2, a. 2 [Mandonnet, 606])[15]

12. See Augustine, *Expos. de Trin.*, XII, 15, 24–25; XIII, 1, 1–2; XIV, 1, 3; XIV, 6, 11.

13. See *II Sent.*, d. 24, q. 2, a. 2; *De ver.*, q. 15, a. 2; *ST*, I, q. 79, a. 9. Superior and inferior reason are not diverse powers; they are the same activity of reason since they bear on the same formal object, *operabilia*. But superior reason and inferior reason are diverse habits since they are operations beginning from diverse principles: superior reasoning proceeds *"ex rationibus aeternis,"* inferior reasoning *"ex rationibus temporalibus"*: see *II Sent.*, d. 24, q. 2, a. 2, ad 5 [Mandonnet, 608–9]. Aquinas grants, however, that reason can have different material (i.e., ontological) objects: "Sed ratio superior et inferior respiciunt diversa obiecta materialiter, non formaliter . . ." *(De ver.*, q. 15, a. 2, ad 13 [Spiazzi, 313]). Whereas "inferior reason" is turned to temporal and material things that are ontologically lower than the soul knowing them, "superior reason" is so-called because its eternal and immaterial objects are ontologically higher than the human soul that knows them. This diverse ontological relation diversifies the functions *(officia)* of superior and inferior reason. But, again, they are but diverse habits of the same one power of reason because of the unity of their formal object; eternal and temporal things are both known (through immaterial forms existing in the intellect of the knower) "secundum communem rationem intelligibilis" (ibid., a. 2 [Spiazzi, 312]). Cf. ibid., ad 4 (313): "Sed aeternae res et temporales sunt diversae genere naturae; non autem quantum ad rationem cognoscibilis. . . ."

14. See *II Sent.*, d. 24, q. 2, a. 2 [Mandonnet, 608]: "Officia autem rationis superioris et inferioris non differunt penes diversam rationem objecti . . ."; *De ver.*, q. 15, a. 2, ad 3 [Spiazzi, 312]: ". . . [ratio] superior ad actus humanos ex libero arbitrio dependente, et per hoc contingentes, quodammodo convertitur. . . ."

15. ". . . ratio enim inferior consiliatur ad electionem tendens ex rationibus rerum temporalium, ut quod aliquid est superfluum vel diminutum, utile vel honestum, et sic de aliis conditionibus quas moralis Philosophus pertractat; superior vero consilium sumit ex rationibus aeternis et divinis, ut quia est contra praeceptum Dei, vel ejus offensionem parit, vel aliquid hujusmodi" *(II Sent.*, d. 24, q. 2, a. 2 [Mandonnet, 606]).

This Augustinian distinction, however, does not clarify the exact character of Aquinas's moral science. Indeed if these are the criteria, Thomistic ethics seems to be an indeterminate mixture of philosophy and theology since it relies on arguments that pertain, apparently in ad hoc fashion, to what Aquinas calls inferior as well as superior reason.[16]

Nonetheless, the Augustinian distinction poses, albeit somewhat obliquely for our purposes, the fundamental issue that confronts us here: any effort to typify Thomistic ethics, whether put in traditional or contemporary terms, must adduce how reason paradigmatically functions in philosophy, theology, and ethics. Often enough, interpretations of Aquinas begin by acknowledging this point, but they just as quickly move forward in quite different directions depending, of course, on the interpreter's paradigm.

To take one recent example, Sofia Vanni Rovighi describes "philosophy in the ambit of Thomistic thought" as "what Thomas thinks that he is able to demonstrate by reason alone and, therefore, what he thinks is also valid for someone who does not accept the Christian faith, [or] biblical revelation."[17] With this definition in mind, Vanni Rovighi easily finds—and is perplexed that another scholar, Wolfgang Kluxen, has somehow not discovered—a readily isolable, straightforwardly philosophical ethics in Aquinas.[18] Kluxen maintains, however, that any such discovery is truly an invention: "philosophical Thomism" is always the *result* of an "act of interpretation" (97), one that, in this instance, faces peculiar difficulties in abstracting the philosophical ethics immanent within Aquinas's theology: "Thomistic ethics as a system is found only in Thomistic theology" (87). The importance of Kluxen's sober and often repeated observation, although it does not finally inhibit him from cautiously projecting a systematic Thomistic philosophical ethics, can hardly be overestimated.

By "systematic ethics" I shall mean, throughout this book, a teleological and eudaimonistic ethics, like that found prototypically in Aristotle's *Nicomachean Ethics* and, more pertinently, in numerous

16. Referring to the secondary or derived moral precepts, Aquinas notes: "Et haec principia determinata pertinent ad rationem superiorem vel inferiorem . . ." (*II Sent.*, d. 39, q. 3, a. 2 [Mandonnet, 999]). But the same characterization applies to the primary precepts of the Natural Law that are indemonstrable or known through themselves *(per se nota)* "either through nature or faith": see *ST,* I–II, q. 100, a. 3, ad 1.

17. Sofia Vanni Rovighi, "C'è un'etica filosofica in san Tommaso d'Aquino?" in *Studi di filosofia medioevale* (Milan: Catholic University of the Sacred Heart, 1978), 129.

18. Cf. Vanni Rovighi, ibid.,129, n. 3; Wolfgang Kluxen, *Philosophische Ethik bei Thomas von Aquin,* 2d ed. (Hamburg: Felix Meiner Verlag, 1980), 20–21, 97–98.

modern scholastic manuals, which methodologically considers, conceptually organizes, and evaluates all morally relevant human ends by reference to some inclusive or dominant end that putatively shapes a good life as well as excellent practical thinking. Such an ethics is "systematic" because it offers a comprehensive understanding of the moral significance of all human actions in terms of that ultimate end.[19] However, the typical move of the scholastic philosophical moralist is to subordinate the ultimate natural end rationally demonstrated in moral philosophy to the supernatural ultimate end affirmed by faith in moral theology.[20]

What scholastic moral philosophy seems to reach, then, might well be called the "penultimate end of man." But I shall argue for the contrary position: a systematic philosophical ethics of this Aristotelian-scholastic kind constitutes, *if really attainable*, a rationally adequate or scientific whole; within it, philosophical reason has actually demonstrated that it has no need or license to look outside its own purview in determining the ultimate end or meaning of human action. Unlike Kluxen, therefore, I shall conclude that the effort to construct a systematically rational but (allegedly) *theologically open-ended* philosophical Thomistic ethics was and remains a theological construction; it can only plausibly stand, as it did with Aquinas, in and for a theology.

Vanni Rovighi's philosophical Thomistic ethics, because she was led to it by identifying philosophy with "pure reason," can be easily subsumed by the present-day notion of "moral theory." Of course, the meaning of the term "theory," as it is used paradigmatically in "scientific theory," is controverted since there is no generally held interpreta-

---

19. Cf. Sancto Schiffini, S.J., *Disputationes philosophiae moralis* (Turin: J. Speirani, 1891), 1: 2: ". . . in Philosophia Morali considerantur hae actiones [humanae] ut ordinabiles ad proprium finem eis a natura praestitutum, qui quidem est bonum per rationem voluntati propositum"; 1: 55: "Quoniam Deus cognoscendus et amandus est ultimus finis totius vitae humanae . . . necesse est dicere, hominem in praesenti aevo huc destinari, ut eam cognitionem et amorem Dei adipiscatur, cuius haec vita est capax . . . Secundum hanc regulam proinde dirigere oportet actiones omnes humanas, et in hoc unice consistere potest vera perfectio nostri generis, ad quam quaecumque non conducunt, apparentia quidem bona erunt, vera autem nullo modo."

20. Cf. Franciscus Suarez, S.J., *Opera omnia*, ed. D. M. André, 2d ed. (Paris: Vivès, 1856), 4: 44b, tract. 1, *De ultimo fine hominis*, disp. 4, "De beatitudine in communi, an sit, et quid sit," sect. 3, n. 4: ". . . facile concedemus naturalem beatitudinem non mereri nunc beatitudinis nomen absolute dictae, et sine aliquo addito diminuente, quia in homine elevato ad finem supernaturalem, illa non habet rationem ultimi termini, seu perfectionis ultimae. . . ."

tion of the nature or function of scientific theories. Are scientific theories, like statements, true or false? Are they descriptive or predictive? Or are they merely logical schema for organizing experimentally derived laws? It should be readily acknowledged, then, that "theory" has no noncontroversial definition. Still, "moral theory" is thought not to be significantly deviant from the general meaning of "theory": with respect to morals, it usually signifies a comprehensive or systematic map of the universal and ultimate principles of morality that normatively guide our rational judgments about the rightness or wrongness of action-types and action-tokens.[21]

Undoubtedly, a "moral theory" is a construction of reason. But the prevailing contemporary presupposition is that philosophy uniquely has the task of constructing it.[22] The history of this presupposition, it is well known, can be traced to the late medieval and early modern split between reason/philosophy and religious faith/theology.[23] Now this presupposition has an important bearing on our question: it does not leave "moral theory" a neutral term as we had provisorily assumed. On the contrary, it seems that if one casually follows contemporary usage, one will presuppose that because Aquinas has a "moral theory," he has a *philosophical* moral theory.

The next step, one anyway that a number of contemporary philosophers have taken, is to assign Thomistic moral theory its proper philosophical subclassification. A surprising variety of labels, however, has been applied. Thomistic moral theory has been called "an impure or mixed agapism . . . [with] a rule utilitarian conception of 'human law,'" a "naturalism," and in contradiction to all the above, a "deontological intuitionism."[24] Other subclassifications have also been attached: the

21. See Ernest Nagel, *The Structure of Science: Problems in the Logic of Scientific Explanations* (New York: Harcourt, Brace, & World, 1961), 117–18; John Rawls, *A Theory of Justice* (Oxford: Clarendon Press, 1972), 51. For six features of moral theories, gleaned from the writing of "antitheorists," see Robert B. Louden, "What Do Antitheorists Mean by *Theory?*" in *Morality and Moral Theory: A Reappraisal and Reaffirmation* (New York and Oxford: Oxford University Press, 1992), 85–98. My description of "moral theory" roughly covers features one, three, and five on Louden's list.

22. To take a prominent example, this unique connection of philosophy with "moral theory" is presupposed by the exclusively philosophical readings contained in *Readings in Ethical Theory*, ed. Wilfrid Sellars and John Hospers (New York: Appleton-Century-Crofts, 1952).

23. Among innumerable studies, see Cornelio Fabro, *God in Exile: Modern Atheism*, trans. Arthur Gibson (New York: Newman Press, 1968).

24. See William K. Frankena, "Love and Principle in Christian Ethics," in *Perspectives on Morality*, 84; "'Ought' and 'Is' Once More," ibid., 136: "[Aquinas] is

moral theory found in the *Summa contra gentiles* is "a deontology based on a distinctive teleology," while the one found in the *Summa theologiae* is a "theory of virtues and vices based on a theory of right reason."[25]

Such variant classifications, however, are not surprising since there are, of course, many types of moral theory, and contemporary meta-ethicians have reached different conclusions about their logical topographies. Even the basic classification of theories as "deontological" or "teleological" has been attacked.[26] Nonetheless, according to a proponent of a Kantian type of deontological theory, a moral theory is "a theory of a system of laws or precepts, binding upon rational creatures as such, the content of which is ascertainable by human reason."[27] The author of this definition, Alan Donagan, acknowledges the rational side of the Judeo-Christian moral tradition; yet he opines that "the ages of faith brought forth the idea of a pure moral philosophy but not the thing" (8). Of course, one might think that the *Nicomachean Ethics* provides, long before the Christian era, the real source of "pure moral philosophy." But according to Donagan, it was not Aristotle, whom he charges with mixing up moral and civic virtue, but Kant who was "the first major philosopher to work out a complete philosophical theory of morality" (8).

Although these certainly are contestable opinions, it is not my intention to challenge anew Donagan's criticism of Aristotle or his high estimation of Kant.[28] For the present inquiry, what Donagan claims about Kant is secondary to what he says about Aquinas. And what does

---

really not an intuitionist but a naturalist in metaethics . . ."; John Patrick Langan, "Desire, Beatitude, and the Basis of Morality in Thomas Aquinas" (Ph.D. diss., University of Michigan, 1979), 403: "Thomas's ethical theory . . . [is] a kind of deontological intuitionism, despite the teleological and naturalistic language in which parts of it are expressed." Frankena, however, makes the interesting remark ("Love and Principle," 87) that his own "quest for philosophical clarity . . . [may] have blurred some [of Aquinas's] theological refinements and subtleties."

25. See Alan Donagan, *Human Ends and Human Actions: An Exploration in St. Thomas's Treatment*, The Aquinas Lecture of 1985 (Milwaukee: Marquette University Press, 1985), 15.

26. See Adrian M. Piper, "A Distinction without a Difference," in *Midwest Studies in Philosophy*, Vol. 7: *Social and Political Philosophy*, ed. Peter A. French, Theodore E. Uehling, Jr., and Howard K. Lettstein (Minneapolis: University of Minnesota Press, 1982), 403–35.

27. Alan Donagan, *The Theory of Morality* (Chicago: University of Chicago Press, 1977), 7.

28. For a spirited defense of Aristotle contra Kant, see Henry B. Veatch, *For an Ontology of Morals: A Critique of Contemporary Ethical Theory* (Evanston, Ill.: Northwestern University Press, 1971). For a criticism of Donagan's Stoic-Kantian

he say about Aquinas? If we had posed our initial question to Donagan—"Is Thomistic ethics a philosophical or a theological 'moral theory?'"—Donagan's answer would have been already given: Aquinas "preferred to treat the moral law theologically" (8).

Donagan correctly notes in passing what I shall consider at length: that Aquinas did not write a "pure moral philosophy." But Donagan's judgment, while it reflects a sympathetic reading of Aquinas, also incorporates the presupposition, which is a commonplace for most contemporary philosophers, that only some *philosophy*, of whatever denomination, can bring forth a complete and fully rational moral theory.

This same commonplace, however, pushes the contemporary interpreter of Aquinas into an unavoidable dilemma: either Aquinas does not have a fully rational "moral theory" or, to the extent that he does, his theory is philosophical. The dilemma entails the conclusion that Aquinas could not have a rational but integrally *theological* "moral theory."

At first hearing, this dilemma may seem artificial, or forced, or just unimportant. Does it not arise only if we are philosophical purists, wielding the definition of "moral theory" too strictly? Surely a more latitudinarian use of the term can be allowed. While "Thomistic moral theory" has a penumbra of strictly theological notions that are dependent solely on religious beliefs and that therefore cannot be fitted into a purely rational philosophical ethics, Aquinas constantly relies on rational demonstrations to establish his basic ethical principles. It can be granted, as Donagan does, that Aquinas's "primary commitment"[29] was to theology. But, nevertheless, who would deny that in the *Summa theologiae* Aquinas provides all the elements of a systematically *rational* moral theory perhaps alongside his "moral theology" which is grounded on religious belief? If so, why refuse that moral theory—despite the title of the book in which it is found—the accolade of "philosophy"?[30] To do so betrays a kind of narrow literalism about Aquinas's own usage.

While such objections, or others like them, are to be anticipated,

---

conception of morality as "impoverished, antipolitical, and abstract" (127): see Jeffrey Stout, *Ethics after Babel: The Language of Morals and Their Discontents* (Boston: Beacon Press, 1988), 124–44.

29. See Alan Donagan, "Thomas Aquinas on Human Action," in *The Cambridge History of Later Medieval Philosophy*, ed. N. Kretzman, A. Kenny, and J. Pinborg, with assoc. ed. E. Stump (Cambridge: Cambridge University Press, 1982), 642.

30. See J. de Vries, S. J., Review of *Philosophische Ethik bei Thomas von Aquin*, by Wolfgang Kluxen, *Scholastik* 40 (1965): 114: "Trotzdem ist im Werk des Thomas

our initial question resists so easy a resolution. Whether our usage be narrow or latitudinarian, the contemporary notion of "moral theory" binds reason ever so tightly to philosophy and ever so loosely to theology. And it is this tight bond that imposes an initial and, if it is not untied, powerful restraint that hinders a historically and doctrinally correct interpretation of Aquinas's theological ethics or moral science. In a general way, Aquinas's theological vocation has often been noticed. But calling Aquinas a "philosophical theologian"[31] ignores a problem that is not merely nominal. Anton Pegis puts the hermeneutical issue far more precisely and significantly: St. Thomas "was not a theologian *and* a philosopher, he was a theologian *even in philosophy.*"[32] If this is true, what, then, is the status of the strictly rational arguments (i.e., those arguments that do not incorporate any revealed doctrine) which can be found in abundance in Thomistic theology? The contemporary presupposition, that reason in some defining fashion belongs to philosophy, makes it difficult to grasp, much less to explore, the doctrinal significance of the fact that Aquinas's ethics is rational and integrally theological.

If we were to adopt contemporary fashion by referring to "Thomistic moral theory," we would, indeed, highlight for our contemporaries the rational character of Thomistic ethics. But using that phrase, in the contemporary philosophical context, would also continually invite misinterpretation. Aquinas did not write, if we judge his work according to his own principles, a moral philosophy but a theological ethics. For this reason, as well as to observe the Aristotelian distinction between the theoretical and the practical sciences, I shall eschew the term "Thomistic moral theory." And I shall tediously reiterate that while Aquinas's moral science or ethics is rational, it is, on that account, no less theological. But this fact and its significance are easy to ignore.

Despite their theological context and the theological service that they render, the integrally or irreducibly theological character of Aquinas's moral principles is sometimes not patent even to attentive readers of Aquinas.[33] Moreover, even when the global theological character

---

eine systematische Philosophie eingeschlossen, und zwar mehr in den theologischen Hauptwerken als in den Aristoteleskommentaren. Insbesondere zeigt die Secunda, dass Thomas eine philosophische Ethik anerkennt."

31. See Alasdair MacIntyre, *Whose Justice? Whose Rationality?* (Notre Dame, Ind.: Notre Dame University Press, 1988), 171.

32. Anton C. Pegis, "After Seven Hundred Years: St. Thomas Aquinas in 1974," *Église et Théologie*, 5 (1974): 144.

33. See Anton C. Pegis, "*Sub Ratione Dei*: A Reply to Professor Anderson," *New*

of Thomistic ethics is acknowledged, there remains considerable disagreement about what it implies. Donagan, for example, claims that "Aquinas implied that his theory of the natural virtues—of common morality—does not logically presuppose his moral theology."[34] Donagan's claim, if it means only that philosophy apart from theology can legitimately consider natural virtues, is neither idiosyncratic nor unusual; many Thomist commentators agree with it.[35] The question, however, is not whether a moral philosophy focused on the natural virtues is logically possible, for Aquinas certainly did not doubt that possibility on either logical or historical grounds,[36] but instead whether *Aquinas's* conception of natural virtue is logically independent of *his* "moral theology." The latter question, if it is not conflated with the first question, calls for sustained consideration and for a careful answer.

Aquinas certainly grants that it is possible and morally salutary for philosophers to consider the moral virtues. But he has a precise understanding of how the philosophers think about moral virtue and why—speaking theologically—they think in the way that they do. For philosophers, the virtuous activity of the moral agent is its own ultimate end. Among the virtues required for a morally virtuous activity, the (practical) intellectual virtue of *prudentia* is preeminent and controlling. Since it governs moral deliberation, choice, and prescription, prudence is the sine qua non for exercising all the moral virtues. But philosophers value prudence so highly because they look at nature not knowing about grace.

The philosophers did not posit virtue unless it be formed by prudence because in the will, in proportion to the ultimate end, and in the essence of the soul, they did not posit any perfection superadded to nature. *(III Sent.,* d. 27, q. 2, a. 4, sol. 3, ad 3 [Moos, n. 182, p. 890][37]

Scholasticism 39 (1965): 143: ". . . a theology of fully demonstrable truths is a phenomenon that modern students [of St. Thomas] find hard to accept."

34. Donagan, *Theory of Morality,* 62.

35. See J. M. Ramírez, O.P., *Bulletin thomiste* 4 (1934–1936), Comptes rendus, 423–32, esp. 432: "La philosophie morale, sans ce complément [théologique] et sans cette subalternation à la théologie . . . est une véritable science morale speculative et pratique. . . ."

36. See *ST,* I–II, q. 63, a. 3: "Obiectum autem virtutum intellectualium et moralium est aliquid quod humana ratione comprehendi potest."

37. "Sed ideo non posuerunt Philosophi virtutem nisi a prudentia formari, quia in voluntate prout est finis ultimi et in essentia animae non posuerunt aliquam perfectionem superadditam naturae" *(III Sent.,* d. 27, q. 2, a. 4, sol. 3, ad 3 [Moos, n. 182, p. 890]).

Grace, however, is exactly what the theologian must consider. The theologian can agree with the philosopher that morality is about action and action is about its end. But the theologian insists that only divinely infused faith provides man with knowledge of the true or ultimately good end at which to aim. Consequently, the theological virtue of faith, which sets the ultimate end of man's actions, has a certain priority (in the order of generation) over all the other virtues: "The acts of all the virtues depend on the act of faith which directs intention" *(III Sent.*, d. 25, q. 2, a. 1, sol. 1 [Moos, n. 61, p. 796]).[38] The act of faith precedes acts of the theological virtues of hope and charity since one must first know the end before one can confidently strive for it or love it.

The act of faith consists in the knowledge of the true that the desire of the good, which is required in all the other virtues, presupposes. *(III Sent.*, d. 23, q. 2, a. 5, resp. [Moos, n. 213, p. 739])[39]

Yet, in the order of perfection, charity, because it actually unites man to God, is the most excellent virtue *(ST,* I–II, q. 62, a. 4).

Theologians consider all of the virtues, whether naturally acquired or supernaturally infused, in relationship to the ultimate end of man, which is eternal life or the vision of God. The vision of God is anticipated in this life through the exercise of the three divinely infused theological virtues. Because they directly bear on man's ultimate end, God, these theological virtues, and among them charity especially,[40] take precedence over any of the other natural or supernatural virtues.

For since the end is the principle in matters of action . . . it is necessary that the theological virtues, the object of which is the ultimate end, be prior to all the other virtues. *(ST,* II–II, q. 4, a. 7)[41]

The theologian, let us notice, does not merely subordinate the humanly acquired moral and intellectual virtues to the divinely infused theological virtues. Aquinas posits[42] divinely *infused* moral and intel-

---

38. "Actus autem omnium virtutum dependent ab actu fidei, quae intentionem dirigit" *(III Sent.*, d. 25, q. 2, a. 1, sol. 1 [Moos, n. 61, p. 796]).

39. "Actus autem fidei consistit in cognitione veri quam praesupponit affectio boni quae in omnibus aliis virtutibus exigitur" *(III Sent.*, d. 23, q. 2, a. 5, resp. [Moos, n. 213, p. 739]).

40. See *De car.*, q. 1, a. 3, ad 17 (Odetto, 762): ". . . ipsa visio [Dei], in quantum est finis ut bonum quoddam, est obiectum caritatis."

41. "Cum enim in agibilibus finis sit principium . . . necesse est virtutes theologicas, quarum obiectum est ultimus finis, esse priores ceteris virtutibus" *(ST,* II–II, q. 4, a. 7).

42. See *III Sent.*, d. 33, q. 1, a. 2, sol. 3; *De virt.*, q. 1, a. 10; *ST,* I–II, q. 51, a. 4; q. 63, a. 3.

lectual virtues that are not mere replicas of the humanly acquired moral and intellectual virtues.[43] Humanly acquired and infused moral virtues can bear on the same material object, but they specifically differ in reference to (1) their formal objects and (2) their ends.[44] In reference to a particular pleasure or pain, reason alone determines the appropriate mean between excess and defect, and thus reason alone determines the formal object of an acquired moral virtue.[45] The formal object or measure of an infused moral virtue is determined by a "divine rule."[46] Aquinas uses (*ST*, I–II, q. 63, a. 4) the example of temperance in regard to food to distinguish naturally acquired from infused moral virtue: what is a reasonable amount of food to eat to preserve the health of the body (= the formal object of the humanly acquired virtue of temperance) does not correspond to the rule that faith requires in regard to fasting and abstinence for the sake of bringing the body into subjection (= the formal object of the infused virtue of temperance).[47]

Nonetheless, why are these divinely infused virtues, which pose a number of problems and puzzles about the relationship between them and the humanly acquired moral virtues,[48] necessary? The theological doctrine that compels Aquinas to introduce infused moral and intellectual virtues into his schematization of the theological and humanly acquired virtues is that the vision of God is an end that transcends the whole order of nature: no natural or humanly acquired virtue can set

43. See *III Sent.*, d. 33, q. 1, a. 2, sol 4 (Moos, n. 74, p. 1031): ". . . virtutes acquisitae et infusae differunt specie, fortitudo scilicet a fortitudine et temperantia a temperantia et sic de aliis. . . ."

44. See *III Sent.*, d. 27, q. 2, a. 4, sol. 1, ad 3 (Moos, n. 162, p. 886): "Formalis autem objecti diversitas est secundum illam rationem quam principaliter attendit vel habitus vel potentia."

45. See *III Sent.*, d. 33, q. 1, a. 3, sol 1 (Moos, n. 92, p. 1035): "Virtutes enim morales sunt circa passiones et operationes, quas oportet dirigere secundum regulam rationis."

46. See *ST*, I–II, q. 63, a. 4; *De virt.*, q. 1, a. 10, ad 8.

47. See *III Sent.*, d. 33, q. 1, a. 2, sol. 4, ad 3 (Moos, n. 78, p. 1031): "Unde etiam aliquid superfluum secundum virtutem civilem est moderatum secundum virtutem infusam, sicut quod homo jejunet et se voluntarie morti offerat propter defensionem fidei."

48. See Gabriel Bullet, *Vertus morales infuses et vertus moral acquises selon saint Thomas d'Aquin* (Fribourg, Switzerland: Éditions Universitaires, 1958); Anthony J. Falanga, *Charity the Form of the Virtues According to Saint Thomas*, Studies in Sacred Theology, Second Series, No. 18 (Washington, D.C.: The Catholic University of America Press, 1948); and George P. Klubertanz, S.J., "Une Théorie sur les vertus morales 'naturelles' et 'surnaturelles,'" *Revue thomiste* 59 (1959): 565–75.

such a supernatural end for man or enable him to attain it by the appropriate supernatural means.[49]

For example: the (practical) intellectual virtue of prudence directs human choices to the ends pursued by a morally virtuous man or woman. But how do we know which human actions lead *to* or lead *away* from the enjoyment of God in the world to come? Humanly acquired prudence, which directs man to his proximate end, "the good of reason in general,"[50] cannot, by definition, direct men to a supernatural end; for this direction, they need a divinely infused form of prudence (ST, I–II, q. 65, a. 2).

In the supernatural order wherein man's ultimate beatitude is found, the theological virtues take the place of the indemonstrable principles of practical reason that prescribe the ends that are innate to human nature.[51] Faith, hope, and charity allow men to know, to persevere in striving for, and to be one with God. Because being united to God, which is the object of charity, is the ultimate good and the subsuming end of all human activities, Aquinas says that divinely infused charity commands all of the other virtues.[52] In the charitable person, charity is the "mover, end, and form"[53] of the theological virtues, the infused intellectual and moral virtues, and (through the mediation of the infused virtues) the humanly acquired intellectual and moral virtues.[54]

49. See ST, I–II, q. 63, a. 3, ad 3: ". . . virtus illorum principiorum naturaliter inditorum, non se extendit ultra proportionem naturae. Et ideo in ordine ad finem supernaturalem, indiget homo perfici per alia principia superaddita."

50. See III Sent., d. 33, q. 2, a. 3, resp. (Moos, n. 198, p. 1057): "Finis autem proximus humanae vitae est bonum rationis in communi."

51. See ST, I–II, q. 63, a. 3: "Loco quorum naturalium principiorum conferuntur nobis a Deo virtutes theologicae, quibus ordinamur ad finem supernaturalem. . . ."

52. See II Sent., d. 26, q. 1, a. 4, ad 5 (Mandonnet, 679): "Caritas enim est forma virtutum ex parte actus, inquantum scilicet omnes actus virtutum in suum finem convocat, eo quod ejus objectum est finis ultimus"; De malo, q. 8, a. 2 (Bazzi-Pession, 599): ". . . tamen secundum quamdam diffusionem sui imperii [caritas] est communis omnibus virtutibus; unde dicitur forma et mater omnium virtutum"; ST, II–II, q. 23, a. 4, ad 2: ". . . quia caritas habet pro obiecto ultimum finem humanae vitae, scilicet beatitudinem aeternam, ideo extendit se ad actus totius humanae vitae per modum imperii, non quasi immediate eliciens omnes actus virtutum."

53. See III Sent., d. 27, q. 2, a. 4, sol. 3 (Moos, n. 173, p. 888): ". . . caritas ad omnes alias virtutes comparatur et ut motor et ut finis et ut forma." Cf. De car., q. 1, a. 3 (Odetto, 761).

54. See III Sent., d. 27, q. 2, a. 4, sol. 3 (Moos, n. 174, p. 889): "Finis autem inferioris potentiae vel habitus ordinatur ad finem superioris, sicut finis militaris ad finem civilis. Unde actus omnium aliarum virtutum ordinantur ad actum caritatis sicut ad finem; et propter hoc dicitur caritas finis praecepti"; De virt., q. 1, a. 10, ad 4 (Odetto, 736): "Cum caritate autem simul infunduntur aliae virtutes; unde actus virtutis acquisitae non potest esse meritorius nisi mediante virtute infusa. Nam

Aquinas compares the role of charity in the order of supernatural morality and the role of prudence in a strictly natural order of morality.[55] When viewed solely in the natural or philosophical order, prudence is the highest form of all the humanly acquired moral virtues inasmuch as prudence directs them all.[56] But the theologian knows that some perfection has been superadded to nature. In the supernatural order of human acts, charity is the form of the divinely infused moral virtues: it directs them "according to the rules of the divine law"[57] to the appropriate supernatural means to attaining man's supernatural end, the vision of God.[58] Charity, in the spiritual life of a man or woman possessing sanctifying grace, is also the form of the acquired virtues, but the latter do not, thereby, lose their natural status. Charity commands but does not replace or radically supernaturalize the natural virtues.[59] To put it precisely, charity is the form of that supernatural prudence which in turn orders the "matter" of the naturally virtuous pursuit of civil goods to the incomparably higher pursuit of the ultimate and supernatural end of man.[60]

---

virtus ordinata in finem inferiorem non facit actu[m] ordinatum ad finem superiorem, nisi mediante virtute superiori. . . ."

55. See *III Sent.*, d. 27, q. 2, a. 3, obj. 3 (Moos, n. 132, p. 880): "Sicut caritas est principalis in gratuitis virtutibus, illa prudentia moralibus . . ."; ad 3 (Moos, n. 139, p. 881): ". . . prudentia est principalis in virtutibus moralibus . . ."; a. 4, sol. 3 (Moos, n. 175, p. 889): ". . . prudentia ponit formam et modum in omnibus aliis moralibus virtutibus. . . . Et ideo caritas est forma aliarum virtutum omnium [quae sunt meritoriae vitae aeternae, secundum quod nunc loquimur de virtutibus], sicut prudentia moralium"; ad 2 (Moos, n. 180, p. 890): "Nec caritas esset virtus si esset sine gratia, sicut nec prudentia si est sine caritate, loquendo de virtutibus infusis ordinatis ad merendum. . . ."

56. See n. 37 *supra.*

57. ". . . secundum rationes legis divinae . . ." *(De virt.*, q. 1, a. 10, ad 8 [Odetto, 736]).

58. See *III Sent.*, d. 27 q. 2, a. 4, sol. 1, ad 2 (Moos, n. 161, p. 886): ". . . virtutes etiam theologicae dirigunt in his quae sunt ad finem, non quidem secundum proprias rationes rerum quae sunt ad finem sed secundum rationem finis . . . inquantum sunt participabiles divinae bonitatis, quae est ultimus finis."

59. The natural virtue, although commanded and informed by charity, also remains proximately specified by its own formal object, which is determined by reason "in ordine ad bonum presentis vitae" *(De virt.*, q. 1, a. 10, ad 8 [Odetto, 736]): "Non igitur temperantia et fortitudo infusae differunt specie ab acquisitis ex hoc quod imperantur a caritate earum actus; sed ex hoc quod earum actus secundum eam rationem sunt in medio constituti, prout ordinabiles ad ultimum finem qui est caritatis obiectum." (ad 10 [Odetto, 737]) Cf. *III Sent.*, d. 23, q. 3, a. 1, sol. 1 (Moos, n. 233, p. 744); d. 27, q. 2, a. 4, sol. 3, ad 5 (Moos, n. 184, p. 891).

60. See *De ver.*, q. 14, a. 5 (Spiazzi, 290): "Quandocumque enim duo sunt principia moventia vel agentia ad invicem ordinata, id quod in effectu est ab agente superiori est sicut formale; quod vero est ab inferiori agente, est sicut materiale."

That charity is the "mover, end, and form" of all the virtues is, of course, a strictly theological claim about how the virtues of a man or woman, who possesses faith and sanctifying grace, are ordered.[61] But Aquinas observes, perhaps somewhat defensively, that even the philosophers hold that true moral virtue must bear on man's ultimate good.[62] In the strict or unconditional sense *(simpliciter)*, then, the only true, complete, and perfect moral "virtues" are those that are aimed at the ultimate supernatural good of man which is set forth, sought, and anticipatorily possessed in the theological virtues.[63] But since only divinely *infused* moral virtues actually enable men to choose the supernatural means that lead to the ultimate, supernatural good, they alone are, *simpliciter*, the true and perfect virtues.[64] In order to possess these unconditionally true and perfect moral virtues, one must possess charity.[65]

Insofar as charity alone enables man to attain his ultimate supernatural end, charity and the divinely infused intellectual and moral virtues that accompany charity necessarily supersede the humanly acquired moral and intellectual virtues in Aquinas's theological schematization of the virtues.[66] Nonetheless, humanly acquired intellectual and moral virtues can be "true virtues," but only in a conditional sense *(secundum quid):* they are virtues that enable the agent to pursue real secondary or particular goods, that is, those various ends of human action that are less than ultimate.[67] These humanly acquired virtues can be possessed, whether by pagans or by believers who have fallen

For an elaboration of the matter-form analogy in interpreting the relationship between the infused and acquired virtues, see Klubertanz, "Théorie sur les virtus morales," 569–75.

61. See *De ver.*, q. 14, a. 5 (Spiazzi, 291): "Et eadem ratione omnes aliae virtutes prout a theologo considerantur; prout scilicet sunt principia actus meritorii."

62. See *ST*, II–II, q. 23, a. 7: ". . . virtus vera simpliciter est illa quae ordinat ad principale bonum hominis. . . ."

63. See *De virt.*, q. 1, a. 10, ad 1 (Odetto, 736): "Unde duplex competit virtus homini; una quae respondet primae perfectioni [secundum capacitatem suae naturae], quae non est completa virtus; alia quae respondet suae perfectioni ultimae [secundum quamdam supernaturalem perfectionem]: et haec est vera et perfecta hominis virtus."

64. See *ST*, I–II, q. 65, a. 2: ". . . solae virtutes infusae sunt perfectae, et simpliciter dicendae virtutes: quia bene ordinant hominem ad finem ultimum simpliciter. . . ."

65. See *ST*, II–II, q. 23, a. 7: "Et secundum hoc simpliciter vera virtus sine caritate esse non potest."

66. See *II Sent.*, d. 26, q. 1, a. 4, ad 5 (Mandonnet, 679): "Unde caritas informat alias virtutes, sicut virtus virtutem. . . ."

67. See *ST*, I–II, q. 65, a 2; II–II, q. 23, a. 8.

into sin, without supernatural charity.[68] When they exist apart from the order of charity, they are not only *conditional* but also *imperfect* virtues. Yet Aquinas stresses that these conditional and imperfect virtues must be aimed at real and not merely apparent goods. Otherwise, they are merely the "false similitude of virtue."[69]

Aquinas, although he preserves a role for the humanly acquired moral virtues,[70] always speaks of them as a theologian. The acts of unbelievers, who lack the theological virtues, as well as the acts of believers, who have lost through sin charity and its accompanying infused moral virtues, can be morally good and virtuous in the natural order but they are not, of course, supernaturally meritorious.[71] Sometimes, however, Aquinas speaks exclusively as a theologian. Since it is not informed by the divinely infused theological virtue of charity, the humanly acquired moral virtue is—for the theologian interested in supernaturally *meritorious* human actions—not only "imperfect" but it is not even a virtue.

> The philosophers do not consider the virtues insofar as they are the principles of the meritorious act. Therefore, according to them, habits that are not formed by charity are able to be called virtues, but not according to the theologians. *(De ver.,* q. 14, a. 6, ad 5 [Spiazzi, 293])[72]

Nonetheless, Aquinas does not negate the moral value or continued presence of mere human virtue for a believer.[73] But Aquinas does not value them because he is somehow speaking as a philosopher who chooses on occasion to ignore the supernatural moral order that results from and is coextensive with the realm of divinely infused charity.[74] Rather, speaking consistently as a theologian, he sees merely

---

68. See *ST,* I–II, q. 65, a. 2, ad 1.

69. ". . . falsa similitudo virtutis . . ." *(ST,* II–II, q. 23, a. 7).

70. The acquired virtues lessen the onslaught of the passions: "Virtus enim acquisita praevalet quantum ad hoc quod talis impugnatio [passionum] minus sentitur" *(De virt.,* q. 1, a. 10, ad 14).

71. See *II Sent.,* d. 41, q. 1, a. 2 (Mandonnet, 1038): ". . . quamvis ab infidelium actibus subtrahatur ista bonitas, secundum quam actus meritorius dicitur, remanet tamen bonitas alia vel virtus politice . . ."; *ST,* I–II, q. 63, a. 2: "Sed virtus humanitus acquisita potest secum compati aliquem actum peccati, etiam mortalis, quia usus habitus in nobis est nostrae voluntati subjectus. . . ."

72. ". . . philosophi non considerant virtutes secundum quod sunt principia actus meritorii: et ideo secundum eos habitus non formati caritate possunt dici virtutes; non autem secundum theologum" *(De ver.,* q. 14, a. 6, ad 5 [Spiazzi, 293]).

73. The lack of the corresponding humanly acquired moral virtue (say, chastity) can be an extrinsic impediment making the exercise of the divinely infused moral virtue more difficult and less satisfying: see *ST,* I–II, q. 65, a. 3, ad 2.

74. Cf. D. Odon Lottin, *Études de morale: Histoire et doctrine* (Gembloux: J.

human virtues as always able to be subsumed into the supernatural moral order established by the theological virtues of faith, hope, and charity.[75] This subsumption is possible because the real goods, which are objects of the humanly acquired moral virtues, are already intrinsically subordinated *in the order of being* to a transcendent or supernatural good.

It is evident that the act of all the other virtues is ordered to the proper end of charity, [to] that which is its object, namely, the highest good. And this is evident about the moral virtues, for virtues of this type are about created goods which are ordered to the uncreated good as to [their] ultimate end. *(De car.,* q. 1, a. 3 [Odetto, 761])[76]

This last text is a striking example of how a theological doctrine undergirds the basic concepts of Aquinas's moral science. Here the doctrine of creation plays an essential role in Aquinas's account of the humanly acquired virtues. The humanly acquired virtues, whose formal objects abstract from any reference to man's ultimate end,[77] focus on *natural* goods.[78] But Aquinas, by introducing the doctrine of creation, provides a novel perspective on these natural goods, one that clearly subordinates the humanly acquired moral virtues of "the philosophers" to the divinely infused moral virtues of the theologian. Natural goods are, in fact, created goods. As objects of choice, created goods are either *real* or *apparent* moral goods.[79] Apart from the order of charity, created goods (whether real or apparent) are chosen in refer-

---

Duculot, 1961), 134: "Quand saint Thomas parle en philosophe . . . il envisage la nature humaine dans sa réalité concrète. . . ."

75. See *De ver.,* q. 14, a. 5, ad 13 (Spiazzi, 292): ". . . in habente caritatem non potest esse aliquis actus virtutis nisi a caritate formatus. Aut enim actus ille erit in finem debitum ordinatus, et hoc non potest esse nisi per caritatem in habente caritatem; aut non est ordinatus in debitum finem, et sic non erit actus virtutis."

76. "Manifestum est autem quod actus omnium aliarum virtutum ordinatur ad finem proprium caritatis, quod est eius obiectum, scilicet summum bonum. Et de virtutibus quidem moralibus manifestum est: nam huiusmodi virtutes sunt circa quaedam bona creata quae ordinantur ad bonum increatum sicut ad ultimum finem" *(De car.,* q. 1, a. 3 [Odetto, 761]).

77. See *III Sent.,* d. 27, q. 2, a. 4, sol. 2 (Moos, n. 164, p. 886): "Ratio autem objecti sumitur secundum proportionem rei circa quam est operatio habitus vel potentiae, ad actum animae in qua sunt habitus vel potentiae."

78. See *III Sent.,* d. 33, q. 2, a. 1, sol. 2 (Moos, n. 145, p. 1047): ". . . virtutes morales perficiunt in vita activa et habent actus suos non circa finem ultimum, sed circa objectum. . . ."

79. See *ST,* II–II, q. 23, a. 7: ". . . si illud particulare bonum non sit verum bonum, sed apparens, virtus etiam quae est in ordine ad hoc bonum non erit vera virtus, sed falsa similitudo virtutis. . . ."

ence to exclusively human ends, the chief of which is the civil good.[80] But the theologian knows that if the created good is in conformity with reason and thus a real moral good, the created good has the intrinsic capacity to be ordered (by an agent possessing the infused theological and moral virtues) to "the ultimate and principal good of man," which is to see God.[81] Incorporated into the order of supernatural faith and charity, humanly acquired virtue, while yet remaining because of its this-worldly end a "conditional" virtue, is made a *perfect* token of its type.[82]

If the particular good is a real good, namely, the preservation of the city, or some such good of this type, it will be a true virtue, but imperfect unless it is referred to the final and perfect good. *(ST,* II–II, q. 23, a. 7)[83]

Now we can draw more accurately the proper Thomistic distinction between a philosophical and a theological point of view on the humanly acquired virtues. The philosopher knows neither grace nor nature apart from grace; he knows only nature. The theologian knows grace and wounded human nature, and the latter can be understood with or without reference to grace.[84] For the theologian, only a divinely infused virtue that allows one to pursue man's ultimate supernatural end is an unconditionally *(simpliciter)* true and perfect virtue. The humanly acquired virtues, since they are focused on real but secondary goods or ends, are true but conditional *(secundum quid)* virtues. The humanly acquired virtues are aimed at the civil good; but apart from the order of grace and charity, these virtues are both *conditional* and *imperfect.* They are "imperfect" by comparison with (1) the unconditionally *(simpliciter)* true and perfect infused moral and intellectual virtues that are aimed at man's supernatural good; and (2) the conditionally *(secundum quid)* true or humanly acquired moral and intellectual virtues that have been perfected by being incorporated

---

80. See *ST,* I–II, q. 63, a. 4: ". . . aliae virtutes acquisitae, secundum quas homo se bene habet in ordine ad res humanas"; *III Sent.,* d. 33, q. 1, a. 2, sol. 4, ad 2 (Moos, n. 77, p. 1031): ". . . per virtutem acquisitam collimitantur circumstantiae secundum proportionem ad bonum civile. . . ."

81. See *ST,* II–II, q. 23, a. 7: "Ultimum quidem et principale bonum hominis est Dei fruitio. . . ."

82. Cf. II–II, q. 4, a. 7: "Et idem potest dici de aliquibus aliis virtutibus: quamvis non sint verae virtutes nisi praesupposita fide. . . ."

83. "Si vero illud bonum, puta conservatio civitatis vel aliquid huiusmodi, erit quidem vera virtus, sed imperfecta, nisi referatur ad finale et perfectum bonum" *(ST,* II–II, q. 23, a. 7).

84. See Etienne Gilson, *The Christian Philosophy of St. Thomas Aquinas,* trans. L. K. Shook, C.S.B. (New York: Random House, 1956), 347.

into the order of charity.[85] In the latter order, the civil good is pursued in subordination to the supernatural good.

How, then, does the theologian regard, *apart from the order of charity*, the humanly acquired virtues, the virtues that are at the center of moral philosophy? Aquinas would certainly grant that a philosophical ethics that knows only the humanly acquired virtues can be logically independent of theology.[86] Moreover, Aquinas does not eliminate the humanly acquired moral virtues from the life of the believer who also possesses infused moral virtues.[87] But neither of these admissions alters the fact that Aquinas himself provides an integrally theological schematization of the humanly acquired moral virtues.[88] To assert, as Donagan does, that the Thomistic theory of the humanly acquired virtues is logically independent of Aquinas's own theology, is to misapprehend *"as philosophy* what St. Thomas wrote as theology."[89] This misapprehension, however, antedates contemporary philosophical notions of "moral theory."

Originating in the split between dogmatic and moral theology that opened toward the end of the sixteenth century, there has been a long history of confusion about the integrally theological character of Thomistic moral science. Gabriel Vasquez, S. J., was perhaps the first but certainly not the last theologian to claim about the *Summa theologiae* that portions of the *Prima secundae* were not theological but properly belonged to moral philosophy.[90] This historical obfuscation of Aquinas

85. See *ST*, I–II, q. 65, a. 2, ad 1; II–II, q. 23, a. 7.

86. See *III Sent.*, d. 27, q. 2, a. 3, ad 5 (Moos, nn. 143–46, p. 882); d. 33, q. 1, a. 4, ad 5 (Moos, n. 126, p. 1041): ". . . Philosophus loquitur de virtutibus acquisitis quae perficiunt hominem in vita civitatis terrenae, in qua vita non habemus aliquam communicationem cum angelis; unde non est simile de illis virtutibus quae perficiunt in vita civili civitatis quae constituitur ex angelis et hominibus."

87. The humanly acquired virtues, unlike the infused moral virtues, do not remain *"in patria"*; they coexist, therefore, in the believer only during this life. See *III Sent.*, d. 33, q. 1, a. 4, resp. (Moos, n. 119, p. 1040).

88. Gilson asks: "As to what moral virtues St. Thomas is actually speaking about in the *Summa*, the answer in principle is simple. He is speaking of the infused supernatural moral virtues and not the acquired natural moral virtues" *(Christian Philosophy of St. Thomas*, 346–47). But Gilson's conclusion is less exclusionary: it is impossible "to disentangle the [infused and acquired natural] virtues in this theological organism so as to arrive at purely natural virtues" (347). Cf. Bullet, *Vertus morales infuses*, 68, n. 3: "[Aquinas's] morale philosophique est *toujours* au service d'une compréhension plus profonde de la morale théologique, de fait donc surnaturelle." But Bullet does not deny "l'existence de principes d'une morale naturelle chez saint Thomas" (ibid.). Klubertanz, "Theorie sur les virtus morales," 575, n. 2, allows that Aquinas's analyses of the natural virtues are formally theological and "matériellement philosophiques."

89. Pegis, *"Sub Ratione Dei,"* 144.

90. For a history of the split, see Jacobus M. Ramirez, O.P., *Opera omnia*, ed.

makes it imperative to consider whether a *philosophical* Thomistic ethics is possible at all. This is the basic question, which motivates this book, that now emerges from our original query about the philosophical or theological character of "Thomistic moral theory." But given the innumerable volumes of philosophical ethics, all pledged by their Thomist authors to be written *"ad mentem divi Thomae,"* this new question may seem otiose. Yet it is widely acknowledged that not every Thomist disciple, including the great commentators, always followed his master faithfully. And it is universally conceded that Aquinas himself never created an explicit philosophical ethics. But can one be constructed from his theological texts? Here the divide opens between eminent interpreters of Aquinas.[91] In this book, I shall come to stand on one side of the divide: I shall examine and reject the usual Thomist starting point of an autonomous, allegedly Thomistic, systematic philosophical ethics.

By way of anticipating the conclusions of this book, I can say that Thomist philosophical ethics is grounded on the concept of the natural end of man: it is this concept that putatively justifies the construction of a systematic moral philosophy that is "perfectly independent in its own domain."[92] Now most, if not all, interpreters would agree that Aquinas speaks of the natural ends of human nature and that the Thomistic view of moral virtue cannot be logically separated from them. Thomist moral philosophers plausibly argue that Aquinas's concept of the natural ends of human action can be extricated from its theological setting. But, in fact, their *systematic* philosophical construction rests on a considerably stronger thesis. Thomist philosophical ethics is about how one attains, through the natural virtues, *the* ultimate natural end of human nature. Inevitably, such a Thomist philosophical ethics preserves the spirit and, usually, as much of the letter of Aristotle as

---

Victorino Rodríguez, O.P. (Madrid: Consejo Superior de Investigaciones Cientificas, 1972), vol. 3, *De hominis beatitudine: In I–II Summae theologiae divi Thomae commentaria (qq. I–V)*, 1, prolegomenum 1, §2, nn. 15–24, pp. 17–42.

91. Cf. Jacques Leclercq, *La Philosophie morale de saint Thomas devant la pensée contemporaine* (Louvain and Paris: Publications Universitaires de Louvain and Librairie Philosophique J. Vrin, 1955), 50: "Celui qui veut donner un cours . . . de morale thomiste est ainsi amené à un travail de reconstitution d'une système . . . qui ne se trouve pas tel quel dans ses écrits [de saint Thomas]. . . ."; Pegis, "*Sub Ratione Dei,*" 145: ". . . if St. Thomas did not create an autonomous philosophy, no one else can do it for him."

92. Venant Cauchy, *Désir naturel et béatitude chez saint Thomas* (Montreal: Fides, 1958), 118. Cf. Ralph McInerny, "Does Man Have a Natural End?" in *The Question of Christian Ethics* (Washington, D.C.: The Catholic University of America Press, 1993), 21–38.

possible.[93] But here we should pause before following the Thomists; we must consider how "the thoroughgoing theocentricity of Thomistic teleology"[94] affects Aquinas's own understanding of the natural ends of human action, including the felicity that comes from the philosophical contemplation of God in this life. Does Aquinas grant that men have, in the sense required by the systematic moral philosophies of the Thomist ethicians, an ultimate natural end? If not, and this ground is thereby removed, what consequence follows for Thomist philosophical ethics? I shall attempt to answer these questions in the last chapter of this book. But the route to the answer will be a long one. It will be necessary to treat in considerable detail various topics in Aristotle's *Nicomachean Ethics* and Aquinas's theological moral science. We need to discern how far Thomistic moral science can be rightly assimilated to the Aristotelian model. It will be crucial, of course, to determine what weight Aquinas affords to the philosophical contemplation of God in elaborating his own doctrine of human happiness.

On the assumption that Aquinas did indeed originally propound only a theological ethics, we can begin again by rephrasing our initial question. The question now is not whether "Thomistic moral theory" is theological or philosophical, but *what obscures the theological character of Thomistic ethics?* This rephrased question, however, is implicated in an even broader issue. Thomistic theology incorporates—so Etienne Gilson famously claimed—Aquinas's "Christian philosophy." But is "Christian philosophy" an oxymoron? This question requires us to recapitulate what may seem a shopworn if not futile debate. Yet the debate bears importantly on the character of Thomistic moral science and is relevant to any considered judgment about the possibility and cogency of an autonomous Thomistic philosophical ethics.

2. *"Christian Philosophy"*

"Christian philosophy," whatever else can be said about it, is a notorious term.[95] Heidegger rejects it out of hand: A "Christian philos-

93. Cf. Kluxen, *Philosophische Ethik*, 148–49, who, with greater historical nuance, characterizes "die 'natürliche' Moral" embedded in Aquinas's theology as treating what is given in the "factual actuality" ("die den tatsächlichen Gegebenheiten") of Aquinas's situation. But "dies tatsächlich die aristotelische ist . . ." (149, n. 25).

94. Oscar J. Brown, *Natural Rectitude and Divine Law in Aquinas* (Toronto: Pontifical Institute of Mediaeval Studies, 1981), 8.

95. For a recent account of the controversy provoked by Gilson, see John F.

ophy" is a round square and a misunderstanding."[96] But Van Steenberghen, Gilson's most implacable critic, is no less dismissive: "A philosophy would cease being a philosophy to the degree that it would
become Christian."[97] Both Heidegger and Van Steenberghen attempt to
cut to the quick of the issue: the notion of a "Christian philosophy"
contradicts the definition of philosophy as a purely rational enterprise.
To them and many others, there seems an inescapable objection to
Gilson: "Christian philosophy" is self-contradictory inasmuch as the
adjective "Christian" appears to incorporate into the nature of philosophy something other than reason.

Indeed, put merely in terms of the usual definition of "philosophy,"
the objection to "Christian philosophy" is, as Gilson himself recognized, cogent.[98] At the same time, a stipulative definition of "philosophy" can hardly be thought to dispose of Gilson's basic contention.
Admittedly, "Christian philosophy" calls for some explanation that
Gilson often reiterated: only this term, he insisted, accurately typifies
some obvious doctrinal novelties in the history of philosophy. "Christian philosophy" refers, in the first place, to the diversity of rational
doctrines found in a variety of patristic and medieval theologians,
whose novel philosophical problems were provoked and whose attempted philosophical solutions were controlled by their Christian
beliefs. Abstracting from this history, Gilson secondarily assigned a
generic or nonhistorical meaning to the term. A "Christian philosophy" arises whenever Christian faith prompts and intrinsically orients
what, nonetheless, is a strictly rational, self-sufficient demonstration
of some philosophical tenet.

In a Christian philosophy, reason takes up and rationally comprehends what faith first believes and points out.

If there exist philosophical systems, that in their principles and methods are purely rational, [but] whose existence would not be explicable

---

Wippel, "Thomas Aquinas and the Problem of Christian Philosophy," in *Metaphysical Themes in Thomas Aquinas* (Washington, D.C.: The Catholic University of
America Press, 1984), 1–33.

96. Martin Heidegger, *An Introduction to Metaphysics*, trans. Ralph Manheim
(New Haven, Conn.: Yale University Press, 1959), 7.

97. Fernand Van Steenberghen, *Introduction à l'étude de la philosophie médiévale* (Louvain and Paris: Publication Universitaires and Beatrice-Nauwelaerts,
1974), 96.

98. See Étienne Gilson, remarks in "La Notion de philosophie chrétienne,"
Séance du 21 mars 1931, Bulletin de la société française de philosophie 31 (1931):
37–93, passim, but esp. 46–47.

without the existence of the Christian religion, then philosophies so defined merit the name of "Christian philosophies."[99]

The demonstrations of a Christian philosophy can range over every field of philosophy but the paradigm case for Christian philosophy is a demonstration of a "saving truth revealed by God and accessible to the light of natural reason."[100] The most basic of such saving truths is, of course, the proposition that "God exists."

Gilson's definition of Christian philosophy has been continuously and sometimes furiously debated since it was first proposed in 1931 at a meeting of the Société Française de Philosophie. The debate, however, incorporates a limited number of moves and they have been repeated many times in the intervening years. I can reduce them to four. The first move, as always, is the most important.

First, opponents of "Christian philosophy" define "philosophy" as solely the construct of an autonomous rationality; then faith, since it is not reason, cannot enter in any fashion into the inner working of "philosophy."[101] In response, the proponents of "Christian philosophy" attempt to relativize this exclusionary definition of "philosophy" as presupposing but one construal of the faith-reason paradigm.

Second, controversy turns to the historical "facts" that allegedly are evidence for "Christian philosophy." In the original debate, Bréhier attempted to show that in the history of medieval philosophy nothing philosophically novel had appeared as the result of any "philosophically positive inspiration" of Christianity.[102] For their part, Gilson and other like-minded historians have responded by drawing up an impressive list of novel philosophical doctrines introduced into the history of philosophy by the positive influence of Christianity. To mention but a few on Owens's recent list, the following philosophical issues are claimed to have been prompted by the theological doctrine of creation: "the problem of change without a subject that changed," "the notions of duration before and after time," and "the beginning and ending of the temporal continuum in either a part or an indivisible."[103] The debate, however, quickly moves beyond this appeal to historical facts.

99. Gilson, "La Notion de philosophie chrétienne," 39.

100. Etienne Gilson, "What Is Christian Philosophy?" in *A Gilson Reader*, ed. Anton C. Pegis (Garden City, N.Y.: Doubleday & Company, 1957), 187.

101. See Van Steenberghen, *Introduction*, 112: "Vérité historique: Le Moyen Age a produit d'authentiques philosophies, qui sont purement rationnelles et ne sont donc pas 'spécifiquement chrétiennes.'"

102. See Bréhier's remarks in "La Notion de philosophie chrétienne," 37–93, passim.

103. See Joseph Owens, C.Ss.R., Introduction to *Towards a Christian Philoso-*

Third, the participants, finding that the historical "facts" are ambiguous or inconclusive, acknowledge that appeal to historical facts cannot actually settle what kind of influence that Christianity had on philosophy. No historian doubts that Christianity has been an extrinsic influence on philosophers. But does history show that Christianity can have an intrinsic relationship to philosophy? Bréhier's contention is that while history may show that Christianity introduced novel doctrines, such doctrines are not intrinsically philosophical; moreover, the history of philosophy gives evidence only of novelties that are not intrinsically Christian.

Fourth, what is the status of this history of philosophy? Opponents of "Christian philosophy" argue that the history of philosophy and the history of Christianity in philosophy are two separate streams that have not come together. But proponents of "Christian philosophy" can respond that the history of philosophy verifies only what the historian already thinks to be the nature of philosophy. They allege, in other words, that the two streams of Christianity and philosophy have not come together in the view of some historians, because, given their "rationalist" definition of "philosophy,"[104] they cannot come together.

Maritain stated the proper counterposition to Bréhier, which Gilson, from a slightly different perspective, embraced. Advocates of "Christian philosophy" can readily admit that philosophy, by its nature, is a strictly rational exercise of intelligence, if they also add—as did Maritain—a nuance: philosophical reasoning always occurs within an existential or historical state.[105]

Maritain's nuance, which entails reinterpreting the faith-reason paradigm, has a radical consequence: a definition of philosophy that abstracts entirely from any historical embodiment of philosophy cannot be the sole criterion by which the term "Christian philosophy" can be judged. Contrary to the rationalist, the philosopher must consider not only the essence of philosophy but its state of existence or historical actuality. As Gilson apophthegmatizes, only philosophers, not philoso-

---

phy, Vol. 21: *Studies in Philosophy and the History of Philosophy*, gen. ed. Jude P. Dougherty (Washington, D.C.: The Catholic University of America Press, 1990), 25. For Maritain's list of Christian philosophical doctrines ("creation," "nature," "subsistent being," and "sin"), see "La Notion de philosophie chrétienne," 63–64.

104. For Bréhier, "[L]a philosophie a pour substance le rationalisme, c'est-à-dire la conscience claire et distincte de la raison qui est dans les choses et dans l'univers" ("La Notion de philosophie chrétienne," 52).

105. See Maritain's remarks in "La Notion de philosophie chrétienne," 59–72, passim. Cf. Jacques Maritain, *An Essay on Christian Philosophy*, trans. Edward H. Flannery (New York: Philosophical Library, 1955).

phy, exist.[106] To consider philosophy as it exists in the philosopher is to recognize that the conceptual propriety of "Christian philosophy" rests on what Gilson took to be an unimpeachable fact of history: Christians have philosophized from a point within Christian faith. To impugn this same fact by denying that Christian philosophers produce Christian philosophy is a jejune maneuver that sacrifices the history of philosophy to an abstract definition of "philosophy" that, despite what it claims, allows little or no appeal to "experience."[107]

Gilson and Maritain, however, did not wish to throw away the standard textbook definition of philosophy; they agreed that philosophy must strive to be—in Aquinas's apt phrase—a "perfect use of reason."[108] But, if it is admitted that philosophy exists only in the mind of philosophers, as the Augustinian tradition has always insisted, then it is a moot question whether there are Christian philosophies or only Christian philosophers.[109] As a recent critic of Van Steenberghen remarks, "To separate the philosopher from philosophy, the cause from the effect, is an abstraction."[110]

These, then, are the basic positions and counterpositions that first surfaced in the French discussions of 1931 and 1933. Van Steenberghen indefatigably rehearsed them for over fifty years.[111] In resolute opposition to Gilson, Van Steenberghen took and held to the position that only the philosopher but not philosophy benefits from Christian revelation. There is, in other words, no intrinsic relationship between Christianity and philosophy.

Van Steenberghen, whose overriding concern was to prevent philosophy from being confused with theology, insisted on sharply delineat-

106. See Gilson, "La Notion de philosophie chrétienne," 47: ". . . la philosophie et la religion n'existent pas, il n'existe que des hommes religieux et philosophes; et de même que l'unité de ces sujets ne nous interdit pas de les analyser en concepts distincts, la distinction de ces concepts ne nous interdit pas de les rapporter a l'unité de leurs sujets."

107. Cf. Van Steenberghen, Introduction, 95: "[Philosophy's] seul ideal est la fidélité à l'experience et à la raison. Elle ne saurait donc être ni grecque, ni allemande, ni juive, ni chrétienne, ni romantique, ni baroque, ni républicaine, ni monarchiste, car aucune de ces valeurs culturelles ne peut être intégrée, à titre d'elemént constitutif et distinctif, dans le travail philosophique comme tel."

108. ". . . perfectum usum rationis . . ." (ST, II–II, q. 45, a. 2). Cf. Gilson, "La Notion de la philosophie chrétienne," 42; Maritain, ibid., 61.

109. See the remarks of Pierre Mandonnet, O.P., and A.-R. Motte, O.P., in "La Philosophie chrétienne: Juvisy, 11 Septembre 1933," Journées d'études de la société thomiste (Tournai, Belgium: Les Éditions du Cerf, 1933), 63, 138.

110. Luigi Bogliolo, La filosofia christiania: il problema, la storia, la struttura, Studi tomistici, vol. 28 (Vatican City: Libreria Editrice Vaticana, 1986), 148.

111. See Fernand Van Steenberghen, "La Conception de la philsophie au moyen

ing the methodological boundaries of an autonomous philosophical rationality, boundaries that were rigorously observed—so he contended—by medieval thinkers. In his view, "Christian philosophy," at least as Gilson first used it, is merely an amputated and misconstrued segment of a particular medieval theology (whether taken from Augustine, Bonaventure, or Aquinas), or, it is a term, in Gilson's later usage, falsely promoting the necessary symbiosis of philosophy with theology.[112] For both historical and doctrinal reasons, Van Steenberghen judged neither of Gilson's uses of "Christian philosophy" defensible.

According to Van Steenberghen, medieval thinkers themselves actually had two, quite distinct conceptions of philosophy that they never confused: "philosophy" was understood in a large and in a strict sense. "Philosophy," in the large sense, is a weltanschauung that can be and was identified with theology: "the [global] Christian vision of the universe and of life."[113] In this large sense, which was almost completely abandoned during the thirteenth century, medieval thinkers frequently spoke about "Christian philosophy." But, in the strict sense (i.e., the sense that derived in the thirteenth century from the Aristotelian philosophical paradigm), "philosophy" is always a methodical, reflexive, critical, systematic, and scientific work of pure reason that must be kept separate from theology. In this latter sense, medieval thinkers never referred to "Christian philosophy." Nor, wrote Van Steenberghen, should we.[114]

âge. Nouvel examen du problème," in *Philosophie im Mittelalter: Entwicklungslinien und Paradigmen*, ed. Jan P. Beckmann, Ludger Honnefelder, Gangolf Schrimpf, and Georg Wieland (Hamburg: Felix Meiner Verlag, 1987), 187–99.

112. See Van Steenberghen, *Introduction*, 73, 96, 108. For Van Steenberghen's view of the evolution and "hardening" of Gilson's ideas on "Christian philosophy," see his "Étienne Gilson, historien de la pensée médiévale," *Revue philosophique de Louvain* 77 (1979): 487–507.

113. Van Steenberghen, *Introduction*, 479.

114. See Van Steenberghen, *Introduction*, 79–85. But it is questionable whether Van Steenberghen always followed his own advice. He remarked that Gilson's effort to draw out "Aquinas's Christian philosophy" would have bewildered Aquinas since for Aquinas "la somme est évidemment une synthèse *théologique*" (*Introduction*, 103). Nonetheless, Van Steenberghen was prepared to claim, without any sense of inconsistency, that it is possible "emprunter à la *Summa theologiae* de Thomas d'Aquin le petit traité *De homine* qui occupe les questions 75 à 90 de la *Prima Pars* . . . car il s'agit là d'un exposé purement philosophique, que l'auteur a insere dans la somme en vertu de sa conception très large de la théologie speculative" ("La Conception de la philosophie," 195).

For the contrary argument, that "there are Thomistic metaphysical reasons why we cannot take the treatise on man in the *Prima Pars* as a philosophy of man" (24), see Anton C. Pegis, "Thomism 1966," in *In Search of Saint Thomas Aquinas*, The

Still, can the legitimacy or illegitimacy of "Christian philosophy" be resolved by distinguishing the large and the strict senses of "philosophy"? This is the lens through which Van Steenberghen viewed the entire problem. He complained that the conference on Christian philosophy, held by the Thomist Society at Juvisy (13 September 1933), was "very confused, and came to no firm conclusion."[115] Presumably the confusion resulted from a lack of common adherence to Van Steenberghen's passionately advocated "strict sense" of philosophy. But, from a Thomistic point of view, that sense is vulnerable to a fundamental criticism.

Owens, in a recent overview of the Gilson-Bréhier debate, attempts to resolve the problem of "Christian philosophy" by distinguishing two different types of concept formation.[116] Following Aquinas, Owens notes that a concept can be abstracted "with precision" or "without precision."[117] Bréhier's and Van Steenberghen's concept of "philosophy" rests on the former type of concept formation, Gilson's on the latter.[118] Taken precisively, "philosophy" abstracts from any of the conditions (in this case, Christian faith) that determine the thinking of the philosopher; taken without precision, those conditions are retained implicitly and indistinctly by "philosophy." In precisive abstraction, "philosophy" is treated like a substance existing in its own right (which it is not); abstracted without precision, "philosophy" is properly treated as an accident in the mind of the philosopher (which, in fact, it is). Owens sticks to the nonprecisive type of abstraction because, by

---

McAuley Lectures for 1966 (West Hartford, Conn.: Saint Joseph College, 1966), 19–31 [also published in Proceedings of the American Catholic Philosophical Association 40–41 (1966): 55–67].

If "on the nature of man St. Thomas was both an Augustinian and an Aristotelian" (Anton C. Pegis, "St. Thomas and the Unity of Man," in Progress in Philosophy, ed. James A. McWilliams, S. J. [Milwaukee: Bruce, 1955], 155), then the rational insights contained in the "petit traité" on man—presuming that they could be developed outside of Aquinas's theology—would provide a perfect example of what Gilson first meant by the generic term "Christian philosophy."

115. Van Steenberghen, "Étienne Gilson, historien," 495.

116. Similarly, Maritain distinguishes between "abstractio totalis," and "abstractio formalis," attributing the scientific (i.e., rationalist) definition of "philosophy" to the latter: see "La Notion de philosophie chrétienne," 60.

117. Owens refers to EE, 2.85–308: see Introduction to Towards a Christian Philosophy, 31, n. 25.

118. Although allowing the legitimacy and even the necessity of the conceptual distinction between "philosophy" and "Christianity," Gilson stresses the role of judgment in uniting them in their subject, the Christian philosopher: "[L]e conceptualisme exprime précisément en concepts distincts des éléments que le jugement rapporte à l'unité du concret" ("La Notion de la philosophie chrétienne," 46).

preserving "the intrinsic bearing of human concepts," it also preserves "what ["philosophy"] requires for real existence and activity."[119]

Owens, however, advances the distinction between the two types of abstraction in order to promote a much larger thesis: that "all the new philosophies from Descartes on are wrong from start to finish" (39). "Cartesian philosophies" favor concepts formed precisively because they falsely start with cognition or language; they are not correctly based, as are Aristotelianism and Thomism, "upon real things known with what they contain implicitly and indistinctly" (132).

Whatever the merits of this thesis, and it is far too sweeping to examine here, Owens's general approach to the debate about "Christian philosophy" is surely the correct one. "Christian philosophy" is a philosophical problem even before it is, in any nonphilosophical sense, a historical problem. But Owens himself recognizes that in defending the propriety of "Christian philosophy," his own philosophical approach, his commitment to a philosophy that is based on "real things," smacks of philosophical dogmatism.[120] But his "dogmatism" is only an aspect of a larger issue, the problem of "philosophical pluralism."

3. "Christian Philosophy" and Philosophical Pluralism

Whether one sides with Bréhier's and Van Steenberghen's, or Gilson's and Owens's, views of "Christian philosophy," the issue is certainly not one that can be decided solely on historical grounds.[121] If more than fifty years of protracted debate have shown anything, they have shown that Aquinas's "Christian philosophy" is as much a philosophical (and perhaps theological) as it is a historical concept.[122]

Van Steenberghen attempted to settle the debate about "Christian

119. Owens, Introduction to *Towards A Christian Philosophy*, 33, 32.

120. See ibid., 39. Cf. Etienne Gilson, *Being and Some Philosophers*, 2d ed., rev. (Toronto: Pontifical Institute of Mediaeval Studies, 1952), vii–xi.

121. See Paul Vignaux, "Philosophie chrétienne et théologie de l'histoire," in *De saint Anselme à Luther* (Paris: J. Vrin, 1976), 55–67, who argues that Gilson correctly states the issue in a footnote in the fourth edition of *Le Thomisme* (published in 1941). Quoting Gilson, Vignaux agrees that "'Christian philosophy' expresses a theological view of an historically observable reality" (56).

122. Anton C. Pegis, "Gilson and Thomism," *Thought* 21 (1946), 442, claims that "as Gilson insists, the real question at issue is whether we can separate a philosophy from the conditions in which it was born and without which it never existed—and not thereby destroy it." But if that is the "real question," it can hardly be answered solely by appealing to history: cf. Joseph Owens, C.Ss.R., "Aquinas and Philosophical Pluralism," in *Thomistic Papers*, ed. Leonard A. Kennedy, C.S.B., and Jack C. Marler (Houston: Center for Thomistic Studies, 1986), 2:133–58.

philosophy" by recalling Aquinas's "teachings relative to the nature, structure, and methods of philosophy."[123] Vigorously championing what he took to be the Thomistic conception of philosophy as a "purely rational" enterprise, Van Steenberghen drew a paradoxical conclusion about the history of philosophy: Hegelian philosophy is the "only type of philosophy that merits being called 'Christian'"[124] because Hegel's system, while theologically heterodox, is a rationalist reconstruction of the entirety of Christian dogma. Nothing less is congruent with the autonomy of philosophy: the proper outcome of "Christian philosophy," if it really is a philosophy, is to swallow its Christianity.

Van Steenberghen's provocative conclusion, however, cannot be proven by some neutral appeal to the history of philosophy, as can be seen if we consider his remarks about Hegel. Van Steenberghen's notion of philosophy is more narrowly or abstractly rationalistic than Hegel's.[125] Hegel, although he attempts to subsume theology into philosophy, nevertheless purports to demonstrate the necessity of reason embodying itself in history and faith, which embodiment is not eliminated but only subsequently rationalized by philosophy. Hegelian reason thus remains internally bound to history and faith, and above all to the history of Christian religious consciousness and its dogmas. In Hegelian terms, philosophical reason must preserve no less than negate what it subsumes; it "cannot therefore stand opposed to positive religion, and to the church doctrine that has still preserved its content."[126] Admittedly, the standard and plausible criticism of the Hegelian philosophy of religion is that it ultimately negates but does not authentically preserve orthodox Christian faith.[127] Van Steenberghen also rejects Hegel, but his rejection pays no real attention to the success or failure of Hegel's own project. Van Steenberghen's rejection turns, once again, on his notion of "philosophy": "A Christian philosophy that would introduce, under any title whatsoever, the data of revelation into the construction of its philosophy, would be a bad philosophy."[128]

123. Van Steenberghen, "Étienne Gilson, historien," 500.

124. Van Steenberghen, Introduction, 96, n. 19.

125. See Bogliolo, La filosofia Christiania, 147, who criticizes Van Steenberghen for remaining "su un piano puramente concettuale senza l'aggancio con la realtà."

126. Georg Wilhelm Friedrich Hegel, Lectures on the Philosophy of Religion, ed. Peter C. Hodgson, vol. 1, Introduction and the Concept of Religion, trans. R. F. Brown et al. (Berkeley and Los Angeles: University of California Press, 1984), 129, n. 40.

127. For a brilliant if not entirely convincing defense of Hegel's Christian orthodoxy, see Emil L. Fackenheim, The Religious Dimension in Hegel's Thought (Bloomington: Indiana University Press, 1971).

128. Van Steenberghen, Introduction, 94.

To be sure, if philosophical reason is kept within Van Steenbergh-en's boundaries, it can have no commerce with Hegelian philosophy which labored to explain that human thought itself is "somehow divine."[129] Hegel's assertion of the divine nature of philosophy, its necessary immersion and subsequent transcendence of history and faith, may well be theologically heterodox, a heterodoxy that signals to the orthodox Christian believer that Hegelian philosophy has somewhere gone astray. But this suspicion is not yet a philosophical critique. A philosophical critique of Hegel, however, misses the mark if it assumes what Hegel would not concede: an ahistorical definition of the boundaries of philosophical reason. Van Steenberghen claims that "the contribution of revelation is occasional, accidental, and remains extrinsic to the philosophical task."[130] This assertion reflects not only Van Steenberghen's understanding of revelation but, even more, his understanding of philosophy. But these, after all, are exactly the narrowly rationalist boundaries of philosophy that Hegel attempted to redraw.[131]

Owens, realizing that the Gilson-Bréhier debate reflects an underlying philosophical issue, includes in his own defense of "Christian philosophy" some comments about "philosophical pluralism." Owens accepts that different philosophies start from their own principles which lead necessarily to their own conclusions. Yet he grants that it is possible and necessary for participants in an actual philosophical debate to talk to each other; the talk, as Owens describes it, seems mostly to consist in understanding how each participant's diverse starting points lead to irreconcilably different conclusions. For Owens admits that once a complete set of principles have been adopted, "there is no strictly philosophical way open for change from that philosophy to one with another basis."[132] Philosophical conversation among the adherents of diverse philosophies consists, therefore, in a reasoned "dogmatism": each participant in the conversation understands the alternative philo-

129. Quentin Lauer, S.J., "Hegel on the Identity of Content in Religion and Philosophy," in *Essays in Hegelian Dialectic* (New York: Fordham University Press, 1977), 157.

130. Van Steenberghen, *Introduction*, 99. Cf. "Étienne Gilson, historien," 504: "Toute intervention *directe* de la révélation dans l'élaboration de la philosophie serait dénaturante et illégitime."

131. A fact that has not escaped other Roman Catholic philosophers. See Georges Van Riet, "The Problem of God in Hegel," *Philosophy Today*, 2, no. 1 (1967): 3–16; and 2, no. 2 (1967): 75–102: "Hegelianism, taken seriously, is an invitation to rethink anew the very delicate relations of reason and faith . . ." (102).

132. Owens, Introduction to *Towards a Christian Philosophy*, 39.

sophical views but keeps his or her own starting point and from that position makes "an epistemological evaluation of the truth or falsity" (39) of the other philosophies.

Now there is much that needs to be considered and spelled out in Owens's succinct version of "philosophical pluralism." He is clearly concerned not to embrace a "relativistic" concept of philosophical pluralism. Owens takes care only to embrace what he labels "historical relativism," a relativism that acknowledges the de facto but not the de jure diversity of philosophical starting points. "Historical relativism" leaves intact "definitely established truths" (40), the truths, presumably, that are taken as definitely established from any given starting point. But Owens's admission that each complete philosophy is necessarily self-enclosed by its own principles would exactly seem to warrant a radical form of philosophical pluralism that is scarcely distinguishable from what he himself would disavow as a "thoroughgoing type of relativism."[133]

Owens, in this context, does not explain why "historical relativism" does not, of necessity, lead to "thoroughgoing relativism." Instead, he refers to the fact that philosophers sometimes "switch philosophies." But Owens's explanation of why they do so is left vague and undeveloped: "If the conclusions reached in the philosophical reasoning begin to appear unacceptable, the dissatisfaction can lead to a reassessing of the starting points and eventually to abandoning them for a new set."[134] Of course, many factors, of entirely different logical types and orders, could lead to such dissatisfaction with one's own conclusions: religious, psychological, social, academic, and presumably philosophical. It is the latter that are of interest here.

Owens, however, calls such a switch a "quantum jump into another philosophical orbit."[135] This metaphor suggests that there is a radical philosophical discontinuity, and consequently no way of rationally plotting the jump between one philosophical position and another. Again, the metaphor hardly supports the notion of a strictly "historical relativism." It suggests, rather, a discontinuous logical jump from

133. Cf. Richard McKeon, "Discourse, Demonstration, Verification, and Justification," in *Demonstration, vérification, justification*, Entretiens de l'Institut International de Philosophie, Liège, Septembre 1967 (Louvain: Editions Nauwelaerts, 1968), 40: "From the standpoint of the meanings given to demonstration, verification, and justification in any one philosophic position, the processes followed and the results alleged in other philosophies use badly organized and unreliable methods to arrive at meaningless results in resolution of misconceived problems."

134. Owens, Introduction to *Towards a Christian Philosophy*, 40.

135. Ibid.

one self-contained perspective to another. But, as one can gather from his other writings, Owens would certainly wish to distance his own account of philosophical pluralism from any relativistic implications. On the contrary, he looks at philosophical pluralism from the standpoint of what Gilson calls a "dogmatic realism."[136]

It is commonly thought among philosophers who are not committed to a radical form of philosophical pluralism that one can advance good reasons why one should "switch" from one philosophy to another. Gilson, and Owens concurring with him, put the matter quite differently: switching philosophies is impossible once one has assumed the starting point of any philosophy. "Every philosophical doctrine is ruled by the intrinsic necessity of its own position and by the consequences which flow from it. . . ."[137]

Owens's conception of the problems inherent in philosophical pluralism recapitulates Gilson's early polemic against "critical realism" and his remarks, at the end of his career, about speech: "Language does not first of all signify thought, but things."[138] Owens also looks at other philosophies, those that begin with thought or speech in separation from real being, as never being able to escape thought or speech.[139] Realism, as it is understood by Gilson and Owens, is dogmatic: it refuses to justify itself "critically." But it is not dogmatic in the sense that their form of realism refuses to give reasons for eschewing a critique of knowledge. Put briefly, it is unnecessary, self-defeating, and self-contradictory for realism to embrace a preliminary critique as though the conclusions of such a critique were somehow more certain than our immediate and foundational knowledge of sensible things.[140] Realism cannot be critically justified and remain authentic

---

136. See Joseph Owens, C.Ss.R., "The Primacy of the External in Thomistic Noetics," *Église et Théologie* 5 (1974): 204: "The philosophers before Descartes were accordingly right in their direct study of real things without benefit of approach through epistemology."

137. Etienne Gilson, *Thomist Realism and the Critique of Knowledge*, trans. Mark A. Wauck (San Francisco: Ignatius Press, 1986), 149–50.

138. Étienne Gilson, *Linguistique et philosophie: Essai sur les constantes philosophiques du langage* (Paris: Librairie Philosophique J. Vrin, 1969), 148.

139. See Owens, "Primacy of the External," 197: nonrealist philosophies have accepted "a starting point that does not allow any philosophically justified exit to anything outside one's own cognition." This position is untenable because it contradicts perception that grasps "distinct objects complete in themselves, and not as modifications of the percipient" (195).

140. See Joseph Owens, C.Ss.R., *Cognition: An Epistemological Inquiry* (Houston, Texas: Center for Thomistic Studies Studies, 1992), 326: "Nothing can be more certain than the tenet of their [sensible things] real existence."

realism.[141] It must start with, and never throw into epistemological jeopardy, "what is primarily perceived in its own existence outside the percipient"[142]—the sensible thing. Now it is just this latter datum that "critical realism" first throws into doubt and then attempts to rectify. It is, for that reason, "a square circle."[143] It attempts to do what is impossible: to move across some epistemological bridge from "cognitional existence to real existence."[144]

Bréhier's and Van Steenberghen's rejoinders to Gilson, as well as Gilson's and Owens's philosophical efforts to justify "Christian philosophy," all involve, implicitly or explicitly, the problem of philosophical pluralism. To simplify that problem, we can say that awareness of philosophical pluralism raises, in turn, the question of whether there are self-enclosed philosophies, each of which writes its own history of philosophy. In their own way, Van Steenberghen, Gilson, and Owens give evidence that there are as many Thomistic histories of philosophy as there are "Thomisms." And, evidently, only some versions of "Thomism" allow for "Christian philosophy."

Different conceptions of "philosophy" underlie and, in fact, generate the diverse historical perspectives in which "Christian philosophy" first emerges.[145] How is this pluralism to be resolved? McKeon argues, with extraordinary historical erudition, that only the "common framework of discourse" adequately assimilates "the frameworks of things, thoughts, actions, and symbols."[146] Owens, with his strong Aristotelian emphasis on the primacy of sensibly known things, rejects such a contention. However, I shall not here attempt to adjudicate the disagreement between McKeon and Owens which does, ultimately, reduce to a dispute about the cognitive primacy and epistemological integrity of

---

141. See Gilson, *Thomist Realism*, 152: ". . . any aspect of a realist philosophy may be subject to criticism except its very realism. This is the true position of dogmatic realism which we defend."

142. Owens, "Primacy of the External," 191.

143. Étienne Gilson, *Le Réalisme méthodique*, 3d ed. (Paris: Chez Pierre Tequi, n.d. [1936]), 83.

144. Owens, *Cognition*, 327.

145. See Richard McKeon, "Truth and the History of Ideas," in *Thought, Action, and Passion* (Chicago: University of Chicago Press, 1954), 88: ". . . the philosophic assumptions of the historian enter into his choice of facts and his use of contexts, and the truth of the history is dependent on the principles to which it has recourse. . . ."

146. See McKeon, "Discourse," 51: cf. Owens, *Cognition*, 322–23: "All three [i.e., things, concepts, and language] offer themselves [as starting points for philosophy] as they stand. Yet they are related to each other in a way that makes things basic, thought a presenting of things, and language an expression of thought."

the sensibly known, extramental existent over and against the primacy of philosophical speech.[147]

To provide a fully developed theory of philosophical pluralism would be a difficult and controversial undertaking.[148] Owens opens a large space for philosophical pluralism by granting that "the combined complexities of things, thought and language are accordingly present in the immediate object from which metaphysics takes its start."[149] At the same time, he narrows that space by denying that "each starting point or set of starting points has equal virtuality for pursuing the metaphysical enterprise" (649). This, however, is a circular claim: it is the principles of a given philosophy that allow one to judge what is the appropriate scope and virtuality of the "metaphysical enterprise," if such an enterprise is allowed at all.[150] Is there, then, any "preestablished priority of being, cause, or rule among things, thoughts, actions, and statements"?[151] Or is each a universal subject matter that includes the others, prior in the sense only that a philosopher can choose to start with one rather than another?[152] There is no doubt what Aquinas's (and following Aquinas, Gilson and Owens's) answer is to a neutral philosophical pluralism that would emphasize the irreducibility of various

147. "Neither existence nor experience is *ab initio* an ordered whole of constituted facts or of spaced or sequential events" (McKeon, "Discourse," 50). Cf. my "Philosophical Pluralism and 'The Internal Evolution of Thomism': Some Realist Animadversions," in *Thomistic Papers*, ed. John F. X. Knasas (Houston, Texas: Center for Thomistic Studies, 1994), 6:195–228.

148. See the elaborate "Inventory of Possible Approaches to a Choice among Rival Philosophical Positions," offered by Nicholas Rescher, in *The Strife of Systems: An Essay on the Grounds and Implications of Philosophical Diversity* (Pittsburgh: University of Pittsburgh Press, 1985), 222. Rescher defends an "orientational pluralism" that views "[philosophical] inquiry as proceeding via a normative stand based on cognitive values" (233).

149. Joseph Owens, "Reality and Metaphysics," *Review of Metaphysics* 25 (1971–1972): 647.

150. The same could be said about the "criterion of truth": see George P. Klubertanz, S.J., "The Nature of Philosophical Inquiry: An Aristotelian View," *Proceedings of the American Catholic Philosophical Association* 41 (1967): 27–38, who claims that, in terms of the criterion of truth, "some philosophies show themselves historically to be more inclusive, more adequate than others" (38).

151. McKeon, "Discourse," 45.

152. See Walter Watson, *The Architectonics of Meaning: Foundations of the New Pluralism* (Albany: State University of New York Press, 1985), 9–10.

Owens, when acknowledging the fact, and indeed the legitimacy of philosophical pluralism, allows that the *objective* epistemological primacy of the sensible existent may be overridden by choice: "Things, thought, and language offer a myriad of starting points. . . . The choice will in practice depend in large part on temperament and upbringing" *(Cognition,* 333).

starting points: "Being [ens] is what the intellect first conceives as the most evident and in which it resolves all concepts."[153]

It is from this starting point, the Thomistic doctrine of the primacy in cognition of sensible beings, that Owens and Gilson argue for "Christian philosophy."[154] Nonetheless, the theme of philosophical pluralism, from whatever point of view it is dealt with and resolved, starts from a commonplace that anyone taking up the theme must consider. What should count as the definition or criterion of philosophical reason is a problem confronting every philosophy but one that cannot be historically or systematically encompassed by any one philosophy. Treated, then, as spinning off the theme of philosophical pluralism, a review of the "Christian philosophy" debate leads to one main conclusion. At the level at which it was first generated, debate about "Christian philosophy" is, in principle, unresolvable. The discussants could and did alternate between (1) definitions of philosophy that stipulate the logical impossibility of religious faith having an intrinsic or constitutive influence on philosophy, and (2) historical examples of philosophies allegedly formed under the tutelage of faith. Contemporary rehearsals of these debates can always fall back on one or the other of these alternatives.[155]

Yet, if the debate is kept at this level, it remains intractable. There is no philosophically neutral, purely historical adjudication of Gilson's claim that a "Christian philosophy" is possible because, at one time or the other, it was actual. What can be historically counted as "an actual philosophy" is not solely dependent on historical criteria. The historical debate, therefore, cannot be directly resolved; resolution comes at

153. ". . . quod primo intellectus concipit quasi notissimum, et in quo omnes conceptiones resolvit, est ens. . . " (De ver., q. 1, a. 1 [Spiazzi, 2]). Cf. Gilson, Thomist Realism, 149: "You must either begin as a realist with being, in which case you will have a knowledge of being, or begin as a critical idealist with knowledge, in which case you never come in contact with being."

154. Gilson offers an existential grounding for "Christian philosophy" in "La Possibilité philosophique de la philosophie chrétienne," Revue des sciences religieuses 32 (1958): 168–96. Thomistic metaphysics is open to revelation and theology because it grasps being as the "actus essendi" that cannot be conceptualized. In general terms, only a philosophy that does not sever reason from intellectual insight into the first principle of being can be "Christian."

155. Although he phrases the matter differently, Wippel ("Problem of Christian Philosophy," 23–24) adheres to the first of them; he insists that the "moment of discovery," which necessarily reflects the historical condition of the Christian philosopher, must be sharply distinguished from a second "moment of proof" which cannot admit a revealed premise into an otherwise philosophical argument. "Christian philosophy" can be applied correctly only to the first moment.

a different level, one that recognizes that the history of philosophy is itself a philosophical construction. In this way, the debate about "Christian philosophy" becomes an oblique statement of the problem of philosophical pluralism. That there is a need, at the very beginning of the discussion, for a lively appreciation of philosophical pluralism can be seen well enough in Van Steenberghen's dubious reduction of "Christian philosophy" to Hegelianism.

Van Steenberghen approached the problem of "Christian philosophy" with a decidedly non-Hegelian notion of philosophy but paradoxically asserted that only a Hegelian notion of philosophy is "Christian" in the required sense. Gilson and Maritain, however, were surely not Hegelians and defended "Christian philosophy" on entirely different grounds. But the Hegelian could just as well retort that Van Steenberghen had failed to consider the pertinent Hegelian question whether reason itself is—in some ontological sense—necessarily historical. Hegel's answer to that question leads to a history of Christian philosophical reason that Van Steenberghen would not recognize either as philosophy or as history. Here philosophical pluralism begins and ends in an evident lack of communication. Yet Van Steenberghen over a lifetime found himself in a cul-de-sac not with Hegel, but with Gilson.[156] What is incontestable is that Gilson and Van Steenberghen did not share the same notion of "philosophy."

First Gilson, and then Maritain, and most recently Owens, have all noted, in very similar terms, that Van Steenberghen's definition of "philosophy" abstracts from the historical, religious, and existential conditions of the philosopher. Their own positions, however, are completely removed from any Hegelian thesis about the historicity of philosophical reason. They are committed, rather, to certain theses about the abstraction of concepts. Philosophy can and cannot be "Christian," depending on whether one illegitimately hypostatizes (so they think) an abstracted concept of "philosophy" divorced from the philosopher.

For our purposes, none of the particular theses of these doughty controversialists needs to be defended since the debate was not about and cannot be resolved in reference to any particular thesis. "Christian philosophy," to use McKeon's terminology, was a "common theme" but not a common set of theses held by the discussants who continuously moved back and forth, as Merleau-Ponty described them, be-

---

156. See Van Steenberghen, "La Conception de la philosophie au moyen âge," 187–99.

tween historical facts and timeless essences or definitions.[157] Owens's recent account is still more illuminating. Is "Christian philosophy" an oxymoron? The question can only be answered by understanding its matrix. A frank recognition of philosophical pluralism highlights not only the competing concepts of "philosophy," but the philosophical character of the "historical facts" that are appealed to. "Christian philosophy" is possible because philosophy is inherently pluralistic whether one understands that pluralism to be merely de facto (Owens) or de jure (McKeon).

Gilson claimed, however, that it was not philosophical theory but history that led him to pose the problem of "Christian philosophy."[158] Yet he too averred that in order to understand the relationship of philosophy to Christianity, "it is necessary to go beyond the level of empiricism" (43). Empiricism, of course, is but one philosophical viewpoint on the history of philosophy. For his part, Gilson did not eschew any movement of philosophical thought between concepts and reality: wisdom consists "in ceaselessly returning to reality in order to express [reality] more and more adequately in concepts" (47). On this realist basis, he commonsensically adhered to what he regarded as the historian's perspective; he put the emphasis on "an indisputably real historical fact."[159] Consequently, Gilson insisted, especially to those colleagues in the Société Française de Philosophie who fastened on the abstract definition of philosophy, that "Christian philosophy" is possible because it has occurred in the history of philosophy.

If one wishes to restore to this notion [of Christian philosophy] its proper sense, it is important to keep it on the plane of concrete reality, especially of history. If there have been philosophies, or systems of rational truths, whose existence would be historically inexplicable without taking into account the existence of Christianity, then these philosophies should bear the name of Christian philosophies. They are philosophies because they are rational, and they are Christian because the rationality that they have produced had not been conceived without Christianity. In order that the relationship between the two elemental concepts be intrinsic, it is not

157. See Maurice Merleau-Ponty, "Everywhere and Nowhere," in *Signs*, trans. Richard C. McCleary (Evanston, Ill.: Northwestern University Press, 1964), 140–46
158. See Gilson, "La Notion de philosophie chrétienne," 72.
159. Gilson, "La Possibilité philosophique," 168. Gilson's espousal of the "simple histoire de la philosophie" (ibid., 176) doubtless reflects his rejection of any epistemological critique in favor of what is often called "naive realism." For recent criticism of Gilson's views, see Patrick Lee, "Etienne Gilson: *Thomistic Realism and the Critique of Knowledge*," *New Scholasticism* 63 (1989): 81–100.

sufficient that a philosophy is compatible with Christianity; it is necessary that Christianity has played an active role in the very constitution of this philosophy.[160]

As a historian, Gilson observed not only the influence of Christian faith on diverse philosophies but put into relief the theological setting in which these Christian philosophies were articulated. From this latter circumstance—their theological nexus, order, and service—arises what Pegis calls the "ambivalence" of medieval Christian philosophies.[161] In the broadest sense, a "Christian philosophy" is any philosophy succored by Christian faith. In a more specific sense, the Christian character of a philosophy appears most vividly when it is evident that it is a by-product of a theology that attempts to rationalize faith. But, to a corresponding degree, the strictly philosophical character of such a Christian philosophy is less vivid. A philosophy that was developed for a theology and stays immersed within that theology is an ambivalent philosophy. For a Christian philosophy to be unambivalently a philosophy, it must be developed independently—outside of its state of service to theology—so that it can be clearly seen in and for itself. In short, it must be autonomous.[162]

4. *Autonomous Thomistic Philosophy*

For his part, Gilson eventually concluded that the dependence of philosophy upon theology was the source of Scholasticism's past vitality and—because theology positively fosters as well as negatively safeguards rationality—he advocated that "scholastic philosophy must return to theology"[163] and remain subordinated to theology if it is to

160. Gilson, "La Notion de philosophie chrétienne," 48. Cf. Etienne Gilson, *The Spirit of Mediaeval Philosophy*, trans. A. H. C. Downes (New York: Charles Scribner's Sons, 1940), 41.

161. See Anton C. Pegis, *The Middle Ages and Philosophy: Some Reflections on the Ambivalence of Modern Scholasticism* (Chicago: Henry Regnery Company, 1963), 71–72: "By as much as it was a theology, there is a sense in which it was not a philosophy: it did not, in fact, have the autonomous state of expression proper to a philosophy." But the same point can be put more reductively: "But what is a philosophy that is part of theology? . . . that philosophy so employed was theology." ("*Sub Ratione Dei:* A Reply," 142–43) Or, put in terms of the object of an intellectual habit, the philosophy that is in Aquinas's theological works "is *formally* theology and *only materially* philosophy" (ibid., 153).

162. See Anton C. Pegis, "Catholic Intellectualism at the Crossroad," in *In Search of Saint Thomas Aquinas*, The McAuley Lectures for 1966 (West Hartford, Conn.: Saint Joseph College, 1966), 7.

163. See Etienne Gilson, "Historical Research and the Future of Scholasticism,"

undergo any healthy development. Gilson followed his own advice; he consistently refused to detach Aquinas's philosophy from its original theological order.[164] The latter order remains the intrinsic condition of the only philosophy that Aquinas wrote.[165]

Nonetheless, Aquinas's own Christian philosophy, which in its original state will always be "the philosophy of and in a scholastic theology,"[166] also remains—in Pegis's sense—ambivalent. It did not attain the full or autonomous development that was due it as a philosophy. And this latter goal—even for those colleagues of Gilson who concur with his theological placement of Aquinas's own philosophy—seems possible and necessary if one is to live in the twentieth century "where human intelligence leads and needs to lead an autonomous life."[167] Owens cautions, however, that while Aquinas may provide the principles for developing an autonomous metaphysics, he himself did not write it, and therefore none of the Thomist constructions of his commentators and disciples can be rightly attributed to him.[168] Gilson's

---

in *A Gilson Reader*, ed. Anton C. Pegis (Garden City, N. Y.: Doubleday & Company, 1957), 165 [originally published in *Modern Schoolman* 29 (1951): 1–10]. Contrary to Gilson, Wippel (following Van Steenberghen) argues that Thomistic philosophy was "the necessary condition for [Aquinas] to develop his theology." ("Problem of Christian Philosophy," 29, n. 80) Cf. Pegis, "*Sub Ratione Dei:* A Reply," 154: ". . . there is no Thomistic philosophy which is a whole *before* it is a functioning part of St. Thomas's theology." But Gilson sometimes suggests that the two disciplines were interdependent: "At the same time, therefore, that historical research justifies, for the middle ages, the saying that *qualis in philosophia talis in theologia,* it invites us to complete it by another one: *qualis in theologia talis in philosophia.* . . . Indeed, these are two formulations of the same truth . . . " ("Historical Research," 162).

164. See Gilson, *The Christian Philosophy of St. Thomas Aquinas*, 3–25, esp. 8, 22.

165. For a lengthy argument contra Gilson that their theological contexts are merely *extrinsic* conditions but not intrinsic constituents of the philosophies of Bonaventure and Aquinas, see John Francis Quinn, *The Historical Constitution of St. Bonaventure's Philosophy* (Toronto: Pontifical Institute of Mediaeval Studies, 1973), esp. 835–36.

166. Pegis, "Thomism 1966," 21.

167. Pegis, "Catholic Intellectualism at the Crossroads," 14.

168. See Joseph Owens, C.Ss.R., *An Elementary Christian Metaphysics* (Milwaukee: Bruce, 1963), vii. For a confident statement of the view that Aquinas's metaphysics, psychology, and ethics can be readily "separated out" from his theology, see Mother Mary Cecelia Wheeler, R.S.C.J., *Philosophy and the "Summa Theologica" of Saint Thomas Aquinas*, Philosophical Studies, No. 169 (Washington, D.C.: The Catholic University of America Press, 1956), 150. For Pegis ("Who Reads Aquinas?" *Thought* 42 [1967]: 488–504), there is no "Thomism" to be extracted from Aquinas, but there are Thomistic metaphysical principles "by which a modern philosopher can create a modern philosophy" (501) because "metaphysics is that part of any philosophy that neither ages nor dies in history" (503).

two distinguished colleagues set a rigorous standard. The would-be-Thomist should be both historically fastidious and philosophically innovative. He must recognize, first of all, that Aquinas's own metaphysics was occasioned by and developed within a theology that attempted to assimilate the historical Aristotle and, in the process, transformed Aristotelianism. Second, the would-be-Thomist must be cognizant that any present Christian philosophy must confront an entirely different range of post-Aristotelian philosophical issues.[169] Finally, the would-be-Thomist must attempt this task by using Aquinas's principles, not just by repeating his words.[170] The task, then, is to develop an autonomous Thomistic philosophy that would still be under the aegis of faith but would no longer be directly serving the needs of a theology focused on Aristotle.[171] "For what St. Thomas did with philosophy when he used it as a theologian cannot be for us a criterion as to how we should practice it when we wish to develop it according to its own specification and for its own purposes."[172]

Pegis and Owens's goals—the contemporary development of Aquinas's Christian philosophy outside of its original theological context—are not widely shared. In an elegiac book, Gilson deplored the fact that Aquinas is no longer the "Doctor Communis" in today's Roman Catholic theological and philosophical community.[173] Pegis contended, reiterating Gilson and Maritain's opinion, that it is not St. Thomas but "modern Thomism that is dying in the world today."[174] Although the scene, however one casts it, has not significantly changed since Gilson surveyed it over twenty years ago, Aquinas's "Christian philosophy" continues to have some adherents, not all of them Roman Catholic, and to inspire a variety of contemporary philosophical reflections. One possibility has been embraced by a number of historically oriented

169. See Anton C. Pegis, *St. Thomas and Philosophy*, The Aquinas Lecture for 1964 (Milwaukee: Marquette University Press, 1964).

170. For a highly personal critique of what he labels "paléo-thomisme," see Fernand Van Steenberghen, "Comment être thomiste aujourd'hui?" *Revue philosophique de Louvain* 85 (1987): 171–97.

171. See Joseph Owens, C.Ss.R., *St. Thomas and the Future of Metaphysics*, The Aquinas Lecture for 1957 (Milwaukee: Marquette University Press, 1957), 51; and Anton C. Pegis, "Thomism as a Philosophy," in *Saint Thomas Aquinas and Philosophy*, The McAuley Lectures for 1960 (West Hartford, Conn.: Saint Joseph College, 1961), 15–30.

172. Anton C. Pegis, "The Middle Ages and Philosophy," *Proceedings of the American Catholic Philosophical Association* 21 (1946): 19.

173. See Étienne Gilson, *Les Tribulations de sophie* (Paris: Librairie Philosophique J. Vrin, 1967).

174. Pegis, "After Seven Hundred Years," 142.

scholars, a suggested project as it were for would-be Thomists. Aquinas articulated his metaphysics within the context of his theology. But if we allow that an autonomous Thomistic metaphysics can be extracted without much difficulty from Aquinas's theology,[175] it might then seem possible or necessary to take a second step: the "extraction" of a systematic philosophical Thomistic ethics.[176] This ethics, presumably, would be of interest to any philosopher and it could provide a much needed bridge between philosophical and theological ethics.

On the surface, this project is hardly new. Over seventy years ago the French Dominican A. D. Sertillanges unhesitatingly extracted what he called "Aquinas's moral philosophy" from Aquinas's theology. Pegis, borrowing Maritain's ironic phrase, referred to any philosophy that was merely lifted from Aquinas as "dead theology."[177] Sertillanges, without considering whether his Thomistic moral philosophy was alive or dead, justified his procedure on the grounds that "Thomistic ethics is only a prolongation of Thomistic metaphysics."[178] Now if Thomistic ethics is merely a prolongation of Thomistic metaphysics, and if the latter can be extracted from its theological setting, it seems reasonable to assume that so can the former. But, even on these eminently reasonable grounds, Sertillanges's metaphysically prolonged ethics cannot be squared with Aquinas. Thomistic ethics is not a "prolongation" of Thomistic metaphysics. On the contrary, Aquinas sharply distinguishes the theoretical science of metaphysics from the practical science of ethics. The two sciences have different ends that correspond to different conceptions of happiness. Moral philosophy is directed toward activity and not contemplation, and accordingly is called a practical and not a theoretical science.

175. See Kluxen, *Philosophische Ethik*, 21: "Es ist zweiflos moglich, die Metaphysik des Thomas als System darzustellen, ohne kunstliche Abstraktion. . . ."

176. See Vanni Rovighi, "C'è un'etica filosofica?" 147–48. Cf. Ralph McInerny, *Aquinas on Human Action* (Washington, D.C.: The Catholic University of America Press, 1992), who sanctions the extraction of Aquinas's "moral philosophy": ". . . those for whom moral theology holds no charm, can nonetheless read with philosophical profit both the [i.e., Aquinas's] commentary on Aristotle's *Ethics* and the moral part of the *Summa theologiae*. . . . [T]here is an extractable philosophical doctrine in the [i.e., Aquinas's] moral theology which, when extracted, could be described both as non-Aristotelian and as moral philosophy. This, it might be said, is the moral philosophy of St. Thomas Aquinas" (162). McInerny's oblique and hedged recommendation doubtless reflects his expert cognizance of the issues surrounding any such attempted philosophical "extraction."

177. Pegis, "After Seven Hundred Years," 144.

178. A. D. Sertillanges, O.P., *La Philosophie morale de saint Thomas d'Aquin*, rev. ed. (Paris: Aubier, 1942), 11.

As is evident in Book X of the *[Nicomachean] Ethics*, philosophers posit a twofold happiness: one is contemplative, the other active. According to this, they distinguish two parts of philosophy, calling moral philosophy practical and natural, and rational philosophy theoretical. *(Expos. de Trin.*, q. 5. a, 1, ad 4 [Decker, 14–18, p. 169])[179]

Twenty-five years ago, Kluxen, although he carefully noted the difficulty of the project, again attempted to disengage—this time, without reducing ethics to metaphysics[180] a strictly philosophical Thomistic ethics that St. Thomas did not write but whose "structure" could be discerned in his "moral theology."[181] One reviewer, who was not alone in praising Kluxen's efforts,[182] lent his enthusiastic approval to this attempt to rescue Thomistic ethics from "le blocage avec théologie."[183] However, Kluxen's views on the possibility of extracting and constructing a systematic natural or (what I shall treat as equivalent) philosophical ethics from Thomistic theology are highly qualified and subtly phrased. He allows that, in its original theological setting, Aquinas's moral science may be called a "system": to repeat an important observation, "Thomistic ethics *as system* is found only in Thomistic theology" (87). From this point, Kluxen proceeds to argue that (1) while there is no "independent system of a natural practical science" in Aquinas's theology, (2) the principles of practical reason cannot be considered to be "senseless in themselves," and (3) hence it would seem that a "higher interpretation" or *"Aufheben"* of Thomis-

179. "Unde cum duplex felicitas a philosophis ponatur, una contemplativa et alia activa, ut patet in X Ethicorum, secundum hoc etiam duas partes philosophiae distinxerunt, moralem dicentes practicam, naturalem et rationalem dicentes theoricam" *(Expos. de Trin.*, q. 5, a. 1, ad 4 [Decker, 14–18, p. 169]).

180. Kluxen argues *(Philosophische Ethik*, 93–101), nonetheless, that Aquinas's ethical synthesis, because it takes a theological point of view surpassing that of any natural ethics, needs—as well as implicitly contains—a "metaphysics of action" that reunites moral precepts to their divine foundations, the God who has revealed Himself as a legislator.

181. See Kluxen, *Philosophische Ethik*, xxxii: "Die philosophische Ethik des Thomas 'steckt' also in der Moraltheologie 'drin', und zwar so, dass sie in der ihr eigenen Struktur nicht unmittelbar abhebbar ist. Es bedarf einer sorgsamen Operation, diese Struktur festzustellen, die philosophischen Aussagen auf sie zu beziehen und so zu bestimmen, was denn eigentlich Thomas selbst als die philosophische Ethik ansah. Das ist die Aufgabe, die zu lösen ist."

182. See V. J. Bourke, Review of *Philosophische Ethik bei Thomas von Aquin*, by Wolfgang Kluxen, *New Scholasticism* 39 (1965): 265–67; and J. de Finance, S.J., Review of *Philosophische Ethik bei Thomas von Aquin*, by Wolfgang Kluxen, *Gregorianum* 46 (1965): 432–33.

183. M. Corvez, Review of *Philosophische Ethik bei Thomas von Aquin*, by Wolfgang Kluxen, *Revue thomiste* 69 (1969): 514.

tic theology could lead to "a *'Systematik'* of natural moral science" (87–88). The philosophical product of this *Aufhebung*, which Kluxen carefully describes as a *"Systematik"* ("systematics"?) rather than as an enclosed and comprehensive *"System"* of "natural moral science," presumably because it must be able to indicate "the limits of its own horizons," is supposed to be open-ended enough for the theologian to show how it can receive its needed conceptual completion in theology. What needs to be completed, of course, is a philosophical ethics which has speculatively understood that the natural desire for *eudaimonia* is to be fulfilled only in knowing God's essence, even as it admits that knowing how such an end may be practically attained is beyond the resources of philosophy.[184]

Now it is this last condition, the self-limitation of philosophical reason that requires a theological completion of the natural (i.e., philosophical) Thomistic moral science, that makes Kluxen's proposal perplexing, ambiguous, and—as I shall argue—philosophically unachievable if not philosophically incomprehensible. It is theology from the outside, not any philosophy from the inside, that can grasp and articulate this self-limitation of "natural moral science." This large conclusion, however, will only emerge from many smaller analyses of Aquinas's moral science.

The general issue, however, can be easily enough raised now. Does the attempt to extract a genuinely philosophical Thomistic ethics from Aquinas's theological ethics, despite the erudition and exegetical subtlety of those who have recently proposed it, actually lead to a conceptual impasse beyond which the philosopher cannot go, an *aporia* in the original sense of the term?[185] We must ask how could a philosopher recognize, in the sense that Kluxen requires, the limitations of man's natural moral science, a conception that turns out to be exactly congruent with a higher or subsuming theological truth about natural morality, and yet have such a recognition remain solely philosophical? As a way of initially locating this *aporia*, consider briefly the encounter of the nonbelieving philosopher with biblical revelation as Leo Strauss brilliantly, albeit controversially, poses it:

. . . as a philosopher, he refuses assent to anything which is not evident to him, and revelation is for him not more than an unevident, unproven

184. See Kluxen, *Philosophische Ethik*, ch. 9, §3, "Das 'Naturverlangen' nach der Gottesschau als spekulativ erfahrbarer Grund des Ordnungsgefüges der unvollkommenen Glückseligkeit," 154–57.

185. See *Metaph.*, II, 1, 995a27–37.

possibility. Confronted with an unproven possibility, he does not reject, he merely suspends judgment . . . [but] the philosopher who refuses to assent to revelation because it is not evident therewith rejects revelation.[186]

Doubtless there are objections that can be brought against this portrayal of the nonbelieving philosopher. According to one modern school of Thomist theologians, the philosopher without faith, contrary to what Strauss apodeictically asserts, could find the fact of a revelation, since it is supported by miracles, to be rationally credible; in other words, it is logically possible for the philosopher to judge with certitude that the miracles establish that the alleged revelation is actually supernatural in origin. Even so, the content of revealed supernatural teachings surpasses the evidentiary value of the accompanying miracles and hence the substance of a supernatural revelation remains, in Strauss's words, philosophically unevident and unproven.[187] We can continue, then, to use Strauss to frame the present issue.

Any theological doctrines that are able to complete philosophical ethics are supernatural truths that divinely infused faith alone can recognize and access. It follows, then, that any philosophical ethics, authentically developed from "below," that is to say, developed without any theological controls, cannot be by design open-ended to the complimentary supernatural truths of theology. Such an ethics can merely turn out, by happy accident, to be open-ended to theology. In fact, it would be more accurate to say that some philosophies are neutral to theology, neither requiring nor contradicting theological doctrines. So described, would not the strictly neutral philosopher judge that any so-called *Aufhebung* of Aquinas's moral science, that conveniently results in a philosophically open-ended ethics, really amounts only to a theological deconstruction of a theological ethics? This, in any case, is the issue that will occupy us at length throughout this book.

Let us assume, however, that Kluxen and other distinguished scholars of a similar persuasion have no interest in extracting a "dead theology" to serve as a philosophy. Rather, they are prepared to treat "Tho-

186. Leo Strauss, "The Mutual Influence of Theology and Philosophy," *Independent Journal of Philosophy* 3 (1979): 113.

187. Cf. Reginald Garrigou-Lagrange, O.P., *De Revelatione per Ecclesiam Catholicam Proposita*, 2 vols., 4th ed., rev. (Rome: Libreria Editrice Religiosa, 1945), 1:493: "Ratio enim ex se sola, consideratione miraculorum potest cognoscere factum revelationis . . . sed ratio ex se sola non potest cognoscere revelationem divinam, ut est supernaturalis quoad substantiam procedens a Deo . . ."; 190: "Hoc supernaturale quoad substantiam est simul supernaturale quoad cognoscibilitatem,

mistic moral theology . . . [as] another and most complicated story."[188] Having put that story aside, they are then able to claim that the principles of Aquinas's moral science permit and can be sustained in an independent or autonomous Thomistic philosophical ethics. Again, let us suppose that this ethics cannot and will not be merely bits and pieces extracted from Aquinas's theology; it needs to be systematically developed. Nonetheless, can we merely put aside Aquinas's "moral theology," so easily? Why and how is a systematic Thomistic moral science theological? Is it theological by its essence or merely by the accident of its historical setting? Or does the pursuit of an autonomous philosophical Thomistic ethics actually contradict the fundamental structure of Thomistic moral science?

These questions lead any interpreter of Aquinas to ponder, as Kluxen took care to do, the status of the moral philosophy allegedly submerged in Aquinas's theology. But especially at this point, one must plot one's own course. Aquinas, however much his theology embodies and depends upon its own rational principles, did not, in fact, provide any explicit guidelines for the autonomous development of what, after all, not he but only some of his readers have called Aquinas's "Christian philosophy."[189] "Christian philosophy," so I have argued, is itself a highly complex philosophical notion that resonates with the problems inherent in philosophical pluralism. It can be expected that an autonomous philosophical Thomistic ethics, if it is regarded as a particular instantiation of "Christian philosophy," will be no less complex and resonant. Still, our questions about the accidentally or essentially theological character of Thomistic moral science, if we wish to use Aquinas's principles to answer them, can only be approached by first attending to what he did talk about.

One way to begin, a way that is perhaps unavoidable for a contemporary philosopher, is to trace how Aquinas coordinates faith and reason with theology and philosophy. But, here as elsewhere, one may know

---

excedens scilicet vires naturales cognoscitivas cuiuslibet naturae intellectualis creatae. . . ."

For an extensive discussion of the role of reason in determining the *credibilia*, see Roger Aubert, *Le Problème de l'acte de foi: Données traditionnelles et résultats des controverses récentes* (Louvain: E. Warny, 1958).

188. Ralph McInerny, *Ethica Thomistica: The Moral Philosophy of Thomas Aquinas* (Washington, D.C.: The Catholic University of America Press. 1982), 123.

189. For significantly different overviews of the hermeneutical questions surrounding Aquinas's philosophical *opuscula* and commentaries on Aristotle, cf. Wippel, "Problem of Christian Philosophy," 24–33; and Joseph Owens, C.Ss.R., "Aquinas as Aristotelian Commentator," in *St. Thomas Aquinas, 1274–1974: Commemorative Studies* (Toronto: Pontifical Institute of Mediaeval Studies, 1974), 1:213–38.

where to begin but not exactly how to proceed. The contemporary interpreter finds an obstacle standing between us and St. Thomas; especially in this instance, what may seem obvious to us must be set aside.[190] Aquinas's distinction between philosophy and theology cannot be approached by way of modern philosophical distinctions between faith and reason. This modern perspective greatly distorts Aquinas.

5. Faith and Reason

The basic modern distinctions between faith and reason have been set—to mention only three stellar figures—by Descartes, Kant, and Hegel. Their notions about theology and its relationship to philosophy, which were propagated by legions of epigones in the seventeenth, eighteenth, and nineteenth centuries, are now taken for granted in the twentieth century.

Descartes, who is usually identified as the immediate progenitor of the distinctively modern outlook,[191] informed the Sorbonne theologians about the proper role of philosophy vis-à-vis theology.

I have always thought that two topics—namely, God and the soul—are prime examples of subjects where demonstrative proofs ought to be given with the aid of philosophy rather than theology.[192]

Because it is a matter of providing rational demonstrations, Descartes assigned to philosophy and not to theology the task of proving God's existence.[193]

Such philosophical proofs, along with the Cartesian confidence in reason, fell into disrepute after Kant's critique. In the Kantian framework, speculative theology has solely a heuristic value for science,

190. See Giuseppe Abbà, *Lex et virtus: Studi sull' evoluzione della dottrina morale di san Tommaso d'Aquino* (Rome: Libreria Ateneo Salesiano, 1983), 88.

191. In fact, Descartes had his own progenitors. But the historical background to the Cartesian approach is less well known. It is found in the sixteenth and seventeenth-century Scholastic philosophical syntheses, notably those produced by the Jesuits of Coimbra (the *Conimbricenses*) and the Carmelites of Alcala (the *Complutenses*) and of Salamanca (the *Salmanticenses*). For different evaluations of their philosophical merits, cf. John Deely, Editorial Afterword, appendix to *Tractatus De Signis: The Semiotic of John Poinsot* (Berkeley and Los Angeles: University of California Press, 1985), 400–402; and Gilson, "Christian Philosophy," 184–85.

192. Rene Descartes, "Dedicatory Letter to the Sorbonne," *Meditations on First Philosophy,* in *The Philosophical Writings of Descartes*, trans. John Cottingham, Robert Stoothhoff, and Dugald Murdoch (Cambridge: Cambridge University Press, 1984), 2:3.

193. See Michael J. Buckley, S.J., *At the Origins of Modern Atheism* (New Haven, Conn.: Yale University Press, 1987), 74–77.

since it promotes (what turns out to be) the endless pursuit of the final cause; but it cannot "expand or correct our knowledge of nature, or in fact of any theory whatever."[194] Dismissing all theoretical proofs for the existence and attributes of God, Kant only allowed that the ultimate rational requirements of morality necessitate a practical faith in God whom we must believe to be the just moral governor of men. Philosophy expresses this faith in an "ethicotheology."[195] Surveying Kant's followers, Friedrich Heinrich Jacobi accurately epitomized what they left to postcritical theology: "It is generally acknowledged [that] God cannot be known, but only believed."[196]

Hegel, who insisted on the speculative riches of orthodox church doctrine, repudiated these Kantian strictures: reason can attain theoretical knowledge of infinite being. But Hegelian dialectical reason (Vernunft), despite its author's own admiration for the rational character of medieval theology, is adamantly philosophical; Hegel defined philosophical reason in contrast to theology's reliance on the understanding (Verstand) which represents rather than conceptually produces or comprehends its object.[197] Theological explanations are at best quasi-rational and at worst pictorial metaphors. Consequently, theology remains, for Hegel as with Kant, in a position inferior to philosophy. In the later nineteenth century, post-Hegelian thinkers—whether they were right-wing friends or left-wing enemies of religious faith—continued to assign revelation, faith, and historical religion to theology; in contrast, reason (i.e., scientific arguments leading to speculative knowledge) belonged exclusively to philosophy.[198]

Historically, there have been many conceptions of how philosophy relates to theology.[199] But the contemporary discussion of the relationship is overshadowed by the dichotomy posed by the great modern

194. Immanuel Kant, Critique of Judgment, trans. Werner S. Pluhar (Indianapolis, Ind.: Hackett, 1987), 377 [Berlin Academy edition, 5:482].

195. See ibid., 380 [Berlin Academy edition, 5:485].

196. Friedrich Heinrich Jacobi, "Open Letter to Fichte," in Philosophy of German Idealism, ed. Ernst Behler (New York: Continuum, 1987), 121.

197. See The Logic of Hegel: Encyclopedia of the Philosophical Sciences, trans. William Wallace, 2d ed., rev. (Oxford: Oxford University Press, 1892), 73–75; Lectures on the Philosophy of Religion, 1: 115–132.

198. See Karl Lowith, From Hegel to Nietzsche: The Revolution in 19th Century Thought, trans. David E. Green (London: Constable, 1965).

199. For some patristic and medieval conceptions of the theology/philosophy and faith/reason distinctions, see Denis J. M. Bradley, "Philosophy and Theology, Western: To Mid 12th Century," in Dictionary of the Middle Ages (New York: Charles Scribner's Sons, 1987), 9:582–90. The modern philosophical history of the problem is expertly covered in James Collins, The Emergence of Philososphy of

philosophers. Descartes, Kant, and Hegel assign faith to theology and reason to philosophy. Read against this background, certain texts of Aquinas appear to fit the modern paradigm. Aquinas says, and never departs from the position, that theology is grounded on faith, philosophy on reason: "Just as sacred doctrine is founded on the light of faith, so philosophy is founded on the light of natural reason" *(Expos. de Trin.,* q. 2, a. 3 [Decker, 15–16, p. 94]).[200] Nonetheless, the modern philosophical disjunction of faith and reason cannot be imposed on Aquinas;[201] it leads to the radical separation of theology from reason, a separation that Aquinas never allows.

Aquinas, on the other hand, never conflates appealing to religious authorities and appealing to rational arguments. Depending on what is controverted, one or the other appeal is called for. If one needs to show that a particular doctrine pertains to the faith, especially against the protestations of a heretic, the theologian must appeal to some religious authority that the heretic recognizes—be it the Old Testament, or the New Testament, or the doctrine of the saints. Faith seeking understanding demands another course. Intellectual understanding of faith is generated by reasoned explanations of why the belief is true. The task of the theologian, especially the master who teaches in the university, is to provide such explanations for his students. Otherwise, they leave the classroom intellectually empty.[202]

Theology, then, is committed to reason but the foundation of theology is revealed doctrine. The second mode of judging [the mode of knowledge] pertains to this [theological] doctrine, inasmuch as it is acquired through study, although its principles are acquired through revelation. *(ST,* I, q. 1, a. 6, ad 3)[203]

Religion (New Haven, Conn.: Yale University Press, 1967). Contemporary issues are astutely analyzed in Richard Swinburne, *Faith and Reason* (Oxford: Clarendon Press, 1981).

200. "Sicut autem sacra doctrina fundatur supra lumen fidei, ita philosophia fundatur supra lumen naturale rationis . . ." *(Expos. de Trin.,* q. 2, a. 3 [Decker, 15–16, p. 94]).

201. On the other hand, James Collins, in "Christian Philosophers and the Modern Turn," in *The Impact of Belief: The New Dialogue of Philosophy and Theology,* ed. George F. McLean (Lancaster, Pa.: Concorde, 1974), 7, emphasizes that modern philosophers' "deep discontent with explaining the faith-philosophy relationship . . . is combined with an intense interest in the human attitude of faith itself."

202. See *Quod.* IV, q. 9, a. 3 (Spiazzi, 83).

203. "Secundus autem modus judicandi [per modum cognitionis] pertinet ad hanc doctrinam, secundum quod per studium habetur, licet ejus principia ex revelatione habeantur" *(ST,* I, q. 1, a. 6, ad 3).

But if theology is founded on revelation and philosophy on reason, it is not faith, according to Aquinas, that *exclusively* distinguishes theology from philosophy. There is a role for belief in both philosophy and theology, and reason, in fact, belongs to theology as much as it belongs to philosophy. Now this kind of conjunction of reason and faith is enough to discomfort both the modern rationalist and the modern fideist.[204] To the modern point of view, which treats faith and reason dichotomously, Aquinas's account of "theological reason" is alien. But in its own terms, the Thomistic account is remarkably coherent. Moreover, it is only when viewed in its own terms that one can simultaneously grasp the theological status and the rational character of Aquinas's moral science.

6. Theology and Moral Science

In the Thomistic context, a moral philosophy is philosophical not because it is rational, but because of the formal point of view from which it derives its unity as a science. Theology has a unique and defining perspective: how things are related to God. Thus, "all things are considered in sacred doctrine under the formality [*ratio*] of God."[205] Thomistic moral science is theological because it considers human actions exactly from this perspective. In the Prologue to the *Prima secundae* of the *Summa theologiae*, Aquinas pointedly asserts that man is created in God's image. This assertion provides the framework for Thomistic ethics: God is the exemplar, man the image. As the image of God, man acts freely and intelligently. In acting in accordance with right reason, man acts virtuously. Nonetheless, the *Secunda secundae*, which treats the various virtues that are the principles of particular actions, begins with a discussion of the *theological virtues:* faith, hope, and charity. This procedure indicates, as I have already discussed, that humanly acquired virtues are to be viewed from the beginning as subordinated to divinely infused virtues. This subordination is essential in the Thomistic scheme of the virtues because only

---

204. It is misleading, I think, to describe Thomistic theology as a "synthesis of two profoundly heterogenous elements, the revealed datum and philosophy." (Van Steenberghen, *Introduction*, 104) In the case of those doctrines that can be grasped philosophically, there is, in fact, no "heterogeneity" between the "elements." Cf. Abbà, *Lex et virtus*, 136: ". . . la teologia tomista e in particolare la *ST.* Non un ibrido di fede e ragione filosofica, ma una scienza nuova; non una filosofia in un contesto teologico, ma una ragione teologica . . . una scienza speculativa su Dio."

205. See *ST,* I, q. 1, a. 7: "Omnia autem pertractantur in sacra doctrina sub ratione Dei."

the theological virtues and the attendant infused intellectual and moral virtues can lead man to his ultimate end.

The perspective of Thomistic moral science, which is set by the theological virtues, corresponds to the sublime end that the Christian moral agent seeks. Aquinas holds to an *eudaimonistic* "moral point of view" but ultimate beatitude is not the philosophical beatitude proposed by Aristotle but eternal union with God through seeing the divine essence.[206] That such a vision is possible, and that indeed it is the only ultimate end toward which man is actually oriented, are truths that only sacred doctrine provides. Thomistic moral science takes this *revelatum* as a premise even as Aquinas labors mightily to show that such an end corresponds to the deepest exigencies of human reason and will. These arguments, as we shall see later in this book, raise the problem of "Christian philosophy" in all of its force. What can an autonomous Thomistic *philosophical* ethics know of a supernatural end that utterly transcends man's metaphysical and moral capacity to achieve?

For the present, though, we can adhere to the strictly theological point of view, that human acts either lead or do not lead to union with God. From this perspective, the immediate or proximate ends of action must be judged as to whether or not they are in harmony with the ultimate end, union with God.

Since things are referred to the ultimate common end through a proper end, the diverse relationship of things to the ultimate end is achieved, therefore, corresponding to the diversity of the proper end. Consequently, it ought to be said that as there is one ultimate end of all things, God, so there is one ultimate end of all that is willed, namely, God. Nonetheless, there are other, proximate ends and if, in regard to these ends, the appropriate relationship of the will to the ultimate end is preserved, the will will be rectitudinous; if it is not preserved, [the will] will be perverse. *(II Sent.*, d. 38, q. 1, a. 1 [Mandonnet, 968])[207]

Aquinas's moral science is theological because it considers what is morally good or bad for man from the standpoint of a man's move-

206. See *ST,* I–II, q. 3, a. 8.

207. ". . . et quia res referuntur ad finem ultimum communem, mediante fine proprio, ideo secundum diversitatem finis proprii efficitur diversa relatio rerum ad finem ultimum. Sic ergo dicendum est quod sicut rerum omnium est unus ultimus finis, scilicet Deus, ita et voluntatum omnium est unus ultimus finis, scilicet Deus; nihilominus tamen sunt alii fines proximi, et, si secundum illos fines servetur debita relatio voluntatis in finem ultimum, erit recta voluntas; si autem non, erit perversa" *(II Sent.*, d. 38, q. 1, a. 1 [Mandonnet, 968]).

ment toward his ultimate end, the beatifying vision of God. But how does one judge whether an action is or is not in conformity with that end?

Aquinas explains that the ultimate norm of what is morally good or bad is the revealed law of God. Nonetheless, the proximate norm, which does not depend on faith in revelation, is human reason. Aquinas finds no conflict between these two norms. On the contrary, "Man is disposed to God through reason which enables him to know God."[208] Human actions that are in accord with human reason are, by that fact, in accord with the will of God.

> It means the same thing [to say] that vice and sin are contrary to the order of human reason and that they are contrary to the eternal law. (ST, I–II, q. 71, a. 2, ad 4)[209]

The larger point is that if some proposition is not in accord with revelation, it cannot be in accord with reason. Underlying these confident assertions of the harmony of faith and reason is a theological notion of reason. In endowing men with reason, God has created in us a "likeness of the uncreated truth."[210] Given that similitude, de facto conflicts between faith and reason can in principle be resolved.

What, then, is the primary role of revelation in determining moral norms? Before answering this specific question, it is necessary, of course, to have some understanding of the fundamental purpose of divine revelation. As it turns out, Aquinas's conception of revelation is directly geared to this specific question: revelation is given so that human beings may learn to desire and to strive to attain their ultimate end, the vision of God. That end needs to be revealed because it surpasses reason.[211]

> The ultimate happiness of man consists in a supernatural vision of God. Man is not able to attain this vision except by way of learning from God the teacher. (ST, II–II, q. 2, a. 3)[212]

208. ". . . homo ordinatur ad Deum per rationem, per quam Deum cognoscere potest . . ." (Quod. II, q. 4, a. 2, ad 4 [Spiazzi, 29]).

209. "Eiusdem rationis est quod vitium et peccatum sit contra ordinem rationis humanae et quod sit contra legem aeternam" (ST, I–II, q. 71, a. 2, ad 4).

210. See De ver., q. 11, a. 1 (Spiazzi, 226): "Huiusmodi autem rationis lumen, quo principia huiusmodi sunt nobis nota, est nobis a Deo inditum, quasi quaedam similitudo increatae veritatis in nobis resultantis."

211. See III Sent., d. 23, q. 1, a. 4, sol. 3; ST, I, q. 1, a. 1; q. 94, a. 3; SCG, I, 5.

212. ". . . ultima beatitudo hominis consistit in quadam supernaturali Dei visione. Ad quam quidem visionem homo pertingere non potest nisi per modum addiscentis a Deo doctore . . . " (ST, II–II, q. 2, a. 3).

7. Revelation and Human Intelligence

To the recipient, revelation is self-confirming; it carries its own certitude because it brings to the believer what Aquinas calls "an interior and intelligible light"[213] that enables the human intellect to glimpse certain superrational truths about God and divine things. Revelation, however, is always conformed to the human mode of knowing, which remains anchored in sensation and imagination.

Unless man is changed to another state, it is necessary that even in knowledge by means of grace, which is through divine revelation, the intellect always has insight through a phantasm. . . . *(De ver.,* q. 18, a. 5 [Spiazzi, 347])[214]

What we know, not how we know, is revealed.[215] In this life, we know God in the way that we know something reflected in a mirror—through an effect:

. . . either through a natural effect as the philosophers came to God by a natural knowledge through the knowledge of creatures; or through a spiritual effect, as in the vision of faith of one who adheres to other things which are revealed through the influence of a spiritual light. . . . *(II Sent.,* d. 23, q. 2, a. 1 [Mandonnet, 573])[216]

While fitted to the human way of knowing things, revelation is profoundly salutary. Its truths enable the ordinary man to compensate for his lack of philosophy and the philosopher to overcome his own moral weaknesses and the obscurities of philosophical knowledge. And philosophical knowledge of God is obscure; it is entirely dependent on the instrumentality of the forms that can be abstracted from sensible things. The Aristotelian intelligence, because it is at home only in the sensible world, can know only the essences of sensible things. While

---

213. See *SCG,* III, 154 (Pera, n. 3258, p. 229): "Quae quidem revelatio fit quodam interiori et intelligibili lumine mentem elevante . . . et de his quae supernaturali lumine apprehendit, certitudinem habet."

214. "Unde nisi homo in alium statum mutetur, oportet quod etiam in cognitione gratiae, quae est per revelationem divinam, semper intellectus inspicit ad phantasmata . . ." *(De ver.,* q. 18, a. 5 [Spiazzi, 347]).

215. See *Expos. de Trin.,* q. 6, a. 3 (Decker, 11–13, p. 221): "Unde quamvis per revelationem elevemur ad aliquid cognoscendum, quod alias esset nobis ignotum, non tamen ad hoc quod alio modo cognoscamus nisi per sensibilia."

216. ". . . sive per effectum naturalem, sicut per cognitionem creaturarum naturali cognitione philosophi in Deum devenerunt; sive per effectum spiritualem, sicut est in visione fidei illius qui adhaeret his quae aliis revelata sunt per influentiam spiritualis luminis . . ." *(II Sent.,* d. 23, q. 2, a. 1 [Mandonnet, 573]).

reason can reach into the supersensible world and know God, it does so only because it can pursue the causal origin of sensible things.[217] It can only know God as First Cause of nature.

Metaphysical knowledge of God is confined to those conclusions that can be derived "through the medium of arguments that proceed from sensible creatures."[218] But, at once, the Thomistic metaphysician stands before an infinite gap that opens between the Creator and His creation.[219] God, whose essence is His existence, does not belong to a genus and, a fortiori, He cannot be conceived as belonging to a genus shared in common with created things, whose essences participate existence. Because God's being and the being of creatures are diverse, metaphysical (as well as revealed) knowledge of God is radically imperfect. From knowing these nonproportionate effects, we know that God is, and through an ascending series of more and more refined negations of creaturely perfections, what He is not. But, in this life, we never can know, not even from revelation, the divine essence.[220] Revelation also is a knowledge of God from effects that are never adequate to their cause.[221]

Our knowledge of the separate substances is subject to the same limitation.[222]

Therefore we know about immaterial forms that they are, and, in place of knowledge of what they are we have knowledge through negation, through causality, and through transcendence. . . . (Expos. de Trin., q. 6, a. 3 [Decker, 11–13, p. 223])[223]

217. See Expos. de Trin., q. 1, a. 4 (Decker, 14–16, p. 76): "Et ideo naturali ratione de deo cognoscere non possumus nisi hoc quod percipitur de ipso ex habitudine effectuum ad ipsum. . . ."

218. ". . . per medium argumentationis ex creaturis sensibilibus procedens . . ." (II Sent., d. 23, q. 2, a.1, ad 1 [Mandonnet, 574]).

219. See I Sent., prologus, q. 1, a. 1 (Mandonnet, 7): "Item, effectus non proportionatus causae, imperfecte ducit in cognitionem suae causae. Talis autem effectus est omnis creatura respectu Creatoris, a quo in infinitum distat."

220. See ST, I, q. 12, a. 13, ad 1: ". . . licet per revelationem gratiae in hac vita non cosgnoscamus de Deo quid est, et sic ei quasi ignoto coniungamur; tamen plenius ipsum cognoscimus, inquantum plures et excellentiores effectus eius nobis demonstrantur; et inquantum ei aliqua attribuimus ex revelatione divina, ad quae ratio naturalis non pertingit, ut Deum esse trinum et unum."

221. See Expos. de Trin., q. 1, a. 2 (Decker, 23–26, p. 65): ". . . alius effectus est, qui deficit a praedicta aequalitate, et per talem effectum non potest comprehendi virtus agentis et per consequens nec essentia eius; sed cognoscitur tantum de causa quod est."

222. See ST, I, q. 84, a. 7, ad 3.

223. "Ita ergo de formis immaterialibus cognoscimus an est et habemus de eis

In short, we can know that the separate substances exist and negatively define some of their properties, but we cannot know their essences.[224] But even in this limited form, metaphysical knowledge of the separate substances and the principles common to all being is difficult to attain because such knowledge is so removed from its origins in sensible things. To the intrinsic limitations of human intelligence, which by its natural principles is confined to sensible things, the philosopher adds his own individual debilities. Like the ordinary man, who has neither the leisure nor the intellectual ability to pursue philosophy, the philosopher can also stumble from the ordinary burdens, passion, stupidity, toil, and fatigue. He can especially go wrong in figuring out the end and purpose of human life.[225]

That men are so misguided on something so fundamental is perplexing. In one sense, nature leads us all in the same direction: all men eagerly desire fulfillment or happiness, that *eudaimonia* that is the goal of all the Aristotelian virtues. But what specific end will fulfill us seems peculiarly elusive. What is the end that will truly fulfill a man throughout and perhaps beyond a lifetime of striving and acting? Aquinas, repeating Augustine, thinks that philosophers have provided a grotesquely large number of contradictory answers to this question. But, for Aquinas, reason's incapacity to grasp man's ultimate end is a sign not only of reason's corrigible mistakes but also of reason's unsurpassable limits. Aquinas argues that men can acquire a knowledge of their true (supernatural) end only through faith.

> Since the end of human life is beatitude, which consists in the full knowledge of divine things, it is necessary, so as to direct human life towards batitude, to have from the very beginning faith in divine things. . . . *(Expos. de Trin.*, q. 3, a. 1 [Decker, 3–5, p. 111])[226]

But this belief is not just a starting point that can, eventually, be abandoned. Neither has the ordinary man clearly imagined nor can any philosopher adequately demonstrate the supernatural end of man. Only the believer, who accepts sacred doctrine, knows that the actual destiny of man is to see God's essence and that here and now God guides men toward this vision.

---

loco cognitionis quid est cognitionem per negationem, per causalitatem et per excessum . . ." *(Expos. de Trin.*, q. 6, a. 3 [Decker, 11–13, p. 223]).

224. See *Expos. de Trin.*, q. 6, a. 3; a. 4, ad 2.

225. See *De ver.*, q. 5, a. 1; q. 6, a. 4; *Expos. de Trin.*, q. 3, a. 1.

226. "Cum ergo finis humanae vitae sit beatitudo, quae consistit in plena cognitione divinorum, necessarium est ad humanam vitam in beatitudinem dirigendam

The ultimate perfection to which man is ordered consists in the perfect knowledge of God which he is not able to attain except through the action and instruction of God who knows Himself perfectly. (De ver., q. 14, a. 10 [Spiazzi, 300])[227]

As a complement to faith, Aquinas demonstrates that this belief is in conformity with human nature since only this end, seeing God Himself, can radically fulfill the deepest human desire for beatitude. To attain this end, however, one must know how to pursue God in this life. To pursue God in this life is to act in a morally good fashion. To act in a morally good fashion is to act rationally. There is, then, an irreducible tie between supernatural beatitude and human rationality. But if so, why and how does morality need faith?

8. Revelation and Morality

For the believer in the biblical God, the Ten Commandments are divinely revealed precepts that tell men how to fulfill God's will. But in Thomistic moral science, there is no question of obeying rules, even divinely revealed rules, solely for the formality of being in conformity with what God or practical reason dictates.[228] Moral precepts are given so that men may become virtuous.[229] And the humanly acquired moral virtues, under the guidance of divinely infused charity, may themselves be directed toward a higher good. By inculcating the virtues, the Decalogue, no less than the commandments of the New Law, teaches fallible men how to attain friendship with each other and God.[230] Precisely as images of God, men through reason and will are united to God, who is infinite intelligence and will.[231] Obedience to the revealed commandments unites man's will to God's will. The Decalogue commands the intellectual virtues, which rightly order reason itself to

statim a principio habere fidem divinorum . . ." (Expos. de Trin., q. 3, a. 1 [Decker, 3–5, p. 111]).

227. "Ultima autem perfectio ad quam homo ordinatur, consistit in perfecta Dei cognitione: ad quam quidem pervenire non potest nisi operatione Dei, qui est sui perfectus cognitor" (De ver., q. 14, a. 10 [Spiazzi, 300]).

228. See ST, II–II, prologus: ". . . tota materia morali ad considerationem virtutum reducta. . . ."

229. See ST, I–II, q. 100, a. 9, ad 2; II–II, q. 112, a. 1, ad 1.

230. See ST, I–II, q. 99, a. 1, ad 2: ". . . ad hoc enim omnis lex tendit, ut amicitiam constituat vel hominum ad invicem, vel hominis ad Deum."

231. See ST, I–II, q. 100, a. 2: "Homo autem Deo conjungitur ratione, sive mente, in qua est Dei imago."

God, and the moral virtues, which subordinate inner passions and outer actions to reason.[232]

In addition to moral precepts, revealed law contains ceremonial and judicial precepts, which God or men appointed by God can command; the latter precepts oblige, not from reason, but from the authority of the divine lawgiver.[233] Aquinas, however, considers these revealed ceremonial precepts to be further specifications or determinations of the moral (i.e., natural) law. Natural law dictates that men worship God; revealed law presupposes this moral precept but directs that worship be conducted according to certain rites *(ST,* I–II, q. 99, a. 3, ad 2).

As an expression of sacred doctrine, biblical morality is revealed morality. But revealed morality is not to be defined in opposition to a morality of reason. On the contrary, Aquinas states that if a revealed precept is to be identified as a moral precept, it is also to be identified as a precept of reason.

In regard to the precepts of any law, some have the power of binding from the very dictate of reason, because natural reason dictates that this ought to be done or to be avoided. And precepts of this type are called moral precepts: human morals are defined as deriving from reason. *(ST,* I–II, q. 104, a. 1)[234]

Revealed morality is rational and is commanded because it is such: "The commandments of the Decalogue are about the things that natural reason dictates."[235] In that sense, revealed law presupposes natural law.[236] Or, as a contemporary philosopher might put it, Aquinas grants that the moral precepts of the revealed law are susceptible to rational justification. If so, the philosopher can agree that the Decalogue, because it is rational, binds all men and not just believers.[237]

For Aquinas, however, the rational character of the Decalogue does

232. See *SCG,* III, 129 (Pera, n. 3010, p. 1910): "Ex praeceptis enim legis divinae mens hominis ordinatur sub Deo; et omnia alia quae sunt in homine sub ratione."

233. See *ST,* I–II, q. 104, a. 4, ad 2: "Sed praecepta judicialia et caeremonialia habent aliam rationem obligationis, non quidem ex ratione naturali, sed ex sola institutione."

234. ". . . praeceptorum cujuscumque legis quaedam habent vim obligandi ex ipso dictamine rationis, quia naturalis ratio dictat hoc esse debitum fieri vel vitari. Et hujusmodi praecepta dicuntur moralia: eo quod a ratione dicuntur mores humani" *(ST,* I–II, q. 104, a. 1).

235. ". . . mandata Decalogi sunt de his quae naturalis ratio dictat . . ." *(De ver.,* q. 14, a. 11. ad 3 [Spiazzi, 303]).

236. See *ST,* I–II, q. 99, a. 2., ad 1: "Sicut enim gratia praesupponit naturam, ita oportet quod lex divina praesupponit legem naturalem."

237. See *ST,* I–II, q. 98, a. 5.

not supersede its revealed status. The Decalogue, as revealed, remains salutary: it overturns immoral customs, fortifies love by obligation, adds reverence for God to natural inclination, and strengthens memory by repetition *(ST,* I–II, q. 98, a. 5). The Decalogue is revealed not because it transcends the limits of moral reasoning, but to save ordinary men from the ordinary forms of moral turpitude that engender the particular misjudgments and mistakes that they could have avoided if they were more virtuous and thus better able to reason correctly.[238]

At this point, Aquinas seems to have moved full circle. He begins by arguing the necessity of revelation for any understanding of man's ultimate (supernatural) goal and the salutary corrective revealed morality exercises over human passions and cares. At the same time, Aquinas grants that the Decalogue contains only rules that reason can also drive. I shall develop Aquinas's doctrine of the primary and derived precepts of the natural law in Chapters 6 and 7. But here I can take note, in an anticipatory way, of Aquinas's position, that revealed morality is grounded in two "most universal" or "most common precepts," namely, the biblical precepts enjoining love of God and of neighbor. Each of these precepts is indemonstrable or immediately known *(per se notum).* For biblical faith that affirms the existence of God, *"Love the Lord your God!"* is the immediate beginning for morality; for reason, *"Love your neighbor!"*[239]

The revealed Decalogue, Aquinas claims, can be equated with the first set of precepts that practical reason can easily deduce from the two most common principles. This Thomistic equation once again raises the issue that we have been considering. Does not the equation of rational and revealed morality license us to call Aquinas's ethics a *philosophical* science of morality? This conclusion seems fully consonant with Aquinas's own claims. Yet to draw it is to misconstrue Aquinas's conception of the relationshp between theology and philosophy.

238. See *ST,* I–II, q. 99, a. 2, ad 2; q. 100, a. 5, ad 1.
239. "God exists" is not a self-evidently true proposition in this life: see *SCG,* I, 10–11. But it can be easily inferred from other propositions. Men have a confused knowledge that God (or the gods) is the source of the order observed in the universe, see *SCG,* III, 38 (Pera, n. 211, p. 44). Hence, "Love the Lord your God!" which is a "self-evident" *("per se notum")* principle for faith, is an easily derived precept of practical reason once the existence of God has been established: see *ST,* I, q. 100, a. 3, ad 1; a. 4, ad 1. For the proper hermeneutical background for understanding the Thomistic connotations of the term *"per se notum,"* the Anselmian question whether the existence of God is "self-evident," see Luca F. Tuninetti, *"Per se Notum": Die logische Beschaffenheit des Selbstverständlichen im Denken des Thomas von Aquin* (Leiden: E. J. Brill, 1996), 11–26. Cf. *De ver.,* q. 10, a. 12.

Although the principles of Thomistic ethics are rational, these moral principles, *in the context of Aquinas's own moral science,* are theological. They fall precisely under a theological category that Aquinas labels the *"revelabilia."* Although accuracy is best served by using this Latin term, we might—in exceedingly awkward English—call this the Thomistic category of *"that-which-is-able-to-be-revealed"* or, put more simply, *"the revealable."*

II

Science and Theology

Whereas theology or, more precisely, *sacred doctrine* "is based on the light of faith," *philosophy* "is based on the natural light of reason."[1] Nonetheless, Aquinas, unlike so many modern philosophers, did not take the global distinction between faith and reason, which he never blurred in regard to the premises of individual arguments, as the *sufficient* criterion for distinguishing theology from philosophy.[2] The contrary, in fact, was the case. Against the background of Aristotle's notion of how sometimes a scientific demonstration can legitimately take an unproven "hypothesis" (ὑπόθεσις) or "postulate" (αἴτημα) as its premise,[3] Aquinas could confidently argue that faith *(fides)* broadly taken cannot be assigned exclusively to theology, nor reason exclusively to the (philosophical) sciences. Still, Aquinas's apologetic on behalf of "scientific theology" is faced with an initial problem that the medieval reading of Aristotle itself posed. Aristotelian science is grounded on certain "common beliefs" (κοιναὶ δόξαι)[4] or axioms that

---

1. See *Expos. de Trin.*, q. 2, a. 3 (Decker, 15–16, p. 94): "Sicut . . . sacra doctrina fundatur supra lumen fidei, ita philosophia fundatur supra lumen naturale rationis. . . ."

2. Cf. *Expos. de Trin.*, q. 2, a. 3, ad 3 (Decker, 4–6, p. 96): ". . . sacramentum fidei pro tanto dicitur liberum a philosophicis argumentis, quia sub metis philosophiae non coartatur. . . ."

3. See *Apo.*, I, 10, 76b23–34; *ELP*, I, 19, 76b23–34, 1–74 (Leonine ed., I, pt. 2, 70a–71b). An "hypothesis" and a "postulate" are both provable propositions that are assumed but not actually proven in certain circumstances (e.g., teaching mathematics to a learner). If the student is inclined to believe the proposition, it is an "hypothesis," if not, a "postulate." "Hypotheses and postulates differ according to the pupil's attitude" (Richard D. McKirahan, Jr., *Principles and Proofs: Aristotle's Theory of Demonstrative Science* [Princeton, N.J.: Princeton University Press, 1992], 46).

4. See *Metaph.*, III, 2, 996b28: λέγω δὲ ἀποδεικτικὰς τὰς κοινὰς δόξας.

Aquinas calls the "common conceptions" *(communes conceptiones)* implanted by nature. Immediately known and self-evidently true to all rational persons,[5] these indemonstrable common conceptions are also called "axioms" *(dignitates)* or "highest universals" *(maxime univer-sales)*[6] since they are the ultimate common principles of demonstration. Used by all the sciences, these principles, although also considered in logic, are common to all things and, therefore, are properly contained in the subject of metaphysics, namely, being and its properties *(passiones)*.[7] Theology, although it appeals to infallible divine truth,[8] does not rest on immediate principles known to be self-evidently true by all men.[9] How, then, can theology be classified as a "science"?[10]

1. Aristotelian Science

Upon examination, the initial opposition between the principles of Aristotelian science and revealed theology is less diametric than it first appears. According to their diverse subjects, sciences are generically different; as they treat of diverse subjects, they have diverse principles. Thus there are two types of immediate or indemonstrable principles: common and proper. For there to be a demonstration in any particular science, its proper first principles, those *positiones* (θέσεις) that define the subject of the science, must be supplied in addition to

5. For Aquinas, an indemonstrable proposition that is immediate (one whose predicate is contained in the *ratio* of its subject) but is not a self-evident axiom known to be true by everyone, is a *"positio."* The latter is assumed but not known to be true by some: see *ELP,* I, 5, 72a14, 131–43 (Leonine ed., I, pt. 2, 25a–b). For Aristotle, θέσεις are the proper indemonstrable principles of the particular sciences, see ch. 4, sec. 3. For the sources in Boethius for the Latin Aristotelian terminology, see Tuninetti, *"Per Se Notum,"* 55–58.

6. See *In Metaph.,* III, lect. 5.

7. See *ELP,* I, 5, 72a14, 128–30 (Leonine ed., I, pt. 2, 25a); I, 20, 72a30, 113–16 (75a).

8. Theological faith, unlike rational beliefs, rests on the *"ipsa veritas prima,"* which is God Himself: see *III Sent.,* d. 23, q. 2, a. 4, sol. 1 (Moos, n. 201, p. 737).

9. See *III Sent.,* d. 24, q. 1, a. 2, sol. 1 (Moos, n. 51, p. 768): "Nec iterum ea quae sunt fidei, ad principia visa reducere demonstrando possumus."

10. Contrary to this medieval preoccupation, contemporary scholars frequently observe that Aristotle's actual scientific investigations do not fit his logical paradigm for science. See W. Wieland, "Aristotle's Physics and the Problem of Inquiry into Principles," in *Articles on Aristotle,* vol. 1, *Science,* ed. Jonathan Barnes, Malcolm Schofield, and Richard Sorabji (London: Duckworth, 1975), 128: "Aristotle never relies (as do the majority of his successors) on pure immediate intuition to legitimize his doctrine of principles."

the self-evident *dignitates* common to all the sciences.[11] Scientific demonstration, wherein the premises of a syllogism are considered to be the causes of its conclusion, is impossible without prior knowledge of both types of these immediate principles; otherwise, science would founder in an infinite regress of premises whose truth needs yet to be demonstrated. Nevertheless, not every Aristotelian science begins with its own immediate proper principles. There are hierarchically subordinated or *subalternate* sciences[12] wherein the lower science begins with a demonstrable but nondemonstrated proper principle (ὑπόθεσις) which Aquinas translates as "*suppositio*":

> . . . [Certain] propositions are called "suppositions." For there are some propositions which can be proved only by the principles of some other science; therefore, they must be supposed in the one science, although they are proved by the principles of the other science. *(ELP,* I, 5, 72a14, 144–49 [Leonine ed., I, pt. 2, 25b; Larcher trans., 22])[13]

Subalternated sciences, then, rest on *suppositiones* which are "accepted as having truth" (ibid.). This acceptation, which is justified by the authority of the higher science, introduces a moment of strictly *natural belief* into the hierarchy of Aristotelian sciences.[14] "Scientific theology" legitimatizes itself by drawing an analogy between itself and the other sciences.[15] Theological demonstrations derive from revealed principles that, in turn, derive from God's own "divine science." Thus theology, although it rests on *supernatural beliefs*, conforms to Aristotle's paradigm of an inferior science accepting its proximate principles from a superior science.[16]

---

11. See *Apo.,* I, 32, 88b25–29; *ELP,* I, 43, 88b25, 299–323 (Leonine ed., I, pt. 2, 165b).

12. *Apo.,* I, 9, 76a22–25 gives as examples of logically subordinated sciences: (1) geometry which provides the immediate principles for mechanics and optics; (2) arithmetic for harmonics. *Apo.,* I, 13, 78b40–79a1 refers to the subordination of nautical astronomy to mathematical astronomy.

13. ". . . alique propositiones suppositiones dicuntur. Sunt enim quaedam propositiones que non possunt probari nisi per principia alterius sciencie, et ideo oportet quod in illa sciencia supponantur, licet probentur per principia alterius sciencie . . ." *(ELP,* I, 5, 72a14, 145–49 [Leonine ed., I, pt. 2, 25b).

14. See *III Sent.,* d. 23, q. 2, a. 4, sol. 1 (Moos, n. 201, p. 737): "Unde voluntas non dat infallibilem veritatem intellectui credenti alia credibilia, sicut dat infallibilem veritatem [credenti] articulos fidei"; *ST,* II–II, q. 4, a. 5, ad 2: ". . . fides de qua Philosophus loquitur innititur rationi humanae non ex necessitate concludenti. . . ."

15. See *Expos. de Trin.,* q. 2, a. 2, ad 7.

16. The inferior science is a πρὸς ἕν equivocal, designated "science" in reference to the superior science: see *Metaph.,* XI, 3, 1060b36–61a7.

There are some [principles] which in the subalternated sciences are supposed and believed from the superior sciences and they are not immediately known except in the superior sciences. *(Expos. de Trin.,* q. 2, a. 2, ad 5 [Decker, 7–9, p. 89])[17]

Aquinas details *(ELP,* I, 25, 78b34–79a13, 1–182 [Leonine ed., I, pt. 2, 89a–92b]) two types of subalternation among the sciences. These types correspond to the two basic conceptual models that dominate Aristotelian logic and physics: genus to species, and form to matter. According to the first type, science B is subalternated to science A if the subject matter of B is a *species* of the subject matter of A. In this fashion, zoology (the science of living bodies) is subalternated to physics (the science of moving bodies). Corresponding to the second type of subalternation, Aquinas mentions, among other examples, the subordination of the observational science of rainbows to optics, and of optics to geometry. These two subalternated sciences are not species of geometry; rather, in them the formal principles of geometry are applied to different matters. Geometry is concerned with lines and magnitude as they determine what Aquinas calls "intelligible matter"; optics deals with lines determined in visual matter; the science of rainbows treats of particular visual lines that result from the convergence of sun and clouds.

Within any given science, Aristotle distinguishes *(APo.,* I, 9, 76a10–13) between two types of scientific demonstrations: the scientist can demonstrate (1) that a fact is or (2) why the fact is the way it is. Aquinas labels the first type of demonstration a *"quia"* demonstration, the second a *"propter quid"* demonstration.[18] A *propter quid* demonstration, which gives knowledge of why something is so, proceeds from the first and immediate causes of a thing. A *quia* demonstration, which proceeds either from mediate causes or from an effect that (in the demonstration) takes the place of the cause, gives knowledge only of the fact that something is the case. A hoary example makes the point clearly enough. In astronomy, the argument that the planets are near because they do not twinkle is a *quia* demonstration; a *propter quid* demonstration establishes that the planets do not twinkle because they are near. In other words, "being near" is the cause of "not twinkling"; "not twinkling" is an effect of "being near."

---

17. ". . . in scientiis subalternatis supponuntur et creduntur aliqua a scientiis superioribus, et illa non sunt per se nota nisi superioribus scientibus" *(Expos. de Trin.,* q. 2, a. 2, ad 5 [Decker, 7–9, p. 89]).

18. See *ELP,* I, 17, 76a9, 65–81 (Leonine ed., I, pt. 2, 64b–65a).

The same distinctions between *quia* and *propter quid* demonstrations apply in the case of diverse but subalternated sciences. Thus the subalternating or superior science (A) provides *propter quid* demonstrations of what is known in the inferior science (B). The inferior or subalternated science (B), inasmuch as it receives its principles from science (A), provides only *quia* demonstrations of the conclusions reached in its own science (B).

In the superior science there is given a *propter quid* demonstration of those things that in the inferior science are known only according to a *quia* demonstration *(Expos. de Trin.,* q. 5, a. 1, ad 5 [Decker, 2-3, p. 171])[19]

In the hierarchy of the sciences already mentioned, optics receives its principles from geometry. Since only geometry grasps the axioms governing magnitude and lines, only geometry can provide the *propter quid* knowledge of the cause of the visual phenomena treated in optics. But once it has received these principles, optics can in turn provide *propter quid* explanations of matters treated in the observational science of rainbows.[20]

On this Aristotelian basis, which encompasses the notion of a hierarchy of subalternated sciences, theology can be meaningfully compared to Aristotelian "science."[21] Theology is a science subalternated to "divine science,"[22] that is, God's own knowledge of Himself, a knowledge which, in part, God has revealed to men.

Our faith thus relates to divine reason by which God knows like the faith of one who takes the principles of a subalternated science from the subalternating science that proves [those principles] through a proper explanation. *(III Sent.,* d. 24, q. 1, a. 3, ad 3 [Moos, n. 63, p. 770])[23]

Yet there is an epistemological difference between theology and any ordinary subalternated science. The subject of optics is subalternated to the subject of geometry. Theology, however, is subalternated to the

---

19. ". . . in superiori scientia assignatur propter quid eorum, de quibus scitur in scientia inferiori solum quia . . ." *(Expos. de Trin.,* q. 5, a. 1, ad 5 [Decker, 2-3, p. 171]).

20. *ELP,* I, 25, 79a10, 148–60 (Leonine ed., I, pt. 2, 91b–92a).

21. See M. R. Gagnebet, O.P., "La Nature de la théologie spéculative," *Revue tho-miste* 44 (1938): 1–39, 235–55, 645–74; Tharcisée Tshibangu, *Théologies positive et théologie spéculative: position traditionnelle et nouvelle problématique* (Louvain and Paris: Publications Université de Louvain and Beatrice-Nauwelaerts, 1965).

22. Aquinas is using *"scientia"* (the discursive knowledge of conclusions) equivocally since God's knowledge of Himself is not mediated: see *SCG,* I, 57.

23. "Unde fides nostra ita se habet ad rationem divinam qua Deus cognoscit,

science of God and the blessed not according to any diversity of their respective subjects but according to their way of knowing. Just as in divine science God knows Himself, so God Himself is the subject of theology. Thus divine science and theology have the same subject. But theology receives the articles of faith from God and knows only imperfectly what God knows perfectly and immediately. When the vision of God is attained, then and only then will the articles of faith be immediately grasped as self-evidently true principles.[24]

The Aristotelian theory of subalternation, once applied to theology, becomes complicated and perhaps overextended. Still, Aquinas's main point holds: there is *natural faith* exercised in science no less than there is reason exercised in theology.

> Understanding is always the first but not always the proximate principle of any science. Sometimes faith is the proximate principle of a science, as is the case in subalternated sciences. . . . Similarly, the proximate principle of this [divine] science is faith, but the first principle is the divine understanding, in which we believe. . . . *(Expos. de Trin.*, q. 2, a. 2, ad 7 [Decker, 21–28, p. 89])[25]

Moreover, Aquinas carefully notes the limits of comparing theology to Aristotelian science. Although he has been accused of doing so, Aquinas does not succumb to the danger of conflating faith and reason[26] but neither does he dismiss—as Erasmus would in the sixteenth century—any commerce between Christ and Aristotle. In the Aristotelian schema scientific conclusions must be ultimately derivable from principles that are immediately known. Only the proximate principles of a subalternated science are methodologically taken as matters of "belief." But, in this life, scientific theology can never reduce its conclu-

---

sicut se habet fides illius qui supponit principia subalternatae scientiae a scientia subalternante quae per propriam rationem illa probavit" *(III Sent.*, d. 24, q. 1, a. 3, ad 3 [Moos, n. 63, p. 770]).

24. See *I Sent.*, prologus, q. 1, a. 3, sol. 2; d. 24, q. 1, a. 2, sol. 1, obj. 2/ad 2; *Expos. de Trin.*, q. 2, a. 2, ad 6.

25. ". . . cujuslibet scientiae principium est intellectus semper quidem primum, sed non semper proximum, immo aliquando est fides proximum principium scientiae. Sicut patet in scientiis subalternatis. . . . Et similiter huius scientiae principium proximum est fides, sed primum est intellectus divinus, cui nos credimus . . ." *(Expos. de Trin.*, q. 2, a. 2, ad 7 [Decker, 21–28, p. 89]).

26. Cf. J.-F. Bonnefoy, O.F.M., "La Théologie comme science et l'explication de la foi selon saint Thomas d'Aquin," *Ephemerides theologicae Lovaniensis* 14 (1937): 421–46, 600–631; 15 (1938): 491–516, esp. 608 [reprinted as *La Nature de la théologie selon saint Thomas d'Aquin* (Paris and Bruges: Librairie Philosophique J. Vrin and Ch. Beyaert, 1939)]; Gagnebet, *Théologie spéculative*, 652.

sions to immediately known principles; it is always dependent on revelation.[27]

Since the ultimate principles of the human sciences are immediately knowable, the human sciences are more rational or cognitive or evidentiary than theology.[28] It has to be admitted that theology, which is grounded on *supernatural faith*, since it lacks "vision," is not a science in Aristotle's strict sense of the term.

> Thus, insofar as it lacks vision, [faith] falls short of the type of cognition that is in science: for science determines the intellect to one thing through the vision and understanding of first principles. *(ST,* I, q. 12, a. 13, ad 3)[29]

On an epistemological scale, faith also resembles doubt, suspicion, and opinion: it does not see what it believes.[30] Faith is only half way between opinion and science.[31] Yet Aquinas contends that faith (and therefore the theology that is based on faith) is more *certain* than any Aristotelian science. This claim, which especially contradicts those modern philosophers who found epistemological certainty only in self-evident intuitions, seems paradoxical. Even in an Aristotelian context, what could be more certain than a scientific demonstration that can be reduced to immediately known principles?[32]

2. "Certitude"

For certitude to be counted as "scientific," it is required that the proposition to which one gives assent be true.[33] But how is the truth of a proposition established? According to the canons of Aristotelian logic, propositions can be known to be true either immediately or mediately: that is, the propositions are either immediately known to be true or have been demonstrated to be true. So distinguished, their truth is

27. See *I Sent.*, prologus, q. 1, a. 5; *Expos. de Trin.*, q. 2, a. 1, ad 5.

28. See *III Sent.*, d. 23, q. 2, a. 3, sol. 3, ad 1 (Moos, n. 158, p. 729): "Certitudo enim scientiae consistit in duobus, scilicet in evidentia, et firmitate adhaesionis. Certitudo vero fidei consistit in uno tantum, scilicet in firmitate adhaesionis."

29. "Et sic, inquantum deest visio, deficit a ratione cognitionis quae est in scientia: nam scientia determinat intellectum ad unum per visionem et intellectum primorum principiorum" *(ST,* I, q. 12, a. 13, ad 3).

30. See *ST,* II–II, q. 2, a. 1.

31. See *III Sent.*, d. 24, q. 1, a. 1, q. 2 (Moos, n. 9, p. 761): "Fides est media inter opinionem et scientiam."

32. See *De ver.*, q. 14, a. 1 (Spiazzi, 281): "In scientia enim motus rationis incipit ab intellectu principiorum, et ad eundem terminatur per viam resolutionis. . . ."

33. See *ELP,* I, 4, 71b25, 194–95; 205–9 (Leonine ed., I, pt. 2, 20b–21a).

grasped by diverse cognitive acts, and so too assent to their truth. According to Aquinas, the first, assent to immediate propositions, accompanies an act of understanding *(intellectus)*, called by analogy with sight "vision" *(visio)*. The second, assent to validly demonstrated, true conclusions, results from an act of reasoning *(ratio)*. The latter is called "scientific assent" *(assensus scientiae)*.[34]

Thus there are indemonstrable principles that are immediately understood and necessarily assented to, and demonstrated conclusions that reason can mediately derive and, by reduction to first principles, know to be certain.

From the certitude of principles to which it assents unchangeably, the intellect proceeds by reasoning to conclusions. The intellect stops with certitude in this knowledge, inasmuch as [conclusions] are reduced to the first principles that are virtually in them. *(III Sent.,* d. 27, q. 1, a. 3, ad 1 [Moos, n. 60, pp. 864–65])[35]

Discursive thought terminates in science, the knowledge of true conclusions that are validly derived from true premises. Yet Aristotle and Aquinas are quick to admit that error is always possible. Dialectical, rhetorical, and eristic arguments must not be confused with science. If the conclusion of a syllogism is not necessary (i.e., not reducible to immediately known first principles), then the conclusion is a matter of contingent opinion and not science.[36]

If there are some conclusions which do not have a necessary connection with the naturally known first principles, such as those that are contingent or matters of opinion, the intellect is not forced to assent to them. *(De malo,* q. 3, a. 3 [Bazzi-Pession, 500])[37]

And these false opinions can be easily incorporated into logically valid syllogisms.[38]

Science, at least as Aristotle paradigmatically describes it, involves

---

34. See *III Sent.,* d. 23, q. 2, a. 2, sol. 1 (Moos, nn. 138–39, p. 725).

35. "Intellectus enim ex certitudine principiorum, quibus immobiliter assentit, procedit ratiocinando ad conclusiones in quarum cognitione certitudinaliter quiescit, secundum quod resolvuntur in prima principia quae in eis sunt virtute" *(III Sent.,* d. 27, q. 1, a. 3, ad 1 [Moos, n. 60, pp. 864–65]).

36. For the Aristotelian and Thomistic theory of scientific demonstration, see Edward D. Simmons, "Demonstration and Self-Evidence," *Thomist* 24 (1961): 139–62.

37. "Si vero sint aliquae conclusiones quae non necessariam cohaerentiam habeant cum primis principiis naturaliter notis, sicut contingentia et opinabilia, non cogitur his intellectus assentire" *(De malo,* q. 3, a. 3 [Bazzi-Pession, 500]).

38. See *Top.,* I, 1.

a chain of syllogistic arguments in which most premises first appear as previously deduced conclusions.[39] These mediate premises are sometimes false. False premises can be generated, of course, by purely formal errors in reasoning, but they derive more radically from faulty inductions arising from a mistaken judgment about some object of perception. In the latter instance, the false premises do not actually embody a universal predicate (one necessarily true of the subject) that can function as the middle term in a subsequent demonstrative syllogism.[40]

If the truth of a premise has not yet been demonstrated, reason continues to inquire about it. Discursive thought goes back and forth between contradictory propositions so long as it must use premises that it regards as doubtful or as opinions.[41] In such cases, the intellect has not yet assented to either of the doubtful propositions. "Assent" is the intellectual act of accepting one of a pair of contradictory propositions.[42] Intellectual certitude results from assenting to or absolutely adhering (rightly or wrongly) to the supposed truth of some judgment.[43] The intellect is certain when it does not waver between contradictory propositions.

"Certitude," then, can be defined as "the fixing of the intellect on one thing."[44] But, so defined, certitude no longer only results from scientific demonstration or self-evidence. It can originate from either a rational demonstration or a willed conviction.[45] In the latter case, certi-

39. The notion of Aristotelian science as an "axiomatized deductive system" may be misleading if, as some contemporary scholars claim, Aristotelian demonstrative syllogisms do not constitute a logic governing scientific discovery but only a logic governing the pedagogical presentation of scientific knowledge: see Jonathan Barnes, "Aristotle's Theory of Demonstration," in *Articles on Aristotle, Science*, 1: 65–87. Contra Barnes, see Michael Ferejohn, *The Origins of Aristotelian Science* (New Haven, Conn.: Yale University Press, 1991), 141, n. 4.

40. See *Apr.*, II, 23, 68b28–29; 24, 69a16–19: cf. *ELP*, I, 27, 79b35–39, 144–93 (Leonine ed., I, pt. 2, 99b–100a); 30, 81a39, 30–70 (109b–110a).

41. See *De ver.*, q. 14, a. 1.

42. See *III Sent.*, d. 23, q. 2, a. 2, sol. 1 (Moos, n. 137, p. 724): "Cum autem ab assentiendo sententia dicatur, quae . . . est determinata acceptio alterius partis contradictionis. . . ."

43. See *De malo*, q. 6, a. 1 (Bazzi-Pession, 561): ". . . assentire non nominat motum intellectus ad rem, sed magis ad conceptionem rei, quae habetur in mente; cui intellectus assentit dum iudicat eam esse veram"; *De ver.* q. 14, a. 1, ad 3 (Spiazzi, 281): ". . . assentire proprie pertinet ad intellectum, quia importat absolutam adhaerentiam ei cui assentitur. . . ."; a. 8, ad 5 (Spiazzi, 296): "Et sic, per hoc quod compositioni factae tamquam verae assentit. . . ."

44. See *III Sent.*, d. 23, q. 2, a. 2, sol. 3, ad 3 (Moos, n. 155, p. 728): ". . . certitudo nihil aliud est quam determinatio intellectus ad unum. . . ."

45. See *ST*, II–II, q. 1, a. 4.

tude does not result from the intrinsic rationality of a demonstration (what Aquinas calls *"evidentia"* or *"manifestatio"*); it refers rather to the voluntary but firm adherence *(inhaesio)* to what is believed.

Aquinas, however, insists that the ultimate certitude of theology results from the divine, not the human, will. God, who may be called the "First Truth," is also the first cause of the firm adherence of the authentic believer. God, not man, is the active cause of faith.

In the revelation of faith, God who has a perfect knowledge is like the agent; man, however, is like the matter receiving the influx of the divine agent. *(ST,* II–II, q. 1, a. 7, ad 3)[46]

Because he is under divine influence, the believer can be more certain than the philosopher or scientist who relies solely on rational evidence. Aquinas underscores the point. He insists that faith can evince a greater degree of certitude than the conclusions of science or even the first principles of reason.[47] But the superior certitude of the believer only reflects the superior strength of God, who causes faith to firmly adhere to what has been revealed.

"Certitude" is able to signify two things: first of all, firmness of adherence; and in regard to this, faith is more certain than all understanding and science, because the first truth, which causes the assent of faith, is a stronger cause than the light of reason. ["Certitude"] also signifies the evidence to which one assents. . . . *(De ver.,* q. 14, a. 1, ad 7 [Spiazzi, 281])[48]

Yet this notion of certitude must be reconciled with a disturbing anomaly: the heretic can adhere no less firmly to falsity than the orthodox believer to truth.[49] "Certitude," defined as conviction, is not self-authenticating; conviction can be of divine or human origin. Religious conviction can go wildly astray. Aquinas attempts to circumvent this issue by denying that heresy is divinely inspired. Because the object of divinely infused faith is the First Truth, it cannot include

46. "In manifestatione autem fidei Deus est sicut agens, qui habet perfectam scientiam ab aeterno; homo autem est sicut materia recipiens influxum Dei agentis" *(ST,* II–II, q. 1, a. 7, ad 3).

47. See *I Sent.,* prologus, q. 1, a. 3, sol. 3 (Mandonnet, 14): ". . . magis enim fidelis et firmius assentit his quae sunt fidei quam etiam primis principiis rationis."

48. ". . . certitudo duo potest importare: scilicet firmitatem adhaesionis; et quantum ad hoc fides est certior omni intellectu et scientia, quia prima veritas, quae causat fidei assensum, est fortior quam lumen rationis, quod causat assensum intellectus vel scientiae. Importat etiam evidentiam eius cui assentitur . . ." *(De ver.,* q. 14, a. 1, ad 7 [Spiazzi, 281]).

49. See *Quod.* VI, q. 4, a. 1 (Spiazzi, 122): ". . . nec minus firmiter inhaeret aliquis veritati quam falsitati. . . ."

anything false.[50] Since heretical beliefs by definition are false they cannot properly arise from "faith."[51] Of course, a man possessing faith may hold a false belief but this belief is to be attributed not to divinely infused faith but to mistaken human conjecture.[52] Heretics, as distinguished from unbelievers who do not assent to Christ, are believers who refuse to assent to those doctrines that have been "truly handed down from Christ" (ST, II–II, q. 11, a. 1). But to count as "heretical," the refusal must derive from pride and cupidity and not just from (morally inculpable) adherence to mistaken human beliefs about Christ's teachings.[53]

While Aquinas does offer criteria for separating authentic from spurious revelation,[54] he does not offer logical or metaphysical criteria that would enable one to prove the dogmas of any particular faith to be true. But Aquinas did not anticipate this burning modern issue because he did not think that the truth of the *articles* of orthodox Christian faith could be proved or disproved: faith accepts these beliefs as true solely on God's testimony to them.[55] Creedal affirmations can be defended against contrary claims only by showing the latter to be false or not necessarily true.[56] Aquinas's attention was focused on an altogether different point: he wanted to show how the habit of faith prevents the believer from falling into heretical views:

For the habit of faith has this power, that through it the intellect of the believer is held back lest he assent to things that are contrary to the faith, just as the chaste man refrains from [actions] that are contrary to chastity. (De ver., q. 14, a. 10, ad 10 [Spiazzi, 301])[57]

Faith, like a moral habit that inclines a man to virtue, inclines by its nature the believer to the truth.[58]

50. See ST, II–II, q. 1, a. 3.
51. See ST, II–II, q. 4, a. 5: "Nam ex ratione ipsius fidei est quod intellectus semper feratur in verum, quia fidei non potest subesse falsum. . . ."
52. See ST, II–II, q. 1, a. 3, ad 3.
53. See ST, II–II, q. 11, a. 1, ad 2.
54. See Aubert, "Le Traité de la foi de S. Thomas," in Le Problème de l'acte de foi, 43–71.
55. See III Sent., d. 25, q. 1, a. 1, sol, 1 (Moos, n. 15, p. 785): "Fides autem non inquirit sed supponit ea quae fidei sunt ex testimonio Dei ea dicentis."
56. See I Sent., prologus, q. 1, a. 3, sol. 2, ad 2 (Mandonnet, 14); De ver., q. 2, a. 1, ad 5; a. 3.
57. "Fidei etiam habitus hanc efficaciam habet, ut per ipsum intellectus fidelis detineatur ne contrariis fidei assentiat; sicut et castitas refrenat a contrariis castitati" (De ver., q. 14, a. 10, ad 10 [Spiazzi, 301].
58. Cf. III Sent., d. 23, q. 3, a. 3, sol. 2, ad 2 (Moos, n. 277, p. 751).

Faith depends upon the first truth. Since the latter is infallible, nothing false is able to fall under faith. *(III Sent.,* d. 24, a. 2, sol. 3, ad 3 [Moos, n. 31, p. 1765])[59]

But how "infallible" is infused faith? Aquinas puzzled over the problem and, although he retained the analogy with moral virtue,[60] he eventually conceded that it took an additional gift of the Holy Spirit to protect the believer from error.[61]

Nonetheless, both the orthodox and the heterodox believer can equally appeal to Aquinas's definition of faith. In the judgment of the orthodox believer, heresy is a merely human belief. Whether or not it involves specious reasoning,[62] heresy is a conviction that has strength only from man's will. Yet every faith remains a matter of willed conviction, no matter what the explanation of its ultimate cause.[63] The contemporary philosopher will be quick to observe that believers of all stripes must admit that there are no strictly rational criteria that by themselves sort out counterfeit from genuine faith.

Aquinas is content to note that the reasons that prompt faith do not bring any vision of what is believed. Faith of any type always stops short of rational proof.[64]

A proof which is taken from the proper principles of a thing makes the thing to be evident. But a proof that is taken from divine authority does not make the thing to be evident in itself. And such is the kind of argument that is put in the definition of faith. *(ST,* II–II, q. 4, a, 1, ad 5)[65]

Admitting that the essentials of faith cannot be proved, medieval theologians, beginning with Augustine, stressed that faith is rooted in the

59. ". . . fides innititur veritati primae.Unde cum illa sit infallibilis, fidei non potest subesse falsum" *(III Sent.,* d. 24, q.1, a. 2, sol. 3, ad 3 [Moos, n. 31, p. 765]).

60. See *ST,* II–II, q. 2, a. 3, ad 2.

61. In *III Sent.,* d. 23, q. 3, a. 3, sol. 2 (Moos, n. 275, p. 751), the believer, because he has infused faith, is said to assent "in no way *[nullo modo]* to those things that ought not to be believed." If he does assent to errors, it is because "he has abandoned the inclination of faith through his own fault" *(III Sent.,* d. 24, q. 1, a. 3, q. 3, sol. 2, ad 3 [Moos, n. 96, p. 776]). Cf. *ST,* I–II, q. 68, a. 2, ad 3; II–II, q. 45, a. 1 which require that wisdom *(sapientia),* as a special gift of the Holy Spirit, be added to the theological virtue of faith in order for the believer to avoid mistakes.

62. See *ST,* II–II, q. 4, a. 5, ad 2.

63. See *III Sent.,* d. 25, q. 2, a. 2, sol. 1 (Moos, n. 96, p. 804): ". . . certitudo fidei est ex voluntate determinante intellectum ad unum. . . ."

64. See *III Sent.,* d. 23, q. 2, a. 2, sol. 1 (Moos, n. 140, p. 725); q. 3, a. 3, sol. 1 (Moos, n. 269, p. 750).

65. ". . . argumentum quod sumitur ex propriis principiis rei facit rem esse apparentem. Sed argumentum quod sumitur ex auctoritate divina non facit rem in se esse apparentem.Et tale argumentum ponitur in definitione fidei" *(ST,* II–II, q. 4, a, 1, ad 5).

believer's will.[66] Aquinas, although he grants that the certitude of faith is noncognitive,[67] attempts to mitigate the voluntaristic side of this tradition.

According to Aquinas, faith does not essentially pertain to the will.[68] Although the act of faith is willed, divinely infused faith, since its object is the First Truth, must be considered a virtue of the speculative intellect.[69] It pertains especially to the intellect because it perfects reason in regard to the truth.[70] Faith is a form of assent and assent is itself an intellectual act.

Nonetheless, this notion of strictly intellectual assent must be altered if it is to apply to faith.[71] Faith is not solely intellectual and neither is the assent of faith.[72] It is not the object believed, since that is

66. See Fr. Candido Arniz, O.P., "Definicion Augustiniano-Tomista del acto de fey," La Ciencia Tomista 80 (1953): 25–74.

67. See III Sent., d. 23, q. 2, a. 3, sol, 1, ad 2 (Moos, n. 173, p. 732): "Fides autem habet certitudinem ab eo quod est extra genus cognitionis, in genere affectionis existens."

68. See ST, II–II, q. 4, a. 4: ". . . illud per se ad fidem pertinet quod pertinet ad intellectum: quod autem pertinet ad voluntatem non per se pertinet ad fidem. . . ."

69. See ST, II–II, q. 4, a. 2, ad 2. But De ver., q. 14, a. 4, adds that faith is only in the speculative intellect because the latter "is subject to the command of the will."

70. See De ver., q. 14, a. 5, ad 11; Expos. de Trin., q. 6, a. 1, ad 4 (Decker, 16–17, p. 213): ". . . cognitio etiam fidei maxime pertinet ad intellectum."

71. The intellectual act of assent (assensus) is distinguished from the volitional act of consent (consensus). According to Aquinas, "assensus" is etymologically derived from "sentire" = "ad aliud sentire" ("to sense toward another"); "consentire" = "simul cum alio sentire" ("to sense simultaneously with another"): see ST, I–II, q. 15, a. 1, ad 3.

Assent does not of itself involve any relationship to another psychological act; in itself, it is just the determination of thought to some one thing. Consent, however, always presupposes a prior cognitive act: first, practical reason (through the act of deliberation [consilium]) judges something to be a good means toward a desired end; then the will, by an act of consent, simultaneously tends toward or is applied to that means. See III Sent., d. 23, q. 2, a, 2, sol. 1, ad 1 (Moos, n. 144, p. 726): ". . . determinatio cogitationis ad aliquid dicitur assensus, quia aliquid non praecedit; determinatio autem voluntatis ad unum, dicitur consensus, quia cogitationem praesupponit, cum qua simul sentit, dum in illud tendit quod ratio bonum esse judicat"; De ver., q. 14, a. 1, ad 3: ". . . sed consentire est proprie voluntatis, quia consentire est simul cum alio sentire; et sic dicitur in ordine vel per comparationem ad aliquid praecedens."

Clearly, Aquinas does not maintain exactly this notion of assent when the latter term is applied to faith. In faith, assent is always necessarily preceded by an act of the will.

72. In Aquinas's Scripta super libros Sententiarum, Abbà finds an Augustinian account of the articles of faith that stresses their cognitive status; I Sent., prologus, q. 1, a. 3, sol. 2, ad. 1 (Mandonnet, 14) states that the articles of faith "through the infused light of faith are 'per se noti' to someone having faith." Supposedly, Aquinas

something precisely not seen,[73] but the will of the believer that moves him to assent.[74] Unlike the Aristotelian scientist, whose intellectual assent is compelled by the rational force of the demonstration,[75] the believer chooses to believe this rather than that to be true. In that sense, the voluntaristic side of faith can never be transcended: "To believe is an intellectual act of assent to divine truth from the command of the will which is moved by God through grace."[76]

Yet faith, while it results from the divine influence, is never merely a voluntaristic assertion or a leap contrary to all rational evidence.[77] The believer always has some reason to think that his belief is true because it has been somehow confirmed by God.[78] Faith, which is more like hearing about something absent than seeing something present, responds to a divinely inspired teacher. The believer, therefore, must think that God speaks through the teacher; otherwise, he would not believe what the teacher says.

> In regard to the reason that induces the will to believing, it is said to be from the vision of something that shows that it is God who speaks in him who preaches the faith. *(III Sent.,* d. 23, q. 3, a. 2, ad 3 [Moos, n. 257, p. 748])[79]

"decisively abandons" *(Lex et Virtus,* 119) this illuminationist viewpoint in his later works in favor of the voluntaristic side of faith. But, although the discussion of faith in *ST,* II–II, qq. 1–7 does not rely on the light metaphor, Abbà exaggerates Aquinas's "considerable evolution" (110). Whether a critical edition of the *Scripta* on Peter Lombard's *Sentences* will introduce a *"quasi"* before the *"per se noti"* of *ad 1* (or some such emendation), and thereby will tone down what are alleged to be "le espressioni dello *Scriptum* quasi incredibili e ardite" (112), remains to be seen. In any case, *solutio* 2 hangs on the proposition that "the articles of faith are infallibly proved [only] in the *'scientia'* of God" (Mandonnet, 13), a tenet that is perfectly in line with the theory of subalternation developed in *Expos. de Trin.,* q. 2, a. 2, ad 7 and *ST,* I, q. 1. (Cf. Abbà, 120.) Similarly, while *III Sent.,* d. 23, q. 2, a. 1, ad 4 (Moos, n. 121, p. 721) states that "the infused light, which is the habit of faith, makes evident *[manifestat]* the articles [of faith]," *ad* 7 of the same text (Mandonnet, 721) also laconically notes that "the knowledge of faith emerges *[procedit]* from the will, because no one believes except by willing."

73. See *ST,* II–II, q. 4, a. 1.

74. See *ST,* II–II, q. 2, a. 1, ad 3: ". . . intellectus credentis determinatur ad unum non per rationem, sed per voluntatem. Et ideo assensus hic accipitur pro actu intellectus secundum quod a voluntate determinatur ad unum."

75. See *ST,* II–II, q. 2, a. 9, ad 2.

76. "Credere est actus intellectus assentientis veritati divinae ex imperio voluntatis a Deo motae per gratiam" *(ST,* II–II, q. 2, a. 9).

77. See *ST,* II–II, q. 1, a. 4, ad 2.

78. See *ST,* II–II, q. 1, a. 4; ad 2; q. 2, a. 10, ad 2.

79. "Quantum vero ad rationem quae inducit voluntatem ad credendum, dicitur

Usually, the veracity of the inspired teacher is confirmed through miracles and prophesy.[80] But miracles and prophesy do not demonstrate the truth of faith nor even compel it.[81] God must always inwardly move the believer to assent; He infuses a supernatural habit of faith that is like a supernatural light illuminating the human mind.[82] The same point can be put in terms of the will. It is only an "interior cause," a grace moving the believer's will, that brings assent. So moved, the believer assents that sacred doctrine is divinely revealed, that it is true, and that it ought to be believed.[83]

For most modern philosophers, "faith" is at best categorized as a species of "opinion." But as Aquinas defines the two terms, there is an important difference between them: opinion, unlike faith, lacks firm assent. Although faith cannot be rationally demonstrated, it is "in some way" a form of knowledge (cognitio).[84] Opinion may favor but finally cannot decide which of two contradictory propositions is true. Belief precisely involves firmly assenting to the truth of a proposition. It occurs when the will, attracted by some good, moves the intellect to assent.

The believer, because he desires the good of eternal life and salvation, chooses to give intellectual assent to doctrines that cannot be rationally proved or disproved. But faith is more than an assent to

---

esse ex visione alicujus quod ostendit Deum esse qui loquitur in eo qui fidem annuntiat" (III Sent., d. 23, q. 3, a. 2, ad 3 [Moos, n. 257, p. 748]).

80. See III Sent., d. 25, q. 2, a. 4, sol. 4 (Moos, n. 82, p. 800): " . . . datum est hominibus facere miracula, ut ostendatur quod Deus per illos loquitur."

81. See III Sent., d. 24, q. 1, a. 3, sol. 2, ad 4 (Moos, n. 64, p. 770); ST, II–II, q. 5, a. 2.

82. See Expos. de Trin., q. 3, a. 1, ad 4.

83. See ST, II–II, q. 6, a. 1. Abbà finds the difference between the theme of divine inspiration (in Aquinas's Scripta super libros Sententiarum of Peter Lombard and in the De trinitate) and the theme of divine revelation (in the Summa theologiae) to be of "great importance" (Lex et Virtus, 129). But this difference in Aquinas's terminology proves to be doctrinally significant only because Abbà interprets "inspiration" as belonging to "the order of subjectivity" and "revelation" to "the order of objectivity." These dichotomous, modern categories seem ill-suited to Aquinas's notion of revelation and faith. In ST, I, q. 1, revelation, which communicates God's self-knowledge (a. 6), is given to human minds (a. 9, ad 2), but is known to be certain in the light of divine science (a. 2, a. 7), and can only be accepted by faith (a. 1). What Question One says of revelation does not significantly differ from earlier discussions of divine inspiration. It is not some "objective" revelation but faith in revealed divine science that constitutes sacred doctrine as a science: cf. pp. 131, 134. Abbà's claim that "For the Summa Theologiae sacred doctrine is [a] science simply because its principles exist" (129) oversimplifies by drawing a sharp contrast between Aquinas's earlier and later accounts where none need be drawn.

84. See III Sent., d. 24, q. 1, a. 2, q. 3 (Moos, n. 44, p. 767): "Ergo ea quae sunt

propositions. One not only believes God by assenting to what He has revealed; one believes *in* God by loving Him who, in the words of the prayer, "can neither deceive nor be deceived."[85] Human beings, left to their own devices, often enough fall into both traps, and Aquinas makes an especially cool assessment of what philosophers have achieved. Few if any philosophers, in striving to know God, have avoided mistakes. Frequently enough, they are expertly wrong about particular arguments. From this standpoint, the history of metaphysics is a history of uncertain conclusions.[86] In contrast to the divinely inspired certainties of faith, both believers and nonbelievers admit that philosophical arguments often go astray. The believer is being both cautious and rational if he continues to adhere to the truth of sacred doctrine even if it is opposed to the conclusion of some alleged demonstration.

In another vein, Aquinas observes that philosophy cannot encompass man's whole pursuit of metaphysical truth. The human story has an existential plot. Every man is vulnerable to illness or some physical incapacity that could deprive him of reason or its continuous function. In such circumstances, faith can sometimes perdure when reason is debilitated. Faith thus can preserve man in the truth when philosophy fails.

The theologian, nonetheless, cannot contradict reason or ignore philosophy. Faith perfectly assents to but does not perfectly understand sacred doctrine. Faith should remain humble because, as Aquinas puts it, thought remains restless.[87] The theologian, if he is humble, will not forget that reason provides, if not greater certitude, at least greater evidence for its tenets.

The certitude which is in science and in understanding is from the very evidence of those things which are said to be certain; the certitude of faith, however, is from the firm adherence to that which is believed. . . . And, therefore, faith has more certitude in regard to the firmness of adherence,

---

fidei aliquo modo cognoscuntur"; *SCG*, I, 5 (Pera, n. 30, p. 7): "Est etiam necessarium huiusmodi veritatem ad credendum hominibus proponi ad Dei cognitionem veriorem habendam." For a vigorous defense of faith as a form of knowledge, see J. F. Ross, "Aquinas on Belief and Knowledge," in *Essays Honoring Allan B. Wolter*, ed. William A. Rank and Girard J. Etzkorn (St. Bonaventure, N.Y.: Franciscan Institute Publications, 1985), 245–69.

85. See *III Sent.*, d. 23, q. 2, a. 2, sol. 2, ad 2 (Moos, n. 149, p. 727); *ST*, II–II, q. 1, a. 2, ad 2.

86. See *SCG*, III, 30.

87. See *De ver.*, q. 14, a. 1., ad 5.

than there is certitude for science or understanding, although in science and understanding there is more evidence for those things that are assented to. *(III Sent.,* d. 23, q. 2, a. 3, sol. 3, ad 3 [Moos, nn. 156–57, pp. 728–29])[88]

Yet faith also demands some rational evidence and coherence. A philosophical argument that allegedly disproves an article of faith should be shown to be invalid or inconclusive.[89] Reason, then, has an ineradicable role in theology and cannot be exclusively assigned to philosophy.

3. The "Subject" of Theology

Philosophy and theology are distinguished by their starting points and their respective points of view, and by the way that they use reason to investigate their respective subjects. "Sacred doctrine," or what modern theologians usually call "sacred theology," originates in revelation. This origin determines the formal object of theology. The purview of sacred doctrine extends to anything that is believed to have been divinely revealed.[90] But revelation has a focus, and so too theology has a primary subject, that which it is primarily about. Aquinas precisely delineates the latter:

> Divine being, as it is knowable through inspiration, is the subject of this science. For everything which is treated in this science is either God or those things which derive from God or which are [ordered] to God. . . . *(I Sent.,* prologus, q. 1, a. 4 [Mandonnet, 16])[91]

The primary subject of sacred doctrine, then, is God: first, God in Himself, and, then, God as the end of creation.

Both the *Summa theologiae* and the *Summa contra gentiles* refer all matters to be investigated to God.[92] This perspective, viewing every-

88. ". . . ideo certitudo quae est in scientia et intellectu, est ex ipsa evidentia eorum quae certa esse dicuntur; certitudo autem fidei est ex firma adhaesione ad id quod creditur. . . . Et ideo fides habet majorem certitudinem quantum ad firmitatem adhaesionis, quam sit certitudo scientiae vel intellectus, quamvis in scientia et intellectu sit major evidentia eorum quibus assentitur" *(III Sent.,* d. 23, q. 2, a. 3, sol. 3, ad 3 [Moos, nn. 156–57, pp. 728–29]).

89. See *ST,* II–II, q. 1, a. 4, ad 2: ". . . non enim crederet nisi videret ea esse credenda, vel propter evidentiam signorum vel propter aliquid huiusmodi."

90. See *ST,* I. q. 1, a. 3: ". . . omnia quaecumque sunt divinitus revelabilia, communicant in una ratione formali obiecti huius scientiae."

91. ". . . ens divinum cognoscibile per inspirationem est subjectum hujus scientiae. Omnia enim quae in hac scientia considerantur, sunt aut Deus, aut ea quae ex Deo et ad Deum sunt . . ." *(I Sent.,* prologus, q. 1, a. 4 [Mandonnet, 16]).

92. See Anton C. Pegis, General Introduction to *On the Truth of the Catholic*

thing "under the aspect of God" *(sub ratione Dei)*,[93] defines them as theological treatises. Since everything that Aquinas investigates in these books is viewed from this angle, everything consequently is theology. This can be seen in the actual order of the treatises.

The *Summa theologiae* treats first of God Himself, the one divine essence in three persons; second, of the movement of rational creatures (angels and men) toward God; and third, of the means whereby men return to God, Christ and the grace of His sacraments.[94] The *Summa contra gentiles*, which is divided into four books, is arranged according to the same theological order: (1) God Himself; (2) God's activities that "pass into" external things (creation and its divine governance); (3) the ordering of creation to God as its final end.[95]

In the *Summa contra gentiles*, however, there is an important internal division: Books I–III treat of matters of faith that can also be rationally demonstrated; Book IV deals with matters of faith that can be known only through faith and for which reason can at best provide analogies. Nonetheless, the *Summa contra gentiles* is not part philosophy and part theology; everything is considered in relationship to God. For example, Book III considers intellectual substances. But Aquinas focuses his investigation on how created intelligences—angels and men—attain the divine end of creation precisely by *knowing* God.[96] These metaphysical discussions do not detract from the theological character of the arguments; they are not, as it has been erroneously claimed, extraneous.[97] Aquinas can consistently hold to this point of view because he thinks that revelation and reason overlap.

4. Reason and Revelation

Sacred doctrine, in fact, contains two kinds of revealed truth *(revelata)* about God and man: (1) truths, held only on the authority of Scripture, that do not contradict but nonetheless entirely surpass reason; and (2) truths that are capable of being revealed *(revelabilia)* and believed *(credibilia)*—because they have been revealed *(revelata)*—but which, either antecedently or subsequently to faith, can also

---

Faith: Summa Contra Gentiles, Book 1: *God* (Garden City, N.Y.: Hanover House, 1955), 15–44.

93. *ST,* I, q. 1, a. 7; Pegis trans.

94. See *ST,* I, q. 2, prologus.

95. See *SCG,* I, 9; II, 5; III, 1; IV, 1.

96. See *SCG,* III, 25.

97. Cf. Bonnefoy, "La Théologie comme science," 501, 513.

be rationally demonstrated.[98] As instances of *revelabilia*, Aquinas usually mentions the doctrines about God's existence, unity, intelligence, and incorporeality.[99] But the category is open-ended.[100]
Faith centers on the first kind of revealed truth.

> That [truth] about God that absolutely exceeds the human intellect pertains essentially to the faith which has been divinely revealed to us. What surpasses the understanding of this or that person, but not of every man, pertains not essentially but accidentally to faith. *(III Sent.*, d. 24, a. 2, sol. 2, ad 2 [Moos, nn. 58–59, p. 769])[101]

What pertains essentially to divinely revealed faith can never be rationally demonstrated: for instance, the Trinity, the Incarnation, and the actually attainable supernatural end of man.[102] For that reason, it is appropriate to label these revealed truths "articles" of faith, and the second kind of revealed truths, those that can be rationally demonstrat-

---

98. See *ST*, I, q. 1, a. 3; ad 2. For Aquinas's use of Maimonides, see P. Synave, O.P., "La Révélation des vérités divines naturelles d'après s. Thomas d'Aquin," in *Mélanges Mandonnet* (Paris: J. Vrin, 1930), 2:327–70.

99. See *III Sent.*, d. 24, q. 1, a. 3, sol. 1 (Mandonnet, n. 82, p. 774); *ST*, II–II, q. 2, a. 4; *SCG*, I, 3.

100. According to Gilson *(The Christian Philosophy of St. Thomas Aquinas,* 94), Aquinas took the *"I Am Who Am"* doctrine of Exodus 3.14 *("haec sublimis veritas")* as part *"*of the revealable which has been revealed." Gilson includes among the *revelabilia* any doctrine that "might well have been revealed but has not been" (11) and suggests that this category might cover those propositions of Thomistic metaphysics that follow from the proposition stating the identity of essence and existence in God and their distinction in creatures. Where Aquinas directly learned this exact doctrine (whether from his own metaphysical exegesis of Exodus or from Avicenna) is a "thorny problem" (94). Recent scholarship has proposed that the source of this doctrine is in a Neoplatonic tradition deriving from Porphyry: see Pierre Hadot, "Dieu comme acte d'être dans le néoplatonisme: A propos des théories d' É. Gilson sur la métaphysique de l'Exode," in *Dieu et l'être: exégèse d'Exode 3,14 et de Coran 20, 11–24*, ed. Centre d'études des religions du livre, CNRS (Paris: Études augustiniennes, 1978), 57–63; and W. J. Hankey, *God in Himself: Aquinas' Doctrine of God as Expounded in the "Summa Theologiae"* (Oxford: Oxford University Press, 1987), 1–17.
Whatever be the source of Aquinas's metaphysical insight, further developments of the essence-existence doctrine should not be aggregated to the category of *revelabilia*. Aquinas characterizes the latter (whether they actually have been or only could have been revealed) as truths necessary for man's salvation or participation in the beatific vision: see *ST*, I, q. 1, a. 1; II–II, q. 2, a. 4, ad 3; *De ver.*, q. 14, a. 10. No such claim can be plausibly made for the subtleties of the essence-existence distinction.

101. "Sic ergo quod simpliciter humanum intellectum excedit ad Deum pertinens, nobis divinitus revelatum ad fidem per se pertinet. Quod autem excedit intellectum hujus vel illius et non omnis hominis, non per se, sed per accidens ad fidem pertinet" *(III Sent.*, d. 24, q. 1, a. 2, sol. 2, ad 2 [Moos, nn. 58–59, p. 769]).

102. See *ST*, II–II, q. 1, a. 6; *De ver.*, q. 14, a. 9.

ed, "preambles" to faith.[103] Such demonstrations are like preambles to faith because they remove logical impediments to faith.[104]

To know something is either to "see" it through an immediate intellectual insight or to grasp it as a conclusion through the mediation of reasoning. Faith, taken strictly, is about those things that, in this life, can never be immediately seen or mediately known. But some beliefs can become objects of knowledge. Thus to the man who can prove them by rational demonstration, the preambles of faith are no longer believed but known.

Nothing prevents these things from being known by those who can demonstrate them and from being believed by those who do not grasp the demonstration. But it is impossible that they are both known and believed by the same person. (*De ver.*, q. 14, a. 9 [Spiazzi, 298])[105]

Precise limits, however, must be observed. If reason is to replace faith, the object of demonstration must perfectly coincide with the object of belief. In demonstrating that cosmological motion entails the existence of the First Unmoved Mover, the philosopher no longer believes precisely in that Prime Mover, the ultimate source of all cosmological motion, whose existence he has just demonstrated. There cannot be faith and philosophical knowledge about exactly the same (formal) object looked at from exactly the same point of view. Here, Aquinas, who is so confident in the power of reason, may appear to sacrifice the certitudes of faith to the vagaries of philosophy.[106] But the problem seems not to have worried Aquinas: in regard to the proposition "The Prime Mover exists," the same man at the same time either *believes* it to be a true proposition or *knows* it to be true proposition, but not both.

103. See *ST,* II–II, q. 1, a. 5, ad 3: ". . . ea quae demonstrative probari possunt inter credenda numerantur, non quia de ipsis sit simpliciter fides apud omnes: sed quia praeexiguntur ad ea quae sunt fidei. . . ."

104. See *ST,* II–II, q. 2, a. 10, ad 2.

105. "Et de his nihil prohibet quin sint ab aliquibus scita, qui horum habeant demonstrationes; et ab aliquibus credita, qui horum demonstrationes non perceperunt. Sed impossibile est quod sint ab eodem scita et credita" (*De ver.,* q. 14, a. 9 [Spiazzi, 298]).

106. See Gilson (55) who accepts Báñez's solution. Báñez asserts that supernatural faith always has a unique formal object. Faith and knowledge correspond to two different intellectual habits; hence, they do not affirm the same formal object even if they touch on the same material object. See Bañes, *Scholastica commentaria,* I, q. 2, a. 2 (ed. Luis Urbano, 110). Accordingly, Báñez allows that the theologian, who demonstrates the proposition "The Prime Mover exists," can continue to assent to this proposition more firmly by faith than by demonstration. Faith, in this case, does not establish the truth of the proposition but adds a supernatural certitude

There are certain things about which even in this life we are able to attain perfect knowledge, such as those things that we are able to prove demonstratively about God; however, in the beginning it is necessary to believe them. . . . *(De ver.,* q. 14, a. 10 [Spiazzi, 300])[107]

Nevertheless, knowledge does not completely replace faith if the metaphysician also happens to believe that the God of faith is the Prime Mover. Then the same man happens to believe a great deal more about the Prime Mover than he can demonstrate: for example, that the Prime Mover is a trinity of divine persons sharing one essence, or that He is provident, and rewards and punishes men.[108]

Faith is not about God in regard to what is naturally known about God, but in regard to what exceeds natural knowledge. *(De ver.,* q. 14, a. 9, ad 5 [Spiazzi, 298])[109]

In any case, the fact that the theologian can demonstrate truths that other men hold only on faith does not turn the theologian into a philosopher.[110] The theologian, of course, can borrow and, in Aquinas's own case, profoundly rework these proofs from the philosophers.[111]

For this is discovered that God is being, and by irrefutable arguments [this] has been proven even by the philosophers. *(De ver.,* q. 10, a. 12 [Spiazzi, 219])[112]

---

about a truth that is known naturally. Báñez and Aquinas, however, are pursuing two different goals. Báñez distinguishes truth and certitude in order to preserve a role for faith in reason. Aquinas identifies the material objects of certain revealed propositions and the material objects of certain philosophically demonstrated propositions in order to establish a role for reason in faith. Cf. *ST,* II–II, q. 5, a. 1: "Sed quantum ad ea quae materialiter credenda proponuntur, quaedam sunt credita ab uno quae sunt manifeste scita ab alio, etiam in statu praesenti. . . ."

107. "Quaedam vero sunt ad quae etiam in hac vita perfecte cognoscenda possumus pervenire sicut illa quae de Deo demonstrative probari possunt; quae tamen a principio necesse est credere" *(De ver.,* q. 14, a. 10 [Spiazzi, 300]).

108. *III Sent.,* d. 25, q. 1, a. 2 (Moos, n. 38, p. 790); *De ver.,* q. 10, a. 12, ad 5 in contrarium (Spiazzi, 221).

109. ". . . quod de Deo non est fides quantum ad id quod naturaliter de Deo est cognitum, sed quantum ad id quod naturalem excedit cognitionem" *(De ver.,* q. 14, a. 9, ad 5 [Spiazzi, 298]).

110. See *SCG,* I, 4.

111. See Joseph Owens, "Aquinas and the Five Ways," in *St. Thomas Aquinas on the Existence of God: Collected Papers of Joseph Owens, C.Ss.R.,* ed. John R. Catan (Albany: State University of New York, 1980), 132–41 [originally published in *Monist* 58 (1974): 16–35].

112. "Invenitur enim hoc quod est Deum esse, rationibus irrefragabilibus etiam a philosophis probatum . . ." *(De ver.,* q. 10, a. 12 [Spiazzi, 219]).

But the theologian, although he may have demonstrative knowledge of these preambles to faith, continues to treat them from the distinctive point of view of theology—insofar as these demonstrable truths are first rendered credible on the basis of revelation. The subject of theology is the *"credibile."*[113]

This theological point of view structures the order of questions treated in the *Summa theologiae*. It dominates, to take one important instance, Aquinas's celebrated five proofs for the existence of God. *ST*, I, q. 1 treats the nature and extent of sacred doctrine. The purpose of sacred doctrine is to teach believers about the nature of God, especially insofar as He is the end of man. But philosophers have also inquired whether the existence of God can be rationally demonstrated. Aquinas rehearses these demonstrations, which would certainly be the first order of business in a philosophical treatment of God, but does so only in Question Two of the *Summa theologiae*. Question Two subsumes questions about demonstrating God's existence under a consideration of the divine essence,[114] a placement that indicates that Aquinas is primarily concerned to establish the rationality of what faith professes than to demonstrate the existence of God to those agnostic philosophers who do not affirm the existence of God.

Indeed, the authority Aquinas cites on behalf of God's existence is not a philosopher but God Himself, that is, the inspired word of God as recorded in Exodus 3.14: the mysterious and intriguing *"I Am Who Am."* Nonetheless, the proposed philosophical demonstrations must stand on their own logical feet; otherwise neither theologians nor philosophers will find them rationally convincing. But *ST*, I, q. 2, for all of its logically rigorous examination of strictly philosophical issues, clearly fits into a theological scheme and has a theological purpose.

Whether or not a philosophy allows that there are valid proofs for the existence of God is a theological touchstone when evaluating any metaphysics. A metaphysics that affirms the proposition "God exists" clears a path toward faith in the supernatural God who transcends such proofs. But the theologian and the philosopher pursue different purposes in constructing such proofs. The theologian, however long he may dwell on strictly metaphysical questions, is eager to incorporate the Prime Mover of the philosophers into the God of faith.[115] He af-

---

113. See *I Sent.*, prologus, q. 1, a. 4 (Mandonnet, 15): ". . . credibile esse subjectum hujus scientiae."

114. See *ST*, I, q. 2, prologus: "Circa essentiam vero divinam, primo considerandum est an Deus sit. . . ."

115. See Gilson, *Elements of Christian Philosophy*, 54.

firms that the God in whom he believes is also the God whose existence philosophy proves. Believing this, the theologian can then subsume the demonstration of God's existence into questions about human happiness and salvation.

The existence of God, by itself, is not an article of faith; but the God
who rewards and punishes and takes care of everything, which is how faith
views the existence of God, is an article of faith. . . . (III Sent., d. 25, q. 1, a.
2, ad 2 [Moos, n. 38, p. 790])[116]

As something believed in, the existence of God implicitly includes
all the articles of faith touching on divine providence and human
salvation.[117] The five ways are of interest to the theologian because
they provide a metaphysical exegesis of sacred doctrine that pro-
claims the existence of God. Such proofs deepen the theologian's
understanding of something that he believes: that the God Who Is
saves men.[118]

5. Philosophy and Theology

Today "philosophical theology" is a commonly used term, but if
this term is to be applied correctly to Aquinas's theology, it cannot be
used to designate any autonomous or separable or even a subordinate
part of Thomistic theology.[119] Theology is a unified science; indeed,
Aquinas claims that, because it shares in divine science, theology has a
higher form of unity than any of the other, solely human sciences.[120]
Although it incorporates rationally demonstrable propositions, Aquinas's theology—given the point of view that it assumes—is homoge-
neously theological; it sees everything "through the light of divine
inspiration."[121] And it is from this source, and not from philosophy,
that it accepts all of its principles.

116. ". . . Deus esse simpliciter non est articulus; sed Deum esse sicut fides
supponit, scilicet habentem curam de omnibus, remunerantem et punientem . . . "
(III Sent., d. 25, q. 1, a. 2, ad 2 [Moos, n. 38, p. 790]).
117. See ST, II–II, q. 1, a. 7: ". . . omnes articuli implicite continentur in aliquibus primis credibilibus, scilicet ut credatur Deus esse et providentiam habere circa
hominum salutem. . . ."
118. See ST, I, q. 2, prologus.
119. See Abbà, Lex et Virtus, 136: "la teologia tomista e in particolare la ST . . .
non una teologia filosofia in un contesto teologico, ma una ragione teologica. . . ."
120. See ST, I, q. 1, a. 3, ad 2: ". . . sic sacra doctrina sit velut quaedam impressio
divinae scientiae, quae est una et simplex omnium."
121. I Sent., prologus, q. 1, a. 2 (Mandonnet, 10): ". . . per ipsum lumen inspira-
tionis divinae. . . ."

This science is able to accept something from the philosophical disciplines, not as though it needed them from some necessity, but in order to manifest better those things which are treated in this science. For it does not accept its principles from the other sciences but immediately from God through revelation. *(ST,* I, q. 1, a. 5, ad 2)[122]

Aquinas grants that some theological propositions can be rationally demonstrated but they remain sacred doctrines. Once again, it is important not to impose the modern paradigm on Aquinas.[123] Rational demonstrations do not turn theology into philosophy. Philosophy and sacred doctrine, even in regard to those doctrines that they share in common, remain generically different.[124] Such doctrines are, first of all, *revelabilia* and it is for that reason that they are included in theology.

Nothing prevents those things that the philosophical sciences treat insofar as they are knowable by the natural light of reason from being considered in another science according as they are known by the light of divine revelation. Hence the theology that pertains to sacred doctrine is generically different from the theology which is set down as a part of philosophy. *(ST,* I, q. 1, a. 1, ad 2)[125]

Although theology—including the *revelabilia* that can be rationally demonstrated—is not philosophy, it is a form of speculative knowledge, indeed the highest wisdom since its indubitable principles derive from God's own self knowledge.

122. ". . . haec scientia accipere potest aliquid a philosophicis disciplinis, non quod ex necessitate eis indigeat, sed ad maiorem manifestationem eorum quae in hac scientia traduntur. Non enim accipit sua principia ab aliis scientiis, sed immediate a Deo per revelationem" *(ST,* I, q. 1, a. 5, ad 2).

123. The modern philosophical appropriation of revealed but fully demonstrable theological truths may have commenced with the fifteenth-century Thomist commentator. In commenting on *ST,* I, q, 1. a. 1, Cajetan introduces a distinction between those revealed truths that can in principle be rationally demonstrated and those that cannot. For Aquinas, both types of revealed truths fall equally under the one science of revealed *sacra doctrina*; for Cajetan, since the two orders of truth are formally distinct, the former is more accurately described as *"demonstrabilia,"* the latter as *"revelabilia."* Gilson maintains ("Note sur le *Revelabile* selon Cajétan," *Mediaeval Studies* 15 [1953]: 203) that Cajetan's distinction is tantamount to denying what Aquinas affirmed, that the *demonstrabilia* are "au sens plein du terme" *revelabilia.* Gilson opines that the next step, ostensibly taken to preserve the formal unity of theology, is "de renvoyer le démontrable à la philosophie où il est chez lui de plein droit" (ibid., p. 204).

124. See *II Sent.,* d. 24, q. 2, a. 2, ad 5 (Mandonnet, 608): "Diversae enim scientiae ex diversis principiis procedunt, etiam si easdem conclusiones demonstrent. . . ."

125. "Unde nihil prohibet de eisdem rebus, de quibus philosophicae disciplinae

In this way sacred doctrine is a science; because it proceeds from principles known in the light of a superior science, namely, the science of God and the blessed. *(ST,* I, q. 1, a. 2)[126]

Aquinas emphasizes not the moral effects but the purely speculative end of theology. But, as I have mentioned, theology overarches the usual division drawn between the speculative and the practical sciences: primarily speculative, it has God as its subject; secondarily practical, it treats human acts insofar as they may be ordered to God.[127]

The *Summa theologiae,* written probably for the benefit of the theological students in the Dominican studium at Santa Sabina in Rome,[128] treats sacred doctrine not as it has been elaborated in piecemeal fashion by previous theologians, but "according to the order of instruction"[129] itself. For both beginners and masters, the order of instruction demands that theology treats everything that it considers in relationship to God.[130]

Theology is principally about God as its subject [but] it includes many things about creatures inasmuch as they are His effects or have some relationship to Him. *(Expos. de Trin.,* q. 5, a. 4 [Decker, 4–6, p. 200])[131]

The unique order that theology follows in its investigations differs from what Aquinas holds to be the properly philosophical investigation of the same things. Whereas the philosopher puts physics before metaphysics,[132] studying natural things before their divine causes, theology reverses the natural order of knowledge and begins with the First

---

tractant secundum quod sunt cognoscibilia lumine naturalis rationis, et aliam scientiam tractare secundum quod cognoscuntur lumine divinae revelationis. Unde theologia quae ad sacram doctrinam pertinet, differt secundum genus ab illa theologia quae pars philosophiae ponitur" *(ST,* I, q. 1, a. 1, ad 2).

126. ". . . sacra doctrina est scientia; quia procedit ex principiis notis lumine superioris scientiae, quae scilicet est scientia Dei et beatorum" *(ST,* I, q. 1, a. 2).

127. See *ST,* I, q. 1, a. 4: "Unde licet in scientiis philosophicis alia sit speculativa et alia practica, sacra tamen doctrina comprehendit sub se utramque. . . ."

128. See Leonard Boyle, O.P., *The Setting of the "Summa Theologiae" of Saint Thomas* (Toronto: Pontifical Institute of Mediaeval Studies, 1982), 19.

129. *ST,* I, prologus: ". . . traduntur secundum ordinem disciplinae. . . ."

130. See *ST,* I, q. 1, a. 7: "De omnibus enim istis tractatur in ista scientia, sed secundum ordinem ad Deum."

131. ". . . theologia est principaliter de deo sicut de subiecto, de creaturis autem multa assumit ut effectus eius vel quomodolibet habentia habitudinem ad ipsum" *(Expos. de Trin.,* q. 5, a. 4 [Decker, 4–6, p. 200]).

132. See *Expos. de Trin.,* prologus (Decker, 4–6, p. 46): "Philosophi enim, qui naturalis cognitionis ordinem sequuntur, praeordinant scientiam de creaturis scientiae divinae, scilicet naturalem metaphysicae."

Cause,[133] the God who has revealed Himself as creator and redeemer. Theology relates everything to this God.

Since they often investigate the same things, the contrast between their two points of view (or formal objects) is essential to the distinction of theology from philosophy.

The consideration of creatures pertains both to theologians and to philosophers but in diverse ways. For philosophers consider creatures insofar as they have a proper nature; hence they inquire after the proper causes and conditions of things. But the theologian considers creatures insofar as they come forth from the first principle and are ordered to the ultimate end which is God. . . . *(II Sent.,* prologus [Mandonnet, 1])[134]

The contrasting points of view are clear, for example, in discussing angels. Theology considers the angels only in relation to God.[135] Metaphysics treats the angels insofar as they are causes of sensible substances.

It necessarily pertains to the same science to consider the separate substances and common being; the latter is the genus and the [separate] substances are the common and universal causes. *(In Metaph.,* prooemium [Cathala-Spiazzi, 2])[136]

Philosophy looks at things from the standpoint of their own natures and ends. Admittedly, philosophy has difficulty in reaching knowledge of these natures and even more difficulty in comprehending the order between them.[137] Usually one knows only the accidents, not the essences, of sensible things, but through such accidents one can some-

133. See *I Sent.,* prologus, q. 1, a. 3, q. 3 (Mandonnet, 12): "[Theologia] . . . est etiam magis dicenda sapientia quam metaphysica, quia causas altissimas considerat per modum ipsarum causarum, quia per inspirationem a Deo immediate acceptam; metaphysica autem considerat causas altissimas per rationes ex creaturis assumptas."

134. "Creaturarum consideratio pertinet ad theologos et ad philosophos, sed diversimodo. Philosophi enim creaturas considerant, secundum quod in propria natura consistunt: unde proprias causas et passiones rerum inquirunt; sed theologus considerat creaturas, secundum quod a primo principio exierunt, et in finem ultimum ordinantur qui Deus est . . ." *(II Sent.,* prologus [Mandonnet, 1]).

135. See *Expos. de Trin.,* q. 5, a. 4, ad 2.

136. "Unde oportet quod ad eamdem scientiam pertineat considerare substantias separatas, et ens commune, quod est genus, cuius sunt praedictae substantiae communes et universales causae" *(In Metaph.,* prooemium [Cathala-Spiazzi, 2]).

137. See *SCG,* IV, 1 (Pera, n. 3340, p. 242): "Sed et si ipsae naturae rerum essent nobis cognitae, ordo tamen earum, secundum quod a divina providentia et ad invicem disponuntur et diriguntur in finem, tenuitur nobis notus esse potest. . . ."

times come to know essences.[138] Consequently, philosophy continues to search for the causes of things, and by looking for their causes, it finally concludes that God is the first cause and ultimate end of all things. God is thus incorporated into metaphysics not as its subject but as the principle and end of its subject. Thomistic metaphysics terminates in demonstrating that there is a first cause and end of its proper subject, being qua being.[139] "Everyone calls" *(ST,* I, q. 2, a. 3) the First Cause "God."

6. Philosophy and Aquinas's Moral Science

Aquinas holds that the moral order is instantiated in a sequence of rational and volitional acts. But the fact that human reason and will *make* the moral order does not entail that this order exclusively or even necessarily falls under a philosophical consideration.[140] For both Aristotle and Aquinas, human choices are precisely *ordered* by the ultimate end being pursued.[141] The distinction, which we have been pursuing, between the formal objects of theology and philosophy should allow us to see clearly the *theological* character of the Thomistic moral order. Aquinas views the human moral order as made in relation to what has been revealed about man's ultimate beatitude and ultimate end—that men, by divine grace, are actually enabled to see God in the heavenly fatherland *(patria).* Given this foundational theological belief, which determines its point of view, Thomistic ethics while rational cannot be accurately characterized as "philo-

138. See *SLA,* I, c. 1, 402b16, 258–60 *(In de An.,* I, lect. 1 [Pirotta, n. 15, p. 5]): ". . . et per ea, scilicet per differencias accidentales, perueniamus in cognitionem essencialium."

139. See *Expos. de Trin.,* q. 5, a. 4 (Decker, 6–9, p. 195): "Sic ergo theologia sive scientia divina est duplex. Una, in qua considerantur res divinae non tamquam subiectum scientiae [= theologia quae in sacra scriptura traditur], sed tamquam principia subiecti, et talis est theologia, quam philosophi prosequuntur, quae alio nomine metaphysica dicitur."

140. *SLE,* I, ante 1094a1, 35–37 *(In Ethic.,* I, lect. 1 [Spiazzi, n. 1, p. 3]) states that "ordo autem actionum voluntariarum pertinet ad considerationem moralis philosophiae." Previously, this order has been identified (ibid., 21–22 [Spiazzi, n. 2, p. 3]) as "ordo quem ratio considerando facit in operationibus voluntatis." Notice that the order is first "considered" then "made" by human reason. Elsewhere, Aquinas explains in detail how the moral order is made: "Primum igitur activum principium in actionibus moralibus est res apprehensa; secundum vis apprehensiva; tertium voluntas; quartum vis motiva, quae exequitur imperium rationis" *(SCG,* III, 10 [Pera, n. 1945, p. 13]). See ch. VI, sec. 11.

141. See *ST,* II-II, q. 11, a. 2: "Electio autem . . . est eorum quae sunt ad finem,

sophical."[142] Only faith, not philosophy, affirms that man can *actually* attain the supernatural vision of God.

Since the perfect beatitude of man consists in the kind of knowledge that exceeds the capacity of every created intellect . . . it was necessary that there be a certain foretaste of this kind of knowledge in man, by which he might be directed to that fullness of blessed knowledge and this takes place through faith. . . . *(SCG*, IV, 54 [Pera, n. 3925, p. 349])[143]

In Aquinas's moral science, human choices are examined as works of reason and will in relation to an end that, although it can be rationally "considered," cannot be cognitively "seen" since it is exclusively an object of faith.[144] Hence the moral *order* "made" by human choices and actions leading to this end falls only under the purview of theology. But the theological character of Aquinas's moral science does not, for Aquinas, derogate its rational character.

Thomistic ethics receives its first principles on supernatural faith. But every subordinate or subalternate Aristotelian science receives, at least proximately, its first principles as matters of natural belief. Aquinas demonstrates that only the vision of God can fulfill man's desire for perfect happiness or beatitude, but these arguments, as we shall learn in subsequent chapters, do not purport to establish that men can actually attain the vision of God. Only faith brings this knowledge. But

---

praesuppositio fine. . . . Unde quod est principale verum habet rationem finis ultimi: quae autem secundaria sunt habent rationem eorum quae sunt ad finem."

142. In his commentary on the *Nicomachean Ethics*, Aquinas takes appropriate pains *not* to read into Aristotle's text any hint of the Thomistic tenet that the eternal law is the source of the *ultimate principles* upon which practical reason relies in commanding the choices that "make" the moral order: see ch. VI, sec.13, esp. n. 370. But this tenet, certainly, plays an essential role in Aquinas's *own* account of how human reason makes the moral order: "Quod autem ratio humana sit regula voluntatis humanae, ex qua eius bonitas mensuretur, habet ex lege aeterna, quae est ratio divina" *(ST*, I–II, q. 19, a. 4). See ch. II, sec. 4: cf. Joseph Owens, C.Ss.R., "Human Reason and the Moral Order in Aquinas," in *Historia: Memoria Futuri*, ed. Réal Tremblay and Dennis J. Billy (Rome: Editiones Academiae Alphonsianae, 1991), 159–77: "As with Aristotle, then, the *whole* moral order was grounded on starting points located within the human person" (162; my italics).

143. "Quia beatitudo perfecta hominis in tali cognitione Dei consistit quae facultatem omnis intellectus creati excedit . . . necessarium fuit quandam huiusmodi cognitionis praelibationem in homine esse, qua dirigeretur in illam plenitudinem cognitionis beatae: quod quidem fit per fidem . . ." *(SCG*, IV, 54 [Pera, n. 3925, p. 349]).

144. Cf. *De ver.*, q. 14, a. 2, ad 9 (Spiazzi, 285): "Dicitur autem fides supra rationem esse, non quod nullus actus rationis sit in fide, sed quia fidei ratio non potest perducere ad videndum ea quae sunt fidei."

once faith guarantees the *factuality* or *actuality* of that end, the business of Aquinas's moral science is to explain how this sublime "beatitude is the reward of virtue."[145]

Thomistic ethics is replete with rational or demonstrative arguments; yet Aquinas did not write—nor apparently was he interested in writing—what he himself would have recognized as "moral philosophy," even if the latter is described as somehow "integrated" into Thomistic theology.[146] The expression is misleading; it would be more accurate to say that Aquinas integrates reason into his theology. This latter way of speaking does not impose the modern philosophical paradigm on Aquinas. The modern paradigm first identifies a rational ethics with a philosophical ethics and then attempts to discover how Aquinas integrated the latter into his theology.[147] This, as is evident from a medieval objection, is not Aquinas's procedure.

The modern disjunction of philosophy (or reasoned arguments) from theology has a medieval counterpart, which insists that if theology uses rationally demonstrative arguments that make no immediate appeal to faith it becomes diluted or impure. Aquinas rejects the objection with a striking metaphor: when the water of philosophical reason is mixed with the wine of theology, the water actually becomes wine.[148]

Described in less metaphorical terms, Aquinas's moral science is, according to its own standards, both rational and theological.[149] It is not a moral philosophy or a theology that somehow incorporates what would otherwise be an autonomous moral philosophy. The "philosophy" (i.e., rational doctrine) that exists in St. Thomas's theology is, in fact, *theology*.

---

145. ". . . beatitudo virtutis est praemium" (*SCG*, IV, 54 [Pera, n. 3928, p. 350]).

146. Cf. Ricardo Marimon Batalló, "Los fundamentos de la etica en Tomas de Aquino," in *Morale et Diritto nella prospettiva tomistica*, Atti dell'VIII Congresso Tomistico Internazionale (Vatican City: Libreria Editrice Vaticana, 1982), 21: "Pero creemos que aun integrada en el conjuto de su teologia, se da en el pensamiento de Tomas una doctrina sistematica de etica filosofica."

147. Reviewing Kluxen's book, Andre Wylleman, *Revue philosophique de Louvain* 62 (1964): 672, states that the problem vis-à-vis Thomistic ethics is "de définir le statut exact d'une réflexion philosophique qui, *tout en restant philosophique*, est rapportée à une théologie" [my italics]. Defined in this way, the problem has no answer, or at least not one that can be attributed to Aquinas.

148. See *Expos. de Trin.*, q. 2, a. 3, ad 5.

149. See Denis J. M. Bradley, "Aristotelian Science and the Science of Thomistic Theology," *Heythrop Journal* 22 (1981): 162–72.

7. Theology and "Sacred Doctrine"

Aquinas's moral science is part of his effort to "investigate the nature and domain of sacred doctrine *[sacra doctrina]*."[150] The meaning of this term, if one prescinds from subsequent controversies, is tolerably clear from Aquinas's scattered remarks.[151] In summary form, "*sacra doctrina*" *can* be defined as the teaching, revealed by Christ to the Apostles, that is contained in Scripture as authoritatively interpreted and promulgated by the Catholic Church in its preeminent creed, the Apostle's Creed.[152] Thus sacred doctrine is a teaching that rests on revelation and presupposes faith. In regard to the knowledge of God, sacred doctrine is a wisdom that remedies the defects of philosophy.

Since philosophy only proceeds through arguments drawn from created beings, it is not adequate for getting to know God. Therefore, it is necessary that there be some higher doctrine which proceeds from revelation, and which remedies the defect of philosophy. *(I Sent.,* prologus, q. 1, a. 1 [Mandonnet, 7])[153]

Aquinas, then, draws a clear contrast between sacred doctrine and the solely rational philosophical sciences. He also precisely distinguishes the supernatural habit of faith (i.e., belief in the articles of faith) from the natural habit of demonstrating the conclusions that can be drawn from the articles or principles of faith.[154] Not every believer but only the scientific theologian possesses the latter noetic habit. Less clear, for some contemporary interpreters, is the distinction that Aquinas draws, if he does draw one, between sacred doctrine and the science of theology.[155] Indeed, no clearly drawn distinction can be found in Aquinas.

---

150. See *ST,* I, q. 1, prologus; trans. Anton C. Pegis, *Basic Writings of Saint Thomas Aquinas* (New York: Random House, 1945), 1: 5.

151. See M.-J. Congar, O.P., Comptes rendus, *Bulletin thomiste* 5 (1937–1939): 490–505; and Weisheipl, "Meaning of 'Sacra Doctrina,'" 49–80.

152. See *III Sent.,* d. 25, q. 1, a. 1, sol. 3; *ST,* II-II, q. 1, a. 9; q. 5, a. 3; III, q. 42.

153. "Cum igitur philosophia non procedat nisi per rationes sumptas ex creaturis, insufficiens est ad Dei cognitionem faciendam. Ergo oportet aliquam aliam doctrinam esse altiorem, quae per revelationem procedat, et philosophiae defectum suppleat" *(I Sent.,* prologus, q. 1, a. 1 [Mandonnet, 7]).

154. See *I Sent.,* prologus, q. 1, a. 3, sol. 2, ad 3; *Expos. de Trin.,* q. 5, a. 4, ad 8.

155. For example, Per Erik Persson, *Sacra Doctrina: Reason and Revelation in Aquinas,* trans. Ross Mackenzie (Oxford: Basil Blackwell, 1970), 72, n. 5, claims that ". . . *sacra doctrina* is a part of *theologia,* viz., that which teaches what is necessary for man's salvation." Persson's interpretation corresponds to the earlier commentary of Sylvius (1581–1649). Aquinas, however, never calls *sacra doctrina* a "part" of theology; rather, he treats what we call "theology" as subordinated to sacred doctrine.

In the Prologue to his writings on the *Sentences* of Peter Lombard, Aquinas states, without distinguishing the two terms, that *sacred doctrine* or *sacred scripture* is a science that uses both religious authorities and rational arguments to destroy errors, to promote morals, and to contemplate the truth.[156] In the Prologue to *Summa theologiae*, I, q. 1, aa. 1–10, Aquinas proposes to investigate "the nature and extent of *sacra doctrina.*" Subsequently, these articles appear to interchange the meaning of the terms "*sacra doctrina*," "*revelatio divina*," "*theologia*," and "*sacra scriptura.*" But how can "sacred doctrine" refer, without equivocation, to revelation (a. 1), scientific theology (aa. 2–8), and sacred scripture (aa. 9–10)? Is it, as Chenu thought, a case of Aquinas's terminology being in arrears of his ideas and actual theological method?[157]

The apparent ambiguity of "*sacra doctrina*" *troubled* the classic Thomist commentators—Capreolus (1380–c. 1444), Cajetan (1469–1534), Báñez (1528–1604), and John of St. Thomas (1589–1644)—all of whom separate, in one way or the other, what Aquinas leaves united.[158] Aquinas, to be sure, makes enough distinctions of his own. Along with Aristotle, he allows that "science" can be used in a wide or a narrow sense. Taken widely, science is any knowledge that is certain; taken less widely, science is the conclusions that necessarily follow from something already known;[159] taken strictly, science demonstrates how an effect derives from a cause whose nature is known.[160] "Theology" too can be used generically or specifically. Used generically, "theology" is a "discourse about divine things" *(sermo de divinis)*[161] or—according to its etymology—a "discourse about God" *(sermo de Deo).*[162] Used specifically, the "theology which pertains to sacred doctrine" or the "theology which is transmitted in scripture" must be distinguished from philosophical theology or metaphysics.[163] The theology that is

156. See *I Sent.*, prologus, q. 1, a. 5.

157. See M.-D. Chenu, O.P., *La Science théologique*, 3d ed. (Paris: J. Vrin, 1957), 79 [= a revised version of "La Théologie comme science au XIIIe siècle," *Archives d'histoire doctrinale et littéraire du moyen âge* 2 (1927): 31–71].

158. See L. Charlier, O.P., *Essai sur le problème théologique* (Thuillies, Belgium: Ramboux-Gallot, 1938), 14–34.

159. See *Expos. de Trin.*, q. 2, a. 2 (Decker, 22–23, p. 86): ". . . ratio scientiae consistat in hoc quod ex aliquibus notis alia necessario concludantur. . . ."

160. See *ELP*, I, 4, 71b29, 238–41 (Leonine ed., I, pt. 2, 21a); 7, 72b23, 83–97 (31b).

161. *In Metaph.*, VI, lect. 1 (Cathala-Spiazzi, n. 1167, p. 298).

162. *I Sent.*, prologus, q. 1, a. 4, (Mandonnet, 15); *ST*, I, q. 1, a. 8.

163. See *ST*, I, q. 1, a. 1, ad 2: "theologia quae ad sacram doctrinam pertinet"; *Expos. de Trin.* q. 5, a. 4 (Decker, 10–11, p. 195): "theologia quae in scriptura traditur." Thus Aristotle, but not Aquinas, can be appropriately called (by Thomistic criteria) a "philosophical theologian."

based on "sacred doctrine" is preeminently "about those things which are above reason."[164] It is a knowledge "not taken from creatures but immediately inspired from the divine light."[165] Finally, theology is best described as a "wisdom" incorporating knowledge both of principles and conclusions. But these well-known distinctions are not exactly to the commentators' point. They were concerned about the scientific status of theology. In the Aristotelian ambiance of the commentators, the term *"sacra doctrina" requires* further clarification. How is sacred doctrine a "science"? This question continues to inspire highly nuanced answers from contemporary interpreters of Aquinas.[166]

Aquinas affirms that sacred doctrine is a science because, like any Aristotelian science, it too argues from principles—in theology's case, the revealed articles of faith—to further conclusions.[167] The classic Thomist commentators fixate on the Aristotelian definition of "science" undergirding Aquinas's claim.[168] The commentators earnestly repeat what Aquinas himself says: Aristotelian "science" is the intellectual habit of deriving conclusions from premises.[169] Capreolus stresses that science is "solely about the conclusions."[170] Cajetan's for-

---

164. ". . . theologia autem est de his quae sunt supra rationem . . ." (*I Sent.*, prologus, q. 1, a. 5 [Mandonnet, 18]).

165. ". . . cognitionem non a creaturis sumptam, sed immediate ex divino lumine inspiratam; et haec est doctrina theologiae" (*I Sent.*, prologus, q. 1, a. 1 [Mandonnet, 8]).

166. Although he does not directly address the question of the "scientific" status of theology, Anton C. Pegis, in "Qu'est-ce que la *Summa Contra Gentiles?*" in *L'Homme devant Dieu: Mélanges offerts au Père Henri de Lubac* (Paris: Aubier, 1964), 2: 169–82, suggests that theology and *sacra doctrina* are distinguished by the "dessein humain" that the theologian imposes on a unitary *sacra doctrina*. This "human design" is a reflection of the theologian's own particular historical circumstances and purposes which can vary from work to work. Thus "la *S.T.* and la *S.C.G.* exposent la même enseignment divin *(sacra doctrina)* en des théologies différentes . . ." (175).

167. See *ST*, I, q. 1, a. 8. Aquinas enumerates fourteen articles of faith (seven referring to the Godhead, seven referring to Christ's humanity) in the Apostles's Creed, but allows that there are different ways of tallying the articles: see *III Sent.*, d. 25, q. 1, a. 2; *ST*, II–II, q. 1, a. 8.

168. Abbà exaggerates in the opposite direction: sacred doctrine has no need of Aristotle to become "scientific"; it is already "a science simply because it teaches a truth, the [revealed] truth about God" (*Lex et Virtus*, 107). Consequently, "ne la fede ne la ragione la fanno scienza, bensì la rivelazione . . ." (138).

169. See *ELP*, I, 4, 71b17, 137–44 (Leonine ed., I, pt. 2, 19b–20a); *I Sent.*, prologus, q. 1, a. 1, q. 3; *SLE*, I, 18, 1101b21, 95–96 (*In Ethic.*, I, lect. 18 [Spiazzi, n. 219, p. 59]); *SLE*, VI, 5, 1140b31, 17–40 (*In Ethic.*, VI, lect. 5 [Spiazzi, nn. 1176–1177, p. 322].

170. See Capreolus, *Defensiones theologiae*, prologi Sent., q. 1, a. 1, quinta conclusio.

mula is lapidary: "Faith is about the articles; science is about the conclusions."[171] But Cajetan also allows that sacred doctrine is a genus (= "revealed knowledge") that contains both faith and theological science as species.[172]

Dominico Báñez, O.P., who vigorously adheres to the Aristotelian line about science, demurs and takes a step beyond Cajetan. Sacred doctrine, because it is a science, refers only to demonstrated conclusions.

Although Cajetan will have said in the preceding article [ST, I, q. 1, a. 1] that by the name of "sacred doctrine," St. Thomas will not have understood a determinate faith or a determinate theology, but will take [the term] indifferently for the doctrine revealed immediately, which is faith, or [for the doctrine revealed] mediately, which is theology, nonetheless, already in this article [ST, I, q. 1, a. 2] "sacred doctrine" is asserted not about faith but about the doctrine which derives from assenting to the conclusions that are deduced from the principles of faith. (Bañes Scholastica commentaria, I, q. 1, a. 2 [ed. Luis Urbano, 18–19])[173]

John of St. Thomas gives the definitive statement of this position. Sacred doctrine should be identified with theology, and theology refers only to the rigorous deduction of the virtually revealed. Moreover, the deduction can include a premise that is drawn not from faith but from reason.

In all its truths, theology proceeds under the same formal object: namely, by considering those things that have been virtually revealed. And it proceeds from either two premises both of which are held by faith, or from one premise that derives from the natural light [of reason]. (Cursus theologici, In primae partis, disp. 2, a. 7 [Solesmes Edition: 1, §6, p. 376])[174]

171. "Fides est de articulis, scientia autem de conclusionibus" (ST, I, q. 1, a . 2; Commentaria Card. Caietani, n. XII [Leonine ed., IV, 11]).

172. See ST, I, q. 1, a. 1; Commentaria Card. Caietani, n. VI (Leonine ed., IV, 7): "Sacra doctrina neque sumitur pro fide ut distinguitur contra theologiam; neque pro theologia, ut distinguitur contra fidem: sed sumitur pro cognitione a Deo revelata, sive formaliter sive virtualiter, ut habet rationem disciplinae et doctrinae, abstrahendo a ratione crediti et sciti."

173. ". . . quanvis Cajetanus . . . dixerit quod nomine sacrae doctrinae non intellexerit d. Thomas fidem determinate, vel determinate Theologiam, sed indifferenter acceperit pro doctrina revelata immediate, qualis est fides; vel mediate, qualis est Theologia; nihilominus jam in hoc articulo sacra doctrina verificatur non de fide, sed de doctrina, quae inclinat ad assensum conclusionum, quae ex principiis fidei deducuntur" (Bañes Scholastica commentaria, I, q. 1, a. 2 [ed. Luis Urbano, 18–19]).

174. ". . . theologia in omnibus suis veritatibus procedit sub eadem ratione formali: scilicet respiciendo illas ut virtualiter revelatas, sive procedatur ex duabus praemissis de fide, sive ex altera luminis naturalis" (Cursus theologici, In primae partis, disp. 2, a. 7 [Solesmes Edition: 1, §6, p. 376]).

Yet Cajetan attends to a problem that Báñez and the subsequent commentators evade. Cajetan's interpretation, although it is more logical than exegetical, attempts to preserve the unity of what Aquinas announces as the subject to be investigated throughout the entire ten articles of *ST*, I, q. 1—*sacra doctrina*—and does so without ignoring the diversity of what Aquinas talks about. By simply identifying sacred doctrine with scientific theology, Báñez collapses the actual subject matters of articles one, nine, and ten. But while Báñez's reading may be rejected, the unity of these ten articles remains problematic.[175] Cajetan falls back on a logical device that does not resolve the inherent tension in the Thomistic concept of a scientific theology. Thomistic usage, which is not fixed, betrays this tension.

Aquinas sometimes precisely restricts even "sacred doctrine" to demonstrated conclusions. For example:

Thus even in this [sacred] doctrine there is not acquired the habit of faith which is, as it were, a habit of principles; but there is acquired the habit of those things which are deduced from these principles and which are valuable in defending them. *(I Sent.*, prologus, q. 1, a. 3, sol. 2 [Mandonnet, 14])[176]

Thus the articles of faith are the revealed principles from which a deductive theological science derives conclusions. Other times, even in the same work, Aquinas is not so restrictive. Theological science can also be said to determine these principles.

It is the case that the habit of faith receives determination from our part. In regard to this determination, faith is said to be acquired through the science of theology which distinguishes the articles [of faith]. . . . *(III Sent.*, d. 23, q. 3, a. 2, ad 1 [Moos, n. 256, p. 748])[177]

175. Weisheipl, who thinks that the scientific character of sacred doctrine "is obvious from the internal nature of faith" (61), argues that in *ST*, I, q. 1 sacred doctrine in nowise refers to "scholastic theology." But Weisheipl minimizes the work of the theologian (cf. "Meaning of 'Sacra Doctrina,'" p. 71); yet, he acknowledges that prior even to the work of the Scholastic theologian, ecclesial creeds are necessary because Scripture itself lacks a manifestly rational order in presenting the truths of faith. Cf. *ST*, II–II, q. 1, a. 9. In opposition to Chenu's interpretation, Abbà warns *(Lex et Virtus*, 100) that Aquinas's problem was not only to bring theology into harmony with Aristotelian science but also to subsume Augustine's notion of science and wisdom.

176. ". . . ita etiam in hac doctrina non acquiritur habitus fidei, qui est quasi habitus principiorum; sed acquiritur habitus eorum quae ex eis deducuntur et quae ad eorum defensionem valent" *(I Sent.*, prologus, q. 1, a. 3, sol. 2 [Mandonnet, 14]).

177. "Et similiter oportet quod fidei habitus determinationem recipiat ex parte nostra, et quantum ad istam determinationem dicitur fides acquiri per scientiam

Herein lies the tension in Aquinas's account of theology. Sacred doctrine, drawing on the Aristotelian model, can be called a "science" yet the "science of theology" can never be made isomorphic with any Aristotelian science. In that sense, theology can be appropriately labeled "a new science."[178]

Faith is determined through the hearing of doctrine which proposes what ought to be held, but which does not prove what is proposed. And, therefore, such a doctrine does not constitute [scientific] knowledge. (III Sent., d. 24, a. 3, sol. 2 [Moos, n. 62, p. 770])[179]

The Summa theologiae, as its preface states, sets forth "those things which pertain to sacred doctrine."[180] Preeminent among the revealed truths of sacred doctrine are those that can only be accepted on faith because they are beyond any man's natural knowledge.

When sacred doctrine is conformed to the model of Aristotelian science, then the multitudinous propositions of sacred doctrine need to be distinguished into principles and conclusions in order for the comparison to hold. But, actually, the theology that is congruent with revealed sacred doctrine cannot be so neatly divided; it does not and cannot perfectly conform to the Aristotelian model.

Science and faith are not [in this respect] similar, because there are not in us some innate natural principles, to which the articles of faith are able to be reduced. The total determination of faith is in us through doctrine. (III Sent., d. 25, q. 2, a. 1, sol. 4, ad 1 [Moos, n. 78, p. 799])[181]

Although Aquinas does not deny that the theologian can syllogize, theological reasoning is not primarily aimed at inventing new conclusions or demonstrating their truth.[182] The division of sacred doctrine into principles and conclusions is at best analogous: the principles are

---

theologicam [theologiae] quae articulos distinguit . . ." (III Sent., d. 23, q. 3, a. 2, ad 1 [Moos, n. 256, p. 748]).

178. See Abbà, Lex et Virtus, 136. But it does not follow, however, that the Aristotelian model can be dismissed as somehow less than fundamental to Aquinas's own purposes.

179. ". . . fides determinatur per auditum doctrinae proponentis quid tenendum sit, sed non probantis propositum. Et ideo scientiam talis doctrina non facit" (III Sent., d. 24, q. 1, a. 3, sol. 2 [Moos, n. 62, p. 770]).

180. ST, prologus: ". . . ea quae ad sacram doctrinam pertinent, breviter ac dilucide prosequi. . . ."

181. "Et ideo non est simile de scientia et fide, quia non sunt innata nobis aliqua principia naturalia ad quae possint reduci articuli fidei, sed tota determinatio fidei est in nobis per doctrinam" (III Sent., d. 25, q. 2, a. 1, sol. 4, ad 1 [Moos, n. 78, p. 799]).

182. See III Sent., d. 23, q. 2, a. 1, ad 4 (Moos, n. 121, pp. 720–21): ". . . inquantum ipsa fides est manifestativa alterius, sive inquantum unus articulus manifestat

"quasi-principles," the conclusions are "quasi-conclusions."[183] Making this division allows the theologian to assemble certain propositions into valid syllogisms, but it does not alter the revealed status of the premises or (in most cases) of the conclusion.[184] In Thomistic theology, the primary task of the demonstrative method is to *clarify* faith by manifesting how one belief follows from another.[185]

Although sacred doctrine uses human reason, it does not do so to prove faith, since that would take away from the merit of belief, but to make clear other things that are set forth in this doctrine. *(ST,* I, q. 1, a. 8, ad 2)[186]

This Thomistic notion of theological reasoning is in conformity with the standard logical distinction between truth and validity. While the validity of any syllogism depends upon the form of the inference, the truth of the conclusion in a valid syllogism follows necessarily only if the premises are true. Demonstration, if it begins with premises held to be true only on revealed faith, can never independently establish the truth of any conclusion of a theological syllogism.[187] For theology, the range of faith is global.

Faith, taken just in itself, adequately extends to everything that goes along with faith or follows it or precedes it. *(III Sent.,* d. 24, a. 2, sol. 2 [Moos, n. 61, p. 769])[188]

From the standpoint of their truth, the distinction between principles (articles of faith) and scientific conclusions is misleading. Although it can have persuasive value, a theological argument, strictly

---

alium, sicut resurrectio Christi resurrectionem futuram; sive inquantum ex ipsis articulis quaedam alia in theologia syllogizantur; sive inquantum fides unius hominis confirmat fidem alterius."

183. See *Expos. de Trin.,* q. 2, a. 2 (Decker, 20–21, p. 87): ". . . ut sic ipsa, quae fide tenemus, sint nobis quasi principia in hac scientia et alia sint quasi conclusiones."

184. Cf. J. M. Ramirez, "De philosophia morali Christiani," *Divus Thomas* 14 (1936): 114, who provides a merely nominal resolution: "[Theological] conclusions themselves are sometimes able to be of the faith, but not formally or reduplicatively as theological conclusions, but as materially or specifically truths elsewhere formally and explicitly revealed."

185. See *III Sent.,* d. 23, q. 2, a. 1, ad 4; *De ver.,* q. 14, a. 2, ad 9; *ST,* I, q. 1, a. 8, ad 2.

186. "Unde tamen sacra doctrina etiam ratione humana: non quidem ad probandum fidem, quia per hoc tolleretur meritum fidei; sed ad manifestandum aliqua alia quae traduntur in hac doctrina" *(ST,* I, q. 1, a. 8, ad 2).

187. See *Expos. de Trin.,* q. 2, a. 2, ad 5.

188. ". . . fides, quantum in se est, ad omnia quae fidem concomitantur vel sequuntur vel praecedunt sufficienter inclinat" *(III Sent.,* d. 24, q. 1, a. 2, sol. 2 [Moos, n. 61, p. 769]).

speaking, is not a demonstration that establishes the truth of its conclusion.

The arguments which are introduced by holy men to prove things that
pertain to the faith are not demonstrations, but they are persuasive statements showing that what the faith proposes is not impossible. Or they
proceed from the principles of faith, namely, from the authority of sacred
scripture. . . . (ST, II–II, q. 1, a. 5, ad 2)[189]

In a theological syllogism, the truth of the conclusion, as much as
its premises, is affirmed only on the authority of biblical revelation.
Faith, not demonstration, thus grounds the truth of the conclusions
reached in a scientific theology.[190] But, using Aristotle's definition of
"science," scientific theology is what follows or what can be logically
derived from the articles of faith.[191] The significance accorded to such
theological demonstrations has varied in the history of Thomist theology. The sixteenth-century Thomist commentators, especially those
engaged in Counter Reformation polemics, stressed the role of demonstration in reaching new conclusions so that they might defend those
Catholic doctrines that had only been "virtually revealed." But their
emphasis even as it explicates also slants Aquinas.[192] Although sacred
doctrine is a wisdom (sapientia) that encompasses principles and conclusions,[193] faith is especially an understanding of principles.[194]

In discussing heresy and disbelief, Aquinas does acknowledge that
reason can draw out propositions that are not explicitly revealed. Once
these implicit truths have been rationally demonstrated, it would be
sinful and possibly heretical to deny them.[195] But in allowing reason a
role, Aquinas highlights faith and ecclesiastical authority; and while he
does not deny, he certainly does not emphasize that reason can draw
out novel theological conclusions. In fact, the modern notion of substantive theological progress in attaining new truths is contrary to the
spirit of what Aquinas says. Aquinas denies that succeeding genera-

189. ". . . rationes quae inducuntur a Sanctis ad probandum ea quae sunt fidei
non sunt demonstrativae, sed persuasiones quaedam manifestantes non esse impossibile quod in fide proponitur. Vel procedunt ex principiis fidei, scilicet ex auctorita-
tibus sacrae Scripturae . . ." (ST, II–II, q. 1, a. 5, ad 2).
190. See Expos. de Trin., q. 2, a. 2, ad 6.
191. See De ver., q. 14, a. 9, ad 3.
192. See Congar, Bulletin thomiste, 5, p. 493, n. 1.
193. See I Sent., prologus, q. 1, a. 3, q. 3, sol. 1.
194. See III Sent., d. 25, q. 2, a. 1, sol. 3 (Moos, n. 70, p. 798); Expos. de Trin., q.
6, a. 1, ad q. 3, ad 1; ibid., ad 4.
195. See I Sent., d. 33, q. 1, a. 5.

tions of Christian theologians have come to a better understanding of the apostolic faith. In regard to the essentials, understanding of the faith actually diminishes because each succeeding generation is increasingly distant from Christ and the apostles "who more fully knew the mysteries of faith."[196] Since nothing can be taken away or added to the articles of faith, succeeding generations of believers must content themselves with drawing out inessential details.[197]

Aquinas ties faith, but only indirectly, to a logic of demonstration. A proposition belongs to faith indirectly when its contrary is opposed to some truth that belongs directly to faith.[198] What is uppermost is that the Church declares that some proposition is to be believed.

> In the faith there are some things which every man is obliged to know explicitly. If he strays from these things, he is regarded as an unbeliever and a heretic if he adds obstinacy [to his error]. . . . And about some things, people have diverse opinions (because some things are [only] contained implicitly in the faith of the Church, as conclusions [are contained] in principles) until such time as the Church determines that something is contrary to the faith of the Church. In this case, it follows that something is directly contrary to faith. *(IV Sent.,* d. 13, q. 2, a. 1, ad 6 [Moos, n. 139, pp. 565–66])[199]

Aquinas himself never forgets the intrinsic limitations of the analogy between theology and Aristotelian science.

> Faith is said to be above reason not because there is no act of reason in faith, but because reasoning about faith is not able to lead to seeing those things which pertain to faith. *(De ver.,* q. 14, a. 2, ad 9 [Spiazzi, 284])[200]

Since the conclusions drawn from the articles are only "quasi-conclusions," it is more accurate to say that the theologian "explicates" the

196. ". . . plenius mysteria fidei cognoverunt" *(ST,* II–II, q. 1, a. 7, ad 4).

197. See *III Sent.,* d. 25, q. 2, a. 2, sol. 1, ad 5 (Moos, n. 102, p. 805).

198. See *ST,* I, q. 32, a. 4: "Indirecte ad fidem pertinent ea ex quibus negatis consequitur aliquid contrarium fidei. . . ."

199. ". . . in fide sunt aliqua ad quae explicite cognoscenda omnis homo tenetur. Unde si in his aliquis errat, infidelis reputatur, et haereticus, si pertinaciam adjungat. . . . Et quia quaedam sunt quae in fide Ecclesiae implicite continentur, ut conclusiones in principiis, ideo in his diversae opiniones sustinentur, quousque per Ecclesiam determinatur quod aliquid eorum contra fidem Ecclesiae est, quia ex eo sequitur aliquid contrarium fidei directe" *(IV Sent.,* d. 13, q. 2, a. 1, ad 6 [Moos, n. 139, pp. 565–66]).

200. "Dicitur autem fides supra rationem esse, non quod nullus actus rationis sit in fide, sed quia fidei ratio non potest perducere ad videndum ea quae sunt fidei" *(De ver.,* q. 14, a. 2, ad 9 [Spiazzi, 284]).

articles of faith by showing how one such article is implicitly contained in another. The real explication of the faith is found in Christ's own life.[201] But the theologian, to be sure, can engage in *"l'explication de texte."* He or she might attempt to show that:

The article about the conception [of Christ] is implicitly contained in the article about the nativity insofar as it is the way toward the nativity. Moreover, the article about the descent to the lower regions [is contained] within the article about the passion, and the article about the ascension [is contained] in the article about the resurrection, because there the victory of the resurrected one is completed. *(III Sent.*, d. 25, q. 2, a. 2, sol. 3 [Moos, n. 116, p. 808])[202]

But such reasoning is not a strict deduction and it obviously occurs within the circle of faith.

Aquinas's moral science falls also within this circle. The proper subject of moral philosophy is human actions and virtues. Human actions should be evaluated in reference to their ends. The ultimate end of human action, so Aristotle argues, is the contemplation of God. On this point, Aristotelian philosophy and Christian faith appear to be in remarkable agreement. But, as Aquinas explains at great length and with great care, there is an even more remarkable divergence between them: "The philosopher and the theologian consider a different good to be ultimate."[203] What, then, is the ultimate good that grounds man's moral efforts? One of the articles of faith teaches that the direct vision of God is man's true end. As it turns out, it is this belief that structures Aquinas's entire moral science.

The theologian considers as the ultimate good that which exceeds the faculty of nature, namely, eternal life. . . . Hence, he does not consider the good in human acts unconditionally, because he does not place the end there, but [he considers them only] in relation to that good which he places as the end. *(De ver.*, q. 14, a. 3 [Spiazzi, 287])[204]

201. See *III Sent.*, d. 25, q. 2, a. 2, sol. 1, ad 5 (Moos, n. 101, p. 805): "Et sic fides implicita explicatur in articulis fidei determinatis. Et haec explicatio completa est per Christum; unde ejus doctrinae quantum ad essentialia fidei nec diminuere nec addere licet. . . ."

202. ". . . quod articulus conceptionis implicite continebatur in articulo nativitatis in quantum est via ad nativitatem; articulus autem de descensu ad inferos, in articulo de passsione; articulus autem de ascensione in articulo de resurrectione, quia ibi terminatur victoria resurgentis" (*III Sent.*, d. 25, q. 2, a. 2, sol. 3 [Moos, n. 116, p. 808]).

203. "Aliud est autem bonum ultimum quod considerat philosophus et theologus" (*De ver.*, q. 14, a. 3 [Spiazzi, 286]).

204. "Sed theologus considerat quasi bonum ultimum id quod est naturae facul-

Now it is just this belief which makes the proposed construction of a "Thomistic philosophical ethics" so problematic an undertaking. The preceding text from the *De veritate* provokes many questions that I shall examine in the remaining chapters of this book. What is the status of the good that the philosophers regard as ultimate? And if that good is not man's real ultimate good, in what sense can the theologian acknowledge the validity of philosophical ethics? Does the construction of an allegedly autonomous Thomistic ethics entail that there is an ultimate earthly good? The issues, as we can already see, are many and complex. We can simplify them somewhat by approaching moral philosophy as Aquinas did, by reading Aristotle through Aquinas's spectacles.

---

tatem excedens, scilicet vitam aeternam, ut praedictum est. Unde bonum in actibus humanis non considerat absolute, quia ibi non ponit finem, sed in ordine ad id bonum quod ponit finem . . ." *(De ver.,* q. 14, a. 3 [Spiazzi, 287]).

III

Aquinas Reading Aristotle

1. Aquinas's Aristotelian "Commentaries"

Of the many different philosophical ethics that have been or could be used to contrast Thomistic theological ethics, only Aristotle's ethics is paradigmatic from Aquinas's own historical and doctrinal perspective. Beginning with his bachelor's lectures (1252–56) on Peter Lombard's *Sentences,* and continuing throughout his later works, Aquinas commanded the entirety of the *Nicomachean Ethics;* it was the counterpoint to everything that Aquinas himself wrote about morality.[1] From our historical perspective too, Aquinas's appropriation of the *Nicomachean Ethics* is a monument in the history of Christian moral speculation. With Aristotle's help, Aquinas was able to recast the medieval Augustinian tradition, with its profound biblical and Neoplatonist spirituality, into an ethics—a rational, humanistic, and theological science[2]—that synthesized and systematized, in remarkably comprehen-

1. The text of the *Nicomachean Ethics* upon which Aquinas comments is a mid-thirteenth century revision of Robert Grosseteste's Latin translation (dated 1246–47). The redactor is anonymous; contemporary scholars no longer identify him with William of Moerbeke. For the host of textual and historical puzzles surrounding Aquinas's commentary, see Vernon J. Bourke, "The Nicomachean Ethics and Thomas Aquinas," in *St. Thomas Aquinas, 1274–1974: Commemorative Studies* (Toronto: Pontifical Institute of Mediaeval Studies, 1974), I: 239–59.

2. For Aquinas's three major systematic accounts of his moral science, see *III Sent.,* d. 33; *SCG,* III, 48–160 (written sometime between 1261 and 1265); and *ST,* Secunda pars (written 1269–72). M.-D. Chenu, O.P., in *Toward Understanding St. Thomas,* trans. A.-M Landry, O.P. and D. Hughes, O.P (Chicago: Henry Regnery, 1964), 271, n. 20, calls the forty-two questions in the *III Sent.,* d. 33 (which correspond to two pages of Peter Lombard's text) "the first treatise of moral theology to have been developed."

sive fashion, Greek philosophical doctrines about earthly virtues and vices and Christian religious beliefs about otherworldly union with God.[3]

Although Aquinas's moral science incorporates Platonic, Neoplatonic, and Stoic elements,[4] the structural and doctrinal influence of Aristotle on Thomistic ethics is pervasive.[5] Aquinas makes a massive number of specific references to Aristotle himself: the *Index Thomisticus* lists 38 references to *"Aristoteles"* and 977 references to *"Philosophus"* in the *Secunda pars* of the *Summa theologiae*.

About Aristotle's influence on Aquinas, then, no one can be in doubt. Nonetheless, that influence can be variously calculated, with the calculation varying according to the interpreter's wish to stress the methodological and doctrinal originality of Thomistic ethics.[6] Such calculations are matters of interpretative nuance and they can hardly be avoided. But every interpretation faces the same initial difficulty: how is Aquinas's way of reading Aristotle to be characterized? In the first place, it is evident that Aquinas's exegesis cannot be easily accommodated to the canons of contemporary textual exegesis. To his "expositions"[7] of Aristotle's texts, Aquinas evidently brings theological preoccupations; indeed, sometimes he explicitly mentions Christian doctrines and sometimes they appear to dominate his exegesis.

To take one instance,[8] Aquinas attributes to Aristotle a notion of

---

3. See D. Odon Lottin, "Pour un commentaire historique de la morale de saint Thomas d'Aquin," in *Psychologie et morale aux xiie et xiiie siècle*, vol. 3, pt. 2: *Problèmes de morale* (Louvain: Abbaye de Mont Cesar; Gembloux: J. Duculot, 1949), 576–601; and Étienne Gilson, *Saint Thomas Moraliste*, 2d ed., rev. (Paris: J. Vrin, 1972), 1–14.

4. See Reginaldo M. Pizzorni, O.P., *Il diritto naturale dalle origini a S. Tommaso d'Aquino*, 2d ed., rev. (Rome: Pontificia Università Lateranense, Città Nuova Editrice, 1985); and Michel Spanneut, *Permanence du Stoïcisme: De Zeno à Malraux* (Gembloux, Belgium: Éditions J. Duculot, 1973), 193–94.

5. For example, see Marie-Noëlle Dumas, "La Definition de la prudence chez Thomas d'Aquin et ses relations avec la definition d'Aristote," *Bulletin du cercle thomiste, Caen*, no. 2 (1978): 19–30; no. 3 (1978): 3–14.

6. Cf. André Thiry, S.J., "Saint Thomas et la moral d'Aristote," in *Aristote et saint Thomas d'Aquin* (Louvain: Publications Universitaires de Louvain; Paris: Éditions Béatrice-Nauwelaerts, 1957), 229–58.

7. *"Expositio"* was first used to label the commentaries in the Venice edition of 1563. The internal division of Aquinas's text into *"lectiones"* was introduced by Paolina Turco in his fourth edition of the commentaries (Venice, 1519). See René-A. Gauthier, O.P., "Saint Thomas et *L'Éthique à Nicomaque*," appendix to *Sententia libri Politicorum, Sancti Thomae Aquinatis opera omnia*, Leonine Edition (Rome: 1971), 48: xxiv.

8. See *In Metaph.*, VI, lect. 1 (Cathala-Spiazzi, n. 1164, p. 354).

creation while he sharply criticizes those interpreters of Aristotle who, presupposing that the heavenly bodies are eternal and subject only to the final causality of the unmoved movers, deny that the heavenly bodies need an efficient cause. Against these other interpreters, Aquinas objects that all finite existents, the heavenly bodies included, must be efficiently caused by a subsistent existent.

Aquinas's benign but blatantly Christian reading of Aristotle, however philosophically defensible in itself, is clearly a theological construction.[9] In the face of such a construction, some contemporary interpreters juxtapose Aquinas's reading of Aristotle with an exegesis that purports to retrieve the authentic doctrine of the historical Aristotle.[10] So juxtaposed, it is easy to show that Aquinas's reading deviates from Aristotle and incorporates what can then be called the non- and perhaps anti-Aristotelian theological preoccupations of Aquinas.[11]

Now this kind of hermeneutics, which is concerned to elucidate the historical Aristotle, is necessary, for it has the undeniable merit of spotting important doctrinal differences between Aristotle and Aquinas. But this hermeneutical method is not philosophically self-sufficient. The contemporary exegete, if he or she is going to understand the limitations of this method, should also ponder how Aquinas himself treats doctrinal conflicts in philosophy. Where the apparent opposition between Aristotle and Christian faith is of great moment, in this case the denial of God's universal creative causality, Aquinas usually notes the conflict and sometimes states what he regards to be the correct philosophical view even if that view is "completely foreign to Aristotle's system."[12] But Aquinas himself does more than merely juxtapose

9. See J. Owens, "The Relation of God to World in the *Metaphysics*," in *Études sur la Métaphysique d'Aristote: Actes du VI Symposium Aristotelicum* (Paris: Librairie Philosophique J. Vrin, 1979), 218, n. 23; and Mark F. Johnson, "Did St. Thomas Attribute a Doctrine of Creation to Aristotle?" *New Scholasticism* 63 (1989): 129–54.

10. See H. W. Jaffa, *Thomism and Aristotelianism: A Study of the Commentary by Thomas Aquinas on the "Nicomachean Ethics"* (Chicago: University of Chicago Press, 1952), 167–88.

11. Among other examples of "Christian readings" of Aristotle, Aquinas notes that nature and natural movements derive from God, the author of nature, whose divine reason *providentially* ordains things (*SLE*, I, 1, 1094a2, 165–75; *In Ethic.*, I, lect. 1 [Spiazzi, n. 11, p. 4]); or Aquinas can claim that God, who is provident and solicitous about human things, *loves* the philosophers most of all, because they engage in the divine activity of contemplation (*SLE*, X, 13, 1179a13, 79–137; *In Ethic.*, X, lect. 13 [Spiazzi, nn. 2133–34, p. 554]). Cf. Bourke, "Nicomachean Ethics," 257.

12. Fernand Van Steenberghen, "The Problem of the Existence of God in Saint

Christian doctrine with Aristotle; the difference between Aquinas and Aristotle first arises at a more basic level. Aquinas is able to oppose specific doctrines of the Christian faith to Aristotelian teaching because he already has a generous conception of the capacity of philosophical reason to correct its own mistakes.

As a theologian, Aquinas reads Aristotle with a spirit confident in both the power of reason and the truth of revelation:

If something is discovered in the sayings of the philosophers that is contrary to faith, this is not philosophy but more an abuse of philosophy [arising] from a defect of reason. And therefore it is possible from the principles of philosophy to refute an error of this kind either by showing that it is altogether impossible or that it not necessary. *(Expos. de Trin.*, q. 2, a. 3 [Decker, 19–23, p. 94])[13]

Aquinas's confidence imposes a certain burden on the theologian, one that Aquinas himself took up. As a defense of theological doctrine, it is legitimate enough to argue that philosophical mistakes are just philosophical mistakes if the theologian also recognizes that such mistakes call for philosophical correction. From the philosophical point of view, reason must overturn or neutralize its own errors. But also for the theologian, if he or she is to show that faith can embrace philosophy, he or she must first show that sound philosophy does not contradict faith.

It was Aquinas's conviction that philosophy can attain truth, and that conviction as much as his theological allegiances led Aquinas to look for and to promote concord between Aristotle and Christian faith. That conviction, whether or not we share it, determined Aquinas's hermeneutical stance toward Aristotle. And it is Aquinas's hermeneutical method and not his faith that provokes so many of our preliminary questions. How should we describe Aquinas's introduction of theological doctrines into his Aristotelian exegesis? Are they casual introjections or deliberate injections? In either case, do they merely color or do they distort Aristotle?

At first, these may appear to be exegetical questions that are generated solely by a laudable effort to keep track of the historical Aristot-

---

Thomas' *Commentary on the Metaphysics* of Aristotle," *Review of Metaphysics* 27 (1974): 568.

13. "Si quid autem in dictis philosophorum invenitur contrarium fidei, hoc non est philosophia, sed magis philosophiae abusus ex defectu rationis. Et ideo possibile est ex principiis philosophiae huiusmodi errorem refellere vel ostendendo omnino esse impossibile vel ostendendo non esse necessarium" *(Expos. de Trin.*, q. 2, a. 3 [Decker, 19–23, p. 94]).

le.[14] Yet what seems to be a sound and even necessary procedure, the textual juxtaposition of the historical Aristotle and Aquinas, has led to paradoxical results: some interpreters affirm the substantial accuracy of the Thomistic commentary, while others flatly deny it.[15] Such contrary evaluations show that interpreters cannot rest content with a methodology that merely juxtaposes Aquinas's commentary and Aristotle's text. The contradictions that such textual juxtapositions generate reveal a latent philosophical as well as a manifest literal sense.[16] In his own exegesis of "Blessed Dionysius," Aquinas, we can observe, was aware of both senses.[17] And Aquinas's reading of Aristotle supports the thesis that the answers to our textual or historical questions depend as much on philosophical as exegetical considerations.[18]

Still, philosophical consideration of Aquinas's exegesis cannot pretend to dispense with an accurate understanding of the literary genre of Aquinas's Aristotelian "commentaries."[19] The editors of the Leonine Edition, departing from modern practice, have abandoned this label; in

14. For a summary of the information we have about Aquinas's own Aristotelian sources, see Daniel A. Callus, O.P., "Les Sources de saint Thomas," in *Aristote et saint Thomas d'Aquin,* 95–174.

15. For Gauthier's unequivocally negative judgment about the exegetical value of Aquinas's commentary, see René Antoine Gauthier and Jean Yves Jolif, *L'Éthique à Nicomaque: Introduction, traduction et commentaire* (Louvain: Publications Universitaires, 1970; Paris: Béatrice-Nauwelaerts, 1970), 1: 131.Cf. Roger Guindon, O.M.I., *Béatitude et théologie morale chez saint Thomas d'Aquin* (Ottawa: Éditions de l'Université d'Ottawa, 1955), 174: [Aquinas's] "prolongements . . . n'empêchent pas saint Thomas de présenter un exposé fidèle à la doctrine d'Aristote"; Dimitrios Papadis, *Die Rezeption der Nikomachischen Ethik des Aristoteles bei Thomas von Aquin: Eine vergleichende Untersuchung* (Frankfurt: R. G. Fischer, 1980), 176: "In grossen und ganzen gibt Thomas in seinem Kommentar die aristotelischen Thesen richtig wieder." Gauthier's criticism, in his appendix to volume 48 of the Leonine edition (p. xxv), is considerably softer: there he states that Aquinas's commentary is flawed as a historical-critical work but allows that Aquinas wanted to produce "un oeuvre de sagesse." For a canvass of nineteenth- and early twentieth-century opinions, see Martin Grabmann, "Die Aristoteleskommentare des Heiligen Thomas von Aquin," in *Mittelalterliches Geistesleben: Abhandlungen zur Geschichte der Scholastik und Mystik* (Munich: Max Hueber Verlag, 1926), 266–313.

16. See McKeon, "Truth and the History of Ideas," 56: "The history of philosophy is itself a form of philosophic inquiry; and, when philosophy is the object of philosophic inquiry, questions of fact are inseparable from philosophic questions."

17. See *In de Div. Nom.,* V, lect. 1 (Pera, n. 630, pp. 234–35) where Aquinas explains Dionysius's pantheistic formula *"Ipse est esse existentibus."*

18. Cornelio Fabro, in "Platonism, Neo-Platonism, and Thomism: Convergencies and Divergencies," *New Scholasticism* 44 (1970): 95, describes Aquinas's exegesis as "intensive," i.e., "not a historical-static type of exegesis, but a speculative-dynamic one."

19. See I. T. Eschmann, O.P., "A Catalogue of St. Thomas's Works: Bibliographi-

the place of "commentary" or "exposition," they have resurrected the term found in the manuscripts, *"sententia."* As the term was used by the medieval masters in the faculty of arts, a *"sententia"* was a summary of the doctrine of a given text, and it was contrasted with an *"expositio"* which was a more detailed textual discussion. Gauthier states that by giving his commentary the title of *Sententia libri ethicorum,* Aquinas wished to exclude a fully critical study of Aristotle's text.[20]

These historical precisions establish that our designation "commentary," or at least some of its contemporary connotations, must be adjusted in order to correspond to the literary genre of what Aquinas actually wrote. But more than a correct designation of the literary genre of Aquinas's writings is needed in order to portray the philosophical scope of Thomistic exegesis. Chenu outlines six features of Aquinas's approach to Aristotle:[21] Aquinas (1) is concerned about the literal meaning of the text, but (2) interprets the text sympathetically; (3) keeps the Aristotelian philosophy "open" by (4) deepening its principles rather than by fastening on Aristotle's actual conclusions; and (5) introduces his own philosophical and theological distinctions in order (6) to clarify Aristotle and to refute unwarranted counter interpretations.

To rephrase Chenu: Thomistic exegesis is in the service of the philosophical truth that can be found—but not exclusively or purely—in the Aristotelian texts; still, it does not ignore or negate that historical objectivity, so important to the contemporary exegete, about the meaning of the *ipsa verba* of the Aristotle. That is, Aquinas was capable of engaging Aristotle on Aristotelian grounds.[22] But, just as certainly, Aquinas read Aristotle as only a Christian theologian could read him.

Yet despite the guidance that Chenu and others have given, interpre-

---

cal Note," in Gilson, *Christian Philosophy of Aquinas,* 381–439; James A. Weisheipl, O.P., "A Brief Catalogue of Authentic Works," in *Friar Thomas D'Aquino: His Life, Thought, and Work* (New York: Doubleday & Company, 1974), 355–405; Jean-Pierre Torrell, O.P. , *Saint Thomas Aquinas,* vol. 1, *The Person and His Work,* trans. Robert Royal (Washington, D.C.: The Catholic University of America Press, 1996), 341–45.

20. See Leonine Edition, vol. 48: xxiv.

21. See Chenu, *Understanding St. Thomas,* 206–14.

22. For example: Aristotle's division *(EN,* VI, 1, 1139a5–15) of the rational part of the soul into two rational subparts, the scientific (τὸ ἐπιστομμονικόν) which knows necessary beings, and the calculative (τὸ λογιστικόν) which knows contingent beings, does not seem consonant with the fundamental division of the soul *(de An.,* III, 4) into active and potential, both of which parts are universal in scope. Aquinas resolves this doubt by distinguishing the scientific knowledge of the uni-

tation of Aquinas's *sententia* on the various works of Aristotle remains fraught with philosophical questions to which scholars have hardly settled on answers. Is Aquinas's exegesis of Aristotle really in service to an original Thomistic philosophy so that they should be included among the "philosophical writings" of Aquinas?[23] Or are they, perhaps to varying degrees, theological works that should be distinguished from a strictly philosophical exegesis of Aristotle?[24]

The divergent responses to these questions reflect different philosophical judgments about Aquinas's philosophical originality, especially in regard to his foundational metaphysical doctrine of being *(esse)*.[25] The latter doctrine especially challenges the historically minded interpreter to evaluate Aquinas's insight into Aristotle and the use to which he put Aristotelian principles. What are the philosophical consequences, for our understanding of both Aristotle and Aquinas, of Aquinas's Aristotelian exegesis? If it is not to be expected that philosophers will reach common answers to this question, the latter nevertheless derives from a commonly recognized source: Aquinas's theological reading of Aristotle.

2. Aquinas's Theological Point of View

In his opening remarks about the *Nicomachean Ethics*, Aquinas's exegesis, it might be thought, already goes egregiously astray. Here Aquinas introjects into his explanation of the lapidary Aristotelian dictum *"Good is what everything desires"*[26] the idea that every particular good *participates* in the highest good: "For nothing is good except insofar as it a certain similitude and participation of the supreme

---

versal principles of contingent beings from the sense knowledge of contingent beings qua contingent. In his exegesis, Aquinas reassigns "calculative reason" to the sensitive parts of the soul and calls it the *"ratio particularis"* or the *"vis cogitativa."* See *SLE*, VI, 1, 1139a11, 190–214 *(In Ethic.*, VI, lect. 1 [Spiazzi, n. 1123, p. 307]).

23. See Van Steenberghen, *Introduction*, 106.

24. Cf. Leon Elders, S.V.D., "Saint Thomas d'Aquin et Aristote," *Revue thomiste* 88 (1988): 357–76; Ioannes Isaac, O.P., "Saint Thomas interprete des oeuvres d'Aristote," in *Scholastica ratione historico-critica instauranda: acta congressus scholastici internationalis* (Rome: Pontificium Athenaeum Antonianum, 1951), 355–63; Joseph Owens, C.Ss.R., "Aquinas as Aristotelian Commentator, in *St. Thomas Aquinas, 1274–1974*, I: 213–38; C. H. Lohr, "The Medieval Interpretation of Aristotle," in *The Cambridge History of Later Medieval Philosophy*, ed. Norman Kretzman, Anthony Kenny, and Jan Pinborg, with assoc. ed. Eleonore Stump (Cambridge: Cambridge University Press, 1982), 80–98.

25. See Fabro, "Platonism, Neo-Platonism, and Thomism," 71.

26. *EN*, I, 1, 1094a3: τἀγαθόν, οὗ παντ' ἐφίεται = *"bonum quod omnia appetunt"* in the Latin translation that Aquinas used.

good."[27] Now here it would be easy to charge Aquinas with seriously distorting Aristotle, perhaps unwittingly conflating him with Plato.[28] This, however, would be an implausible charge: Aquinas's remark, it can be shown, is not inadvertent or insouciant. He is fully aware that Aristotle, whom Aquinas takes to be affirming the existence of a separate goodness,[29] rejects the Platonic corollary, which is the mainstay of the Platonic doctrine of participation, that this absolute and separate goodness is a separate *form* shared in and common to all instances of goodness. In his earlier comment on *Metaph.*, I, 9, 991a9–10,[30] Aquinas accurately rehearses Aristotle's general criticism of the Platonic separation of the ideas from their sensible instantiations: the separate universal form provides no help in understanding the participating sensible particulars if, as claimed, the latter share the same form. In this instance, the reduplication of the same separate and nonseparate form is unnecessary and unexplanatory.[31]

In line with this criticism, Aquinas's Aristotle firmly maintains that there is a certain good "separated from the entire universe," but that this good must be placed "in a different order of goodness" from all other (sensible) goods.[32] Consequently, Aristotle rejects the second of a pair of (allegedly) contradictory Platonic theses that (1) this separated

27. ". . . nihil est bonum, nisi inquantum est quaedam similitudo et participatio boni summi . . ." *(SLE,* I, 1, 1094a2, 178–80; *In Ethic.*, I, lect. 1 [Spiazzi, n. 11, p. 5]).

28. See Arthur Little, S.J., *The Platonic Heritage of Thomism* (Dublin: Golden Eagle Books, 1950), 286.

29. Calling things "good" by reference to a (separate) good is, in Aristotle's terminology, a πρὸς ἕν equivocal expression; for Aquinas, the same expression is said *"secundum analogiam."* See *EN*, I, 6, 1096b27; *SLE*, I, 7, 1096b26, 206–7 *(In Ethic.*, I, lect. 7 [Spiazzi, n. 96, p. 25]); Gauthier-Jolif, II, 1: 45–47.

30. Aquinas's *Sententia super metaphysicam* is difficult to date, perhaps 1268–72, but the commentary on Book I is early [Torrell: 1270-71] and almost certainly antedates the *SLE:* see Weisheipl, *Friar Thomas,* 379–80.

31. See *In Metaph.*, I, lect. 15 (Cathala-Spiazzi, n. 225, p. 67): "Unde Aristoteles ostendens quod ideae ad nihil possunt sensibilibus utiles esse, destruit rationes Platonis de positione idearum."

32. See *SLE*, I, 6, 1096a17, 91–92 *(In Ethic.*, I, lect. 6 [Spiazzi, n. 79, p. 21]); *SLE*, I, 7, 1096a34, 18–42 *(In Ethic.*, I, lect. 7 [Spiazzi, n. 84, p. 23]). In *EN*, I, 6, 1096b30–31, however, Aristotle assigns the whole topic of the separate good to another science, presumably metaphysics. Gauthier-Jolif (II, 1: 41) read *EN*, I, 6, 1096a33–34 as an argument against the separation of the idea of the good. *Metaph.*, XII, 10, 1075a14, however, allows that there could be ("probably be" in the revised Oxford translation) both a separate and an immanent good in the universe. Aquinas, commenting on the latter passage, transforms the metaphysical issue by adding that the good of order in the universe depends upon the order in the intellect and will of the separate good, i.e., of the separate Prime Mover: see *In Metaph.*, XII, lect. 12 (Cathala-Spiazzi, n. 2631, p. 612).

good is absolute (per se) but, nonetheless, (2) "an idea common to all [particular] goods."[33] Aquinas's Aristotle regards the separate good not as the universal form of all goods, but as their principle and end.[34]

On this point, nonetheless, there is an important difference between the Thomistic Aristotle and the textual Aristotle. Aquinas repeats but does not dwell on Aristotle's remark *(EN, I, 6, 1096b34)*, so devastating to Christian faith, that even if there is a separate, absolute good, it could not be attained or possessed by human beings. But Aquinas does take pains to mitigate Aristotle by adding the nuance that men cannot possess the separated good "in this life."[35] That nuance leaves open, of course, whether the separated good can be possessed in some other life.

What I wish to emphasize, however, is not Aquinas's concern to graft Christianity onto Aristotle, but the care that Aquinas takes not to conflate the metaphysical doctrines of Plato and Aristotle. Specifically, Aquinas does not remake Aristotle, however congruent such a transformation might be with Aquinas's Christian beliefs, into an adherent of the Platonic theory of participation which identifies, albeit ambiguously, the lesser perfection in the immanent (participating) form and the perfection in the transcendent (participated) form.[36] What, then, are we

33. See *SLE*, I, 7, 1096b8, 89–105 *(In Ethic.*, I, lect. 7 [Spiazzi, n. 89, p. 24]).
34. See ibid., 1096b26, 203–6 *(In Ethic.*, I, lect. 7 [Spiazzi, n. 96, p. 25]).
35. See ibid., 8, 1096b30, 26–31 *(In Ethic.*, I, lect. 8 [Spiazzi, n. 98, p. 26]).
36. The ambiguity results from the apparent contradictions in what Plato says about the immanence and transcendence of the separate forms. Cf. *Phaedo,* 100d7: "by the beautiful all beautiful things are beautiful"; *Timaeus,* 52a: "[the separate form] does not pass into another." Joseph Owens, C.Ss.R., *A History of Ancient Western Philosophy* (New York: Appleton-Century-Crofts, 1959), remarks that "Plato himself shows no consciousness of vacillating between an immanent and a transcendent theory of the Ideas" (228). Cf. Leo Sweeney, S.J., "Participation in Plato's Dialogues," *New Scholasticism* 62 (1988): 131, n. 7, who calls the transcendent form "an 'extrinsic formal' cause" that at once remains transcendent and yet is "the immanent source of perfection in multiple participants" (131).

Among others, David Ross, in *Plato's Theory of Ideas* (Oxford: Clarendon Press, 1951), attempts to resolve the contradiction by the distinction (unambiguously stated in *Tim.*, 50c5) between the transcendent idea and its copies (μιμήματα): "What is present in the particular thing is not, strictly speaking, the Idea, but an imperfect copy of the idea" (30). For a survey of the issue and the attendant secondary studies, see W. K. C. Guthrie, *A History of Greek Philosophy,* Vol. 4: *Plato: The Man and His Dialogues, Earlier Period* (Cambridge: Cambridge University Press, 1975), 353–56; and Vol. 5, *The Later Plato and the Academy* (Cambridge: Cambridge University Press, 1978), 41–42, 268. Aquinas, who is aware of Plato's vacillation, adopts and adapts this solution: he also posits that the immanent form resembles its exemplar cause, but Aquinas places the divine idea *in the divine mind:* see *In* Metaph., I, lect. 15 (Cathala-Spiazzi, nn. 232–33, pp. 68–69). Furthermore, the Thomistic divine ideas "are not really distinct from the divine essence" *(ST,* I, q. 44, a. 3).

to make of Aquinas's reference to "participation" at the beginning of his commentary on the *Nicomachean Ethics?* Aquinas could not have plausibly attributed the doctrine of participation to Aristotle who repudiated it as so many "empty words and poetical metaphors,"[37] but neither can Aquinas's remark be regarded as his own personal turn toward a strictly Platonic doctrine. Although some volumes of the *Corpus Platonicum* were available to Aquinas (notably a translation of Calcidius's commentary on the *Parmenides*),[38] the Plato with whom Aquinas contended was, for the most part, Aristotle's redaction of Plato and Aquinas closely followed Aristotle's interpretation and criticism of that Plato.[39] Nonetheless, Aquinas's introductory remark does introduce something philosophically alien into the Aristotelian text, even if nothing of Plato is foisted on Aristotle. On the contrary, there is weighty evidence indicating that Aquinas intended to open the Aristotelian ethics to a *non-Platonic* theory of participation in the separate good. Yet this latter assertion surely courts scholarly repudiation.

Since the beginning of this century, passionate efforts have been expended both to prove and to disprove if not the Platonic then the Neoplatonic character of the Thomistic doctrine of participation.[40] Everything depends, to be sure, on how one characterizes the Neoplatonic doctrine of participation, and the history of Neoplatonism is long and convoluted. Hadot, who has diligently tracked the Neoplatonic sources of Marius Victorinus, Augustine, and Boethius, maintains that "to participate" (μετέχειν) signifies, according to the Neoplatonist understanding of that term, "to receive a form that is the reflection of a transcendent form."[41] "Reflection" is a metaphysically obscure word,

---

37. *Metaph.*, I, 9, 991a22 (rev. Oxford trans.). Cf. *In Metaph.*, I, lect. 15 (Cathala-Spiazzi, n. 231, p. 68): ". . . est simile metaphoris quas poëtae inducunt, quod ad philosophum non pertinet. Nam philosophus ex propriis docere debet."

38. See R. Kiblansky and H.-D. Saffrey, *"Le Corpus Platonicum medii aevi,"* in Henri D. Saffrey, *Recherches sur la tradition platonicienne au moyen âge et à la renaissance* (Paris: Librairie Philosophique J. Vrin, 1987), 27–42.

39. Cf. *Metaph.*, I, 6, 988a9–10 (rev. Oxford trans.): ". . . for the [Platonic] Forms are the causes of the essence of all other things"; *In Metaph.*, I, lect. 10 (Cathala-Spiazzi, n. 169, p. 49): ". . . quia species quas posuit 'sunt aliis,' idest sensibilibus causae eius 'quod quid est,' idest causae formales. . . ."

40. For an invaluable survey of the all the *"Platonici"* texts in Aquinas, see R. J. Henle, S.J., *Saint Thomas and Platonism: A Study of the Plato and Platonic Texts in the Writings of Saint Thomas* (The Hague: Martinus Nijhoff, 1956), xvii–xviii.

For a recent bibliography of the Neoplatonic sources and influences on Aquinas, see Christina D'Ancona Costa, ed. and trans., Introduction, in *Tommaso D'Aquino, Commento al Libro delle Cause* (Milan: Rusconi, 1986), 123–62.

41. Pierre Hadot, "L'Être et l'étant dans le néoplatonisme," in *Études néo-platoniciennes*, ed. Jean Trouillard et al. (Neuchatel: La Baconnière, 1973), 30. Cf.

but Hadot uses it to indicate the ontological communality (i.e., the imperfect formal identity) of the participated and participating forms. Hadot's interpretation corresponds with Aquinas's understanding of Plato and the "Neoplatonists."

> The Platonists . . . have placed separate entities existing in themselves, which are participated by composite things. So before singular men which participate humanity, they devised a separate man existing without matter, in which singular men are said to participate . . . and [they said] similar things about wisdom in itself and being in itself. *(In de Div. Nom.,* V, lect. 1 [Pera, n. 634, p. 235])[42]

The Platonist doctrine of participation means, for Aquinas, that "the separate forms are the principles of the forms that are in matter"; and, although the separate forms are subsistent, "they immediately cause the forms of sensible things."[43] In short, Aquinas accepts Aristotle's version of the immanence of the Platonic forms: the separate forms are the forms of sensible things.[44]

Aquinas's immediate sources of Neoplatonic doctrine were the *De divinis nominibus* of Dionysius (who was probably a sixth-century Syrian monk) and the Proclean excerpts, the *Liber de causis,* which were in circulation in Arabic by the tenth century.[45] Earlier medievals (and

---

Henle, *Saint Thomas,* 375: "[Platonic] participation . . . must be conceived as an immediate, direct relationship within the order of formality"; G. H. Allard, "The Primacy of Existence in the Thought of Eriugena," in *Neoplatonism and Christian Thought,* ed. Dominic J. O'Meara (Albany: State University of New York Press, 1982), 89: "One can scarcely be mistaken in asserting that Neoplatonism—whether it be Christian or not—is fundamentally an "essentialist" philosophy. . . ."

42. ". . . Platonici . . . posuerunt separata per se existentia, quae a compositis participantur; sicut ante homines singulares qui participant humanitatem, composuerunt hominem separatum sine materia existentem, cuius participatione singulares homines dicuntur . . . et similiter per se sapientiam et per se esse" *(In de Div. Nom.,* V, lect. 1 [Pera, n. 634, p. 235]).

43. See *SCG,* III, 24 (Pera, n. 2047, p. 30): "Et quantum ad hoc verificatur dictum Platonis, quod formae separatae sunt principia formarum quae sunt in materia: licet Plato posuerit eas per se subsistentes, et causantes immediate formas sensibilium. . . ."

44. See *De ver.,* q. 10, a. 6. (Spiazzi, 201): "Quidam enim, ut Platonici posuerunt formas rerum sensibilium esse a materia separatas. . . . Sed haec positio a Philosopho sufficienter reprobata est; qui ostendit quod non est ponere formas sensibilium rerum nisi in materia sensibili . . ."; *SCG,* III, 69 (Pera, n. 2433, p. 94): ". . . Plato posuit species rerum sensibilium esse quasdam formas separatas, quae sunt causae essendi his sensibilibus, secundum quod eas participant."

45. For historical, textual, and doctrinal information about these two works, see Ceslaus Pera, O.P., Petrus Caramello, and Carolus Mazzantini, introductions and notes, in *In librum beati Dionysii de divinis nominibus expositio* (Turin: Marietti, 1950), vii–liv; *In librum de causis expositio,* 2d ed. (Turin: Marietti, 1972), vii–lviii;

Albert the Great as late as 1271) had erroneously attributed the latter
to Aristotle. Given the tension in Plato's own account,[46] it is hardly
surprising that Neoplatonic formulae about the immanence and transcendence of the forms need to be adjusted to the individual authors
who played endless variations on this theme.[47] Nevertheless, if Hadot's
general characterization is correct—and it fits well with the views of
other scholars[48]—it can be shown that the Thomistic theory of participation, which also incorporates the Aristotelian conception of act, cannot be reduced to the ontological doctrine found in its Neoplatonic
sources, whether remote or proximate,[49] even if the Thomistic theory
was "stimulated" by Neoplatonism.[50] On the contrary, the Thomistic
understanding of being is profoundly different from the Platonist or
Neoplatonist doctrines.[51]

H. D. Saffrey, O.P., Introduction in *Sancti Thomae de Aquino super librum de
causis expositio* (Fribourg: Société Philosophique; Louvain: Éditions E. Nauwelaerts,
1954), xv–xxxix.

46. See Cornelio Fabro, C.P.S., *Participation et causalité selon s. Thomas
d'Aquin* (Louvain and Paris: Publications Universitaires de Louvain and Éditions
Béatrice-Nauwelaerts, 1961), 114: "Le drame du platonisme réside dans l'impos-
sibilité de parvenir à une détermination positive du rapport de participation. . . ."

47. For Iamblichus's notion of transcendent or unparticipated forms, see R. T.
Wallis, *Neoplatonism* (New York: Charles Scribner's Sons, 1972), 126–27.

48. See Giovanni Reale, *A History of Ancient Philosophy*, Vol. 4: *The Schools of
the Imperial Age*, ed. and trans. John R. Catan (Albany: State University of New
York, 1990), 220, 362; Anton C. Pegis, "The Dilemma of Being and Unity," in *Essays
in Thomism*, ed. Robert E. Brennan, O.P. (New York: Sheed and Ward, 1944), 173;
James McEvoy, "The Divine as the Measure of Being in Platonic and Scholastic
Thought," in *Studies in Medieval Philosophy*, ed. John F. Wippel (Washington, D.C.:
The Catholic University of America Press, 1987), 85–116.

49. For Aquinas's interpretation of Dionysius, see Michael B. Ewbank, "Remarks
on Being in St. Thomas Aquinas' *Expositio De Divinis Nominibus*," *Archives
d'histoire doctrinale et littéraire du moyen âge* 56 (1989): 123–49; for his interpretation of the *Liber de causis*, see D'Ancona Costa, Introduction, sec. IV, "Il commento
di san Tommaso al 'Liber de Causis,'" 78–120.

50. See Fabro, "Platonism, Neo-Platonism, and Thomism," 90.

51. For an account that stresses the uniqueness of the Thomistic metaphysical
doctrine, see Joseph Owens, C.Ss.R., "Diversity and Community of Being in St.
Thomas Aquinas," in *St. Thomas Aquinas on the Existence of God*, ed. John R.
Catan (Albany: State University of New York Press, 1980), 97–131 [originally pub-
lished in *Mediaeval Studies* 22 (1960): 257–302]. Cf. Rudi A. Te Velde, *Participation
and Substantiality in Thomas Aquinas* (Leiden: E. J. Brill, 1995), 256: ". . . the
Neoplatonic concept of participation undergoes a fundamental transformation in
Aquinas."

For the opposite approach, see Klaus Kremer, *Die neuplatonische Seinsphilosophie und ihre Wirkung auf Thomas von Aquin* (Leiden: E. J. Brill, 1966). Kremer's
Neoplatonic *reductio* of Aquinas precisely hinges on "die Identifizierung Gottes mit
dem esse commune" (310), an identification that Aquinas excludes by his firm

Still, there are Thomistic texts that have a strong Neoplatonic flavor and appear to invite a Neoplatonic explanation along the usual lines of formal causality. Such an explanation turns on the ontological identity of the participated and participating forms.[52] For example:

As this man participates human nature, so every created being participates, if I may speak in this way, the nature of being; because only God is His being. . . . (ST, I, q. 45, a. 5, ad 1)[53]

Read by itself, this text seems to imply that as human nature is identical in all humans, so too being is somehow identical in God and creatures. But Aquinas mentions that this statement is "a way of speaking,"[54] which in turn strongly suggests that some important qualifications are needed.

Indeed, drastic qualifications are necessary because of Aquinas's unequivocal assertion that divine being is unique and individuated in and of itself because it is subsistent:

---

distinction between *ens commune* and its universal causes or principles. See *In Metaph.*, prooemium; *Expos. de Trin.*, q. 5, a. 4 (Decker, 195). Cf. J. Owens, C.Ss.R., "The Intelligibility of Being," *Gregorianum* 36 (1955): 173; Te Velde, *Participation and Substantiality*, 188–94.

In reviewing Kremer's book, A. Solignac, S.J., in "La Doctrine de l'*esse* chez saint Thomas, est-elle d'origine néo-Platonicienne?" *Archives de philosophie* 30 (1967): 439–52, recognizes that Neoplatonizing interpretations of Aquinas run against *De pot.*, q. 7, a. 2, ad 4 (Pession, 192), which flatly repudiates the proposed identification of God and *esse commune*: "Esse divinum, quod est eius substantia, non est esse commune, sed est esse distinctum a quolibet alio esse." Other Thomistic texts clearly reiterate the same distinction: see *In de Div. Nom.*, V, lect. 2 (Pera, n. 660, p. 245); *ST*, I, q. 3, a. 4, ad 1; *SCG*, I, 26. Nonetheless, Solignac attempts to bring together the two orders of efficient and formal causality, in order to rediscover in the Thomistic synthesis "a prolongation of neo-Platonism" (451).

For a detailed examination of Kremer's "radical misinterpretation" (p. 85): see Fabro, "Platonism, Neo-Platonism, and Thomism," 69–100, who, nevertheless, continues to hold that the Thomistic doctrine of *esse* "shows itself . . . to be a clear Neo-Platonic derivation . . ." (71). More precisely, Fabro claims that "[l]a source principale de la notion thomiste d'*esse* intensif est donc avant tout le mystérieux Auteur des *Areopagitica*" (*Participation et causalité*, 229). For incisive criticism of Fabro's own use of Aquinas's texts, see Henle, *Saint Thomas and Platonism*, xix–xx, 302–3, and "A Note on Certain Textual Evidence in Fabro's *La Nozione Metafisica de Participazione*," *Modern Schoolman* 34 (1957): 265–82.

52. See Fabro, *Participation et causalité*, 115: "Ainsi l'Eidos platonicien est 'le veritable être' de l'étant."

53. "Sed sicut hic homo participat humanam naturam, ita quodcumque ens creatum participat, ut ita dixerim, naturam essendi: quia solus Deus est suum esse . . ." (*ST*, I, q. 45, a. 5, ad 1).

54. See *In de Div. Nom.*, V, lect. 5 (Pera, n. 630, p. 235): ". . . *Ipse est esse existentibus*, non quidem ita quod ipse Deus sit esse formale existentium, sed eo

The being of God is distinguished and individuated from any other being *[esse]*, through this [fact] that it is subsistent being in itself and [it] does not come to some nature which is distinct *[aliud]* from its being. *(De pot.,* q. 7, a. 2, ad 5 [Pession, 192])[55]

Consequently, the divine form, whether it be described as being itself or goodness itself, "cannot be received in another."[56] The Neoplatonic tendency, however, is to reduce diversity to unity by treating emanated beings as a diminished grade or an imperfect receptacle of divine being.[57]

Aquinas nonetheless lauds the Platonist effort to derive created being and goodness from the First Principle as metaphysically correct and consonant with Christian faith. While acknowledging that the *Platonici* affirm that the Good or the One is the "highest God,"[58] he also carefully notes that they regard sensible beings as a diminished instantiation of the second ranking divinity, subsistent Being.[59] In Neoplatonism the two tenets go together, but the latter has a peculiar importance for Aquinas. Aquinas, of course, rejects the Platonist subordination of Being to the Good and the One.[60] But quite apart from the

---

modo loquendi utitur quo Platonici utebantur qui esse separatum dicebant esse existentium. . . ."

55. ". . . ipsum esse Dei distinguitur et individuatur a quolibet alio esse, per hoc ipsum quod est esse per se subsistens, et non adveniens alicui naturae quae sit aliud ab ipso esse" *(De pot.,* q. 7, a. 2, ad 5 [Pession, 192]).

56. ". . . non potest recipi in alio" *(ST,* I, q. 3, a. 2, ad 3).

57. Aquinas quotes *(In de Causis,* prop. 24, lect. 24 [Pera, n. 396, p. 125; Saffrey, 121]) Proposition 142 from Proclus's *Elements of Theology:* "The gods are present in the same way to all things, but not every thing is present to the gods in the same way" (Omnibus quidem dii assunt eodem modo, non autem omnia eodem modo diis assunt). But Aquinas quickly adds (ibid. [Pera, n. 399]) that "[i]t is necessary to say that the first diversity in things, according to which they have diverse natures and powers, is not from some diversity in the recipients, but from the First Cause."

58. See *In de Causis,* prop. 3, lect. 3 (Pera, n. 66, p. 20; Saffrey, 18): "Ultimum autem quod ab omnibus participatur et ipsum nihil aliud participat, est ipsum Unum et Bonum separatum quod dicebat Summum Deum et primam omnium Causam"; *In de Div. Nom.,* XI, lect. 4 (Pera, n. 931, p. 346): "Sub bono autem [Platonici] ponebant esse. . . ."

59. See *In de Div. Nom.,* XI, lect. 4 (Pera, n. 931, p. 346): ". . . Platonici, ponentes ideas rerum separatas, omnia quae sic in abstracto dicuntur, posuerunt in abstracto subsistere causas secundum ordinem quemdam. . . . Et ideo dicebant sub summo Deo, esse quamdam divinam substantiam quae nominatur per se esse . . ."; *De sub. Sep.,* c. 17 (Spiazzi, n. 147, p. 50): "In quo removet opinionem Platonicorum, qui ponebant quod ipsa essentia bonitatis erat summus Deus, sub quo erat alius Deus, qui est ipsum esse. . . ."

60. See *In de Div. Nom.,* V, lect. 1 (Pera, n. 633, p. 235): "Ipsum autem esse inter alios Dei effectus est principalius et dignius. Ergo Deus, qui a nobis nominari non

precise ontological order of Platonic polytheism, he firmly disavows any tendency to identify divine being and created being as an intellectual perversity.[61]

This criticism, which is unusually severe but redolent of Aquinas's Christian faith, expresses a basic metaphysical tenet that divides the Platonist and the Thomistic theories of participation. Aquinas interprets the derivation of created beings from the First Principle in terms of causal *dependency:* that is, the First Principle is the final and efficient cause of created beings.[62] So, while Aquinas allows that created beings participate in the divine being, since God efficiently causes their being, divine being is "pure subsistent being" that must always be distinguished from created being.[63] Unlike what the Platonists think, things do not participate in being in the way that white things participate in the universal form of whiteness.[64] Aquinas denies that being is a common form.[65]

Aquinas, however, grants that all created beings fall under the concept of *"esse commune"* but firmly denies, it should be noted, that God is subsumed into this concept. God, rather, is the transcendent

---

potest nisi per suos effectus, convenientissime nominatur nomine entis"; ibid. (Pera, n. 635, pp. 235–36): "Quod autem per se esse sit primum et dignius quam per se vita et per se sapientia . . . prius enim intelligitur aliquod ens quam unum, vivens, vel sapiens"; ibid., (Pera, n. 639, p. 236): ". . . Deus, qui est per se bonitas et primo proponens idest tribuens rebus creatis hoc donum quod est per se esse, laudatur hoc nomine, quod est quasi a digniore et prima suarum participationum."

61. See *In de Div. Nom.*, prooemium (Pera, p. 2); I, lect. 2 (Pera, n. 52, p. 18).

62. See *SLE*, I, 6, 1096a17, 87–90 *(In Ethic.*, I, lect. 6 [Spiazzi, n. 79, p. 21]): ". . . Aristoteles non intendit improbare opinionem Platonis quantum ad hoc quod ponebat unum bonum separatum a quo dependerent omnia bona . . . ad quod totum universum ordinatur, sicut exercitus ad bonum ducis."

63. "Proclus" (see *In de Causis*, prop. 4, lect. 4 [Pera, 27; Saffrey, 26]), who clearly preserves the transcendence of the Good or One over Being, identifies Being *(esse)* as the *"prima rerum creaturum."* Aquinas, however, uses Dionysius to reinterpret this thesis: as Dionysius reduces all the separate Platonic hypostases to the one (Christian) God, Aquinas reduces Proclus's first creature, Being, to God by identifying God as *"esse purum subsistens."* (See *In de Causis*, prop. 4, lect. 4 [Pera, nn. 102–3, p. 28; Saffrey, 29].) Thus Proclus's "first creature" becomes for Aquinas "the being participated in the first grade of created entity" (esse participato in primo gradu entis creati [ibid., n. 102]). Cf. Fabro, *Participation et causalité*, 231–43, who aptly remarks that Aquinas is engaging in "la interprétation et non plus exégèse de critique textuelle" (243).

64. See *In de Causis*, prop. 3, lect. 3 (Pera, n. 80, p. 21; Saffrey, 22): ". . . Si albedo simplex esset causa omnium alborum in quantum sunt alba, non autem aliquid albedine participans. Secundum hoc ergo Platonici ponebant quod id quod est ipsum esse est causa existendi omnibus. . . ."

65. See *II Sent.*, d. 17, q. 1, a. 1, sol. (Mandonnet, 414): ". . . ita etiam non est

cause of *esse commune.*[66] Moreover, in his later works Aquinas stresses that *esse commune* exists only in the mind. If God were identified with *esse commune,* then God too would exist only in the mind.[67] There can be no question, then, of identifying divine being and the being of creatures. In simple terms, being is not a genus or common form that they share.[68]

Unlike Neoplatonic theories, the Thomistic doctrine of participation brings into the forefront of the discussion efficient, not formal, causality.[69] Nothing less than the Christian doctrine of creation is at issue. Aquinas carefully points out that formal causality presupposes a matter that can be informed, whereas the absolute production of created *esse* presupposes nothing from the side of the creature.[70] According-

---

necessarium, si in anima est natura intellectualis et in Deo, quod sit eadem intellectualitas utriusque per essentiam, vel quod per quam eamdem essentiam utrumque dicatur ens."

66. See *In de Div. Nom.,* V, lect. 2 (Pera, n. 660, p. 245): ". . . omnia existentia continentur sub ipso esse communi, non autem Deus, sed magis esse commune continetur sub eius virtute. . . ."

67. See *SCG,* I, 26 (Pera, n. 241, p. 37): "Multum igitur minus et ipsum esse commune est aliquid praeter omnes res existentes nisi in intellectu solum. Si igitur Deus sit esse commune, Deus non erit aliqua res nisi quae sit intellectu tantum."

68. See *SCG,* II, 52. For a discussion of how the divine idea, as the exemplar cause, plays a role in the Thomistic doctrine of participation, see John F. Wippel, "Thomas Aquinas and Participation," in *Studies in Medieval Philosophy,* 156–58; "Thomas Aquinas, Henry of Ghent, and Godfrey of Fontaines on the Reality of Nonexisting Possibles," in *Metaphysical Themes in Thomas Aquinas* (Washington, D.C.: The Catholic University of America Press, 1984), 163–89.

69. See *In de Div. Nom.,* I, lect. 2 (Pera, n. 52, p. 18): "[Deus] . . . qui est principium agens et causa fontalis omnis vitae et substantiae . . ."; *ST,* I, q. 44, a. 1, ad 1: ". . . quia ex hoc quod aliquid per participationem est ens, sequitur quod sit causatum ab alio"; *De sub. Sep.,* c. 3 (Spiazzi, n. 58, p. 25): "Omne autem participans aliquid, accipit id quod participat, ab eo a quo participat: et quantum ad hoc, id a quo participat, est causa ipsius."

On the historical emergence of the notion of efficient causality and its relationship to the Islamic and Christian doctrines of creation, see Étienne Gilson, "Notes pour l'histoire de la cause efficiente," *Archives d'histoire doctrinale et littéraire du moyen âge* 29 (1962): 7–31.

On whether Plato incorporates the notion of efficient cause into his theory of participation, cf. Sweeney, "Participation in Plato's Dialogues," who argues that Plato, in the *Parmenides,* "joined participation explicitly with exemplarity and efficiency" (141); Fabro, *Participation et causalité,* 187: "Plato avait en vue explicitement une causalité efficiente"; and Henle, *Saint Thomas and Platonism,* 375: "[Platonic] participation, therefore, must be conceived as an immediate, direct relationship within the order of formality."

70. See *In de Causis,* prop. 18, lect. 18 (Pera, n. 345, p. 104; Saffrey, 104).

ly, the Thomistic God, first of all, "is not the essential but the causal being of all [created] things."[71]

The Godhead is called the being of all things as their efficient and exemplar cause but not as being their essence. *(ST,* I, q. 3, a. 8, ad 1 [Pegis trans.])[72]

Second, Aquinas concludes that divine being and created being are absolutely diverse and not relatively different.[73] Because God is His being, He is diverse from any entity that has being.

The Thomistic notion of an absolute diversity of being, as placed between the primary and secondary instances of being, is not congruent with Neoplatonic doctrine as we can historically reconstruct it, and more importantly, as Aquinas himself understood the doctrine of the *Platonici.*[74] The latter, according to Aquinas, assert the transcendence of the First Principle over being not the transcendence of infinite, subsistent, pure existence *(esse purum subsistens)* over every created entity *(ens)* which participates being.

The first cause, according to the Platonists, is above being insofar as the essence of goodness and unity, which the first cause is, exceeds even separate being. . . . But according to the truth of the matter, the first cause is above being insofar as it is infinite existence itself; that which finitely participates existence is said to be "a being." *(In de Causis,* prop. 6, lect. 6 [Pera, n. 175, p. 47; Saffrey, 47])[75]

In his commentary on Dionysius's *On the Divine Names* (written ca. 1261), Aquinas attempts to disengage Dionysius's formula, "God Himself is the being of existing things" *(Ipse est esse existentibus),* from what appears to be its obvious Platonist sense. The formula, Aquinas insists, is not "pantheistic" and therefore should not be interpreted to mean that:

71. "Deus est esse omnium non essentiale, sed causale" *(I Sent.,* d. 7, q. 1, a. 2 [Mandonnet, 198]). Cf. *In de Div. Nom.,* V, lect. 3 (Pera, n. 672, p. 250): ". . . divina essentia est principium omnium existentium. . . . Principium quidem est omnium, sicut causa factiva rerum. . . ."

72. ". . . deitas dicitur esse omnium effective et exemplariter: non autem per essentiam" *(ST,* I, q. 3, a. 8, ad 1).

73. See *I Sent.,* d. 7, q. 1, a. 2, ad 3 (Mandonnet, 198): ". . . ita etiam Deus et esse creatum non differunt aliquibus differentiis utrique superadditis, sed seipsis: unde nec proprie dicuntur differre, sed diversa esse: diversum enim est absolutum, sed differens est relatum. . . ."

74. See Anton C. Pegis, "Cosmogony and Knowledge," *Thought* 18 (1943): 642–64, esp. 662; 19 (1944): 269–90; and 20 (1945): 473–98.

75. "Causa autem prima, secundum Platonicos quidem, est supra ens in quan-

. . . God Himself is the formal being of existing things; rather [Diony-sius] uses this way of speaking, which the Platonists used who said that separate being is the being of existing things. Insofar as there are composite beings through participation in the abstract, the [separate beings] are participated. And this must be understood causally. . . . *(In de Div. Nom., V, lect. 1 [Pera, n. 630, p. 235])*[76]

This and other texts indicate that, long before writing the commentary on the *Nicomachean Ethics*,[77] Aquinas had already disassociated his own doctrine of participation from "Neoplatonism." The Thomistic account assimilates "the complex pattern of the four [Aristotelian] causes."[78] In that account, the efficient and final cause are clearly distinguished from the formal cause, and the exemplar cause is kept sharply separate from the immanent form of the thing.

God is not able to have some relation to us except through the mode of [being a] principle. Although there are four causes, He is not our material cause. But He does relate to us in the mode of an efficient cause and final [cause], and in the mode of an exemplar form although not in the mode of an inherent form. *(I Sent., d. 27, q. a. 5 [Mandonnet, 445])*[79]

Since the form that inheres in a creature cannot be identified with its transcendent analogue (the corresponding divine idea), God cannot be properly called "our essence" or "our substance" or "our wisdom." When such expressions are used by Christian authors, Aquinas advises that they are to be explained away rather than extended. Yet he is not prepared to jettison the notion of exemplar causality. Freed from the Platonist theory of separate forms, exemplar causality remains metaphysically useful since it helps explain how God acts as an intelligent efficient cause. To say that God acts intelligently is to say that God,

---

tum essentia bonitatis et unitatis, quae est causa prima, excedit etiam ipsum ens separatum. . . . Sed secundum rei vertitatem causa prima est supra ens in quantum est ipsum esse infinitum, ens autem dicitur id quod finite participat esse . . ." *(In de Causis,* prop. 6, lect. 6 [Pera, n. 175, p. 47; Saffrey, 47]).

76. ". . . Sed *Ipse est Esse existentibus,* non quidem ita quod ipse Deus sit esse formale existentium, sed eo modo loquendi utitur quo Platonici utebantur qui esse separatum dicebant esse existentium, inquantum compositiva per participationem abstractorum participantur. Et quod causaliter sit intelligendum . . ." *(In de Div. Nom.,* V, lect. 1 [Pera, n. 630, p. 235]).

77. Relevant texts, as listed by Henle and as dated in Weisheipl's and Torrell's chronologies, can be found in: *De veritate,* 1258–59; *Summa contra gentiles,* 1258–65; *Summa theologiae,* prima pars, 1266–68; *De substantiis separatis,* circa 1271.

78. Henle, *Saint Thomas and Platonism,* 379.

79. ". . . Deus non potest habere aliquam relationem ad nos, nisi per modum principii. Cum autem causae sint quatuor, ipse non est causa materialis nostra; sed

like an artisan, acts with a model in mind.[80] That model can be an idea of a divine property. If, for example, God causes a man to be wise, the divine wisdom then can be said to be the exemplar of that inherent human wisdom.[81]

Aquinas did not change his attitude toward Platonic exemplarism when he wrote his commentary on the *Nicomachean Ethics*. Writing about the same time (1271–73) as he wrote the latter, Aquinas asserts— one should say definitively reasserts—that the "basis of the [Platonic] position does not have any force."[82] Again, in a context that explicitly refers to the Platonic theory of formal participation, Aquinas denies that God participates in being; God is His Being.[83] Equivalently, he affirms over and against the *Platonici* that the formal goodness of created things is created and not divine goodness.[84] Plato's opinions, more-over, can be saved only by a radical reorientation of his metaphysical theory away from formal to efficient causality.[85]

If the first goodness is the effective cause of all goods, it must imprint its likeness upon the things produced; and so each thing will be called good by reason of an inherent form . . . and because of the first goodness taken as the exemplar and effective cause of all created goodness. In this fashion, the opinion of Plato is able to be upheld. *(De ver.*, q. 21, a. 4 [Spiazzi, 382])[86]

---

se habet ad nos in ratione efficientis et finis et formae exemplaris, non autem in ratione formae inhaerentis" *(I Sent.*, d. 27, q. 1, a. 5 [Mandonnet, 445]).

80. See *In Metaph.*, I, lect. 15 (Cathala-Spiazzi, n. 232, p. 68): "Hoc enim videtur opus exemplaris, idest utilitas, quod artifex respiciens ad exemplar inducat simili-tudinem formae in suo artificio"; *I Sent.*, d. 38, q. 1, a. 1 (Mandonnet, 899): ". . . inquantum scientia Dei est sicut exemplar per modum artis rerum, sic dicitur men-sura earum. . . ."

81. See ibid.: ". . . quia per ejus sapientiam efficitur in nobis sapientia exemplata a sua sapientia, per quam sapientes sumus formaliter."

82. "Huius autem positionis radix invenitur efficaciam non habere" *(De sub. sep.*, c. 2 [Spiazzi, n. 50, p. 23]).

83. See *In de Div. Nom.*, VI, lect. 2 (Pera, n. 690, p. 245).

84. See *ST*, I, q. 6, a. 4.

85. *In de Causis*, prop. 1, which examines the principle "*The influence of the first cause comes first and recedes last*," Aquinas notes that Proclus's examples are taken from the order of formal causes, but argues that the principle applies original-ly to efficient causes and derivatively to formal causes: see Pera, lect. 1, nn. 32–35, p. 6; Saffrey, 8.

86. ". . . unde si prima bonitas sit effectiva omnium bonorum, oportet quod similitudinem suam imprimat in rebus effectis; et sic unumquodque dicetur bonum sicut forma inhaerente . . . et ulterius per bonitatem primam, sicut per exemplar et effectivum omnis bonitatis creatae. Quantum ad hoc opinio Platonis sustineri po-test" *(De ver.*, q. 21, a. 4 [Spiazzi, 382]).

The Thomistic theory of participation, which "completely trans-form[s] the Greek doctrine of participation"[87] and, therefore, cannot be reduced to its historical sources,[88] is not easy to define.[89]

Perhaps the simplest definition relies on an analogy suggested by the etymology of *participare:* the relationship between part and whole.

To participate is, as it were, to have a part; and therefore when some particular thing receives that which universally pertains to another, it is said to participate it. *(In de Hebd.*, lect. 2 [Calcaterra, n. 24, p. 396])[90]

But, as this definition itself shows, Aquinas was aware that, historically considered, the doctrine of participation first arose in regard to the (Platonic) problem of predicating universals: man participates in "animal," Socrates participates in "man."[91]

However, the problem of predicating universals is not the metaphysical axis upon which the Thomistic doctrine turns. Being, its ultimate cause and intrinsic structure in finite things, is the central issue in the Thomistic theory of participation.[92] Since being is found in all things, which yet remain distinct from one another, Aquinas argues that all things must participate being from some unitary source.[93] Against this background, Aquinas finds that predication reveals a deeper distinction in the being of things between *esse* and *essentia.*

Whenever something is predicated of another through participation, then it is the case that the thing is outside that which is participated.

---

87. Joseph Owens, C. Ss.R., "The Causal Proposition—Principle or Conclusion?" *Modern Schoolman* 32 (1955): 263.

88. Cf. Fabro, *Participation et causalité*, 196, n. 40: ". . . bien que la notion thomiste de participation provienne . . . du platonisme, elle adopte et s'assimile essentiellement la métaphysique de l'acte aristotélicien."

89. See Owens, "The Causal Proposition," 262, n. 52.

90. "Est autem participare quasi partem capere; et ideo quando aliquid particulariter recepit id quod ad alterum pertinet universaliter, dicitur participare illud" *(In de Heb.*, lect. 2 [Calcaterra, n. 24, p. 396]).

91. See *In de Heb.* (Calcaterra, lect. 2, n. 24, p. 396): ". . . Sicut homo dicitur participare animal, quia non habet rationem animalis secundum totam communitatem; et eadem ratione Socrates participat hominem. . . ."

92. Wippel, "Aquinas and Participation," 147–48, finds three different senses of "participating being": finite things are said to participate in: (1) *esse commune*, (2) *esse subsistens*, (3) and in their own *actus essendi*. The second usage, however, is "the ultimate metaphysical explanation" of the other two.

93. See *De pot.*, q. 3, a. 5 (Pession, 49): "Cum ergo esse inveniatur omnibus rebus commune, quae secundum illud quod sunt, ad invicem distinctae sunt, oportet quod de necessitate eis non ex se ipsis, sed ab aliqua una causa esse attribuatur."

And, therefore, in any creature, the creature itself which has being is other than its very being. *(Quod.* II, q. 2. a. 2 [Spiazzi, 24])[94]

Whether "participation is more fundamental than the doctrine of *esse*"[95] is a moot point for contemporary scholars. Contrary to Fabro's position, Owens argues forcefully that Aquinas grounds the doctrine of participation in the essence-existence distinction. But the latter, as a real distinction validly applied to things, can only follow upon the proof that God exists as pure subsistent being.[96]

According to Owens, *ST,* I, q. 44, a. 1 provides a normative version of the Thomistic argument. In that text Aquinas sketches the following sequence of propositions: (1) that God is *Ipsum Esse Subsistens;* (2) that there can only be one *Ipsum Esse Subsistens;* (3) that in all other beings, therefore, there is a "real" distinction between *essentia* and *esse.* Each of these propositions needs to be demonstrated but, once demonstrated, they support the further conclusion (4) that all created beings are being by participation.

Owens's reconstruction of the metaphysical framework for the Thomistic doctrine of participation has been challenged.[97] For in other texts (e.g., *SCG,* II, 52) Aquinas argues in reverse order (going from the participated character of finite being to the essence-existence distinction), or, as seems the case in *Quod.* II, q. 2, a. 1, relies on both forms of the argument.[98] Whether one sides with Owens or his challengers, there remain stable elements in the Thomistic doctrine of participa-

---

94. "Quandocumque autem aliquid praedicatur de altero per participationem, oportet ibi aliquid esse praeter id quod participatur. Et ideo in qualibet creatura est aliud ipsa creatura quae habet esse, et ipsum esse eius . . ." *(Quod.* II, q. 2, a. 2 [Spiazzi, 24]).

95. George Lindbeck, "Participation and Existence in the Interpretation of St. Thomas Aquinas," *Franciscan Studies* 17 (1957): 114, n. 117. Lindbeck follows Fabro, *Participation et causalité,* 194: "Car l'acte d'*esse,* concept proper du thomisme . . . est dominé par et fondé sur la notion de participation." Cf. Joseph Owens, C.Ss.R., "Aquinas on Knowing Existence," in *Aquinas on the Existence of God,* 20–33, esp. his comments on Fabro, 32.

96. Owens, "The Causal Principle," 265–70.

97. For controversy about Owens's position, see Joseph Owens, C.Ss.R., "Quiddity and Real Distinction in St. Thomas Aquinas," *Mediaeval Studies* 27 (1965): 1–22 and "Stages and Distinction in *De Ente:* A Rejoinder," *Thomist* 45 (1981): 99–123; and John F. Wippel, "Aquinas's Route to the Real Distinction: A Note on *De ente et essentia,*" *Thomist* 43 (1979): 279–95 [reprinted in *Metaphysical Themes,* 107–32].

98. For an examination of these texts, see John F. Wippel, "Essence and Existence in Other Writings," in *Metaphysical Themes,* 133–61, and "Thomas Aquinas and Participation," 117–58.

tion that must be taken into consideration from whatever angle it is approached.[99] For Aquinas, every created being is an *ens* having *esse*, an existential composition of some *essentia* and *esse*, wherein both principles are efficiently caused by God. Irreducibly composite, finite beings "participate" *esse* but they "do not participate being *[esse]* according to the universal mode of being as it is found in the First Principle."[100] God alone is *Ipsum Esse Subsistens*; therefore, only in God is *esse* a nature. As participated, therefore, existence is not a nature but the actuation of a nature.[101] Nothing in Neoplatonism corresponds to the latter tenet.[102]

Nonetheless, historical scholarship has established that, however novel their Thomistic combination and meaning,[103] Neoplatonism certainly contributed some of the semantic elements of Aquinas's theory of participation. Hadot finds that the distinction between the infinitive and participial forms of Being (i.e., between εἶναι and οὐσία) first appears in Western philosophy in an anonymous commentary on Plato's *Parmenides* that Hadot attributes to Porphyry.[104] In this text, the First Principle is not "beyond being." Unlike Plotinus, the anonymous commentator is prepared to identify the One and Being, designating the latter, significantly, by means of the infinitive as "to-be-itself" (αὐτὸ τὸ εἶναι). Pure to-be-itself then can be characterized as pure activity (αὐτὸ τὸ ἐνέργειν). The second hypostasis is designated by means of the participial form; it has or participates being (μετέχειν). Yet it is no less significant, at least from a Thomistic metaphysical perspective, that the anonymous commentator (whom Hadot identifies as Porphyry) does not diversify the being of the first and second hypostases: on the

99. See especially *Q. de an.*, q. 6, ad 2 (Robb, 112) for a succinct statement of Aquinas's mature doctrine of participation.

100. ". . . non participant esse secundum universalem modum essendi, secundum quod est in primo principio . . ." *(De sub. sep.*, c. 8 [Spiazzi, n. 88, p. 34]).

101. See Owens, "Diversity," 106–7.

102. See Fabro, *Participation et causalité*, 169: ". . . l'esse comme positivité absolue et acte de toute forme est la nouveauté de la métaphysique de saint Thomas. . . ."

103. See M.-D. Roland-Gosselin, O.P., Le *"De ente et essentia" de s. Thomas d'Aquin* (Paris: Librairie Philosophique J. Vrin, 1948), 14: ". . . la distinction de forme et d'être est loin d'avoir dans le néo-platonisme, une importance égale à celle que lui donnera saint Thomas." For short doctrinal histories of the essence-existence distinction, see Étienne Gilson, *History of Christian Philosophy in the Middle Ages* (New York: Random House, 1955), 420–27, and John F. Wippel, "Essence and Existence," in *Cambridge History of Later Medieval Philosophy*, 385–410.

104. See Hadot, "L'être et l'étant," 32, for the relevant lines from the commentary. The full text of the latter can be found in Pierre Hadot, *Porphyre et Victorinus* (Paris: Les Etudes augustiniennes, 1968), 2: 98 ff.

contrary, the commentator states that τὸ εἶναι is double and that the One which is pure Being (εἶναι) is, in some way, the Idea of Being (ἰδέα τοῦ ὄντος), that is, the Idea of those entities that have being.

The semantic similarities between this anonymous Neoplatonic theory and the Thomistic theory of Being are apparent. Central to each is the distinction between the infinitive (εἶναι/*esse*) and participial (ὄν/ *ens*) forms of Being. But the metaphysical differences between the two theories can hardly be overlooked or collapsed.[105] Hadot, without specifically mentioning Aquinas (although he presumably has Aquinas in mind), denies that the Neoplatonic commentator is opposing essence and existence: "[L]'Être pur n'est pas un exister pur."[106] The commentator's opposition, rather, is in "the order of determination," between εἶναι as pure indetermination and ὄν as the first determination. In spelling out the equation, *pure being = pure activity = pure indetermination*, Hadot has precisely located the doctrinal chasm that separates the Neoplatonic commentator and Aquinas. For Aquinas, the divine *Ipsum Esse Subsistens* contains the perfection of being. Analogously, God is the most "determinate" of all beings.[107] He lacks no perfection found in finite beings: "The perfections of every thing pertain to the perfection of being."[108] God is being; finite entities merely participate being.[109] Pure existence is what gives actuality to any and every form.[110] It is from this angle that we can now return, after this long excursus, to our original query: What is the meaning and significance of Aquinas's remark at the beginning of the *Sententia libri Ethicorum*?

However one characterizes its historical provenance,[111] Aquinas's reference to the doctrine of participation at the beginning of his commentary projects the entire Aristotelian ethics against a novel metaphysical background, one that cannot be correctly characterized as

105. See Pierre Aubenque, "Gilson et la question de l'être," in *Étienne Gilson et nous: la philosophie de sa histoire*, ed. Monique Couratier (Paris: J. Vrin, 1980), 88, 92, n. 56.

106. Hadot, "L'Être et l'étant," 34.

107. See *SCG*, I, 23 (Pera, n. 214, p. 33): "Nihil enim est formalius aut simplicius quam esse."

108. *ST*, I, q. 4, a. 2. For similar texts, see Owens, "Diversity," 252, n. 26.

109. See *ST*, I, q. 4, a. 3, ad 3: ". . . Deus est ens per essentiam, et alia per participationem."

110. See *ST*, I, q. 4, a. 1, ad 3: ". . . unde ipsum esse est actualitas omnium rerum, et etiam ipsarum formarum."

111. Cf. Cornelio Fabro, "The Intensive Hermeneutics of Thomistic Philosophy: The Notion of Participation," *Review of Metaphysics* 27 (1974): 470: ". . . the Thomistic notion of participation constitutes in a most intensive sense (Hegelian) the *Aufhebung* of the opposition between Plato and Aristotle."

Platonic, or Aristotelian, or Neoplatonic, or Avicennian.[112] In short, we can only consider Aquinas as viewing Aristotle's ethics against an original Thomistic metaphysical background that is pithily characterized in Aquinas's dictum:

The substantial being of a thing is not an accident, but the actuality of every existing form. *(Quod.* XII, q. 5, a. 1 [Spiazzi, 227])[113]

Why, at the beginning of his commentary on the *Nicomachean Ethics,* did Aquinas introduce what we can now recognize to be the extraordinarily transformed Platonist theme of participation? The only sound answer is that he meant to signal his own doctrinal point of view. The participationist theme, which relocates the Aristotelian ethics, corresponds to the metaphysical background of the theological ethics in the *Summa theologiae* that Aquinas was developing simultaneously with his Aristotelian commentary.[114]

All things desire God as their end in desiring any good whatsoever, whether by an intellectual, or sensual, or natural appetite which is without knowledge. Nothing has the essence of the good and the desirable except that it participates in some likeness of God. *(ST,* I, q. 44, a. 3)[115]

According to this Thomistic doctrine, God is the universal good and everything else is good through participation in the divine, universal good.[116] The inference that Aquinas draws for Aristotelian ethics is a

112. See Bourke, "Nicomachean Ethics," 239–59; and Paul Merken, "Transformation of the Ethics of Aristotle in the Moral Philosophy of Thomas Aquinas," in *Atti del congresso internazionale, Tommaso d'Aquino nel suo settimo centenario,* Vol. 5: *L'Agire morale* (Naples: Edizioni Domenicane Italiane, 1977), 151–62.

113. ". . . esse substantiale rei non est accidens, sed actualitas cuiuslibet formae existentis . . ." *(Quod.* XII, q. 5, a. 1 [Spiazzi, 227]).

114. If Gauthier's arguments are correct, then Aquinas completed the *Prima pars* of the *Summa theologiae* by 1268, wrote the *Secunda pars* from 1269 to 1272, and finished the *Prima secundae* by 1270. Falling exactly within this period, the *Sententia libri ethicorum* was written in 1271, or by early 1272: see Weisheipl, *Friar Thomas,* 361, 380; Torrell, 227. For arguments contra Gauthier and a different dating of the *Sententia libri ethicorum,* see Bourke, "Nicomachean Ethics," who places its composition between 1261 and 1264. The doctrinal comparison, however, would remain unaffected by this changed dating; the main points of the Thomistic theory of participation can be already found in Aquinas's commentary on Dionysius's *De divinis nominibus,* written about 1261.

115. ". . . omnia appetunt Deum ut finem, appetendo quodcumque bonum, sive appetitu intelligibili, sive sensibili, sive naturali, qui est sine cognitione: quia nihil habet rationem boni et appetibilis, nisi secundum quod participat Dei similitudinem" *(ST,* I, q. 44, a. 3).

116. See *ST,* I–II, q. 9, a. 6: ". . . Deus, qui est universale bonum. Omne autem aliud bonum per participationem."

radical one. Since the goodness of the good man is a participation in divine goodness,[117] his virtues can be understood as a "similitude and participation in future beatitude."[118]

In the *Primae secundae* of the *Summa theologiae*,[119] Aquinas realigns the Aristotelian pursuit of happiness by tying earthly happiness to heavenly bliss: "[T]here is some happiness in this life because it has some similitude to true happiness."[120] The realignment draws on the different meanings of the Thomistic doctrine of participation. There are, Aquinas acknowledges, earthly goods worth pursuing. But earthly goods are imperfect; nonetheless, they *participate* in a perfect good. Earthly goods *derive* from the cause of their goodness, God. What can be achieved by the pursuit of earthly goods, imperfect beatitude, can only be viewed as a participation in the perfect beatitude of the life to come. Earthly beatitude, philosophical contemplation of divine things, is an imperfect *reflection* or an *imitation* of perfect beatitude, the direct vision of God in the world to come. Finally, even the eventual possession of perfect beatitude is itself but a participation in God's beatitude: "God is beatitude though His essence."[121] The blessed *share* in what God is in Himself.

The Thomistic doctrine of participation has other implications. It permits or, better put, *forces* Aquinas to surmount a certain dualism in Aristotle; Aquinas is able to ground and to unify in the transcendent good at least two of the Aristotelian forms of life that otherwise fall asunder. The *Nicomachean Ethics*, while championing its own conception of supreme human fulfillment, accepts the possibility of discrete ways of life with irreducibly divergent ends: men pursue pleasure, politics, or divine contemplation, but in doing so they are traveling on different paths that never meet. Only their desire for *eudaimonia* is common, not their actual ends. Aristotle takes for granted that no single account or explanation can be given of the goodness of these diverse ends.[122] But, metaphysically speaking, Aquinas could not have

117. See *ST*, II–II, q. 23, a. 2, ad 1: ". . . bonitas qua formaliter boni sumus est participatio quaedam divinae bonitatis. . . ."

118. ". . . in virtutibus est quaedam similitudo et participatio futurae beatitudinis" (*ST*, II–II, q. 129, a. 7, ad 3).

119. See *ST*, I–II, q. 2, a. 6; q. 3, a. 1; a. 6; q. 5, a. 3.

120. ". . . in hac vita esse aliquam beatitudinem, propter aliquam similitudinem verae beatitudinis" (*ST*, I–II, q. 5, a. 3, ad 3).

121. "Deus est beatitudo per essentiam suam" (*ST*, I–II, q. 3, a. 1).

122. See *EN*, I, 6, 1096b24–25 (rev. Oxford trans.): "But of honour, wisdom, and pleasure, just in respect of their goodness, the accounts are distinct and diverse." In his commentary, Aquinas accurately reproduces this Aristotelian tenet: see *SLE*, I, 7, 1096b21, 151–67 (*In Ethic.*, I, lect. 7 [Spiazzi, n. 94, p. 25]).

left these strings loose. There remains a Thomistic if not an Aristotelian knot to tie. Because two of these ways of life, the political and the philosophical, actually pursue some authentic good, each must somehow be grounded in the good. But how is that possible?

According to Aquinas, "[T]he supreme good itself is in some way desired in every [particular] good."[123] In the Thomistic metaphysical setting, Aquinas can claim that God, who is not always explicitly acknowledged as man's end and whose nature, even when He is acknowledged, utterly exceeds the positive comprehension of the human intellect, is nonetheless the ultimate end that actually moves every man's will.[124] The desire for the perfect good, which in truth can only be identified with God, is built into human nature by God.[125] Of course, all cognizable finite ends can also be desired as good, but they are good only because they participate in His infinite goodness.[126] The diversity of human ends thus gives way to a deeper unity in the pursuit of goodness, appropriate to a universe where no created good can be taken away or added to the one God who is the essence of goodness.[127]

Aquinas's reading of Aristotle has an advantage; it surmounts, in advance as it were, the contemporary exegetical dilemma about Aristotelian man's ultimate end, whether it should be regarded as *exclusive* or *inclusive* of all other goods. The latter question cannot be sustained against the background of Aquinas's doctrine of participation. God, in the Thomistic metaphysical context, is an inclusive good.

Any good whatsoever that is added to God does not make any increase in goodness, since that [additional good] is not good except through this fact that it participates the divine goodness. *(SLE, I, 9, 1097b16, 192–95; In Ethic., I, lect. 9 [Spiazzi, n. 115, p. 31])*[128]

123. ". . . ipsum summum bonum quodammodo appetitur in quolibet bono" *(SLE, I, 1, 1094a2, 180–81; In Ethic., I, lect. 1 [Spiazzi, n. 11, p. 5]).*

124. See *IV Sent.*, d. 49, q. 1, a. 3, sol. 1, ad 1 (Vivès, 11, p. 173): "Et sicut bonum, communiter loquendo, est per se objectum voluntatis; ita et summum bonum est ultimus voluntatis finis, per se loquendo: sed hoc vel illud bonum ponitur ut ultimus voluntatis finis et principale eius objectum quasi per accidens."

125. See ibid., sol. 2: "Unde cum ex impressione primae causae, scilicet Dei, hoc animae insit ut bonum velit; et perfectum bonum tamquam finem ultimum appetat. . . ."

126. See *SCG*, III, 17; 21; *ST*, I–II, q. 2, a. 8, ad 3.

127. See *SLE*, X, 2, 1172b28, 105–8 *(In Ethic.*, X, lect. 2 [Spiazzi, n. 1972, p. 515]): ". . . ipsi autem essentiae bonitatis nihil potest apponi, quod sit bonum alio modo, quam participando essentiam bonitatis. . . ."

128. ". . . ita enim quodcumque bonum connumeratum Deo non facit aliquod augmentum bonitatis, quia non est bonum nisi per hoc, quod participat bonitatem divinam" *(SLE, I, 9, 1097b16, 192–95; In Ethic., I, lect. 9 [Spiazzi, n. 115, p. 31]).*

Unlike the limited and possibly incompatible ways of life confronting the Aristotelian moral agent (and it is this incompatibility that generates the contemporary interpreter's dilemma), the pursuit of various finite ends, saving sinful ones, neither adds nor takes away from the beatitude that man finds in his ultimate end, God, who is the source of all participated goodness.[129] In short, the Thomistic pursuit of the supreme and transcendent good, although not compatible with a life devoted to sensual pleasure, is compatible with either the active or the contemplative lives. The two lives, however, are not of equivalent value. Whereas the happiness of the active life disposes one toward perfect beatitude, the imperfect happiness of the contemplative life, as a similitude thereof, marks a certain beginning of future or perfect beatitude.[130]

The introduction of the participation theme, as well as other themes that could be adduced to indicate where Aquinas transposes Aristotle's doctrine (say, in regard to the eternity of the world or the animation of the heavens), is a good example of the theological subtlety of Aquinas's exegesis. Yet Aquinas's exegesis is not dominated by the naive wish to Christianize Aristotle. Rather, Aquinas looks beyond what Aristotle says to the philosophical problems that he raises and to the Aristotelian solutions proposed. Aristotle is "the Philosopher," but philosophical reason can and should transcend the boundaries set by Aristotle. This, certainly, is how Aquinas regards Aristotelian metaphysics and Aristotelian psychology.[131] And he has exactly the same attitude about Aristotle's ethics: the *Nicomachean Ethics* is the historical paradigm of a philosophical ethic but it is not philosophically definitive. Yet, if this is Aquinas's approach to Aristotle, it still leaves open the question of how Aquinas subsumes the concept of the moral good into his *theological* ethics.

3. Ethics in a Theological Context

In the *Summa theologiae*, Aquinas develops his moral science as a part of a much larger study, the study of God as the beginning and end

129. See *SLE*, X, 13, 1179a22, 133–34 (*In Ethic.*, X, 13 [Spiazzi, n. 2134, p. 554]): "[Deus] . . . qui est fons omnium bonorum"; *SCG*, III, 59 (Pera, n. 2348, p. 79): "Perfectio autem esse intelligibilis est cum intellectus ad suum ultimum finem pervenerit. . . ."

130. See *ST*, I–II, q. 69, a. 3: "Beatitudo autem contemplativa, si sit perfecta, est essentaliter ipsa futura beatitudo: si autem sit imperfecta, est quaedam inchoatio eius."

131. Cf. Elders, *"Thomas et Aristote,"* 374, who maintains, in specific opposi-

of creation. The *Secunda pars*, accordingly, treats morality as "the motion of the rational creature to God."[132] In this theological context, the Aristotelian virtue of practical wisdom (φρόνησις) takes on a heightened significance: *phronesis/prudentia* is now viewed as an instrument of divine providence and not as merely the expression of human foresight. Nonetheless, the theologian can only speak of divine providence by analogy with the human form of providential knowledge. In human affairs, providence or foresight *(providentia)* allows one to see what is to be done beforehand.

In coordinating definitions of *"prudentia"* found in Cicero, Aristotle, Andronicus of Rhodes, and other traditional authors, Aquinas specifies three different senses of the "parts" of prudence: (1) *integral* parts, or parts that actually constitute a whole (the bricks of a house); (2) *universal* or *subjective* parts, which are species of which the whole can be predicated ("'Man' is an 'animal'"); (3) and *"potential* parts,"* or parts that share in the power of the whole without being constitutive or universal parts (e.g., the vegetative and sensitive souls which share in the power of the rational soul). Personal ethics, household management, military science, and politics are the major species or subjective parts of prudence. Since they do not bear on the principal act of prudence (prescription) but on its secondary acts, Aquinas classifies the Aristotelian virtues of εὐβουλία (good deliberation), σύνεσις (understanding of things that can be deliberated about), and γνώμη (right judgment about the equitable) as *potential* parts of prudence: they are "virtues distinct from each other and from prudence."[133] *Providentia* (foresight), however, is the principal *integral* part of prudence;[134] it enables a man to direct himself and others to their proper ends.[135]

God, then, is said to be "provident" because He orders creation to its ultimate end, the divine goodness itself. The eternal law is the divine order for creation, as that order first exists eternally in God's mind. Divine providence, although not identical with the eternal law, is in-

---

tion to Owens, that Aquinas's anthropology, metaphysics of being, and ethics "découlent des principes posés par Aristote."

132. ". . . de motu rationalis creaturae in Deum . . ." *(ST,* I, q. 2, prologus).

133. ". . . virtutes et ab invicem et a prudentia distinctae . . ." *(III Sent,* d. 33, q. 3, a. 1, sol. 3 [Moos, n. 281, p. 1075]).

134. See *III Sent.,* d. 33, q. 3, a. 1 sol. 1 (Moos, n. 270, p. 1074): ". . . providentia est completiva et formalis pars prudentiae . . ."; *ST,* II–II, q. 49, a. 6, ad 1: " . . . providentia est principalior inter omnes partes prudentiae . . . ."Cf. *III Sent.,* d. 33, q. 3, a. 1, sol. 1–3 (Moos, nn. 268–288, pp. 1073–76).

135. See *ST,* I, q. 22, a. 1: "Ratio autem ordinandorum in finem, proprie providentia est."

stantiated in the eternal law. The eternal order of creation exists in
God's mind as the order of the divine ideas that are the models or
exemplars of created things. According to the standard interpretation
of Aquinas's doctrine of divine ideas,[136] God knows as many individuated divine exemplars as there are individuated created things that imitate the exemplars.[137] The standard interpretation recommends itself
since Aquinas certainly holds that God's knowledge extends to the
individual things in the world that He creates.[138] But so interpreted, the
doctrine of divine ideas introduces the notorious problem of how one is
to preserve the divine simplicity in the face of the multiplicity of
divine ideas. Aquinas claims that God knows these individuals *(singularia)* by knowing His own essence which is absolutely one. In knowing the divine essence, God also knows how His essence can be imitated in multiform ways by creatures. The multiplicity of the divine ideas
arises in the divine intellect because God compares His own essence to
the creatures that can participate in the divine essence.[139]

Aquinas, however, is aware of the tension between these claims
about the unity of the divine essence and the multiplicity of the divine
ideas. He distinguishes between the divine essence itself and God's

136. See L. B. Geiger, O.P., "Les Idées divines dans l'oeuvre de s. Thomas," in *St.
Thomas Aquinas, 1274–1974,* 1: 175–209.

James Ross, in "Aquinas's Exemplarism; Aquinas's Voluntarism," *American
Catholic Philosophical Quarterly* 64 (1990): 171–98, challenges the standard interpretation, the "photo-exemplarism" as he calls it, that identifies "the possibles"
with an infinite plurality of actually individuated divine ideas. According to Ross,
"Aquinas's metaphysics requires that no reality *ante res* be attributed to mere
possibilities" (175). Consequently, in knowing the divine essence, God knows "the
possibles" that are created only eminently, virtually, and indeterminately: cf. *De
ver.,* q. 3, a. 6. Even "absolute possibility" is a *result* of creation; it is consequent
upon God's willing to create the order of nature that He actually creates (cf. *De pot.,*
q. 3, a. 1, ad 3): see 179–80. Ross admits (189), however, that his voluntarist
interpretation must be harmonized with texts referring to a realm of absolute
possibility that extensionally corresponds to the infinite scope of (individuated?)
divine ideas: see, for example, *ST,* I, q. 25, a. 3. Moreover, if "the plurality of [divine]
ideas is denominative from the things made" (Ross, 182), the plurality of the ideas
is, according to Aquinas, the cause of the plurality of things: ". . . quamvis pluralitas
idearum attendatur secundum respectus ad res; non tamen pluralitas rerum est
causa pluralitatis idearum, sed e contrario . . ." (*I Sent.,* d. 36, q. 2, a. 2, ad 3
[Mandonnet, 842–43]).

137. A divine idea is an *exemplar* if it pertains to divine practical knowledge: it
is a model of a thing that God will make. A divine idea is a *ratio* if it pertains to
God's theoretical knowledge of things that are possible but that He will not make:
see *ST,* I, q. 15, a. 3.

138. See *I Sent.,* d. 36, q. 1, a. 2; *ST,* I, q. 15, a. 3.

139. See *ST,* I, q. 15, a. 2, ad 3.

knowledge of the divine essence. The divine ideas do not name or refer to the unitary divine essence itself, which is the infinite and simple plenitude of being that can be imitated in diverse modes by creatures, but to the divine essence as God *knows* Himself to be imitable:[140] "This name 'idea' names the divine essence insofar as it is the exemplar imitated by a creature."[141] Aquinas takes pains to stress that God's act of knowing is unitary; what He knows is multiple. God knows all the modes in which He can be imitated. The diversity in things consequently depends upon the diversity of their exemplars as known by God.[142]

Nonetheless, does not God's knowledge of the multiple divine ideas fragment, as indeed the Neoplatonists thought,[143] the absolute unity and simplicity of God? If the divine ideas "do not fall outside the divine knowledge,"[144] how is it that when God understands the divine ideas "no multiplicity is attached to His substance"?[145] Aquinas's explanation is that God knows an actual plurality of divine exemplars through the one act of knowing His self-same essence.[146] What is the ontological status of this plurality? In denying that the divine ideas are really or ontologically distinct from the divine essence, Aquinas draws upon the distinction between a real relationship *(relatio realis)* and a relationship of reason *(relatio rationis)*.[147] The latter relationship is not in the natures of the things being compared but only in the apprehension of the reason doing the comparison. The divine ideas, unlike the relation-

140. ". . . et ex hoc sunt plures rationes ideales, secundum quod Deus intelligit essentiam suam ut imitabilem per hunc vel per illum modum. Ipsae enim rationes imitationis intellectae, seu modi, sunt idea; idea enim . . . nominat formam ut intellectam, et non prout est in natura intelligentis" *(I Sent.,* d. 36, q. 2, a. 2 [Mandonnet, 842]).

141. "Unde cum hoc nomen 'idea' nominet essentiam divinam secundum quod est exemplar imitatum a creatura . . ." *(I Sent.,* d. 36, q. 2, a. 2 [Mandonnet, 842]).

142. See *I Sent.,* d. 36, q. 2, a. 2, ad 3 (Mandonnet, 843): "Intellectus enim divinus est causa rerum; distinctio autem idealium rationum est secundum operationem intellectus divini, prout intelligit essentiam suam diversimode imitabilem a creaturis"; *SCG,* I, 54 (Pera, n. 452, p. 66): "Quia vero propria ratio unius distinguitur a propria ratione alterius; distinctio autem est pluralitatis principium: oportet in intellectu divino distinctionem quandam et pluralitatem rationum intellectarum considerare, secundum quod id quod est in intellectu divino est propria ratio diversorum."

143. For the differences between Christian and Greek philosophical doctrines of providence, see Gilson, "Christian Providence," in *Spirit of Mediaeval Philosophy,* 148–67.

144. Hankey, *God in Himself,* 101.

145. See *ST,* I, q. 14, a. 4: "Unde patet quod per hoc quod Deus dicitur intelligens, nulla multiplicitas ponitur in eius substantia."

146. See *ST,* I, q. 15, a. 3.

147. See *ST,* I, q. 28, a. 1.

ships between the three divine persons, are not "real relations"; they are "logical relations," that is, relations that exist in the divine intellect only because God chooses to compare His essence *qua imitable* to the many creatures that can imperfectly imitate it.[148]

According to the analogy of the intellect generating an intelligible word, the Father is said, in orthodox Trinitarian doctrine, to generate the Son. The relations between Father and Son, paternity and filiation, are real relations. But the intellect-word model does not apply to the divine ideas; otherwise we could not distinguish, as neatly as Aquinas does, the real relationship between Father and Son and the logical relationship between God and the divine ideas.[149] Presumably we should think, since a logical relationship only arises from reason observing two *understood* things, that God compares the *idea* of the divine essence qua imitable to the *idea* of a thing that imitates the divine essence. But Aquinas says *(ST,* I, q. 15, a. 2, ad 3), perhaps elliptically, that God compares His essence with things.

The distinction between real and logical relations, when applied to the divine ideas, certainly generates as many puzzles as it solves,[150] but I shall not delve into them here. My precise topic is the *analogy* that Aquinas draws between human and divine providence. Focusing on this topic, I should note that Aquinas does not equate the eternal law (= the idea of the order among the divine ideas or exemplars) and divine providence. Aquinas identifies divine providence, again in line with human providence, as God's *act of directing or ordering* creation to the end set forth in the eternal law.[151] Since God is the creator of all things and the universal cause of all being, then all things, men included, must be subject to divine providence.[152]

Human providence is but one type of particular cause (namely, a cause that acts freely) that falls under God's universal providence. Theology thus subsumes human providence, which is particular, under divine providence, which is universal.

Since the act of free choice is reduced to God as to [its] cause, it is necessary that those events that occur from free choice are subject to

148. See *ST,* I, q. 15, a. 2, ad 3.

149. See *ST,* I, q. 28, a. 1, ad 4.

150. See Christopher Hughes, "Identity and the Trinity," in *On a Complex Theory of a Simple God: An Investigation in Aquinas' Philosophical Theology* (Ithaca, N.Y.: Cornell University Press, 1989), 186–240.

151. See *I Sent.,* d. 39, q. 2, a. 2; *De ver.,* q. 5, a. 1; *ST,* I, q. 22, a. 1.

152. See *ST,* I, q. 22, a. 2: ". . . omnia, inquantum participant esse, intantum subdi divinae providentiae."

divine providence. For the providence of man is contained under the providence of God as a particular cause [is contained] under a universal cause. *(ST,* I, q. 22, a. 2, ad 4)[153]

Although he subordinates human freedom to God's infinite causal power, Aquinas attempts to preserve contingent or free human choices.[154] The concept of divine providence involves, of course, the intractable problem of reconciling divine necessity and created contingency: men fall under divine providence, however paradoxical it may seem, inasmuch as they are self-directing.[155] Men are created with intellects and wills so that what divine providence ordains in regard to human actions comes about through contingent human choices.[156]

The task of reconciling the two causal orders, divine and human, belongs to the business of metaphysics and not ethics.[157] Common morality presupposes that human affairs are subject to human providence. Human providence is expressed in choices that, because they are free, can be appropriately evaluated as morally good and bad, can be subjected to approbation and blame, and consequently can be given reward and punishment both human and divine.

Thomistic theology treats the theme of free human choice—its psychological principles and the conditions under which it is inhibited—as the prolegomenon to moral science. But ethics, while it presupposes some knowledge of the soul and its powers,[158] does not require the complete sciences of psychology and metaphysics; it needs only those psychological and metaphysical principles that explain how men attain their final end, happiness.[159] Ethics thus properly focuses on the virtues

153. "Sed quia ipse actus liberi arbitrii reducitur in Deum sicut in causam, necesse est ut ea quae ex libero arbitrio fiunt, divinae providentiae subdantur: providentia enim hominis continetur sub providentia Dei, sicut causa particularis sub causa universali" *(ST,* I, q. 22, a. 2, ad 4).

154. See *In Metaph.,* VI, lect. 3 (Cathala-Spiazzi, n. 1222, p. 308): ". . . cum de divina providentia loquimur, non est dicendum solum, hoc est provisum a Deo ut sit, sed hoc est provisum a Deo, ut contingenter sit, vel ut necessario sit. . . . Quod autem sit necessarium vel contingenter, dependet ex causa altiori, quae est causa entis inquantum est ens. . . ."

155. See *De ver.,* q. 5, a. 5 (Spiazzi, 98): "Et ideo humani actus sub divina providentia cadunt hoc modo quod ipsi provisores sunt suorum actuum. . . ."

156. For Aquinas's effort to reconcile human freedom and divine necessity, see *ST,* I, q. 19, a. 8; I–II, q. 10, a. 4; *SCG,* I, 67; III, 90–94.

157. See *De ver.,* q. 6, a. 3; esp. ad 3.

158. See *SLA,* I, c. 1, 402a4, 122–24 *(In de An.,* I, lect. 1 [Pirotta, n. 7, pp. 3–4]): "Si uero attendatur quantum ad moralem, non possumus perfecte ad scienciam moralem peruenire nisi sciamus potencias anime. . . ."

159. See *SLE,* I, 1, 51–54 *(In Ethic.,* I, lect. 1 [Spiazzi, n. 3, p. 3]): ". . . Subiectum moralis philosophiae est operatio humana ordinata in finem vel etiam homo prout

and human action[160] and develops specifically moral criteria to distinguish human actions into good and bad.[161]

4. Eternal Law and Natural Law

Aquinas compares *(De ver.,* q. 5, a. 1) the eternal law in the mind of God and the natural law in the minds of men. The eternal law consists of the divine ideas that are the exemplars and ends of creation; these ideas are the principles of divine providence. In reference to them, God providentially orders creation and moves it to its end.[162] The natural law consists of the innate first principles of practical reason. In the sphere of human providence, the natural law has a function similar to that of the eternal law. The first principles of practical reason prescribe the fundamental ends that human action should realize.

The analogy is based on the functional similarity between the eternal law in the mind of God and the natural law in the minds of men.[163] But while the analogy displays, it does not establish the theonomous character of these practical principles. Some stronger connection is needed: Aquinas adverts to the causal relation between the eternal law and the natural law. As divinely caused, the first practical principles are said to participate in the eternal law.[164] Aquinas explains this ontological participation by showing that the natural law has God as its efficient cause and the eternal law as its exemplar and final cause.[165] God as the creator of nature imprints the natural law on the human mind. Through the first principles that are imprinted on practical reason, man is divinely ordered to his natural end.[166]

---

est voluntarie agens propter finem"; *SLE,* I, 2, 1094a28, 138–40 *(In Ethic.,* I, lect. 2 [Spiazzi, n. 27, pp. 7–8]): ". . . actus in quantum sunt voluntarii pertinent ad materiam moralem et sunt ordinabiles ad finem humanae vitae. . . ."

160. *SLE,* I, 19, 1102a23, 75–76 *(In Ethic.,* I, lect. 19 [Spiazzi, n. 228, p. 62]): ". . . in hac scientia contemplandum est de anima gratia horum, id est virtutum et actuum hominis, de quibus est hic principalis intentio . . ."; *ST,* I–II, q. 6, prologus: "Moralis igitur consideratio, quia est humanorum actuum. . . ."

161. See *ST,* I–II, qq. 18–21.

162. See *ST,* I–II, q. 93, a. 1.

163. See *De ver.,* q. 5, a. 1, ad 6: "Lex enim aeterna est consideranda in Deo, sicut accipiuntur in nobis principia operabilium naturaliter nota, ex quibus procedimus in consiliando et eligendo: quod est prudentiae, sive providentiae. . . ."

164. See *ST,* I–II, q. 91, a. 2.

165. Divine providence is the efficient cause of the human intellect and its intrinsic principles; knowing God is the end of intellectual activity. See *De ver.,* q. 5, a. 1, ad 7.

166. See *ST,* II–II, q. 62, a. 3.

Aquinas's assertion *(De ver.,* q. 5, a. 1) that the natural law participates the eternal law is a conclusion drawn from the causal relationship that Aquinas posits between man and God. Men act in accordance with practical reason. But God, in accordance with the divine ideas in the divine mind, is the efficient cause of the human mind. Thus the innate practical principles that direct human action reflect the order of creation first instantiated in the eternal law. But the Thomistic doctrine of participation does not license any immediate knowledge of the eternal law.[167]

The eternal law exceeds natural reason. And therefore the knowledge of human acts insofar as they are regulated by the eternal law, exceeds natural reason. . . . *(ST,* II–II, q. 8, a. 3, ad 3)[168]

Such knowledge of the eternal law is impossible because it would be equivalent to immediate cognition of the divine essence, and it is not possible, in this life, to know the divine essence.

The eternal law is the divine idea of the order among the divine ideas, which order is the exemplar of the order of creation. Although Aquinas argues that what God knows is multiple (i.e., the divine ideas are multiple), he wishes to preserve the unity and simplicity of God. God remains in Himself absolutely simple and one. Aquinas denies, therefore, that the divine ideas are really distinct from the divine essence.[169] Since men cannot comprehend, even with the help of revelation, the divine essence, so too the eternal law, inasmuch as it is really identical with the divine essence, is equally unknowable in this life.[170]

Inasmuch as practical reason immediately governs human actions and its own basic principles are not derived from theoretical principles, Thomistic practical reason can be regarded as *logically* "autonomous." Autonomous knowledge of basic practical principles is an innate feature of rational human nature.

The natural law is nothing other than the concept that is naturally innate to man, by which he is directed to acting appropriately in [his]

167. See *I Sent.,* d. 19, q. 5, a. 3, ad 2; *ST,* I, q. 15, aa. 1–3; q. 44, a. 3; I–II, q. 91, a. 1.

168. "Lex autem aeterna excedit naturalem rationem. Et ideo cognitio humanorum actuum secundum quod regulantur a lege aeterna, excedit rationem naturalem . . ." *(ST,* II–II, q. 8, a. 3, ad 3).

169. See *ST,* I–II, q. 15, a. 1: "Unde idea in Deo nihil est aliud quam Dei essentia."

170. See *ST,* II–II, q. 173, a. 1: "Non est autem possibile quod aliquis videat rationes creaturarum in ipsa divina essentia, ita quod eam non videat"; *III Sent.,* d. 23, q. 2, a. 3, sol. 3, ad 2 (Moos, n. 187, p. 734): "Sed ad visionem articulorum

proper actions, whether [these actions] pertain to him from his generic nature, such as procreating, eating, and [other actions] of this sort, or from his specific nature, such as reasoning and similar actions. *(IV Sent.*, d. 33, q. 1, a. 1 [Vivès, 11, p. 140])[171]

Nonetheless, Thomistic natural law ethics is a part of the Thomistic theology of creation as that is understood by means of the metaphysical doctrine of participation. The principles of the natural law are viewed *"sub ratione Dei"*: they are immediately grounded in practical reason and mediately, through its exemplar, in the divine mind. From this theological vantage point, God is seen to be the creator of the human mind and the structure of practical reason is explained by reference to the eternal law in the divine mind. Accordingly, Aquinas's natural law ethics can also be described as metaphysically "theonomous" in character.

In its Thomistic theological setting, the law of practical reason is not opposed to a revealed or divine law whose authority immediately derives from its divine author. Because the natural law mediately (via the innate principles of practical reason that participate the eternal law) and the revealed or divine law immediately (through divine authority) are both grounded in the eternal law, the two laws are in harmony. Against the background of Aquinas's metaphysical doctrine of participation, practical reason can be both logically autonomous and metaphysically dependent on the divine mind. Of course, the principles of practical reason are the proximate, not the ultimate, rules of Thomistic morality. But Thomistic practical reason, when it is assigned the task of figuring out what morality requires, ultimately draws its conclusions from its own basic intrinsic principles. In such considerations, the eternal law remains the ontological foundation of the natural law, but it is neither the logical nor the epistemological criterion governing practical reasoning.

Thomistic natural law ethics is often hailed as an expression of the logically and epistemically "autonomous" functioning of practical reason. But even if it is appropriate to use this term, it is not correct to regard Aquinas's natural law ethics, in its Thomistic setting, as an autonomous *philosophical* science. In fact, the interpretation of Tho-

---

[fidei] neque lumen intellectus agentis sufficit, neque lumen fidei." See *ST,* I–II, q. 93, aa. 2–3.

171. "Lex ergo naturalis nihil est aliud quam conceptio homini naturaliter indita, qua dirigitur ad convenienter agendum in actionibus propriis, sive competant ei ex natura generis, ut generare, comedere, et hujusmodi; sive ex natura speciei, ut ratiocinari, et similia" *(IV Sent.*, d. 33, q. 1, a. 1 [Vivès, 11, p. 140]).

mistic moral science as an autonomously rational philosophical ethics provokes an exaggerated and dubious counterclaim that the subordination of natural law to the eternal law renders Thomistic moral science completely oriented toward moral "heteronomy."[172] Both terms, it is clear, have misleading connotations; according to their modern usage, neither "autonomy" nor "heteronomy" accurately places Thomistic natural law theory on its own metaphysical center. From its own theological standpoint, which ontologically grounds human reason by viewing it as a participation in the eternal law, it would be more accurate and more illuminating to call Thomistic natural law ethics a "theonomous" moral science. Yet this term, no less than the other two, needs to be understood precisely. Used with any historical accuracy, it should connote not a modern contraction or subversion of reason to religious authority but a medieval expansion of the scope of Aristotelian practical reason.

172. See Paul-M. Van Overbeke, O.P., "La Loi naturelle et le droit naturel selon s. Thomas," *Revue thomiste* 57 (1957): 60, n. 1: "Il ne saurait donc être question d'autonomie; toute la perspective de la doctrine de saint Thomas est orientée vers l'héteronomie."

IV

Aristotle: Practical Wisdom

1. Reason and Desire

In the prefatory remarks of his commentary to the *Nicomachean Ethics*, Aquinas explains how ethics differs from the other Aristotelian sciences. Diverse sciences have diverse subjects.[1] The "subject" *(subiectum)* of a science is that whose causes and qualities we seek to know through investigation.[2] What, then, is the *subject* of moral philosophy?[3] According to Aquinas, moral philosophy has as its subject human action insofar as it is ordered to an end; or, what Aquinas takes to be roughly equivalent, the subject of moral philosophy may be said to be man insofar as he is acting voluntarily for an end.[4] This subject can be described even more precisely by reference to the specific operations of man's cognitive and appetitive powers: in these psychological terms, moral philosophy considers how human reason, through its own deliberations, and human will, through free choice, order human actions to

1. See *ELP*, I,15, 75b10, 109–11 (Leonine ed., I, pt. 2, 58a); *I Sent.*, prologus, q. 1, a. 4; *Expos. de Trin.*, q. 5, a. 1.

2. See *In Metaph.*, prooemium (Cathala-Spiazzi, 2).

3. In Aquinas's usage, a science has a *subiectum*; a power or a habit has an *obiectum*: "Sic enim se habet subiectum ad scientiam, sicut obiectum ad potentiam vel habitum" *(ST,* I, q. 1, a. 8). Since the *subiectum* of a science is the genus under which all things in the science are considered, the *subiectum* is equivalent to the formal object of a power: see *ST,* I, q. 1, a. 3; a. 7; *I Sent.*, prologus, q. 1, a. 4.

4. See *SLE*, I, *ante* 1094a, 51–54 *(In Ethic.*, I, lect. 1 [Spiazzi, n. 3, p. 3]): ". . . Subiectum moralis philosophiae est operatio humana ordinata in finem vel etiam homo prout est voluntarie agens propter finem." Cf. *EN*, III, 3, 1112b31–32: ἄνθρωπος εἶναι ἀρχὴ τῶν πράξεων; *SLE*, III, 12, 1114a4, 35–36 *(In Ethic.*, III, lect. 12 [Spiazzi, n. 508, p. 145]): ". . . ratio et voluntas, quae sunt principia humanorum actuum. . . ."

their proper ends.[5] In making these and similar formulations,[6] Aquinas assumes that Aristotle takes practical reason to be the source of the human act and the moral goodness inherent in these acts.[7]

Aquinas uses causal language to explain how reason is the source of morality: when the agent wills to act, practical reason *makes* or *causes* the moral order instantiated in human action.[8] Since Kant, philosophers have frequently contended that practical reason, because it is causative, is self-grounded or radically autonomous.[9] But, for Aquinas, that practical reason makes the moral order is compatible with the fact that the principles of the human moral order preexist in the mind of God.[10] The first principles of practical reason participate in divine reason. By thus aligning his ethics with the metaphysical doctrine of participation,[11] Aquinas is able to give a theonomous account of practical reason.[12] The Thomistic formula is that right human reason is the proximate and homogeneous rule of morally good human actions; divine reason is the supreme and transcendent rule.[13]

5. See *SLE*, I, *ante* 1094a, 35–37 *(In Ethic.*, I, lect. 1 [Spiazzi, n. 2, p. 3]): "... ordo autem actionum voluntarium pertinet ad considerationem moralis philosophiae ..."; *SLE*, I, *ante* 1094a, 39–43 *(In Ethic.*, I, lect. 1 [Spiazzi, n. 2, p. 3]): "Sic igitur moralis philosophiae, circa quam versatur praesens intentio, proprium est considerare operationes humanas secundum quod sunt ordinatae ad invicem et ad finem."

6. See *ST*, I–II, q. 58, a. 2: "... omnium humanorum operum principium primus ratio est: et quaecumque alia principia humanorum operum inveniantur, quodammodo rationi obediunt. ..."

7. See *EN*, IX, 8, 1168b35–1169a1; *SLE*, II, 1103b31, 48–50 *(In Ethic.*, II, lect. 2 [Spiazzi, n. 257, p. 74]): "... operatio hominis sit bona ex hoc quod est secundum rationem rectam, perversitas enim rationis repugnat naturae rationis"; *III Sent.*, d. 23, q. 2, a. 3, q. 2 (Moos, n. 167, p. 731): "Cognitio practica est causa cognitorum."

8. See *SLE*, I, *ante* 1094a, 21–22 *(In Ethic.*, I, lect. 1 [Spiazzi, n. 1, p. 3]): "Tertius autem est ordo quam ratio considerando facit in operationibus voluntatis . . . ." Cf. *ST*, II–II, q. 83, a. 1: "... ratio speculativa est apprehensiva solum rerum; ratio vero practica est non solum apprehensiva, sed etiam causativa"; *De ver.*, q. 1, a. 2 (Spiazzi, 50): "Intellectus enim practicus causat res, unde est mensuratio rerum quae per ipsum fiunt. ..."

9. For Kant's notion of the autonomy of pure practical reason, as expressed in the mere form of universal self-legislation, see *Critique of Practical Reason*, trans. Lewis White Beck (New York: Liberal Arts Press, 1956), 33–35 [= pp. 33–35, vol. 5, Prussian Academy edition].

10. See ch. 2, p. 89, n. 142.

11. See *I Sent.*, d. 29, q. 5, a. 2 (Mandonnet, 491–92): "... nihilominus tamen quaelibet res participat suum esse creatum, quo formaliter est, et unusquisque intellectus participat lumen per quod recte de re judicat, quod quidem est exemplatum a lumine increato."

12. See *ST*, I–II, q. 19, a. 4: "... multo magis dependet bonitas voluntatis humanae a lege aeterna, quam ratione humana. ..."

13. See *ST*, I–II, q. 71, a. 6: "Regula voluntatis humanae est duplex. Una, proprin-

From his own historical perspective, Aquinas's paradigm of "autonomous practical reason" (if we may use this Kantian term loosely and anachronistically) was Aristotle's philosophical ethics. Aquinas understands, correctly enough, that Aristotle's moral philosophy determines what is morally right or wrong only in reference to the reasoned choices of the practically wise man (φρόνιμος) who, preeminently, is a politician. Beyond what the *phronimos* takes to be the good of the polis, Aristotle makes no appeal to any higher moral standard, natural or divine.[14] Yet Aquinas's theological ethics, which does appeal to a divine standard (the eternal law in the divine mind), concedes nothing of imminent human rationality to Aristotle.[15]

Of course, the theonomous grounding of Thomistic moral reasoning will seem to contradict the autonomy of practical reason if this notion is linked to Kant's critique of "heteronomous morality," which is blatantly, although perhaps inconsistently, antitheological.[16] Kant explicitly pits the a priori autonomy of practical reason against any appeal to God as divine judge or "the Holy One of the gospel" as moral example.

---

qua et homogenea, scilicet ipsa humana ratio; alia vero est prima regula, scilicet lex aeterna, quae est quasi ratio Dei"; II–II, q. 17, a. 1: "Humanorum autem actuum . . . duplex est mensura: una quidem proxima et homogenea, scilicet ratio; alia autem est suprema et excedens, scilicet Deus."

14. See *EN*, I, 2, 1094b7–11; *Pol.*, I, 2, 1253a20–30. Cf. Martin Rhonheimer, *Praktische Vernunft und Vernünftigkeit der Praxis: Handlungstheorie bei Thomas von Aquin in ihrer Entstehung aus dem Problemkontext der aristotelischen Ethik* (Berlin: Akademie Verlag, 1994), 406: "Erst die Theorie menschlicher Existenz in der durch richtige Gesetze geordneten Polis ist die definitive aristotelische Antwort darauf, *wie* man zur Tugend und damit auch zur Phronesis gelangen kann."

15. For a study emphasizing that human reason is the proximate rule of Thomistic morality, see P. Léonard Lehu, *La Raison, règle de moralité d'après Saint Thomas* (Paris: Librairie Lecoffre, 1930). Lehu notes (8) that while *"ratio"* refers both to the faculty and to the exercise of the faculty, Aquinas primarily identifies the *"recta ratio"* of moral reasoning with the product of practical reason, the prescriptive *"dictamen"* embodied in a law: cf. *ST*, I–II, q. 92, a. 2.

16. See Immanuel Kant, *Religion within the Limits of Reason Alone*, trans. Theodore M. Greene and Hoyt H. Hudson (New York: Harper & Row, 1960), 158, who takes the following proposition as "a principle requiring no proof": "Whatever, over and above good life-conduct, man fancies that he can do to become well-pleasing to God is mere religious illusion and pseudo-service to God." Since men make "God according to moral concepts," alleged revelations must first be submitted to our independently derived moral ideals: see p. 157.

Nonetheless, as was recognized by his contemporaries, Kant's notion of radical evil threatens the autonomy of the will and undermines the separation of moral philosophy and theology. See Jean-Louis Bruch, *La Philosophie religieuse de Kant* (Paris: Aubier, 1968): "Toute la philosophie kantienne aboutit ainsi à une théologie, et à une théologie qui accuse les limites de l'homme" (262).

Kant argues, on the contrary, that God must judge our goodness in accordance with the moral law as we must judge Jesus a person worthy to be imitated because he fulfills our ideal of moral perfection.[17] But in the Thomistic context, wherein divine reason is the first cause and ontological exemplar of practical reason, the Kantian anxiety over moral heteronomy can hardly arise. Aquinas holds that practical reason, which is the proximate but secondary cause of moral goodness, is, in regard to human actions, the *homogeneous* rule of morality.[18] Moreover, to adopt the Kantian perspective is surely to view Aquinas from the wrong end of the historical telescope. Aquinas was able to develop a rational theological ethics because, first of all, he significantly expanded the range of practical reason beyond its original Aristotelian boundaries. To use an ambivalent term whose meaning needs to be carefully specified, Aquinas was a greater "rationalist" than Aristotle.

What are the boundaries of Aristotelian practical reason? Or to put the question in more precise Aristotelian terms, how does Aristotle's practically wise man, the *phronimos*, reach the normative premises (the universal propositions about what is good and bad) that govern his moral reasoning?[19] This is the question that sets the topic of the present chapter. In the next chapter, I shall examine what Aquinas says about the first principles of practical reason. To anticipate matters a bit, Aquinas attempts to locate and illumine the undiscovered or obscured intellectual origin of Aristotelian practical wisdom (φϱόνησις).

---

17. See *Groundwork of the Metaphysics of Morals*, trans. H. J. Paton (New York: Harper and Row, 1964), 76, 107 [= pp. 408, 439, Prussian Academy edition].

18. See *ST*, I–II, q. 19, a. 4, obj. 2: ". . . lex aeterna non est homogenea voluntati humanae"; ad 2: ". . . mensura proxima [i.e., ratio humana] est homogenea mensurato: non autem mensura remota."

19. Aristotle identifies *(EN,* III, 4, 1113a33) the *phronimos* himself as the rule (χανών) or measure (μέτϱον) of what is morally good and bad. Arguably, the universal premises that the *phronimos* uses in his moral reasoning resemble, at least partially, what contemporaneously are called "moral rules": "For phronesis is imperative [ἐπιταχτιχή]; its end is what ought or ought not to be done" *(EN,* VI, 10, 1143a8–9). But for an influential statement of the (allegedly irreducible) differences between the principles of an Aristotelian-type "virtue ethics" and the obligatory precepts of a Kantian-type "rule ethics" see G. E. M. Anscombe, "Modern Moral Philosophy," *Philosophy* 33 (1958): 1–19; reprinted in *The Is-Ought Question: A Collection of Papers on the Central Problem in Moral Philosophy*, ed. W. D. Hudson (London: Macmillan Press, 1969), 175–95. Contra Anscombe, see Donagan, *The Theory of Morality:* "The conception of morality as virtue is not an alternative to a conception of it as law . . . to each precept of moral virtue . . . there is a precept of moral law that is its counterpart . . ." (3). Donagan quotes (245, n. 5) Aquinas approvingly: "Si igitur loquamur de actibus virtutum inquantum sunt virtuosi, sic omnes actus virtuosi pertinent ad legem naturae" *(ST,* I–II, q. 94, a. 3).

Without denying or ignoring that Aristotle draws attention to the emotive side of morality, Aquinas emphasizes that knowledge and a knowing pursuit of the "ultimate and best end" are called for if one is to lead a well-ordered life: It is required that all human life be ordered to the ultimate and best end. For the rectitude of human life, it is necessary, therefore, to have knowledge.

It is required that all human life be ordered to the ultimate and best end. For the rectitude of human life, it is necessary, therefore, to have knowledge of the ultimate and best end of human life. *(SLE,* I, 2, 1094a22, 67–71; *In Ethic.,* I, lect. 2 [Spiazzi, n. 23, p. 7])[20]

According to the Thomistic standard, the first principles setting the ends of man's morally correct choices must clearly reflect not only the morally good habits of the *phronimos* but the very nature of practical reason itself. By comparison with Aristotle, Aquinas emphasizes our cognitive grasp of the basic ends of human life. Accordingly, Aquinas leaves no room for thinking that moral principles can be solely grounded in acquired personal habits or social conventions, however morally excellent. But does Aquinas's cognitivist outlook accurately reflect the tenor of Aristotle's own ethical doctrine? The answer, to be sure, depends on balancing various texts of Aristotle. Where does Aristotle finally locate the *ground* of morality, in reason or in properly habituated emotions?[21]

In this chapter, then, I shall be looking at Aristotle but with an eye fixed on Aquinas and with an ear tuned to some recent discussions of the origin and scope of Aristotelian moral principles. Contemporary scholarship, for all of its fine siftings of Aristotle's texts, does not escape perennially revisable views of his ethical doctrines. But continual revision is not only possible but likely because there are, in addition to the interpreter's variant and changing philosophical predilections about the nature of morality, basic Aristotelian motifs about the relationship between practical reason and emotional habituation that need to be but cannot be easily harmonized. No reading of the *Nicomachean Ethics* founders for lack of nuances in the texts themselves;

---

20. ". . . Sed tota humana vita oportet quod ordinetur in ultimum et optimum finem humanae vitae; ergo ad rectitudinem humanae vitae necesse est habere cognitionem de ultimo et optimo fine humanae vitae" *(SLE,* I, 2, 1094a22, 67–71; *In Ethic.,* I, lect. 2 [Spiazzi, n. 23, p. 7]).

21. Cf. Rhonheimer, *Praktische Vernunft,* 421: "Die aristotelische Ethik ist also eine Theorie des tugendhaften Menschen und somit eine Theorie der affektiven Bedingungen für die Garantierung der praktischen Unfehlbarkeit des logos. . . ."

the problem, rather, is to give a coherent account of them. It should be forthrightly acknowledged that, independent of any consideration of Aquinas's view of Aristotle, any systematic reconstruction of what Aristotle says about the foundations of ethical reasoning is difficult and will remain controvertible.[22] On any synoptic reading, there will remain a number of ambiguous, apparently contradictory texts, whether or not one set of texts, the one that is uncongenial to a proposed interpretation, is declared "a lapse on Aristotle's part."[23] We can also note that Aquinas, unlike some contemporary interpreters, tries to keep hold of both sets of texts. Certainly the underlying philosophical question—whether moral virtue is ultimately rooted in practical reason or habituated emotion—does not escape him. But here, as with other important issues, Aquinas avoids overt eisegesis.

How can the doctrinal tension in the Aristotelian texts be characterized? On the one hand, Aristotle, presupposing that the virtuous man's morally correct ends have already been fixed by his *"prerational habits,"* straightforwardly affirms that *phronesis* ascertains only the correct means to attain those ends.[24] This conception of practical wisdom is tied to what I shall call the "narrow view" of deliberation and choice. On the other hand, Aristotle also often suggests that moral habits are only virtuous to the extent that they work with (as distinguished from merely being in conformity with) reason.[25] And *perhaps* once he states *(EN,* VI, 9, 1142b33) that the virtue of *phronesis* involves having an immediate cognitive comprehension of the true ends of human life. If the latter is the case, then Aristotelian practical reason is not confined solely to determining the means to prerationally grounded, emotionally generated, habitual ends. For many contemporary philosophers, deliberation about and choice of different ends are essential components in their notion of autonomous moral rea-

22. For two recent statements of the cognitivist and emotivist themes that are the source of doctrinal tensions in Aristotle's ethics, see Richard Sorabji, "Aristotle on the Role of Intellect in Virtue," in *Essays on Aristotle's Ethics,* ed. Amélie Oksenberg Rorty (Berkeley and Los Angeles: University of California Press, 1980), 201–19; and David Wiggins, "Deliberation and Practical Reason," ibid., 221–40.

23. H. H. Joachim, *Aristotle, The Nicomachean Ethics: A Commentary,* ed. D. A. Rees (Oxford: Clarendon Press, 1951), 218.

24. See *EN,* VI, 12, 1144a7–8; 13, 1145a4–6. Cf. *SLE,* VI, 11, 1145a2, 179–81 *(In Ethic.,* VI, lect. 11 [Spiazzi, n. 1289, p. 347]): ". . . virtus moralis ordinat ad finem, prudentia autem dirigit circa ea quae sunt ad finem."

25. See *EN,* III, 8, 1117a8–9; VI, 13, 1144b26–28. Cf. *SLE,* VI, 13, 1144b25, 107–12 *(In Ethic.,* VI, lect. 11 [Spiazzi, n. 1284, pp. 346–47]): "Non enim solum hoc habet virtus moralis quod sit secundum rationem rectam . . . Sed oportet ulterius dicere quod virtus moralis est habitus cum ratione recta. . . ."

son;[26] hence they find especially troubling those statements of Aristotle that restrict deliberation and choice, and consequently *phronesis*, solely to knowledge of the means to predetermined ends.[27] But, supposing that we can put aside any extraneous contemporary aversion to Aristotle's restrictive statements, it will still be far from clear what scope Aristotle actually assigns to *phronesis*. Does the Aristotelian virtue of practical wisdom include the cognitive grasp of ends as well as means? Aquinas, at least on one occasion in his commentary, seems ready to think so.

In one significant but opaque text, Aristotle states:

> If, then, it is characteristic of men of practical wisdom to have deliberated well, excellence in deliberation will be correctness with regard to what conduces to the end *of which* practical wisdom is the true apprehension. *(EN, VI, 9, 1142b31–33 [rev. Oxford trans.])*[28]

The text, which seems to contradict what Aristotle elsewhere says about *phronesis* being right knowledge of the *means*, is opaque because it is grammatically ambiguous: the "of which" (οὗ) can be attached either to the whole of the antecedent phrase, "what conduces to the end," or solely to its last word, "the end."[29] Aquinas, however, did not find the text ambiguous: on his reading what should be strictly called

26. See Wiggins, "Deliberation and Practical Reason," 234: "The unfinished or indeterminate character of our ideals and value structure is constitutive both of human freedom and . . . of practical rationality itself." For a more radical statement of the same view, but one that rejects "the very idea of a paradigm human being" (35), see Richard Rorty, *Contingency, Irony, and Solidarity* (Cambridge: Cambridge University Press, 1989). Donagan, in *Moral Theory*, 224–39, provides a well-argued version of the alternative (i.e., Kantian) conception of practical reason.

27. Among others, see *EN*, III, 3, 1112b11–12; IV, 7, 1141b8–9; VI, 12, 1144a7–8; 13, 1145a5–6.

28. εἰ δὴ τῶν φρονίμων τὸ εὖ βεβουλεῦσθαι, ἡ εὐβουλία εἴη ἂν ὀρθότης ἡ κατὰ τὸ συμφέρον πρὸς τὸ τέλος, οὗ ἡ φρόνησις ἀληθὴς ὑπόληψίς ἐστιν *(EN*, VI, 9, 1142b31–33). Cf. *SLE*, VI, 8, 1142b31–33 *(In Ethic.*, VI, lect. 8, Textus Aristotelis [Spiazzi, n. 880, p. 333]): "Si utique prudentium bene consiliari, eubulia erit utique rectitudo quae secundum conferens ad finem cuius prudentia vera suspicatio est."

29. Rackham, noting that Aristotelian *phronesis* explicitly "deals with means, not ends" hesitates, saying that the object of ἀληθής ὑπόληψις is "probably not" τὸ τέλος, see Aristotle, *The Nicomachean Ethics*, trans. H. Rackham, vol. 19, The Loeb Classical Library (Cambridge, Mass.: Harvard University Press, 1968), 356. John Burnet, *The Ethics of Aristotle* (London: Methuen & Co., 1900), 227, n. 7, states apodeictically that "[i]t is not *phronesis* but *orexis* which makes us aim at the good, and it is not *phronesis* but *ethos* which makes our good the true good" (127, n. 7). For arguments why the text of *EN*, VI, 9, 1142b32–33 should be emended to refer to the general end (and not any particular ends) of human life and why *phronesis* cannot on grammatical grounds be restricted (contra Walter, Burnet,

"prudentia" (as distinguished from *"euboulia"* = right deliberation about means) is the virtue that rightly comprehends the "universal end of the entirety of life."[30]

Aquinas's reading of *EN*, VI, 9, 1142b31–33, which grants Aristotelian *phronesis/prudentia* a universal, end-encompassing scope, is quite in line with the overall interpretations of Aristotelian *phronesis* that have been propounded in recent years by a growing number of Anglophone scholars.[31] But on this precise issue, whether *phronesis* is confined to right judgments about means or also cognitively *originates* right judgments about ends, there is no definitive Aristotelian text (assuming that 1142b31–33 is irremediably ambiguous) which, by itself, can be said to resolve the question.[32] Contemporary scholars, the ones who are troubled by Aristotle's restrictive characterizations of *phronesis*, take a different tack. Admitting that no one text definitively resolves the issue, they argue for the end-inclusive scope of *phronesis* by filling in and expanding on the implications of Aristotle's portrait of the practically wise man.

The *phronimos*, these scholars point out, pursues morally virtuous

---

Rackham, Greenwood, et al.) only to the means, see Gauthier-Jolif, II, 2: 518–19. For even more strenuous arguments contra Gauthier-Jolif, see Pierre Aubenque, "La Prudence Aristotélicienne porte-t-elle sur la fin ou sur les moyens?" *Revue des études grecques* 78 (1965): 40–51.

30. See *SLE*, VI, 8, 1142b28, 184–89 *(In Ethic.*, VI, lect. 8 [Spiazzi, n. 1233, p. 335]): "Quia, cum prudentia sit bene consiliari, oportet quod eubulia simpliciter sit rectitudo consilii in ordine ad illum finem circa quem veram aestimationem habet prudentia simpliciter dicta, et hic est finis communis totius humanae vitae. . . ."

31. Among others, see D. J. Allan, *The Philosophy of Aristotle*, rev. ed. (Oxford University Press: London, 1963), 180–81; John Cooper, *Reason and Human Good in Aristotle* (Cambridge, Mass.: Harvard University Press, 1975), 64; Anthony Kenny, *Aristotle's Theory of the Will* (New Haven, Conn.: Yale University Press, 1979), 107; Troels Engberg-Pedersen, *Aristotle's Theory of Moral Insight* (Oxford: Clarendon Press, 1983), 196; Norman O. Dahl, *Practical Reason, Aristotle, and Weakness of the Will* (Minneapolis: University of Minnesota Press, 1984), 39–40; and Nancy Sherman, *The Fabric of Character: Aristotle's Theory of Virtue* (Oxford: Clarendon Press, 1989), 88.

32. See Joseph Owens, "The Grounds of Ethical Universality in Aristotle," in *Aristotle: The Collected Papers of Joseph Owens*, ed. John R. Catan (Albany: State University of New York Press, 1981), 163, who by way of conclusion about the general thrust of the argument of the *Nicomachean Ethics* affirms that "[t]here can hardly be any doubt that men can deliberate about the choice of a life of pleasure, or of public standing, or of contemplation. . . . Both ends in particular (whether ultimate or non-ultimate) and means are the objects of choice." For Rhonheimer *(Praktische Vernunft*, 417–18, esp. n. 25.), the question of how we *know* how to distinguish right from wrong ends is not an explicit theme for Aristotle, who deals with this question only in a dialectical and general fashion when discussing the different forms of life.

ends but does so not only by force of prerational habituation; rather, the *phronimos* is practically wise because he has an unerring epistemic grasp on what is *true* in the practical sphere.[33] Such knowledge, they go on to argue, would be truncated if it did not sometimes include correct deliberation about and right choice of ends,[34] and these deliberations and choices cannot be ultimately determined by the moral agent's antecedent desires and habits. The practically wise man, according to Aristotle's portrait, is not wise merely because he happens to desire the true ends of action for himself. Aristotle observes that Pericles is commonly thought to be a *phronimos* because he intellectually "sees" (θεωϱεῖν) what is good for himself and for mankind.[35] This knowledge, whether or not popular opinion is correct to attribute it to Pericles, can only arise from the ability of the *phronimos* to make right judgments about which ends are universally worthy of pursuit, and such judgments require deliberating about alternative ends.

Still, the ground of these right judgments about the ends of human life remains obscure in the Aristotelian texts that describe the range of *phronesis*. In explaining the correct moral orientation of the *phronimos*, Aristotle often adverts to, indeed emphasizes, the necessity of right desires and good habits. Inordinate love of pleasure, we are informed, makes the majority of men and women fools about what is genuinely good and bad.[36] The possession of right desires and good habits that marks the virtues, as the possession of bad desires and habits marks the vices, is the beginning of Aristotelian practical wisdom.[37] The good man, in response to his circumstances, feels the right pleasures and pains.[38]

Aristotle unwaveringly asserts that the intellectual virtue of *phronesis* presupposes and rests upon the moral virtues; the latter set the good ends to which the former figures out the right means.[39] But with this apparent subordination of *phronesis* to moral virtue, there emerge

33. See *EN*, VI, 6, 1141a3–5 (rev. Oxford trans.): "If, then, the states by which we have truth and are never deceived about things that cannot—or can—be otherwise are knowledge [ἐπιστήμη], practical wisdom [φϱόνησις], philosophic wisdom [σοφία], and comprehension [νοῦς]. . . ."

34. See Sherman, *Fabric of Character*, 89: "That first principles *(archai)* in ethics come to those who have adequate experience (1142a15–19) suggests that part of that experience consists precisely in making deliberative choices . . . [that] qualify and refine ends. . . ."

35. See *EN*, VI, 5, 1140b6–8.

36. See *EN*, III, 4, 1113a33–b2.

37. See *EN*, III, 5, 1114b30–1115a2.

38. See *EN*, VI, 1, 1121a3–4.

39. See *EN*, VI, 12, 1144a6–9.

the Aristotelian doctrinal ambiguities, which contemporary academic studies belabor, about the priority of prerational desires and habits (including those that can be inculcated by laws) over the moral agent's own rational deliberations and choices.[40] Aristotle's position is that the first principles of moral action, the ends that the agent pursues, are set by the *habituated emotions* of the agent, and that these ends, like the hypotheses or foundational premises of mathematical demonstrations, are not themselves rationally derived or demonstrated. Morally good ends or true first principles, however, are inculcated and protected by virtue and destroyed by vice.[41]

Aquinas reiterates the point very clearly: not reason but our habits determine which ends we pursue.

Just as in mathematics principles are not taught through reasoning, neither is the end in matters of action taught through reasoning. But man through the habit of virtue, either natural or acquired through custom, attains the right estimation about the principle of things to be done, which is the end. *(SLE, VII, 8, 1151a11, 126–32; In Ethic., VII, lect. 8 [Spiazzi, n. 1431, p. 383])*[42]

For the moment, let us leave aside the distinction between the types of habits to which both Aristotle and Aquinas advert: habits can be *acquired* or *natural*. Although this distinction, in an expanded form, plays a crucial role in determining the Thomistic boundaries of *prudentia*, it is not this distinction but Aristotle's fundamental conception of *phronesis* that first provokes scholarly puzzlement.

In what sense can Aristotle's *phronimos* rationally deliberate about which ends to pursue if his reasoning works only on the assumption that he is, in fact, already pursuing right ends? One interpreter objects that if this is Aristotle's doctrine, it leads to a "desperate situation" where "virtue is needed in order to find out what virtue is."[43] But even

40. See *EN*, X, 9, 1180a13–18.

41. See *EN*, VII, 8 1151a15–19 (rev. Oxford trans.): "For excellence and vice respectively preserve and destroy the first principle, and in actions that for the sake of which is the first principle, as the hypotheses are in mathematics; neither in that case is it reason that teaches the first principles, nor is it so here—excellence either natural or produced by habituation [ἀρετὴ ἢ φυσικὴ ἢ ἐθιστή] is what teaches right opinion about the first principle."

42. "Sicut enim in mathematicis principia non docentur per rationem, sed statim intellecta creduntur, ita etiam in agibilibus fines non docentur per rationem, sed per habitum virtutis sive naturalis sive per assuetudinem acquisitae consequitur rectam aestimationem circa principium agibilium quod est finis" *(SLE, VII, 8, 1151a11, 126–32; In Ethic., VII, lect. 8 [Spiazzi, n. 1431, p. 383])*.

43. C. J. de Vogel, "On the Character of Aristotle Ethics," in *Schriften zur*

if the situation is not so desperate, Aristotle does couple desire and reason too tightly for one prominent, cognitivist strain of contemporary moral theorizing. The principles of Aristotelian practical wisdom spell out what is "good or bad for man,"[44] but the contemporary cognitivist ethician cannot know about, much less justify, what is "good or bad for men" solely by appealing to the desires, habits, and pursuits of the conventionally virtuous man. Some account must also be provided to show "how an [Aristotelian] agent reasons about the ends of good living"[45] independently of what he or she is already doing.

Perhaps, though, the cognitivist ethician's puzzlement about the rational grounds of morality can be dismissed as only his or her present-day problem and not Aristotle's.[46] To take a parallel issue, it is clearly erroneous to assume that Aristotle's account of morality must incorporate (say, in good Stoic or, more likely, Kantian fashion) impersonal and unconditionally universal principles binding practical reason as such.[47] Aristotle himself is content to reach moral principles that are (epistemically) relative to the agent's own moral virtues[48] and which, even for the morally virtuous agent who is capable of grasping them, are principles that only hold "for the most part." In short, Aristotle's positive moral principles are general rather than strictly universal or exceptionless. Still, it would be no less a mistake to dismiss the cognitivist ethician's anxiety too quickly. Aristotle himself recognizes that the ends of the morally good agent must be reasonable[49] and, moreover,

---

aristotelischen Ethik, ed. Christian Mueller-Goldingen (Hildesheim: Georg Olms Verlag, 1988), 277. De Vogel contends that nature and not the *phronimos* sets moral norms, but this, I shall argue, is Aquinas's, not Aristotle's, position.

44. *EN,* VI, 5, 1140b5.

45. Sherman, *Fabric of Character,* 57.

46. Cf. Rhonheimer, *Praktische Vernunft,* 413: "Die Frage einer im modernen Sinnenormativen Ethik ist hingegen diejenige nach den *kognitiven Prinzipien* des richtigen Handelns. Genau diese Frage gehört nun *nicht* zum "Thema" der aristotelischen Ethik. Ihr Thema sind vielmehr die *affektiven Prinzipien* des richtigen Handelns. . . ."

47. Joseph Owens, C.Ss.R., "Christian Conscience vs. Aristotelian Right Reason," in *Towards a Christian Philosophy,* 150, observes that it is impossible to determine whether the Aristotelian appeal to "right reason" (ὀρθὸς λόγος) as the norm for human conduct is an appeal to a standard accepted only by Aristotle's circle or to a standard accepted more widely. In either case, the appeal involves reference to a consensus and to what finally, then, would be a conventional standard.

48. See *EN,* III, 4, 1113a15-33.

49. See *EN,* VI, 5, 1140b16-21 (rev. Oxford trans.): "For the principles of the things that are done consist in that for the sake of which they are to be done. . . . Practical wisdom, then, must be a reasoned and true state of capacity to act with regard to human goods."

"reasonable" in a strong sense of the term: moral virtue is not merely "in accordance with right reason" (κατὰ τὸν ὀρθὸν λόγον) but in "the presence of right reason" (μετὰ τοῦ ὀρθοῦ λόγου).[50]

Phronesis, it should not be forgotten, is an intellectual virtue. If so, the contemporary interpreter remains well within the Aristotelian ambit in demanding that the moral goodness of the agent's ends be rationally grounded. But if (in line with Aristotle's analogy about mathematical hypotheses) a rational demonstration of these ends is neither possible nor required, should we then infer that practical intellectual intuition supplies self-evidently true principles (= self-evidently good ends) for the Aristotelian *phronimos?* This inference, a few interpreters maintain, follows from what Aristotle says about the structure of reasoning about ends:[51] in practical reasoning, deliberate or intermediate ends can only be justified by reference to some ultimate ends whose truth and goodness are in need of no further deliberation or justification. But why are such ends in need of no further rational justification? No text in the *Nicomachean Ethics* unequivocally states that our intellectual grasp of such ultimate ends originates rather than merely parallels or follows our desire for them.[52] There remain, then, numerous questions about how, according to Aristotle, the *phronimos* knows what are the right ends to pursue.

Aristotle admits that it is difficult to provide exact explanations or accounts (λόγοι) of justice and goodness and happiness.[53] This admission, of course, is relevant to our own query. Does the *Nicomachean Ethics* provide a precise enough and deep enough account of the cognitive side of morality? Did Aristotle have the conceptual resources to do so?[54] Despite all the praise that he pours on the intellectual virtue of

50. *EN*, VI, 13, 1144b26–27 (rev. Oxford trans.).
51. See *EN*, I, 7, 1097a15–b6. Cf. Cooper, *Reason and Human Good*, 60–64.
52. Cf. *EN*, VI, 2, 1139a22–26.
53. See *EN*, I, 3, 1094b14–17; 1095a18–23.
54. See Paul Schuchman, *Aristotle and the Problem of Moral Discernment* (Frankfort: Peter D. Lang, 1980), 133, who argues for the necessity of "the perspective of transcendental method" (as elaborated by Bernard Lonergan, S.J.) to provide the "proper concepts" that will clarify "[Aristotle's] momentous insight into practical thinking." Schuchman, however, turns Aristotle's practical science into a theoretical science with Heideggerian overtones: the *Nicomachean Ethics* is supposedly a metaphysical anthropology that seeks to explain the "ontological structure of human *praxis*" in order to answer the question about the meaning of being human "in all that we do." See 124–27. But whereas Schuchman thinks that "a highly abstract and ontological account is . . . most necessary for an adequate understanding of Aristotle's doctrine of *phronesis*," (131), Aristotle clearly holds the opposite view: "*Phronesis* and wisdom [σοφία] . . . each is the excellence [ἀρετή] of a different part of the soul . . . wisdom will contemplate [θεωρήσει] none of the things

phronesis, Aristotle does not ground, in any unambiguous fashion, the moral principles of the *phronimos* in either reason or intellectual intuition as both may be clearly distinguished from desire.[55] Accordingly, in many scholarly redactions of Aristotle's ethics, desire plays as big if not a bigger role than reason in determining what principles the *phronimos* holds.[56] But does Aristotle actually espouse, as we have been assured, "a deterministic psychology of action" in which framework "all action proceeds from desire"?[57]

Many of Aristotle's explicit statements do leave the moral agent, including the *phronimos*, habitually wishing to pursue certain ends,[58] and these wishes, since they are set by the childhood education of his desires, fears, angers, and habits,[59] appear to fall outside of the agent's own rational deliberations and choices.[60] If so, these ends, as some readers of Aristotle have observed, are not rationally grounded by the moral agent himself and are perhaps even immune to rational suasion.[61] This latter observation expresses, indeed, a contemporary bias

that will make a man happy for it is not concerned with any coming into being" *(EN*, VI, 11, 1143b14–17; b19–20 [rev. Oxford trans.]).

55. See *EN*, VI, 2, 1139a31–33 (Rackham trans.): "Now the cause [ἀρχή] of action [πρᾶξεως] . . . is choice [προαίρεσις] and the cause of choice is desire [ὄρεξις] and reasoning [λόγος] directed to some end."

56. One recent example: David Charles, *Aristotle's Philosophy of Action* (Ithaca, N.Y.: Cornell University Press, 1984), 184–85, attempts to distinguish "Moderate Desire" from "Extreme Desire" explanations of how the *phronimos* sets his goals. The "Extreme-Desire" explanation is extreme because it denies that reason in any way sets ends. By comparison, a "Moderate Desire" explanation is moderate because it allows that practical reason can at least sort out which of an agent's conflicting ends is better in view of his or her conception of an overall best life. But Charles has propounded a distinction without a significant difference if the conception of an overall best life is indeed "constrained (and in a large measure determined) by the set of general desires [the *phronimos*] already has" (184). Although Charles appeals to *EN*, X, 4, 1175a12–15 to support his "Moderate Desire" theory, Aristotle forcefully rejects (1175a18) the notion that life is for the sake of pleasure. Life is for the sake of activity and pleasure is *concomitant* with activity: see Gauthier-Jolif, II, 2: 843. Cf. *SLE*, X, 6, 1175a18, 198–205 *(In Ethic.,* X, lect. 6 [Spiazzi, n. 2037, p. 527]): ". . . videtur tamen principalius esse operatio quam delectatio . . . ipsa operatio, quae delectat sicut quiddam conveniens, videtur per prius appetibilis quam delectatio."

57. D. J. Allan, "The Practical Syllogism," in *Autour d'Aristote* (Louvain: Publications Universitaires de Louvain, 1955), 333.

58. Ends can be defined as what we wish for: see *EN*, III, 2, 1111b26–27.

59. See *EN*, II, 1, 1103b2–5.

60. See *EN*, III, 5, 1114b30–1115a3.

61. See Bernard Williams, *Ethics and the Limits of Philosophy* (Cambridge, Mass.: Harvard University Press, 1985), 38: "[Aristotle] gives an account of moral development in terms of habituation and internalization that leaves little room for

in favor of rational self-determination. Aristotle, for his part, admits that philosophical discussions of virtue do not change a man's character, because he holds that prerational habits and intelligent choices are mutually determining. Does Aristotle's account of their mutual determination leave practical reason subordinated to prerational habituation? Aristotle, while he may not answer this question to the full satisfaction of contemporary philosophers, nonetheless affirms (*EN*, II, 4, 1105a33) that the morally good man (σπουδαῖος) must act firmly (βεβαίως) and immovably (ἀμετακινήτως), but also that he cannot act merely from unreflective habits. A morally good man is a *phronimos* because he acts from habits that embody knowledge and deliberation.

Yet Aristotelian morality seems bereft of a secure foundation in reason if we are content to accept what Aristotle baldly contends, that "we do not deliberate about ends, but about means" and that choice (προαίρεσις) only "deals with means to ends."[62] These and similar texts, which restrict the scope of *phronesis*, are the crux of contemporary scholars searching for a firm cognitive ground of Aristotelian morality.[63] If they are interpreted narrowly, Aristotle's *explicit* dicta would rob the moral agent of any cognitive assessment and rational choice about the rightness of his goals. Aristotle assumes that the virtuous man, through the good fortune of his upbringing and temperament, is, as a matter of fact, pursuing the right goals. But, then, is the Aristotelian *phronimos* making moral evaluations and pursuing goals that rest solely on conventional attitudes and sentiments?

Presumably, the *phronimos*, because he is wise, must know something beyond what convention dictates. But from the contemporary philosophical point of view, which dramatizes the need to justify (perhaps because it is feared that all of them are nonrational) competing societal conventions, the Aristotelian *phronimos* could not be said to know the rightness of the goals that he actually pursues unless those goals and their alternatives can be rationally adjudicated. In short, no matter how high the conventional moral standard is set in classical culture,[64] if it lacks an independent rational justification, the standard

---

practical reason to alter radically the objectives that a grown-up person has acquired."

62. *EN*, III, 3, 1112b33–34; 1113a12–14 (Rackham trans.).

63. See Sarah Waterlow Broadie, "The Problems of Practical Intellect in Aristotle's *Ethics*," in *Proceedings of the Boston Area Colloquium in Ancient Philosophy*, ed. John J. Cleary (Lanham, Md.: University Press of America, 1988), 3: 229–52; Henry S. Richardson, "Commentary on Broadie," ibid., 3: 253–61.

64. See Leo Strauss, "On Aristotle's Politics," in *The City and Man* (Chicago: Rand McNally & Company, 1964), 25: "The morally good man is the properly bred

will be, for many contemporary philosophical readers of Aristotle, deficient and arbitrary. But the predilections of contemporary ethical cognitivism can lead to exaggerations that surely do distort Aristotle's own position. For example, one interpreter is eager to show that Aristotelian *phronesis* permits the moral agent to subject his or her ends to a "continual re-evaluation."[65]

It would be fruitless, however, to continue contrasting Aristotle and contemporary views of morality if one presupposes either that Aristotle must and can be brought in line with contemporary views or that no light at all can be shed on Aristotle from "modern conceptions of action and its elements."[66] Neither of these presuppositions illumines or resolves the tensions that are to be found in Aristotle's texts. Yet, if we do find that the Aristotelian texts on the range of *phronesis* are not symphonic,[67] then any effort to harmonize them involves reconstructing the doctrine of *phronesis* in the *Nicomachean Ethics*. But, before attempting such a reconstruction, we should first interrogate Aristotle's texts. How far do the Aristotelian moral agent's deliberations and choices extend? And if the *phronimos* does somehow grasp the true ends of human action, does he do so through right emotional habituation, indemonstrable moral intuition, or reasoned arguments? Or to recast the question in the normative Platonic terms, does the *phronimos* have knowledge of (ἐπιστήμη) and not merely right opinion (ὀρθὴ δόξα) about first principles?

In the rest of this chapter, I shall review, without any pretense of putting to rest, this complex topic which, beginning with the debate between Adolf Trendelenburg and Julius Walter,[68] has preoccupied Aristotelian scholars since the latter half of the nineteenth century.[69]

---

man, the well-bred man. Aristotle's political science is addressed only to such men. The sphere of prudence is then closed by principles which are fully evident only to gentlemen."

65. See Sarah Broadie, *Ethics with Aristotle* (Oxford: Oxford University Press, 1991), 245.

66. Emmanuel M. Michelakis, *Aristotle's Theory of Practical Principles* (Athens: Cleisiounis Press, 1961), 50.

67. See Pierre Aubenque, *La Prudence chez Aristote* (Paris: Presses Universitaires de France, 1963), 116–17: ". . . dans la description de l'*eubolia*, il range pêle-mêle le caractère moral de la fin et le discernement du moyen le plus convenable. . . ."

68. See Adolf Trendelenburg, *Historische Beiträge zur Philosophie*, 3 vols. (Berlin: G. Bethge, 1856–1867); and Julius Walter, *Die Lehre von der praktischen Vernunft* (Jena: Mauke, 1874). Trendelenburg stresses that practical reason (i.e., *nous*) immediately determines "den richtigen Zweck" (2: 379); in response, Walter argues that the "Willen oder Charakter des Handelnden" (271) determines which ends are pursued.

69. For the history of the discussion, see Gauthier-Jolif, II, 2: 563–78; Schuch-

The exercise, though it has often been and likely will continue to be repeated because of the importance of the topic for any moral theory, is useful here because it provides a good backdrop against which to expose Aquinas's treatment of the philosophical issues latent in Aristotle's texts. To formulate the larger issue in the somewhat darker tones of contemporary metaethics, Aquinas was aware of what we identify as the tension between Aristotle's cognitivist and emotivist views about the grounding of moral principles.

If there is truth and falsehood in morals as in other domains, it is because we can make cognitive assertions about what is morally good and bad. Aquinas remarks that practical wisdom *(prudentia)*, although about contingent things, is one of "the intellectual virtues about which we truly say that falsehood never underlies them."[70] In order to strengthen the cognitive dimension of *prudentia*, Aquinas undergirds Aristotelian practical wisdom with a set of fixed, universal, cognitive but practical principles. These principles provide the framework of Aquinas's theological ethics: the first principles of practical reason, which are the object of a natural disposition or habit of the human intellect called "*synderesis*," participate the eternal law in the mind of God.

The doctrine of *synderesis*, as historians of medieval theology have long known, distinguishes Aquinas's and Aristotle's respective conceptions of practical reason.[71] Nonetheless, Aquinas directs the doctrine of *synderesis* toward the resolution of a doctrinal tension that he finds in Aristotle's account of the origin of moral principles. The same tension between the cognitivist and emotivist strands in Aristotle's doctrine of *phronesis* leads contemporary interpreters to expand Aristotle's portrait of the *phronimos*. In aligning Aquinas and contemporary interpreters of Aristotle, my intention is not to defend the acuity or relevance of Aquinas's Aristotelian exegesis,[72] though en passant I shall

---

man, *Problem of Moral Discernment*, 99–112; and Beatriz Bossi De Kirchner, "On the Power of Practical Reason," *Review of Metaphysics*, 43 (1989), 47, n. 1.

70. ". . . virtutes intellectuales quibus ita verum dicimus quod eis numquam subest mendacium . . ." *(SLE*, VI, 5, 1140b31, 40–42; *In Ethic.*, VI, lect. 5 [Spiazzi, n. 1178, p. 322]).

71. D. Odon Lottin, "Syndérèse et conscience aux xiie et xiii siècles," in *Psychologie et morale aux xiie et xiiie siècles*, Vol. 2: *Problèmes de morale*, Pt. 1 (Louvain: Abbaye du Mont César, 1948), 106, finds that the term *"synderesis"* first appears in the commentary on Peter Lombard's *Sententia*, written (ca. 1160–65) by a certain Magister Udo. Peter Lombard uses *(Libri IV Sententiarum*, lib. 2, d. 39; Quaracchi edition, 517) Jerome's term *"scintilla conscientiae"* (which had been taken up by the school of Anselm of Laon) to refer to the innate principle of reason that not even Cain's sin could eradicate: "Do good; hate evil."

72. For a moderately negative view of Aquinas's redaction of the Aristotelian

make a case for both,[73] but to expose some of the theological interests and commitments that Aquinas incorporates into his commentary on the *Nicomachean Ethics*.

Aquinas's exegesis, although it does not develop the imaginative and sometimes textually overblown portraits of the *phronimos* favored by contemporary scholars, does reflect the commonly understood need to escape the explicit boundaries in which Aristotle confines *phronesis*. Aquinas rescues Aristotelian *phronesis* from any ambiguous conjunction and perhaps subordination to desire and acquired habituation[74] by anchoring prudential reasoning in a set of universal, immediate, primary principles that structure and direct practical reason, principles that, in turn, are said to participate in the divine mind itself. Certainly nothing directly or explicitly corresponds to this Thomistic doctrine in the *Nicomachean Ethics*.[75] But it remains to be seen whether Aquinas's conception of *synderesis* blatantly contradicts basic Aristotelian tenets about the inexactitude and restricted truth of moral principles.[76]

---

doctrine of *phronesis*, see T. H. Irwin, "The Scope of Deliberation: A Conflict in Aquinas," *Review of Metaphysics* 44 (1990): 21–42, who argues that Aquinas fails "to articulate a part of the Aristotelian position" (22) about practical wisdom—namely, that Aristotle does allow the *phronimos* to deliberate about ends. But since Aquinas assimilates Aristotelian *phronesis* to his own theological notion of *synderesis*, there is a strong reason for him not to expand the scope of deliberation. *Synderesis* gives the *phronimos* a set of natural or fixed ends whose goodness is assured without deliberation.

73. For an extended contemporary discussion of Aristotelian *eudaimonia* that, in its main contentions about the preeminence and moral rectitude of the contemplative life, is remarkably in harmony with Aquinas's view of Aristotle, see Richard Kraut, *Aristotle on the Human Good* (Princeton, N.J.: Princeton University Press, 1989).

74. See *EN*, X, 8, 1178a17–20: ". . . the first principles of *phronesis* are in accordance [κατά] with the moral virtues and the standard [τὸ δ' ὀρθόν] of the moral virtues is in accordance [κατά] with *phronesis*. The moral virtues, which are connected with the passions, must be related to our composite nature."

75. Cf. Rhonheimer, *Praktische Vernunft*, 473: "Gibt est aber auch eine unmittelbare, jedem zugängliche *praktische Erkenntnis* der Prinzipien? Dast is bei Aristoteles weniger klar, es gehört ja auch nicht zum eigentlichen Thema seiner Ethik."

For reasons that I will spell out in Chapter 5, I do not share the view of Kenny (*Aristotle's Theory of the Will*, 151–52) that there is a strict parallelism, from what we can discern in the Aristotelian texts about *nous*, between the insight into the universal and indemonstrable theoretical principles and insight into the (defeasible) general principles of practical reasoning. This parallelism, however, is exactly what Aquinas asserts.

76. Cf. Leo Strauss, *Natural Right and History* (Chicago: University of Chicago Press, 1950), 163–64.

2. *Aristotle: Practical Reasoning*

As Aristotle describes it, practical reasoning, whether of the morally good or bad agent, typically involves wishing for some end (βούλησις) and consequently deliberating about (βούλευσις) and choosing (προαίρεσις) what to do in order to achieve that end.[77] Deliberative reasoning, which figures out how to attain an end, presupposes some end to deliberate about.[78] These ends can either be something made or something done, that is, either a product or an action.[79] In both cases, Aristotle identifies the *end* that the agent seeks to produce or accomplish as the starting point or principle (ἀρχή) of practical reason (πρακτικὴ διάνοια).[80] Aquinas's summary comment emphasizes the end-directed character of practical reason and the analogy that, given this teleological character, can be drawn between theoretical syllogisms and the quasi-syllogistic forms of practical reasoning:

It is manifest that principles of practicable matters are the ends for which the practicable matters are done. The ends in relation to practicable matters are like principles in demonstrations. . . . *(SLE, IV, 4, 1140b11, 127–30; In Ethic., VI, lect. 4 [Spiazzi, n. 1170, p. 320]])*[81]

The moral status of these practical ends—how the Aristotelian *phronimos* cognitively grasps their moral goodness (i.e., how he knows that it is rationally justified to desire them[82])—needs to be examined. For

77. See *EN*, III, 5, 1113b3–4; VI, 1, 1139a13–14, 22–27; 9, 1142b16–20. Although it is true that Aristotle does not in *EN*, III explicitly distinguish theoretical and practical reason, Allan inexplicably asserts that "deliberation is not a distinctive operation of the *practical* reason" ("Practical Syllogism," 328). Cf. *EN*, III, 3, 1112a30–31 (Rackham trans.): "We deliberate about things that are in our control and are attainable by action. . . ."

78. See *EN*, VI, 2, 1139a35–36; 1139b2–5; 5, 1140b15–16; 9, 1142b28–31.

79. Practical reason encompasses both making and doing. But making is not an end in itself; the product made is. Good actions, or more generally, acting well, is an end in itself: see *EN*, VI, 2, 1139a35–1139b5. Aquinas comments that the artisan works only for some definite end (making a knife or a house) but adds significantly that practical reason in regard to action extends to the "universal end": see *SLE*, VI, 2, 1139a35, 186–92 *(In Ethic., VI, lect. 2 [Spiazzi, n. 1136, p. 311]).*

80. See *EN*, VI, 2, 1139a31–36.

81. "Manifestum est enim quod principia operabilium sunt fines cuius gratia fiunt operabilia, qui ita se habent in operabilibus sicut principia in demonstrabilibus . . ." *(SLE, IV, 4, 1140b11, 127–30; In Ethic., VI, lect. 4 [Spiazzi, n. 1170, p. 320]).*

82. See *EN*, II, 1, 1103b31–32, which refers to right actions in a global sense, i.e., without distinguishing between ends and means. *EN*, VI, 2, 1139a30–31 views (more typically) the "truth" of practical reasoning in relation to the means: assuming that the agent's end is right, and therefore that the agent's desire (for the end) is right,

the most part, practical reasoning (whether of the technical or the moral kind) is not and often cannot be put into proper syllogistic form.[83] But on the assumption that the morally good man's pursuits are indeed good, Aristotle regards such good ends as having a function in valid moral reasoning like the principles in theoretical demonstrations. Ends that are desired (because they are thought to be *good* and *possible*) can be formalized by being incorporated into the universal premise of (what commentators usually call) "the practical syllogism."[84]

The end of practical reasoning differentiates theoretical and practical reasoning. Theoretical and practical syllogisms do not lead to the same type of conclusion: a theoretical syllogism affirms as its conclusion the *proposition* that follows from its two premises; the conclusion of a quasi-syllogistic instance of practical reasoning, as Aristotle identifies it, is the *performance* of a particular action.[85] This claim, that the practical conclusion is not a proposition, is somewhat paradoxical since it, of course, weakens the allegedly syllogistic character of practical reason.[86] But since Aristotle explicitly allows for both immediate and future action to follow as the conclusion of practical reasoning,[87] the practical syllogism may also be interpreted as affirming a propositional conclusion but a proposition that either prompts (immediately or in the future) an action.[88] While this intimate connec-

---

"practical truth" then signifies truth about the means in "conformity with right desire" about the end. Cf. *SLE*, VI, 2, 1139a27, 104–6 *(In Ethic*, VI, lect. 2 [Spiazzi, n. 1130, p. 310]): "Sed bonum practici intellectus non est veritas absoluta, sed veritas confesse se habens, id est concorditer, ad appetitum rectum. . . ."

83. For a detailed study of the logical problems attendant on any attempt to reduce practical reasoning to valid syllogistic forms, see Kenny, "Practical, Technical, and Ethical Syllogisms," in *Aristotle's Theory of the Will*, 111–24.

84. See *MA*, 6, 700b20–30; 701a25. The non-Aristotelian term, "the practical syllogism" has its closest counterpart in Aristotle's expression οἱ συλλογισμοὶ τῶν πρακτῶν (*EN*, VI, 12, 1144a31–32).

85. See *EN*, VII, 3, 1147a27–28; 1147b9–11; *de An.*, III, 11, 434a16–21; *MA*, 7, 701a9–11. In the last text, Aristotle notes that an action follows as the conclusion of practical reasoning if "there is nothing to compel or prevent [it]" (rev. Oxford trans.). The condition implicitly allows for a future action.

86. See Allan, "Practical Syllogism," 326, who, commenting on *de An.*, III, 11, 434a16–21, states without further clarification that "the conclusion [of the practical syllogism] is, of course, not another judgment, but the performance of the action. . . ."

87. See *Rh.*, II, 19, 1392b15–20; 1393a1–5; Sherman, *Fabric of Character*, 58–61.

88. *EN*, VII, 3, 1147a26–31 does not deny that we have a propositional conclusion in the example given of a practical syllogism (viz., "This sweet thing is to be tasted"); the text stresses only that the conclusion will be, in the case of the incontinent man, immediately acted upon.

tion of the conclusion with particular actions is a well enough established feature of Aristotelian practical reasoning,[89] interpreters dispute just about everything else in explaining the structure of "the practical syllogism."[90] But this is to be expected since Aristotle left no fully developed examples of such practical syllogisms. And when the commentators try to construct them, they discover that unpacking Aristotle's allusive examples generates, more often than not, many premises that cannot be easily poured into the mold of a single valid syllogism.

Nonetheless, Aristotle states that, typically, practical reasoning,[91] or what can be construed as the paradigm of a morally practical syllogism, begins with a universal premise specifying an end or good that is desirable and desired: "The end (i.e., what is best) is of such and such a nature"[92] or "Such and such a kind of man should do such and such a kind of act."[93] And he labels both the universal (or, in the commentators" terminology, the "major") premise as well as the particular (or the so-called "minor") premise an opinion (δόξα).[94] In regard to moral opinions, the universal premise states a judgment that prescribes (by using terms expressing necessity or obligation) some general end that is to be pursued,[95] an end that the agent has come to know inductively from the "moral facts" that he recognizes.[96] The particular premise embodies an opinion about a sensible particular or singular: that *this action x*, which the agent here and now is poised to do, is a token of the *Action X* (mentioned in the universal premise) that is a good to be pursued.[97]

Although Aristotle seems to regard the universal premise as relatively unproblematic, I shall come soon enough to the many questions that can be raised about the "moral inductions" that lead to knowledge

---

89. See *EN*, VI, 8, 1142a25: τὸ γὰρ πρακτὸν τοιοῦτον.

90. For a discussion of the lacunae in Aristotle's account of practical reasoning, and how the various commentators have filled in those lacunae, see W. F. R. Hardie, "Note on the Practical Syllogism," in *Aristotle's Ethical Theory* (Oxford: Clarendon Press, 1968), 240–57.

91. Aristotle's examples of the practical syllogism are not usually examples of moral reasoning. For examples of nonmoral, practical reasoning, see the suggested major premises for practical syllogisms in *EN*, VI, 7, 1141b18 (rev. Oxford trans.): "Light meats are digestible and wholesome"; VI, 8, 1142a23 (rev. Oxford trans.): "All water that weighs heavy is bad."

92. *EN*, VI, 12, 1144a32–33 (rev. Oxford trans.).

93. *De An.*, III, 11, 434a17 (rev. Oxford trans.).

94. See *EN*, VII, 3, 1147a25.

95. See *EN*, VI, 10, 1143a7–9.

96. See *EN*, I, 4, 1095b6: ἀρχὴ γὰρ τὸ ὅτι.

97. See *de An.*, III, 11, 434a18; *EN*, VII, 3, 1147a5–7; 1147b9–10.

of the general end that is prescribed in the universal premise. For the moment, though, let us look at the particular or minor premise of the practical syllogism. Aristotle notes that moral reasoning must incorporate in its minor premise a proposition about a singular action so that it can prompt, in its conclusion, a singular action.[98] Actions are individuated by their performance. But Aristotle seems to elide the singularity of the action referred to in the minor premise and the conclusion with the radical individuality of an action already performed.

As an example, we can construct the following practical syllogism from Aristotle's account of temperance (σωφροσύνη) and intemperance (ἀκρασία). The temperate man (ὁ ἐγκρατής), who neither embraces nor eschews pleasure *tout court*,[99] would reason: (1) No shameful pleasure should be pursued by a temperate man; (2) Tasting this sweet but shamefully pleasant thing is not to be pursued by me who am a temperate man; (3) Therefore, I ought not to eat this sweet but shamefully pleasant thing.[100] Here, obviously, the temperate man's conclusion is not an action but the abstention from an action. But in the case of the acratic or intemperate man (ὁ ἀκρατής), while the universal premise forbidding shameful pleasures is ever present and operative during his reasoning process, passion drags the particular or "last premise" (ἡ τελευταία πρότασις), the one derived from sensation, "like a slave" (*EN*, VII, 1, 1145b24; 3, 1147b16–17). It is the particular or last premise that rules over action.[101]

Nonetheless, given Aristotle's distinction (*EN*, VII, 6, 1150b19–23) between the impetuous acratic agent and the weak acratic agent,[102] ἡ τελευταία πρότασις would be more usefully translated as "the last proposition" so that it may refer either to the particular (i.e., minor) premise or to the particular proposition that concludes the acratic man's practical syllogism.[103] The acratic man who is impetuous either

98. See *EN*, VII, 3, 1147a3–4: πρακτὰ γὰρ τὰ καθ' ἕκαστα. In moral reasoning, however, the particular premise of the practical syllogism is not a particular theoretical proposition but a particular prescription or prohibition of an action–token that falls under the prescription or prohibition of the action-type referred to in the universal premise: see *de An.*, III, 11, 434a18.

99. See *EN*, VII, 9, 1151b21–22.

100. See *EN*, VII, 3, 1147a25–1147b3. I have simplified matters by combining two particular propositions in the minor premise.

101. See *EN*, VII, 3, 1147b9–10: ἡ τελευταία πρότασις αἰσθητοῦ καὶ κυρία τῶν πράξεων.

102. The distinction (*EN*, VII, 7, 1150b19) is between impetuousness (προπέτεια) and weakness (ἀσθένεια) as distinct types of ἀκρασία.

103. See Kenny, *Aristotle's Theory of the Will*, 164. Cf. Joseph Owens, "The Acratic's 'Ultimate Premise' in Aristotle," in *Aristotle's Werk und Wirkung*, ed.

altogether lacks the particular premise, or, if he has it, lacks genuine knowledge of it since he knows the particular premise only in the way a drunken or sleeping man knows something.[104] The acratic man whom passion renders truly "weak" both has and knows the minor premise but he lacks the ability to stand by or to enact the particular conclusion that he has drawn from the universal and particular premises.[105] The "weakwilled" acratic man (as we might describe him) eats the shameful but pleasantly sweet thing even though he knows quite well that he ought not to eat things of this type or, more to the point, this particular thing.

Although interpreters disagree about the exact particularity of the action referred to in the minor premise,[106] Aquinas takes the referent to be a singular (i.e., individuated) action:

> Prudential reasoning ends, as though at a particular conclusion, in a particular action, to which it applies a universal cognition. . . . The singu-

Jürgen Wiesner (Berlin and New York: Walter de Gruyter, 1985), 376–92, who, identifying ἡ τελευταία πρότασις (1147b9) with the minor premise, argues that the acratic man is always aware (in some psychological sense) of the particular premise but that this psychological awareness does not count as a case of "genuine moral knowledge" (387, n. 11) because the acratic man de facto does not effectively subsume the particular premise under his habitually held universal premise. Owens is perhaps led to equate the particular proposition with only the minor premise, and subsequently to distinguish the constant psychological awareness from the intermittent moral knowledge of the particular premise, an unusual distinction that does not easily fit what Aristotle describes as the "weak-willed" man's failure to instantiate his *conclusion*, because Owens so strictly identifies the conclusion of the practical syllogism with the actual performance of the action: see 387, n. 13.

104. See *EN*, VII, 3, 1147b9–12.

105. See *EN*, VII, 7, 1150b19–22.

106. For an extended argument that the minor premise of a practical syllogism refers to a specific *type* of thing (one that is more specific than the generic thing referred to in the major premise) rather than to a spatial-temporal particular, see Cooper, *Reason and Human Good*, 27–46. Aquinas, however, thinks that the minor premise of the Aristotelian practical syllogism does refer to a spatial-temporal particular: i.e., it refers to a token not a type, what Aristotle calls *(Apo.,* I, 31, 87b30) τόδε τι καὶ ποῦ καὶ νῦν. Cooper, then, is in disagreement with Aquinas as to what, for Aristotle, is the object of perception. Cooper claims that "Aristotle holds, correctly, that the object of perception is never a concrete particular . . ." (43, n. 53). For arguments contra Cooper, see Fred D. Miller, "Aristotle on Rationality in Action," *Review of Metaphysics* 38 (1984): 499–520; and Daniel T. Devereux, "Particular and Universal in Aristotle's Conception of Practical Knowledge," *Review of Metaphysics* 39 (1986): 483–504.

For Aquinas, sensing quasi-universal qualities necessarily entails sensing a spatially and temporally particular substance: ". . . non enim obiectum per se sensus est substancia et quod quid est, set aliqua sensibilis qualitas . . . huiusmodi autem qualitates afficiunt singulares quasdam substancias in determinato loco et tempore

lar conclusion [,therefore,] is syllogistically derived from a universal and a singular proposition. *(ST,* II–II, q. 49, a. 2, ad 1)[107]

Aquinas's interpretation of the "singular proposition" embodied in the minor premise squares with Aristotle's reiterated assertion that practical wisdom *(phronesis)* preeminently applies to "singular things" (τὰ καθ' ἕκαστα).[108] From the standpoint of practical wisdom, knowledge of the singular thing, since it is closer to action, is more important even than knowledge of the universal.[109] In regard to practical reasoning, it is the premise that is κατὰ μέρος or περὶ τῶν καθ' ἕκαστα [110] (i.e., the particular premise) which, in conjunction with desire, activates the agent. Still, Aristotle provides only an outline of the structure of moral reasoning,[111] and this outline does not fully explain how the Aristotelian agent comes to formulate a true particular premise in reasoning about an action that is to be done or not done.

In the first place, the particular premise cannot be proven to be true

---

existentes; unde necesse est quod id quod sentitur sit *hoc aliquid,* scilicet singularis substancia, et sit alicubi *et nunc,* scilicet in determinato loco et tempore " *(ELP,* I, 42, 87b28, 86–88 (Leonine ed., I, pt. 2, 158b).

But Aquinas, it must be noted, also allows that sense apprehends the universal "in a certain way": "Manifestum est enim quod *singulare sentitur,* proprie et per se, sed tamen *sensu* est quodam modo etiam ipsius *universalis:* cognoscit enim Calliam non solum in quantum est Callias, sed etiam in quantum est hic homo . . . *(ELP,* II, 20, 100a16, 258–62 [Leonine ed., I, pt. 2, 246a–b]).

Cf. Jonathan Barnes, *Aristotle's Posterior Analytics* (Oxford: Clarendon Press, 1975), 185: ". . . the [Aristotelian] act of perception is necessarily tied to some individual time and place"; and Mario Mignucci, *L'argomentazione dimostrativa in Aristotele: Commento agli Analitici Secondi* (Padua: Editrice Antenore, 1975), 1: 599: ". . . la facoltà sensitiva in atto (ἡ κατ' ἐνέργειαν αἴσθησις) termina ai singolari (τὸ καθ' ἕκαστον). . . ."

107. ". . . ratio prudentiae terminatur, sicut ad conclusionem quandam, ad particulare operabile, ad quod applicat universalem cognitionem. . . . Conclusio autem singularis syllogizatur ex universali et singulari propositione" *(ST,* II–II, q. 49, a. 2, ad 1).

108. See *EN,* VI, 7, 1141b14–16.

109. See *EN,* VI, 7, 1141b20–22; *SLE,* VI, 6, 1141b14, 164–69 *(In Ethic.,* VI, lect. 6 [Spiazzi, n. 1194, p. 327]).

110. See *EN,* VII, 3, 1147a2; 1147a25–26.

111. See, e.g., *EN,* VII, 3, 1147a29–32: (1) All sweet things ought to be tasted; (2) This particular thing is something sweet; (3) I ought immediately to taste this sweet thing. Cf. *de An.,* III, 11, 434a17–19; *SLA,* III, 10, 434a16, 128–33 *(In de An.,* III, lect. 16 [Pirotta, n. 845, p. 198]): "Ratio autem practica quedam est uniuersalis et quedam particularis (uniuersalis quidem sicut que dicit quod oportet talem tale agere, sicut quod oportet filium honorare parentem; ratio autem particularis, quod hoc quidem talem et ego talis, puta quod ego filius hunc honorem nunc debeo exhibere parenti). . . ."

by a prior demonstration.[112] We cannot, for example, deduce from any universal premise (in the previous example, "One ought not to pursue shameful pleasures") and its antecedents or corollaries that the proposition stating that "*This* particular action (eating *this* particular sweet thing) is a prohibited act of pursuing something pleasant but shameful" is a true proposition. Particular actions insofar as they are particular are accidental, and for that reason cannot be known scientifically:[113] they "do not fall under any art or set of precepts."[114]

It is the latter circumstance that robs moral reasoning of any pretension to being a strict scientific demonstration. But particular actions, while they fall outside the necessities that ground scientific certitude,[115] can be known by perception (αἴσθησις);[116] they fall, in Aquinas's phrase, "under the senses."[117] Not deduction, then, but some kind of immediate sensible cognition of the particular action is required to know that this action is a token of the prescribed act of protecting the innocent. *Nous* (νοῦς) answers to this requirement.

In the Aristotelian corpus, "*nous*" has a wide range of meanings.[118] As a psychological or metaphysical term, "*nous*" refers in a general way to the intellectual power (δύναμις) of the rational soul. In the logical and ethical works, "*nous*" refers more specifically to an intellectual disposition or habit (ἕξις).[119] But in *EN*, VI, 11, 1143a35–b3, the intellectual habit is specified by two different objects: (1) universal

---

112. See *EN*, VI, 8, 1142a25–30.

113. See *EN*, IX, 2, 1165a12–14; *Rhet.*, I, 1356b2–3 (rev. Oxford trans.): ". . . individual cases are so infinitely various that no knowledge of them is possible."

114. *EN*, II, 2, 1104a7 (rev. Oxford trans.): "precepts" = "professional teachings" (παραγγελίαν).

115. See *SLE*, IX, 2, 1165a12, 87–99 (*In Ethic.*, IX, lect. 2 [Spiazzi, n. 1779, p. 469]): ". . . rationes quae sunt circa actiones et passiones humanas non possunt habere aliquid determinatum secundum certitudinem. . . ."

116. See *EN*, VI, 8, 1142a27; VII, 3, 1147a26.

117. "[Particularia enim et contingentia] . . . cadunt sub sensu," *SLE*, VI, 5, 1140b31, 16–17 (*In Ethic.*, VI, lect. 5 [Spiazzi, n. 1175, p. 322]). Cf. *EN*, VI, 3, 1139b21–22; 8, 1142a26–27. Gauthier-Jolif, II, 2: 538, n. 1143b3 comment that the minor premises is a "judgment of sense" which need not be confined, as Aristotle's own examples show, to moral matters.

118. See James H. Lesher, "The Meaning of NOUS in the *Posterior Analytics*," *Phronesis* 18 (1973): 44–68; and W. K. C. Guthrie, *A History of Greek Philosophy*, Vol. 6: *Aristotle: An Encounter* (Cambridge: Cambridge University Press, 1981), 192–94, 308–30.

119. See *de An.*, II, 2, 413b24; 4, 415a16–22; III, 4, 429a10; 429a22–25; *Metaph.*, VI, 1, 1025b22; XII, 3, 1070a26: νοῦς = power (δύναμις) or part (μόριον) of the human soul that is able to think and judge; *de An.* III, 5, 430a14–15: the distinction between passive and active νοῦς; 430a18: active νοῦς = activity (ἐνέργεια); 430a22–23: νοῦς is

indemonstrable, primary definitions (ὅροι); and (2) the last and contingent fact (τὸ ἔσχατον καὶ ἐνδεχόμενον). Both (a) and (b) are said to be "ultimates" (ἔσχατα) inasmuch as neither of them is attained by any process of rational demonstration (i.e., by λόγος). But how can an immaterial universal and a sensible particular fall under the same intellectual habit? Are the two objects of *nous* compatible? At first glance, it would seem not.

In *EN*, VI, 8, 1142a25, Aristotle states, according to the usual modern redaction of the verb in the text, that "*phronesis* is opposed to *nous*" (ἀντίκειται μὲν δὴ τῷ νῷ).[120] In line with this opposition, Aristotle appears to deny that *nous* is in any way tied to the perception (αἴσθησις) of particulars. In this text, perhaps because he is focusing on particular actions rather than on theoretical principles,[121] Aristotle attributes the quasi-perceptual grasp of particulars to *phronesis* rather than to *nous*. This denial of or, more accurately, silence about the perceptual side of *nous* strongly suggests, of course, that *nous* only intuits, in a nonsensible or quasi-Platonic fashion, immaterial universals. But this inference would be mistaken. Aristotle's ambivalence is more terminological than doctrinal. At *EN*, VI, 11, 1143b5, he attributes to *nous* the same connection between perception and knowledge of sensible particulars that he attributes to *phronesis* at *EN*, VI, 8, 1142a25–27.[122] The opposition between *nous* and *phronesis*, in short, should not be hardened: *EN*, VI, 11, 1143a25 states that *nous* and *phronesis* refer to the same thing.

Nonetheless, one could correctly claim that the preeminent function of *nous* is to intuit the universal, immediate, or indemonstrable principles (ἀρχαί) and primary definitions (ὅροι πρῶτοι) that ground *theoretical* syllogistic demonstrations.[123] And it can be granted that as Aristotle uses this polyvalent term, the function of *nous* in practical reasoning

---

"separated" (χωρίσθεις) and may or may not be identified with divine νοῦς; *Apo.*, II, 19, 100b5: νοῦς = an active disposition/habit (ἕξις) whereby we intuitively and infallibly grasp truth; *Apo.*, II, 19, 100b12; *EN*, VI, 8, 1142a26; 11, 1143b2–3: νοῦς has as its object the indemonstrable definitions (ὅροι) and principles (ἀρχαί) as well as contingent particular actions.

120. Cf. Allan, "Practical Syllogism," 329: "The word ἀντίκειται in 1142a25 means not so much 'is opposed as corresponds to, thought *[sic]* with a difference.'" But Allan gives no philological evidence for this assertion.

121. See Michelakis, *Aristotle's Theory*, 78.

122. Cf. *Apo.*, I, 18, 81a40–b9; *de An.*, III, 4, 429b20 (rev. Oxford trans.) which refers to "the same power in a different state." Thus *nous* "is an awareness of a particular as instantiating a relevant universal" (C. D. C. Reeve, *Practices of Reason: Aristotle's Nicomachean Ethics* [Oxford: Clarendon Press, 1992], 58).

123. See *Apo.*, I, 23, 84b37–85a1; *EN*, VI, 6, 1141a7–8. The latter text also con-

seems quite different: *nous* intuits the sensible particular.[124] *Nous* thus provides the immediate "opinion" (δόξα), derived from sensation, about the nature of the particular action to which, presumably, the minor premise refers in a practical syllogism.[125] In practical reasoning, Aristotelian *nous* grasps (by some kind of act of perception[126]) "the last and contingent [action],"[127] that is, the action that is or is not to be done.

The dual and apparently contradictory function of *nous*, the fact that it immediately cognizes or intuits both universals and sensible singulars, has complicated efforts to understand Aristotle's theory of moral reasoning.[128] But unless one foists on Aristotle a Platonic opposition between sensible individuals and immaterial universals, Aristotle does not contradict himself when assigning intuitive knowledge of singulars and universals to *nous*.[129] For even the immediate knowledge of indemonstrable theoretical principles is grounded inductively in the sense awareness of singulars.[130] As is the case with all Aristotelian universals, then, knowledge of the singular sensible action is the source of our knowledge of universal moral principles. The Aristotelian universal, however, covers what are today called "general" as well as "exceptionless" moral principles.[131]

Aristotle, unfortunately, leaves vague what kind of perception is to

---

trasts *nous* and *phronesis*, assigning knowledge of the first principles to the former and not to the latter.

124. See *EN*, VI, 10, 1143a35–b5.

125. See *EN*, VII, 3, 1147b9–10: ἡ τελευταία πρότασις δόξα αἰσθητοῦ . . .

126. See *EN*, VI, 11, 1143b5: τούτων οὖν ἔχειν δεῖ αἴσθησιν, αὕτη δ᾽ ἐστὶ νοῦς.

127. *EN*, VI, 11, 1143b2 = τοῦ ἐσχάτου καὶ ἐνδεχομένου.

128. Cf. *EN*, I, 3, 1094b14–22; II, 9, 1109b15–23; VI, 6, 1140b31–1141a1; 11, 1143a32–b5. The last passage has proved especially difficult to fathom: see Takatura Ando, *Aristotle's Theory of Practical Cognition* (The Hague: Martinus Nijhoff, 1971), 193–208. It is difficult to determine what is Aristotle's main point. Is he contrasting theoretical deductions that reason *from* a universal with practical inductions that reason *to* a universal? See *EN*, 1143b3–5; 1139b28–31. For an extended and subtle defense of the latter interpretation, see Dahl, *Practical Reason*, 228–36.

129. For a strongly anti-Platonic version of Aristotelian "intuitionism," see Enrico Berti, "The Intellection of 'Indivisibles' According to Aristotle, *De Anima* III 6," in *Aristotle on Mind and the Senses*, ed. G. E. R. Lloyd and G. E. L. Owen (Cambridge: Cambridge University Press, 1978), 141–63. Cf. Lesher, "Meaning of *NOUS*," 44–45.

130. See *Apo.*, II, 19, 100b4–5. Cf. *ELP*, II, 20, 100b3, 282–85 (Leonine ed., I, pt. 2, 246b): "Quia igitur uniuersalium cognitionem accipimus ex singularibus, concludit manifestum esse quod necesse est prima uniuersalia principia cognoscere per inductionem."

131. Cf. C. C. W. Taylor, "Aristotle's Epistemology," in *Companions to Ancient Thought*, Vol. 1: *Epistemology*, ed. Stephen Everson (Cambridge: Cambridge University Press, 1990), 136, who argues that Aristotle "tends to assimilate" the practi-

be attributed to *nous* or *phronesis*.[132] While acknowledging that *phronesis* does not operate by means of an external sense or even by means of an internal or imaginative sense, he offers only the lame explanation that *phronesis* belongs to a different form or kind (εἶδος) of sense: it exercises, in other words, a unique kind of perception.[133] But, despite all of Aristotle's emphasis on its perceptual character, the intuitive act of *phronesis*, considering its precise object, cannot be plausibly maintained unless it involves some form of intellectual intuition and judgment of the singular action.[134] The Latin names of the alleged sense in question suggest as much: *"vis cogitativis," "vis aestimativis,"* and *"ratio particularis."* In any case, the *phronimos* must make intellectual judgments[135] about the actual moral character of the contingent, singular action.[136] Though Aristotle does use the perceptual analogy (*EN*, VI, 11, 1143b13–14), the moral character of an action, however that connects with its sensible qualities, cannot be seen with a physical or even with an imaginary eye. All that one can say is that these immediate judgments of the moral character of particular actions, since they are noninferential, are *like* perceptual intuitions.

---

cal functioning of *nous* to the quasi-perceptual knowledge of "instances of moral concepts" and not, as in its theoretical function, to the intuition of "exceptionless generalizations." But since Aristotle firmly holds that some actions are always bad, he clearly allows there are at least "exceptionless" or (in contemporary logical usage) *universal* negative principles.

132. According to *EN*, VI, 8, 1142a28–29, the perception does not belong to one of the five special senses but it is like the perception whereby we grasp that a mathematical figure is, for example, a triangle. Aquinas explains (*SLE*, VI, 7, 1142a25, 231–55; *In Ethic.*, VI, lect. 7 [Spiazzi, n. 1214, p. 331]) that the sense in question is not one of the proper senses (sight or hearing) but an "interior sense, by which we perceive that which is able to be imagined *[imaginabilia]*" (249–50). It is this interior sense that operates when we imagine geometrical figures: see *de An.*, II, 6, 418a–17. The interior sense pertains to prudence (*SLE*, VI, 7, 1142a25, 255–65; *In Ethic.*, VI, lect. 7 [Spiazzi, n. 1215, p. 331]); is a sensory power of judgment (*SLE*, VI, 9, 1143b11, 239–51; *In Ethic.*, VI, lect. 9 [Spiazzi, n. 1255, p. 339]); and can be called an "intellectual sense" even though it intuits sensible particulars: "Unde hic sensus vocatur intellectus, qui est circa sensibilia vel singularia" (*SLE*, VI, 9, 1143a35, 184–85; *In Ethic.*, VI, lect. 9 [Spiazzi, n. 1249, p. 338]). The name of the sense in question is the *"vis cogitativis"* or *"vis aestimativis"* or *"ratio particularis"* (182–84).

133. See *EN*, VI, 8, 1142a29–30, where Aristotle distinguishes the perception of *phronesis* from its closest analogue, the imaginative perception of a mathematical figure.

134. Cf. *ST*, II–II, q. 49, a. 2, ad 3: ". . . recta aestimatio [prudentiae] de fine particulari et intellectus dicitur, inquantum est alicuius principii; et sensus, inquantum est particularis . . . Sed de sensu interiori quo de particulari iudicamus."

135. See *EN*, II, 9, 1109b23; IV, 5, 1126b4.

136. What Gauthier-Jolif denominate "les valeurs morales singulières" (II–2: 537).

Aristotle's texts on the intuitive dimensions of practical reasoning are more puzzling, at least for most contemporary scholars, than Aquinas's redaction of them suggests. Among many points at issue, what does *nous* grasp that is then formalized in the particular premise: (1) a singular action? or (2) a singular proposition about a singular action? or (3) a type of action?[137] By comparison with contemporary views, Aquinas's interpretation of Aristotle is schematic and straightforward.[138]

Aquinas states that Aristotelian *nous* grasps "extremes" (τὰ ἔσχατα = *extrema*): namely, indemonstrable, universal definitions (ὅροι = *termini*). But *phronesis/prudentia* may also be said to grasp another kind of indemonstrable extreme: the singular action *(singularis operabilis).*[139] Both ultimates or extremes are, in different senses, "principles," and for that reason both can appropriately be considered to fall under *nous.* Aquinas says, rather vaguely, that Aristotelian *phronesis* is receptive of, or united to, or coheres with theoretical *intellectus* because *prudentia* also possesses indemonstrable knowledge of a principle—in this case, insight into the singular action that functions as a principle (i.e., a "beginning") for the agent choosing what to do or not to do.[140]

In *ST,* II–II, q. 49, a. 2, Aquinas expounds an answer to a question

137. Dahl argues that *nous* grasps "a single proposition indicating what is to be done in a specific situation" (280, n. 14) and thus implicitly grasps a general principle and not just "the bare fact that an action is to be done" (232). Accordingly, Dahl opposes (279, n. 12) Cooper *(Reason and Human Good,* 33–43) who maintains that *nous* grasps types of particular actions rather than individual actions themselves.

Halfway closer to Aquinas's view, Engberg-Pedersen, in *Aristotle's Theory,* 199–200, n. 5, emphasizes that *phronesis* "is concerned with genuine particulars" but adds the caveat that these particulars are known through experience and habituation and not "some mysterious capacity for intuition" (211).

Sherman, *Fabric of Character,* who notes (29) that virtue and vice affect our perceptual awareness of particulars, also quite correctly argues (40–41) for a perceptual moment in formulating the major premise.

Gauthier-Jolif assign the apprehension of the major premise to "l'intellect pratique" and the minor premise to what they call "l'intelligence pratique," which is alleged to be "une qualité particuliere distincte de l'intellect pratique" (II–2:538).

138. See *SLE,* VI, 9, 1143a35–b5, 152–86 *(In Ethic.,* VI, lect. 9 [Spiazzi, nn. 1247–49, p. 338]).

139. Cf. *EN,* VI, 8, 1142a25–27.

140. See *SLE,* VI, 7, 1142a25, 235–38 *(In Ethic.,* VI, lect. 7 [Spiazzi, n. 1214, p. 331]): ". . . tam scientia quam prudentia sunt suceptibiles, vel attingibiles secundum aliam litteram, intellectui, idest habent aliquam cohaerentiam [Spiazzi: convenientiam] cum intellectu, qui est habitus principiorum." The corresponding text in the Latin translation of Aristotle ("Susceptibiles [vel: Attingibiles] quidem igitur intellectui") is found in the revised edition of Grosseteste used by Aquinas: see Gauthier-Jolif, II, 2: 504. Contemporary translations of 1142a25, as I have noted, read: *"Phronesis* stands opposite [ἀντίκειται] *nous"* (Rackham trans.).

that the Aristotelian texts do not raise: does *nous* have immediate cognitive insight into the primary or indemonstrable universal principles of practical reason? Aquinas's answer is that *intellectus* has a universal object in both the theoretical and practical spheres of reasoning. In both of these spheres, the operation of Thomistic *intellectus* lead to immediate or self-evident *(per se nota)* universal or exceptionless principles. However, there is also a particular operation of *intellectus* in the practical sphere. In regard to the intuition of singulars, whereas Aristotle leaves the relationship between *nous* and *phronesis* clouded, Aquinas states definitively that the act of *intellectus* that intuits the moral character of a singular action is an integral part of prudence. By the particular operation of *intellectus*, that is, by its operation in reference to a singular action that is to be done or not done, the prudent man has right cognitive insight into some singular or particular end.[141]

In his commentary on *EN*, VI, 10, 1143a35–b5,[142] however, Aquinas gives a cautious and correctly restricted account of the universal role that Aristotelian *nous* plays in the practical sphere. In the sphere of theoretical reason, *nous/intellectus* grasps the first or indemonstrable terms and universal principles that function as the ultimate major premises of theoretical syllogisms. These principles are constitutive of theoretical reason and are said to be "immobile" since knowledge of them "is not able to be removed from man."[143] In the sphere of practical reasoning, however, *nous/intellectus* bears solely on the contingent singular action-token that is embodied in the minor premise of the practical syllogism. But Aquinas in nowise claims that—for Aristotle—*nous* grasps first or immediate universal practical principles.

Instead, Aquinas remarks, glossing a phrase of Aristotle, that contingent singular actions are "principles in the mode of a final cause."[144] In the Aristotelian context, final causes are indeed principles. But how a singular action can be considered a "final cause" calls for further clari-

141. Cf. *ST*, II–II, q. 49, a. 2, ad 1: "Hoc autem primum singulare est aliquis singularis finis. . . . Unde intellectus qui ponitur pars prudentiae est quaedam recta aestimatio de aliquo particulari fine."

142. See *SLE*, VI, 9, 1143a35–b5, 152–86 *(In Ethic.,* VI, lect. 9 [Spiazzi, nn. 1247–49, p. 338]).

143. See *SLE*, VI, 9, 1143a35, 161–64 *(In Ethic.,* VI, lect 9 [Spiazzi, n.1247, p. 338]): ". . . [principia indemonstrabilia] quae sunt prima cognita et immobilia, quia scilicet eorum cognitio ab homine removeri non potest. . . ."

144. ". . . principia ad modum causae finalis" *(SLE*, VI, 9 1143a35, 173; *In Ethic.,* VI, lect. 9 [Spiazzi, n. 1248, p. 338]). Cf. *EN*, VI, 11, 1143b4: ἀρχαὶ γὰρ τοῦ οὗ ἕνεκα αὗται.

fication. Obviously, Aquinas is not thinking in terms of the means-end model of action. What, in fact, he is referring to is the knowledge of a universal in and through a singular. But before we take up this topic, it would be useful to have an overview of the role of indemonstrable principles in Aristotle's theory of reasoning.

3. Indemonstrable Principles

According to Aristotle's paradigm, reason is most visible in a syllogistic demonstration, that is, in the process of formally inferring a conclusion from two premises.[145] A syllogistic demonstration has as its end the attainment of scientific knowledge (ἐπιστήμη).[146] Scientific reasoning is the process of validly deriving a universal and necessary conclusion from true, universal, and necessary categorical propositions that function as premises since they share a common middle term.[147] Science thus results from syllogistic demonstrations in the first figure, syllogisms that Aristotle calls "perfect" because their conclusions have a transparent or self-evident necessity.[148]

Syllogisms, drawn from all three Aristotelian figures, can be fashioned into interestingly long chains. A syllogistic chain is formed when syllogisms are linked together so that the conclusions of an antecedent syllogism function as the premises of a subsequent one. But Aristotle contends that, if stable definitions are to be attached to things, the chain cannot be infinite. Actual demonstrations, like actuality itself, are finite: "[O]ne cannot go through infinitely many things in thought" *(Apo.,* I, 22, 83b6–7 [rev. Oxford trans.]). No matter how long the syllogistic chain, it leads back to primary, indemonstrable premises, that is, principles (ἀρχαί) whose truth is immediately known because there is an immediate connection between their subject and predicate terms.[149]

145. For the relationship between informal and formal reasoning, see Jonathan Lear, *Aristotle and Logical Theory* (Cambridge: Cambridge University Press, 1980), 10–14.

146. See *Apr.,* I, 1, 24a18; 4, 25b27; 23; *Apo.,* I, 2, 71b17–19. Cf. *ELP,* I, 1, prooemium, 134–35 (Leonine ed., I, pt. 2, 7b): ". . . finis autem demonstratiui sillogismi est acquisitio sciencie. . . ."

147. The scientific syllogism is the traditional "Barbara" syllogism with the additional specification of the necessity of the propositions: "All A is necessarily B"; "All B is necessarily C"; "All A is necessarily C." See *Apo.,* I, 14.

148. Syllogisms in the other two figures can be reduced to ones in the first figure: see *Apr.,* I, 1, 24b18–26. For the history of the interpretation of the term "perfect syllogism" see Günther Patzig, *Aristotle's Theory of the Syllogism,* trans. Jonathan Barnes (Dordrecht, Holland: D. Reidel, 1968), 43–87.

149. See *Apr.,* II, 16, 64b35–36; *Apo.,* I, 22, 84a30–31; 84b36–37; II, 19, 99b20–21.

Although it is difficult to provide a coherent schematization of Aristotle's variant statements about the ultimate principles of syllogistic reasoning,[150] I shall attempt to summarize what Aristotle says in *APo.*, I, 1, 71a11–17; 2, 72a14–24; 9, 76a32–38; 10, 76b11–16; 32, 88b27–29. Aristotelian syllogistic is grounded in primary, indemonstrable, or immediate principles (αἱ πρῶται ἀρχαί αἱ ἄμεσαι)[151] that are of two basic kinds:[152] (1) common principles (κοιναὶ ἀρχαί) = common axioms (κοινὰ ἀξιώματα)[153] which, since they are required for knowledge of anything, are used by all the sciences;[154] (2) proper principles (ἴδιαι ἀρχαί) of the particular sciences = theses (θέσεις)[155] which are subdivided into (a) indemonstrable definitions (ὅροι, ὁρισμοί)[156] and (b) indemonstrable suppositions (ὑποθέσεις)[157] which since they take one or the other of a pair of contradictory propositions, are affirmations or negations. Hypotheses say that something is or is not.[158]

The model for the syllogistic chain that Aristotle has in mind is probably a (pre-Euclidean) version of an axiomatized geometry, despite the fact that the latter cannot be logically fitted to the former: see Alfonso Gómez-Lobo, "Definitions in Aristotle," in *Studies in Aristotle*, ed. Dominic O'Meara (Washington, D.C.: The Catholic University of America Press, 1981), 25–46, esp. 28–30.

150. In Aristotle's terminology, the following are prima facie equivalent: τὰ πρῶτα (the primitives) = αἱ ἀρχαί (the principles) = ἄμεσα καὶ ἀρχαί (immediate principles); ἀρχὴ ἀποδείξεως (principle of demonstration) = ἄμεσος πρότασις (immediate proposition) = ἄμεσον ἀναπόδεικτον (undemonstrated immediate), see *Apo.*, I, 2, 72a6–7; 72b19–20; II, 18, 99b21.

For Aristotle's terminological "fluctuations," see Mignucci, *L'argomentazione dimostrativa*, commentary on texts from *Apo.* cited above.

151. *Apo.*, II, 19, 99b21.

152. See *Apo.*, I, 10, 76a38; 32, 88b27–28.

153. = "dignitas vel maxima propositio" *(ELP,* I, 5, 72a14, 105 [Leonine ed., I, pt. 2, 24b]).

154. According to Aquinas, these axioms, whose truth is known to all, are taken from metaphysics: "Vnde et huiusmodi principia omnes sciencie accipiunt a methaphisica, cuius est considerare ens simpliciter et ea que sunt entis" *(ELP,* I, 5, 72a14, 128–30 [Leonine ed., I, pt. 2, 25a]).

155. = "positio" *(ELP,* I, 5, 72a14, 100 [Leonine ed., I, pt. 2, 24b]).

156. See *Apo.*, II, 10, 94a, 9–10: ὁ δὲ τὸν ἀμέσων ὁρισμὸς θέσις ἐστὶ τοῦ τί ἐστιν ἀναπόδεικτος.

157. = "suppositio" *(ELP,* I, 5, 72a18, 158–59 [Leonine ed., I, pt. 2, 25b]). Cf. 72a14–24 and 76b23–34; the latter text refers to "hypotheses" that are provable and, in which case, are not to be identified with the hypotheses that are the ultimate immediate principles governing deductions. See ch. 2, n. 1.

158. Hypotheses are standardly interpreted as existential assumptions about the objects that fall under the genus denoting the subject of a science. See *Apo.*, I, 1, 71a11–12: cf. J. M. Le Blond, *Logique et méthode chez Aristote* (Paris: J. Vrin, 1939), 96, n. 1: "ὑπόθεσις, affirmation d'existence"; and Ross, *Analytics*, 504–5, nn. 11–17. For more recent interpretations stressing the existential character of hypotheses, see Jaakko Hintikka, "On the Ingredients of an Aristotelian Science," *Noûs* 6 (1972):

This summary, however, is too tidy because it does not consider what Aristotle leaves rather obscure: the relationship between these various principles (ἀρχαί) and syllogistic demonstrations. While it is clear from Aristotle's account that hypotheses function as indemonstrable premises that support syllogistic reasoning,[159] axioms seem to be rules of inference or even so-called transcendental principles that do not actually appear as premises in syllogisms.[160] According to Aquinas, the difference between axioms and indemonstrable hypotheses and postulates is that an axiom must satisfy both logical and epistemological criteria: a common axiom is an immediate principle that is both necessary through itself and appears (δοκεῖν) to be necessary.[161] The role of definitions in scientific demonstration is more problematic.[162]

55–69: "[T]he only ultimate existential assumption needed in a science concerns the existence of the members of the genus which is its subject matter" (63–64); and Michael Ferejohn, *Origins of Aristotelian Science,* who stresses that definitions, unlike hypotheses, "lack existential force" (40). Nonetheless, Mignucci, *L'argomentazione dimostrativa,* argues that this existential interpretation presents "gravi difficoltà" (36): inasmuch as Aristotle does not explicitly distinguish predicative from existential propositions, "la ὑπόθεσις è qui definita come una θέσις che esprime un enunciato esistenziale come anche un'attribuzione predicativa" (37). Cf. *Apo.,* I, 10, 76b12–13; 76b39–77a3; II, 2, 91a1–2.

For an important argument (based on the Euclidean prototype) that hypotheses are *not* first-order existential statements but singular identity or instantiation statements of the form "This X is an F," see Alfonso Gómez-Lobo, "Aristotle's Hypotheses and the Euclidean Postulates," *Review of Metaphysics* 30 (1977): 430–39. For Gómez-Lobo's extended arguments against the "venerable tradition" of existential exegesis (35), see "The So-Called Question of Existence in Aristotle, *Apo.,* 2. 1–2," *Review of Metaphysics* 34 (1980): 71–89. Cf. McKirahan, "Existence Claims," in *Principles and Proofs,* 122–32: "Existence claims [i.e., hypotheses] prove to be the existential underpinning that gives definitions a grip on reality" (124).

159. See *Apo.,* I, 10, 76b35–37.

160. See *Apo.,* I, 11, 77a10–11: cf. Ross, *Analytics,* 60; Mario Mignucci, *La theoria Aristotelica della scienza* (Florence: G. C. Sansonie Editore, 1965), 264: ". . . principi comuni trascendentali . . ."; and idem., *Argomentazione Dimostrativa,* 136–43.

161. Cf. *Apo.,* I, 10, 76b23–24: Οὐκ ἔστι δ' ὑπόθεσις οὐδ' αἴτημα, ὃ ἀνάγκη εἶναι δι' αὐτὸ καὶ δοκεῖν ἀνάγκη; *ELP,* I, 19, 76b23, 18–26 (Leonine ed., I, pt. 2, 70b–71a): "Considerandum namque est quod communes animi conceptiones aliquid habent commune cum aliis principiis demonstrationis et aliquid proprium: commune quidem habent, quia necesse est tam ista quam alia principia per se esse uera; proprium autem est horum principiorum quod non solum necesse est ea per se esse uera, sed etiam necesse est uideri quod per se sint uera: nullus enim potest opinari contraria eorum."

McKirahan, in *Principles and Proofs,* 45–46, interprets 76b23–24 as referring to the indemonstrable hypotheses that are the immediate *proper* principles of a science.

162. "Definition" is usually taken to translate two Aristotelian terms, ὅρος and ὁρισμός, both of which Aristotle distinguishes from ὑπόθεσις see *Apo.,* I, 2, 72a20–

Definitions are not quantified statements—they are neither singular nor universal—[163] whereas syllogistic premises are quantified.[164] Nonetheless, Aristotle clearly licenses some definitions to function as indemonstrable premises in a chain of scientific syllogisms.[165] The license presupposes some distinction, although Aristotle does not use the exact expression (and it is not relevant in regard to mathematical objects) between "nominal and real definitions,"[166] at least in regard to the definitions that are used in the natural sciences.[167] Nominal defini-

---

21 (ὁρισμός); 9, 76b35 (ὅρος). Apo., I, 10, 76b35 states that definitions (ὅροι) are not hypotheses (ὑποθέσεις), and not therefore premises (προτάσεις). But Apo., II, 17, 99a22–23 states that "all sciences are generated through ὁρισμοί" and II, 3, 90b24 states that ὁρισμοί are the "principles of demonstration" (ἀρχαί τῶν ἀποδείξεων). Although the exegesis of these texts is extremely knotty, if these ὁρισμοί are to be viewed as ultimate syllogistic premises, it is because an ὁρισμός can be identified as a "real definition" = definiens setting forth the essence of the definiendum (90b30); ὅροι (at 76b35), although Aristotle's usage is not self-explanatory, would then correspond to "purely nominal" definitions (Ross, Analytics, p. 55) or meaningful "terms" (Mignucci) but terms which cannot be used as ἀρχαί or indemonstrable premises since they do not actually set forth what the thing (i.e., the definiendum) essentially is: cf. Apo., II, 7, 92b5–8.

Cf. Joachim, Commentary, 197, n. 1: "The term ἀρχή, when used strictly, is confined to assumptions ὅτι ἔστι: i.e., it includes ὑποθέσεις and ἀξιώματα, but excludes mere definitions of meaning"; Mignucci, L'argomentazione dimostrativa, 1: 212: ". . . nel nostro testo [76b35] ὅρος non significa 'definizione', bensì 'termine'. . . ."

163. See Apo., I, 10, 77a3–4.

164. See Apo., I, 2, 72a21: cf. Mignucci, L'argomentazione dimostrativa, 33–37; and Hippocrates G. Apostle, Aristotle's Posterior Analytics (Grinnell, Iowa: Peripatetic Press, 1981), 89–91, nn. 29–31. Gómez-Lobo, "Definitions," dispels these perplexities by contending that mathematical definitions, as they are found in Euclid, lay down the necessary and sufficient conditions for X to be identified as F; hence definitions are unquantified. A Euclidean/Aristotelian hypothesis, however, instantiates the definition: it "assumes that a given individual in fact satisfies those [definitional] conditions" (33). Aquinas distinguishes between immediate principles and immediate propositions; definitions are immediate principles but they are also virtual propositions. In actual propositions, definitions can be premises: see ELP, I, 5, 72a18, 171–82 (Leonine ed., I, pt. 2, 26a–b).

165. See de An., I, 402b25–26; Top., I, 8, 103b7–12; Apo., I, 14, 79a28–29; II, 3, 90b3–7: cf. Mignucci, L'argomentazione dimostrativa, 38.

166. Cf. Apo., II, 10, 93b29–31; 38–39. Aristotle appears to distinguish three kinds of real definitions corresponding to different stages of scientific inquiry: see Apo., II, 10, 94a11–14. Cf. Robert Bolton, "Definition and Scientific Method in Aristotle's Posterior Analytics and Generation of Animals," in Philosophical Issues in Aristotle's Biology, ed. Allan Gotthelf and James G. Lennox (Cambridge: Cambridge University Press, 1987), 145–46.

167. See Hintikka, "Aristotelian Science," esp. 66–69. Ferejohn, Origins of Aristotelian Science, while accusing Hintikka of embracing a "strict syllogisticism" (41) that allegedly contradicts Hintikka's distinction between nominal and real definitions, separates ὅροι that are prescientific (nominal?) from those definitional ἀρχαί

tions, to simplify Aristotle's account somewhat, signify the meaning of a word but do not signify what a thing essentially is.[168]

However, nominal definitions, although they cannot function as the premises of scientific demonstrations, are useful inasmuch as they can initiate scientific inquiry: nominal definitions of "X" allow one to ask of "X", "If X is?," that is, to inquire whether "X" is instantiated. If "X" is instantiated, further inquiry leads to the question "What is X?" which Aristotle regards as equivalent to "Why is X?," the answer to which is a real definition of "X" inasmuch as it demonstrates the cause of X.[169] But if the nominal definition of "X" is not instantiated, no question much less answer is forthcoming about the nature of X.[170]

Real definitions, then, are universal affirmative propositions that define the essences or fundamental attributes of things that we know through perception;[171] they are propositions about the essences of the extralinguistic facts from which the definitions are drawn and to which they refer.[172] In syllogisms, real definitions are used as the middle term that explains why something is what it is.[173] In *APo.*, II, 8 93a29–36, Aristotle gives us an imaginative example of how we might come to know an *immediate*, real definition—the definition of "lunar eclipse" —in the science of astronomy.[174] If we were on the moon, and if we were to see the earth move between us and the sun, then we would immediately know both that there is (on the earth) an eclipse of the moon and what is its cause: blockage of the sun's light by the earth. The latter phrase expresses the real immediate definition of "lunar

---

(= ἄμεσοι = ἄτομοι) that come from perceptual acquaintance with existing particulars. Only definitions that express the universal immanent in particulars (real definitions?) can function as premises in a syllogistic demonstration: see 52–61.

168. See *Apo.*, II, 6, 92b5–8; 8, 93b30–31. For a more nuanced account, see Gómez-Lobo, "Definitions," who finds "three different kinds of nominal definitions . . . implicitly distinguished by Aristotle" (41).

169. See Gómez-Lobo, "Definitions," 34–36, 44.

170. See *Apo.*, II, 8, 93a24–27.

171. See *Apo.*, I, 75b1; II, 3, 90b3–4.

172. See Mignucci, *La theoria Aristotelica*, 273, n. 62: "Dal punto di vista aristotelico . . . la definizione . . . esprime sempre la realtà oggettiva indicata dalle parole"; and Ferejohn, *Origins of Aristotelian Science*, 58: ". . . knowledge of definitional ἀρχαί is derived ultimately from multiple "perceptions" (αἴσθησις) of sensible particulars. . . ."

173. See *Apo.*, II, 2; II, 9, 93b22.

174. For a more typical, mathematical example of the definition of an essence that is immediately posited, see Aristotle's reference (*Apo.*, I, 10, 76b4–5) to the indemonstrable hypotheses of arithmetic (unit) and geometry (point and line). Given these hypotheses, the sciences demonstrate the essential attributes of numbers and figures: see *Metaph.*, V, 29, 1025a1–17.

eclipse," a definition that is known through perception to be immediately instantiated, and that can be used therefore as an indemonstrable premise in the science of astronomy.[175]

For our present purposes the complexities in and debates about the role of immediate propositions in Aristotelian syllogistic may at this point be set aside. Here we need only remind ourselves that Aristotle compares the ends (= principles) that structure moral reasoning with the hypotheses of mathematical science. There are subtle difficulties involved in interpreting how the elements of Aristotelian syllogistic and Euclidean geometry are to be correlated,[176] but the main point of Aristotle's comparison is, surely, that a hypothesis whether in mathematics or ethics is an ἀρχή or immediate beginning: its truth is assumed, not proven. But the word "hypothesis," as it is used in ordinary speech, connotes that such a principle, although assumed to be true, may or may not be actually true. This ordinary usage is, indeed, important for understanding ethical hypotheses. Unlike the hypotheses of arithmetic and geometry (and the *immediate* real definitions of the physical sciences) which are seen to be immediately instantiated, and therefore can be immediately known to be true,[177] a moral agent's hypotheses (i.e., his or her goals) may or may not be actually in accord with right reason. The agent's ends, in short, might be "false hypotheses." Later, we shall come back to this comparison of mathematical and moral hypotheses in order to determine more precisely its significance for Aristotelian ethics. For the moment, however, we must look at Aristotle's explanation of how indemonstrable first principles are known.

4. Knowledge of First Principles

Aristotle states that immediate principles (ἀρχαί) are attained through the psychological processes of perception (αἴσθησις) and the psychological-logical process of induction (ἐπαγωγή), and (what is especially important in the formulation of moral principles) the education or habituation (ἐθισμός) of the emotions.[178] Since it is a basic tenet of Aristotelian noetic theory that "it is impossible to consider the universal [τὰ καθόλου] except through induction" (*APo.*, I, 18, 81b2),[179]

175. For a helpful discussion of the lunar eclipse reference and other examples, see Bolton, "Definition and Scientific Method," 120–66.

176. See Gómez-Lobo, "Aristotle's Hypotheses and the Euclidean Postulates," 430–39.

177. See *Apo.*, I, 10, 76b39–77a1; II, 9, 93b24–25.

178. See *EN*, I, 7, 1098b3–4.

179. ἀδύνατον δὲ τὰ καθόλου θεωρῆσαι μὴ δι' ἐπαγωγῆς (*Apo.*, I, 18, 81b2). Cf.

Aristotle is consistent in maintaining that induction (ἐπαγωγή) is the source of whatever is universal in moral knowledge.[180] But in explaining how the moral agent induces his or her moral principles, Aristotle lays particular stress on the personal and cultural habituation of the agent making the induction.[181] As we have noted, on Aristotle's *explicit* account, knowledge of moral principles appears to have an emotional rather than an intellectual ground: morally good habits, which allow the agent to adhere to the mean between emotional excess and defect, are the necessary condition for the exercise of the intellectual virtue of *phronesis*. They make it possible for the *phronimos* to make correct inductions.

What, in brief, does Aristotle mean by "induction" (ἐπαγωγή)? Aristotle closely links induction and *nous*.[182] The basic Aristotelian use of ἐπαγωγή combines the vague notion of an advance in thought with the more precise notion of cognitively grasping a universal in a singular.[183] Induction thus involves both a heuristic process or enumeration of singulars and an immediate insight into what has been discovered as common in the singulars. To induce is "to grasp,"[184] through a process of discovery, the common form that is instantiated in many singulars. The form is grasped by *subtracting* what is unique from what is common to a class of sensible individuals.[185]

Metaph., I, 1, 981a5–7 (rev. Oxford trans.): "And art arises, when from many notions gained by experience one universal judgement about similar objects is produced"; *In Metaph.*, I, lect. 1 (Cathala-Spiazzi, n. 18, p. 9): "Nam sicut ex multis memoriis fit una experimentalis scientia, ita ex multis experimentis apprehensis fit universalis acceptio de omnibus similibus."

180. See *EN*, VI, 3, 1139b28–29 (rev. Oxford trans.): "Now induction is of first principles and of the universal and deduction proceeds from universals. . . ."

181. Burnet's commentary *(Ethics of Aristotle*, 39) on *EN*, I, 7, 1098b3–4 suggests that Aristotle actually separates induction (ἐπαγωγή), perception (αἴσθησις), and habituation (ἐθισμός), and Burnet apparently assigns knowledge of moral principles (only?) to the latter. Aquinas suggests a similar division of labor: see *SLE*, I, 11, 1098a33, 106–15 *(In Ethic.*, I, lect. 11 [Spiazzi, n. 137, p. 36]) which correlates induction with imagination as it is used in mathematics, perception with the natural sciences, and custom with ethics. But such an exclusive division runs contrary to what Aristotle says elsewhere and Aquinas does not maintain it in his commentary. See *Apo.*, I, 18, 81a37–81b9; II, 19, 100a1–b17, which incorporate perception and habituation into the inductive process. Cf. Dahl, *Practical Reason*, 256, n. 12; and Reeve, *Practices of Reason*, 60–61.

182. See *Apo.*, II, 19, 100a3–100b16; *EN*, VI, 11, 1143b5.

183. For Aristotle's different uses of ἐπαγωγή, see W. D. Ross, *Aristotle's Prior and Posterior Analytics* (Oxford: Clarendon Press, 1949), 47–51, 481–87.

184. "to grasp" = λαβεῖν *(Apo.*, I, 5, 74a7): gnomic aorist second infinitive expressing no note of time.

185. On the difference between Aristotle's concept of *subtraction* (ἀφαίρεσις)

Aristotle is well aware of the so-called logically perfect induction,[186] an induction that is made only after one has enumerated the common characteristics of all the relevant individual cases, but he readily allows that inductions leading to principles (ἀρχαί) can be based on insight into several cases and perhaps (in the case of the primary definitions of mathematics) into only one instance, that is, into the hypothesis that instantiates the definition.[187] In any case, induction always involves the perception of the sensible singular.[188] But it is the intellectual insight or grasping of the common form that counts.[189] From the perceptual (heuristic) experience of however many sensible singulars, *nous* provides a (cognitively) immediate insight or intuition into the common form that is instantiated in a class of sensible singulars composed of matter and form.

Since the identical form is instantiated in all the members of its class, it can be applied through a universal definition to all the relevant material singulars. The Aristotelian universal, however, exists only in knowing. *Knowing* is either universal or singular. Actual knowledge is always knowledge of the form in one sensible singular, that is, of a *this* (τόδε τι) composed of matter and form;[190] universal knowledge through the identical form is potential knowledge of the other material singulars that instantiate the form.[191]

In the *Nicomachean Ethics*, "faculty psychology" and "virtue theory" go hand in hand to explain how the *phronimos* reaches universal moral knowledge.[192] All human agents, inasmuch as they share a rational human nature, have the power of *nous*. But the *phronimos* also has what all men do not have, the right emotional habituation toward morally good actions that is the basis for his insight into the morally beautiful and ugly. Because the *phronimos* has the right starting points,

---

and the Scholastic notion of *abstraction*, see Joseph Owens, *The Doctrine of Being in the Aristotelian Metaphysics: A Study in the Greek Background of Mediaeval Thought*, 3d ed., rev. (Toronto: Pontifical Institute of Mediaeval Studies, 1978), 382–85; M.-D. Philippe, O.P., "Ἀφαίρεσις, πρόθεσις, χωρίζειν dans la philosophie d'Aristote," *Revue thomiste* 48 (1948): 461–75.

186. See *Apr.*, II, 23, 68b27–29; 24, 69a16.

187. See *Apr.*, II, 23, 68b29; *Metaph.*, VI, 1, 1025b14–16.

188. See *Apo.*, I, 13, 78a34; 18, 81b5–6 (rev. Oxford trans.): ". . . it is impossible to get an induction without perception—for of particulars there is perception. . . ."

189. See *Apo.*, I, 5, 74a30–32.

190. On the vexing Aristotelian doctrine of form as itself a τόδε τι that is prior both to the material singular and the universal, see Owens, *Doctrine of Being*, 335–37, 360–62, 386–95, 427–31.

191. See *Metaph.*, XIII, 10, 1087a10–25.

192. See *Apo.*, I, 33, 89b7–9; *EN*, VI, 11, 1143a35–b5.

the right habits or pattern of morally good actions, he is able to induce the correct universal moral principles.

Aristotle identifies the starting points of moral reasoning with the contingent, singular actions that the agent actually performs; the latter are "the starting-points of that for the sake of which" *(EN,* VI, 11, 1143b4 [rev. Oxford trans.]).[193] The latter phrase is elliptical. How can a singular action be a starting point? I have already mentioned Aquinas's explanation: singular actions are first principles "in the mode of a final cause":

> Singulars of this type, those that we say intellect is about, are principles of the end; that is, they are principles in the mode of a final cause. *(SLE,* VI, 9, 1143a35, 168–73; *In Ethic.,* VI, lect. 9 [Spiazzi, n. 1248, p. 338])[194]

Now Aristotle is sometimes charged with collapsing all moral reasoning into the model of technical or productive reasoning. But neither Aristotle nor Aquinas are merely restating the evident fact that individual actions are the means to reach an end. Here they are making an epistemic point: in Aristotle's words, "The universal is from the particular."[195] But in making particular moral judgments, the reverse point is more relevant: a singular action is performed or not performed because it instantiates a universal end that marks a virtue or a vice.[196]

The background (to *EN,* VI, 11, 1143b4) is provided by Aristotle's doctrine that through the perception and memory (i.e., from the experience) of singulars of the same type, "the one apart from many" comes "to rest in the [rational] soul."[197] Material singulars of the same species instantiate the form by which the species is denoted. In the present context, what must be stressed is Aristotle's assertion that it is impossible to know the universal except through induction from a sensible

---

193. ἀρχαί γὰρ τοῦ οὗ ἕνεκα αὗται *(EN,* VI, 11, 1143b4).

194. ". . . haec autem singularia, quorum dicimus esse intellectum huiusmodi, principia eius sunt quod est cuius gratia, id est sunt principia ad modum causae finalis" *(SLE,* VI, 9, 1143a35, 168–73; *In Ethic.,* VI, lect. 9 [Spiazzi, n. 1248, p. 338]).

195. ἐκ τῶν καθ' ἕκαστα γὰρ τὰ καθόλου *(EN,* VI, 11, 1143b4–5) = "universals are reached from particulars" (rev. Oxford trans.). Cf. *SLE,* VI, 9, 1143a35, 173–75 *(In Ethic.,* VI, lect. 9 [Spiazzi, n. 1249, p. 338]): "Et quod singularia habent rationem principiorum, patet quia ex singularibus accipitur universale. . . ."

196. See *EN,* VI, 7, 1141b15; 11, 1143b10. Cf. *SLE,* VI, 9, 1143b9, 220–22 *(In Ethic.,* VI, lect. 9 [Spiazzi, n. 1253, p. 339]): ". . . in operativis demonstrationes et procedunt ex his, scilicet singularibus, et dantur de his, scilicet de singularibus."

197. See *Apo.,* II, 19, 100a1–b5 (rev. Oxford trans.). Aquinas contrasts the existential and cognitive status of universals: ". . . dicit esse unum *praeter multa,* non quidem secundum esse, set secundum considerationem intellectus qui considerat naturam aliquam . . ." *(ELP,* II, 20, 100a7, 178–81 [Leonine ed., I, pt. 2, 245a]).

singular.[198] This familiar but, admittedly, difficult doctrine about universal knowledge[199] must guide any explanation of how the *phronimos* reaches a knowledge of universal moral principles. For Aristotle, there is no incompatibility between cognitive insight into a universal and induction of that universal from a number of singular actions; the latter is the propaedeutic to insight or the way of discovering the universal.[200] As we can only know a universal through a singular that instantiates it, so through experience and insight into some singular actions, we grasp a universal or a type of action as morally good or bad. Thus a moral agent induces a universal moral principle enjoining or prohibiting some universal end in the same epistemic way that he induces any other universal proposition.[201]

Aquinas's commentary expands Aristotle's terse reference to the universal-singular relationship. A singular action is the starting point by which the agent gains knowledge of some universal end that is to be pursued. But the way we come to know a universal is by considering it apart from the sensible composites that instantiate it. Induction, as Aquinas explains at length in his commentary on the *Posterior Analytics*,[202] plays an essential role in deriving a universal from our experience of what is common to many material singulars:

> Induction is introduced for the purpose of knowing some principle and some universal in what we reach through experience of singulars. . . . *(SLE, VI, 3, 1139b25, 87–90; In Ethic., VI, l.3 [Spiazzi, n. 1148, p. 315])*[203]

Aristotle, however, makes the somewhat confusing claim, although we have no exact Platonic citation to support his claim,[204] that he

---

198. See *Apo.*, I, 18, 81b2: ἀδύνατον δὲ τὰ καθόλου θεωρῆσαι μὴ ἐπαγωγῆς.

199. See *Metaph.*, XIII, 10, 1087a10–15.

200. See Alexander Grant, *The Ethics of Aristotle*, 4th ed., rev. (London: Longmans, Green, and Co., 1885; reprinted, New York: Arno Press, 1973), 1: 394; Gauthier-Jolif, II–2: 490, nn. 1141a7–8.

201. There are, then, strong reasons for rejecting the sense-intellect dualism implied by Kenny's assertion *(Aristotle's Theory of the Will*, 234) that "the ultimate premises of ethical reasoning are acquired not by sense-perception . . . but by ethical intuition." Cf. *ELP*, I, 30, 81b2, 68–70 (Leonine ed., I, pt. 2, 110b): "Sic igitur uniuersalia ex quibus demostratio procedit, non fiunt nobis nota nisi per inductionem"; II, 20, 100a10, 212–13 (Leonine ed., I, pt. 2, 245b): ". . . habitus principiorum fiunt in nobis a sensu preexistente."

202. See *Apo.*, I, 18, 81a40–b10; *ELP*, I, 30, 81a38–b5, 1–102 (Leonine ed., I, pt. 2, 109a–110b).

203. "Inductio autem inducitur ad cognoscendum aliquod principium et aliquod universale, in quod devenimus per experimenta singularium . . ." *(SLE*, VI, 3, 1139b25, 87–90; *In Ethic.*, VI, lect. 3 [Spiazzi, n. 1148, p. 315]).

204. *Rep.*, VI, 510b deals with dialectical assumptions not with inductive pre-

accepts Plato's distinction between arguments that *start from* first principles and arguments that *lead to* first principles.[205] But whether or not this Platonic distinction is apposite, Aristotle's doctrine is that deductions begin with the universals that have been inductively attained.[206] The universal principles of science, contrary to the Platonic ontology, remain dependent on an induction that is rooted in sensation. Ethical principles are similarly grasped as instantiated in singular actions. Universal ends are known inductively: the universal principle setting forth some end to be pursued or eschewed by considering what is common about the individual cases that have been seen to be morally good or bad. Since these principles are reached inductively, experience and age are essential if one is to make correct moral judgments.

Following Aristotle, Aquinas also presupposes that just as there is an essential link between *intellectus* (with its quasi-perceptual intuition) and induction in the formulation of theoretical principles, there is no less tight a link between *intellectus* (or *prudentia*) and induction in formulating principles in the practical sphere of morality. If we learn from experience that this herb made us well, we can then formulate the proposition that this type of herb cures.[207] In the same fashion, practical reason, from the immediate *noesis/intellectus* of the moral character of singular actions, inductively reaches universal practical principles.[208] From Aristotle's remarks, which are more suggestive than developed, we can draw a kind of outline, doubtless full of logical blanks, of how such principles are formulated.

From the immediate insight that "this lie A," and "this lie B," and "this lie C" are morally shameful and not to be done, we induce the principle that "Lying is morally shameful (αἰσχρόν) and base (φαῦλον) and not to be done." Once formulated, such moral principles can function as the universal premises of moral syllogisms. Such principles direct us to choose or to eschew a singular action-token about which we are deliberating here and now.

I have already adverted to the criticism that Aristotle assigns two quite incompatible tasks to *nous*, namely, immediate cognition of uni-

---

mises. Both Grant (1: 432) and Burnet (*Ethics of Aristotle*, 17) think that Aristotle is giving a personal recollection of Plato's teaching.

205. See *EN*, I, 4, 1095a30–b1.

206. See *EN*, VI, 3, 1139b27–30; *Apr.*, II, 23, 68b15 (rev. Oxford trans.): ". . . deduction springs out of induction. . . ." Cf. *SLE*, VI, 3, 1139b25, 98; *In Ethic.*, VI, lect. 3 (Spiazzi, n. 1148, p. 315): ". . . principiorum syllogismi sit inductio."

207. See *ELP*, II, 20, 100a6, 154–57 (Leonine ed., I, pt. 2, 245a).

208. See *SLE*, VI, 9, 1143a35–b5, 152–86 (*In Ethic.*, VI, lect. 9 [Spiazzi, nn. 1247–49, p. 338]).

versals and singulars. This objection, however, seems to assign to theoretical *nous* a quasi-Platonic intuition of nonsensible universals. In the theoretical sphere, *nous* grasps the universal, immediate, indemonstrable axioms and primary definitions (πρῶτοι ὅροι) that are the principles (ἀρχαί) of theoretical syllogisms. But these universal, theoretical definitions must also be instantiated and grasped in some sensible singular.[209] In the practical sphere, *nous* has an indemonstrable "perception" of the moral character of the singular action that is embodied in the particular premise and conclusion.[210] But may we assume that from a singular action *nous* is able to induce a moral universal that can be predicated without exception of all singular action-tokens of that apparent action-type? In fact, Aristotle does not make this assumption and we shall look shortly at his reasons for not doing so.

Aristotle observes that *nous* is both the beginning (ἀρχή) and the end (τέλος) of practical demonstrations.[211] Aquinas interprets this cryptic remark to mean that the particular action that *nous* grasps is both a beginning and an end in moral demonstrations.[212] Both theoretical and practical demonstrations employ universals that have been understood in and through a singular; but moral reasoning must end by choosing to do or not to do a singular action. The latter choice involves subsuming a singular action (the one referred to by the particular premise), which because of its character *nous* grasps here and now as to be done or not done, under a universal moral principle. Since such choices whether to do or not to do the singular action referred to in the particular premise can be formalized as the conclusion of the practical syllogism, moral reasoning may be said to be both proceeding from and demonstrating a singular action. This latter feature of practical demonstrations distinguishes them from theoretical demonstrations that reach universal conclusions.

Of course, many contemporary philosophical objections could be raised against the Aristotelian doctrine that *nous* intuits the moral character of singular actions.[213] Contemporary epistemologists are in-

209. To say that "in its theoretical employment *nous* grasps the *conclusion* of an inductive inference to a universal principle" (Dahl, *Practical Reason*, 232) seems irreconcilable with the noninferential character of *nous*.

210. See *EN*, VI, 11, 1143a35–1143b3.

211. See *EN*, VI, 12, 1143b9–11 (rev. Oxford trans.): "Hence comprehension [νοῦς] is both beginning and end; for demonstrations are from these and about these [particulars]."

212. Cf. Burnet, *Ethics of Arisotle*, 281, who thinks that Aristotle is propounding a "strange doctrine" about theoretical demonstrations.

213. For the prototypical, nineteenth-century Utilitarian attack on intuitionism

clined to throw intuitionist doctrines out of court if they appeal to allegedly incorrigible or infallible reports about the "appearances" of sense data to a percipient.[214] It is well known, however, that when Aristotle argues against the Skeptics, he vigorously defends the infallibility of sense knowledge: in regard to its proper sensible objects (καθ' αὐτὰ αἰσθητά), "perception is always free from error" *(de An.*, III, 3, 427b12 [rev. Oxford trans.]).[215] This "anti-Skeptical" attitude toward the veridicality of perception resurfaces in the *Nicomachean Ethics.* While Aristotle certainly rejects any universal ethical "infallibilism"— a badly habituated moral agent will surely have incorrect moral intuitions—he does hold for the moral infallibility of *phronesis.* When exercising that virtue, the *phronimos* will make infallible moral judgments since *phronesis* never leads into falsehood.[216] But while acknowledging the difficulties that our fallibilist contemporaries have with an infallibilist Aristotle, let us grant that sensible intuition remains a defensible epistemological notion, and that, by extension, ethical intuitionism also remains an open possibility.[217] Even on this benign assumption, numerous difficulties are posed for contemporary ethical theory by the

---

in ethics, see Henry Sidgwick, *The Methods of Ethics,* 7th ed. (London: Macmillan and Company, 1907; reprinted, Indianapolis: Hackett, 1981). For more recent anti-intuitionist arguments, based on the psychological "queerness" of the alleged intuitive moral faculty and the ontological "queerness" of its alleged "non-natural" object, see J. L. Mackie, *Ethics: Inventing Right and Wrong* (Middlesex, England: Penguin Books, 1977), 38–42. For the doctrinal vicissitudes of twentieth-century intuitionism in response to such attacks, see Mary Warnock, *Ethics since 1900,* 2d ed. (London: Oxford University Press, 1966).

214. For a recent summary of these fallibilist counterarguments to intuitionism, see Keith Lehrer, *Theory of Knowledge* (Boulder and San Francisco: Westview Press, 1990), 51–54.

215. Terence H. Irwin, in *Aristotle's First Principles* (Oxford: Clarendon Press, 1988), 314–15, argues that Aristotle's infallibilist view of sense awareness cannot be reconciled with his other views about dialectical method and perceptual realism. Accordingly, Irwin reads *Metaph.,* IV, 5, 1010b14–25 as a more appropriate defense of the infallibility of what "appears" to the percipient and not of the senses vis-à-vis empirical things. For an elaborate discussion of Aristotle's distinction between proper and common *sensibilia,* see Andreas Graeser, "On Aristotle's Framework of Sensibilia," in *Aristotle on Mind and the Senses,* 69–97.

216. See *EN,* VI, 5, 1141a2–3.

217. For arguments that all basic ostensive statements about the empirical world can be justified by *fallible* intuitions, but not the de facto contradictory statements about alleged moral or religious intuitions, see Anthony Quinton, *The Nature of Things* (London and Boston: Routledge & Kegan Paul, 1973), 119–42. Contrariwise, see Mark Platts, "Moral Reality," in *Essays in Moral Realism,* ed. Geoffrey Sayre-McCord (Ithaca, N.Y.: Cornell University Press, 1988), 282–300, for arguments in favor of a "pluralistic" form of ethical intuitionism that allows for moral conflicts. For an overall "Cartesian" defense of noninferential or intuitive

Aristotelian *perceptual* analogy. In the Aristotelian context, where the character and ends of a rightly habituated moral agent are highlighted, moral goodness and badness can hardly be regarded, in accordance with the views of some contemporary intuitionists, as "nonnatural properties." But if they are to be considered natural properties of actions and persons, they are more plausibly regarded not as directly perceived qualities but as supervenient properties that, in conjunction with some underlying perceptual qualities, can only be known intellectually, whether through intuition or, more plausibly, *practical* judgment.[218]

Nonetheless, in its own context, Aristotle's perceptual metaphor cannot be discarded: while providing an independent basis for moral judgments, it connects (by analogy) the operation of *nous* in the practical sphere with the normative intellectual pattern of experience, induction, and insight in the natural sciences. Aristotelian intuitions or insights, whether in the natural sciences or in ethics, are not a priori. In short, without sensible experience, there can be no *phronesis*.

Nous, or at least the exercise of *nous*, makes its appearance at a certain stage in the life of a man or a woman. Aristotle refers to the truth contained in the undemonstrated sayings of old folks. Since induction depends upon experience, it is understandable that the sayings of old folks contain much truth: experience enables them to see things correctly.[219]

There is an obvious problem, however, about making all of our moral principles dependent upon inductive insight into our experience. What if our experience is morally defective or perverse? If it is, then what we can induce from our experience will be similarly defective or perverse. In the formation of the moral agent's outlook, inductive insight leading to the explicit formulation of universal moral principles comes relatively late on the scene; unlike mathematical insights, moral insights presuppose that the agent has habits and because of these habits considerable experience of pursuing and avoiding certain ends. By inducing the universal from the singular, the agent is able to en-

---

knowledge of self-evident "fundamental ethical propositions," see Panayot Butchvarov, *Skepticism in Ethics* (Bloomington: Indiana University Press, 1989).

218. See Henry Veatch, *For an Ontology of Morals: A Critique of Contemporary Ethical Theory* (Evanston, Ill.: Northwestern University Press, 1971), 108–10. On the logical puzzles connected with the notion of supervenient properties, see Simon Blackburn, "Supervenience Revisited," in ed. Sayre-McCord, *Essays in Moral Realism*, 59–75; and Robert L. Arrington, *Rationalism, Realism, and Relativism: Perspectives in Contemporary Moral Epistemology* (Ithaca, N.Y.: Cornell University Press, 1989), 142–52.

219. See *EN*, VI, 11, 1143b12–14.

shrine these habitual ends in explicitly stated principles. But, in the ordinary course of life, the agent's goals or ends are first set, rightly or wrongly, by his or her education, his or her habituation in pleasure and pain.[220] Our ends, then, appear good or bad according to our character.[221] Accordingly, induction discerns the patterns set by our character but it does not set our character.[222]

Induction presupposes the pattern of the agent's actions.[223] Of course, the *phronimos* transcends unthinking habit; he has insight into what he does and the insight can be enshrined in moral principles. But knowing what one is doing is not the same as knowing that what one is doing is morally good. Inductive insight does not enable the moral agent to rise above his prerational habituation about what seems good and bad and to make judgments about what actually is good or bad.[224] Aristotle says comfortingly that for the truly good man, what seems good is actually good.[225] Aquinas repeats Aristotle's tenet but explains further that the good man *"sees"* what is true in singular actions because his moral virtues provide him with the right comprehension of the end.[226] But this familiar doctrine, again, makes practical reason dependent on moral virtue: the first principles for the ordinary moral

220. See *EN*, II, 3; VI, 12, 1144a30-37; VII, 8, 1151a15-20.

221. See *EN*, III, 5, 1114b1-3.

222. See *EN*, I, 4, 1095b5-10.

223. Michelakis, in *Aristotle's Theory*, 18, reports that, according to Maier, "... ἐθισμός results from a repeated application of ἐπαγωγή." But this assertion, as Michelakis recognizes, is a mistake. Induction presupposes repeated cognition of singulars with something in common. Ἐθισμός is what results from habits; habits result from repetition of actions of a certain type; hence, induction presupposes ἐθισμός: cf. *EN*, II, 1, 1103a31-32; III, 2, 1112a1-3. For his part, Michelakis treats ἐθισμός as an epistemological springboard for knowing moral principles that are somehow grounded independently of the moral agent. Aristotle's point, however, is that an agent's habits ground his or her moral principles because ἐθισμός sets the ends that are the agent's moral principles: αἱ μὲν γὰρ ἀρχαὶ τῶν πρακτῶν τὸ οὗ ἕνεκα τὰ πρακτά (*EN*, VI, 5, 1140b16-17). It is an understatement, therefore, to describe virtue as primarily preserving "a general psychological habituation for understanding" (Michelakis, 20). Virtue has a stronger role, for it preserves the good ends actually being pursued by the agent: see *EN*, VII, 8, 1151a15-16.

224. Cf. Engberg-Pedersen, *Aristotle's Theory*, 218, who claims that *"phronesis* contains a whole body of theory that will provide genuine justification. . . ." But this claim requires Engberg-Pedersen to introduce "three conceptions or levels of moral goodness" (224) into Aristotle's account of *phronesis*.

225. See *EN*, III, 4, 1113a29-30. Cf. *SLE*, III, 10, 1113a25, 59-61 (*In Ethic.*, III, lect. 10 [Spiazzi, n. 493, p. 139]): "Et dicit quod studioso, id est virtuoso, est voluntabile id quod est voluntabile secundum veritatem, id est simpliciter bonum. . . ."

226. See Aquinas, *SLE*, III, 10, 1113a29, 87-89 (*In Ethic.*, III, lect. 10 [Spiazzi, n. 494, p. 139]): "Et hoc plurimum differt studiosus ab aliis quod in singulis operabilibus videt quid vere sit bonum. . . ."; *SLE*, VI, 10, 1144a28, 239-42 (*In Ethic.*, VI, lect.

agent and the *phronimos* are the habitual ends that direct their practical reasoning. In the case of an immoral man, his vicious habits lead him astray. He is reasoning in pursuit of bad ends:

> Vice, the opposite of virtue, perverts the judgment of reason, and causes deception about ends, which practical principles are about. *(SLE, VI, 11, 1144a28, 244–46; In Ethic., VI, lect. 11 [Spiazzi, n. 1274, p. 344])* [227]

In regard to the justification of these good ends, Aristotle's account is vague and incomplete and as it stands unsatisfactory. Moral insight or intuition, although not in any way disconnected from experience or ordinary psychological processes, carries the burden of proof. Old folks, the well-brought-up young men who are suitable students of ethics, and, more importantly, the *phronimos*, have the moral eyes to see things correctly.[228] But they see things correctly because they have been, due to their virtuous habits, pursuing the right ends. We have not escaped that circle that Aquinas finds in Aristotle's text between right reason and habituated right desire. But perhaps Aristotle's *phronimos* does not really fall back, in any way that a contemporary philosopher might find epistemologically odd or interesting, on autonomous moral intuitions.[229] It is frequently charged, after all, that Aristotle uncritically takes for granted the moral worth of the conventional ends enshrined by his own culture. If so, do the "intuitions" of the *phronimos* rest on anything more than his (or Aristotle's) cultural biases? This charge, although Aristotle's attitude about the credibility of universally held moral opinions is less naive than is sometimes supposed,[230] is worth considering.

Aristotle repeats several times that ethical instruction is profitably addressed only to well-brought-up or virtuous men with considerable experience of political life.[231] Presumably these men, because they are well brought up, already have the right opinion about the goodness of the ultimate end to be pursued by the *phronimos*, the life of morally

---

10 [Spiazzi, n. 1274, p. 344]): "Sed quod hoc sit optimum, non apparet nisi bono, id est virtuoso, qui habet rectam existimationem de fine, cum virtus moralis faciat rectam intentionem finis. . . ."

227. ". . . malitia opposita virtuti pervertit iudicium rationis et facit mentiri circa fines, qui sunt [circa] practica principia . . ." *(SLE, VI, 11, 1144a28, 244–46; In Ethic., VI, lect. 11 [Spiazzi, n. 1274, p. 344]).*

228. See *EN*, I, 4, 1095b5–9.

229. See Richardson, "On Broadie," 254.

230. See *EN*, X, 2, 1173a2–3 (rev. Oxford trans.): "For we say that which everyone thinks really is so; and the man who attacks this belief will hardly have anything more credible to maintain instead."

231. See *EN*, I, 4, 1095a1–5; 1095b1–8; VI, 8, 1142a5–23.

virtuous political activity.[232] This presupposition, in any case, helps explain why Aristotle also does not offer any detailed theoretical account of how *nous* enables the *phronimos* to grasp the goodness of those particular actions leading to or constituting this end. The goodness of these particular actions is self-evident in the light of the habituation that governs choices directed toward this end.[233] Any further epistemological investigation of how the goodness of particular actions can be intuited, or any general defense of intuition, would not be germane in the context of the *Nicomachean Ethics* since they are not needed to settle any moral controversy.[234]

We can return now to Aristotle's comparison *(EN,* VII, 8, 1151a15–17) of an agent's habitual ends with the indemonstrable hypotheses of a mathematical demonstration; both sets of hypotheses are "assumed" or taken to be true but not proven.[235] The comparison with mathematical reasoning can be extended to include the initial, unproven definitions of ethics. Thus, it "is well said" that "good" is defined as "that at which all things aim" *(EN,* I, 1, 1094a3). But for human beings, "good" is more properly defined as "happiness" (εὐδαιμονία) or its equivalents "living well" (εὖ ζῆν) or "doing well" (εὖ πράττειν). *"Eudaimonia,"* by definition, is what all men naturally seek. But in what end or ends is happiness really instantiated? Men pursue quite different ends that they assume will make them happy. But these "hypotheses," which are thought to instantiate happiness, are open to dispute. Some ends[236] are not actually morally good.[237]

232. See *EN,* I, 5, 1095b29–31; X, 7, 1178a9–14.

233. See *EN,* III, 1, 1111b4–6; 5, 1113b3–6.

234. See *EN,* I, 6, 1096b30–31.

235. "To assume" (from *ad* + *sumere),* and its derivatives, is the standard English translation of Aristotle's verb λαμβάνειν. The latter has as its primary signification "to take" as do the English and Latin terms. Thus principles and hypotheses can be "assumed" or perhaps "taken for granted" without prejudice to their truth. Cf. *Apo.,* I, 10, 76b33–34: ὅτι δ' ἔστι, τὰς μὲν ἀρχὰς ἀνάγκη λαμβάνειν.

236. In regard to the word "end" Bonitz notes (p. 753, b49) that τὸ τέλος is frequently used as a synonym of τὸ ἀγαθόν, τὸ ἄριστον, and τὸ βέλτιστον. To refer to a morally bad end, Aristotle sometimes uses τὸ σκοπός: see *EN,* VI, 12, 1144a26–27; *Pol.,* VIII, 6, 1341b15. But the usage is not consistent. Aristotle also uses τὸ σκοπός interchangeably with τὸ τέλος *(EE,* I, 2, 1214b7; *Pol.,* 7, 12, 1331b28); in distinction from τὸ τέλος to indicate that the bearing or object of a virtue is τὸ τέλος *(MM,* I, 18, 1190a16); in a morally neutral sense inasmuch as virtue must determine the rightness of τὸν σκοπόν *(EN,* VI, 12, 1144a8); and to refer to an intrinsic condition of virtuous activity *(EN,* VI, 1, 1138b22). Pierre Aubenque, in "La Prudence Aristotélicienne," 46, n. 3, claims that "le mot τέλος n'est jamais employé par Aristote pour désigner une fin *mauvaise.* . . ." But this is erroneous: ἀλλὰ τὸ τέλος ἔθεντο φαῦλον *(Pol.,* VII, 12, 1331b34).

237. See *EE,* I, 2.

The mathematical analogy, therefore, is apt only if we interpret it in the light of Aristotle's distinction between *indemonstrable* and *unproven* hypotheses: the former hypotheses (= mathematical hypotheses) are indemonstrable as such; the latter are hypotheses that are indemonstrable relative to what an individual can prove or has actually proven.[238] "Moral hypotheses" belong to the latter type of hypothesis: people do act without feeling the need to justify, or, in some cases, being able to justify the general ends that they are pursuing. They just assume that attainment of these ends will bring *eudaimonia*.[239]

When talking about how moral agents act, Aristotle does not consider how the ends of action are to be morally justified; he states simply that agents pursue or avoid certain ends that, because they are concomitants of their virtues and vices, are assumed by the same agents to be good or bad.[240] Aristotle's labeling an agent's habitual ends "hypotheses" is congruent with what I refer to as "the narrow view" of Aristotle's notion of deliberation (βούλευσις) and choice (προαίρεσις). Moral hypotheses are relative hypotheses; they are unproven assumptions relative to some individual moral agent. The distinction between the absolute hypotheses of mathematics and the relative hypotheses of moral reasoning becomes clearer when we consider the scientific character of ethics.

5. Is Aristotle's Ethics a "Science"?

Moral and political reasoning embody what Aristotle calls "*phronesis*," which medieval translators rendered as "*prudentia*," although many contemporary English-language translators prefer to translate the Greek term (φρόνησις) by "practical wisdom" rather than "prudence." Whichever translation is favored, Aristotle delineates *phronesis* by comparing it with four other intellectual dispositions or habits (ἕξεις): (1) art (τέχνη), (2) science (ἐπιστήμη), (3) wisdom (σοφία), and

238. See *Apo.*, I, 10, 76b27–29 (rev. Oxford trans.): "Whatever a man assumes without proving it himself although it is provable—if he assumes something that seems to be the case to the learner, he supposes it (and it is a supposition not *simpliciter* [οὐχ ἁπλῶς ὑπόθεσις] but only in relation to the learner). . . ."

239. See *EN*, I, 3, 1095a14–22.

240. Cf. *EN*, VII, 8, 1151a15–19; *SLE*, VII, 8, 1151a11, 126–32 (*In Ethic.*, VII, lect. 8 [Spiazzi, n. 1431, p. 383]): "Sicut enim in mathematicis principia non docentur per rationem, sed statim intellecta creduntur, ita etiam in agibilius fines non docentur per rationem, sed per habitum virtutis sive naturalis sive per assuetudinem acquisitae consequitur rectam aestimationem circa principium agibilium quod est finis."

(4) intellectual intuition or insight (νοῦς).[241] In this text, *"nous"* is not used generally to refer to the intellect as a distinct power of the rational soul, but precisely to refer to the intellectual disposition or habit that cognitively grasps the principles of Aristotelian demonstrative science.[242] Aristotelian theoretical science is grounded in universal, primary, and immediate or indemonstrable principles. *Nous ("intellectus"* in Aquinas's Latin translation) is the intellectual habit that has as its object these primary principles.[243] Because Aristotle contrasts the immediate cognition of *nous* with the mediate or discursive syllogistic attainments of reason, Aquinas explains that the first principles are known through "their own proper terms."[244] Contemporary commentators sometimes refer to these indemonstrable principles that *nous* grasps as "self-evidently" true propositions. But the modern notion of self-evidency, whose connotations are deeply colored by the Cartesian notion of a direct inspection of the contents of a mind methodically severed from the world,[245] can be seriously misleading when applied to Aristotle.[246] Similar reservations, which I shall men-

241. See *EN*, VI, 3, 1139b15–17. *EN*, VI, 5, 1141a5 drops τέχνη; *EN*, VI, 12, 1144a2 reduces these four to two intellectual virtues, σοφία (the virtue of the theoretical intellect) and φρόνησις (the virtue of practical intellect). Cf. Gauthier-Jolif, II, 2: 450–52, 490.

242. See *SLE*, VI, 5 1140b31, 50–54 *(In Ethic.,* VI, lect. 5 [Spiazzi, n. 1179, p. 322]): "Accipitur autem hic intellectus non pro ipsa potentia intellectiva, sed pro habitu quodam quo homo ex virtute luminis intellectus agentis naturaliter cognoscit principia indemonstrabilia."

243. See *EN*, VI, 5, 1141a7–8.

244. See *Apo.*, I, 3, 72b18–25. Cf. *ELP*, I, 7, 72b23, 88–91 (Leonine ed., I, pt. 2, 31b): ". . . ipsa autem principia inmediata non per aliquod medium extrinsecum cognoscuntur, set per cognitionem propriorum terminorum. . . ."

245. For the idealist consequences of this kind of intuition, see David Weissman, *Intuition and Ideality* (Albany: State University of New York Press, 1987).

246. Cf. Martha C. Nussbaum, *The Frailty of Goodness: Luck and Ethics in Greek Tragedy and Philosophy* (Cambridge: Cambridge University Press, 1986), who, drawing on the work of other revisionist scholars (see bibliography n. 27, p. 480), rejects the idea, held "by centuries of commentators" (254), that Aristotelian theoretical sciences require "either intuition or extra-experiential truth" (251). But, if "intuition" is to be thus yoked to "extra-experiential," what Nussbaum rejects is the modern conception of "intuition" that has been read into Aristotle. For a view, which focuses on the primacy of being and which runs counter to Nussbaum's own alternative (but, again, decidedly modern) notion, that the first principles of Aristotelian science have a "Kantian kind of non-hypothetical status" (255), see Owens, *Doctrine of Being,* 285–87; and Thomas V. Upton, "Aristotle on Hypothesis and the Unhypothesized First Principle," *Review of Metaphysics* 39 (1985): 283–301. In a similar vein, Irwin, in *Aristotle's First Principles,* 133, asserts that Aristotle's first principles are self-evident because they must "satisfy a metaphysical realist conception of truth."

tion in the next chapter, apply to the logical characterization of these principles as "analytic principles."

Aristotle's consistent doctrine is that the indemonstrable principles that ground demonstration are known experientially and inductively: the universal must be first apprehended and known through a sensible singular that is a composite of form and matter.[247] Yet these universal, immediate principles are necessary. Thus, contrary to everything that a Humean philosophy might allow, *nous* grasps through sensible experience that necessity which is the hallmark of Aristotelian science.[248] But precisely in regard to the necessity of their ultimate principles, and therefore to the necessity of their conclusions, a major fault line appears to separate the Aristotelian theoretical sciences and the practical science of ethics.

The divide opens in *EN*, VI, 6, 1140b31–1141a8, where Aristotle apparently rejects the possibility of a demonstrative science of ethics. Scientific knowledge is about what is universal, necessary, and invariant (τὰ μὴ ἐνδεχόμενα); hence, it cannot be had of things that vary (τὰ ἐνδεχόμενα), that is, things that are capable of being other than what they are at the moment when they are being observed. Such variable things fall under the scope of opinion (δόξα).[249] The objects of scientific knowledge, however, must be unchanging or necessary, and thus they must also be eternal (1139b22–23). From necessary and eternal things (or from the necessary features of changing things), necessary and universal principles may be inductively attained. This is the case in the three theoretical sciences of physics, mathematics, and metaphysics.[250]

The subjects of these three theoretical sciences are differentiated by their relationship to matter which accounts for the varying degree of exactness attainable in each of the sciences.[251] Physics deals with mov-

---

247. See *Apo.*, II, 19,100a15–b5. Cf. *SLE*, VI, 3, 1139b25, 87–90 (*In Ethic.*, VI, lect. 3 [Spiazzi, n. 1148, p. 315]): "Inductio autem inducitur ad cognoscendum aliquod principium et aliquod universale, in quod devenimus per experimenta singularium . . ."; *ELP*, II, 20, 100a10, 212–13 (quoted in n. 201 above).

248. Cf. the objection against Aristotle, that "perception is incapable of discriminating necessary from contingent truths," raised by Taylor, in "Aristotle's Epistemology," 128.

249. See *Metaph.*, VII, 15, 1039b32–1040a1 (Tredennick trans.): "If, then, the demonstration and definition of necessary truths requires scientific knowledge [ἐπιστημονικόν] . . . So too demonstration and definition cannot vary thus, but it is opinion that deals with that which can be other than as it is [τὸ ἐνδεχομένου]. . . ."

250. See *Metaph.*, VI, 1, 1025b26–1026a20.

251. See *Metaph.*, II, 3, 995a14–17 (rev. Oxford trans.): "The minute accuracy [ἀκριβολογία] of mathematics is not to be demanded in all cases, but only in the

ing things that can be truthfully known only as existing in matter; accordingly, the definitions of natural things, which abstract from singular sensible matter, must make reference to universal sensible matter. But a mathematical definition, though its object exists in matter, truthfully abstracts from universal as well as singular sensible matter; it refers solely to quantity apart from any sensible qualities, or to what both Aristotle and Aquinas call "intelligible matter."[252] Metaphysics treats of beings (or the categories or properties of being) that are (or can be) altogether separated from matter of any kind.[253]

Because the objects of mathematics and metaphysics are known apart from any sensible matter, accounts or explanations in these sciences attain a greater degree of epistemic exactness and accuracy (ἀκριβολογία) than in physics.[254] However, physics, though its definitions of species must include reference to the common sensible matter of the *definienda*, attains a greater degree of exactitude than ethics. Physics is not concerned with knowledge of the singular material thing in the way that ethics does ultimately aim to provide a normative account of the singular action. Ethics is knowledge about the moral virtues so that one can act in a morally virtuous fashion.[255] But every action is a singular which, because intellect cannot grasp its determinate particular matter, cannot be exactly described or de-

---

case of things which have no matter. Therefore its method is not that of natural science; for presumably all nature has matter."

252. See *Metaph.*, VI, 1, 1025b30–34 (rev. Oxford trans.): "Of things defined, i.e., of essences, some are like snub, and some like concave. And these differ because snub is bound up with matter . . . while concavity is independent of perceptible matter [ἄνευ ὕλης αἰσθητῆς]; *Metaph.*, VII, 10, 1036a9–12 (rev. Oxford trans.): "And some matter is sensible [αἰσθητή] and some intelligible [νοητή] . . . intelligible matter being that which is present . . . in the objects of mathematics." Cf. *In Phys.*, II, lect. 3 (Maggiòlo, n. 161, p. 83): "Potest igitur intelligi quantitas sine materia subiecta motui et qualitatibus sensibilibus . . . non autem a materia intelligibili . . ."; *In Metaph.*, VI, lect. 1 (Cathala-Spiazzi, n. 1161, p. 297): "In hoc ergo differt mathematica a physica, quia physica considerat ea quorum definitiones sunt cum materia sensibili. . . . Mathematica vero considerat ea, quorum definitiones sunt sine materia sensibili"; VII, lect. 9 (n. 1468, p. 358): ". . . res naturales habent in sui definitione materiam sensibilem, et in hoc differunt a mathematicis"; (n. 1470, p. 359): ". . . materia sensibilis in communi est ratio speciei."

253. See *In Phys.*, I, lect.1 (Maggiòlo, nn. 1–2, p. 3); *In Metaph.*, XI, lect. 7 (Cathala-Spiazzi, n. 2264, p. 536).

254. See *Metaph.*, II, 3, 995a14–17 (quoted n. 251 above); *In Metaph.*, II, lect. 5 (Cathala-Spiazzi, n. 336, p. 94): "Et quia tota natura est circa materiam, ideo iste modus certissimae rationis non pertinet ad naturalem philosophum." Cf. *Metaph.*, XI, 7, 1064b5–6 (rev. Oxford trans.): ". . . each [of the three theoretical] sciences is called better or worse in virtue of its proper object."

255. See *EN*, II, 2, 1103b26–31; X, 9, 1179a35–b2.

fined.[256] (The singular, as such, is grasped only through sense and imagination.) Thus ethics remains an inexact science given its practical goal: an account or explanation of what singular action must be done.

"Scientific propositions" are, by Aristotle's stringent criteria, universal and necessary propositions. But a universal and necessary proposition can only be demonstrated by valid syllogistic inference from universal and necessary premises. Such premises, in turn, must be ultimately derived from universal and necessary indemonstrable principles.[257] Aquinas sums up, very accurately, Aristotle's stringent conception of a scientific demonstration: the demonstrative syllogism goes from necessary premises to necessary conclusions.[258]

Demonstrative sciences treat things that are eternal and unchanging,[259] and scientific demonstrations start from necessary premises that generate necessary conclusions.[260] Since necessary universal principles are inductively derived from what is universal and necessary in things, the Aristotelian stringent criteria for "science" entail, in reverse order, that only universal and necessary things can be the objects of scientific demonstration.[261] Because *phronesis* is focused on contingent, singular actions, Aristotle assigns it to that power of the rational soul that is defined in terms of contingent and varying objects: *phronesis* is a good disposition or virtuous habit of the calculative faculty (τὸ λογιστικόν).[262] But this classification of *phronesis* also undermines the scientific character of ethics. Ethics, to the extent that it depends upon *phronesis*, cannot attain the status of a science if *phronesis* focuses exclusively on contingent, singular actions (1140b2–3). Singular, contingent things fall outside the domain of scientific knowledge.[263] Aquinas puts the point about *phronesis* forcefully:

256. See *Metaph.*, VII, 10, 1035b34–1036a5: ὁ δὲ λόγος ἐστὶ τοῦ καθόλου . . . τῶν καθ᾽ ἕκαστά τινος ἢ αἰσθετοῦ ἢ νοητοῦ . . . τούτων δὲ οὐκ ἔστιν ὁρισμός. . . .

257. See *Apo.*, I, 4, 73a24; 5, 74a5.

258. See *SLE*, VI, 3, 1139b25, 100–101 (*In Ethic.*, VI, lect. 3 [Spiazzi, n. 1148, p. 315]): ". . . [syllogismus] demonstrativus, qui ex necessariis necessaria concludit."

259. See *EN*, VI, 3, 1139b22–24.

260. See *Apo.*, I, 6, 74b5 (rev. Oxford trans.): ". . . demonstrative understanding depends on necessary principles . . ."; 75a11–13 (rev. Oxford trans.): ". . . if a man understands demonstratively . . . it is clear that he must have his demonstration through a middle term that is necessary too. . . ."

261. See *EN*, VI, 3, 1139b23.

262. See *EN*, VI, 1, 1139a12–16.

263. Cf. *EN*, VI, 3, 1139b21–22 (rev. Oxford trans.): ". . . of things capable of being otherwise we do not know, when they have passed outside our observation, whether they exist or not"; *SLE*, VI, 3, 1139b18, 60–62 (*In Ethic.*, VI, lect. 3 [Spiazzi,

Prudence deals with the ultimate point, that which is singular, because that which is able to be done is [a] singular. Thus it is clear that prudence is not science. *(SLE,* VI, 7, 1142a23, 226–30; *In Ethic.,* VI, lect. 7 [Spiazzi, n. 1213, p. 331])[264]

Aristotle himself acknowledges that it is just this requirement for a necessary and universal object (from which a necessary universal proposition can be inductively grasped) that ethics is unable to meet. Neither *phronesis* nor art can inductively grasp necessary universal principles because they are always dealing "with things that can be otherwise,"[265] that is, contingent actions and products. How, though, are we to reconcile the present characterization of the domain of *phronesis* with the expanded portrait of the *phronimos?* According to the latter, *phronesis* brings cognitive certitude about what is morally good and bad. But what kind of moral knowledge can the *phronimos* acquire if *phronesis* is restricted to contingent singulars?

Aristotle makes the notorious admission that general accounts of "matters concerned with conduct and questions of what is good for us," especially as they bear on the moral evaluation of particular cases, "have no fixity, any more than matters of health."[266] They "have nothing fixed" (οὐδὲν ἑστηκὸς ἔχει), we are told, because the object of a moral judgment, the singular action, sometimes fluctuates in its moral goodness. The fluctuation is so pervasive that some people (mistakenly) conclude that we can only use conventional standards (νόμοι) to identify what is good (τὰ καλά) and just (τὰ δίκαια).[267] The fluctuating subject matter of our moral judgments is the source of the fluctuation in our moral principles.[268] These principles or basic moral propositions fluctuate in regard to their being true. They are true only "for the most part" (ὡς ἐπὶ τὸ πολύ),[269] which means, strictly speaking, they are sometimes false when stated as fixed principles.

---

n. 1145, p. 315]): ". . . Sed quando [contingentia] fiunt extra speculari, id est quando desinunt videri vel sentiri, tunc latent utrum sint vel non sint. . . ."

264. ". . . prudentia autem extremi, id est singularis, quia est operabilis quod est singulare. Et sic patet, quod prudentia non est scientia" *(SLE,* VI, 7, 1142a23, 226–30; *In Ethic.,* VI, lect. 7 [Spiazzi, n. 1213, p. 331]).

265. *EN,* VI, 4, 1140a1–2 (rev. Oxford trans.). Cf. *SLE,* VI, 5, 1140b31, 27–32; *(In Ethic.,* VI, lect. 5 [Spiazzi, n. 1177, p. 322]): ". . . prima autem demonstrationum non sunt demonstrabilia. . . . Quod autem non sit horum principiorum ars vel prudentia, patet per hoc quod hae duae virtutes sunt circa ea quae contingit aliter se habere. . . ."

266. *EN,* II, 2, 1104a3–5 (rev. Oxford trans.).

267. See *EN,* I, 3, 1094b14–16.

268. See *EN,* I, 3, 1094b19–21; 7, 1098a25–29.

269. *EN,* I, 3, 1094b21.

A fixed moral principle is one that is universally true or exceptionless; it covers every member of a class of actions.[270] Aristotle means to
distinguish (though not always unhesitatingly) between fixed negative
and fixed positive moral principles. His treatment of universal negative
precepts rests on the generic consideration of actions. There are exceptionless universal *prohibitions* that fixedly forbid, even at the price of a
terrible death, certain action-types, no matter what the extenuating
circumstances of their action-tokens. Thus any further possible dis-
crimination among the singular actions of the proscribed class is morally irrelevant and out of bounds. Under no further (narrowing) description can adultery, murder, and thievery be considered morally good and
praiseworthy. It is always wrong to commit such actions *(EN, II, 6,
1107a14–15)* even if we mitigate our moral condemnation of someone
forced by humanly unendurable threats to do them.[271]

In regard to a positive moral principle, the action-type that falls
under it is less determinately fixed. There are no exceptionless positive
principles enjoining actions that, in a generically fixed way, are always
morally good. Aristotle allows that positive principles, by reference to
the morally relevant features of subsets of particular actions falling
under the principle, can be indefinitely narrowed in scope. That is,
there are always more narrow action-types that prove to be exceptions
to the principle drawn more widely.

For Aristotle, the difficulty is that no fixed *positive* principle can
anticipate or reach down with sufficient precision or exactitude to the
contingently determinate, singular actions that here and now are the
object or target of moral judgments.[272] This is so because it is impossible to give an exact account of a singular action. Although prima facie
they are tokens of the same type, singular actions within a class, because of their contingently determinate matter, are not necessarily
informed by the ethical universal, and hence it is impossible to frame
universally true or fixed propositions about them.[273] Law sheds light on

270. See *Apo.*, I, 4, 73b26–28; II, 12, 96a8–10.
271. See *EN*, III, 1, 1110a19–b1. Aristotle, nonetheless, betrays some hesitation
(cf. 1110a26–27): some acts we *perhaps* (ἴσως) should never allow ourselves to be
forced to do. But does this mean that we should never murder or never murder (like
Euripides's Alcmaeon) our *mother*?
272. Cf. *Pol.*, II, 8, 1269a11–12 which poses the problem in terms of the universality of written laws vis-à-vis singular actions: καθόλου γὰρ ἀναγκαῖον γραφῆναι,
αἱ δὲ πράξεις περὶ τῶν καθ᾽ ἕκαστόν εἰσιν. In some instances, then, the laws need to
be changed (1269a12–13).
273. See *EN*, V, 10, 1137b19. For the biological background to the notion of
matter being resistant to form, see Reeve, *Practices of Reason*, 17–22.

morality. In regard to particular cases, the universal laws of legal justice (νόμοι) are defective because of their very universality; they always need to be rectified by equity (τὸ ἐπιεικές), that is, by the particular judgments of the equitable man.[274]

Principles such as "Honor your father and mother above all others," "Do not break off relations with your friends," "Return borrowed property," and the like are not, Aristotle remarks, always universally true or exceptionless principles;[275] they, and presumably all of the other conventional moral principles like them, do not cover every particular instance when we are called upon to choose some action. Which conventional moral principles should be regarded as holding only "for the most part"? Aristotle does not give a list of which actions should *always* (as distinguished from a few actions that he claims should *never*) be chosen. A list of what one should always do, for example, "Always tell the truth," would be futile; justified deviations from such (allegedly universal) positive principles depend upon our "perception" of the particular facts. But the issue is left conceptually murky and perhaps morally ambiguous.[276] Aristotle merely hints that exceptionally noble ends as well as exceptionally painful consequences can sometimes justify deviations from our positive moral principles.[277]

Aristotle's general viewpoint, however, is not ambiguous. Under an indefinite number of morally relevant particular circumstances, each of our positive moral principles, however more and more narrowly specified to cover already discovered exceptions, will prove to have further exceptions.[278] Sometimes it may, indeed, be more important, or noble, or morally necessary to give money to a friend than to repay a loan to a creditor. Most of the time, but not always, the normative proposition that "One ought to return borrowed property" is true and holds, but not if the owner of the borrowed knife has become crazed and is bent on stabbing someone as soon as you return the knife. But if there are no exceptionless positive moral principles, that is, no principles that enjoin all the singular action-tokens that apparently belong to

274. See *EN*, V, 10, 1137b26–30.

275. See *EN*, IX, 2–3.

276. Aquinas glosses over the Aristotelian question of when we should put aside our positive moral principles. While noting that *"particulares sermones"* are more *"efficaciores"* in guiding particular actions, Aquinas makes what in this context is the misleading claim that they are also "veriores quia accipiuntur secundum id in quo universales sermones verificantur" *(SLE, II, 8, 1107a28, 23–25; In Ethic.,* II, lect. 8 [Spiazzi, n. 334, p. 95]).

277. See *EN*, II, 9,1109b14–22; III, 1, 1110a29–b1.

278. See *EN*, I, 10, 1101a24–28; *Rh.,* I, 13, 1374a30–35.

the same action-type, moral insight must actually grasp something that proves to be logically more restricted than the unconditional universal that necessarily "belongs to its subject in every case."[279]

Aristotle thinks that moral insight usually results in a general normative proposition, that is, one that holds only "for the most part" (ὡς ἐπὶ τὸ πολύ). However, a general proposition, which applies only to most of the members of a class, fits comfortably enough with Aristotle's vaguer definition of a "universal" (καθόλου) as "that which is by its nature predicated of a number of things" (Int., 7, 17a39-40 [rev. Oxford trans.]).[280] This definition is vague inasmuch as it does not specify that a universal entails a universally quantified proposition of the form "All Fs are necessarily x." Positive moral principles, like the laws enacted by legislatures, cover only the great *majority* of apparently similar cases, that is, cases that, apart from some distinguishing contingent feature, would otherwise be similar to all the members of the same (larger) class.[281] *For the most part*, one ought to repay one's debts before endowing one's friends, honor one's father before all others, and return borrowed property. But not always.

General moral principles, although they nearly always hold, have exceptions; they do not—unlike universal principles—unconditionally bind moral agents who must make particular moral judgments. Aristotle describes in metaphorical terms the inherent problem of universal moral principles. A universal moral principle is like a rigid rule or a measure that sometimes is too rigid to be useful. Moral philosophers should look to the builders on the isle of Lesbos; they measure by using a leaden rule that can be bent to the shape of a particular uneven stone. Like this flexible leaden rule, general (as opposed to universal) moral principles can be understood flexibly, that is, as holding only "for the most part." To apply a general moral principle flexibly is to know when it does not apply. In such cases, the principle is "bent" to the shape of the singular or particular action, that is, to the particular judgment of the moral agent who finds this action to be an exception to the principle.[282]

Stated less metaphorically, a general moral principle is too inexact to be applied truthfully to those actions that are exceptions to the

---

279. See *Apo.*, I, 4, 73b26-27: καθόλου δὲ λέγω ὃ ἂν κατὰ παντός τε ὑπάρχῃ καὶ καθ' αὐτὸ καὶ ᾗ αὐτό.

280. λέγω δὲ καθόλου μὲν ὃ ἐπὶ πλειόνων πέφυκε κατηγορεῖσθαι (*Int.*, 7, 17a39-40).

281. See *EN*, V, 10, 1137b13-17.

282. See *EN*, II, 7, 1107a28-32; V, 10, 1137b29-32.

principle. A particular action as particular is contingently determinate. Of course, both universal and general moral principles can be given further and further specification. But the process of specifying narrower and narrower moral principles, by making morally relevant subdivisions among the members of a larger class of actions, is endless. The contingent but morally significant features that account for the actual moral character of singular actions are potentially infinite, and therefore all the morally relevant subdivisions of a general (positive) principle can never be exhaustively specified.[283] This has led some interpreters to emphasize what they call Aristotelian "particularism."

For Aristotle, knowing whether any moral principle is relevant to a particular case (i.e., knowing whether this action falls under a given principle) requires a quasi-perceptual judgment about the actual moral character of the singular action.[284] Making correct moral judgments about singular actions is more like the application of an empirically acquired medical skill than deducing conclusions from the universal principles of the art or science of medicine.[285] In medicine, it is the individual man who must be cured; in morality, the singular action must be pursued or avoided. In both cases, skill in applying general principles has a perceptual basis and can only be acquired from experience.[286]

Yet Aristotle recognizes that in stressing the importance of the experiential knowledge of the singular action, the reach of moral principles is also being shortened. Making moral judgments, by the standards of a demonstrative science, is an imprecise business: such judgments must focus on contingent singular actions that do not neatly fall under general principles. The more tailored our judgments are to the particulars, the better and more true they are: particular judgments, which often can be exceptions to general principles, are more likely to correspond to the actual moral character of the singular actions that are the objects of our ongoing deliberations and prospective choices.[287] Aristotle, accordingly, deflates the "science" of ethics. Since general positive moral

283. See *Metaph.*, III, 4, 999a26–28 (on the impossibility of knowing singular things that are potentially infinite in number); *EN*, I, 11, 1101a24–28 (on the moral relevance of individual differences); *Rh.*, I, 13, 1374a29–33 (on the impossibility of making universal laws to cover all the morally different individual cases).

284. See *EN*, IV, 5, 1126b2–4.

285. See *EN*, X, 9, 1180b7–9. Cf. Daniel T. Devereux, "Particular and Universal in Aristotle's Conception of Practical Knowledge," *Review of Metaphysics* 39 (1986): 483–504.

286. See *Metaph.*, I, 1, 981a24; *EN*, X, 9, 1181a2–1181b7.

287. See *EN*, II, 7, 1107a29–32.

principles, however usually correct, cannot secure the knowledge of the moral character of singular actions, ethics, which above all is a practical science aimed at enabling agents to act,[288] can at best be put in outline form. Experience fills in the outline: it allows the moral agent to develop his or her quasi-perceptual skill in sizing up individual cases and in applying and disregarding general principles aptly.[289]

Aquinas was fully aware of the implications of Aristotle's own view: according to the stringent Aristotelian criteria, ethics is not a "science." Aristotle, it is true, understands that both physics and ethics treat changing, contingent things. Yet the two cases are not exactly parallel. In a much stricter sense of the term, physics is possible as a "science."[290] Natural things, though contingent, because they are subject to physical generation and corruption, do have necessary and universal principles (i.e., matter, form, and privation) that apply to all mobile beings qua mobile.[291] Physics deals with enmattered things but considers them only insofar as they have universal sensible matter. But ethics is a practical "science" dealing, unlike physics, with "contingents insofar as they are contingents, that is, particulars."[292] Aquinas thus decisively separates the subject matter of Aristotelian ethics from the necessity inherent in the cognitive objects of physics as well as metaphysics and mathematics. By reason of the radical contingency of the precise object of moral judgment, the goodness and badness of the *singular* action, the moral philosopher cannot induce or apply necessary or exceptionless (positive) principles.

Moral philosophers may continue, of course, to fashion formally valid syllogistic deductions by stating their general principles in the form of universally quantified propositions, but ethics cannot be, speaking strictly, a demonstrative science.[293] From moral principles

288. See *EN*, I, 3, 1095a5–6.

289. On the need for experience in relationship to practical wisdom, see *EN*, VI, 8, 1142a12–16.

290. See *Phys.*, II, 3, 194b15–23. Cf. *In Phys.*, II, lect. 5 (Maggiòlo, n. 176, pp. 91–92): ". . . hoc negotium quo intendimus de natura tractare, non ordinatur ad operationem, sed ad scientiam: quia nos non possumus facere res naturales, sed solum de eis scientiam habere."

291. See *Phys.*, I, 7.

292. See *EN*, VI, 3, 1139b22–23; 4, 1140a1–2 (rev. Oxford trans.): ". . . the object of knowledge [τὸ ἐπιστητόν] is of necessity [ἐξ ἀνάγκης]. . . . Among things that can be otherwise [τοῦ δ' ἐνδεχομένου] are included both things made and things done [πρακτόν]. . . ." Cf. *SLE*, VI, 3, 1140a1, 154–56; *In Ethic.*, VI, lect. 3 (Spiazzi, n. 1152, p. 316): "Unde et solae scientiae practicae sunt circa contingentia in quantum contingentia sunt, scilicet in particulari. . . ."

293. See *EN*, VI, 5, 1140a33–34 (rev. Oxford trans.): ". . . there is no demonstra-

that the moral philosopher knows to hold "only for the most part," no necessary conclusions follow. Aquinas accurately repeats this standard Aristotelian doctrine about the demonstrative or scientific syllogism:[294]

> It is not possible to demonstrate from principles that are contingent, since everything that follows from those principles could be otherwise. *(SLE*, VI, 4, 1140a31, 53–57; *In Ethic.*, VI, lect. 4 [Spiazzi, n. 1164, p. 319])[295]

Yet contingent actions, although not objects of scientific knowledge in the strict sense, do remain intelligible in the Aristotelian context. Aquinas, however, does not accept Aristotle's explanation of how we know contingent actions: he repudiates the Aristotelian division *(EN,* VI, 1, 1139a5–12) of the rational soul into two parts, the scientific (τὸ ἐπιστημονικόν) which bears on necessary things, and the calculative (τὸ λογιστικόν) which bears on contingent things.[296] Aquinas instead argues that the same intellectual power extends to both necessary and contingent beings since the intellect extends universally to "that which is."[297]

According to Aquinas, Aristotle's division is mistaken because it conflates contingency and particularity whereas the two should be distinguished. Aquinas holds that it is possible to have scientific knowledge of contingent things but not qua particular. In Aquinas's precise terms, one must distinguish the scientific *"universales rationes immutabiles"* of contingent things from the non-scientific *"intentiones particulares"* of contingent things. Physics rests on the "immutable, uni-

tion of things whose first principles might be otherwise. . . ." Cf. *SLE*, VI, 3, 1139b25, 98–101 *(In Ethic.*, VI, lect. 3 [Spiazzi, n. 1148, p. 315]): "Non autem quilibet syllogismus est disciplinalis, quasi faciens scire, sed solus demonstrativus qui ex necessariis necessaria concludit."

294. Cf. *EN*, VI, 5, 1140a34–35 (rev. Oxford trans.): ". . . there is no demonstration of things whose first can be otherwise (for all such things might actually be otherwise)"; *SLE*, VI, 3, 1139b18, 56–58 *(In Ethic.*, VI, lect. 3 [Spiazzi, n. 1145, p. 315]): "Huiusmodi autem certitudo, quod scilicet non possit aliter esse, non potest haberi circa contingentia aliter se habere"; *SLE*, VI, 3, 1140a1, 144–46 *(In Ethic.*, VI, lect. 3 [Spiazzi, n. 1152, p. 316]]): ". . . contingentium cognitio non potest habere certitudinem veritatis repellentem falsitatem. . . ."

295. ". . . demonstratio non potest esse de his quorum principia contingit se aliter habere, quia si principia possunt aliter se habere, omnia quae ex principiis illis consequuntur possunt aliter se habere . . ." *(SLE*, VI, 4, 1140a31, 53–57; *In Ethic.*, VI, lect. 4 [Spiazzi, n. 1164, p. 319]).

296. See *SLE*, VI, 1, 1139a11, 203–10 *(In Ethic.*, VI, lect. 1 [Spiazzi, n. 1123, p. 307]).

297. See *SLE*, VI, 1, 1139a11, 183–84 *(In Ethic.*, VI, lect. 1 [Spiazzi, n. 1122, p. 307]): "Obiectum autem intellectus proprium est quod quid est."

versal concepts" of contingent and changing beings.[298] But intellectual knowledge of a contingent being qua particular must be mediated by a sensible power, albeit a sensible power with a peculiar affinity and proximity to reason, the *ratio particularis* or *vis cogitativa*.[299] And it is on this sensible power that we rely when we deliberate about and choose singular actions.[300]

Aristotle's analysis of action highlights deliberation about and choice of particulars. The efficient cause of a singular action is a choice on the part of the agent.[301] Human choices, however, are contingent; the "same" action could have been otherwise, that is, it could have had a different moral character.[302] Aristotle draws attention to the motive of the agent. The actual moral character of a singular action depends upon the motive of the agent.[303] Accordingly, two men can perform conventionally courageous acts. But the courage of the courageous man must be distinguished from the courage of the profligate man who is motivated by lust and not honor. The bold acts of the profligate man are not genuinely courageous acts however they appear to an external observer.[304]

The contingency of the moral character of singular actions, which embodies contingent human choices, helps explain the inexactitude of ethics, or why moral principles apply only "for the most part." Aquinas explains:

> For the principle of the active sciences is in the agent, not in his actions or in his morals. This principle is 'prohairesis,' that is, 'electio.' For what can be done is the same as what can be chosen. (*In Meta.*, VI, lect. 1 [Cathala-Spiazzi, n. 1154, p. 296])[305]

---

298. See *SLE*, VI, 3, 1139b18, 68–73 (*In Ethic.*, VI, lect. 3 [Spiazzi, n. 1146, p. 315]): "Potest autem et de generabilibus et corruptibilibus esse aliqua scientia, puta naturalis; non tamen secundum particularia quae generationi et corruptioni subduntur, sed secundum rationes universales quae sunt ex necessitate et semper."

299. See *ST*, I, q. 78, a. 4, ad 5.

300. Cf. *SLE*, VI, 4, 1140a31, 65–68 (*In Ethic.*, VI, lect. 4 [Spiazzi, n. 1165, p. 319]): ". . . quod agibilia de quibus est consilium et circa quae est prudentia, contingit aliter se habere, et circa talia non est scientia."

301. See *EN*, III, 1, 1110a17–18; VI, 2, 1139a31–32.

302. This Aristotelian observation, refined as the distinction between the *finis operantis* and *finis operis* (or, equivalently, between the object of the interior and the exterior act of the will), becomes central in the Thomistic theory of moral evaluation: see *ST*, I–II, q. 18, a. 6.

303. Cf. *ST*, I–II, q. 18, a. 4 which treats of the fourfold goodness or badness of an action: ontological, generic, circumstantial, and particular. The last depends upon the agent's particular end or motive.

304. See *EN*, III, 8, 1117a1–2.

305. "Nam principium activarum scientiarum est in agente, non in ipsis action-

Aquinas, however, is prepared to move ethics closer to physics. His commentary leaves open, purposely, whether ethics, like physics, might not also have a knowledge of actions at the generic level (i.e., qua contingent but not qua singular) that would allow exceptionless *positive* moral principles. But Aquinas is eager to draw a parallel between theoretical and practical reason, both of which, he maintains, ground quasi-innate, *necessary*, universal principles.[306]

Nonetheless, Aristotle's positive moral principles remain grounded in singular contingent actions. Since the principles that can be drawn from these actions are only true "for the most part," the conclusions of moral arguments, even when the arguments are put in syllogistic form, fall outside the scope of scientific demonstration strictly defined. Aristotelian ethics therefore cannot be assimilated to the model of Aristotelian physics.

It is widely recognized, however, that Aristotle allows a less stringent notion of demonstrative science. He relaxes the criterion that "[demonstrative] knowledge is belief about things that are universal and necessary."[307] There can be, of course, no science about things that are radically fortuitous or merely accidental.[308] But there can be sciences whose principles and conclusions hold "for the most part," that is, with comparatively rare exceptions.[309] This latter description exactly fits the principles and conclusions of ethics which are about contingent actions. Since ethics is a practical and not a theoretical science, it is especially appropriate to relax the criterion. So too moral hypotheses are not exactly like strict scientific hypotheses. Whereas the theoretical hypotheses of mathematics and the other sciences need not and cannot be proven because they are absolutely indemonstrable,[310] moral

---

ibus, sive moribus. Hoc autem principium 'est prohaeresis' idest electio. Idem enim est agibile et eligibile" (*In Metaph.*, VI, lect 1 [Cathala-Spiazzi, n. 1154, p. 296]).

306. See *SLE*, VI, 2, 1139a27, 134–38 (*In Ethic.*, VI, lect. 2 [Spiazzi, n. 1132, pp. 310–11]): "Dicendum est ergo quod intellectus practicus principium quidem habet in universali consideratione et secundum hoc est idem subiecto cum speculativis, sed terminetur eius consideratio in particulari operabili."

307. *EN*, VI, 6, 1140b31 (rev. Oxford trans.).

308. On the accidental (τὸ δὲ συμβεβηκός) as contrary to what is always (ἀεί) or to what is for the most part (ὡς ἐπὶ τὸ πολύ), see *Metaph.*, VII, 2, 1027a25–28. Cf. XI, 8, 1065a4–6.

309. See *Metaph.*, VI, 2, 1027a20–21 (rev. Oxford trans.): ". . . for all science [ἐπιστήμη] is either that which is always or of that which is for the most part." Cf. *Apo.*, I, 30, 87b19–22; II, 12, 96a17–19. The contrary to "what holds for the most part" = the "comparatively rare": see *Top.*, II, 6, 112b10–11 (rev. Oxford trans.).

310. See *Apo.*, I, 9, 76a16–17; 20.

311. See *EN*, X, 9, 1180b, 20–23 (rev. Oxford trans.): ". . . if a man does wish to

hypotheses are agent-relative. As "the narrow view" of deliberation and choice makes evident, the ordinary moral agent takes for granted the ends that he is pursuing; he does not attempt to demonstrate their truth or goodness. But this is not to deny that the demonstration could be and needs to be supplied by the moral philosopher who seeks scientific knowledge of the universal.[311]

---

become master of an art or science he must go to the universal [τὸ καθόλου], and come to know it as well as possible; for . . . it is with this that the sciences are concerned."

V

Aristotle: Deliberation and Choice

1. *"The Narrow View"*

In modern scholarship, what I have been calling the "narrow view" of Aristotelian practical reason was prominently expounded in the nineteenth century by Walter, popularized at the beginning of the twentieth century by Burnet, and more recently defended by Aubenque.[1] According to the narrow view, deliberation (βούλευσις) and choice (προαίρεσις), and consequently practical wisdom (φρόνησις), the virtue of practical reason of which deliberation and choice are constituent psychological acts, are not, at least in the *Nicomachean Ethics*, about the ends of human action but are all exclusively about means to such ends.[2] True, the narrow view has been dismissed as a total misunderstanding of the Aristotelian doctrine of *phronesis*.[3] Yet Aristotle's texts, those in which he explicitly defines the scope of *phronesis*, and confines it to correct deliberation and choice about means, do generate a problem that can perhaps be resolved but not peremptorily dismissed.[4] Despite these restrictive texts, how can practical wisdom fail to include deliberation and choice about the ends of action?

1. See Walter, *Die Lehre von der praktischen Vernunft*, 470–72; Burnet, *Ethics of Aristotle*, 227, nn. 7, 17; Aubenque, *La Prudence*, 122: "Ce qui frappe ici, c'est l'absence de toute référence à la fin (dont la visée est certes présupposée par le choix, mais ne le constitue pas). . . . "

2. See *EN*, III, 3, 1112b12–13 (βούλευσις); 1111b27 (προαίρεσις); VI, 12, 1144a8–9 (φρόνησις). See *EE*, II, 10; *MM*, I, 17, 1189a1–b25. Cf. *EE*, I, 2, 1214b7–11 which clearly allows for *choice* of ends.

3. See Gauthier-Jolif, II, 2:576–77.

4. See *EN*, VI, 13, 1145a4–6: "Choice will not be right without practical wisdom any more than without virtue: the [latter] makes one do the end; the [former] makes

Aristotle contrasts *(EN,* III, 5, 1113b3–4) both "deliberation" (βού-λευσις) and "choice" (προαίρεσις) with "wish" (βούλησις). The contrast drawn is dichotomous: we wish about but we do not deliberate about or choose the end (τὸ τέλος); we deliberate about and choose but we do not wish about the means to the end (τὰ πρὸς τὸ τέλος).[5] Aristotle never explicitly rejects this dichotomy between means and ends which leaves deliberation and choice exclusively focused on "means."[6] But it is important to note that Aristotle allows that deliberation can be either about those means that pertain to the unconditioned or ultimate end (πρὸς τὸ τέλος τὸ ἁπλῶς) of human action or about those things that pertain to a particular end (πρὸς τι τέλος).[7]

By way of example, Aristotle refers *(EN,* III, 11, 1112b13–14) to doctors, orators, and statesmen who (qua doctor, qua orator, qua statesman) take for granted and do not deliberate about the respective ends of their arts: promoting the health of the patient, convincing their audience, and making laws.[8] These are all examples of particular ends that

---

one do the means." Gauthier-Jolif explain (II, 2:560, n. 1145a4–6) that *phronesis* knows the end but that virtue makes this knowledge effective by desiring the end. But this explanation cannot be plausibly derived from the text itself. Aquinas takes the text at face value: ". . . virtus moralis ordinat ad finem, prudentia autem dirigit circa ea quae sunt ad finem" *(SLE,* VI, 11, 1145a2, 179–81; *In Ethic.,* VI, lect. 11 [Spiazzi, n. 1289, p. 347]).

5. The medievals made the distinction between *voluntas* (= βούλησις) and *electio* (= προαίρεσις), a technical precision of considerable importance both in psychology and ethics. Aquinas, commenting on *EN,* III, 4, 1113a15 *(SLE,* III, 10, 1113a15, 1–19; *In Ethic.,* III, lect. 10 [Spiazzi, n. 488, p. 139]), specifies that *voluntas* bears on the end; elsewhere *(SLE,* III, 1, 1109b30, 9–10; *In Ethic.,* III, lect. 1 [Spiazzi, n. 382, p. 111]) he explicitly contrast *voluntas* and *electio,* and assigns *electio* (choice) to the means.

In Thomistic ethics, for an action to be morally good, both the means chosen and the end intended must be morally good: ". . . si finis intentus est malus, voluntas mala est, quantumque sit bonum, illud ad talem finem ordinatur . . . tunc non sequitur, si finis [volentis] est bonus quod voluntas sit bona; quia potest esse id quod est volitum malum . . . " *(II Sent.,* d. 38, q. 1, a. 5 [Mandonnet,979]). See *ST,* I–II, q. 58, a. 4.

6. See *EN,* III, 3, 1112b32–34; 5, 1113b3–4; VI, 12, 1144a34–36. But how are we to interpret "means"? A number of scholars argue that τὰ πρὸς τὸ τέλος (= "means") can be taken, on linguistic and doctrinal grounds, to include the constituent parts of the end as well as the instrumental or causal conditions for attaining the end: see, e.g., J. L. Ackrill, "Aristotle on *Eudaimonia," Proceedings of the British Academy* 60 (1974): 339–59 [reprinted in *Schriften zur aristotelischen Ethik,* ed. Christian Mueller-Goldingen (Hildesheim: Georg Olms Verlag, 1988), 335–55]; Cooper, *Reason and Human Good,* 19–22.

7. See *EN,* VI, 9, 1142b30–35.

8. Despite the important distinction Aristotle draws *(EN,* VI, 4, 1140a1–3) between making (ποίησις) and doing (πρᾶξις), his examples are often models of

an agent can produce because he has a particular skill (τέχνη). In contrast, the man who is thought to have practical wisdom, Pericles for instance,[9] deliberates well about those actions that are conducive (whether instrumentally or constitutively) to attaining the ultimate end, "the good life in general"[10] or *eudaimonia.*[11]

Some contemporary readers are quick to criticize Aristotle's outlook as an "ideology," an uncongenial "aristocratic conservatism."[12] Whether or not such criticisms are historically and methodologically myopic,[13] Aristotle's moral elitism cannot be doubted. Although everyone does wish to be happy or blessed,[14] not everyone is or can aspire to be a Pericles. In Aristotle's opinion, *phronesis* about how to attain happiness is as rare as the end that it seeks is utterly common. But given the rarity and importance of *phronesis,* it is even more troubling that Aristotle could confine practical wisdom to functioning on only one side of the means-end dichotomy. Aristotle repeatedly states that right habituation or moral virtue sets the good man's ends. The man who has moral virtue requires *phronesis,* so it seems, only in order to know how properly to carry out deliberations and choices about means to these good ends.[15]

To take one example, we can look at *EN*, VI, 2, 1139a21–33 to learn how Aristotle's dichotomous means-end formula for *phronesis* structures his analysis of morally good actions. Aristotle claims that the function of practical reason is to reach the truth about human actions.

---

technical rather than moral reasoning, perhaps because the former so clearly involves reasoning about (strictly instrumental) means. These technical examples lead Gauthier-Jolif to complain that Aristotle degrades the intrinsic worth of morally good actions by making them instrumental means of attaining *eudaimonia:* see II, 1:6–7, n. 1094a16–18.

9. See *EN*, VI, 5, 1140b8–9.

10. πρὸς τὸ εὖ ζῆν ὅλως *(EN*, VI, 4, 1140a28); rev. Oxford trans.

11. See *EN*, I, 4, 1095a15–20. For the conceptual equivalence in Aristotle's epoch of "living well" (εὖ ζῆν), "doing well" (εὖ πράττειν), and "happiness" (εὐδαιμονία), see Gauthier-Jolif, II, 1:27, n. 1095a19–20.

12. Ellen Meiksins Wood and Neal Wood, *Class Ideology and Ancient Political Theory: Socrates, Plato, and Aristotle in Social Context* (New York: Oxford University Press, 1978), 223.

13. See Giovanni Reale, *A History of Ancient Philosophy,* Vol. 2: *Plato and Aristotle,* 5th Italian ed., ed. and trans. John R. Catan (Albany: State University of New York Press, 1990), 325: "In general, the many and fine analyses of the various aspects of individual ethical virtues made by Aristotle remain, mostly, on a purely phenomenological level. . . . "

14. See *EN*, III, 5, 1113b16. *Eudaimonia,* since we necessarily seek it, is not something that we choose: see *EN*, III, 2, 1111b26–27.

15. See *EN*, VI, 12, 1144a7–9; 1144a20–22.

There are, according to Aristotle, wrong and right desires. A morally good choice results from right desire and reason. Right desire of the end is the presupposition for practical reason choosing the right means. Subsequently, right desire will follow reason in desiring precisely these means.[16] Aquinas comments that, although the prudent man knows both the good and the bad for man,[17] *"prudentia"* only reasons about how to attain good ends.[18] Built into Aristotle's definition of *"phronesis"* is the qualification that *phronesis* commands only those actions that are right because they are the means to ends that it is right to desire.[19]

On the narrow view of deliberation, Aristotle severely contracts the all-encompassing, Socratic scope of human choices: not knowledge and rational deliberation (nor their contrary, ignorance) but the agent's moral character, whether good or bad, sets his or her ends.[20] Thus the narrow view entails depreciating the value of ethical arguments. It seems that the good man, without any significant need of or any attention to reasonable arguments about his goals, pursues out of prerational habit what is good and just, and the bad man, because of his habits, does exactly the opposite.[21] Good experiences, not good arguments, open the eyes of the *phronimos* to what is good.[22]

In his commentary, Aquinas often repeats without any hesitation what I have been calling the "narrow view," that men's ends are set by their prerational habits and not by their rational deliberations or choices. If one's habits are good, so are one's ends; bad ends, however, undercut one's capacity to reason about means.

> Moral virtue determines the right intention of the end . . . vice, the opposite of virtue, perverts the judgment of reason and makes [the judgment of reason] to be deceived in regard to ends, which practical principles are about. *(SLE*, VI, 10, 1144a28, 241–46; *In Ethic.*,VI, lect. 11 [Spiazzi, nn. 1273–74, p. 344])[23]

---

16. See *EN*, VI, 2, 1139a24–25.

17. See *SLE*, VI, 4, 1140b6, 32–33 *(In Ethic.*, VI, lect. 4 [Spiazzi, n. 1167, p. 319]): ". . . prudentia sit habitus activus circa hominis bona et mala."

18. See *SLE*, VI, 4, 1140a28, 29–31 *(In Ethic.*, VI, lect. 4 [Spiazzi, n. 1163, p. 319]): ". . . quia ratiocinari de his quae pertinent ad malum finem est contrarium prudentiae. . . . "

19. See *EN*, VI, 10, 1143a5–10.

20. See *EN*, III, 4, 1113a23–30; VI, 12, 1144a20–22; 1144a31–36. Cf. *Laches*, 199d.

21. See *EN*, VI, 12, 1143b21–24; VII, 3, 1145b23–28.

22. See *EN*, VI, 11, 1143b13–14.

23. ". . . virtus moralis faciat rectam intentionem finis . . . malitia opposita virtuti pervertit iudicium rationis et facit mentiri circa fines, qui sunt [circa] prac-

Accordingly, Aquinas also confines deliberation and choice to the means by which these preordained ends can be achieved.[24] The prudent man deliberates, judges, and prescribes—but only about means.[25]

While granting that virtue and vice play an important role in determining our pursuits, the contemporary moral theorist will be eager, as were the Stoics, to ask not only whether we can deliberate about ends as well as means, but whether we ever directly deliberate about being virtuous in the sense of choosing to make virtue our end. Aristotle, however, does not explicitly ask this latter question, although in the context of his convoluted argument *(EN*, III, 5, 1113b3–1114b25) on behalf of the voluntariness of both virtue and vice, it might seem especially appropriate for him to do so and to answer it affirmatively. The argument, however, is ambiguous and parts of it perhaps contradict other texts. Nonetheless, *EN*, III, 5, 1113b6–7, which states that the virtues are exercised in reference to the means, appears to make the virtues themselves elective; similarly, 1114b20–21, 1114b32–1115a1 claim that the virtues and vices are voluntary since, at least in the beginning, we are their "masters" (κύριοι). To be a "master" of virtue and vice suggests that we can choose to be virtuous or not. Aristotle's own conclusion (11–14b16–17), however, is irritatingly vague: we are partly responsible for pursuing the ends that we do in fact pursue because we are responsible (partly responsible?) for our virtues and vices. Do ends, then, partly fall under deliberation and choice?

Aquinas, however, takes the narrow view in interpreting this argument: the virtues are voluntary because they bear on the means that alone are the object of deliberation and choice.[26] Prima facie, one can hardly object to Aquinas's exegesis. The rejection of the narrow view, as one can discern from the translations of contemporary exegetes, relies in some cases as much on philosophical as linguistic consider-

---

tica principia . . ." *(SLE*, VI, 10, 1144a28, 241–46; *In Ethic.*, VI, lect. 11 [Spiazzi, nn. 1273–74, p. 344]).

24. See *SLE*, III, 5, 1111b26, 180–82 *(In Ethic.*, III, lect. 5 [Spiazzi, n. 446, p. 126]): ". . . sed electio est solum eorum quae sunt ad finem, non autem ipsius finis, quia finis praesupponitur ut iam praedeterminatus. . . ."

25. See *SLE*, VI, 10, 1144a6, 151–58 *(In Ethic.*, VI, lect. 10 [Spiazzi, n. 1269, p. 343]): "Duo enim sunt necessaria in opere virtutis [scilicet] quorum unum est ut homo habeat rectam intentionem de fine, quod quidem facit virtus moralis, in quantum inclinat appetitum in debitum finem; aliud autem est quod homo bene se habeat circa ea quae sunt ad finem, et hoc facit prudentia, quae est bene consiliativa et iudicativa et praeceptiva eorum quae sunt ad finem"; *SLE*, VI,, 11, 1145a2, 179–81 *(In Ethic.*, VI, lect. 11 [Spiazzi, n. 1289, p. 347]): ". . . quia virtus moralis ordinat ad finem, prudentia autem dirigit circa ea quae sunt ad finem."

26. See *SLE*, III, 11, 1113b3, 14–21 *(In Ethic.*, III, lect. 11 [Spiazzi, n. 496, p. 141]).

ations.[27] Now this modest conclusion should help us to recognize that Aquinas's effort to realign Aristotle, by introjecting the medieval doctrine of *synderesis*, although this introjection is not embraced by contemporary interpreters, is not so exegetically deviant as is sometimes suggested. The basic differences between Thomistic and contemporary readings of Aristotle reflect the different philosophical preoccupations of the readers.

The argument of *EN*, III, 5, 1113b3–6 presupposes the close connection between choice and voluntariness that Aristotle establishes in *EN*, III, 2, 1112a14–17. The latter text embodies the conclusion that although not all voluntary actions are chosen, every choice is voluntary. Since deliberation precedes choice, deliberating about doing something is at least a sign that the ensuing action will be voluntary. Aristotle, however, wants to show that virtue and vice are voluntary. A contemporary reader might readily suppose that the easiest way to prove that they are voluntary is to show that virtue and vice are appropriate matters to deliberate about and choose as *ends*. But this is not, as we have seen, the argument that Aristotle presents.

While Aristotle grants that virtue and vice are "in our power," he does not explicitly say or unambiguously imply that they are voluntary because virtue and vice are ends that we can directly deliberate about and choose apart from or in contradiction to our prerational habituation.[28] Rather, he says that the *actions* that we deliberate about are voluntary. He contends (1113b5–6) that because the acts (ἐνέργειαι) of the virtues and vices are about (περί) these voluntary actions, so too

27. How, for example, are we to translate *EN*, VI, 12, 1144a 20: τὴν μὲν οὖν προαίρεσιν ὀρθὴν ποιεῖ ἡ ἀρετή? Cf. Gauthier-Jolif (I, 2:181; II, 2:549, n. 1144a19) who interpret προαίρεσις as "intention qui porte sur une fin" and the literal "Now excellence makes the choice right" of the revised Oxford translation which remains neutral as to whether or not προαίρεσις bears on the end. In this instance, however, Gauthier-Jolif echo Aquinas's exegesis. The Latin text of VI, 10, 1144a20 is neutral: "Electionem quidem igitur rectam facit virtus. " But Aquinas explains: ". . . virtus moralis facit electionem rectam, quantum scilicet ad intentionem finis . . ." (*SLE*, VI, 10, 1144a11, 200–201; *In Ethic.*, VI, lect. 10 [Spiazzi, n. 1271, p. 343]).

28. Aristotle comes close to suggesting that vice can be directly chosen as an "end-in-itself" in distinguishing the profligate or intemperate man (ἀκόλαστος) from the acratic or morally impotent man who lacks self-control (ἀκρατής): see *EN*, VII, 3, 1146b22–24; 4, 1148a16–22. The profligate man chooses to yield to his appetites for natural bodily pleasure, even when his appetites are weak, because he thinks that it is always right to pursue such pleasures. The acratic man knows that it is not right, but lacking self-restraint, succumbs now and then to the intense pleasures of the moment. But it would be a mistake to think that Aristotle's profligate man chooses what is vicious from a lucidly intellectual motive; the profligate is not a fallen angel choosing evil out of pride or a defiant, modern Prometheus rejecting a heteronomous-

the virtues and vices are voluntary. Aristotle's point is that the voluntariness of virtue and vice derives from voluntary actions that are virtuous or vicious. But the point is left unexplained: perhaps Aristotle means that virtues and vices are instantiated in these voluntary actions.

As I have indicated, *EN*, III, 5, 1113b5–6 could be read as evidence for Aristotle's tacit acknowledgment that the virtues and vices do not mechanically determine our choices in regard to already (prerationally) fixed ends; on the contrary, the voluntariness of the virtues and vices is itself mediated by our choices and, it would seem, that our ends inasmuch as they are set by our virtues and vices must be similarly mediated by deliberation and choice. What are we, then, to think about the immediate voluntariness of virtue and vice: can they be directly chosen as ends? Although this may not be a question explicitly posed by Aristotle, he does speak about doing virtuous deeds for the sake of what is morally noble (καλόν).[29] So why, if we can deliberate about and choose ends, can we not deliberate about and choose virtue and vice as themselves formal ends?[30]

Nonetheless, Aristotle in explaining the voluntariness of virtue in *EN*, III, 5, 1113b3–14 holds fast to the means-end dichotomy; he reiterates at the beginning of the argument (1113b3–4) that deliberatively chosen (i.e., voluntary) actions are about the means to our ends. In

---

ly imposed moral law. On the contrary, there is an almost unconscious quality to the viciousness of the Aristotelian ἀκόλαστος since his practical reasoning has been corrupted by a lifetime of bad habits: see *EN*, VII, 6, 1150a1–3; 7, 1150a13–16; 8, 1150b36; 1151a13. The reference to habituation, then, remains central in Aristotle's explanation of why the ἀκόλαστος chooses as he does: see *EN*, III, 12, 1119a24–28. Cf. Joseph Owens, "The Acratic's 'Ultimate Premise,'"384.

29. See *EN*, III, 7, 1115b11–13 (rev. Oxford trans.): the brave man faces fearful things "as he ought and as reason directs, and he will face them for the sake of what is noble [τοῦ καλοῦ ἕνεκα], for this is the end of excellence [ἀρετῆς]."

30. See Broadie, *Ethics with Aristotle*, 63–64. Broadie, however, absorbs Aristotelian *praxis* into an almost Deweyian version of *techne*: she contends that the Aristotelian agent's pursuit of ends "entails continual re-evaluation in the light of means" and she denies that "[Aristotelian] virtue reveals to the agent which of various possible ends is the right one to aim for" (245). The plausibility of this view is undermined by Broadie's assertion that Aristotelian virtue has a purely formal function: "virtue ensures that whatever is aimed for is aimed for rightly at any stage" (ibid.).

Aristotelian virtue, however, determines not only how an agent should pursue things under a set of circumstances but what things generically should be pursued. The good man is the individual measure of what is good, but because he is virtuous he is enabled to judge according to the truth in things. Some ends are intrinsically noble, and for that reason deserve to be and need to be chosen for their own sake;

1113b3–6, Aristotle is completely silent about whether the agent ever deliberates about or chooses ends and whether virtue and vice are themselves ever directly chosen as ends. All that he says is that virtue and vice are voluntary because they are connected to our voluntary choice of means to ends. This connection is itself problematic. How is this text to be reconciled with Aristotle's insistence that because virtue and vice set our ends, the sphere of our voluntary choices in regard to means is also set?[31] Or is it a blatant contradiction, as some interpreters have concluded, for Aristotle to allow that virtue and vice bear on both means and ends?[32] At this point, Aristotle's doctrine seems obscure or muddled.

Aquinas's commentary avoids all of these questions; he remarks that virtuous actions are about freely chosen means and only as a consequence of these choices may virtue itself be said to be voluntary:

[Aristotle] first says that, since willing is about the end and deliberation and choice are about the means, it follows that actions which are about the means are voluntary, since choice is a voluntary act. . . . But virtuous actions are about the means. Therefore, they are voluntary. And as a consequence, it is the case that virtue itself is voluntary and in us, that is, it exists in our power. (SLE, III, 11, 1113b3, 14–24; In Ethic., III, lect. 11 [Spiazzi, n. 496, p. 141])[33]

Now this comment and many other of Aquinas's restatements of Aristotle are respectful of the original Aristotelian dichotomy between wishing for ends and deliberating and choosing (solely) about the means. It may be thought, of course, that Aquinas is being far too respectful since he nowhere ventures to observe that it is in anyway wrongheaded of Aristotle to confine *phronesis* to knowledge of the means. But the fact is that Aquinas reiterates the narrow view of

others are intrinsically bad and can never be chosen under any circumstances. Except for the rare exception, what is intrinsically noble may and should be pursued in almost all circumstances; there are no circumstances, however, in which what is intrinsically bad should be pursued. For all practical purposes, then, the intrinsically noble and the intrinsically bad set "unrevisable" ends. See *EN*, III, 4, 1113a30–1113b1; II, 4, 1105a34; 1107a8–27.

31. See *EN*, VI, 2, 1139a33–34; 5, 1140b16–20; 12, 1144a20–22; 13, 1145a4–6.

32. See Gauthier-Jolif, II, 1:212–13, n. 1113b5–6; W. K. C. Guthrie, *A History of Greek Philosophy*, Vol. 6: *Aristotle: An Encounter* (Cambridge: Cambridge University Press, 1981), 359.

33. "Dicit ergo primo quod, cum voluntas sit de fine, consilium autem et electio de his quae sunt ad finem, consequens est quod operationes quae sunt circa haec, scilicet circa ea quae sunt ad finem, sint secundum electionem et per consequens quod sint voluntariae, quia electio voluntarium quoddam est . . . Sed operationes

deliberation and choice in the *Summa theologiae* where he is not commenting on Aristotle.[34]

One exception, however, must be noted. In response to an objector who is upholding the narrow view, Aquinas himself states, as though it involves no departure from Aristotle's doctrine, that *prudentia* includes deliberation about ends.[35] Is this an exegetical inconsistency that cannot be convincingly reconciled with Aquinas's repeated statements of the narrow view of Aristotelian *phronesis*, or is Aquinas stating his own view but without directly contradicting Aristotle? But what, then, is Aquinas's view of the scope of *prudentia?* For the moment the apparent contradiction in Aquinas's view of *prudentia* must give way to the primary question. Is the narrow view of Aristotelian *phronesis*, as it has been claimed, a seriously mistaken view? Or is it the case that the Aristotelian *phronimos* is a moral paradigm precisely because Aristotle, his restrictive statements not withstanding, portrays the *phronimos* as preeminently skillful in deliberating and choosing ends?[36]

2. The Expanded View of Aristotelian "Phronesis"

First of all, we need to explain why the narrow view of *phronesis* is a mistake according to a number of contemporary interpreters of the *Nicomachean Ethics*. On the narrow view, Aristotelian moral agents are confined to the pursuit of ends that are determined by their virtues and vices. This confinement, however, has a consequence that is as unavoidable as it is unpalatable to many contemporary moral theorists. If the morally good man or woman, as well as the morally bad man or woman, can never step back from the ends that he or she happens to be pursuing and consider whether these ends are truly worthwhile, then they remain "Humean prisoners"[37] of their temperaments, habits, and

---

virtutum sunt circa praedicta. Ergo sunt voluntariae. Et per consequens oportet quod etiam ipsa virtus sit voluntaria et in nobis, id est in potestate nostra existens" (*SLE*, III, 11, 1113b3, 14–24; *In Ethic.*, III, lect. 11 [Spiazzi, n. 496, p. 141]).

34. See *ST*, I, q. 113, a. 1, ad 2; q. 22, a. 1, ad 3; I–II, q. 57, a. 5; II–II, q. 47, a. 6.

35. See *ST*, I–II, q. 66, a. 3, ad 3: ". . . prudentia non solum dirigit virtutes morales in eligendo ea quae sunt ad finem, sed etiam in praestituendo finem."

36. See Nancy Sherman, "Character, Planning, and Choice in Aristotle," *Review of Metaphysics* 39 (1985): 105.

37. For a modified Humean reading of Aristotle, see Engberg-Pedersen, *Aristotle's Theory*, 267–68, who does argue (195), however, that the virtue of εὐβουλία (excellence in deliberation) covers deliberation about the end, i. e., about living well in general. For an extended anti-Humean interpretation, see Dahl, *Practical Reason*, esp. 93–99.

desires. Now it is just this alleged subordination of reason to desire that urgently prompts many scholars to contend that any interpretation that prohibits deliberation about ultimate ends is a radically mistaken view of Aristotle.[38]

To get practical reason free of this straitjacket, the sphere of deliberation and choice, as it is originally delineated in the third book, needs to be expanded, and Aristotle offers hints how to do so in the sixth and seventh books of the *Nicomachean Ethics*.[39] Many recent interpreters are eager to follow suit.[40] But how far can the Aristotelian concepts of *bouleusis* and *prohairesis* be opened up?[41] As one might expect, different interpreters press Aristotle's texts to different lengths. In order to reduce a plethora of detailed scholarly discussions to their schematic importance, I shall consider three steps that may be taken by which the "narrow view" is left behind to be replaced by what I am tagging by contrast the expanded or "the wide view" of Aristotelian *bouleusis* and

38. See D. J. Allan, "Aristotle's Account of the Origin of Moral Principles," *Proceedings of the XIth International Congress of Philosophy*, Vol. 12: *History of Philosophy: Methodology, Antiquity, and the Middle Ages* (Amsterdam and Louvain: North Holland and Editions E. Nauwelaerts, 1953),120–27. Dahl, *Practical Reason*, 38–39, interpreting *EN*, VI, 2, 1139a24–25, argues that (1) desire is right if it is in accord with reason; and (2) as desire (ὄρεξις) bears on ends, so—if it is to be right—must reason.

In reference to the same text, Aquinas merely observes *(SLE*, VI, 2, 1139a21, 71–75; *In Ethic.*, VI, lect. 2 [Spiazzi, n. 1128, p. 310]) that reason and desire are in harmony when appetite pursues what reason affirms to be good. Aquinas allows, however, that the desirable *(appetibile)*, and therefore desire *(appetitum)*, moves the practical intellect. See *SLA*, III, c. 9, 433a14, 67–71 *(In de An.*, III, lect. 15 [Pirotta, n. 821, p. 195]): ". . . quia enim ipsum appetibile mouet, quod est primum consideratum ab intellectu practico, propter hoc dicitur intellectus practicus mouere, quia scilicet eius principium, quod est appetibile, mouet." But Aquinas firmly distinguishes between rational and non-rational desire and thus avoids the Humean subordination of reason to desire: the will is "intellectus appetitus" whose object is "bonum secundum communem boni rationem" *(ST*, I, q. 59, a. 4).

39. The chronology of these books, however, is problematic. Aubenque, following Gauthier-Jolif, considers them to be transposed from the *Eudemean Ethics* and therefore earlier than *EN*, III: see Aubenque, *La Prudence*, 141. For that reason, Aubenque argues that the narrow view is Aristotle's considered and final view. Aristotle, in other words, contracts rather than expands his original view of βούλευσις and προαίρεσις.

40. But not all: Guthrie, *History*, 6: 347, n. 3, remains nicely skeptical about the contemporary attempt to expand *phronesis* beyond the mere "intuition of particulars and discovery of means."

41. Sherman, *Fabric of Character*, argues that the Aristotelian concept of βούλευσις includes the idea that the *phronimos* can revise his ends but admits that "Aristotle's examples of deliberation do not adequately reveal the complexity of acting from character" (76).

prohairesis. The steps discuss: (1) the logic of deliberative choices, (2) the cognitive character of *phronesis*, and (3) the purpose of the overall argument of the *Nicomachean Ethics*. The steps are calibrated, rather loosely, to Aquinas's exegesis, which also departs from the letter of Aristotle's text, but in a different direction, by grounding *phronesis/ prudentia* in the intellectual habit of *synderesis*.

(1) The first step away from the narrow view is to recognize (as Aquinas does) the logical structure of deliberation: an agent deliberates in order to chose to act so that he or she may attain an end.[42] The logical structure of deliberation is such that it cannot be endless.[43] If an agent deliberates on any given occasion, he or she necessarily takes some end for granted.[44] But, then, it can certainly be allowed that, on another occasion, the same end can be regarded as a means:[45] it may itself be held up for discussion and deliberation in regard to some higher, (and in this context) fixed end.

What we are elaborating, of course, is the concept of an *intermediate* end. Aristotle evidently understood and used the basic concept. His hierarchical arrangement of the sciences presupposes that there are intermediate ends. The subordinate arts and sciences have their own intrinsic but subordinate ends. Political science, however, is "architectonic": it sets the final goal of the subordinate arts such as bridle making, horsemanship, household economy, oratory, and military strategy.[46] Political science is architectonic because it understands how to attain the ultimate end of human activities: *eudaimonia*, the end that is never sought for the sake of anything else.[47] It is not even proper to

42. See *SLE*, III, 8, 1112b15, 39–41 (*In Ethic*, III, lect. 8 [Spiazzi, n. 475, p. 134]): ". . . supposito aliquo fine, prima intentio consiliantium est qualiter, id est quo motu vel actione, possit perveni ad illum finem. . . ."

43. See *SLE*. III. 8, 1112b33, 123–25 (*In Ethic.*, III, lect. 8 [Spiazzi, n. 480, p. 134]): ". . . consilium habet terminum vel statum ex parte finis. Et dicit quod operationes omnes sunt aliorum gratia, id est finium. Unde de ipso fine non est consilium, sed de his quae sunt ad finem."

44. See *EN*, III, 3, 1112b11–20; *EE*, II, 10, 1227a6–18. Cf. *SLA*, III, c. 9, 433a14, 57–60 (*In de An.*, III, lect. 15 [Pirotta, n. 821, p. 195]): ". . . cum enim uolumus aliquid deliberare de agendis, primo supponimus finem et deinde procedimus per ordinem ad inquirendum illa que agenda sunt propter finem. . . ."

45. See L. H. G. Greenwood, *Aristotle Nicomachean Ethics, Book Six: With Essays, Notes, and Translation* (Cambridge: Cambridge University Press, 1909),44–48; and Engberg-Pedersen, *Aristotle's Theory*, 212. Cooper's claim that "a fixed end is itself never deliberated about" (*Reason and Human Good*, 14) does not entail that any particular end is always fixed. Only the ultimate end, *eudaimonia*, is set.

46. See *EN*, I, 1, 1094a7–1094b4.

47. See *EN*, I, 6, 1096b17–19: wisdom, sight, certain pleasures, and honor are chosen for themselves as well as chosen (1097b2–6) as means to happiness.

say that we choose *eudaimonia;* it is a goal that we wish for but one not in our control since our pursuit of *eudaimonia* is set by nature and not by choice.[48]

Indeed, Aristotle thinks that, except for *eudaimonia*, all ends (including the moral virtues themselves) are "intermediate":[49] everything can be seen as a means toward (or a constituent of) *eudaimonia*. This notion of *eudaimonia* as the ultimate fixed end has an advantage: by reaffirming the standard of means-end reasoning, it preserves the rational character of deliberation and yet it allows for deliberation about all other (subordinate) ends that could ever be considered important (e.g., health) either as means toward or a constituent of *eudaimonia*.[50]

Still, the narrow view of deliberation cannot be overturned solely by adverting to the logical possibility that at different times every penultimate end can also be regarded as a means, and therefore can be really mulled over. The basic contemporary objection to the narrow view is not that it misconstrues the logic of deliberation but that it does not recognize the moral necessity of deliberating about ends.

On the narrow view of deliberation, it is difficult to explain how the virtuous man's pursuit of morally good ends depends not only on right desire (i.e., desire directed by moral virtue) but also truly derives from practical reasoning. Aquinas draws attention to the apparent circularity of Aristotle's position: practical reason is right when it is in conformity with right appetite but right appetite is right because it is in conformity with practical reason.[51] Although Aquinas and not Aristotle worries about this circle,[52] Aquinas's observation is relevant. How can we know

48. See *EN*, III, 2, 1111b28–30.

49. The concept of an intermediate end undergoes a rather significant development in Aquinas's commentary: it leads to an *"agens perfectissmum."* See *SLE*, I, 9, 1097a24, 79–135 *(In Ethic.*, I, lect. 9 [Spiazzi, nn. 108–10, p. 30]) where Aquinas explains that "the grade of ends is proportioned to the grade of the agent" (l. 79) and thus assimilates Aristotle's perfect good to the Christian God who as "the most perfect agent" is both final and efficient cause.

50. See Greenwood, *Book Six*, 44: *"Phronesis* may be defined as the intellectual *arete* that leads to knowledge of the good things to do as means to the great end of man which is *eu zen* or *eupraxia* or *eudaimonia."*

51. Cf. *EN*, VI, 2, 1139a25–26, 30–31 (Rackham trans.): "... desire must pursue the same things that [reasoning] affirms ... [the function] of the practical intelligence is the attainment of truth corresponding to right desire"; *SLE*, VI, 2, 1139a27, 109–14 *(In Ethic.*, VI, lect. 2 [Spiazzi, n. 1131, p. 310]): "Nam, si veritas intellectus practici determinatur in comparatione ad appetitum rectum, appetitus autem rectitudo determinatur per hoc quod consonat rationi verae, ut prius dictum est, sequitur quaedam circulatio in dictis determinationibus."

52. The interpretation of *EN*, VI, 2, 1139a21–26 depends on whether Aristotle (in line with the official means-end formula of *EN*, III, 5, 1112b11–12) is confining

what appetites (about means) are morally right unless we can, independent of our appetites, rationally assess the rectitude of our ends?[53]

Aristotle does not take up the question. Instead, he warns that since
an agent's ends are set by his virtues and vices, philosophical arguments alone cannot convince a morally bad agent, given his pernicious
habits, to change his usual pursuits.[54] The morally bad man has been
corrupted by pleasure and pain; he is not able to form correct judgments about which ends are truly good. In contrast, the good man's
virtuous habits, which allow him to control his attachment to pleasure
and fear of pain, allow him to develop the right *opinion* (ὀρθοδοξεῖν)
about which ends to pursue.[55] Specifically, the virtue of moderation or
temperance (σωφροσύνη) keeps him rightly directed.[56]

In commenting on *EN*, IV, 2, 1139a21–26, Aquinas breaks out of this
desire-reason circularity by distinguishing natural from acquired desires. Acquired desires are desires for certain means; they are consequent upon reason's deliberations and reason judges their rectitude.
Acquired habitual desires are right when they are in accord with reason's choice of means. Natural desire, however, is for the end of human
action since "the end for man is determined by nature."[57] Whereas
Aristotle stresses that reason is right when it is in accord with right
habituation, Aquinas's point of view is that reason is right when it is in
accord with natural desire.[58]

---

true reasoning (ἀληθὴς λόγος) to means and right desire (ὄρεξις ὀρθή) to ends. The
phrase "desire must pursue the same thing as *logos* affirms" (1139a25–26) is ambiguous: it may mean that desire, in addition to first fixing the end, must also come to
bear on those means that reason chooses, or that both desire and reason must fix on
the same end. The latter interpretation is obviated by 1139a32–33 which confines
deliberative *logos* to the means. Gauthier-Jolif (II, 2:446–48), while noting the re-
striction placed in the latter text, nonetheless argue that reason bears on both
means and end. Their argument, however, is not exegetical but doctrinal; they
appeal to "la veritable portée de la psychologie aristotélicienne de la décision . . ."
(447). Aquinas, while noting the ambiguity in Aristotle's text, interprets it narrowly: reason bears on the means; desire bears on ends and means, but differently for
each. Desire for the end is natural and precedes reason; desire for the means follows
upon reason's deliberations. See *SLE*, VI, 2, 1139a27, 109–27 (*In Ethic.*, VI, lect. 2
[Spiazzi, n. 1131, p. 311]).

53. See *EN*, X, 7, 1178a17–18 (Rackham trans.): ". . . the first principles which
prudence [φρόνησις] employs are determined by the moral virtues. . . ."

54. See *EN*, I, 3, 1095a9; X, 9, 1179b20–30.

55. See *EN*, VII, 8, 1151a18–19.

56. See *EN*, VI, 5, 1140b11–13.

57. ". . . finis autem determinatus est homini a natura . . ." (*SLE*, VI, 2, 1139a27,
116–17; *In Ethic.*, VI, lect. 2 [Spiazzi, n. 1132, p. 311]).

58. Aristotle leaves unsettled whether natural virtues set the right ends of human action: see *EN*, VII, 8, 1151a17–18.

Aquinas assumes that there are various natural or fixed ends of human action.[59] Without providing a detailed list of man's fixed ends, Aquinas is content to report that they correspond to man's natural inclinations.[60] In Chapter 6, I shall develop the theological context in which Aquinas views human nature and its fixed ends. Now, however, I shall just note that, for Aquinas, rational choices about means are right if they are also "natural," that is, if they do not violate the order of fixed ends that nature sets for us.

Aquinas contends, then, that appetite must conform to the norm of right reason in regard to the means but, conversely, right reason must conform to the norm of natural appetite in regard to natural ends. In both cases, nature's ends remain the measure for both appetite and practical reason: "The rectitude of the [natural] appetite in regard to the end is the measure of truth in practical reason."[61] Since nature assures the rightness of appetite in regard to fixed or natural ends, practical reason can then be assigned the task of determining what are the right means to these fixed ends as well as to determining those intermediate ends that are not fixed by nature itself. Desire for ends that are not in harmony with the fixed or natural ends is unnatural or vicious desire.[62]

Aristotle's position, however, is more fluid than Aquinas's commentary suggests and than the Thomistic theology of natural ends could allow.[63] But Aquinas does not elevate nature above reason: the ordered inclinations of nature, and especially rational human nature, reflect the wisdom of nature's creator.[64] Aristotle, by contrast, is arguing in a

---

59. See *ST*, II–II, q. 47, a. 15: "Fines autem recti humanae vitae sunt determinati. Et ideo potest esse naturalis inclinatio respectu horum finium. . . ."

60. See *ST*, I–II, Q. 94, a. 2.

61. ". . . rectitudo appetitus per respectum ad finem est mensura veritatis in ratione practica . . ." *(SLE*, VI, 2, 1139a27, 120–22; *In Ethic.*, VI, lect. 2 [Spiazzi, n. 1131, p. 310]).

62. See *ST*, I–II, q. 71, a. 1: "vitium enim uniuscuiusque rei esse videtur quod non sit disposita secundum quod convenit suae naturae. " The desire, however, can be "natural" in that it follows "inclinationem naturae sensitivae" but "unnatural" (in the normative sense of the term) because it is "contra ordinem rationis" *(ST*, I–II, q. 71, a. 2, ad 3). That which is "contra ordinem rationis proprie est contra naturam hominis" *(ibid.*, c.).

63. See *ST*, I–II, q. 71, a. 2, ad 4: "Lex autem aeterna comparatur ad ordinem rationis humanae sicut ars ad artificiatum."

64. See *I Sent*, d. 42, q. 2, a. 1 (Mandonnet, 988): ". . . quidquid perfectionis in creatura est, totum est exemplariter eductum ex perfectione Creatoris . . ."; *In Phys.*, II, lect. 4 (Maggiòlo, n. 171, p. 87): ". . . ab aliquo principio intellectivo tota natura ordinatur ad finem suum, ut sic opus naturae videatur esse opus intelligentiae . . ."; *SCG*, III, 64 (Pera, n. 2394, p. 87): "Ordo autem rerum causatarum secun-

strictly practical context; he is assigning moral responsibility. Aristotle holds that men are responsible for their habits and character. But in refuting the Socratic contention that no one is voluntarily vicious, Aristotle leaves *(EN,* III, 5, 1114a30–1114b25) the issue of man's natural end open: he does not settle whether man has a natural end but argues (1114b17–18) instead that whether or not man's end is set by his natural temperament, both the virtuous and the vicious man voluntarily choose the means to the end; therefore, vice is as voluntary as virtue. Aquinas, however, reads Aristotle's text in a way that makes it compatible with the Thomistic theological conception of nature; Aquinas interprets it as a straightforward assertion that nature rightly sets man's ends.[65]

Despite the ambiguity of many of the Aristotelian texts, it is clear that Aristotle thinks that human choices are determined by both reason and desire.[66] But Aristotelian practical reason, especially among contemporary moral theorists who repudiate the notion of natural human ends, will seem dangerously subordinated to nonrational habits, and, as a consequence, human freedom will seem unacceptably compromised if we are not explicitly allowed to deliberate about our overall aims.[67] Perhaps our concern to deliberate about ends reflects a significant difference between Aristotle's cultural outlook and our own,[68] but there are the unavoidable, modern "meaning of life" questions,[69] and we need to learn whether Aristotle allows that our basic goods, if

---

dum distinctionem naturarum et gradum ipsarum, procedit ex divina sapientia . . ."; *ST,* I, q. 105, a. 6, ad. 1: ". . . naturae ordo sit a Deo rebus inditus. . . ."

65. See *SLE,* III, 13, 1114b12, 145–49 *(In Ethic.,* III, lect. 13 [Spiazzi, n. 524, p. 149]): "Similis enim ratio est quod ambobus, scilicet et virtuoso et vitioso, insit finis a natura vel qualitercumque aliter ei videatur, quantum ad apprehensionem, et adiaceat, quantum ad appetitum."

66. See *EN,* VI, 2, 1139a21–26. Cf. Greenwood, *Book Six,* 43: ". . . good *logos* and good *orexsis* about the same thing combine to form a good *prohairesis* which gives rise to a good *praxis.*"

67. See Stuart Hampshire, *Morality and Conflict* (Oxford: Basil Blackwell, 1983), 155: ". . . human nature, conceived in terms of common human needs and capacities, always underdetermines a way of life . . . [whereas] a human person hesitates between two contrasting ways of life, and sets of virtues, and he has to make a very definite, and even final, determination between them."

68. See George Boas, *Rationalism in Greek Philosophy* (Baltimore: Johns Hopkins University Press, 1961), 216: "There can be little doubt that to Aristotle the life of the Athenian gentleman was in no need of critical appraisal. It was a standard by which all life could be judged."

69. See Julius M. E. Moravscik, "On What We Aim At and How We Live," in *The Greeks and the Good Life,* ed. David J. Depew (Indianapolis: Hackett, 1980), 198–235.

they are not implanted in us by nature as Aquinas assumes, do depend on us choosing them.[70]

(2) The second step away from the narrow view is to consider whether the Aristotelian doctrine of practical wisdom does recognize and does provide a way to fulfill the moral requirement, enjoined so strongly by modern and contemporary philosophers, that we deliberate about ends. This need, it can be fairly maintained, is not just a modern burden placed on Aristotle. There are good Aristotelian reasons to overcome the narrow view. Only by expanding the scope of deliberation, so that it becomes a "wide view" that explicitly (and perhaps paradigmatically) includes ends, can we guarantee what Aristotle himself says about a good action, that it is "a combination of intellect and character,"[71] and about true virtue, that it (as distinguished from a merely natural predisposition toward virtue) cannot exist without practical wisdom.[72]

The contemporary interpreter, who is convinced that our character must result from our choices about ends as well as means, can usefully pursue the implications of what Aristotle says about the relationship between moral virtue and the ends that are presupposed by deliberation and choice.[73] Aristotle's dichotomous formula is that ends are wished for but not deliberated about or chosen;[74] yet he holds that men are responsible for their habits and characters,[75] and therefore responsible for what ends seem to them to be good and bad. Here Aristotle is again moving in a circle.[76] Our virtuous and vicious habits (i.e., our character) set our ends, and therefore the range of our characteristic

---

70. See *EN*, III, 5, 1114b12–25.

71. *EN*, VI, 2, 1139a35 (rev. Oxford trans.).

72. See *EN*, VI, 13, 1144b15–17.

73. See *EN*, III, 3, 1112a1–2 (rev. Oxford trans.): ". . . for by choosing what is good or bad we are men of a certain character. . . ."

74. See *EN*, III, 5, 1113b2.

75. See *EN*, III, 5, 1114a11–12 (Rackham trans.): ". . . it is unreasonable to say that a man who acts unjustly or dissolutely does not wish to be unjust or dissolute. . . ."

76. There are many such conceptual circles in Aristotle's ethics. Owens, "Christian Conscience vs. Aristotelian Right Reason," 150–73, asserts that the circularity of the Aristotelian ethics "could hardly pose even a theoretical problem" (156) about how moral habituation could first begin. Just as the cosmos moves in eternal cycles, so too cultures eternally rise and fall; there will always be men to habituate the succeeding generation. Nonetheless, the cyclical character of nature and culture does not guarantee the rectitude of the habituation that is inherited. As Owens notes, Aristotle designed laws "to educate a better generation" (157). The point could be put more strongly. Aristotle saw what was basically wrong with the Greek

choices about how to achieve those ends; but our choices also determine our character (which is constituted by repeated choices), and
therefore our ends.

Is this an unbreakable circle? Everything, of course, depends on the
strength of our childhood habituation.[77] Aristotle's observations,
though undergirded by a metaphysical comparison, are—for him—
commonsensical: men find it difficult to change their habits because a
habit is "like nature."[78] Although the acratic man can, with great
difficulty, overcome his intermittently bad actions, men with permanently diseased characters (the unjust and the profligate addicted to
the pleasures of drink and sex) have lost the power to change since
their intellects have been corrupted.[79] But Aristotle's pessimism about
the morally bad man is outweighed by an extraordinary confidence in
the virtuous man. The morally virtuous or moderate man (ὁ ἐπιεικής),
unlike every practicing Christian, does not need to repent seven times
daily: Aristotle's virtuous man is steadfast in virtue. Whereas the
acratic man wavers, the truly virtuous man never falls, and therefore,
so to speak, never needs to repent.[80]

At this point, Aristotle's description of the virtuous man, which
echoes the famous paean of Simonides, probably seems, for our contemporaries, more metaphysical than commonsensical.[81] But the interpreter, one eager to expand the range of *bouleusis* and *prohairesis*, need
not tarry over the cultural relativity of Aristotelian common sense.[82]
The interpreter can open a modest escape from the circle, which is
more psychological than logical, that seems to vitiate the Aristotelian

---

cultural tradition: it embodies truths but, in greater measure, myths and, presumably, outright falsehoods: see *Metaph.*, XII, 8, 1074b1-4.

77. See *EN*, II, 1, 1103b22-25.

78. *EN*, VII, 10, 1152a31 (rev. Oxford trans.). See *SLE*, III, 15, 1115b20, 97-99 (*In
Ethic.*, III, lect. 15 [Spiazzi, n. 549, p. 156]): "... movet enim habitus ex consuetudine
causatus per modum naturae eo quod consuetudo est sicut quaedam natura. . . ."

79. See *EN*, III, 5, 1114a19-21; VII, 6, 1150a1-3; 8, 1150b29-35.

80. See *EN*, IV, 9, 1128b28-29; IX, 4, 1166a29. Although Aristotle adds the qualification, "so to speak" (ὡς εἰπεῖν) in 1166a29, Aquinas further weakens Aristotle's
unswervingly virtuous man: the virtuous man because he "always acts according to
reason does not easily [need to] repent [non de facili paenitet]" (*SLE*, IX, 4, 1166a27,
164-65; *In Ethic.*, IX, lect. 4 [Spiazzi, n. 1809, p. 477]).

81. See *EN*, I, 11, 1100b34-1101a3. For the poem of Simonides, see Gauthier-
Jolif, II, 1:81, n. 1100b21.

82. Cf. Grant, *Ethics of Aristotle*, 2:219-20, which contrasts the Greek and the
Semitic points of view; and MacIntyre, *Whose Justice?* 90: "Aristotle's account of
the good and the best cannot but be an account of the good and the best as it is
embodied in a *polis*."

doctrine about the overriding importance of character.[83] As Aristotle describes the role of habituation (ἦθος), a man's habits threaten to ensnare and effectively to eliminate, even though they only arise from, his self-determining choices. But while Aristotle might think that character is destiny, he does not allow that nature determines a man's moral character; moral virtues and vices, as distinguished from bestial behavior reflecting a depraved nature or from morbid behavior caused by pathological conditions, are habits that are generated by the repetition of ordinary human acts.[84]

Aristotle holds that men and women, by the choices that they make, are responsible for their characters, since otherwise virtue and vice would not be fully voluntary, and therefore not subject to praise or blame. Although Aristotle does not draw the easily inferred corollary, it must be logically possible and therefore, under some set of specifiable conditions, psychologically possible at some time, for Aristotelian agents to choose the ends and goals that direct their lives.[85]

Acts can be chosen for "their own sakes"[86] or for some other motive. The alternative, however, makes sense only if the agent is free to choose ends. This claim commits us to a libertarian view of Aristotle. And the libertarian view, it has to be admitted, is problematic. Any Christian theological or modern philosophical emphasis on *free choice* is conspicuously absent in Aristotle's discussion of voluntary actions. A voluntary agent is indeed the principle or *arche* of his or her actions,[87] and choice involves preferring one thing over another, but Aristotle has no explicit word for "free choice." The concept, though, seems implied by and is perhaps sometimes confused with the notion of voluntariness.[88] Aristotle's explanation *(EN, VI, 2, 1139a31–33)* that

---

83. See *EN*, VI, 1139a33–35: "There is no choice without intellect and thought and a certain disposition of character, for there is no doing well and its opposite in the sphere of action without thought and character."

84. See *EN*, II, 1, 1103a17–19; 1103b21–22; VII, 5, 1148b17–18; 1148b31–32; 5, 1149a16–18.

85. See *EN*, III, 1, 1110b25–30, which suggests that there is a morally blameworthy ignorance in the *choice* of bad ends. For other texts whose "cumulative evidence" indicates that *prohairesis* can apply to ends as well as means, see Ross, *Aristotle*, 307, n. 39. Cf. *SLE*, III, 5, 1111b29, 192–97 *(In Ethic.*, III, lect. 5 [Spiazzi, n. 447, p. 126]) which implies that choice, inasmuch as it must focus on what is possible for us, can focus on ends as long as they are not set "by nature."

86. See *EN*, II, 4, 1105a31–32.

87. See *EN*, III, 3, 1112b31–32: ἄνθρωπος εἶναι ἀρχὴ τῶν πράξεων.

88. See *EN*, III, 1, 1110a17–18: ". . . when the *arche* of an action is in oneself, it is in one's own power both to do it and not to do it"; 5, 1113b20–21: ". . . [actions] the *archai* of which are in us are from us and are voluntary."

the efficient cause of an action is the choice made by the agent, which choice, in turn, is caused by desire and reason, does not sufficiently clarify matters.

Aristotle's official doctrine about choice is that because we desire a certain end, we reason about the choices that would enable us to attain that end.[89] Now it just this doctrine that lends support to the opinion, forcibly argued at the beginning of the century by Loening[90] and subsequently reiterated, that Aristotle's theory of voluntariness is not only compatible with "some version of psychological determinism"[91] but is a "deterministic psychology of action"[92] which negates his implicit "belief in free choice."[93] On this view, Aristotelian choices are the proto-Humean slaves of desire.[94] The agent's strongest desire directs his or her deliberation and choices since "choice is deliberative desire (βουλευτικὴ ὄρεξις) of things in our power" *(EN,* III, 3, 1113a10–11).[95]

To mount a full-fledged libertarian reading of the *Nicomachean Ethics* would take us too far afield;[96] at the philosophical level, it would

89. See *EN,* VI, 2, 1139a31–33 (Rackham trans.): "Now the cause of action (the efficient, not the final cause) is choice, and the cause of choice is desire and reasoning directed to some end." See *Metaph.,* VI, 1, 1025b23–25 (rev. Oxford trans.): ". . . the principle [ἀρχή] of action is in the doer—viz. choice[προαίρεσις], for that which is done and that which is chosen are the same."

90. Richard Loening, *Die Zurechnungslehre des Aristoteles* (Jena: 1903; reprint, Hildesheim: Georg Olms, 1967), 273–318.

91. Broadie, *Ethics with Aristotle,* 130.

92. Allan, "Practical Syllogism," 333.

93. Gauthier-Jolif, II, 1:219. That Aristotle implicitly affirms free choice follows from his express conviction that some actions are in our power to do or not to do: see *EN,* III, 1, 1110a17–18; 5, 1113b7–8; *EE,* II, 6, 1222b41–1223a9. Although Aristotle does sometimes conflate freedom with voluntariness (see *EN,* III, 1, 1110a17–18), Allan ("Practical Syllogism") appears to deny that Aristotle had any belief in free choice because there is no Aristotelian concept of a separate faculty of "will, i. e., of a self which can intervene to curb or deflect the desires" (335). Allan, if we ignore this anachronistic reference to an interventionist "self," does not clarify what notion of "will" he is refusing Aristotle: spontaneity, or an act of introspective self-determination, or rational desire? Moreover, I am unable to understand one of Allan's exegetical remarks, which apparently is meant to be an argument against attributing "free choice" to Aristotle: "When *eph hemin* is used in its primary sense, before the choice, it is not the single action which is 'in our power,' but 'to do this or not to do it'" (335). See Kenny, *Aristotle's Theory of the Will,* vii–x, for suggested links between Aristotelian and contemporary notions of volition.

94. See David Hume, *A Treatise of Human Nature,* Book II, Part 3, Section 3 (Garden City, N. Y.: Doubleday & Company, 1961), 374: "I shall endeavour to prove *first,* that reason alone can never be a motive to any action of the will. . . ."

95. Cf *EN,* VI, 2, 1139b4–5: διὸ ἢ ὀρεκτικὸς νοῦς ἡ προαίρεσις ἢ ὄρεξις διανοητική.

96. See Gauthier-Jolif, II, 1: 212; II, 2: 445–46, n. 1139b4–5.

engage us, perhaps in a uselessly anachronistic fashion, in post-Aristotelian, theologically inspired disputes about "free will" or "free choice." Against a Humean version of the supremacy of desire, I shall simply counterpose Aristotle's clear acknowledgment *(de An.*, II, 9, 443a6–8) that agents are not always pushed around by their desires. Reason can triumph over desire. The basic defense of an Aristotelian notion of "free choice," to the extent that there is an analogue to that concept in the *Nicomachean Ethics,* is what we have been engaged in: showing that Aristotelian practical reason is not solely confined to deliberation and choices about means but that it embraces deliberation and choice of ends.

If Aristotelian practical reason does embrace ends, then an Aristotelian agent, one anyway who is not completely ruined and spoiled by irrational pleasures,[97] is able to reeducate his or her desires. Practical reason thus becomes the teacher of desire and does not remain just its slave. And this is sufficient freedom of choice to enable us to escape the narrow view.

It would be, however, a gross exaggeration of Aristotle's libertarian tendencies to suggest that Aristotelian practical reason is the unconditional master of human choices. Post-Aristotelian theories of free choice usually focus on the causal indeterminacy of the choice, that is, its freedom from any antecedent, determining efficient cause. Aristotle's attention was more directed to the final causes that practical reason establishes. The actual choices of an agent are not necessitated by the ends that practical reason takes to be truly good or bad. The Aristotelian agent is able to know the better and do the worse. But there is no Aristotelian analogue to the post-Christian freedom to do evil in order to affirm man's groundless or radical freedom.

The Aristotelian agent's freedom and the checks upon it are conditioned by rather domestic passions. The acratic person's occurrent choices can be out of step with his habitual choices; they can be blocked or overwhelmed by passion and thus no longer free. Through a pattern of vicious choices, the profligate man (ἀκόλαστος) has lost the right principle; he thinks it right to pursue pleasure above all else. Consequently, his habitual ends contradict what practical reason requires and he no longer knows the better.[98]

An acratic agent sometimes displays his or her knowledge of the morally better when choosing a morally good action "for its own

---

97. See *EN*, X, 5, 1176a21.
98. See *EN*, VII, 8, 1151a19–26.

sake." The latter motive, as it happens, determines all the choices of the *phronimos*. *Phronesis* is said to be the right principle (ὀϱθὸς λόγος) governing human actions.[99] But in *EN*, VI, 12, 1143b18–28 Aristotle raises the objection as to how *phronesis* adds to the good man's prerational habituation toward noble and just deeds. In reply to this question, Aristotle explains (1144a19) that *phronesis* is the virtue that enables the good man to choose to do good deeds (i.e., those actions that instantiate or lead to the good end set by moral virtue) for their own sake.

Phronesis is the addition to his morally good habits that enables the truly good man (σπουδαῖος) in acting virtuously not only to act "from choice"[100] of the means but "for the sake of the acts themselves."[101] Could the *phronimos* do actions for their own sake if he were incapable of deliberating and judging about the ends instantiated in or sought through virtuous actions?[102] Without that assumption, much of what Aristotle says about appetites sharing in the rational principle of the soul would make little sense.[103]

Aristotle insists that we only deliberate about things that (we think) are "under our control" (τῶν ἐφ' ἡμῖν).[104] This feature of deliberation throws into relief the difference between the *phronimos* and the unjust man.[105] Unlike the unjust and self-indulgent man, the *phronimos* has virtuous habits that enable him to keep his passions (desire, fear, longing, etc.) under rational control.[106] Our passions, though they result from bodily modifications, are "in the soul"; they incline us toward or lead us away from certain ends.[107] To say, however, that the *phronimos*

99. See *EN*, VI, 13, 1144b26–27.

100. διὰ πϱοαίϱεσιν (*EN*, VI, 12, 1144a19). But given that the virtuous man is supposed to act willingly and not out of ignorance (see *EN*, VI, 12, 1144a15), there is no reason to think that Aristotle is not here using πϱοαίϱεσις to indicate a decision, nor to think that the decision reduces to merely the habitual desire to act virtuously: cf. Gauthier-Jolif, II, 2:549, n. 1144a19.

101. *EN*, VI, 12, 1144a20 (rev. Oxford trans.). Aquinas refines the motive of the good man: the prudent man, who finds virtuous actions pleasing, acts "propter amorem ipsorum operum iustitiae" (*SLE*, VI, 10, 1144a11, 192–93; *In Ethic.*, VI, lect. 10 [Spiazzi, n. 1271, p. 343]).

102. Consequently, if the end "is not immediately in our power" (Gauthier-Jolif, II, 1:195, n. 1111b29–30), we should conclude then it must be mediately in our power.

103. See *EN*, I, 13, 1102b13–1103a7.

104. *EN*, III, 3, 1112a31 (Rackham trans.).

105. See *EN*, III, 5, 1114a13–22.

106. See *EN*, II, 4, 1105b21–28.

107. See *EN*, II, 4, 1105b19–25; IV, 9, 1128b13–15; X, 8, 1178a14–20.

has his passions under control does not mean that he deliberates about his passions. The *phronimos* deliberates about those ends to which he is inclined or disinclined by his passions. Because he is not led by his passions, the *phronimos* can choose his goals.[108]

This aspect of the *phronimos* becomes visible by clarifying the implication of Aristotle's remark about choosing actions "for the sake of the actions themselves" *(EN, VI, 12, 1144a19–20* [Rackham trans.]). But while we may legitimately tease this remark, we cannot find any direct support for our position in the text itself. Aristotle states (1144a20) that while "virtue makes the choice right" (τὴν μὲν οὖν προαίρεσιν ὀρθὴν ποιεῖ ἡ ἀρετή), some other power (δύναμις) does what is needed to carry out that choice. Although 1144a20 has been interpreted to mean that there is actual *prohairesis* of ends,[109] the text itself does not explicitly mention ends, and therefore it can hardly be regarded as an explicit license for abandoning the official means-end formula. Admittedly, 1144a20 is puzzling in that it attributes "choice" to virtue,[110] but interpreted conservatively, we are still in the ambit of the narrow view of deliberation and choice. In this case, virtue (ἀρετή) is said to "choose" right ends but only the other power (presumably *prohairesis* in its restricted sense) properly makes "choices" and this power continues to bear solely on the means.

This, in any case, is how Aquinas explains *EN, VI, 12, 1144a20:*

> Moral virtue makes right choice in regard to the intention of the end, but those things that are naturally fitted to be done for the end do not pertain to moral virtue, but to some other power, that is to some other operative principle which discovers ways leading to the end. . . . *(SLE, VI, 10, 1144a11, 200–205; In Ethic.,* VI, lect. 10 [Spiazzi, n. 1271, p. 343])[111]

While developing Aristotle's reply to the question raised at *EN, V I, 12, 1143b18–28* (Why is *phronesis* necessary if the good man makes right

---

108. See *EN,* III, 8, 1117a4–8.

109. See Gauthier-Jolif, II, 2:549, n. 1144a19.

110. Cf. Grant, *Ethics of Aristotle,* 1:184, n. 8, who says that there is "some confusion" in 1149a20, and refers to *EE,* II, 11, 1227b25–1228a1 "where *prohairesis* is said to imply both end and means." The latter text, however, while it mentions the *prohairesis* of ends (1228a1), sustains the essential feature of the narrow view: *logos* is applied to the means but virtue, not *logos,* is the cause of "choosing" some good end (1227b23–24).

111. ". . . virtus moralis facit electionem rectam, quantum scilicet ad intentionem finis, sed ea quae nata sunt fieri propter finem non pertinent ad virtutem moralem, sed ad quandam aliam potentiam, id est ad quoddam aliud operativum principium, quod ingeniatur vias ducentes ad finem . . ." *(SLE, VI, 10, 1144a11, 200–205; In Ethic.,* VI, lect. 10 [Spiazzi, n. 1271, p. 343]).

choices by nature?), Aquinas stays in the ambit of the narrow view.[112] Moral virtue perfects the appetitive part of the soul by inclining desire to a good end; prudence perfects the rational part of the soul by rightly disposing the agent to the means that lead to a noble end.[113] This reluctance to expand the scope of *prudentia* is somewhat perplexing since, at an earlier point in his commentary, Aquinas does give reason a bigger role and even appears to reverse the official relationship between reason and desire: choice is said to be the appetite of the means that are for the end proposed by reason. Appetite, now we are told, clearly follows the lead of reason that sets ends.[114]

Nonetheless, Aristotle's answer to the objector who questions the necessity of *phronesis* suggests that *phronesis* does enable the good man to do something beyond what his virtuous habits and desires already prompt. The *phronimos* is not merely clever (δεινός) in his pursuits, since the clever man can pursue either good or bad ends with equal efficiency.[115] Quite unlike the clever man, the *phronimos* is noble because he pursues noble ends intelligently.[116] Doing good acts intelligently involves choice: one must choose them "for the sake of the acts themselves" (*EN*, VI, 12, 1144a21 [Rackham trans.]). One can argue that, by analogy, it also should be the mark of the good man to pursue good ends not merely because he is habituated to desire them, but because he judges and chooses those good ends for their own sake.[117] Otherwise, the ends of the good man would merely be accidentally in accord with practical wisdom; Aristotle, however, emphasizes that true virtue is not only in conformity with (κατά) but on account of or resulting from (μετά) right reason.[118]

Moreover, there is the one text,[119] to which I have already referred,

112. See *SLE*, VI, 10, 1144a6, 151–68 (*In Ethic.*, VI, lect. 10 [Spiazzi, n. 1269, p. 343]).

113. *Phronesis*, which regards the means that lead to a good end, presupposes but is also to be distinguished from shrewdness (δεινότης), which is merely the ability to settle on the means to any end, be it good or bad: see *EN*, VI, 12, 1144a24–28; *SLE*, VI, 10, 1144a22, 208–24 (*In Ethic.*, VI, lect. 10 [Spiazzi, n. 1272, p. 343]).

114. See *SLE*, VI, 2, 1139a31, 157–60 (*In Ethic.*, VI, lect. 2 [Spiazzi, n. 1133, p. 311]): ". . . est enim electio appetitus eorum quae sunt ad finem, unde ratio proponens finem et ex eo procedens ad ratiocinandum et appetitus tendens in finem comparantur [Spiazzi: comparatur] ad electionem per modum causae."

115. See *EN*, VI, 12, 1144a23–27.

116. See *EN*, VI, 12 1144a20–30.

117. Aquinas, in noting that moral virtue inculcates right desires about ends, attributes to prudence "the rectitude of judgment" (*rectitudo judicii*) about such ends: see *SLE*, VI, 4, 1140b21, 157 (*In Ethic.*, VI, lect. 4 [Spiazzi, n. 1172, p. 320]).

118. *EN*, VI, 13, 1144b26–27.

119. Included in MS *Kb* that Bekker follows in the Berlin Academy edition.

where arguably Aristotle does more than hint about the expanded range of *phronesis*. He makes the remark, one that has exercised many a scholar, that *phronesis* has "the true apprehension of the end":

> If, then, it is characteristic of men of practical wisdom to have deliberated well, excellence in deliberation [εὐβουλία] will be correctness with regard to what conduces to the end of which practical wisdom is the true apprehension [ἀληθὴς ὑπόληψις]. *(EN,* VI, 9, 1142b31–33 [rev. Oxford trans.])

On this reading, the text—assuming that it is not lifted from a corrupt manuscript or that it does not suffer from irredeemable grammatical ambiguity about the object of *phronesis*—is not logically compatible with the narrow view of Aristotelian deliberation (βούλευσις).[120] How could the *phronimos* have "true apprehension" of the end if excellent deliberation (εὐβουλία) is confined to determining only the means toward those ends that are predetermined by his own acquired tastes and habits? For if the wise man's ends were beyond deliberation, they would fall outside the purview of practical wisdom and it would then be impossible for the *phronimos* to know in any rational way that his own ends are true and right.[121] Such ignorance is contrary to the spirit if not the letter of what Aristotle affirms:[122] the true *phronimos*, the man who is expert in deliberation, is capable of hitting "the best for man of things attainable by action."[123] This implies, of course, that there are good, and better goals, and perhaps a best goal to pursue, and, as Aristotle takes for granted, that all of this has to be decided about if both cities and individuals are to attain the highest form of human flourishing.[124]

Nonetheless, many scholars have found *EN,* VI, 9, 1142b33 to be an

120. See infra p. 169, n. 26, cf. Miller, "Aristotle on Rationality,"502, n. 5; Dahl, *Practical Reason,* 38–39; Engberg-Pedersen, *Aristotle's Theory,* 96; R. A. Gauthier, Comptes rendus Bibliographiques, no. 47, in *Revue des études grecques* 76 (1963): 265–68. For a vigorous rebuttal of this interpretation, especially for arguments contra Gauthier, see Aubenque, "La Prudence Aristotélicienne," 40–51.

121. Aquinas notices the problem. Commenting on Aristotle's remark that "sensation originates no action" *(EN,* VI, 2, 1139a18–20 [rev. Oxford trans.]), he explains that "it is manifest that truth pertains neither to sense nor to appetite" *(SLE,* VI, 2, 1139a18, 61–62; *In Ethic.,* VI, lect. 2 [Spiazzi, n. 1127, p. 310]). In other words, the truth of the end can only be grasped intellectually.

122. See *EN,* VI, 13, 1144a8–9.

123. *EN,* VI, 7, 1141b12–14 (rev. Oxford trans.). I am drawing upon Engberg-Pedersen's translation and exegesis (see *Aristotle's Theory,*190–91) of this text. The *phronimos* is στοχαστικός—rationally "able to hit" the end as well as the means.

124. See *Pol.,* VII, 12, 1331b27–30.

obscure text—suggestive but not definitively establishing that Aristotle extends *bouleusis* to the ends of action. Aquinas's commentary on this text does not explicitly break with the narrow view of deliberation; it too is ambiguous about the exact range of *euboulia*. He allows that *prudentia* (but not precisely *euboulia*) has the right estimation of the end:

> *"Euboulia"* in an unqualified sense is rightness of deliberation in relation to that end about which prudence, speaking absolutely, has the true estimation of value, and this is the universal end of the whole of life. . . . *(SLE,* VI, 8, 1142b28, 185–88; *In Ethic.,* VI, lect. 8 [Spiazzi, n. 1233, p. 335])[125]

Nonetheless, if the contemporary interpreter takes *EN,* VI, 13, 1144b30, which states that virtue is "on account of reason" (μετὰ λόγου), as a license to include ends in the range of "choice" or *bouleusis,* the interpretation will fit with what Aristotle says elsewhere. In *De Anima,* III, 7, 431a15–17, Aristotle breaks cleanly with the narrow view of deliberation. He acknowledges that pleasure and pain make the soul pursue or avoid an object. Yet practical reason can also judge that an object is good or bad and, as a consequence of that judgment, pursue or avoid the object.[126] Aristotle specifies (contrary to what medieval thinkers would later claim) that desire arises solely in the nonrational part of the soul; nonetheless, it can be subjected to reason. *Bouleusis* is just such a rational desire: it is a wish for an end that results from desire subject to rational calculation.[127] Reason guarantees the authenticity of the wish: *"bouleusis,"* as Aristotle defines it, is for a real and not merely an apparent good. The good man wishes rightly because he wishes for what is good by nature.[128]

(3) The third step toward an expanded view of *phronesis* is a giant step that takes us far beyond individual texts, wherein we can gather

---

125. ". . . eubulia simpliciter sit rectitudo consilii in ordine ad illum finem circa quem veram existimationem habet prudentia simpliciter dicta, et hic est finis communis totius humanae vitae . . ." *(SLE,* VI, 8, 1142b28, 185–188; *In Ethic.,* VI, lect. 8 [Spiazzi, n. 1233, p. 335]).

126. See *Metaph.,* XII, 7, 1072a27–28 (rev. Oxford trans.): "The primary objects of desire and of thought are the same. For the apparent good is the object of appetite, and the real good is the primary object of wish. "

127. See *de An.,* III, 9. 432b5–433a8. But *Pol.,* VII, 15, 1334b20–25 puts βούλησις in the nonrational part of the soul. For the distinction between Aristotelian βούλησις and the Scholastic notion of an intrinsically rational desire *(voluntas),* see Gauthier-Jolif, II, 1:192–94.

128. See *EN,* III, 4, 1113a21: εἶναι φύσει βουλητόν.

Aristotle's hints and draw inferences that run counter to the narrow view. When one considers the overall purpose of the *Nicomachean Ethics*, there is a much larger reason for abandoning the narrow view of *bouleusis* and *prohairesis*. Aristotle's analysis of *phronesis* presupposes what is an evident and foundational principle for his *eudaimonism*: that we do not deliberate about or choose to be happy. Our wish to be happy is not under our control; it is a fact of human nature.[129] What, then, is the point of Aristotle's extended query in which he examines the three main, but incompatible, ways of life: the vulgar pursuit of pleasure, the aristocratic pursuit of political honor and prestige, and the ever so rare, quasi-divine pursuit of philosophical contemplation? Aristotle assumes that each of them can be and has been identified with happiness;[130] he attempts therefore to settle in which way of life *eudaimonia* is to be truly found. If ways of life were beyond rational deliberation and choice, then Aristotle's discussion would be otiose.

There are, however, limitations to what ethical instruction can accomplish. By itself, it cannot make men morally good. Men become virtuous by acting in a virtuous fashion.[131] The ideal audience for ethical instruction is a group of well-brought-up, experienced but relatively young men—men who are about to enter full swing into the political life.[132] According to the tenets of his own ethical theory, Aristotle must assume that a well-brought-up man knows, by proper habituation, what is morally good, but that what he lacks and needs to get is some rational justification for his opinions.[133] But the *Nicomachean Ethics* is not just an attempt to justify what those with good moral habits already recognize. The young politicos, those anyway to whom Aristotle could profitably speak, would already recognize, since they are well brought up and mature enough to have drawn some conclusions, that the end of the political life is not honor and prestige but that which is worthy of being honored, namely, works of moral beauty and justice.[134] But what they would not already recognize (if we are not to regard the *Nicomachean Ethics* as a redundant exercise) is the superior nobility of the philosophical life; indeed, they probably have the wrong opinion about its value since they are not themselves

---

129. See *EN*, III, 2, 1111b29–30.
130. See *EN*, I, 5, 1095b20: most men preferring (προαιρούμενοι) a life of pleasure, choose it in preference to any other end.
131. See *EN*, II, 4, 1105b2–5.
132. See *EN*, I, 3, 3, 1095a2–3; 4, 1095b5–6.
133. See *EN*, I, 4, 1095b1–10.
134. See *EN*, I, 3, 1094b15; 5, 1095b23–31; X, 9, 1179b23–26.
135. See *EN*, X, 6, 1176b26–27; 7, 1177b4–25.

philosophers.[135] Yet it should not be imagined that Aristotle was trying to revive the Platonic dream of transforming a group of politicians into philosophers.[136] The aim of the *Nicomachean Ethics*, it can hardly be stressed enough, is eminently practical.[137] Aristotle, from the Platonic point of view, tries to do the second best thing: he tries to convert politicians into becoming the type of politician who would honor and make room for the philosopher in their state.[138] In order to do that, the politicians, who must busy themselves in pursuing a strictly human good, need to know which way of life is objectively best.[139] Like Pericles, the wise politician will deliberate about ends.[140]

Aristotle, it is well known, identifies political knowledge (πολιτική) and practical wisdom (φρόνησις): they are the same intellectual disposition or habit (ἕξις), differing only in that the former deals with state affairs of the city and the latter with the affairs of the individual agent.[141] This identification strengthens the supposition that Aristotelian *phronesis* (and not only Aristotle's metaethical analysis) includes some political discussion and deliberation about the end of "the good life in general,"[142] that is, about the end that best instantiates *eudaimo-*

---

136. For an interpretation of Aristotle that stresses the anti-Platonic discontinuity between the philosopher and the politician, see Trond Berg Eriksen, *Bios Theoretikos* (Oslo: Universitets-forlaget, 1976),174–82. On the other end of the spectrum, Kraut, *Aristotle on the Human Good*, 49–62 attempts to show that since the politician exercises practical reason, he too shares (but in a lesser degree than the philosopher who exercises theoretical reason) in the contemplative happiness of the gods.

137. See *EN*, II, 2, 1103b26–27.

138. Cf. *Laws*, V, 739b–740a. On the Platonic notion of guardians who are not philosophers but who have the right opinions, see *Laws*, I, 632C. For a discussion of the "second-best" Platonic polis, where philosophers are not kings but are recognized and have a role in framing the constitution, see Erich Voegelin, *Order and History*, Vol. 3: *Plato and Aristotle* (Baton Rouge: Louisiana State University Press, 1957), 217–23; and Leo Strauss, *The Argument and the Action of Plato's Laws* (Chicago: University of Chicago Press, 1975), 74–75.

139. See *Pol.*, VII, 2, 1324a17–35; *EN*, I, 13, 1102a7–26; X, 8, 1178a9–14.

140. See *EN*, VI, 9, 1142b31–33.

141. See *EN*, VI, 8, 1141b23–24. For Aquinas, prudence and political wisdom are the same habit "secundum substantiam" (i. e., generically) since both are forms of right reason "circa humana bona vel mala." The specific difference, the difference "secundum rationem," is taken from their objects—the good or bad of one man as distinguished from the good or bad "totius multitudinis civilis": see *SLE*, VI, 7, 1141b23, 24–30 *(In Ethic.*, VI, lect. 4 [Spiazzi, n. 1196, p. 329]).

142. *EN*, VI, 4, 1140a28. Cf. *EN*, VI, 9, 1142b29–31 (my trans.): "Deliberative excellence [εὐβουλία] in general is that which is correct about the end in general . . ." ["Excellence in deliberation in the unqualified sense, then, is that which succeeds with reference to what is the end in the unqualified sense . . ." (rev. Oxford trans.)].

nia.[143] This apprehension of the best end, which is necessary if there is to be excellence of deliberation about the means,[144] is attained by considering and rejecting some or other possible constituents of the best end attainable by action.[145]

To lend further support to a nonrestrictive interpretation of deliberation and choice, one can draw out the implications of Aristotle's description of the legislator (νομοθέτης). By comparison with the legislator, the politician (πολιτικός) is like a manual laborer, concerned with the nuts and bolts of politics, those immediately practical matters surrounding the issuance of particular decrees.[146] The legislator, who is at the acme of practical wisdom, has a role that transcends the politician's;[147] he is the "architect of the end" (τοῦ τέλους ἀρχιτέκτων) who determines, in regard to pleasure and pain, what is unqualifiedly good or bad.[148] But who could be properly called an "architect of the end," a man capable of sorting out in some absolute way good and bad pleasures, unless he were capable of knowing and judging, and thus deliberating about, and finally choosing among ultimate ends? The honorific title hardly makes sense without that presupposition.[149]

Such, then, are some of the arguments, which I have schematized in three steps, that lead many contemporary interpreters away from the narrow view of deliberation and choice. One further observation: perhaps the contemporary scholarly concern to have choice bear on ends is but a muted echo of the urgent religious need felt by the medieval theological commentators to clarify Aristotle in the light of the Christian preoccupation about choosing between God and the world.[150] No such choice, of course, confronted Aristotle, nor, we should add, does it confront most contemporary interpreters of Aristotle. Nonetheless, contemporary scholars have reached, by projecting a

143. But here Aquinas again holds to the narrow view: see *SLE*, VI, 4, 1140a28, 36–38 (*In Ethic*, VI, lect. 4 [Spiazzi, n. 1163, p. 319]); ". . . quod ille sit totaliter et simpliciter prudens qui est bene conciliativus de his quae pertinent ad totam vitam."

144. See Cooper, *Reason and the Human Good*, 61–62.

145. See *EN*, VII, 1, 1145b2–7.

146. See *EN*, VI, 7, 1141b28.

147. See *EN*, I, 2, 1094a28–1094b7. Aristotle is the philosopher who teaches would-be legislators. But unlike the philosopher, the legislator and politician are wholly consumed by political matters: see *Pol*. III, 1, 1274b37.

148. *EN*, VII, 11, 1152b2.

149. See *SLE*, VII, 11, 1152b6, 39–44 (*In Ethic.*, VII, lect. 11 [Spiazzi, n. 1472, p. 393]): "Ad philosophum enim moralem pertinet considerare felicitatem, sicut ultimum finem . . . ergo ad moralem philosophum pertinet determinare de delectatione."

150. See Gauthier-Jolif, II, 1:201–2.

few and admittedly somewhat inconclusive texts against the larger Aristotelian background, a view of Aristotelian *bouleusis* that parallels, in effect, the notion of choice *(electio)* that Aquinas's develops in the *Summa theologiae.*

According to Aquinas, "choice" *(electio)* can bear on every intermediate end and even, in a certain way, on the ultimate end. The ultimate end can be characterized as the attainment of *eudaimonia* (rendered either as *felicitas* or *beatitudo)*, which is equivalent to the attainment of a perfect or complete good.[151] But this notion of the complete good must be specified. How and in what is *eudaimonia* realized? The answer to this question, which provides the specification of *eudaimonia,* is a matter for deliberation and its pursuit a matter of choice.[152] Men have to choose between the pursuit of riches or pleasure or some other end.

Aquinas's explicit doctrine of "choice" mirrors the strategy by which Aristotle reaches the overall conclusion of the *Nicomachean Ethics.* We do not choose *eudaimonia* as opposed to some alternative notion of man's ultimate end. Rather, Aristotle analyzes the various ultimate ends that can be plausibly identified with *eudaimonia:* pleasure, political activity, and contemplation.[153] These are both ends in themselves and possible instantiations (whether singly or in some combination) of the ultimate end. Aristotle's analysis of these possible ends is conducted in the light of strictly formal criteria: which of the ends is most self-sufficient, perfect, complete, and independent of external aids? These criteria allow Aristotle to classify the life of philosophical contemplation as the highest form of *eudaimonia,* and the life of virtuous political activity as a penultimate form of *eudaimonia.* Both ways of life, for an agent not irretrievably trapped by vicious habits, are ultimate ends that can be and need to be deliberated about and chosen.

3. *"Phronesis" and the Ultimate End of Human Life*

Aristotle's account of the relationship between reason and morally correct appetites and habits leaves us with many questions that reappear when we examine more closely how the Aristotelian *phronimos* attains knowledge of the correct *ultimate* end of human life. According to Cooper, it is quite beyond "reasonable doubt" that the *phronimos* knows "by some kind of intellectual intuition what the correct

---

151. See *ST,* I–II, qq. 12–13.
152. See *ST,* I–II, q. 1, a. 5; a. 7.
153. See *EN,* I, 7, 1097b2.

ultimate end is."[154] The intuition, however, cannot be a priori. Aristotle rejects any view of human character that includes the notion that some men are born with a vision of what is morally good, and therefore naturally pursue the right ultimate end.[155] He firmly maintains that men are responsible for how they see the good because of how they act. The moral intuition of what is the ultimate good, if it can be correctly labeled an "intuition," arises only from the experience of doing good acts.[156] But why does one person but not another have the correct intuition into the goodness or badness of particular acts? Aristotle emphasizes that virtuous habituation is a condition sine qua non for the good man attaining his correct insight, but we have also seen that this answer involves a ambiguous, circular relation between desire and reason.[157]

Aristotle, despite these obscurities, is tolerably clear about how knowledge of particular actions leads to knowledge of universal moral principles. Greenwood notices, along with a number of other scholars, that Aristotle ties intuitive *nous* to induction (ἐπαγωγή) and, in particular, to the inductive attainment of moral principles.[158] Greenwood, though, ties the knot too tightly; he maintains that "the grand universal judgment of the nature of the final end"[159] (i.e., the end that specifies *eudaimonia*) is also reached by induction. But this is surely incorrect. A distinction should be made between the inductive attainment of universal moral principles (such as "Killing an enemy's children is ignoble and wrong") and the allegedly inductive grasp of the ultimate end. A great deal of theoretical argumentation, which will of course involve some induction from experience, is needed before one can conclude which one of Aristotle's three basic ways of life is truly *eudaimonic*.

While it can be easily maintained that ordinary experience and induction leads to the knowledge of universal moral principles,[160] even

---

154. Cooper, *Reason and Human Good*, 64.

155. See *EN*, III, 5, 1114b5–16.

156. See *EN*, VI, 12, 1144a31–34.

157. Cf. Joseph Owens, "The *Kalon* in Aristotelian Ethics," in O'Meara, ed., *Studies in Aristotle*, 261–77, who leaves the question of the relationship between intuition and right habituation unsettled: "The person properly brought up either recognizes at once or can be readily shown what is right or wrong in ordinary conduct" (268).

158. For a powerful interpretation along these lines, see Dahl, *Practical Reason*, 41–60, 227–36.

159. Greenwood, *Book Six*, 70.

160. See *EN*, VI, 7, 1141b14–15, which affirms that "phronesis is not only of the universal" (οὐδ᾽ ἐστιν ἡ φρόνησις τῶν καθόλου μόνον).

the *phronimos* must be shown by philosophical demonstration that contemplation is the true ultimate end of human life. That, after all, is the purpose of the philosophical teaching spelled out in the *Nicomachean Ethics.*[161] There are, of course, more politicians than philosophers. But the ordinary politician does not come to grasp the true end of political life (noble works and just deeds) by a process of induction from how men usually lead the political life. By definition, "ordinary politicians" are the ones pursuing the ordinary political awards: honor and prestige. But the politician who possesses *phronesis* is certainly superior to the ordinary politico. Could such a *phronimos* reach through his own reflective experience, without benefit of the philosopher's teaching, the knowledge of the right end of political life? Aristotle seems to think that this insight into the value of justice and noble works is not, in fact, so rare among men of action.[162] What, then, can the philosopher offer to such a practically wise politician?

On the assumption that Aristotelian moral agents can deliberate about ends, we need, therefore, to distinguish the deliberation of the *phronimos* not only from the deliberation of the ordinary politician but also from that of the philosopher. The philosophical criteria that Aristotle uses to sort out the best form of life are certainly not the first principles of ordinary moral agents but neither are they the criteria used in the more accurate and more profoundly developed moral reasoning of the *phronimos.*[163] Ordinary moral agents deliberate badly about the ultimate end of life; they are deceived by what is apparently but not really good: pleasure, wealth, and honor.[164] The *phronimos*

161. In commenting on *EN*, VI, 7, 1141b14–15, Greenwoood *(Book Six,* 44) asserts that "of course" the general principle, which Aristotle leaves unstated, but upon which "all the reasoning of the truly *phronimos* must ultimately be founded" is the principle that eudaimonia = theoretical contemplation. Greenwood thus equates the "truly *phronimos*" with the philosopher who has argued for the identification of *eudaimonia* and theoretical contemplation. But even if the philosopher and not the virtuous politician has the highest form of *phronesis,* it would be too great a stretch to maintain that there can be no "true" *phronesis* antecedent to philosophical deliberation and decision about the ultimate end. The students who come to get ethical instruction must already be practically virtuous in order to profit from their philosophical lessons. The fact that they would bother to sit at the feet of an Aristotle reveals that they already possess enough practical wisdom to know that politics is about justice and not just about honor and prestige. See *EN,* I, 3, 1095a1–12.

162. See *EN,* I, 5, 1095b29–31.

163. See Sherman, *Fabric of Character,* 10, n. 7, who maintains, against Cooper, that dialectical argument is continuous with the moral agent's deliberative choices, so that both are simultaneously necessary if the *phronimos* is to reach an adequate conception of happiness.

164. See *EN,* I, 4, 1095a20–25.

deliberates well about these things. He is a man of action; he seeks his happiness in the political life. But unlike the ordinary politician, the *phronimos* has come to realize that moral virtue (acting justly for the well-being of the *polis*) and not honor is the end of the political life. He does not need the philosopher in order to understand this dimension of "true politics." He has learned this from his own experience which has been guided and colored by his virtuous habits.

EN, VI, 10–11, 1143a1–1143b17 sketches but does not provide a fully developed account of how the *phronimos* comes to grasp the universal principles of morality. First, Aristotle fills out the picture of the *phronimos*. He incorporates into the notion of *phronesis* a number of subordinate conventional virtues which also were featured in the pre-Aristotelian philosophical tradition:[165] understanding (σύνεσις), which judges about other mens' opinions on practical matters; right judgment (γνώμη) about matters of justice; and intuition or insight (νοῦς) into particular actions. Aristotle explains, in short, how the elements of practical wisdom, the virtues subordinate to it, enable the *phronimos* to grasp and to effect true and right particular actions. In the first place, *phronesis* comes only with experience. The man who has been properly educated into the values of his own culture is aware of what, to him, are obvious "facts" that function as starting points for his moral reasoning.[166] He believes that this particular action is good and is to be done. But while the good man first derives his goals from education and habituation, age and repeated experiences permit him, by an induction, to grasp the universal (i.e., the universal end) that he has been implicitly pursuing. He "sees," eventually, that this *type* of action is to be done.[167]

Deliberating about what to do is, of course, an important part of a moral agent's "experience."[168] When deliberating about what to do, a moral agent can make a mistake about either the universal principle or the particular action. In regard to the universal, one may hold a wrong view about the (moral) type of the agent or the (moral) type of the action deliberated about. In regard to the particular, one may misjudge whether this particular action falls under the moral type.[169] The *phronimos*, however, has knowledge of both universal and particulars. Genu-

---

165. See Burnet, *Ethics of Aristotle*, 278–81, notes.

166. See *EN*, I, 4, 1095b1–10.

167. See *EN*, VI, 3, 1139b25–31; VI, 7, 1141b15.

168. See *EN*, VI, 7, 1141b8–9: ἡ δὲ φϱόνησις πεϱὶ τὰ ἀνθϱώπινα καὶ πεϱὶ ὧν ἔστι βουλεύσασθαι.

169. See *EN*, VI, 8, 1142a0–22; VII, 3, 1147a5–8.

ine practical wisdom *(phronesis)* is never involved in falsehood; it is a habit that attains truth in accordance with reason.[170]

What, though, guarantees that *phronesis* always attain the correct universal principles? From the extent texts all that we can safely infer is that the Aristotelian *phronimos* correctly apprehends the true or morally virtuous ends of human action, that these ends are attained without any great difficulty or effort, and that his knowledge of them is a matter of practical and not theoretical wisdom.[171] In concrete cases, the *phronimos* because of his correct habituation has immediate insight into what actions would be noble or ignoble,[172] and noble actions, Aristotle assures us, necessarily promote the common good.[173]

Precisely at this point, Aquinas appeals to the indemonstrable, universal principles of practical reason with which the agent is naturally endowed:

> The perfection of moral virtue of which we are now speaking, consists in this: that the appetite is regulated in accordance with reason. The first principles of reason, however, are naturally implanted in us in regard to both practical and speculative matters. Therefore, just as through principles already known, a man makes himself actually know by discovery, so too by acting in accordance with the principles of practical reason, a man makes himself actually virtuous. *(SLE*, II, 4, 1105b5, 99–106; *In Ethic.*, II, 4 [Spiazzi, n. 286, p. 81])[174]

In no text does Aristotle either explicitly refer to or explicitly reject such indemonstrable, necessary, universal moral principles.[175] But we know that Aristotle thought that moral universals (i.e., positive moral principles) hold only "for the most part"; they have exceptions.[176] In

170. See *EN*, VI, 5, 1140b6–7; 1140b20.

171. See *EN*, VI, 5, 1140a24–29; 7, 1141a29–30.

172. See Owens, "The *Kalon* in Aristotelian Ethics," 274: moral obligation is a matter of immediately recognizing what is concretely right or fitting, i. e., having an intuition into "the intrinsic nature of the *kalon*" (275).

173. See *EN*, IX, 8, 1169a8–11.

174. ". . . perfectio virtutis moralis, de qua nunc loquimur, consistit in hoc quod appetitus reguletur secundum rationem; prima autem rationis principia sunt naturaliter nobis indita, ita in operativis sicut in speculativis, et ideo, sicut per principia praecognita facit aliquis se scientem in actu, ita agendo secundum principia rationis practicae facit aliquis se virtuosum in actu" *(SLE*, II, 4, 1105b5, 99–106; *In Ethic.*, II, 4 [Spiazzi, n. 286, p. 81]).

175. Cf. Engberg-Pedersen, *Aristotle's Theory*, 37–62, who finds two intuitive universal principles of "nobility and utility" that govern the sharing of natural goods by the *phronimos*.

176. See *EN*, X, 9, 1180b7–25.

exceptional cases, it is important to know not to apply the otherwise relevant principle.

Aristotle sticks close to the experience of the *phronimos* even though he occasionally propounds single "theoretical" arguments. Aristotelian ethics takes the standpoint of practical wisdom; it is a practical not a theoretical science. Theoretical wisdom (σοφία) does not study how we become happy because it does not study objects that come into being, and happiness comes into being as a concomitant of certain activities.[177] Ethics is a practical science that aims to make men good.[178] Since practical wisdom and moral virtue necessarily go together,[179] Aristotle appropriately directs moral agents to look to the virtuous man as the "norm and measure"[180] of ethical truth.

Is there any other criterion? Or must the Aristotelian philosopher be content with looking solely to the virtuous man as the measure? If so, there is an unavoidable question for the contemporary reader of Aristotle. How does Aristotle prove, if he does, that the standard set by the good man is not merely conventional, perhaps reflecting just Aristotle's refinement of Greek cultural standards of praise and blame?[181] Habituation or the "facts" that habituation makes evident are the starting points for the bad man as well as for the good man. What is it that provides ultimate justification for the principles of the conventionally good man? Contemporary moral theory is mired in endless theoretical

177. See *EN*, VI, 12, 1143b19–21: the emphasis is on the distinction between *sophia* and *phronesis*. The latter knows the means to happiness, thus leaving some room for relevant theoretical reflection about human ends inasmuch as such ends can be examined from the standpoint of man's psychological constitution; hence the need for the politician to have some theoretical knowledge of the soul and its powers. See *EN*, I, 13, 1102a23–26; *Top.*, II, I, 1099. But questions about how to *become* happy belong strictly in the domain of practical knowledge: see IX, 9, 1169b30–31. Cf. *SLE*, VI, 10, 1143b19, 22–24 *(In Ethic.*, VI, lect. 10 [Spiazzi, n. 1258, p. 342]): ". . . sapientia autem nullius generationis, id est operationis, est considerativa, cum sit de primis principiis entium."

178. See *EN*, II, 2, 1103b27–30. Aquinas adds that a strictly theoretical knowledge of ethics does not greatly perfect the intellect because ethics studies "variabilem veritatem contingentium operabilium" *(SLE*, II, 2, 1103b26, 33; *In Ethic.*, II, lect. 2 [Spiazzi, n. 256, p. 73]). Ethics as a practical science is valuable because it is *"utilis."*

179. See *EN*, VI, 13, 1144b30–32.

180. *EN*, III, 4, 1113a33. See *EN*, II, 6, 1107a1–2; VI, 5, 1140a24–25.

181. See Joseph Owens, "Nature and Ethical Norm in Aristotle," in *Aristotle: The Collected Papers of Joseph Owens*, 166: "With correct habituation, any [Aristotelian] man is able to make the decision that his fellow citizens will universally regard as correct in moral matters." For a critique of Aristotle's "very specific Greek ideal" (150), see Hampshire, *Morality and Conflict*, who contends that it is rationally impossible to eliminate alternative ways of life with alternative internal schemes of virtues and vices.

debates about the justification of moral principles. Perhaps Aristotle takes the correct alternative route in assuming that the habits and opinions of the morally good man are a sufficient criterion for practical wisdom.[182] But to decide that moral opinions have no further theoretical justification is to destine Aristotelian ethics, and not only the practical deliberations of the Aristotelian moral agent, to moving in a circle of strictly practical beliefs and opinions. This is not likely to prove satisfactory to most contemporary moral philosophers who, despite the many problems that are attendant upon theoretical justifications of ethical principles, are painfully aware that competing circles of moral opinion and practice divide our own culture.

Aristotle, who considered himself obliged to subordinate the metaphysical opinions of friends to the untrammeled pursuit of truth,[183] was no less critical about de facto moral beliefs. The truth or falsity of an individual's ethical beliefs must be rationally tested and only some current opinions can be left standing.[184] Practical reason aims at what is objectively good and true: "In conduct our work is to start from what is good for each and make what is good in itself good for each."[185]

By his habits, the good man is properly aimed and has the right opinions about certain ends to be pursued, but there are *reasons* to be adduced in support of the good man's habits and opinions.[186] Experience is essential but it is not everything even in politics; legislators need to exercise intelligence (διάνοια) and critical judgment in framing a constitution.[187] But these kind of critical judgments are certainly an exercise of practical intelligence;[188] they are exactly what we would expect from the *phronimos* who knows what the overall good is for the city.[189] The arguments of the *Nicomachean Ethics* remain within the realm of practical intelligence, of what is accessible to the *phronimos*. But notwithstanding the fundamentally practical character of ethics,[190] there is

182. See Joseph Owens, "The Aristotelian Conception of the Sciences," in *Aristotle: The Collected Papers of Joseph Owens*, 28: "The notion that a science can find its principles in the habituation of the doer or producer . . . offers a fruitful solution to difficulties arising from [present-day] notions of ethics as a theoretical science of norms. . . ."

183. See *EN*, I, 6, 1096a11–16.

184. See *EN*, VII, 1, 1145b1–5.

185. *Metaph.*, VII, 4, 1029b5–7 (rev. Oxford trans.). Cf. *EN*, VII, 14, 1154a22–25.

186. See *EN*, I, 4, 1095b7.

187. See *EN*, X, 9, 1180b35–1181b12. Politicians do not exercise διάνοια: see 1181a2–3.

188. See *EN*, X, 9, 1180b28.

189. See *EN*, X, 9, 1180b13–16.

190. See *EN*, X, 8, 1179a35–1179b2.

room and perhaps need, so Aristotle suggests when he rejects the Eudoxian identification of good with pleasure and other such doctrines, for theoretical arguments about what is objectively good.[191]

Such arguments, which are not developed in any detail in the *Nicomachean Ethics*, would be theoretical inasmuch as they would focus on the exigencies of human nature[192] interpreted in terms of metaphysical and psychological distinctions about actions, passions, and qualities.[193] These arguments, though they are not focused on the language of morals, are like "metaethical arguments"; they are aimed not at making people act in morally virtuous fashion but at determining the theoretical framework in which to view ultimate human happiness.[194] One such argument, for example, might attempt to prove the theoretical principle "That which perfects a being's activities perfects its life and is therefore not only a desirable but a good thing to pursue."[195]

4. Dialectic and Ethics

On one long-standing and plausible reading, of which Burnet has been the most influential exponent in English-language scholarship,[196] Aristotle defends his basic ethical principles dialectically.[197] A dialectical argument does not begin by alleging indemonstrable or intuitive

191. See *EN*, X, 2, 1172b9–18.

192. See Owens, "The Grounds of Ethical Universality in Aristotle," 154: "The location of the supreme good in the activity that conforms with the best and most complete virtue is based upon a theoretical study of human nature and its resultant actions."

193. See, e. g., the discussion of pleasure in *EN*, X, 4, 1174a13–1175a2.

194. See *EN*, I, 3, 1095a6–7; 13, 1102a5–10, 24–27; VI, 2, 1139a27–29.

195. Cf. *EN*, X, 4, 1175a16–17.

196. See Burnet, *Ethics of Aristotle*, xxxix–xlvi. Cf. T[erence] H. Irwin, "First Principles in Aristotle's Ethics," in *Midwest Studies in Philosophy*, Vol. 3: *Studies in Ethical Theory*, ed. Peter A. French, Theodore E. Uehling, Jr., and Howard K. Wettstein (Minneapolis: University of Minnesota Press, 1980), 252–72; "Aristotle's Methods of Ethics," in O'Meara, ed., *Studies in Aristotle*, 193–223.

197. See Aristotle's discussion of incontinence (ἀκρασία) in *EN*, VII, 1, 1145b2–7 (rev. Oxford trans.) which begins with a statement of the dialectical method: "We must, as in all other cases, set the phenomena before us and, after first discussing the difficulties, go on to prove, if possible, the truth of all the reputable opinions. . . ."

Aristotle uses dialectic to defend the theoretical principle of contradiction: see *Metaph.*, IV, 4, 1006a11–22. But, in this latter instance, the dialectical defense runs clearly parallel to an assertion of the immediacy of the principle: "And it will not be possible for the same thing to be and not to be, except in virtue of an ambiguity . . ." (1006b19–20 [rev. Oxford trans.]).

For the metaphysical considerations grounding the indemonstrability of the

principles but neither is its beginning merely provisional or sophistic;[198] rather, it "reasons from reputable opinions" (ἐνδόξα),[199] preferably those held by the best of "experienced and older people,"[200] and appeals to other common beliefs to support these principles. But Aristotle, as Irwin points out, does not appeal only to common *moral* beliefs,[201] since that would be too small a dialectical circle, but to common *nonmoral* beliefs. By exposing the congruity between certain moral opinions and certain authoritative and reputable opinions about nonmoral issues, the moral philosopher is implicitly relying on a kind of "coherence theory" of truth to support his specifically ethical opinions.

The *Nicomachean Ethics* begins by accepting common and, for Aristotle, rather banal moral opinions: that happiness *(eudaimonia)* is the final good for man and that man finds his happiness in his highest activity.[202] But these beliefs are not just isolated opinions since they can be shown to harmonize or to be compatible with other common, nonmoral beliefs—about life, about human nature, about characteristic human activities, and about the teleological character of rational agency. In turn, the moral agent's nonmoral beliefs cannot be adequately justified (i.e., shown to be true) except through scientific demonstrations in psychology, physics, and, finally, in metaphysics.[203] What Aristotle's doctrine of happiness presupposes is that "the intellect [νοῦς] more than anything else is man."[204] In order to show the latter, we must have a metaphysical understanding of human nature.

The dialectical defense of Aristotle's basic ethical principles leads back to the theoretical sciences but this defense demands only that moral beliefs be congruent with, not immediately deducible from or reducible to, metaphysical principles.[205] Metaphysics or wisdom, be-

---

principle of non-contradiction, see Thomas V. Upton, "Psychological and Metaphysical Dimensions of Non-Contradiction in Aristotle," *Review of Metaphysics* 36 (1983): 591–606.

198. See Greenwood, *Book Six,* 127–44, who argues that Aristotle never adopts "even temporarily any view that is not actually his own" (138).

199. *Top.,* I, 1, 100a28–29 (rev. Oxford trans.). See *EN,* I, 4, 1095a28–30. At the practical level, the perceived harmony of an opinion with the "facts" renders the opinion credible and efficacious: see *EN,* X, 1, 1172b6.

200. *EN,* VI, 11, 1143b12 (rev. Oxford trans.).

201. See, e.g., the appeal to and the need to clarify what men "mean by justice" in *EN,* IV, 8, 1128b5–9.

202. See *EN,* I, 4, 1095a15–20; 7, 1097b22.

203. See *EN,* I, 8, 1098b15–20; I, 13, 1102a22–23 (rev. Oxford trans.): "The student of politics, then, must study the soul. . . ."

204. *EN,* X, 7, 1178a6–7 (Rackham trans.).

205. See *EN,* I, 8, 1098b9–1099a1. Concerned to protect Aristotle from a "fallacious naturalism," Alfonso Gómez-Lobo, "The Ergon Inference," *Phronesis* 34

cause it is knowledge of the most noble objects, is superior to *phronesis*,[206] but Aristotle never states that we need metaphysics in order to ground our moral principles.[207] Still, metaphysics and physics give knowledge of natures, and especially psychology, which gives knowledge of human nature, is relevant to the clarification and justification of our moral beliefs and judgments. In short, while Aristotle never attempts to deduce the principles of ethics from either metaphysical or psychological principles, and hence he is not guilty of any is-ought violations, there are many allusions to such principles in the *Nicomachean Ethics*. Aristotle's assumption is that ethics, though an independently grounded practical science, is in harmony with the principles of the theoretical sciences of which metaphysics is supreme. Aquinas, as we shall see, takes the same point of view.

Needless to say, the interpreter who adopts this position can find in Aristotle merely an outline of this "coherence theory" of moral and metaphysical truth.[208] But to the extent that such coherence can be displayed, scientific confirmation of ethical principles is possible, and Aristotle's ethics can be said to transcend its initial dependence on cultural habituation, right opinions, and moral intuitions.[209]

(1989): 170–84, argues convincingly that Aristotle "does not infer the notion of the human good [solely] from facts about human nature" (170). The Aristotelian argument, as he reconstructs it, includes an evaluative premise containing the term "good." But Gómez-Lobo's suggested evaluative principle seems (if the fact-value distinction is to be equated, as is usual, with the is-ought distinction) to lack any prescriptive or moral force. "For any x, if x has an *ergon* y, then x will be a good x, if and only if x produces good instances of y" (182). In any case, without specifying exactly (see 173) how this principle is known to be true (by induction?—see *EE*, II, 1, 1219a91), Gómez-Lobo labels it a commonsensical rather than a metaphysical principle. But does Gómez-Lobo's position entail that the Aristotelian moral philosopher can only fall back on commonsense moral intuitions in attempting to justify basic moral principles? Cf. *EN*, I, 8, 1098b9–10 and *EE*, II, 1, 1219a34–1219b1–5, which contrasts current opinion and scientific conclusions deduced from premises.

206. See *EN*, VI, 13, 1145a6–11.

207. J. Donald Monan, *Moral Knowledge and Its Methodology in Aristotle* (Oxford: Clarendon Press, 1968), however, first finds a "radical difference" (114) and then a "conflict" (150) or "dissidence" (151) between the *implicit* "speculative psychology" (107) underlying the *ergon* argument (which he discerns in Books I and X of the *Nicomachean Ethics*) and Aristotle's explicitly non-metaphysical doctrine of *phronesis* which highlights "the contingent, individualized *prakton agathon*." Monan resolves the contradiction by proposing another hypothesis about Aristotle's "development." This developmental hypothesis, in favor of the maturity of the *phronesis* doctrine found in the "common books," leads Monan to reject any Scholastic effort "to weld together a Protreptican summit of contemplation and a lower range moral life" (151).

208. See Gauthier-Jolif, I, 1:61.

209. See *EN*, I, 9, 1099b25–26. For different reasons, Gauthier-Jolif, II, 1:23–25,

5. Aligning Aristotle and Aquinas

Although I shall defer a detailed treatment of Thomistic natural law principles until Chapters 6 and 7, I can now align Aristotle's and Aquinas's conception of the ground of morality. Aristotle asserts that genuine *phronesis*, although about things that fluctuate in their moral goodness, can never be directed, unlike mere cleverness, to any morally bad ends. At the same time, he repeatedly makes the point that our moral principles or ends are set by our prerational acquired habits. Now if this is the ultimate source of our principles, then even the morality of the *phronimos* seems to lack any adequate cognitive foundations. Undoubtedly, the *phronimos* has a good character; Aristotle declares the latter a necessary condition for the exercise of *phronesis*.[210] Because he has a morally good character, the *phronimos* is then able through rational calculation to aim at what, for man, is the best of the things attainable by action.[211] This is knowledge of what practicable good (πρακτὸν ἀγαθόν) is best for the human species. Aristotle, however, concurs *(EN,* 5, 1140a26; 8, 1141b33) with popular opinion that the *phronimos* must also know how to reach what is best for himself. Now it may be that what is best for the human species is always what is best for the individual. But how does the *phronimos* know this? Moreover, it is reasonable to assume that, even among the *phronimoi*, there will be some difference in what is good for each, and hence some difference in the ends that each ought to pursue. Aquinas suggests as much.[212] The point, then, is how does the moral character of the *phronimos* settle which end, among rationally competing ends, that he should pursue? It seems implausible that this kind of decision can be rightly made solely on the basis of one's habitual preferences.

Perhaps, "in the best Platonic and Socratic tradition,"[213] Aristotle merely took for granted and hence felt no need to "thematize" that

argue that Aristotelian moral philosophy is "une connaissance *originale,* ni dialectique ni science, mais sagesse . . . " (25).

210. See *EN,* VI, 13, 1144b30–32: "δῆλον οὖν ἐκ εἰρημένων ὅτι οὐχ οἶόν τε ἀγαθὸν εἶναι κυρίως ἄνευ φρονήσεως, οὐδὲ φρόνιμον ἄνευ τῆς ἐθικῆς ἀρετῆς."

211. Cf. *EN,* VI, 7, 1141b12–14: "ὁ δ' ἁπλῶς εὔβουλος ὁ τοῦ ἀρίστου ἀνθρώπῳ τῶν πρακτῶν στοχαστικὸς κατὰ τὸν λογισμόν."

212. Cf. *SLE,* VI, 6, 1141a22, 57–62 *(In Ethic.,* VI, lect. 6 [Spiazzi, n. 1187, p. 326]): ". . . sed id quod est prudens oportet quod sit alterum apud diversos propter hoc quod prudentia dicitur secundum proportionem et habitudinem ad aliquid. Ille enim qui potest bene speculari singula quae pertinent ad seipsum dicitur esse prudens et tali conceditur sive attribuitur prudentia." Cf. *SLE,* VI, 4, 1140b11–b21, 126–63 *(In Ethic.,* VI, lect. 4 [Spiazzi, nn. 1170–72, p. 320]).

213. Rhonheimer, *Praktische Vernunft,* 418.

right reason can universally apprehend and prescribe the highest moral good for man and for himself.[214] Nonetheless, what Aristotle does thematize is not easily reconcilable with this tradition: an anti-Socratic insistence on the priority of the prerational side of the virtues, that is, of the psychological and epistemic determinacy of a child's emotional habituation for an adult's rational deliberation and choice.[215] It is this theme that makes the rational ground of morality recede in the *Nicomachean Ethics*. Aristotle's explicit texts leave obscure whether it is *phronesis* or moral virtue that enables the *phronimos* to grasp the right final ends of human action. Does a man have any effective rational choice of the ultimate ends that determine his character, or does his childhood or prerational character determine his ends and define the sphere of his rational choices?[216] As an abundant secondary literature testifies, the cognitivist/emotivist tension in Aristotle's doctrine cannot be eliminated solely on the basis of the Aristotelian texts bequeathed to us. Scholars who wish to eliminate this tension and to provide Aristotelian morality with strong cognitive foundations are forced to read between Aristotle's lines. Reading between the lines, they can then claim either that *phronesis*, through deliberative reasoning, or that practical *nous*, through immediate intellectual intuition, cognitively grasps the true basic ends or end of human action. Still, each of these alternatives is vulnerable to criticism.

If we choose to remain within the limits set by the texts and not to read between the lines, as I think Aquinas finally did not, we are left with an unresolved tension in Aristotelian morality. On the one hand, Aristotle repeatedly emphasizes that the moral principles of the *phronimos* are grounded in his morally virtuous character. On the other hand, we lack solid textual evidence for equating the functions of theoretical and practical *nous*. But it is just this unresolved tension about the cognitivist/emotivist sources of moral virtue that enlivens Aristotle's ethics. The exercise of practical reason remains subject to the vagaries of human character. Aristotle seems to accept that the emotive distortions to which practical reasoning is subject will inevitably be played out in the lives and decisions of moral agents. Philosophical ethics can diagnose but cannot retrospectively correct men's characters.

In terms of the Aristotelian paradigm, correct moral reasoning must begin and, in a certain sense, can only end with the beliefs of well

---

214. Cf. *EN*, IX, 8, 1169a17–18 (rev. Oxford trans.): ". . . for the intellect [νοῦς] always chooses what is best, and the good man [ἐπιεικής] obeys his intellect."
215. See *EN*, VI, 13, 1144b25–30.
216. See *EN*, III, 7, 1114b1–3; VI, 13, 1144b4–5.

brought up people.[217] The beliefs, and the moral principles that enshrine those beliefs, reflect a pattern of life that is not necessitated by human nature but by human culture. Against bad character, Aristotle offers only long-term, preventive medicine. In a good *polis*, the legislators can pass laws that sanction a social order that sustains the right domestic education in pleasure and pain. Aristotle identifies this right childhood habituation as the necessary condition for the emergence of the *phronimos*.[218]

Aquinas recognizes that the primacy of habituated emotion is the central feature in Aristotle's account of moral reasoning; he comments, without flinching, that everything depends on childhood habituation since we more firmly retain what was first imprinted on us.[219] Accordingly, Aquinas usually takes the Aristotelian restrictions on *phronesis* at face value; he reiterates, without hinting at any serious objection, the doctrine of those texts that confine *phronesis* to judgments about means.[220] But, so restricted, the scope of Aristotelian *phronesis* is undoubtedly smaller than that of Thomistic practical reason. Aristotle states *(EN,* VI, 1141a 7-8) that *"nous* is of the [theoretical] principles."[221] Aquinas extends the operation of *nous* to the practical order. And it is this unequivocal extension that allows Aquinas to ground morality in intellect rather than rightly habituated emotion.

In its practical function, Aquinas claims that *nous* intuits, through the sensible or experiential activation of the innate habit of *synderesis,* "the universal principles of the natural law."[222] What is remarkable is that Aquinas, at least in his early commentary on Peter Lombard, also purports to find the doctrine of *synderesis* in Aristotle:

Hence, just as there are the innate principles of demonstrations in the speculative reason, so there are innate ends, connatural to man, in the

---

217. The universal or major premises of a practical syllogism is a "belief" or an "opinion": ἣ μὲν γὰρ καθόλου δόξα *(EN,* VII, 3, 1147a25).

218. See *EN,* VI, 8, 1142a8–10.

219. See *SLE,* II, 1, 1103b22, 173–75 *(In Ethic.,* II, lect. 1 [Spiazzi, n. 254, p. 71]): ". . . non parum differt quod aliquis statim a iuventute assuescat vel bene vel male operari, sed multum differt, quin potius totum ex hoc dependet; nam ea quae nobis a pueritia imprimuntur, firmius retinemus."

220. See *SLE,* VI, 10, 1144a6, 151–58 *(In Ethic.,* VI, lect. 10 [Spiazzi, n. 1269, p. 343]); VI, 11, 1145a2, 179–80 *(In Ethic.,* VI, lect. 11 [Spiazzi, n. 1289, p. 347]); X, 12, 1178a10, 42–47 *(In Ethic.,* X, lect. 12 [Spiazzi, n. 2114, p. 550]).

221. νοῦν εἶναι τῶν ἀρχῶν *(EN,* VI, 6, 1141a7–8).

222. See *In II Sent.,* d. 7, q. 1, a. 2 (Mandonnet, 185): "In synderesi autem sunt universalia principia iuris naturalis; unde oportet quod remurmuret omni ei quod contra ius naturale fit. Sed tamen istud murmur est actus naturae."

practical reason. In regard to these ends, there is not an acquired or an infused habit, but a natural habit [called] *"synderesis,"* in the place of which the Philosopher (in Book VI of the *Ethics*) posits the understanding *[intellectus]* [of first principles] in practical affairs. *(III Sent.*, d. 33, q. 2, a. 4, sol. 4 [Moos, n. 242, p. 1066])[223]

However, in the commentary on the *Nicomachean Ethics*, and in other mature works, Aquinas is more restrained. He refers to but does not directly attribute the doctrine of practical *nous* or its refinement, the doctrine of *synderesis*, to Aristotle.[224] This exegetical restraint is certainly called for since Aristotle makes no mention of any universal, innate, indemonstrable principles of practical reason. As Aquinas's careful exegesis of the *Nicomachean Ethics* evidences, Aristotle discusses only the indemonstrable and necessary principles of theoretical reason.[225] The obvious explanation for what some interpreters regard as a lacuna in Aristotle's account is that, given what Aristotelian ethics is about, there is no need for or even possibility of such indemonstrable, universal, and necessary practical principles. Aristotle's doctrine is clear: only the theoretical sciences deal with necessary things.[226] Ethics, as a subdivision of politics, is a practical science aimed at making people virtuous; more precisely, ethics, like *phronesis*, is about human actions and human goods, both of which are variable or can be otherwise than they are.[227] The contingency of singular actions, about which we must make moral judgments, obviates any deductive moral science in the strict sense of the term. *Phronesis* is a form of opinion (δόξα)

223. "Unde sicut in ratione speculativa sunt innata principia demonstrationum, ita in ratione practica sunt innati fines connaturales homini; unde circa illa non est habitus acquisitus aut infusus, sed naturalis sicut *synderesis*, loco cujus Philosophus in VI *Eth.* (ζ2, 1139ᵃ, 18; l. 2, b), ponit *intellectum* in operativis" *(III Sent.*, d. 33, q. 2, a. 4, sol. 4 [Moos, n. 242, p. 1066]). But rather than to Moos's reference, it is more likely that Aquinas is referring to *EN*, VI, 11, 1143a35.

224. See *SLE*, II, 4, 1105b5, 101-6 *(In Ethic.*, II, lect. 4 [Spiazzi, n. 286, p. 81]); *SLE*, V, 12, 1134b19, 49-57 *(In Ethic.*, V, lect. 12 [Spiazzi, n. 1018, p. 280]); *SLE*, VI, 11, 1144b1, 30-33 *(In Ethic.*, VI, lect. 4 [Spiazzi, n. 1277, p. 346]). Cf. *SLA*, III, c. 9, 433a26, 109-10 *(In de An.*, III, lect. 15 [Pirotta, n. 826, p. 195]); *ST*, I, q. 79, a. 12. In the latter text, Aquinas mentions the Aristotelian doctrine that there is a habit of self-evident theoretical principles, but does not claim that Aristotle refers to the habit of self-evident practical principles.

225. See *SLE*, VI, 7, 1142a25, 231-55 *(In Ethic.*, VI, lect. 7 [Spiazzi, n. 1214, p. 331]).

226. See *EN*, VI, 3, 1139b22-24: ἐξ ἀνάγκης ἄρα ἐστὶ τὸ ἐπιστητόν.

227. See *EN*, I, 4, 1095a16; II, 2, 1103b26-31; VI, 4, 1140a1-2; 5, 1140b20-21; 7, 1141b11-12; 10, 9, 1179b1-2. The question of whether to assimilate ethical inquiry to an exercise of practical reason arises because both deal with actions that can be otherwise: Τοῦ δ' ἐνδεχομένου ἄλλως ἔχειν ἔστι τι καὶ ποιητὸν καὶ πρακτόν ... *(EN,*

about moral variables.[228] Aquinas comments, in line with what he takes to be Aristotle's doctrine, that the scientific part of the soul "in no way pertains to practical matters."[229] Now, while this proves to be an over-statement of Aristotle's position, since Aristotle does include ethics among the sciences,[230] Aquinas is being precise: Aristotle confines practical reason, since it deals with contingent things, to the *logistikon* or calculative part of the soul (τὸ λογιστικόν) in distinction to the *epistemonikon* or scientific part of the soul (τὸ ἐπιστημονικόν).[231]

Although he rejects the Aristotelian division of the rational soul into these two parts,[232] Aquinas draws attention to the less strict sense in which Aristotelian moral principles are called "scientific principles." Aristotelian positive moral principles hold "for the most part" because they deal with things that can be otherwise. Aquinas fully understands Aristotle's problem with universal moral principles. That problem, let us recall, is to explain how universal or fixed moral principles can be applied to contingent, singular actions that have no fixed moral character.[233] Moral reasoning that uses such universal moral principles suffers from an inherent defect: universal principles cannot reach down to the particular contingent action that must be prescribed or proscribed. The actual moral character of the particular cases remain indeterminate in reference to the fixed universal principle.[234] Even

VI, 4, 1140a1–2). Of course, the assimilation is plausible only if *phronesis* involves more than just deliberation about means: cf. Anagnostopoulos, *Aristotle on the Goals and Exactness of Ethics*, 66–101.

228. See *EN*, VI, 5, 1140b27: ἥ τε γὰρ δόξα περὶ τὸ ἐνδεχόμενον ἄλλως ἔχειν καὶ ἡ φρόνησις."

229. ". . . quia scientificum nullo modo ad praxim pertinet . . ." (*II Sent.*, d. 24, q. 2, a. 2, ad 2 [Mandonnet, 606]). See *SLE*, VI, 1, 1139a8, 119–20 (*In Ethic.*, VI, lect. 1 [Spiazzi, n. 1116, p. 306]): ". . . sit diversum genus partium animae rationalis quo cognoscit necessaria et contingentia."

230. *MM*, I, 1, 1183a33–36 refers to "political science" (ἡ πολιτικὴ ἐπιστήμη); *Metaph.*, IV, 2, 1026b4, *Top.*, VI, 6, 145a15 and VIII, 1, 157a10 to "practical science" (ἡ πρακτική); and *Rhet.*, I, 4, 1359b10 to the "sciences of logic and ethics" (τῆς περὶ τὰ ἤθη πολιτικῆς). In the *EN*, Aristotle nowhere uses the term "moral science" (ἡ ἠθική), but *Apo.*, I, 33, 89b9 employs the term "moral theory" (τὰ δὲ ἠθικῆς θεωρίας).

231. See *EN*, VI, 1, 1139a5–16.

232. See *SLE*, VI, 1, 1139a11, 150–214 (*In Ethic.*, VI, lect. 1 [Spiazzi, nn. 1119–23, pp. 306–7]).

233. See *EN*, VI, 1, 1138b, 22–34; 3, 1139b20–25. See *SLE*, VI, 1, 1138b25, 53–55 (*In Ethic.*, VI, lect. 1 [Spiazzi, n. 1111, p. 305]): ". . . sed solum ille qui hoc commune habet, non propter hoc sciet amplius procedere ad operandum. . . ."

234. See *SLE*, II, 2, 1103b34, 57–60 (*In Ethic.*, II, lect. 2 [Spiazzi, n. 258, p. 74]): ". . . omnis sermo qui est de operabilibus . . . debet tradi tipo, id est exemplariter, vel similitudinarie, et non secundum certitudinem. . . ."

when "narrowed down," universal principles cannot always cover the singular and really disparate cases which, prima facie, fall under an existing principle.

In all cases, though, what is needed is a way to make correct moral judgments about singular actions. Aquinas accepts Aristotle's contention that in order to make correct particular moral judgments, *phronesis/prudentia* must intervene.[235] In developing his solution to this problem, Aristotle falls back on an analogy taken from the practice of medicine. Like a doctor successfully treating an individual patient, because he knows how to apply the medical art, the morally astute person, who has the right general principles, must still make prudent judgments about particular cases which are said, in Aquinas's exaggeration of Aristotle, to be "infinitely" varied.[236]

Aquinas sympathetically and accurately rehearses Aristotle's remarks about the difficulty and fallibility of moral reasoning about particular cases.[237] Although what is by definition an "unjust" action should never be done ("One ought never *to steal*"), the positive rules of natural justice do not apply in a few cases (e.g., "Deposits ought always to be returned"). Moreover, Aquinas incorporates into his own moral science the Aristotelian tenet that moral principles hold only "for the most part." He does not dispute that some derived (what we may label "tertiary") precepts hold only "in most cases" *(ut in pluribus)*.[238] Nonetheless, Aquinas wants to guarantee that there are not only general principles (ones that hold "for the most part") but also exceptionless or universal moral principles.

Aquinas argues that the primary precepts of the natural law, which are positive as well as negative,[239] are universally true: for example, "One ought not to do harm to another" or "One ought to return benefits to one from whom one has received benefits."[240] Such principles are

235. See *III Sent.*, d. 33, q. 3, a. 1, sol. 1 (Moos, n. 270, p. 1073): "Quia enim prudentia circa particularia operabilia est, in quibus universalia principia dirigunt propter eorum contingentiam et varietatem, oportet, sicut dicitur de scientiis in libro *Post.* (7. 75a, 38s.), ex eodem genere principia accipere, ut ex similitudine aliorum factorum de his quae facere oportet, recte ratiocinetur prudens. . . ."

236. See *SLE*, II, 2, 1103b34, 76–77 *(In Ethic.*, II, lect. 2 [Spiazzi, n. 259, p. 74]): "Quia causus [Spiazzi: causae] singularium operabilium variantur infinitis modis."

237. See *SLE*, V, 12, 1134b33, 180–207 *(In Ethic.*, V, lect. 12 [Spiazzi, nn. 1028–29, p. 281]).

238. See *ST*, I–II, q. 94, aa. 4–5; q. 100, a. 8.

239. See *ST*, I–II, q. 100, a. 4, ad 2: ". . . praecepta affirmativa distinguuntur a negativis, quando unum non comprehenditur in alio. . . ."

240. Cf. *ST*, I–II, q. 100, a. 7. Universal negative precepts oblige always at every

the immobile foundations of practical reasoning.[241] Furthermore, there are some quasi-immediate or instantly *(statim)* deduced secondary precepts of the natural law, equivalent to the divinely revealed Ten Commandments,[242] which apply to everyone without exception. They are exceptionless because such precepts delineate the very order of virtue and justice.[243] When carefully analyzed, apparent exceptions—biblical cases of (allegedly) morally justified murder, fornication, or theft—turn out *not* to be action-tokens of those forbidden action-types. Hence, there are no real exceptions either to the primary or the basic secondary precepts of practical reasoning.[244]

Clearly enough, Aquinas intends to put limits on what we call "moral particularism" and what he called the defeasibility of moral principles, that is, that there are no universal moral principles that hold in all relevantly similar cases.[245] But Aquinas sets a precise limit to the infallibility of moral agents and the indefeasibility of moral principles. The moral understanding *(intellectus)* of all practically rational agents maintains an infallible hold only on the indemonstrable primary precepts. We cannot err about such basic principles as "No one is to be harmed" or "Something unjust is not to be done."[246] However, passion, as too often happens, can deflect practical reasoning even in regard to the easily derived secondary precepts of the natural law. But for other reasons our best efforts at reasoning often go astray because of

---

time and in every place (= *"ad semper"*); universal positive precepts oblige always but not at every time and in every place (= *"semper"*). See *ST*, II–II, q. 140, a. 2, ad 2: ". . . pracepta affirmativa, etsi semper obligent, non tamen obligant ad semper, sed pro loco et tempore."

241. See *ST*, I–II, q. 94, a. 4: ". . . lex naturae, quantum ad prima principia communia, est eadem apud omnes et secundum rectitudinem, et secundum notitiam"; a. 5: ". . . quantum ad prima principia legis naturae lex naturae est omnino immutabilis."

242. See *ST*, q. 100, a. 4: ". . . praecepta ad decalogum pertinent, quorum notitiam homo habet per seipsum a Deo. Huiusmodi vero sunt illa quae statim ex principiis communibus primis cognosci possunt modica consideratione . . ."; a. 6: ". . . praecepta decalogi dantur de his quae statim in promptu mens hominis suscipit."

243. See *ST*, q. 100, a. 8.

244. For this strategy, which preserves the exceptionless character of the Ten Commandments, see *ST*, I–II, q. 100, a. 8, ad. 3. Cf. *I Sent.*, d. 47, q. 1, a. 4, which allows for a quasi-miraculous divine dispensation from (only) those precepts of the natural law that bear on the secondary end of the law, the relationship of one human being to another, but not on the primary end, the relationship of man to God. In this text, Aquinas argues that God can preserve the latter even as He dispenses from the former.

245. See *III Sent.*, d. 37, q. 1, a. 3.

246. See *SLA*, III, c. 9, 433a26, 106–9 *(In de An.*, III, lect. 15 [Pirotta, n. 826, p. 195]): ". . . non enim erramus circa prima principia inoperabilibus, cuiusmodi sunt: Nulli nocendum esse, Non esse aliquid iniuste agendum, et similia. . . . "

the very difficulty of the matters that need to be reasoned about. The subject matter that falls under the largest class of narrow or more determinate moral precepts, the tertiary moral precepts, is opaque even to moral experts whose passions are well under control. In short, putting our passions aside, we still have trouble with our moral deductions from the primary principles:

> Just as in speculative [demonstrations], there is not able to be error in the understanding of principles but only in the deduction of conclusions from principles, so too in practical [demonstrations], the understanding is always right, but reason [can be both] right and not right. (II Sent., d. 24, q. 3, a. 3 [Mandonnet, 624])[247]

Aquinas schematizes three grades or levels of moral precepts (ST, I–II, q. 100, a. 11). At the first level stand the exceptionless, first, indemonstrable, or immediate (per se nota) principles. From these, the Thomistic moral agent can instantly and easily derive a set of exceptionless secondary moral principles. In drawing these secondary principles or first "conclusions,"[248] moral reasoning attains the natural law precepts that are equivalent to the revealed Ten Commandments. Yet sinful men, captives to their passions, sometimes fail to draw these easy conclusions. Errors arising from properly epistemic puzzles typically occur at the tertiary level of moral precepts. But one might say that most of our interesting and challenging moral issues are about matters that are intrinsically difficult even for virtuous moral experts.[249] It is in this third rank, too, that we find the moral principles that have exceptions, that is, that hold only "ut in pluribus." These latter are equivalent to Aristotle's general principles but now they are being viewed as somehow derived from the universal or unchanging principles of synderesis. And so viewed, Aquinas confidently strengthens Aristotle's distinction between legal and natural justice.[250]

---

247. ". . . unde sicut in speculativis in intellectu principiorum non potest esse error, sed in deductione conclusionum ex principiis, ita etiam in operativis intellectus semper est rectus, sed ratio recta et non recta" (II Sent., d. 24, q. 3, a. 3 [Mandonnet, 624]).

248. See ST, I–II, q. 104, a. 4, ad 2: ". . . praecepta decalogi sunt prima in genere moralium . . . et ideo convenienter alia praecepta moralia secundum ea distinguuntur."

249. See ST, I–II, q. 100, a. 1: "Quaedam enim sunt in humanis actibus adeo explicita quod statim, cum modica consideratione, possunt approbari vel reprobari per illa communia et prima principia. Quaedam vero sunt ad quorum iudicium requiritur multa consideratio diversarum circumstantiarum, quas considerare diligenter non cuiuslibet, sed sapientum. . . ."

250. See SLE, V, 12, 1143b19, 45–75 (In Ethic., V, lect. 12 [Spiazzi, nn. 1018–19, p. 280]).

Aquinas's schema of precepts—immediate and exceptionless primary precepts, instantly and easily derived quasi-immediate conclusions or exceptionless secondary precepts, and difficult-to-derive and defeasible tertiary precepts—shifts the focus away from Aristotle's almost exclusive interest in fallible moral reasoning and defeasible moral principles. In the Thomistic schema, the natural inclination of the will and the innate intellectual habit of *synderesis*, not acquired moral virtue, are the foundations of moral reasoning.[251] In itself, the will has

251. Despite Aquinas's repeated statements to the contrary (e. g., *De ver.*, q. 5, a. 1 [Spiazzi, p. 89]: "Prudentia praecise dirigit in his quae sunt ad finem . . ."), Irwin thinks ("The Scope of Deliberation," 21–42), in line with his view of Aristotle, that Thomistic prudence should also apply right deliberation and choice not only to means but to ends, or otherwise we will be at a loss to explain the essential role that choice plays in genuine moral virtue. Moral virtue entails not only that we have the right ends but that we make the right choices in the right way, and the latter entails having "the appropriate motive for choosing the virtuous action" (29). Irwin seeks support for the latter claim from Aquinas who acknowledges that we must will the good for the sake of the good: see *ST*, I–II, q. 19, a. 8, ad 3: "Sed ad hoc quod sit voluntas bona, requiritur quod sit boni sub ratione boni; idest quod velit bonum, et propter bonum." But, according to Irwin, prudence is responsible for the virtuous man's right motive or "true conception of the ends worth pursuing" (30).

The term "motive," however, must be applied with care to the Thomistic account of action. The agent's motive is the proper object and end of the will (see *De malo*, q. 14, a. 3; *ST*, I–II, q. 72, a. 9); it is identified as the "*finis operantis*," the remote end that the agent intends. (See *ST*, II–II, q. 141, a. 6, ad 1; *II Sent.*, d. 1, q. 2, a. 1; d. 36, q. 1, a. 5, ad 5; d. 40, q. 1, a. 2.) But, for Aquinas, the ultimate right end that determines whether a particular act falls under a moral virtue is that we intend to act, in regard to our appetites, in accordance with practical reason: see *ST*, I–II, q. 59, a. 4. Now this universal end of the virtues Aquinas attributes not to prudence but to *synderesis*: see *ST*, II–II, q. 47, a. 7: ". . . conformari rationi rectae est finis proprius cuiuslibet moralis virtutis. . . . Et hic finis praestitutus est homini secundum naturalem rationem: naturalis enim ratio dictat unicuique ut secundum rationem operetur"; *III Sent.*, d. 33, q. 2, a. 3 (Moos, n. 198, p. 1057): "Rectitudo autem rationis naturalis est. Unde hoc modo praestitutio finis ad naturalem rationem pertinet et praecedit prudentiam, sicut intellectus principiorum scientiam."

Irwin's exegesis of Aquinas (28–30) conflates judgment and choice. In the order of reason, the practical syllogism concludes with a prudential judgment, and that can be understood to embody the agent's conception of how rightly to pursue a good end in the *particular* case: see *III Sent.*, d. 33, q. 2, a. 1, sol. 3 (Moos, n. 281, p. 1076): "Perfectio autem rationis practicae, sicut et speculative, consistit in duobus, scilicet in inveniendo et judicando de inventis." Right judgment, not choice, "focuses on the right means" (28); "choice" *(electio)* is the *volitional* act whereby the agent finally accepts and adheres to whatever judgment presents as the best means to an end: see *ST*, I, q. 83, a. 3, ad 2. Although the reciprocal causality of intellect and will is especially profound in choice, Aquinas, despite what he occasionally and loosely says, does not regard choice as properly an act of prudence: see *III Sent.*, d. 33, q. 2, a. 4, sol. 4, ad 2 (Moos, n. 245, p. 1067); *De ver.*, q. 22, a. 15, ad 2, ad 3. Nor does he exclusively bind moral virtue to choice. Moral virtue

a natural inclination to certain basic ends that is prior to any intellectual grasp of these ends.[252] As a power joined to intellect, the innate tendency of the will is naturally in conformity with reason. But, in another sense, the practical intellect conforms to the will. The ends that are innate to practical intellect are the ends that the will naturally desires. Our intellectual grasp of these basic, or natural, or fixed ends pertains to the sensibly activated habit of *synderesis*. The indemonstrable principles of *synderesis* prescribe that the naturally desired ends are to be pursued. They can be pursued only if the other human powers are made subject to reason through the moral virtues. Thus the primary rational precepts of *synderesis* can be said to set forth the ends of the moral virtues.[253] In regard to these basic ends, the exercise of prudence presupposes the will's natural inclination toward them, the practical intellect's immediate prescriptive *knowledge* of them, and the virtuous habituation of the lower appetites in conformity with the primary dictates of practical reason.[254] Thinking prudentially about the *means* whereby to attain these natural ends results in a determinate moral desire for them.[255]

With these precisions in place, Aquinas is able to stress—but now without danger of resurrecting Aristotle's unresolved cognitivist-emotivist dilemma about the foundations of morality—that prudence (as well as counsel and choice) is properly about the means to ends.[256] Of

---

inclines to those basic ends fixed by practical reason as a result of nature and not of prudence or choice: see *III Sent.*, d. 33, q. 2, a. 3 (Moos, n. 199, p. 1057): "Sed haec inclinatio in finem illum pertinet ad virtutem moralem quae consentit in bonum rationis per modum naturae."

252. See *III Sent.*, d. 33, q. 2, a. 4d, co. (Busa, p. 386a): ". . . naturalis inclinatio ad finem aliquem est ex praestituente naturam, qui talem ordinem naturae tribuit: ideo naturalis inclinatio voluntatis ad finem non est ex ratione. . . ."

253. See *III Sent.*, d. 33, q. 2, a. 3, co. (Busa, 384c): "Rectitudo autem rationis naturalis est; unde hoc modo praestitutio finis ad naturalem rationem pertinet, et praecedit prudentiam, sicut intellectus principiorum scientiam . . ."; *ST*, II–II, q. 47, a. 6, ad 1: ". . . virtutibus moralibus praestituit finem ratio naturalis quae dicitur synderesis. . . ."

254. See *ST*, II–II, q. 47, a. 6, ad 3: ". . . finis non pertinet ad virtutes morales tanquam ipsae praestituant finem: sed quia tendunt in finem a ratione naturali praestitutum"; *III Sent.*, d. 33, q. 2, a. 5, ad 6 (Moos, n. 263, p. 1070): ". . . prudentia procedit ad electionem et consilium de his quae sunt ad finem, ex fine; et ideo dicuntur fines aliarum virtutum esse principia prudentiae. Hi tamen fines praeexistunt in ratione essentialiter; quia ad hoc tendit virtus moralis ut appetitus rationi concordet."

255. See *III Sent.*, d. 33, q. 2, a. 3, ad 3.

256. See *ST*, II–II, q. 47, a. 1, ad 2: "Unde patet quod ea quae considerat prudentia ordinantur ad alia sicut ad finem."

course, "means" *(ea quae sunt ad finem)* should not be interpreted too narrowly.[257] Aquinas uses the term to refer to (1) the instrumental means as that is understood in ordinary means-end reasoning;[258] (2) the instantiation of a virtue in an appropriate action (one that is between excess and defect);[259] (3) a proximate end that is subordinate to or a constituent of the ultimate end. In the latter case, we can properly be said to deliberate about and choose these proximate ends, inasmuch as they are *sometimes* regarded as means to reach the ultimate end.[260] Here Aquinas fully rejoins Aristotle: the more basic of these proximate ends will be set by our prerational habituation. Genuine prudential deliberation and judgment about the means to these proximate ends presupposes that moral virtue has already set the right target of these deliberations. Hence our appetitive choice of these means can be said to be guided by moral virtue as well as by prudential reasoning.[261] Of course, not all (perhaps not most) of our proximate ends have been set by our childhood habituation. But it is no less an act of prudence "to perceive" and to judge correctly the singulars through which we induce those deliberative ends characteristic of rational adults.[262]

By contrast, we do not deliberate about our primary or fixed ends.[263] In this sphere of the primary and indemonstrable precepts, Thomistic *prudentia* is properly the servant of *synderesis*, not of moral virtue.[264]

---

257. See Jean Porter, *The Recovery of Virtue: The Relevance of Aquinas for Christian Ethics* (Louisville, Ky.: Westminster Press, 1990), 156–62.

258. See *III Sent.*, d. 33, q. 2, a. 3 (Moos, n. 203, p. 1058): ". . . in virtutibus moralibus est finis determinatus, non autem viae ad finem, qui potest medium inveniri in diversis diversimode."

259. See *ST*, I–II, q. 66, a. 3, ad 3: ". . . prudentia non solum dirigit virtutes morales in eligendo ea quae sunt ad finem, sed etiam in praestituendo finem. Est autem finis uniuscuiusque virtutis moralis attingere medium in propria materia: quod quidem medium determinatur secundum rectam rationem prudentiae. . . ."

260. See *III Sent.*, d. 33, q. 2, a. 3, co. (Busa, 384c): ". . . inclinatio in finem dicitur electio, inquantum finis proximus ad finem ultimum ordinatur"; *ST*, I–II, q. 6, a. 2: ". . . apprehensio fine, aliquis potest, deliberans de fine et de his quae sunt ad finem, moveri in finem vel non moveri"; q. 14, a. 2: ". . . quod accipitur ut finis in una inquisitione, potest accipi ut ad finem in alia inquisitione. Et sic de eo erit consilium."

261. See *III Sent.*, d. 33, q. 2, a. 3 (Busa, 384c): ". . . praestitutio finis praecedit actum prudentiae et virtutis moralis; sed inclinatio in finem, sive recta electio finis proximi, est actus moralis virtutis principaliter, sed prudentiae originaliter"; *ST*, II–II, q. 47, a. 4: "Ad prudentiam autem pertinet . . . applicatio rectae rationis ad opus, quod non fit sine appetitu recto."

262. See *ST*, II–II, q. 47, a. 3, ad 3: ". . . prudentia non consistit in sensu exteriori . . . sed in sensu interiori, qui perficitur per memoriam et experimentum ad prompte iudicandum de particularibus expertis."

263. See *ST*, II–II, q. 47, a. 15: "Fines autem recti humanae vitae sunt determinati."

264. See *III Sent.*, d. 33, q. 2, a. 4, sol. 4 (Moos, n. 242, p. 1066): "Unde sicut in

The primary and immediately known principles of practical reason direct us to man's natural or basic ends; these indemonstrable principles are as immediately seen to be true as the ends that they enjoin are immediately desired as good. However, Aristotle's ethics focuses on the agent's acquired habits and grounds the rightness of his moral reasoning in his good character. That the *phronimos* works only with acquired moral principles goes hand in hand with Aristotle's insistent focus on the particularity and contingency of the object of *phronesis*.[265] By considering such objects, the *phronimos* attains principles that hold only "for the most part."

For the contemporary interpreter, this focus can raise the specter of Aristotelian "ethical relativism." But the "relativistic" side of the *Nicomachean Ethics* need not be exaggerated; nor, consequently, Aquinas's alleged correction thereof.[266] Yet there remains a question of how congruent is the Thomistic doctrine of *sydneresis* with the Aristotelian theme that prudential moral reasoning uses premises that are only true "for the most part" (ὡς ἐπὶ τὸ πολύ [*EN*, I, 3, 1094b21]) since it must deal with particular things whose goodness fluctuates (1094b16).[267] Does the Thomistic doctrine of *synderesis* represent not only a difference in orientation and emphasis but is it, as has been charged, a gross contradiction of Aristotle?[268]

In response to this charge, a caveat about Aristotelian moral "particularism" is first in order. For all of his undoubted emphasis on the contingent moral character of the singular action, Aristotle does not deny the importance of general moral principles. General principles (stated in the practical syllogism in the form of universally quantified propositions) remain necessary even as they are not, if used apart from moral insight into particulars, sufficient for making right particular moral judgments. In regard to the exceptions that limit the scope of

---

ratione speculativa sunt innata principia demonstrationum, ita in ratione practica sunt innati fines connaturales homini; unde circa illa non est habitus acquisitus aut infusus, sed naturalis, sicut synderesis. . . ."

265. See Thiry, "Thomas et la moral d'Aristote," 229–58; Livio Melina, *La conoscenza morale: Linee di reflessione sul Commento di san Tommaso all'Etica Nicomachea* (Rome: Città Nuova Editrice, 1987), 74.

266. Cf. Thiry, "Saint Thomas et la morale d'Aristote," 236, who remarks that Aquinas (in the *Summa theologiae*) "atténue la saveur relativiste" of the *Nicomachean Ethics*.

267. For a remarkably painstaking and illuminating examination of Aristotle's theme of the inexactness of moral reasoning and the fluctuating character of moral goods, see Anagnostopoulos, *Aristotle on the Goals and Exactness of Ethics*.

268. See Jaffa, *Thomism*, 185–86; Gauthier-Jolif, I, 1: 275–80.

general positive moral principles, Aristotelian "particularism" in ethics is not about the logical eliminability or epistemic futility of general positive moral principles. It is about the difficulty of knowing whether, *in a few cases*, we can correctly subsume a singular action under the apparently relevant general principle that we do already possess. Second, although it is not perhaps an Aristotelian "theme," Aristotle does acknowledge that there are some universal or exceptionless (albeit negative) moral principles that bind in all cases. In regard to actions whose very names imply that they are "intrinsically bad," there is no mean that can be identified as virtuous.[269] These types of action—explicitly, adultery, theft, and murder—are always wrong and never to be done.[270] At this point, at least, there is no conflict between the Thomistic doctrine of *synderesis* and Aristotle.

To a great extent Aquinas is merely trying to shore up the *cognitive* foundations of Aristotelian *phronesis*.[271] On the cognitive foundations of indemonstrable primary principles, he relocates but does not eliminate the cognitivist-emotivist theme in regard to secondary and tertiary moral precepts. How does the Aristotelian moral agent *cognitively* grasp his primary principles? It is this question that obviously troubled Aquinas. Aquinas agreed that many of our proximate or nonbasic ends are indeed set by our acquired habits, and that these ends will be good only if we are morally virtuous. Moral virtue thus sets some of the proximate ends that prudential reasoning attempts to attain through some means. Aristotle also has a notion of natural goods (τῇ φύσει ἀγαθόν), such as life or friendship, that every human agent desires.[272] But Aquinas, in contrast to Aristotle, highlights the few basic ends that are fixed by nature. He attributes our knowledge of basic ends to an innate cognitive habit that is not rooted in our acquired character but is given with and through nature.[273] This natural cognitive habit needs merely to be activated by the experience of the basic goods. But, once

269. See *EN*, II, 6, 1107a22–25. Presumably, however, even if one knows these universally binding negative propositions, it may be difficult to identify that this act is a token of a certain (forbidden) type: cf. *EN*, V, 9. 1137a9–17.

270. Cf. *EN*, II, 6, 1107a17: ἁπλῶς τὸ ποιεῖν ὁτιοῦν τούτων ἁμαρτάνειν ἐστίν.

271. See *ST*, II–II, q. 47, a. 6, ad 3: "Sed synderesis movet prudentiam, sicut intellectus principiorum scientiam."

272. See *EN*, IX, 9, 1170a13–b10.

273. See *SLE*, II, 4, 1105b5, 99–106 (*In Ethic.*, II, lect. 4 [Spiazzi, n. 286, p. 81]); quoted *supra*, 231, n. 174. Cf. *II Sent.*, d. 39, q. 1, a. 1 (Busa, 239b): "Unde quaedam inclinationes virtutum sive aptitudines praeexistunt naturaliter in ipsa natura rationali, quae virtutes naturales dicuntur, et etiam per exercitium et deliberationem complentur . . . ideo homo naturaliter in bonum tendit . . . velle bonum homini sit naturale. . . ."

activated, *synderesis* sets the primary ends of both moral virtue and prudential reasoning.

That Aquinas, in developing and emphasizing this distinction between natural and acquired habits, is responding to a problem in Aristotle cannot be doubted. Aristotle does recognize that practical reasoning has principles, the ends for the sake of which we act, and he does not suggest that all ends are of equal rectitude.[274] On the contrary, *phronesis* grasps only the right ends, the ends that, it is claimed, are good for man. For his part, Aquinas explains where *phronesis* gets knowledge of these ends. He synthesizes the Aristotelian doctrine of *phronesis* with a conception of practical *nous* that is nowhere explicitly found in the Aristotelian texts. Aristotle is silent about attributing to *nous* any knowledge of universal, indemonstrable practical principles.

Every interpreter who reads Aristotle with Aquinas's doctrine of *intellectus practicus* in mind must venture an explanation of Aristotle's silence about indemonstrable universal practical principles. I have argued that, in regard to indemonstrable exceptionless negative principles, the Thomistic doctrine of *synderesis* does not contradict Aristotle. But, then, is Aristotle's silence about indemonstrable, exceptionless positive principles an empty conceptual space that needs to be filled by Aquinas? So Rhonheimer contends.[275] Let us prolong this hermeneutical metaphor of an empty space. This conceptual space, if we think that there is one and that Aquinas filled it, was certainly not filled, as Rhonheimer forthrightly acknowledges, by materials taken solely from Aristotle.[276] But if this conceptual space is to have any determinate coordinates, one must assume that an Aristotelian space can only be filled by Aristotelian material. Otherwise, the empty space cannot be seen in Aristotle; it opens only to the Thomistically minded historical interpreter.

In his excellent and important monograph, Rhonheimer speaks at length about explicit "Aristotelian themes"; the *Nicomachean Ethics*

274. See *EN*, VI, 5, 1140b16–17 (rev. Oxford trans.): "For the principles of things done consist in that for the sake of which they are to be done" (αἱ μὲν γὰρ ἀρχαὶ τῶν πρακτῶν τὸ οὗ ἕνεκα τὰ πρακτά).

275. See Rhonheimer, *Praktische Vernunft*, 482–83: "Eine solche Theorie universaler praktischer Prinzipien fiele zwar auf eine Leerstelle der aristotelishen Ethik, bildete aber eine mit ihr und den in ihr involvierten Dimensionen praktischer Erkenntnis durcharus kompatibile Möglichkeit."

276. See Rhonheimer, *Praktische Vernunft*, 506: "Wenn also Thomas von einem 'naturalis intellectus principiorum' und von den universalen praktischen Prinzipien als einen 'naturaliter cognitum' spricht, so widerspricht das in keiner Weise den aristotelischen Ausführungen, sondern *ergänst* diese auf einer anderen Ebene."

explicitly thematizes how practical reason can be crippled and limited by morally bad emotions; accordingly, it subordinates the operation of *phronesis* to moral virtue and does not explore the ultimate cognitive source whereby the *phronimos* knows which ends to pursue. Nonetheless, Rhonheimer contends that Aristotle's account of *phronesis* implicitly presupposes the role of practical *nous*,[277] a doctrine that Aristotle supposedly retained as a member of the Socratic-Platonic moral tradition. Consequently, Rhonheimer is able to view Aquinas as merely expanding and making explicit what Aristotle left implicit.[278] However, there is little direct textual evidence for attributing this presupposition to Aristotle and it is not primarily found, as Rhonheimer acknowledges, in the *Nicomachean Ethics*.[279] Thus what textual evidence there is remains inconclusive and controversial.

Rhonheimer's interpretation, moreover, has a philosophical consequence that in turn tends to cast doubt on his hermeneutical perspective. If the Aristotelian account does presuppose a Socratic-Platonic doctrine of practical *nous*, this presupposition entails, whether the doctrine is regarded as implicit or not, that *phronesis* is subordinated to a more fundamental form of intellectual insight.[280] As a consequence, the interpreter must systematically relocate and perhaps depreciate the

277. See Rhonheimer, *Praktishe Vernunft*, 20: "... ist die aristotelische Ethik ja wesentlich eine Theorie der *affektiven Bedingungen* des 'kata logon prattein,' wobei Aristoteles eben immer *voraussetzt*, dass 'der Intelleckt immer richtig ist' und 'dass der logos stets das Beste vorschreibt.'"

278. See Rhonheimer, *Praktishe Vernunft*, 164–72, 418. For the alleged Platonic background, see *Phaedo*, 65c–663.

279. See *de An.*, III, 10, 433a27: νοῦς μὲν οὖ· πᾶς ὀρθός; *MM*, II, 7, 1206b12–13: τὸν μὲν λόγον προστάττειν ἀεὶ τὸ βέλτιστον. Cf. *EN*, I, 13, 1102b14–16: τοῦ γὰρ ἐγκρατοῦς καὶ ἀκρατοῦς τὸν λόγον καὶ τῆς ψυχῆς τὸ λόγον ἔχον ἐπαινοῦμεν· ὀρθῶς γὰρ καὶ ἐπὶ τὰ βέλτιστα παρακαλεῖ. Rhonheimer rightly calls *(Praktishe Vernunft*, 20, n. 61) the italicized phrase at 1206b12–13, and its equivalent at 1102b15–16, a "formulierung." But the formula, in context, hardly seems to support Rhonheimer's contention that Aristotle implicitly holds that practical *nous* grasps the basic ends: "Speaking generally, it is not the case, as others think, that reason [ὁ λόγος] is the principle and guide to excellence, but rather the feelings [τὰ πάθη]" *(MM*, II, 7, 1206b17–19). At 433a27, νοῦς refers to the νοῦς δὲ ἕνεκά του λογιζόμενος καὶ ὁ πρακτικός (433a14) which is διάνοια πρακτική (433a18) about means to ends that have been set by appetite. Cf. *In de An.*, III, lect. 15 (Pirotta, n. 826, p. 195): "Et dicit quod *omnis intellectus est rectus* quod intelligendum est de intellectu principiorum: non enim erramus circa prima principia in operabilibus ... sicut nec erramus circa prima principia in speculatiuis."

280. Cf. Rhonheimer, *Praktische Vernunft*, 482: "Wenn aber der 'nous tôn archôn' im Akt der Phronesis impliziert ist, dann heisst das eben auch, dass die Phronesis bezüglich der Prinzipien auch kognitiv durch den 'nous' geleitet ist."

significance of the variable human goods, and the moral judgments made about them. Then, for the interpreter, the ultimate object of moral judgment (as Aquinas's schema of three levels make explicit) can no longer be considered to be the human goods that fluctuate and can be otherwise. This revision, however, is difficult to reconcile with Aristotle's overall portrait of the *phronimos* who is pictured as rightly inducing his moral principles (solely?) from these contingent goods.

Of course, Aristotle acknowledges that the natural goods—honor, wealth, bodily vigor, bodily pleasures, good luck, and power[281]—correspond to certain features of human nature, and are, indeed, goods. Ordinary men compete over natural goods because they mistakenly regard them as the highest goods. But they are not. Accordingly, nothing in Aristotle's portrait of the *phronimos* implies that his primary moral principles are grounded in or are primarily aimed at fostering these natural goods.[282] The truly good man (σπουδαῖος) seeks what is morally noble (καλόν) before all else.[283] And what is morally noble involves seeking virtue for its own sake as the most beautiful and highest good, that is, seeking virtue independently of whether being virtuous gives access to the natural goods.[284]

In discussing the relationship between natural and moral virtue, Aristotle denies that a natural virtue (φυσικὴ ἀρετή), which he regards merely as a physical disposition (φυσικὴ ἕξις), has any moral value or import apart from how the *phronimos* uses it.[285] *Phronesis* directs natural virtues to a morally good end because the *phronimos*, who acts for the sake of the morally noble (τὸ καλόν), is already morally virtuous. Lacking *phronesis*, another man can just as easily go morally astray

281. See *EN*, IX, 8, 1168b16–17; *EE*, VII, 15, 1248b28–29.

282. Cf. *EE*, VII, 15, 1248b39–1249a2 (rev. Oxford trans.): ". . . there are some who think one should have excellence [ἀρετή] but only for the sake of the natural goods, and so such men are good (for the natural goods are good for them), but they have not nobility and goodness."
The noble man pursues moral virtue as the highest good "for its own sake" not in order to attain the natural goods: see 1248b34–37.

283. See *EN*, IX, 8, 1169a31–32: εἰκότως δὴ δοκεῖ σπουδαῖος εἶναι, ἀντὶ πάντων αἱρούμενος τὸ καλόν.

284. See *EN*, IX, 8, 1168b25–30. However, the deontological sense of "pursuing virtue for virtue's sake" is considerably softened (and perhaps overturned) by Aristotle's remark (1169a11–13) that being virtuous brings benefits or is useful to both the virtuous man and the community. It is useful to the virtuous man because acting virtuously is a dimension of his own *eudaimonia*. For a discussion of this issue, see Engberg-Pedersen, *Aristotle's Theory of Moral Insight*, 37–42.

285. This is not to say that natural virtues *become* moral virtues. Cf. Rhonheimer, *Praktische Vernunft*, 482–83, n. 97: "Die natürlichen Tugend den werden nicht ohne 'nous' zur eigentlichen Tugend."

because he is led by his natural dispositions. The foolhardy man, unlike the courageous man, feels no fear and therefore takes irrational risks. In short, popular opinion is mistaken in thinking that the natural virtues ground the moral virtues. One may or may not be simultaneously equipped with all the natural dispositions to moral virtue. No matter, *phronesis* by itself guarantees that one possesses *all* the genuine moral virtues.[286]

Rhonheimer's interpretation leaves us wondering why Aristotle (deliberately?) did not explicitly articulate and explore the parallel function of practical *nous* when the latter function, if there were one, would surely alter our view of the moral truths that hold only "for the most part." If Aristotle had presupposed that *practical nous* can attain apodeictic universal principles, would he not have drawn the portrait of the *phronimos* differently? These contemporary questions, let us admit, allow only controversial answers; they merely guide and reflect our reading of Aristotle. They lead me to think, however, that it is more plausible to regard Aquinas's doctrine of *synderesis* not as filling in a space left empty in Aristotle but as filling in a space that only opens in Thomistic moral science. In Aquinas, there is a space for *synderesis* because of the radically non-Aristotelian problem that he faced.[287] Aquinas's problem is theological: the Ten Commandments are universal exceptionless moral principles binding all men. So much is a matter of biblical faith. Consequently, Aquinas attempted "to see" philosophically a stable economy of providentially ordered natural human goods. For the theologian, only that economy is the real ground of the rationally constituted moral order.[288] And it is this natural economy that must be freely affirmed and sustained as the basis for the merely contingent ends that engage human deliberation and choice.

Now it is hardly surprising that Aquinas, who believed in an unchanging revealed moral code, sought to transcend the vagaries of Aristotelian moral reasoning which remains subject to an all too human order. The social and psychic distortions that so often afflict the moral reasoning of most individuals prompted Aquinas to argue for the moral appropriateness *(convenientia)* of a divinely revealed moral law.[289] The

---

286. See *EN*, VI, 13, 1144b30–1145a6.

287. Cf. Gauthier-Joliff, II, 2:563–64.

288. Cf. *III Sent.*, d. 33, q. 2, a. 3, co. (Busa, 384c): ". . . rectitudo electionis est in aliis virtutibus a prudentia, sicut rectitudo in intentione naturae est ex sapientia divina ordinante naturam."

289. See *ST*, I-II, 91, a. 4: "Ut ergo homo absque omni dubitatione scire possit quid ei sit agendum et quid vitandum, necessarium fuit ut in actibus propriis dirigeretur per legem divinitus datam, de qua constat quod non potest errare."

Aristotelian focus on emotional habituation allows the moral philosopher to see deeply but not deeply enough into the ultimate ground of morality. *Phronesis* needs to be bolstered by *synderesis*.[290] As a natural habit of practical intellect, it can provide the immutable cognitive ground that Aristotelian morality ostensibly lacks.[291]

The doctrine of *synderesis* can be philosophically defended by reference to human nature and its necessary ends. In one sense, this natural human teleology is an entirely Aristotelian notion, and, in principle, it is entirely accessible to philosophical reasoning.[292] But philosophical reasoning about the right ends of human action is itself burdened by human sinfulness.[293] Aquinas's argument in favor of the immutable primary principles of morality is an outstanding example of "Christian philosophy"; the principles of *synderesis* are the foundations for a moral philosophy but one inspired by faith.[294] In using the *Nicomachean Ethics* as the matrix for his own doctrine of *synderesis*, Aquinas transforms more than develops Aristotelian moral philosophy.[295] What enabled Aquinas to see something about human nature and the foundations of practical reasoning that Aristotle, so far as we can tell, did not see and perhaps could not see? As portrayed by Aristotle, the *phronimos* pursues ends that are supposedly good for men in general. Yet Aristotle shows little or no concern to expose the ultimate cognitive source of the virtuous man's knowledge of this universal human good. Aquinas, on the other hand, believed that whatever fell under human

---

290. See Thiry, "Saint Thomas et la morale d'Aristote," 243, n. 43: "Cette liason de la syndérèse et de la prudence est la solution proprement Thomiste de l'aporie bien connu de l'ethique d'Aristote . . . *sophia-phronesis*. . . ."

291. See *II Sent.*, d. 24, q. 3, a. 3 (Mandonnet, 625): ". . . in anima est aliquid quod est perpetuae rectitudinis, scilicet synderesis. . . ."

292. Cf. *ST,* I–II, q. 100, a. 11: "Sed praecepta moralia ex ipso dictamine naturalis rationis efficaciam habent, etiam si nunquam in lege statuantur."

293. See *ST,* I–II, q. 100, a. 5, ad 1: ". . . praecepta decalogi referuntur ad praecepta dilectionis. Fuit autem dandum praeceptum homini de dilectione Dei et proximi, quia quantum ad hoc lex naturalis obsurata erat propter peccatum: non autem quantum ad dilectionem sui ipsius, quia quantum ad hoc lex naturalis vigebat."

294. Cf. *ST,* I–II, q. 71, a. 6: ". . . a theologis consideratur peccatum praecipue secundum quod est offensa contra Deum: a philosopho autem morali, secundum quod contrariatur rationi"; q. 104, a. 1, ad 3: ". . . etiam in his quae ordinant ad Deum, quaedam sunt moralia, quae ipsa ratio fide informata dictat: sicut Deum esse amandum et colendum."

295. Cf. *II Sent.*, d. 24, q. 2, a. 4 (Mandonnet, 613): ". . . lex naturalis nominat ipsa universalia principia juris; synderesis vero nominat habitum eorum, seu potentiam cum habitu; conscientia vero nominat applicationem quamdam legis naturalis ad aliquid faciendum per modum conclusionis cujusdam."

reason is somehow contained within the divine order.[296] Even more to the point, Aquinas believed that the precepts of divine law expose what right reason itself should be able to grasp.[297]

For the Christian believer, God has revealed in the immutable commandments given to Moses what is universally good for men.[298] Because of the Gospel, what is good for men can be simply put: that they become friends with each other and with God.[299] For the Christian theologian, the various human goods are merely features within the economy of God's creation. That creation is providentially ordered toward charity human and divine. The theologian must assume that practical reason, whereby man is enabled to order his own affairs, also falls under divine providence. As a created instrument, practical reason participates in the eternal law and, in this fashion, human providence is subsumed under divine providence.[300] It is in this heuristic context that Aquinas ponders the ground and scope of practical reason.[301]

Beneath the contingent matters that are the objects of human choices, Aquinas discerns a stable order of natural human tendencies and ends that reflects the intention of God for His creation.[302] The Thomistic doctrine of *synderesis* highlights and builds on these natural ends. In doing so, we can say that Aquinas *restructured* the foundations of Aristotelian moral reasoning.[303] Aquinas was prompted to look for the cognitive ground of truly universal moral principles because Christian

296. See *ST*, I–II, q. 72, a 4: "Quaecumque enim continentur sub ordine rationis, continentur sub ordine ipsius Dei. . . ."

297. See *ST*, I–II, q. 100, a. 2: "Et ideo lex divina praecepta proponit de omnibus illis per quae ratio hominis est bene ordinata."

298. See *ST*, I–II, q. 103, a. 3: ". . . lex vetus dicitur esse in aeternum, secundum moralia quidem, simpliciter et absolute"; II–II, q. 140, a. 2: ". . . lex divina perfecte informat hominem de his quae sunt necessaria ad recte vivendum."

299. See *ST*, I–II, q. 99, a. 1, ad 2: ". . . sicut ut Apostolus dicit, I ad Tim. 1, 5, *finis praecepti caritas est:* ad hoc enim omnis lex tendit, ut amicitiam constituat vel hominum ad invicem, vel hominis ad Deum. Et ideo tota lex impletur in hoc uno mandato, *Diliges proximum tuum sicut teipsum,* sicut in quodam fine mandatorum omnium. . . ."

300. See *ST*, I–II, q. 91, a. 2: "Unde cum omnia quae divinae providentiae subduntur, a lege aeterna regulentur et mensurentur . . . manifestum est quod omnia participant aliqualiter legem aeternam. . . ."

301. See *ST*, I–II, q. 71, a. 6, ad 4: "Si autem referatur ad ius naturale, quod continetur primo quidem in lege aeterna, secundario vero in naturali iudicatorio rationis humanae, tunc omne peccatum est malum quia prohibitum: ex hoc enim ipso quod est inordinatum, iuri natuali repugnat."

302. See *ST*, I–II, q. 26, a. 1.

303. Cf. *ST*, I–II, q. 100, a. 1: ". . . omne autem rationis humanae iudicium aliqualiter a naturali ratione derivatur; necesse est quod omnia praecepta moralia pertineant ad legem naturae, sed diversimode."

theology affirms the universally binding character of the Ten Commandments. Whatever Aristotelian analogues there are to the Thomistic infallible rational insight into universal, exceptionless, positive, moral principles, an insight that Aquinas explicitly grants to all rational agents, the act of *synderesis* certainly exceeds in scope, firmness, clarity, and significance the "true apprehension" of Aristotle's *phronimos*. But, again, God's providential order is the central issue in Aquinas's thinking about the stable principles of morality:

> The precepts of the Decalogue contain the very intention of the legislator, namely, God. . . . And, therefore, the precepts of the Decalogue are never able to be remitted. *(ST,* I–II, q. 100, a. 8)[304]

The theologian, believing in the immutability of the Decalogue, asks a further question. Since all of human life falls under divine providence, how does natural or merely human morality instantiate *in its own order* the immutable divine intention for mankind?[305] Man's love of self is only too evident; it is the love of neighbor and God that is obscured by sin. Nonetheless, human nature remains good. By what means, then, does practical reason grasp the universal or exceptionless moral principles that promote *natural* friendship between man and man, and man and God? This is the theological question that guided Aquinas's investigation into the cognitive source of Aristotle's natural moral principles. His answer to this question, which had a precedent in Albertus Magnus's exegesis of the *Nicomachean Ethics,* cannot be found—as Aquinas doubtless knew—in the letter of Aristotle's ethics. But the question itself, Aquinas also must have known, transcends the spirit of Aristotle's ethics.

---

304. "Praecepta autem decalogi continent ipsam intentionem legislatoris scilicet Dei . . . Et ideo praecepta decalogi sunt omnino indispensabilia" *(ST,* I–II, q. 100, a. 8).

305. Cf. *ST,* I–II, q. 97, a. 1, ad 1: ". . . naturalis lex est participatio quaedam legis aeternae . . . et ideo immobilis perseverat. . . ."

VI

Practical Reason: The Primary Source of Natural Law

1. Practical Reason and Natural Law

The exact relationship between metaphysics and ethics has proved difficult to delineate in regard to both Aristotle and Aquinas. Thiry, for example, asserts that Aristotle in the *Nicomachean Ethics* "refuses to treat the question of the relationships between metaphysics and ethics."[1] Now it is true that Aristotle does not directly treat this question, but one cannot legitimately regard his silence as a "refusal." Thiry, for his part, does not adequately consider whether a dialectical defense of ethical beliefs could lead, eventually, to a mediated metaphysical defense of ethical beliefs. But Thiry also finds in Aquinas's conception of practical reason, by contrast with what he thinks to be the lacuna in Aristotelian doctrine, a "revelation" of that Absolute Good "which is the soul of all morality."[2]

Thiry's Thomistic "revelation," even if that hyperbolic term is discounted, seems to ground practical reason in a theological or a metaphysical principle. But does such a grounding entail or require that the basic Thomistic moral principles can be or must be immediately deduced from metaphysical or theological propositions about the Absolute Good? The answer to this question, which touches on some important issues in contemporary metaethics, sets various, allegedly historical, interpretations of Aquinas at odds.

Because of the controversy about the metaphysical foundations of the natural law, we need to attend especially to two features of the

---

1. Thiry, "Saint Thomas," 236–37.
2. Ibid., 238.

Thomistic doctrine: (1) the natural law is the law of practical and not theoretical reason; (2) the natural law is prescriptive.

(1) Aquinas identifies *(ST,* I–II, q. 99, a. 3, ad 2) the primary principles of practical reason with the universal or "most common precepts of the law of nature" *(communissima praecepta legis naturae).*[3] In accordance with one of the main connotations of the term "natural," these principles may be identified as precepts of the natural law because they prescribe the very ends to which the will is *ordered* or *inclined* by nature.[4] Both speculative and practical reason have ends upon which the will naturally bears.[5] Practical reason, however, is the source of natural law precepts not because it operates in conjunction with volition but because it alone has action as its defining *end.* The end of practical reason is to pursue or to flee something. Natural law precepts prescribe what we must fundamentally pursue and proscribe what we must fundamentally avoid when choosing to act.

Although the mind is the principle of an action, still the mind itself as it is absolutely considered (that is, speculative reason) moves nothing, because [speculative reason] says nothing about initiating or fleeing . . . and thus it is not the principle of any action but only that [mind] which is for the sake of something, the [mind] which is ordered to some particular action as to an end. And this is the practical mind or reason. . . . *(SLE,* VI, 2, 1139a35, 174–77; *In Ethic.,* VI, lect. 2 [Spiazzi, n. 1135, p. 311])[6]

(2) Unlike certain contemporary varieties of "ethical naturalism" and "descriptivism," Aquinas does not think that the natural law can

---

3. Cf. *ST,* I–II, q. 90, a. 1: "Et huiusmodi propositiones universales rationis practicae ordinatae ad actiones, habent rationem legis"; q. 93, a. 1, ad 1: "Et secundum hoc, large accipiendo, praeceptum, universaliter lex praeceptum dicitur"; ". . . praecepta legis naturae hoc modo se habent ad rationem practicam, sicut principia prima demonstrationum se habet ad rationem speculativam." Similarly, see *II Sent.,* d. 24, q. 2, a. 3; *De ver.,* q. 16, aa. 1–3; *ST,* I, q. 79, a. 12.

4. See *III Sent.,* d 20, q. 1, a. 1, sol. 1, ad 1 (Moos, n. 19, p. 613): ". . . naturale dicitur dupliciter. Uno modo id quod consequitur ex principiis speciei. . . . Alio modo dicitur naturale id ad quod natura est ordinata . . ."; *In de Div. Nom.,* X, lect. 1 (Pera, n. 858, p. 321): ". . . ipsae naturales inclinationes rerum in proprios fines, quas dicimus esse naturales leges. . . ."

5. See *III Sent.,* d. 23, q. 2, a. 3, sol. 2 (Moos, n. 182, p. 733): ". . . conjunctio intellectus ad voluntatem non facit intellectum practicum, sed ordinatio ejus ad opus; quia voluntas communis est et speculativo et practico. Voluntas enim est finis. Sed finis invenitur in speculativo et practico intellectu."

6. ". . . quamvis mens sit principium actus, tamen mens ipsa, secundum se absolute considerata, id est ratio speculativa, nihil movet, quia nihil dicit de [initando] et fugiendo . . . et sic non est principium alicuius actus, sed solum illa quae est gratia huius, id est quae ordinatur ad aliquod particulare operabile sicut ad finem; et

be reduced to descriptions of how men have acted, or are acting, or, even less, to predictions of how men will act to realize certain states of affairs that are regarded as desirable or good solely because of their natural properties.[7] A natural law is a "precept of the law of nature";[8] it enjoins how men *should* act in order to make or preserve the moral order, that is, the rational ordering of human affairs through the exercise of the moral virtues.[9] The primary precepts of the natural law immediately enjoin what ought to be done and what ought not to be done through freely chosen human actions.[10]

Prescriptions, taken broadly, can cover the whole range of human activities. There are prescriptions about telling the truth or building houses. But we need to distinguish precepts that are about "doing" rather than "making." Precepts governing things to be done *(agibilia)* immanently perfect the agent as distinguished from precepts that regulate the artistic and technological production of things external to the agent *(factibilia)*.[11] Action-guiding precepts can be moral or ceremonial or judicial. Moral precepts are precepts whose obligatoriness immediately derives from practical reason itself; ceremonial and judicial precepts, which have authority from a divine or human institution, further determine the moral precepts by regulating divine worship and our actions toward our neighbors.[12] Thus the natural law, which is the immediate prescriptions of practical reason, consists solely of moral precepts: "What natural reason dictates is a moral precept."[13] A moral

---

haec est mens vel ratio practica . . ." *(SLE,* VI, 2, 1139a35, 174–77; *In Ethic.,* VI, lect. 2 [Spiazzi, n. 1135, p. 311]).

7. See W. D. Hudson, "The Intuitionist Theory," in *Modern Moral Philosophy,* 2d ed. (New York: St. Martin's Press, 1983), 65–105, esp. 65–87.

8. ". . . praeceptum legis naturae . . ." *(Quod.* VII, q. 7, a. 1, resp. [Spiazzi, 150]). See *ST,* I–II, q. 92, a. 1: ". . . Sicut enuntiatio est rationis dictamen per modum enuntiandi, ita etiam lex per modum praecipiendi"; ad 1: ". . . large accipiendo praeceptum, universaliter lex praeceptum dicitur."

9. See *ST,* I–II, q. 99, a. 5: "Debitum autem morale est duplex; dicta enim ratio aliquid faciendum vel tanquam necessarium; sine quo non potest est ordo virtutis; vel tanquam utile ad hoc quod ordo virtutis melius conservetur."

10. See *De malo,* q. 2, a. 1 (Bazzi-Pession, 466): "Unde et in ratione naturali et etiam in lege divina, ex quibus nostri actus regulari debent, quaedam praecepta negativa, quaedam affirmativa continentur."

11. See *De ver.,* q. 5, a. 1.

12. See *ST,* I–II, 104, a. 1: ". . . praeceptorum cuiuscumque legis quaedam habent vim obligandi ex ipso dictamine rationis, quia naturalis ratio dictat hoc esse debitum fieri vel vitari. Et huiusmodi pracepta dicuntur *moralia:* eo quod a ratione dicuntur mores humani"; q. 101, a. 1: ". . . caeremonialia praecepta determinant praecepta moralia in ordine ad Deum, sicut iudicialia determinant praecepta moralia in ordine ad proximum."

precept enjoins some good that ought freely to be done or prohibits some evil that ought freely to be avoided by an agent acting in accordance with the dictates of practical reason.[14]

Thomistic natural law precepts, unlike what is maintained by certain varieties of contemporary "prescriptivism,"[15] are cognitive: they are not grounded exclusively in emotion or attitude.[16] On the contrary, Thomistic natural law precepts are first of all expressions of practical reason. Yet, in the Thomistic conception of the order of reciprocal psychological acts, for every intellectual act there is always a corresponding volitional act. Practical reason is practical because it directs the truth that it knows to doing something, to an *"opus."*[17] And, as I shall spell out in the next chapter, the agent cannot pursue this *opus* apart from his or her volitional response to what practical reason presents as true.[18] Still, even the strongest form of Thomistic prescriptions, "commands" (which are imperatives that directly convey a volitional impetus to a particular act), only arise as a consequence of rational *judgments* about how (i.e., by what means) certain ends or goods are to be pursued.

2. Metaphysics and Ethics

Although Aquinas identifies the natural law with the most basic precepts of practical not theoretical reason,[19] Gilson cautions that "the

13. ". . . illud ejus quod naturalis ratio dictat, praeceptum morale est . . ." *(In III Sent.,* d. 37, q. 1, a. 5, sol 2 [Moos, n. 94, p. 1252]). Cf. *IV Sent.,* d. 1, q. 2, a. 5, ad 3 (Moos, n. 318, p. 67): ". . . hoc praeceptum non sit morale, quia naturalis ratio illud non dictat. . . ."

14. See *ST,* I–II, q. 100, a. 1: ". . . cum moralia praecepta sint de his quae pertinent ad bonos mores; haec autem sunt quae rationi congruunt . . ."; *Quod.* VII q. 7, a. 1, ad 3 (Spiazzi, p. 151): ". . . omnia praecepta cuiuslibet legis sunt ordinata ad aliquod bonum inducendum, vel malum tollendum. . . ."

15. See Hudson, "Prescriptivism," in *Modern Moral Philosophy,* 155–248, esp. 163–64, 206–9.

16. See *III Sent.,* d. 33, q. 3, a. 1, sol. 3 (Moos, n. 281, p. 1075): "Ad rationem enim pertinet praecipere quod faciendum est."

17. See *III Sent.,* d. 22, q. 2, a. 3, sol. 2 (Moos, n. 177, p. 732): "Quandoque autem verum quod in se consideratur, potest ut regula operis considerari. Et tunc intellectus speculativus fit practicus per extensionem ad opus."

18. See *II Sent.,* d. 24, q. 3, a. 1 (Mandonnet, 617): ". . . actus appetitivarum virtutum motus vocantur, non autem proprie actus apprehensivarum. . . . Appetitus autem rationalis est qui consequitur apprehensionem rationis, et hic dicitur motus rationis, qui est actus voluntatis"; *De malo,* q. 16, a. 6 (Bazzi-Pession, 680): "Sed appetere finem et movere in ipsum praecipue convenit voluntati. . . ."

19. See *ST,* II–II, q. 47, a. 6: "Sicut autem in ratione speculativa sunt quaedam ut

study of ethics is not able to be isolated from that of metaphysics in the system of St. Thomas Aquinas."[20] Gilson's claim, and others similar to it, introduces us to a present-day controversy about the relationship between Thomistic metaphysics and ethics.[21] Among other issues, the controversy has revived Hume's question: Can moral principles (since they contain "oughts") be validly derived from factual propositions (i.e., descriptions) about nature and man?[22] Hume's answer, at least according to the received interpretation, is that they cannot be validly derived.[23]

Gilson, of course, is not party to the recent controversy among students of Aquinas;[24] nor, for that matter, did he exactly anticipate it. He was concerned to locate Aquinas's discussion of morality in the overall structure of the *Summa theologiae*. But in characterizing Thomistic ethics as part of the study of creation, Gilson asserts that "the study of morality reduces to this metaphysical question":[25] How does God direct intellectual creatures, men endowed with reason and choice, who are themselves self-directing? Now Gilson's assertion is troublesome because it is ambiguous: it can mean either that (1) ethics, insofar as it reduces to metaphysics, must explain how God directs self-directing men; or that (2) ethics can be reduced to this metaphysical issue without leaving any moral (i.e., nonmetaphysical) remainder.

The second interpretation, although it offers an implausibly reductionist view of Thomistic ethics, is nevertheless logically compatible with Gilson's view of "the moral good as a particular case of the good

---

naturaliter nota, quorum est intellectus . . . ita in ratione practica praeexistunt quaedam ut principia naturaliter nota, et huiusmodi sunt fines virtutum moralium, quia finis se habet in operabilibus sicut principium in speculativis. . . ."

20. Gilson, *Saint Thomas moraliste*, 17.

21. See Janice L. Schultz, "Is-Ought: Prescribing and a Present Controversy," *Thomist* 49 (1985): 1–23, and "Thomistic Metaethics and a Present Controversy," *Thomist* 52 (1988): 40–62; McInerny, "Ethics and Metaphysics," in *Aquinas on Human Action*, 193–206.

22. See *A Treatise of Human Nature*, Bk. III, Pt. I, Sect. 1 (ed. L. A. Selby-Bigge, 469).

23. For a revisionist interpretation of Hume, arguing that Hume permits "ought" to be validly derived from "is," see A. C. MacIntyre, "Hume on 'is' and 'ought,'" in *The Is/Ought Question*, ed. W. D. Hudson (London: Macmillan Press, 1969), 35–50.

24. For two contrary views of Aquinas's natural law doctrine, the first stressing the prescriptive and the second the descriptive character of natural law, cf. Alfonso Gómez-Lobo, "Natural Law and Naturalism," *Proceedings of the American Catholic Philosophical Association* 59 (1984): 232–49; Errol Harris, "Natural Law and Naturalism," *International Philosophical Quarterly* 23 (1983): 115–24.

25. Gilson, *Saint Thomas moraliste*, 18.

in general."[26] In other formulations, which again are logically open to a reductive metaphysical reading, Gilson explains why Thomistic ethics "cannot be isolated from metaphysics":[27] "Practical reason measures the goodness of [human] acts by their conformity with the essence of man."[28] This latter formulation makes a certain portrait of the human essence the ultimate norm of ethical judgments. According to one critic,[29] Gilson's norm requires that we have a theoretical (metaphysical) knowledge of human nature before we can justify our practical (moral) judgments about the goodness and badness of actions. If so, then Gilson effectively reduces practical to theoretical reason.[30]

Nonetheless, it is unjustifiable to press Gilson's formulations so far, since he nowhere states that prescriptive moral principles reduce without logical remainder to descriptive metaphysical principles. Moreover, Gilson refers to Aquinas's distinction between theoretical and practical reason: he explicitly notes that there are nonderivable or immediate prescriptive principles of practical reason.[31] Still, one can fairly hold that Gilson's account as well as other standard accounts of Thomistic practical principles do leave a number of difficult issues unexplored and in need of clarification.[32]

In the Humean wake, many questions have been raised about the systematic relationship between Thomistic metaphysical and ethical doctrines that cannot be directly answered from Aquinas's texts.[33] In

---

26. Ibid., 96. Cf. *De virt.*, q. 1, a. 2 (Odetto, 712): ". . . bonum quod convertitur cum ente, non ponitur hic in definitione virtutis; sed bonum quod determinatur ad actum moralem."

27. Gilson, *Saint Thomas moraliste*, 17.

28. Étienne Gilson, "De la nature du principe," in *Constantes philosophiques de l'être* (Paris: Librairie Philosophique J. Vrin, 1983), 105: "La raison pratique mesure la bonté des actes aux rapports qu'ils soutiennent avec l'essence de l'homme. . . ."

29. See Théo G. Belmans, O. Praem., "Au croisement des chemins en morale fondamentale," *Revue thomiste* 89 (1989): 254–55.

30. See Théo G. Belmans, "Le 'Volontarisme' de saint Thomas d' Aquin," *Revue Thomist* 85 (1985): 193, n. 71, who criticizes Gilson for loosing sight of the "caractère pratique" of the moral good.

31. See Gilson, *Saint Thomas moralist*, 102–3.

32. See Jacques Maritain's equivocal remarks in *An Introduction to the Basic Problems of Moral Philosophy*, trans. Cornelia N. Borgerhoff (Albany, N.Y.: Magi Books, 1990). Maritain claims that moral good "signifies a certain particular analogue of ontological good" (33); yet moral good "remains ontological by nature, a particularized ontological good" (34), but it is not the case that "the passage from metaphysical or transcendental good to moral good takes place by a simple logical particularization" (ibid.).

33. For a controversial exploration of the relationship between natural law ethics and metaphysics, see Henry B. Veatch, *Swimming against the Current in Con-*

the Thomistic context, the central connection between metaphysics and ethics seems to be, as Maritain suggested, the *analogy* that Aquinas draws between moral goodness and ontological goodness.[34] The terms in which the analogy is framed can only be understood against the background of Aquinas's metaphysical doctrine: as with natural things, human acts that lack the "fullness of being" lack goodness. But the meaning of the "fullness of being," as the phrase is applied to human acts, must be precisely determined not in the ontological order but "in the order of reason."[35] In the latter order, a human act has "fullness of being," and hence moral goodness, if and only if the agent's end and the act's object and circumstances are *rationally justifiable.*

The entire goodness of moral virtue is derived from the rightness of reason. Therefore, the good comes along with moral virtue inasmuch as [the latter] follows right reason; the bad, however, [comes along with] the opposite vice, namely, excess, and inasmuch as [vice] falls back from right reason. *(SLE,* II, 7, 1107a, 113–18; *In Ethic.,* II, lect. 7 [Spiazzi, n. 326, p. 92])[36]

In this chapter, however, I shall only refer obliquely to this analogy, but I shall directly examine, albeit summarily, three facets of the contemporary question of how Thomistic metaphysics and ethics are related: (1) Does the science of metaphysics provide the principles of ethics? (2) Is the moral good reducible to the transcendental or ontological good? (3) In what sense does the operation of practical reason presuppose the operation of theoretical reason?

The first of these questions can be best approached by attending to the precise Thomistic hierarchy of the sciences and by avoiding loose

---

temporary Philosophy: Occasional Essays and Papers, Studies in Philosophy and the History of Philosophy, vol. 20, gen. ed. Jude P. Dougherty (Washington, D.C.: The Catholic University of America Press, 1990).

34. See *ST,* I–II, q. 18, a. 1. For an analysis of sinful actions that makes extensive use of the analogy between metaphysical and moral evil, see *De malo,* q. 2. But the dissimilarities between the two are no less important than the similarities: ". . . deformitas peccati non consequitur speciem actus secundum quod est in genere naturae; sic autem a Deo causatur; sed consequitur speciem actus secundum quod est moralis, prout causatur ex libero arbitrio . . ." *(De malo,* q. 3, a. 2, ad 2 [Bazzi-Pession, 498]).

35. *ST,* I–II, q. 18, a. 1, ad 3. Cf. a. 5: "In actibus autem humanis bonum et malum dicitur per comparationem ad rationem. . . ."

36. ". . . tota bonitas virtutis moralis dependet ex rectitudine rationis, unde bonum convenit virtuti morali secundum quod sequitur rationem rectam, malum autem convenit utrique vitio, tam superabundanti quam deficienti et in quantum recedit a ratione recta . . ." *(SLE,* II, 7, 1107a, 113–18; *In Ethic.,* II, lect. 7 [Spiazzi, n. 326, p. 92]).

descriptions of how Thomistic metaphysics grounds ethics.[37] Thomistic ethics, everyone can agree, is replete with metaphysical vocabulary and metaphysical doctrines. Nonetheless, Aquinas explicitly denies that metaphysics encompasses or reaches down to or provides the proper principles of ethics; instead, he consistently "grounds" basic moral principles only by identifying them with the epistemically *immediate* and *infallible* dictates of practical reason.[38] In effect, those authors who argue for the logical dependency of the principles of ethics on metaphysics or, epistemically, for the radical metaphysical contextualization of moral principles reorganize Aquinas's schema of the sciences.[39]

Aquinas delineates a hierarchy of subalternating speculative sciences (metaphysics, physics, and mathematics, and the various intermedi-

37. Cf. Eleonore Stump and Norman Kretzmann, "Being and Goodness," in *Being and Goodness: The Concept of the Good in Metaphysics and Philosophical Theology*, ed. Scott MacDonald (Ithaca, N.Y.: Cornell University Press, 1991), 99: "Aquinas's ethics is embedded in his metaphysics . . ."; Vernon J. Bourke, *St. Thomas and the Greek Moralists*, Aquinas Lecture for 1974 (Milwaukee: Marquette University Press, 1974), 8: "The philosophical base of the ethical theory of St. Thomas is metaphysics"; and Reginaldo Pizzorni, *Il diritto naturale dalle origini a S. Tommaso d' Aquino*, 2d ed. (Rome: Pontificia Università Lateranense, Città Nuova Editrice, 1985): ". . . l'etica presuppone la metafisica, perché il *dovere*, oggetto della morale e del diritto, non è che un aspetto, un riflesso dinamico dell'*esse*, oggetto della metafisica. . . ."

Rather than metaphysics *grounding* ethics, or ethics *presupposing* metaphysics, it would be more accurate to describe Thomistic ethics as *incorporating* Aquinas's metaphysical doctrine, especially about the nature of intellect and will, as they are understood to be the ontological causes of human action. Cf. Horst Seidl, "*Natürliche Sittlichkeit und Metaphysische Voraussetzung in der Ethik des Aristoteles und Thomas von Aquin*," in *The Ethics of St. Thomas Aquinas*, ed. L. J. Elders, S.V.D., and K. Hedwig (Vatican City: Libreria Editrice Vaticana, 1984), 95: "Bei näherer Betrachtung zeigt sich nämlich, dass Thomas wie auch Aristoteles von der ethischen Struktur menschlichen Handelns ausgehen, die als solche noch kein metaphysische ist, wenn sie auch letztlich metaphysische Prinzipien voraussetzt (wie übrigens jeder Sachverhalt einer Einzeldisziplin)."

38. See *I Sent.*, prologus, q. 1, a. 2: ". . . metaphysica, quae considerat omnia inquantum sunt entia, non decendens ad propriam cognitionem moralium vel naturalium"; *De malo*, q. 3, a. 12, ad 13 (Bazzi-Pession, p. 516): ". . . ad synderesim pertinent universalia principia iuris naturalis circa quae nullus errat. . . ."

39. Cf. Henry B. Veatch, "Can John Finnis Bring Off a Revival of Natural Law?" in *Swimming against the Current*, 289: ". . . in the *De Veritate* [q. 1, a. 1; q. 21] . . . St. Thomas seems to give the unmistakable impression that ethics must discover its own principles directly in being and in the context of the discipline of metaphysics. . . ." However, this impression is considerably diminished if one notes that, in these questions, St. Thomas does not specifically address the issue of *bonum moralis*; here, the "*bonum* . . . [that] is intelligible only in terms of . . . *ens*" (ibid.) is the ontological or transcendental good.

ate sciences that fit under physics and mathematics)[40] wherein the
higher science provides principles for the lower. But Aquinas does not,
unlike the later Scholastics (notably, John of St. Thomas and the Salmanticenses[41]), put ethics into this hierarchy.[42] Ethics usefully draws
upon the theoretical sciences, especially psychology which is subalternated to physics, but it is not logically or epistemically dependent
upon either theoretical science for its principles.[43]

In the opinion of Aquinas's Dominican contemporary, Robert Kilwardby (d. 1279), if ethics received its principles from either psychology or metaphysics, it would abandon its own subject matter, voluntary human actions.[44] Kilwardby's view is consistent with Aquinas,
who maintains that ethics is a practical or active science that has its
principle in human choice and not the natural properties of things.[45] As
a practical science, one that is not subalternated to any theoretical
science but commences from its own immediate principles, ethics is
first in its own order and is, in that precise sense, an independent
science. It begins with its own, peculiar, practical understanding of the
moral good.[46]

40. See *In Phys.*, I, lect. 1 (Maggiòlo, nn. 2–4, pp. 3–5); II, lect. 3 (nn. 163–65, p.
84); *In Metaph.*, I, lect. 2 (Cathala-Spiazzi, n. 47, p. 14); III, lect. 6 (n. 396, pp. 111–
12); VI, lect. 1 (nn. 1145; 1149; 1155; 1159, pp. 295–97); *SLA*, I, c. 2, 403a3, 8–10 (*In
de An.*, I, lect. 2 [Pirotta, n. 16]); *De ver.*, q. 9, a. 1, ad 3; *Expos. de Trin.*, q. 2, a. 2, ad
5; q. 5, a. 1, ad 5. Cf. *ELP*, I, 25; 43.

41. See J.-M. Ramírez, O.P., review of *Distinguer pour unir, ou les degrés du
savoir*, by Jacques Maritain, in *Bulletin thomiste* 4 (1934–1936): 425; and Joseph
Owens, review of *Lex et Libertas: Freedom and Law According to St. Thomas
Aquinas*, ed. L. J. Elders and K. Hedwig, in *Thomist* 52 (1988): 541.

42. See *Expos. de Trin.*, q. 5, a. 1, ad 5, where the practical sciences of medicine,
alchemy, and agriculture, because they are based on the *natural properties* of things,
are said to be subalternated to the theoretical science of physics. But moral goodness,
for Aquinas, is not a natural property of actions: "Fines autem morales accidunt rei
naturali; et e converso ratio naturalis finis accidit morali" (*ST*, I–II, q. 1, a. 3, ad 3).

43. See *SLE*, I, 19, 1102a13–23, 58–85 (*In Ethic.*, I, lect. 19 [Spiazzi, nn. 227–28,
p. 62]); *SLA*, I, c. 1, 402a4, 113–31 (*In de An.*, I, lect. 1 [Pirotta, n. 7, p. 3]).

44. See Robert Kilwardby, O.P., *De ortu scientiarum*, ed. Albert G. Judy, O.P.
(Toronto: British Academy and the Pontifical Institute of Mediaeval Studies, 1976),
141, nn. 404–5: ". . . metaphysica . . . Si etiam voluntates consideret, non excedit in
eis terminos naturae. Ethica autem considerat voluntarias operationes et mores ut
sunt ad virtutem vel ab illa, et voluntatem ipsam non habet considerare ut natura
est. . . . Et ideo non potest subalternari metaphysicae. . . . Sed nec [ethica] potest
subalternari aliis speculativis, quia omnes considerant veritatem quae inest rebus
naturalibus secundum quod naturae sunt, et dico modo *naturale* prout dividitur
contra *voluntarium*."

45. See *Metaph.*, VI, 1, 1025b22–24; *In Metaph.*, VI, lect. 1 (Cathala-Spiazzi, n.
1154, p. 296).

46. Cf. Wolfgang Kluxen, "Metaphysik und praktische Vernunft: *Über ihre*

3. The Practical Sciences

The fact that ethics is grounded independently of metaphysics can be explained in terms of the differences between the *principles, subjects,* and *ends* of the two sciences.[47] First, the two sciences have different principles or starting points. The starting point of the metaphysical knowledge of being is knowledge of sensible substance or sensible entity (οὐσία); the focal meaning of being, however, is found in the separate and primary entities, the unmoved movers.[48] Human choice, since it is the efficient (i.e., moving) cause of the moral character of our habits and actions, is the principle of ethics.[49] Second, metaphysics is the universal science: its subject, "being qua being," encompasses all beings insofar as they are beings.[50] Ethics, however, is a science confined to a genus of being: it considers the good and bad qualities of animated beings who are able to make choices.[51] Put more precisely, ethics is focused on men's morally good and bad habits. Third, and the most important difference, the ends of the two sciences differ: metaphysics pursues truth; ethics, while we must assume that it is interested in knowing certain truths about man and human affairs, nonetheless has as its defining end the promotion of good ac-

---

Zuordnung bei Thomas von Aquin," in *Thomas Von Aquin: 1274/1974* (Munich: Kösel-Verlag, 1974), 87: "Vor allem ist ihre Selbständigkeit gegenüber der Metaphysik gewahrt: Die praktische Erkenntnis ist unmittelbar auf ihren gegenstand bezogen und nicht durch Vermittlung einer metaphysischen Erkenntnis des 'Guten an sich.'"

47. This clarification or ordering of the sciences falls under metaphysics not moral science: "Sicut Philosophus dicit in principio Metaphysicae, sapientis est ordinare. Cuius ratio est quia sapientia est potissima perfectio rationis, cuius proprium est cognoscere ordinem" *(SLE, I, ante* 1094a1, 1–4; *In Ethic.,* I, lect. 1 [Spiazzi, n. 1, p. 3]). Cf. *Metaph.,* IV, 2, 1004a3–6: the divisions of philosophy correspond to the divisions of οὐσία. Thus discussion of *ens* and its relationship to *bonum moralis,* as the latter pertains to the category of "quality," properly falls under metaphysics: see *In Metaph.,* V, lect. 16 (Cathala-Spiazzi, n. 1000, p. 264).

48. See *Metaph.,* IV, 2, 1003b5–10.

49. See *Metaph.,* VI, 1, 1025b23–25 (rev. Oxford trans.): ". . . the principle of action is in the doer—viz. choice, for that which is done and that which is chosen are the same"; XI, 7, 1064a14–15 (rev. Oxford trans.): "And similarly in practical science the movement is not in the thing done, but rather in the doers." Cf. *In Metaph.,* VI, lect. 1 (Cathala-Spiazzi, n. 1154, p. 296): "Nam principium activarum scientiarum est in agente, non in ipsis actionibus, sive moribus. Hoc autem principium 'est prohaeresis,' idest electio."

50. See *Metaph.,* VI, 1, 1026a31–32.

51. See *Metaph.,* V, 14, 1020b24–25. Cf. *In Metaph.,* V, lect. 16 (Cathala-Spiazzi, n. 1000, p. 264): "Sed tamen bene et male maxime pertinet ad qualitatem in rebus animatis; et praecipue in habentibus 'prohaeresim' idest electionem."

tions.[52] Because of their diverse ends, the two sciences are differently denominated:[53] metaphysics is θεωρητικὴ διάνοια and ethics is πρακτικὴ διάνοια; in Aquinas's Latin terminology, metaphysics is a *"scientia theorica"* and ethics is a *"scientia activa."*[54]

The sharp distinction drawn in some texts between the ends of the theoretical and the practical sciences may seem to compromise the truth value of the Aristotelian practical sciences. Is truth solely the prerogative of the Aristotelian theoretical sciences? Aristotle's logical definition of "truth" ("To say that what is is, and what is not is not, is true"[55]) is a criterion that could apply to propositions in both theoretical and practical sciences. But his metaphysical criterion of truth seems confined to the theoretical sciences. From a metaphysical perspective, to know the truth about a being is to know the causes of that being.[56] Since eternal and necessary beings are the causes of changing beings, the principles of eternal beings are paradigmatically "true."[57]

Nonetheless, despite his metaphysical identification of truth with eternal or necessary beings,[58] Aristotle allows that there can be practical truths about contingent choices and actions:[59] an agent can know what is the morally good thing to do in a given circumstance if he or she reasons in accordance with right desires.[60] A truth about what morally good action should be done is a practical truth (ἡ ἀλήθεια πρακτική),[61] not a theoretical truth: it is a truth about a moral good that should be enacted through human choice.

The *Nicomachean Ethics*, in which Aristotle deliberately excludes

---

52. See *Metaph.*, II, 1, 993b20–21 (rev. Oxford trans.): "For the end of theoretical knowledge is truth, while that of practical knowledge is action. . . ."

53. See *Expos. de Trin.*, q. 5, a. 1, ad 4 (Decker, 8–10, p. 169): ". . . oportet accipere distinctionem eorum ex fine, ut theoricum dicatur illud, quod ordinatur ad solam cognitionem veritatis, practicum vero, quod ordinatur ad operationem."

54. Cf. *Metaph.*, VI, 1, 1025b25 (rev. Oxford trans.): ". . . all thought is either practical [πρακτική] or productive [ποιητική] or theoretical [θεωρητική] . . ."; *In Metaph.*, VI, lect. 1 (Cathala-Spiazzi, n. 1155, p. 296): ". . . omnis scientia est aut activa, aut factiva, aut theorica. . . ."

55. *Metaph.*, IV, 7, 1011b26 (Tredennick trans.).

56. For the connection of "being" and "truth" and "cause," see *Metaph.*, I, 3, 983b1–5. Cf. *Metaph.*, II, 1, 993b23–24 (Tredennick trans.): "But we cannot know the truth apart from the cause."

57. See *Metaph.*, II, 1, 993b26–31.

58. See *Metaph.*, IX, 10, 1051b15–17. Cf. *ST*, I–II, q. 57, a. 5, ad 3: ". . . nullus habitus speculativus contingentium est intellectualis virtus sed solum est circa necessaria."

59. See *EN*, VI, 2, 1139b12.

60. See *EN*, VI, 2, 1139a25–31.

61. *EN*, VI, 2, 1139a26–27.

extraneous theoretical discussions about the nature of the intellect or soul,[62] maintains the standpoint of the moral agent who possesses *phronesis:* its defining end is not theoretical but practical.[63] Even the first Latin commentators on the *Nicomachean Ethics*, who otherwise are only half-faithful Aristotelians,[64] acknowledge that ethics, in terms of its end *as used*, is a practical science.[65] Indeed, in various classifications, ethics remained throughout the Middle Ages a practical science.[66] Aquinas's position, however, is unambiguous and perfectly Aristotelian: the practical sciences have as their proper subjects what men make and do. Ethics is a practical science because it instructs men how to act rightly.[67]

Nonetheless, the practical status of Thomistic ethics seems, for some contemporary interpreters, problematic.[68] Their perplexity arises because Aquinas, while holding to the basic Aristotelian distinction between theoretical and practical sciences, allows for a third kind of science: a theoretical science that is "in a way speculative and in a way practical."[69] This third kind of science is "quasi-practical" because of its subject: it considers things made by human agents, *operabilia*. Yet it is a theoretical science because of its mode and end: it considers *operabilia* either (1) in a theoretical manner (by being engaged in a strictly logical exercise of defining terms); or (2) in regard to a theoretical end

62. See *EN*, I, 13, 1102a23–26.

63. See *SLE*, I, 11, 1098a29, 70–95 (*In Ethic.*, I, lect. 11 [Spiazzi, n. 136, p. 36]).

64. For these first commentaries, see Gauthier *SLE*, praefatio, 236*.

65. Reflecting current theological-metaphysical discussions of the *good*, Kilwardby, (pseudo-) Peckham, and Albert the Great, along with several anonymous commentators, divide Aristotle's unified practical science by distinguishing the theoretical end of ethics as taught *(docens)*, knowledge of *felicitas*, from the practical end of ethics as used *(utens)*, namely, "*ut boni fiamus*": cf. Albertus Magnus, *Super Ethica*, prologus, aa. 3–4 (Kübel, vol. 14, pt. 1, pp. 3–4). For a thorough discussion of these commentators, see Georg Wieland, *Ethica—Scientia Practica: Die Anfänge der philosophischen Ethik im 13.Jahrhundert* (Münster: Aschendorf, 1981), 52–129.

66. For a general view of the medieval distinction between the theoretical and practical sciences, see James A. Weisheipl, "Classification of the Sciences in Mediaeval Thought," *Mediaeval Studies* 27 (1965): 54–90.

67. See *In Metaph.*, XI, lect. 7 (Cathala-Spiazzi, n. 2253, p. 535): "Est ergo scientia activa, ex qua instruimur ad recte exercendum operationes, quae actiones dicuntur; sicut est scientia moralis. Factiva autem scientia est, per quem recte aliquid facimus; sicut ars fabrilis, et alia huiusmodi."

68. For a convincing defense of the irreducibly practical status of Aquinas's moral science, see Richard P. Geraghty, *The Object of Moral Philosophy According to St. Thomas Aquinas* (Washington, D.C.: University Press of America, 1982).

69. ". . . aliqua [scientia] vero secundum quid speculativa et secundum quid practica" (*ST*, I, q. 14, a. 16).

(one that is indifferent to any kind of enactment of the practical truths attained).[70]

Does Aquinas, as Cajetan, John of St. Thomas, and Maritain maintain, place ethics in this third category of "quasi-practical sciences"?[71] Is Thomistic ethics, according either to its mode or its end, a theoretical science? If so, this theoretical science of ethics would have to be distinguished not only from actual practical knowledge but also from habitual practical knowledge that intends to realize an end but not now. On behalf of this interpretation, one might appeal to the fact that Aquinas allows for a theoretical science of *operabilia:* although "the matter of the speculative sciences ought to be things that do not come into being through our activity,"[72] nonetheless "we are able to have a speculative knowledge of those things whose causes are in us."[73] For example, an artist can consider how something could be made without ever intending to make it.[74] Such knowledge remains "virtually practical," but because it does not have action as its end it can be correctly identified as "speculative in a certain way" *(quodammodo speculativa).*[75]

Thus Aquinas allows that we can consider the ends of action without intending to actualize those ends.[76] A theoretical "philosophy of action" is possible: it is knowledge of human action pursued for its own sake, independent of its significance for practical endeavors.[77] A theoretical science of action would seek to understand the volitional motions of the human body.[78] In an Aristotelian context, it would be a

70. See *De ver.*, q. 2, a. 8; q. 3, a. 3.

71. See Jacques Maritain, "'Speculative' and 'Practical,'" appendix in *The Degrees of Knowledge*, trans. Gerald B. Phelan (New York: Charles Scribner's Sons, 1959), 456–64.

72. "Speculativarum vero scientiarum materiam oportet esse res quae a nostro opere non fiunt . . ." *(Expos. de Trin.*, q. 5, a. 1 [Decker, 14–15, p. 164]).

73. "Unde et de eis quorum causae sunt in nobis, possimus habere speculativam scientiam . . ." *(De ver.*, q. 3, a. 3, ad 4 [Spiazzi, 69]).

74. See *De ver.*, q. 2, a. 8.

75. See *De ver.*, q. 3, a. 3.

76. See *De pot.*, q. 1, a. 6, ad 11 (Pession, 20): "Patet enim in artifice creato quod excogitat aliquas operationes quas nunquam operari intendit."

77. In Thomistic terms, contemporary theoretical investigations of action tend to be *"speculativa tantum" (De ver.*, q. 3, a. 3 [Spiazzi, 69]); they draw logical distinctions in order to highlight the "conceptual schemes," or the "logical form of action sentences," or the "event ontologies" that are used to interpret actions; see Alvin I. Goldman, *A Theory of Human Action* (Princeton, N.J.: Princeton University Press, 1970), v–vi; Donald Davidson, *Actions and Events* (Oxford: Clarendon Press, 1980), xi–xvi.

78. For a discussion of an analogous case, the "philosophy of man," which is taken to be a philosophical science requiring a unique combination of theoretical

part of psychology, which in turn is a theoretical science subalternated to physics.[79]

Aquinas, however, repeatedly defines "ethics" as a strictly practical science in reference to the ends that the agent intends to accomplish: "In the moral sciences, the end is not cognition, but action."[80] Ethics cannot be disengaged from the actual or habitual attempt to accomplish certain ends of human action.[81] Therefore, no theoretical science of operabilia, although such a science is indeed possible within the canon of Thomistic sciences, can be identified with Thomistic ethics.[82]

In the Nicomachean Ethics, Aristotle discusses certain topics that may seem theoretical because remote from the immediate ends of action: for example, his discussion of human voluntariness or happiness develops numerous conceptual distinctions. Still, Aristotle holds that such logical exercises retain their practical end.[83] They are aimed at getting men to act virtuously in pursuit of the ultimate end, eudaimonia or the life of theoretical contemplation. By way of comparison, Aquinas notes that medicine also has a "theoretical part," say, the examination of the chemical properties of certain plants. Yet this does not change the operational end of the science (healing the sick); medicine remains, therefore, a practical science. The same criterion applies to the theoretical part of ethics. Since its end is practical, ethics, notwithstanding its apparently theoretical parts, is a practical science.[84]

Aquinas preserves Aristotle's contrast between the end of ethics and

---

and practical sciences (viz., physics, metaphysics, and ethics): see Joseph Owens, C.Ss.R., "The Unity in a Thomistic Philosophy of Man," Mediaeval Studies 25 (1963): 54–82.

79. See de An., I, 1, 403a27–28; 403b11–12; Metaph., VI, 1, 1026a5–6.

80. ". . . in scientiis moralibus finis non est cognitio, sed opus . . ." (III Sent., d. 35, q. 1, a. 3, sol. 2 [Moos, 1184]).

81. See SLE, I, 1, ante 1094a, 51–53 (In Ethic., I, lect. 1 [Spiazzi, n. 3, p. 3]): ". . . Subiectum moralis philosophiae est operatio humana ordinata in finem . . ."; SLE, II, 2, 1103b26, 18–19 (In Ethic., II, lect. 2 [Spiazzi, n. 255, p. 73]): ". . . in scientiis operativis, quorum finis est operatio. . . ."

82. Maritain, however, contends that although ethics is "not a purely speculative knowledge," it is a "speculatively practical knowledge" of operabilia which needs to be supplemented and brought closer to practice by a "practically practical knowledge" and, finally, by prudence; see Degrees of Knowledge, 317–18, 460. Cf. Geraghty, Object of Moral Philosophy, 47: "What Maritain calls speculatively practical science . . . is really speculative through and through according to the conception of St. Thomas."

83. See EN, I, 3, 1095a5–6: τὸ τέλος ἐστὶν οὐ γνῶσις ἀλλὰ πρᾶξις.

84. See Expos. de Trin., q. 5, a. 1, ad 4 (Decker, 9–11, p. 170): "Unde non oportet, ut si alicuius activae scientiae aliqua pars dicatur theorica, quod propter hoc illa pars sub philosophia speculativa ponatur."

the end of any theoretical science: ethics is not about contemplating truths but about enacting them.[85] The latter formula accurately expresses the purpose of the *Nicomachean Ethics:* Aristotle states that we study the virtues in order to acquire them.[86] But Aquinas sometimes draws a sharper line than Aristotle between universal and particular practical knowledge.[87] Ethics is a science inasmuch as it validly draws universal conclusions from universal premises. Universal conclusions are about types of good and bad actions. But another kind of knowledge, expressive of a particular virtue, is required to effect a contingent, singular action.

> Although moral science is truly aimed at action, that action is not an act of science but it is more an act of virtue. . . . *(Expos. de Trin.,* q. 5, a. 1, ad 3 [Decker, 20–22, p. 168])[88]

Aquinas assigns this task, effecting a morally good action, to the intellectual virtue of prudence. Prudence, which is rooted in both reason and right appetite, directs deliberation, judgment, and choices about singular actions.[89] But, for Aquinas, the distinction drawn be-

---

85. See *SLE,* II, 2, 1103b26, 21–25 *(In Ethic.,* II, lect. 2 [Spiazzi, n. 256, p. 73]): ". . . praesens negotium, scilicet moralis philosophiae, non est propter contemplationem veritatis sicut alia negotia scientiarum speculativarum, sed est propter operationem. . . ."

86. See *EN,* II, 2, 1103b26–29. Cf. *SLE,* II, 2, 1103b26, 25–28 *(In Ethic.,* II, lect. 2 [Spiazzi, n. 256, p. 73]) ". . . non enim in hac scientia scrutamur quid sit verus ad hoc solum ut sciamus huius rei veritatem; sed ad hoc, quod acquirentes virtutem, boni efficiamur."

87. See *De virt.,* q. 1, a. 1, ad 1 (Odetto, 723): ". . . Philosophus ibi loquitur de scientia practica; sed prudentia plus importat quam scientia practica: nam ad scientiam practicam pertinet universale iudicium de agendis. . . . Sed ad prudentiam pertinet recte iudicare de singulis agibilibus, prout sint nunc agenda. . . ." Cf. *In Metaph.,* II, lect. 2 (Cathala-Spiazzi, n. 290, p. 84): "[Scientiae practicae] non enim considerant causam veritatis secundum se et propter se, sed ordinando ad finem operationis, sive applicando ad aliquod determinatum particulare, et ad aliquod determinatum tempus."

88. "Scientia vero moralis quamvis sit propter operationem, tamen illa operatio non est actus scientiae, sed magis virtutis . . ." *(Expos. de Trin.,* q. 5, a. 1, ad 3 [Decker, 20–22, p. 168]).

89. See *SLE,* VI, 7, 1141b29, 90–95 *(In Ethic.,* VI, lect. 7 [Spiazzi, n. 1200, p. 329]): ". . . omnia ergo de quibus hic fit mentio in tantum sunt species prudentiae in quantum non in ratione sola consistunt, sed habent aliquid in appetitu; in quantum enim sunt in sola ratione, dicuntur quaedam scientiae practicae, scilicet ethica, yconomica et politica"; *SLE,* I, 1, 1094a1, 142–45 *(In Ethic.,* I, lect. 1 [Spiazzi, n. 8, p. 4]): "Nam facit autem mentionem de prudentia, quae est in ratione practica sicut et ars, quia per prudentiam proprie dirigitur electio"; *In Metaph.,* I, lect. 1 (Cathala-Spiazzi, n. 11, p. 7): "In hominibus quidem est prudentia secundum quod ex ratione deliberat quid eos oporteat agere. . . ."

tween moral science and prudence does not compromise the practical character of ethics. Since its end remains practical, the science of ethics retains its practical character. Ethics seeks the truth but conditionally: its end is truth that can be ordered through the exercise of prudence to some particular good action.

4. Ethics and the "Metaphysics of Action"

Moral precepts enjoin the goods and prohibit the evils that can be accomplished through human action. Aquinas develops the role of these practical principles against the background of what has been called his "metaphysics of action."[90] Metaphysics is the science of being qua being. But being itself is diverse, and this diversity is revealed by the different modes of predicating.[91] *Action* is one of the Aristotelian-Thomistic ultimate predicates or categories of being.[92] The category is constituted by the predication of motion in reference to the source of the motion.[93] Accordingly, the Thomistic network of synonymous definitions that bind "good" *(bonum)*, "end" *(finis)*, "desirable" *(appetibilis)*, and "perfection" *(perfectio)* do not capture only semantic or analytic truths about the network of synonymous predicates that are applied to "action" but point out the essential properties of *action* as a category or ultimate mode of being. By drawing on Aquinas's scattered remarks about the ontological ingredients of action, we can fill in the background that allows for a properly metaphysical interpretation of the *ends* that fall under the first principle of practical reason.[94]

90. See Kluxen, "Metaphysik und praktische Vernunft," 87–88, and *Philosophische Ethik bei Thomas von Aquin*, 121.

91. See *In Metaph.*, V, lect. 9 (Cathala-Spiazzi, n. 890, p. 238): ". . . ens contrahatur ad diversa genera secundum diversum modum praedicandi, qui consequitur diversum modum essendi. . . ."

92. See *In Metaph.*, V, lect. 9 (Cathala-Spiazzi, nn. 890–93, pp. 238–39). Cf. John F. Wippel, "Thomas Aquinas's Derivation of the Aristotelian Categories (Predicaments)," *Journal of the History of Philosophy* 25 (1987): 13–34.

93. See *In Metaph.*, XI, lect. 9 (Cathala-Spiazzi, n. 2313, p. 547): "Similiter motus, secundum quod praedicatur de subiecto in quo est, constituit praedicamentum passionis. Secundum autem quod praedicatur de eo a quo est, constituit praedicamentum actionis."

94. Among others, see *In de Div. Nom.*, III, lect. 1 (Pera, n. 227, p. 75): ". . . bonum habet rationem finis; finis autem, primo, habet rationem causae"; *De malo*, q. 1, a. 1 (Bazzi-Pession, 447): ". . . appetibile habet rationem finis"; ibid.: "Quod autem habet rationem appetibilis, habet rationem boni"; a. 2 (Bazzi-Pession, 451): ". . . id quod est secundum se appetibile, est secundum se bonum. Hoc autem est finis"; a. 2, ad 14 (Bazzi-Pession, 453): ". . . non solum id quod est perfectum, habet rationem boni, sed

First of all, ethics treats of the human agent who acts.[95] But human actions can be more precisely grounded by reference to the soul's powers of intellect and will.[96] Consequently, a human action can be defined as the intentional pursuit (i.e., the volitional pursuit) of an intellectually grasped *end*.[97] "End," then, can be defined as "that towards which the force of the agent tends."[98] Because an end is seen to be good, it is known to be desirable *(appetibile)* and hence known precisely as an end.[99] But an agent actually pursues an end (through the choice of appropriate means) because that good is *desired* by the agent.[100] As the desire in question can be natural, sensitive, or intellectual, so too goods can be natural, sensible, or intelligible.[101]

Among philosophers, the question continually arises whether the agent desires the end because it is good or whether the end is good because the agent desires it. Aquinas's texts seem contradictory: on the one hand, the Thomistic agent regards an end as desirable because he

etiam id quod est in potentia ad perfectionem . . ."; q. 2, a. 4 (Bassi-Pession, 473): ". . . bonum importat quamdam perfectione . . ."; *ST*, I, q. 5, a. 1: "Sed bonum dicit rationem perfecti, quod est appetibile; et per consequens dicit rationem ultimi"; a. 2: "Bonum, autem cum habeat rationem appetibilis, importat habitudinem causae finalis . . ."; a. 4: ". . . bonum sit quod omnia appetunt, hoc autem habet rationem finis; manifestum est quod bonum rationem finis importat"; ibid.: "In causando autem, primum invenitur bonum et finis, qui movet efficientem . . ."; ibid.: ". . . ratio boni, per quam in ente perfectio fundatur"; ad 1: "Nam bonum proprie respicit appetitum: est enim bonum quod omnia appetunt"; q. 5, a. 5: ". . . unumquodque dicitur bonum, inquantum est perfectum: sic enim est appetibile . . ."; a. 6: "Nam bonum est aliquid, inquantum est appetibile, et terminus motus appetitus"; q. 6, a. 1: "Unumquodque autem appetit suam perfectionem"; a. 2, ad 2: ". . . cum dicitur bonum est quod omnia appetunt, non sic intelligitur quasi unumquodque bonum ab omnibus appetatur; sed quia quidquid appetitur, rationem boni habet."

95. See *SLE*, I, 3, 1094b11, 61–62 *(In Ethic.*, I, lect. 3 [Spiazzi, n. 35, p. 10]): "Nam scientia moralis est de actibus voluntariis . . . "; V, 14, 1136b, 176–77 (V, lect. 14 [Spiazzi, n. 1063, p. 291]): ". . . principium actionis est in agente, quod pertinet ad rationem voluntarii. . . ."

96. See *II Sent.*, d. 24, q. 1, a. 2 (Mandonnet, 593): "Sic enim est in potentiis animae, quod cum omnes ab essentia animae oriantur, quasi proprietates ab essentialibus rei. . . ."

97. See *SCG*, III, 2 (Pera, n. 1868, p. 3): ". . . omne agens in agendo intendit aliquem finem"; *III Sent.*, d. 27, q. 1, a. 4 (Moos, 871): ". . . finis ratio proprie respicit motum et operationem et ordinem rei ad rem, et non esse rei absolute." Cf. *ST*, I–II, q. 1, a. 1; q. 6, aa. 1–2; q. 12, a. 1; a. 5.

98. ". . . hoc dicimus esse finem in quod tendit impetus agentis . . ." *(SCG*, III, 2 [Pera, n. 1869, p. 3]).

99. See *De malo*, q. 1, a. 1 (Bazzi-Pession, 447): ". . . appetibile habet rationem finis. . . ."

100. See *De pot.*, q. 3, a. 15, ad 10 (Pession, 85): "Bonitas enim mediante voluntate operatur, in quantum est eius obiectum vel finis. . . ."

101. See *Quod.* IV, q. 11, a. 1; *ST*, I–II, q. 30, a. 1.

has first grasped it as good,[102] while on the other hand anything that satisfies desire is regarded as a good.[103] We can resolve the paradox if we recall that, from the point of view of desire, whatever is desired is "good" because it is desired. But Aquinas considers this to be an accidental sense of "good."[104] Although something is *denominated* "good" because it is desired,[105] Aquinas undoubtedly maintains, despite some ambiguous formulations,[106] that desire essentially follows upon the apprehended goodness of the end. Desire, in other words, does not constitute the good.[107] Because what is good is choiceworthy and lovable, we choose it and love it.[108]

Moral precepts enjoin those actions that enable us to pursue the intellectually desirable; the intellectually desirable is that which follows upon the rational judgment as to what is good.[109] In prescribing action toward certain ends, practical reason spontaneously apprehends them as desirable or good and to be pursued because these ends are

102. See *SLE*, III, 13, 1114a31, 12–15 *(In Ethic.*, III, lect. 13 [Spiazzi, n. 515, p. 147]): ". . . ad hoc igitur quod aliquid appetatur, praeexigitur quod apprehendatur ut bonum, et inde est quod unusquisque desiderat id quod apparet sibi esse bonum"; *ST*, I–II, q. 34, a. 2, ad 2: "Finem autem contingit esse bonum et malum; quamvis nunquam sit finis nisi secundum quod est bonum quod hunc."

103. See *SCG*, III, 3 (Pera, n. 1880, p. 5): "Hoc autem est de ratione boni, ut terminet appetitum. . . ."

104. See *III Sent.*, d. 27, q. 1, a. 3 (Moos, n. 62, p. 865): "Sed quia delectatio etiam potest amari ut quoddam bonum, ideo contingit per accidens ut aliquis amor ex delectatione causetur, sicut actus ab objecto vel fino."

105. See *SLE*, I, 1, 1094a2, 153–160 *(In Ethic.*, I, lect. 1 [Spiazzi, n. 9, p. 4]): "Prima autem non possunt notificari per aliqua priora, sed notificantur per posteriora, sicut causae per proprios effectus. Cum autem bonum proprie sit motivum appetitus, describitur bonum per motum appetitus, sicut solet manifestari vis motiva per motum. Et ideo dicit quod philosophi bene enuntiaverunt bonum esse id quod omnia appetunt."

106. Cf. *ST*, II–II, q. 122, a. 6: "Bonum autem de se habet rationem concupiscibilis."

107. See *II Sent.*, d. 31, q. 1, a. 3 (Mandonnet, 530): ". . . bonum est objectum voluntatis et desiderii, eo modo aliquid est adamandum quo est bonum"; *III Sent.*, d. 27, q. 1, a. 1 (Moos, n. 12, p. 854): ". . . appetitus omnino imbuitur forma boni quod est sibi objectum, compacet sibi in illo et adhaeret ei quasi fixum in ipso. . . ."

108. See *SLE*, IX, 7, 1168a5, 73–74 *(In Ethic.*, IX, lect. 7 [Spiazzi, n. 1846, p. 485]): ". . . unumquodque enim inquantum est bonum est, bonum autem est eligible et amabile."

109. See *SLA*, III, c. 9, 433b13, 191–194 *(In de An.*, III, lect. 15 [Pirotta, n. 831, p. 196]): "In motu igitur animalis, movens quod non movetur, est bonum actuale, quod movet appetitum prout est intellectum vel imaginatum"; *Quod.* IV, q. 11, a. 1 (Spiazzi, 85): "Motus autem superioris appetitus, id est voluntatis, consequens iudicium rationis . . ."; *ST*, I–II, q. 19, a. 1, ad 3 ". . . bonum per rationem repraesentatur voluntati ut obiectum . . ."; q. 58, a. 2: ". . . appetitus est principium humani actus secundum quod participat aliqualiter rationem. . . ."

naturally *perfective* of the agent.[110] Now any agent necessarily pursues its proper good and its proper good is what promotes the agent's own self-perfection.[111] But Aquinas does not speak of self-perfection as itself the ultimate end knowingly pursued by the human agent. Self-perfection, rather, is the concomitant of pursuing the universal human good, happiness *(beatitudo)*, which is the ultimate end necessarily willed by every rational agent.[112] A human agent also necessarily pursues those ends that are viewed as the necessary means to, or the necessary constituents of, happiness. But most of the ends that an agent pursues are optional: they are not intrinsically required for happiness, and hence the agent grasps them as self-perfecting goods yet as goods to be done freely or by choice.[113]

5. Ontological and Moral Goodness

In order to understand why ethics does not reduce to metaphysics, we need to advert to Aquinas's often drawn distinction between *transcendental* and *moral* goodness.[114] In turn, this distinction rests upon

110. See *ST,* I, q. 5, a. 1, ad 1: "Sed bonum dicit rationem perfecti, quod est appetibile: et per consequens dicit rationem ultimi."

111. See *De virt.,* q. 1, a. 6 (Odetto, p. 722): "Per naturalem appetitum homo inclinatur ad appetendum proprium bonum . . ."; *ST,* I, q. 48, a. 1: ". . . bonum est omne id quod est appetibile: et sic, cum omnis natura appetat suum esse et suam perfectionem, necesse est dicere quod esse et perfectio cuiuscumque naturae rationem habeat bonitatis."

112. See *II Sent.,* d. 25, q. 1, a. 3, ad 2 (Mandonnet, 652): "Nulla autem operatio humana est finis ultimus nisi per accidens, inquantum scilicet fini ultimo conjungit . . ."; *ST,* I, q. 82, a. 1: ". . . voluntas ex necessitate inhaereat ultimo fini, qui est beatitudo. . . ."

113. See *De ver.,* q. 22, a. 2; *ST,* I–II, q. 10, aa. 2–3.

114. See *ST,* I–II, q. 1, a. 3, ad 3: "Fines autem morales accidunt rei naturali; et e converso ratio naturalis finis accidit morali"; q. 18, a. 5, ad 3: ". . . actus coniugalis et adulterium, secundum quod comparantur ad rationem, differunt specie . . ."; q. 54, a. 3, ad 2: ". . . bonum commune omni enti non est differentia constituens speciem alicuius habitus . . ."; q. 55, a. 4, ad 2: ". . . bonum quod ponitur in definitione virtutis, non est bonum commune, quod convertitur cum ente, et est in plus quam qualitas; sed est bonum rationis . . ."; *De pot.,* q. 9, a. 7, ad 5 (Pession, 243): ". . . bonum quod est in genere qualitatis, non est bonum quod convertitur cum ente, quod nullam rem supra ens addit; bonum autem quod est in genere qualitatis, addit aliquam qualitatem qua homo dicitur bonus . . ."; *De virt.,* q. 1, a. 2, ad 2 (Odetto, 712): ". . . bonum quod convertitur cum ente, non ponitur hic in definitione virtutis; sed bonum quod determinatur ad actum moralem."

Failure to distinguish precisely between ontological/transcendental goodness and moral goodness leads Mondin to misconstrue the subordination of ethics to metaphysics: "Nella concezione tomistica dell'essere la subordinazione del bene all'essere e quindi della morale alla metafiscia è ancor più accentuata che in Aristo-

Aquinas's prior conception of the relationship between being and transcendental goodness.[115] Here I must attempt to encapsulate in a few sentences Aquinas's metaphysical doctrine about the relationship between these two *transcendentia*, being *(ens)* and good *(bonum)*.[116] Speaking metaphysically, "being and goodness are unconditionally interchangeable in every genera" because "every being insofar as it is a being, is good."[117] In reality, then, being *(ens)* and good *(bonum)* are the same but they differ in their meaning *(ratio)*. "Good" adds to "being" the *ratio* of being "perfect" and "desirable."[118] It adds, moreover, the *ratio* of being related to something "perfective."[119] A being perfects another being inasmuch as it is the end of that being.[120] So, finally, it is the "perfective" that adds to "being" the *rationes* of "good," "desirable," and "end."[121]

Speaking morally, however, "being is not unconditionally inter-

---

tele, Platone e i Neoplatonici. E non si tratta semplicemente di una subordinazione logica ma anche ontologica, reale" (Battista Mondin, "Ermeneutica, metafisica, e analogia in s. Tommaso d'Aquino," *Divus Thomas,* 12 (1995): 149. Hence, Mondin is "somewhat perplexed" why Aquinas himself did not grasp the "utility" of "una metafisica della persona umana" "per orientare l'uomo nella sua condotta morale" (155-56). The utility, however, turns into a necessity: "In effetti si possono fissare solide basi per l'agire umano soltanto se si chiarisce il mistero della persona . . ." (156).

115. See David M. Gallagher, "Aquinas on Goodness and Moral Goodness," in *Thomas Aquinas and His Legacy,* ed. David M. Gallagher, Studies in Philosophy and the History of Philosophy, vol. 28, gen. ed. Jude P. Dougherty (Washington, D.C.: The Catholic University of America Press, 1994), 37-60.

116. See especially *De ver.,* q. 21, aa. 1-3. For a summary of Aquinas's doctrine, see Owens, "Transcendentals," in *An Elementary Christian Metaphysics,* 111-27. On Suarez's replacement of *"transcendentia"* by *"transcendentalis,"* see ibid.,111, n. 1.

117. ". . . ens et bonum convertuntur simpliciter et in quolibet genere . . ." *(De malo,* q. 2, a. 5, ad 2 [Bazzi-Pession, 478]); ". . . omne ens, inquantum est ens, est bonum" *(ST,* I, q. 5, a. 3).

118. See *ST,* I, q. 5, a. 4: "Sic autem non addit aliquid bonum super ens; sed rationem tantum appetibilis et perfectionis . . ."; q. 16, a. 4: ". . . ratio autem boni consequitur esse, secundum quod est aliquo modo perfectum; sic enim appetibile est"; *De ver.,* q. 1, a. 1 (Spiazzi, 3): "Convenientiam ergo entis ad appetitum exprimit hoc nomen bonum. . . ."

119. See *De ver.,* q. 21, a. 3, ad 2 (Spiazzi, 380): ". . . bonum non solum habet rationem perfecti, sed perfectivi . . ."; a. 6 (Spiazzi, 387): "Respectus autem qui importatur nomine boni, est habitudo perfectivi. . . ."

120. See *De ver.,* q. 21, a. 2 (Spiazzi, 378): ". . . ratio boni in hoc consistat quod aliquid sit perfectivum alterius per modum finis."

121. See *ST,* I, q. 5, a. 1: "Sed bonum dicit rationem perfecti, quod est appetibile . . ."; a. 2: "Bonum autem, cum habeat rationem appetibilis, importat habitudinem causae finalis. . . ."

changeable with the moral good."[122] The moral good is goodness in the order of human reason: it is the goodness of an action that is in accordance with reason, or the goodness of an agent who acts rationally.[123] Hence, there are important distinctions to be made between ontological and moral goodness, and between ontological and moral evil. Ontological evil is the *privation* of a good that duly belongs to a nature; moral evil, however, is not so much a privation as it is a *contrary* to moral goodness. Moral evil arises from the will choosing a determinate good that is *contrary* to the good that reason requires.[124] Moral good and moral evil thus constitute different species of actions.[125]

The distinction between transcendental/ontological and moral goodness is necessary and important in a theology committed to the belief in the goodness of creation: immoral actions, that is, actions, whether in regard to ends or means, that are contrary to reason, do not have moral goodness. Yet immoral actions remain actions, and thus they have being and ontological goodness.[126] Because they have some ontological goodness, immoral actions continue to fall under divine causality. For example: procreation is a moral evil if it involves adulterous sexual intercourse, but sexual reproduction remains an ontological or natural good for any animal; for that reason, God can infuse the rational soul into the offspring of an adulterous union.[127]

122. See *De malo*, q. 2, a. 5, ad 2 (Bazzi-Pession, 478): "Sed verum est quod ens simpliciter non convertitur cum bono moris. . . ."

123. See *De malo*, q. 7, a. 6 (Bazzi-Pession, 579): "Est autem aliquis actus moralis per hoc quod est a ratione et voluntate ordinatus et imperatus"; *III Sent.*, d. 33, q. 1, a. 1, sol. 1 (Moos, n. 22, p. 1019): "Bonum autem ad quod humanae virtutes proxime ordinantur est bonum rationis, contra quam esse est malum hominis . . ."; sol. 2 (Moos, n. 32, p. 1021): ". . . bonum moris consistit in ipso operante."

124. See *De malo*, q. 1, a. 1, ad 4 (Bazzi-Pession, 447): ". . . in moralibus magis quam in naturalibus malum contrarium bono dicitur, quia moralia ex voluntate dependent . . ."; q. 2, a. 5, ad 3 (Bazzi-Pession, 478): ". . . bonum et malum in moralibus oppununtur contrarie, et non secundum privationem et habitum. . . . Sed malum in natura consequitur privationem simpliciter . . ."; *De virt.*, q. 1, a. 1, ad 5 (Odetto, 709): ". . . actus vitiosus directe tollit actum virtutis per modum contrarietatis. . . ." Cf. *ST*, I-II, q. 18, a. 1, which treats moral evil as a privation in an action.

125. See *ST*, I, q. 48, a. 1.

126. See *IV Sent.*, d. 49, qq. 3, a. 4, sol. 1 (Vivès, 11, p. 516): ". . . omnis actio quantum ad hoc quod habet de natura actionis est bona . . ."; *De malo*, q. 1, a. 1, ad 9 (Bazzi-Pession, 448): ". . . quod quidquid est ibi de actione vel motione pertinet ad virtutem boni . . ."; q. 2, a. 4 (Bazzi-Pession, 474): ". . . actus humanus in quantum est actus, nondum habet rationem boni vel mali moralis . . . quod est secundum rationem esse. . . ."

127. See *ST*, I, q. 118, a. 2, ad 5.

In order to understand how we can choose what is morally evil, the distinction between the moral good and the transcendental/ontological good needs to be coordinated with a further distinction that Aquinas makes between *real* and *apparent* goods.[128] The object of the will is the good as intellectually apprehended. But the apprehended good can be either a real or merely an apparent good. The real good of a thing is whatever is in agreement with the thing's form.[129] An apparent good is an evil, whether ontological or moral, that is erroneously judged to be in agreement with the thing's form, and therefore as somehow falling under the character or notion *(ratio)* of the good.[130]

Now the form of man is the rational soul; hence, the moral good is found in those ends that are in accord with this form, that is, in accord with practical reason.[131] Moral good and evil properly fall within the sphere of practical reason.[132] Ends and the actions whereby we instantiate or attain them are morally good or evil.[133] Real moral goods actually are, whereas apparent moral goods only appear to be but really are not, in accord with practical reason.[134] Moral evil, however, is never directly chosen; it is chosen because, in some way or other, it appears morally good.[135] But while real moral goods can be ordered to man's ultimate good, the vision of God, apparent moral goods lead away from that ultimate good.[136] Ends or means that are really morally bad can *seem* morally good because our judgments are inculpably mistaken or, more

128. See *De malo*, q. 11, a. 1 (Bazzi-Pession, 617): "Sicut autem est duplex bonum, unum quod est vere bonum, et aliud quod est apparens bonum, propter hoc quod est secundum quid bonum (non enim est vere bonum quod non est simpliciter bonum) ita etiam est duplex malum: quoddam quod est vere et simpliciter malum, et quoddam quod est apparens et secundum quid malum, et simpliciter est vere bonum"; SLE, I, 3, 1094b11, 62–63 *(In Ethic.,* 1, lect. 3 [Spiazzi, n. 35, p. 10]): ". . . voluntatis autem motivum est non solum bonum, sed apparens bonum. . . ."

129. See *ST,* I–II, q. 18, a. 5: "Unicuique enim rei est bonum quod convenit ei secundum suam formam; et malum quod est ei praeter ordinem suae formae."

130. See *ST,* I–II, q. 8, a. 1: "Ad hoc igitur quod voluntas in aliquid tendat, non requiritur quod sit bonum in rei veritate, sed quod apprehendatur in ratione boni . . . finis est bonum vel apparens bonum."

131. See *De virt.,* q. 1, a. 7, ad 5 (Odetto, 723): ". . . verum intellectus practici est bonum, quod et finis operationis. . . ."

132. See *ST,* I–II, q. 18, a. 5; q. 19, a. 1, ad 3.

133. See *ST,* I–II, q. 18, a. 6.

134. See *ST,* I–II, q. 27, a. 1, ad 1; q. 29, a. 1, ad 2; q. 34, a. 2; II–II, q. 35, a. 1.

135. See *II Sent.,* d. 38, q. 1, a. 5, ad 3 (Mandonnet, 979): ". . . quamvis omnis voluntas bonum appetat, non tamen appetit semper quod est vere sibi bonum, sed id quod est apparens bonum . . ."; *ST,* I–II, q. 74, a. 1: "Sed quia aliquod malum est apparens bonum, ideo voluntas aliquando appetit aliquod malum."

136. See *ST,* II–II, q. 23, a. 7.

frequently, our judgments about particular actions are culpably irrational because they are made under the sway of the passions, especially concupiscence or the intemperate desire for bodily pleasures.[137] In the latter case, it is our disordered will that is the source of our false judgments.

That which is not a true good, appears good in two ways. Sometimes [it appears good] from a defect of the intellect, as when someone has a false opinion about doing something (as it is evident in him who thinks fornication not to be a sin) or in him who does not have the use of reason. Such a defect arising on the part of the intellect diminishes or totally excuses the fault. On other occasions, however, it is not a defect on the part of the intellect, but more on the part of the will. For as a person's character is, he perceives the end in the same way, as it is said in *Ethics* III [chapter 5]. We know by experience that something good or evil seems otherwise to us depending on what we love and hate. Therefore, when someone is inordinately inclined to something, the judgment of the intellect in a particular choice is impeded by the inordinate affection. Thus vice is not principally in [the realm] of cognition but affection. *(De malo,* q. 2, a. 3, ad 9 [Bazzi-Pession, 472])[138]

With Aristotle, Aquinas distinguishes the intemperate man (ἀκόλαστος = *intemperatus)* who deliberately chooses immoral pleasure and the incontinent man (ἀκρατής = *incontinens)* who weakly succumbs to pleasure.[139] The incontinent person succumbs to sensible pleasure out of powerful natural desire or concupiscence; his weakness mitigates his moral failure.[140] Acting from natural desire, the inconti-

---

137. See *IV Sent.,* d. 49, q. 3, a. 4, sol. 1, ad 2 (Vivès, 11, p. 517); *De malo,* q. 11, a. 1; 15, a. 4.

138. ". . . quod id quod non est vere bonum, apparet bonum dupliciter. *Quandoque* quidem ex vitio intellectus, sicut cum habet falsam opinionem aliquis de aliquo agendo, ut patet in eo qui putat fornicationem non esse peccatum, vel etiam in eo qui non habet usum rationis; et talis defectus ex parte intellectus proveniens diminuit culpam, vel totaliter excusat. *Aliquando* autem non est defectus ex parte ipsius intellectus, sed magis ex parte voluntatis; qualis enim est unusquisque, talis et finis videtur ei, ut dicitur III *Ethic.* [cap. v]. Experimento enim cognoscimus quod aliter videtur nobis bonum aliquid vel malum circa ea quae amamus et ea quae odimus. Et ideo cum aliquis est inordinate affectus ad aliquid, impeditur iudicium intellectus in particulari eligibili ex inordinata affectione. Et sic principaliter vitium est non in cognitione, sed in affectione" *(De malo,* q. 2, a. 3, ad 9 [Bazzi-Pession, 472]).

139. See *EN,* VII, 7, 1150a25–31.

140. See *SLE,* VII, 7, 115a27, 119–21 *(In Ethic.,* VII, lect. 7 [Spiazzi, n. 1412, p. 378]): "Et inde est quod intemperatus qui non vincitur passione, sed ex electione peccat, est deterior incontinente qui concupiscentia vincitur."

nent man is full of regrets since he does not adequately deliberate about and properly choose the sensible pleasure to which he succumbs. By contrast, the intemperate man chooses to pursue pleasure as an end in itself.[141] Such men have mistakenly judged pleasure to be the only good worth pursuing or, at least, the only good that they are capable of pursuing. Having made this judgment, they pursue pleasure as though it were always a real, and, not as it more often is, merely an apparent *moral* good.[142] But what about the dedicated pursuit of sensible pleasure makes this pursuit appear to be in accordance with practical reason? Aquinas's answer plumbs the psychological depths of fallen mankind: many men and women seek pleasures not just because they are animals naturally drawn to sensible satisfactions, but because they, lacking the virtues, are unable to attain spiritual delights and, *faute de mieux*, they turn to sense pleasure as a "medicine against manifold sorrows and sadnesses."[143]

Desire can corrupt our judgments about the real moral character of the general ends that we pursue and the particular means that we choose in order to achieve those ends.[144] But concupiscence can be satisfied only by the pleasure that comes with possessing the desired object.[145] Ends that satisfy desire, by the very fact that they are able to satisfy desire, are ontological goods;[146] they also may appear, if we are bent on the satisfaction of our desires, to be morally good. Now such apparent moral goods are not, as Aquinas uses the term, real moral goods.[147] They are, in fact, moral evils.

141. See *SLE*, III, 5, 1111b9, 51–52 (*In Ethic.*, III, lect. 5 [Spiazzi, n. 435, p. 125]).

142. See *SCG*, III, 3 (Pera, n. 1884, p. 5); 4 (n. 1893, p. 7); 6 (n. 1905, p. 8); 9 (n. 1928, p. 10).

143. See *ST*, I–II, q. 31, a. 5, ad 1: ". . . homines indigent delectationibus ut medicinis contra multiplices dolores et tristitias: et cum plures hominum non possint attingere ad delectationes spirituales quae sunt propriae virtuosorum, consequens est quod declinent ad corporales."

144. See *ST*, I–II, q. 27, a. 4, ad 2: "Sed desiderium alicuius rei potest esse causa ut res alia ametur"; q. 32, a. 3, ad 3: ". . . omne concupitum est delectabile concupiscenti. . . ."

145. Cf. *SLE*, III, 5, 1111b17, 116–19 (*In Ethic.*, III, lect. 5 [Spiazzi, n. 441, p. 125]): "Concupiscentia semper est cum delectatione, scilicet propter praesentiam rei concupitae, vel cum tristitia, propter eius carentiam. . . ."

146. See *De malo*, q. 2, a. 4 (Bazzi-Pession, 474): ". . . cognoscere mulierem suam et cognoscere mulierem non suam, sunt actus habentes obiecta differentia secundum aliquid ad rationem pertinens . . . quae tamen differentiae per accidens se habent si comparentur ad vim generativam, vel etiam ad vim concupiscibilem."

147. See *ST*, I–II, q. 18, a. 4, ad 1: ". . . bonum ad quod aliquis respiciens operatur, non semper est verum bonum; sed quandoque verum bonum, et quandoque apparens. Et secundum hoc, ex fine sequitur actio mala."

Not only is the good desired, but even the apparent good. Since every enjoyment from the fact that it is an enjoyment, is a good. However much it is rendered bad by something added to it, an enjoyment is and is able to appear good, and as a consequence is able to be desired. But it is thus desirable to one not having right judgment; but to one having right judgment some enjoyments are not desirable. Accordingly, the prudent and temperate man does not desire intemperate enjoyments. *(IV Sent.,* d. 49, q. 3, a. 4, ad 2 [Vivès, 11, pp. 516–17])[148]

Aquinas allows, of course, that real moral goods can satisfy desire,[149] but it is not the satisfaction of desire but being concordant with right reason that is the marker for the real moral good.[150] Only an end that is, however desirable it may be, in accord with reason is morally good.[151] In pursuing even a good end, only an action that fully meets the criteria set for action by practical reason counts as genuinely morally good.[152] External or bodily actions, because they are voluntary, fall within the sphere of morality and must be morally evaluated.[153] An action is morally good when the action's object and circumstances, and the agent's end when performing the action, is in conformity with reason.[154]

---

148. ". . . non solum appetitur bonum, sed etiam apparens bonum. Quia autem omnis delectatio ex hoc quod est delectatio, bona est; quantumcumque ex aliquo adjuncto efficiatur mala, habet unde apparere possit bona, et per consequens unde possit appeti; et sic appetibilis est non habenti rectum judicium: sed habenti rectum judicium delectationes quaedam appetibiles non sunt; sicut prudens et temperatus non appetit delectationes intemperati" *(IV Sent.,* d. 49, q. 3, a. 4, ad 2 [Vivès, 11, pp. 516–17]).

149. *ST,* I–II, q. 34, a. 1: ". . . ita et in moralibus est quaedam delectatio bona, secundum quod appetitus superior aut inferior requiescit in eo quod convenit rationi. . . ."

150. See *ST,* I–II, q. 34, a. 2, ad 1: ". . . non omne delectabile est bonum bonitate morali, quae attenditur secundum rationem."

151. See *SCG,* III, 9 [Pera, n. 1928, p. 10]: "Oportet igitur quod a fine rationis dicantur aliqua in moralibus bona vel mala"; *ST,* I–II, q. 18, a. 5, ad 1: ". . . bonum, inquantum est secundum rationem, et malum, inquantum est praeter rationem, diversificant speciem moris."

152. See *ST,* I–II, q. 34, a. 1: "Bonum enim et malum in moralibus dicitur secundum quod convenit rationi vel discordat ab ea. . . ."

153. See *ST,* I–II, q. 74, a. 1: "Cum autem proprium sit actuum moralium quod sint voluntarii . . ."; a. 2: "Actus autem voluntarii dicuntur non solum illi qui eliciuntur a voluntate, sed etiam illi qui a voluntate imperantur. . . ."

154. See *De malo,* q. 7, a. 4 (Bazzi-Pession, 575): ". . . actus moralis dicitur bonus vel malus ex genere secundum suum obiectum. Supra hanc autem bonitatem et malitiam potest ei duplex bonitas et malitia advenire: uno quidem ex intentione finis, alia ex circumstantia."

6. Moral Goods and the First Practical Principle

The first principle of practical reason prescribes that *"Good is to be done and to be pursued and evil is to be avoided."* As stated, Aquinas does not build into the precept any explicit reference to the distinction between ontological/transcendental and moral goodness or to the distinction between real and apparent moral goodness. These distinctions, nonetheless, clarify the meaning and scope of this principle. So I shall advert to them here. We can begin by noting how an action is necessarily constituted: an action must embody the agent's intentional pursuit of an end in order to be identified as an action.[155] That the end of an action is some *ontological* good is entailed by the (real) definitions of "being," and "good," and "end." Aquinas defines "end" as "that which is sought or desired by those things that have not yet attained the end."[156] What is sought and desired as an end is some kind of *being.* Every being, and hence every end, has ontological goodness: "Everything that is discovered to have the nature of an end has the nature of a good."[157] Since they fall under some genera of being, morally evil ends always have ontological goodness.[158]

The first practical principle does not specify which are the ends that it is morally good to pursue; it does not set forth which of the many possible ends of human action are in accordance with reason. The first practical principle merely prescribes that good is an end to be pursued. It does *not*, we should note, prescribe that moral goodness (i.e., having one's will fixed on doing what is in accordance with reason) is itself the only good end that is to be pursued. Moral goodness, therefore, is only one among other goods that it is morally good to pursue.[159]

Moreover, Aquinas states that the first practical principle is founded *(fundatur)* on the general meaning *(ratio)* of "good": "good is what

155. See *ST,* I–II, q. 1, a. 1: "Illae ergo actiones proprie humanae dicuntur, quae ex voluntate deliberata procedunt"; a. 3, ad 2: "... finis secundum quod est prior in intentione . . . Secundum hoc pertinet ad voluntatem. Et hoc modo dat speciem actui humano sive morali."

156. "... [finis] sit appetitum vel desideratum ab his quae finem nondum attingunt . . ." *(De ver.,* q. 21, a. 2 [Spiazzi, 378]).

157. "... id quod invenitur habere rationem finis, habet et rationem boni" *(De ver.,* q. 21, a. 2 [Spiazzi, 378]).

158. See *SCG,* III, 11 (Pera, n. 1957, p. 15): "... malum moris est in bono naturae ..."; *ST,* I, q. 105, a. 5: "Cum enim omnis operatio sit propter aliquod bonum verum vel apparens; nihil autem est vel apparet bonum nisi secundum quod participat aliquam similitudinem summi boni, quod est Deus. ..."

159. See *ST,* I–II, q. 3. a. 4, ad 5: "Voluntas autem bona ponitur in numero bonorum quae beatum faciunt."

everything seeks."[160] This, of course, is the metaphysical definition of the "good." Should we conclude that "good" as it falls under the *simplex conceptio* of practical intellect is exclusively the ontological or transcendental good?[161] Or, since we are dealing with practical intellect's apprehension, is this good more precisely characterized as "premoral" because "it is merely the object of the will's spontaneous movement?"[162] Again, if we pursue this line of questioning in regard to the second operation of the intellect, is the first practical principle aptly called a "transmoral" principle?[163] Or, more radically, is the first practical principle a nonmoral principle that merely specifies the criteria identifying a "human act" as any "bodily act that instantiates the intelligent pursuit of a desired end or good"?[164]

These questions, which require that practical intellect be first directed to the transcendental good, seem to presuppose that it is theoretical reason as such (and not a person capable of reasoning theoretically and practically) that "passes over" to practical reason. Certainly, Aquinas allows that human actions can be considered from a metaphysical point of view;[165] so considered, they themselves always have some ontological goodness and are always aimed at some ontologically good end.[166] But we can never derive the moral good solely from an apprehension of the ontological/transcendental goodness of actions or their ends.

The human act, insofar as it is an act, does not yet have the character of moral good or evil, unless something is added that contracts it to a species. For although the act has some aspect of the good from the fact that it is a

160. See *ST,* I–II, q. 94, a. 2: ". . . primum principium in ratione practica est quod fundatur supra rationem boni, quae est, *Bonum est quod omnia appetunt."*

161. See Johann Schuster, S.J., "Von den ethischen Prinzipien: Eine Thomasstudie zu S. Th. I*a*II*ae*, q. 94, a. 2," *Zeitschrift für katholische Theologie* 57 (1933): 54–55: "Es wurde die Frage aufgeworfen, ob dan *bonum* hier im streng ethischen Sinne als *bonum honestum* oder nur im allgemeinsten Sinne des *bonum transcendentale* zu fassen sei. Wenn der Wertbegriff der allereste in der *apprehensio practica* sein soll, so kann doch, wie es scheint, nur an die unbestimmte Werthaftigkeit oder das *bonum transcendentale* gedacht sein."

162. Servais Pinckaers, O.P., Notes and appendices to Saint Thomas d'Aquin, *Somme théologique: Les Actes humains,* Vol. 1, *1ᵃ–2ᵃ, questions 6–17,* French trans. by H.-D. Gardeil, O.P. (Paris: Desclée & Cie; Rome: Tournai, 1962), 312.

163. See Grisez, "The First Principle," 186. Cf. *The Way of the Lord Jesus,* Vol. 1: *Christian Moral Principles* (Chicago: Franciscan Herald Press, 1983), 178–82.

164. Cf. Donagan, *Theory of Morality,* 61.

165. This consideration preoccupied the seventeenth-century theologians who debated which criterion formally determines that a human act is also a moral act; see Ramirez, *De actibus humanis,* 4: pars 2, q. 18, §1, nn. 661–670, pp. 502–7.

166. See *III Sent.,* d. 41, q. 1, a. 2 (Mandonnet, 1038): ". . . omnis actus, inquan-

human act, and further from the fact that it is a being, it does not have the [aspect] of the moral good which follows from being in accord with reason. *(De malo,* q. 2, a. 4 [Bazzi-Pession, 474])[167]

Theoretical reason can describe or explain (in metaphysics or psychology) the mutual role that the intellect and the will plays in knowing the moral good.[168] Here, for example, is a detailed *theoretical* explanation of the moral good that explains very precisely why ontological and moral goodness cannot be conflated. The moral good is uniquely discovered in beings capable of intelligently willing and choosing:

Although good is convertible with being, it is discovered in a special mode in things that are ensouled and have choice. . . . The reason for this is that "good" is designated under the aspect of "end." Therefore, although [good] is discovered in everything in which there is an end, it is more particularly discovered in those things which appoint an end for themselves and which know the concept of the end. Thus it is the case that eliciting habits are assigned a species from the end; and for this reason "good" and "evil" are constitutive differences of these habits, not as ["good" and "evil"] are universally taken, but in the way just described. *(II Sent.,* d. 27, q. 1, a. 2, ad 2 [Mandonnet, 699])[169]

"Good is to be done and to be pursued, and evil is to be avoided" is the first of the "self-evident" principles governing human choices. Aquinas attributes these *per se nota* practical principles to the intellectual habit of *synderesis.*[170] As Aquinas defines it, *"synderesis"* is a habit of

---

tum est actus, habet quamdam essentialem bonitatem, secundum quod omne ens bonum est; sed in aliquibus superadditur quaedam bonitas ex proportione actus ad debitum objectum, et secundum hoc dicitur actus bonus ex genere. . . ."

167. ". . . actus humanus in quantum est actus, nondum habet rationem boni vel mali moralis, nisi aliquid addatur ad speciem contrahens; licet etiam ex hoc ipso quod est actus humanus, et ulterius ex hoc quod est ens, habeat aliquam rationem boni, sed non huius boni moralis quod est secundum rationem esse . . ." *(De malo,* q. 2, a. 4 [Bazzi-Pession, 474]).

168. See *De virt.,* q. 1, a. 7 (Odetto, p. 723): ". . . verum intellectus practici est bonum, quod et finis operationis: bonum enim non movet appetitum, nisi in quantum est apprehensum."

169. ". . . quamvis bonum convertatur cum ente, tamen quodam speciali modo invenitur in rebus animatis et habentibus electionem. . . . Cujus ratio est, quia bonum dicitur ex ratione finis; et ideo quamvis inveniatur in omnibus in quibus est finis, tamen specialius invenitur in illis quae finem sibi praestituunt, et intentionem finis cognoscunt; et inde est quod habitus electivi ex fine speciem sortiuntur; et propter hoc horum habituum 'bonum' et 'malum' sunt differentiae constitutivae, non quidem prout communiter sumuntur, sed per modum jam dictum" *(II Sent.,* d. 27, q. 1, a. 2, ad 2 [Mandonnet, 699]).

170. See *II Sent,* d. 24, q. 2, a. 3 (Mandonnet, 610): ". . . ratio practica ab

practical reason by which we have immediate insight that certain goods are to be pursued: *"Synderesis* always tends towards the good."[171] These immediate goods are the basic or universal ends of *voluntary* or human actions because they correspond to our natural inclinations. As objects of the will, they are, undoubtedly, moral goods.

Not every good is a desirable one that moves [the agent to act], but [only] the good that can be done, which is the good as it is applied to action. . . . *(SLA,* III, c. 9, 433a26, 124–26; *In de An.,* III, lect. 15 [Pirotta, n. 827, p. 195])[172]

It is a mistake, therefore, to think that the first *practical* principle focuses on the ontological goodness of human ends and actions.[173] The mistake arises from interpreting the first practical principle from the standpoint of metaphysics and not ethics. To interpret it metaphysically is to turn the first practical principle into a theoretical principle. Practical reason, however, *prescribes* rather than *describes* the "good" that is the end of various human actions; the perfective good in question is the good that is the correlate of natural desire.[174] If we are mindful of the prescriptive character of the first practical principle, then we can readily understand that it enjoins doing ends under the aspect of their *moral goodness.*[175]

Prescriptions guide human choices; human choices are about human actions that bear on the means to some end.[176] Since all human

---

aliquibus principiis per se notis deducatur ut quod est malum non esse faciendum, praeceptis Dei obediendum fore, et sic de aliis: et horum quidem habitus est synderesis."

171. ". . . Synderesis semper in bonum tendit" *(II Sent.,* d. 24, q. 2, a. 3 [Mandonnet, 610]).

172. ". . . non autem omne bonum est appetibile et mouens, sed bonum agibile, quod est bonum applicatum ad operationem" *(SLA,* III, c. 9, 433a26, 124–26; *In de An.,* III, lect. 15 [Pirotta, n. 827, p. 195]).

173. Cf. Schuster, "Von den ethischen Prinzipien," 55: "Ein *praeceptum legis* ist doch nur für vernünftige Geschöpfe im eigentlichen Sinne denkbar. Erst rech gilt das für die spezielleren Gesetze, *quae ratio practica naturaliter apprehendit esse bona humana.* Diese sind aber im strengen Sinn ethische Güter"; Kluxen, "Metaphysik und praktische Vernunft," 86: "Dabei ist zugleich klar, dass das hier angesprochene Gute nicht ein metaphysisch Allgemeines, sondern das *menschliche,* vom Menschen zu erbringende Gute ist."

174. Cf. Martin Rhonheimer, *Praktishe Vernunft,* 547: "Dieser 'perfektive' Gehlat des Guten, so muss dies jedoch präzisiert werden, kommt dem Guten zu, insofern es eben das Korrelat zum Streben ist, und nicht umgekehrt."

175. See *ST,* I–II, q. 60, a. 1: "Manifestum est autem quod in moralibus ratio est sicut imperans et movens; vis autem appetitiva est sicut imperata et mota."

176. See *SLE,* III, 6, 1112a3, 62–65 *(In Ethic.,* III, lect. 6 [Spiazzi, n. 452, p. 128]): "Electio praecipue respicit actiones nostras, eligimus enim quod accipiamus hoc vel

ends have some ontological goodness, the only good that can be prescribed per se is not the ontological good but the moral good that can
be realized solely through human choices that are in accord with practical reason.[177] Human choice as such always involves human actions
that are morally good or bad.[178] But moral good or evil is, first of all, a
quality of the will.[179] External actions have moral goodness or badness

fugiamus vel quicquid est aliud quod ad actiones nostras pertinet . . ."; *ST*, I–II, q. 13,
a. 4: ". . . electio semper est humanorum actuum."

177. See *De malo*, q. 3, a. 2, ad 2 (Bazzi-Pession, 498); quoted *supra* n. 34.

178. Grisez contends ("The First Principle," 184) that the ends covered by the
first practical principle "are not primarily [moral] works that are to be done" but
(nonmoral) "substantive goods" (such as "self-preservation, the life and education of
children, and knowledge") that are to be pursued. More recently, he explains *(The
Way of the Lord Jesus*, 124) that "substantive or nonreflexive goods," which "are not
defined in terms of choosing," must be distinguished from (moral) "reflexive or
existential goods" which do involve choice. Aquinas, however, observes that the
pursuit of any human good requires choice and thus actions: "Finis autem vel est
actio, vel res aliqua. Et cum res aliqua fuerit finis, necesse est quod aliqua humana
actio interveniat . . ." (*ST*, I–II, q. 13, a. 4). In the Thomistic context, such human
goods as living, preserving oneself, procreating and educating children, and knowing, can hardly be understood as nonmoral but *eudaimonic* goods that are somehow
substantively constituted apart from human choices and actions: "Quod autem
eligitur, est aliquod particulare operabile" *(SCG*, III, 55 (Pera, n. 3282, p. 233). If self-
preservation, for example, is viewed merely as a kind of metabolic response to
biological threats, then it is being viewed not as an *actus humanus* but as an *actus
hominis*. And the latter cannot be enjoined by a precept of practical reason: see *ST*,
I–II, q. 2, a. 5; q. 3, a. 2, ad 1.

In a Thomistic context, any alleged distinction between the moral and the
nonmoral ends of human action must be congruent with Aquinas's distinction
between *finis ut res* and *finis ut adeptio/possessio/fruitio*, i.e., between *beatitudo
finis cuius* and *beatitudo finis quo:* see *ST*, I–II, q. 3, a. 1. The former is not but the
latter is a "moral good." The pursuit of *attaining* a perfect good or happiness in
general *(adeptio finis beatitudinis)*, which everyone naturally or necessarily wills,
is not a matter of choice: see *ST*, I, q. 82, a. 1, esp. ad 3. But the pursuit of *attaining*
every determinate form of beatitude, including possessing or enjoying God, does
involve human choice: see *IV Sent.*, d. 49, q. 1, a. 3, sol. 3; *ST*, I–II, q. 5, a. 8. Of
course, God, as *beatitudo increata*, is not an end *(res/finis cuius)* that is constituted
by the human choice to pursue Him; as infinitely transcending the whole order of
human action, God in Himself can be appropriately called a "transmoral good." But
what practical reason enjoins as a basic good to be done is attaining and possessing
God by *worshiping* Him and *obeying* Him: see *SCG*, III, 119 (Pera, n. 2914, p. 177):
"Et quia etiam quodam naturali instinctu se obligatum sentit ut Deo suo modo
reverentiam impendat, a quo est sui esse et omnis boni principium"; *I Sent.*, d. 47,
q. 1, a. 4, ad 2 (Mandonnet, 1074): ". . . est conveniens legi naturae, quae dictat
omne illud esse faciendum quod est ordinatum et praeceptum a Deo." Cf. *supra*, ch.
1, n. 145. Attaining, possessing, or enjoying God (= *beatitudo creata*) are actions of
the soul that are moral goods because they are actions done in accordance with
human practical reason.

179. See *SCG*, III, 9 (Pera, n. 1928, p. 10): ". . . aliquid ad genus moris pertinet,

because they embody the moral goodness or badness of the ends that are the objects of the human will intending them.[180] Moral goods are those ends and means that are intended in accordance with practical reason.

Practical reason, although it can err in its judgments about particular goods or be disrupted by passion in reference to particular choices, is infallibly correct in its universal judgments.[181] Thus the judgments of *synderesis* only enjoin *real* moral goods.[182] Actions are morally good inasmuch as they aim at the intelligible good that practical reason presents to the will.[183] But every human action, inasmuch as it is voluntary, aims at some apparent moral good, whether that end proves to be rationally justifiable or not.[184] The first practical principle, to be sure, is not a criterion that enables us to distinguish between real and apparent moral goods.[185] Apparent as well as real moral goods fall, de facto, under the aegis of the first principle of practical reason.[186] But this is not, in the Thomistic context, an anomaly. The first practical principle is a *generic* moral principle prescribing that what is morally good is to be done and to be pursued. In conformity with this universal

quod est voluntarium"; ". . . vitium morale in sola actione consideratur, non autem in aliquo effectu producto . . ."; *ST*, I–II, q. 19, a. 1, ad 3: ". . . bonum per rationem repraesentatur voluntari ut obiectum; et inquantum cadit sub ordine rationis, pertinet ad genus moris, et causat bonitatem moralem in actu voluntatis.

180. See *SCG*, III, 10 (Pera, n. 1946, p. 13): "Nihil autem ad malitiam moralem pertineret si actus exterior deficiens esset defectu ad voluntatem non pertinente: claudicatio enim non est vitium moris, sed naturae."

181. See *De malo*, q. 3, a. 12, ad 13 (Bazzi-Pession, 516); quoted above, n. 36; q. 16, a. 6, ad 6 (Bazzi-Pession, 681): ". . . voluntas non movetur a bono nisi in quantum est apprehensum: unde non potest deficere ab appetitu boni, nisi etiam subsit defectus aliquis circa apprehensionem; non quidem quantum ad universalia principia, quorum est synderesis, sed quantum ad particularia eligibilia."

182. See *De ver.*, q. 24, a. 8.

183. See *SCG*, III, 10 (Pera, n. 1949, p. 14): "Cum igitur voluntas tendit in actum mota ex apprehensione rationis repraesentantis sibi proprium bonum, sequitur debita actio."

184. See *SCG*, III, 4 (Pera, n. 1893, p. 7): "Sed omne agens per intellectum tendit ad aliquid secundum quod accipit illud sub ratione boni. . . ."

185. See *De malo*, q. 8, a. 2 (Bazzi-Pession, 598): ". . . Si appetitus feratur in aliquod bonum naturaliter desideratum secundum regulam rationis, erit appetitus rectus et virtuosus; si vero transcendat regulam rationis vel ab ea deficiat, erit utrobique peccatum."

186. See *II Sent.*, d. 39, q. 2, a. 1 (Mandonnet, 991): ". . . quamvis velle bonum homini sit naturale, nihilominus tamen potest malum velle, non inquantum est malum, sed inquantum existimatur bonum"; *ST*, I–II, q. 8, a. 1: "Ad hoc igitur quod voluntas in aliquid tendat, non requiritur quod sit bonum in rei veritate, sed quod apprehendatur in ratione boni. . . ."

directive of practical reason, we need to determine which of our freely chosen ends are real moral goods. But the specific *differentia* in the genus "moral actions," which allow us to distinguish ends that are *real* moral goods from ends that are only *apparent* moral goods (but which are, in fact, real moral evils), can only be set by additional and more determinate moral principles.

7. Theoretical Explanations of Practical Goods

In pursuing the basic ends that practical reason prescribes, the moral agent undoubtedly acts against a background of commonsensical theoretical knowledge about the world and man.[187] For example, if men could read minds, would there be any practical reason to enjoin truth telling? Or if men felt no pain and had indestructible bodies, would there be any occasion or reason to prohibit inflicting bodily injury on our fellow humans? What, though, is the epistemic relationship between this rudimentary factual or theoretical knowledge about the nature of the world and man, and the practical knowledge that certain basic ends are *prescribed*? There is not, in Aquinas's account, any epistemic need to deduce the latter from the former. We have an immediate knowledge of these fundamental precepts because they correspond to the innate inclinations of human nature.[188]

Aquinas, as noted, metaphysically gears our understanding *(intellectus)* of the basic practical principles to a teleology of natural human inclinations and ends.[189] But this teleology, as Aquinas utilizes it, provides only a "reflexive" explanation for why practical intellect has an immediate epistemic grasp of the universal precepts governing human action.[190] In today's philosophical context, the theoretical notion of a

187. See *ST,* I–II, q. 14, a. 6: "Hujusmodi autem principia quae in inquisitione consilii supponuntur, sunt quaecumque sunt per sensum accepta, utpote quod sit panis, vel ferrum; et quaecumque sunt per aliquam scientiam speculativam vel practicam in universali cognita, sicut quod moechari est a Deo prohibitum, et quod homo non potest vivere nisi nutriatur nutrimento convenienti. Et de istis non inquirit consiliator."

188. Cf. *SCG*, III, 128 (Pera, n. 3011, p. 191): "Homines ex divina providentia sortiuntur naturale iudicatorium rationis ut principium propriarum operationum. Naturalia autem principia ad ea ordinantur quae sunt naturaliter. Sunt igitur aliquae operationes naturaliter homini convenientes, quae sunt secundum se rectae, et non solum quasi lege positae."

189. See *Quod.* VII, q. 7, a. 1 (Spiazzi, 150): "Illa enim sunt de lege naturali ad quae homo ex suis naturalibus inclinatur."

190. Cf. Rhonheimer, *Praktische Vernunft,* 549: "Ethisch normative Aussagen beziehen sich immer auf eine Reflexion über den (präskriptiven) Akt der praktis-

natural teleology of basic human desires is likely to be as, if not more, controversial than what it is meant to explain, epistemically immediate practical principles.[191] In any case, Aquinas, unlike some of his contemporary admirers, did not think the truth of epistemically immediate practical precepts needs to be metaphysically *justified* by deducing them from theoretical propositions about natural human inclinations.[192] Efforts to do so seem, inevitably, to subsume practical into

---

chen Vernunft. Auch eine reflexe Theorie des 'Naturgesetzes' bezieht sich auf menschliche Güter ("bona humana"), wie sie in ursprünglich *praktischer* Weise der Vernunft gegenständlich sind; sie sind also nicht aus theoretischen Aussagen über die menschliche Natur abgeleitet."

191. On the questions whether there is such a natural teleology of basic human desires, and whether it can ground a set of universal ethical principles, cf. Henry Veatch, "Variations, Good and Bad, on the Theme of Right Reason in Ethics," *Monist* 66 (1983): 49–68; Bernard Williams, "Foundations: Well-Being," in *Ethics and the Limits of Philosophy* (Cambridge, Mass.: Harvard University Press, 1985), 30–53. For an overview of the general epistemological issues surrounding epistemic "foundationalism," see Robert Audi, "The Foundationalism-Coherentism Controversy: Hardened Stereotypes and Overlapping Theories," in *The Structure of Justification* (Cambridge: Cambridge University Press, 1993), 117–64.

192. See Alvin Plantinga, "Reason and Belief in God," in *Faith and Rationality*, ed. Alvin Plantinga and Nicholas Wolterstorff (Notre Dame, Ind.: University of Notre Dame Press, 1983), 16–93, esp. Part II, "Aquinas and Foundationalism," 39–63. Cf. Henry B. Veatch, "Natural Law and the 'Is'-'Ought' Question: Queries to Finnis and Grisez," in *Swimming against the Current*, 293–311, who proposes that, in order to understand that the basic human goods "objectively" ought to be done, these goods "must be understood as beings" (308).

The question that prompts Veatch's proposal is why "we ought to be inclined towards" (308) the goods to which we are de facto inclined? In answering this question, "it is precisely metaphysics that here takes over, in order to clarify and render intelligible that first principle of ethics or of practical reason . . . that good is to be done and pursued" (308–9). Aquinas, however, never asked, nor did he have reason to ask, why *ought* we to follow our natural inclinations. Our basic or natural inclinations (as distinguished certainly from any acquired inclinations) direct us to the necessary ends of human action; because these ends are necessary, reason immediately grasps such ends as "due," i.e., as necessarily to be done: "Intantum ergo aliquid cadit sub praecepto inquantum habet rationem debiti . . . Per se quidem debitum est in unoquoque negotio in quod est finis, quia habet rationem per se boni . . ." (*ST*, II–II, q. 44, a. 1); "Quod autem aliquid debeat fieri, hoc provenit ex necessitate alicuius finis" (I–II, q. 99, a. 1).

The ends that self-evidently ought to be pursued are, Aquinas explains, goods that we naturally desire: "Sed quia naturalis inclinatio ad finem aliquem est ex praestituente naturam qui talem ordinem naturae tribuit, ideo naturalis inclinatio voluntatis ad finem non est ex ratione, nisi forte secundum naturalem communicantiam qua fit ut appetitus rationi conjunctus naturaliter tendat ad conformandum se rationi sicut regulae; et ex hoc est quod voluntas est natualiter inclinata ad finem, qui naturaliter est rationi inditus" (*III Sent.*, d. 33, q. 2, a. 4, sol. 4 [Moos, n. 243, p. 1066]). Presumably, though, a metaphysical explanation or defense of

speculative reason, to transform the practical principles into conclusions, and to substitute less evident theoretical arguments for the more evident practical principles.[193]

In the Thomistic picture of how we know the world, both theoretical and practical reason begin from a set of *per se nota* principles. The term *"per se notum,"* which probably originated with Boethius, had in the complex Latin tradition of assimilating Aristotle, a variety of connotations.[194] But in the Thomistic context, the primary precepts of the natural law are the practical principles or *immediately known propositions* that are peculiar to practical reason. It has often been noted, however, that Aquinas draws a parallel between reason's use of indemonstrable theoretical and indemonstrable practical principles.[195] And in this parallelism there is a first and a second line of parallel principles. Aquinas typically schematizes reason's use of immediate practical principles as the *second* use of *principia per se nota* which runs parallel to reason's *first* use of immediate theoretical principles.[196] This schematization suggests that reason's use of the *per se nota* theoretical principles has a certain logical or metaphysical priority over reason's use of the *per se nota* practical principles.[197] The priority of the *per se nota* theoretical principles is congruent with the Thomistic metaphysical tenet that *ens* is prior to *bonum* and that the principle of contradiction is the absolutely first principle.[198] This priority holds across the

---

natural desire, will be less evident than what, because of the promptings of natural desire, we grasp as self-evidently something to be done. Practical reason begins with and does not deduce these natural ends.

193. Cf. Bourke, *St. Thomas and the Greek Moralists*, 24: "Existing things regulate speculative reason; speculative reason, thus rectified regulates practical reasoning."

194. For an up-to-date historical survey of the Latin and especially Boethian mediation of Aristotle, see Tuninetti, *"Per Se Notum."*

195. See Schuster, "Von den ethischen Prinzipien," 45: "Die ethischem Prinzipien gehen den theoretischen Prizipien *(in demonstrativis)* parallel."

196. See *II Sent.*, d. 24, q. 2, a. 3 (Mandonnet, 610): ". . . Sicut enim ratio in speculativis deducitur ab aliquibus principiis per se notis quorum habitus intellectus dicitur, ita etiam oportet quod ratio practica ab aliquibus principiis per se notis deducatur ut quod est malum non esse faciendum, praeceptis Dei obediendum fore, et sic de aliis: et horum quidem habitus est synderesis."

197. See McInerny, *Aquinas on Human Action*, 198–206, for how *per se nota* practical principles may be ordered among themselves and in relation to antecedent *per se nota* theoretical principles.

198. See *I Sent.*, d. 8, q. 1, a. 2 (Mandonnet, 198): ". . . Sic simpliciter et absolute ens est prius aliis [nominbus]. . . . Alia vero quae diximus, scilicet bonum, verum et unum, addunt super ens . . . bonum [addit] relationem ad finem . . ."; d. 19, q. 5, a. 1, ad 2 (Mandonnet, 488): ". . . bonitas dicit rationem per quam essentia ordinatur ad

categories: in every category the transcendental (ontological) "good" is convertible with but subsequent to "being," including the moral goodness that, speaking metaphysically, is merely a quality of the will.[199] For the metaphysician, the moral goodness and badness of acts always presupposes their ontological goodness.[200]

Nonetheless, we should not read into the moral agent's practical understanding of goodness a metaphysical conception of moral goodness.[201] Aquinas never states or implies that the moral agent when reasoning practically must first derive his knowledge of the good to be done from some prior theoretical understanding of good; much less does Aquinas require that the ordinary moral agent have a rudimentary theoretical "notion of morality."[202] Against all these requirements, one can only repeat what Aquinas says often and clearly: *synderesis*, the intellectual habit whereby every moral agent has an immediate knowledge of the first practical principles, is "in a certain way innate

---

appetitum . . ."; *De ver.*, q. 1, a. 1 (Spiazzi, 3): "Convenientiam ergo entis ad appetitum exprimit hoc nomen *bonum*"; *ST*, I, q. 5, a. 2: ". . . ens secundum rationem est prius quam bonum"; *In Metaph.*, IV, lect. 6 (Cathala-Spiazzi, n. 603, p. 167): ". . . ipsa [impossibile est esse et non esse simul] enim est naturaliter principium et dignitas omnium dignitatum."

199. See *ST*, I, q. 5, a. 4, ad 3; *De ver.*, q. 21, a. 2, ad 6.

200. See *ST*, I–II, q. 18, a. 5, ad 2. However, showing that a desired good is an *ens* and thus is a *transcendental* good (in some category of *ens*) does not show that it is an "objective" *moral* good that *ought* to be desired. Adulterous sexual intercourse as well as marital sexual intercourse are both ontological/transcendental goods if compared to the generative power or the concupiscible appetite; the two acts are morally different only *"secundum quod sunt actus rationis" (De malo*, q. 2, a. 4 [Bazzi-Pession, 474]). Unlike ontological good, moral good and evil are not first found "externally" or "*in rebus*," but "*in executione operis*," i.e., in the human will, and by derivation from the will, in human actions; "*in apprehensione*" moral good and evil are first found in the *ends* of human action but only inasmuch as the latter are or are not in accordance with reason; see *De malo*, q. 2, a. 4 (Bazzi-Pession, 472). Cf. a. 3 (471): ". . . actus exteriores non sunt secundum se mali, sed secundum quod ex corrupta intentione vel voluntate procedunt."

201. Cf. Kluxen, *Philosophische Ethik bei Thomas von Aquin*, 57: "Wenn es seine Prinzipien in der Synderesis hat, kann es sie nicht von einer spekulativen Wissenschaft empfangen. Das 'Warum' menschlichen Handelns muss in der praktishen Wissenschaft selbst aufgewiesen werden."

202. Cf. Janice L. Schultz, "St. Thomas Aquinas on Necessary Moral Principles," *New Scholasticism* 62 (1988): 150–78, who seems not to distinguish the ordinary moral agent's indemonstrable knowledge of *per se nota* practical principles from the philosopher's theoretical reconstruction of the foundations of moral reasoning: "[T]o understand the [*per se notum* practical] principle as moral one would also have to grasp the notion of morality as concerned with human completion" (174, n. 79).

to our mind."[203] It is from these "innate" principles of *synderesis* that practical reason *begins*.[204]

In fact, the primary and immediate practical principles are more epistemically connatural to man than even the logically prior and immediate theoretical principles.[205] The practical principles have *epistemic* priority in human cognition. Anyone who reasons about anything implicitly uses the immediate principles of demonstration that ground the sciences. But anyone who acts (and everyone, in fact, does so act) explicitly recognizes and pursues, although sometimes by choosing means that are not in accordance with right practical reason, the necessary ends or natural goods that are essential for human flourishing.[206]

Theoretical knowledge of the good is a matter of knowing the true definition of "good" apart from any practical reasoning about acting.[207] But no matter what theoretical knowledge one has of the good, *only* practical or prescriptive knowledge of the good moves the moral agent to act.[208] Practical reason alone is aimed at acting and thus only practical reason gives rise to "practical science" *(scientia practica)*.[209] How-

---

203. "Synderesis . . . qui est quodammodo innatus menti nostrae ex ipso lumine agentis, sicut habitus principorum speculativorum . . ." *(II Sent.,* d. 24, q. 2, a. 3 [Mandonnet, 610]).

204. See *ST,* I–II, q. 100, a. 1: "Sicut omne iudicum rationis speculativae procedit a naturali cognitione primorum principiorum, ita etiam omne iudicium rationis practicae procedit ex quibusdam principiis naturaliter cognitis . . ."; *Ad Ephes.,* IV, lect. 6 (Cai, n. 232, p. 57): ". . . ita quod actio ordinetur secundum rationis, et haec, scilicet ratio, iudicet secundum intellectum rectum, vel synderesim. . . ."

205. See *ST,* II–II, q. 47, a. 15: "Quantum igitur ad universalem cognitionem, eadem ratio est de prudentia et de scientia speculativa. Quia utriusque prima principia universalia sunt naturaliter nota . . . nisi quod principia communia prudentiae sunt magis connaturalia homini. . . ."

206. See *ST,* I–II, q. 100, a. 1.

207. See *De ver.,* q. 3, a. 3, ad 9 (Spiazzi, 69): ". . . unde et bonum potest considerari cognitione speculativa, prout consideratur veritas eius tantum: sicut enim definimus bonum et naturam eius ostendimus; potest etiam considerari practice, si consideretur ut bonum; hoc autem est, si consideretur in quantum est finis motus vel operationis."

208. See *ST,* I, q. 79, a. 11, ad 1: ". . . intellectus practicus est motivus, non quasi exequens motum, sed quasi dirigens ad motum. Quod convenit ei secundum modum suae apprehensionis"; *SLA,* III, 7, 432b26, 273–276 *(In de An.,* III, lect. 14 [Pirotta, n. 815, p. 19]): ". . . Sic igitur manifestum est quod intellectus, speculative considerando aliquid agibile, non mouet. Ex quo patet quod intellectus speculatiuus nullo modo mouet"; *II Sent.,* d. 38, q. 1, a. 3 (Mandonnet, 974): ". . . unde judicium fugae et prosecutionis ad intellectum practicum pertinet; non autem ipsa prosecutio vel fuga. Intellectus autem speculativus neque fugit aut prosequitur, neque etiam aliquid de fugiendo et prosequendo dicit . . . ."

209. See *De ver.,* q. 6, a. 1, ad 7 (Spiazzi, 114): ". . . quamvis scientia inquantum est scientia, non respiciat facienda, tamen scientia practica respicit facienda. . . ."

ever, we should not drop Thomistic ethics on one side of the great Kantian divide between theoretical and practical reason.[210] The immaterial objects of theoretical reason are more intrinsically intelligible than the objects of practical reason (singular human actions). But Thomistic practical reason is genuinely cognitive. Aquinas's considered position is that the human soul has only one power of reason with two different uses,[211] theoretical and practical, which result in two habits distinguished by their different ends.[212] But these habits are rooted in the same power and have the same object: *truth*. Only practical reason, however, is causative;[213] it knows truth under the aspect or condition of its being intelligently and rightly desired, as a good that is to be done.[214]

It is in reference to the *ends* of reasoning that we should understand Aquinas's description of practical reason as an "extension" of theoretical reason.[215] Reason, except by metonymy, does not pass from being theoretical to being practical;[216] it is the end that one pursues in reason-

210. See Henry B. Veatch, "Kant and Aquinas: A Confrontation on the Contemporary Metaethical Field of Honor," *New Scholasticism* 48 (1974): 73–99; and McInerny, *Aquinas on Human Action*, 184–206.

211. See *II Sent.*, d. 24, q. 2, a. 2 (Mandonnet, 606): ". . . ratio superior, prout contra inferiorem dividitur, non distat ab ea sicut speculativum et practicum, quasi ad diversa objecta respecta . . ."; *III Sent.*, d. 23, q. 2, a. 3, sol. 2 (Moos, n. 179, p. 723): ". . . intellectus practicus et speculativus non sunt diversae potentiae, sed *differunt fine. . . .*"

For an account of the historical development of Aquinas's doctrine, see John E. Naus, S.J., *The Nature of the Practical Intellect According to Saint Thomas Aquinas* (Rome: Libreria Editrice dell' Università Gregoriana, 1959), 17–34.

212. See *ST*, I, q. 79, a. 11.

213. See *ST*, II–II, q. 83, a. 1: ". . . ratio vero practica est non solum apprehensiva, sed etiam causativa."

214. See *SLE*, VI, 2, 1139a22, 104–6 (*In Ethic.*, VI, lect. 2 [Spiazzi, n. 1130, p. 310]): "Sed bonum practici intellectus non est veritas absoluta, sed veritas confesse se habens, id est concorditer, ad appetitum rectum . . ."; *III Sent.*, d. 23, q. 2, a. 3, sol. 2 (Moos, n. 176, p. 732): ". . . intellectus *speculativus* considerat verum absolute, *practicus* autem considerat verum in ordine ad opus"; *In Metaph.*, II, lect. 2 (Cathala-Spiazzi, n. 290, p. 84); "Non enim [practici] considerant causam veritatis secundum se et propter se, sed ordinando ad finem operationis. . . ."

215. See *III Sent.*, d. 23, q. 2, a. 3, sol. 2 (Moos, n. 177, p. 732): "Et tunc intellectus speculativus fit practicus per extensionem ad opus"; *ST*, I, q. 79, a. 11; ". . . intellectus speculativus per extensionem fit practicus."

216. Cf. Cornelio Fabro, "La dialettica d'intelligenza e volontà nella costituzione esistenziale dell'atto libero," in *Etica e società contemporanea*, Studi tomistici, vol. 48 (Vatican City: Libreria Editrice Vaticana, 1992), 34: "Quindi possiamo dire che fra l'apprehensione degli oggetti universali cioè l'*ens*, l'*unum*, il *verum*, il *bonum*, e il *finis in communis*, c'è un' 'interim' in cui la volontà 'sceglie' e trasmette all' intelletto l'oggetto della sua scelta per procedere al suo conseguimento. E' il passaggio dall'*intellectus speculativus* all'*intellectus practicus*." In speaking in this

ing that is theoretical or practical. Human agents, on the other hand, do constantly pass from theoretical speculation to practical pursuits. But we do not need, in each case, to think first theoretically and then practically about something; we can just begin to think practically about doing something.[217] In beginning to think practically, reason is already "extended" to the realm of human action.[218] In other words, the only good that immediately falls under the practical intellect is the good that is to be done.[219]

Speculative intellect knows "good" as contained under its own proper object, that is, under the nature of "truth" taken unconditionally (sub ratione veri absolute), without any relation to action. Speculative intellect reflexively grasps truth as its own perfective good.[220] Now practical reason also prescribes what are, de facto, perfective goods for man. But the agent's immediate practical knowledge of these perfective goods is not his theoretical understanding (if, indeed, he has any) that "good" is somehow ontologically perfective or even explicitly that a particular good is "ontologically perfective."[221] However rudimentary, this latter notion is a theoretical insight that is not epistemically presupposed or required in order to know the ends that practical reason immediately prescribes.[222]

---

fashion, Fabro makes relationship to will distinguish practical from speculative reason: cf. III Sent., d. 23, q. 2, a. 2, sol. 2 (Moos, n. 182, p. 733), quoted above, n. 5.

217. See ST, I–II, q. 74, a. 7: ". . . Sicut enim ratio speculativa iudicat et sententiat de rebus intelligibilibus, ita ratio practica iudicat et sententiat de agendis."

218. See De ver., q. 14, a. 4 (Spiazzi, 289): "Sed intellectum practicum oportet esse proximam regulam operis, utpote quo consideretur ipsum operabile, et rationes operandi, et causae operis"; De virt., q. 1, a. 7, ad 1 (Odetto, 724): "Intellectus autem practicus ordinatur sicut in finem in alium exteriorem actum: non enim consideratio de agendis vel faciendis pertinet ad intellectum practicum nisi propter agere vel facere."

219. See ST, I, q. 79, a. 11, ad 2: ". . . ita obiectum intellectus practici est bonum ordinabile ad opus. . . ."

220. See De ver., q. 21, a. 3, obj. 4 (Spiazzi, 379): "Sed verum est quoddam particulare bonum, est enim bonum intellectus . . ."; ad 4 (180): ". . . verum dicitur esse quoddam bonum particulare, in quantum habet esse in aliquo speciali perfectibili. . . ."

221. See ST, I–II, q. 69, a. 3, ad 2: ". . . in his quae pertinent ad activam vitam, cognitio non quaeritur propter seipsam, sed propter operationem. . . ." Cf. McInerny, Aquinas on Human Action, 191–92: "When something is grasped as good, it is grasped as something and as perfective or fulfilling of us in some way . . . this is not a full-blown and generalized knowledge of things or self, but it is nonetheless theoretical and presupposed by . . . the practical judgment that this is good for me."

222. See SLE, III, 8, 1112b11, 11–15 (In Ethic., III, lect. 8 [Spiazzi, n. 473, p. 133]): "Cum autem consilium sit quaedam inquisitio practica de operabilibus, necesse est quod, sicut in inquisitione speculativa supponuntur principia et quaedam alia in-

Practical reason has certain innate ends that are known immediately.[223] It is the fact of having natural inclinations, not the metaphysical explanation of the fact (however enlightening that might be in some theoretical context), that is the starting point for practical reason.[224] Impelled and directed by natural inclinations, practical intellect conceptualizes certain goods and judges that they are ends to be pursued. Practical intellect's precepts are thus immediately grounded in the natural *desire* of the goods that are de facto perfective not in the theoretical concept of the perfective good.[225] Our basic prescriptive or practical knowledge of the good expresses our cognitive grasp of what we human agents ought to do because of what we actually and necessarily desire to do.[226]

Just because the primary or common practical principles are not and do not need to be deduced from any more basic principles, they are to be clearly distinguished from the easily inferred secondary precepts, and the more difficult to derive tertiary precepts. By definition, tertiary natural law precepts do not immediately focus on basic goods but what can be considered, perhaps in a quite extenuated way, congruent with the basic goods. Such precepts, therefore, must be argued for by those who are wise in moral matters.[227] Abstruse theoretical considerations, and not just commonsensical knowledge of the world, will surely play an important role in such arguments.[228]

---

quiruntur, ita etiam in consilio fiat"; *ST,* II–II, q. 47, a. 6: ". . . ita in ratione practica praeexistunt quaedam ut principia naturaliter nota, et huiusmodi sunt fines virtutum moralium, quia fines se habet in operabilibus sicut principium in speculativis. . . ."

223. See *III Sent.,* d. 33, q. 2, a. 4, sol. 4 (Moos, n. 242, p. 1066): "Unde sicut in ratione speculativa sunt innata principia demonstrationum, ita in ratione practica sunt innati fines connaturales homini; unde circa illa non est habitus acquisitus aut infusus, sed naturalis, sicut synderesis."

224. See *SCG,* III, c. 123 (Pera, n. 2965, p. 184): "Leges autem positae oportet quod ex naturali instinctu procedant, si humanae sunt: sicut etiam in scientiis demonstrativis omnis humana inventio ex principiis naturaliter cognitis initium sumit."

225. See *SLA,* III, c. 9, 433a14, 53–57 (*In de An.,* III, lect. 15 [Pirotta, n. 821, p. 195]): ". . . id autem cuius est appetitus, scilicet appetibile, est principium intellectus practici; nam id quod est primo appetibile est finis a quo incipit consideratio intellectus practici. . . ."

226. Cf. Klaus Riesenhuber, *Die Transzendenz der Freiheit zum Guten* (Munich: Berchmanskilleg Verlag, 1971), 74: "Das Streben wird daher durch die Erkenntnis der praktishchen Vernunft ermöglicht."

227. See *ST,* I–II, q. 100, a. 11.

228. For example, see Aquinas's discussion of the moral fault attached to various kinds of lies in *ST,* II–II, q. 109, a. 1; q. 110, a. 1. On the need for the prudent man to take counsel, see *ST,* I–II, q. 57, a. 6; II–II, q. 47, a. 8.

Other universal, posterior principles, whether of speculative or practical reason, are not had through nature but through discovery according to the way of experience or through instruction. *(ST*, II–II, q. 47, a. 15)[229]

The Thomistic tenet that there are *per se nota* universal precepts is congenial with those contemporary metaethical theories that emphasize, as part of a strategy to avoid the is-ought barrier, the *logical* autonomy of practical reason's inferences:[230] since there are immediate or underived universal natural laws that are *ab initio* prescriptive, Thomistic ethics circumvents the *logical* barrier that is central to the Humean controversy.[231] Hence the Thomistic ethician, whether or not he or she regards the fact-value disjunction as metaphysically untenable,[232] is not required to deduce a proposition containing an "ought" from propositions that only contain "is," at least not on Aquinas's account.[233]

8. Indemonstrable Practical Principles

In exploring the terrain of practical reason, Aquinas identifies *(ST*, I–II, q., 94, a. 2, ad 1) the first principle of practical reason: "Good is to be

229. "Sed alia principia universalia posteriora, sive sint rationis speculativae sive practicae, non habentur per naturam, sed per inventionem secundum viam experimenti, vel per disciplinam" (*ST*, II–II, q. 47, a. 1).

230. See R. M. Hare, "Descriptivism," in *The Is/Ought Question*, 240–58. Cf. Gerald Dworkin, "Autonomy, Science, and Morality," in *The Theory and Practice of Autonomy* (Cambridge: Cambridge University Press, 1988), 48–61.

231. Cf. *ST*, I–II, q. 58, a. 5: "Circa principia quidem universalia agibilium, homo recte se habet per naturalem intellectum principiorum, per quem homo cognoscit quod nullum malum est agendum. . . ."

232. Aquinas's metaphysical doctrine about man's natural teleology is certainly relevant to any consideration of the modern fact/value disjunction which, often enough, is taken to underlie the is/ought logical barrier. For Aquinas, it is clear that the natural ends of human action, in consonance with the exigencies of human nature, are ontologically perfective goods. But the basic ends of human action are uniquely realized only through reasonable and free choices on behalf of goods that are rationally prescribed. Accordingly, man's naturally desired ends are perfective goods that can be characterized as both "descriptively natural" (= goods that correspond to natural inclinations) and "prescriptively moral" (= goods enjoined by practical reason). Are there, then, "moral facts" built into human nature or, if we wish to equate issues, "moral oughts" built into the human "is"? See Henry Veatch, "Natural Law and the 'Is'-'Ought' Question," *Catholic Lawyer* 26 (1981): 251–65. Thomistic answers to these questions require carefully distinguishing our underived epistemic awareness of the first practical principles from any metaphysical explanation *subsequently* offered for that immediate awareness: cf. Rohnheimer, *Praktische Vernunft*, 551.

233. Cf. *ST*, I–II, 104, a. 1: ". . . naturalis ratio dictat hoc esse debitum fieri vel vitari."

done and to be pursued, and evil to be avoided" *(Bonum est faciendum et prosequendum, et malum vitandum).* Attention has often rested on the grammatical form of the first principle. It is a declarative sentence with the verb "is" in the indicative mood followed by the gerundives or verbal adjectives "to be done," "to be pursued," and "to be avoided," all of which are passive in meaning. As is well known from Latin grammar, the nominative case of the gerundive is a verbal adjective that is used to express obligation and necessity. Hence, an indicative sentence containing a gerundive can be used to prescribe.[234] But while an indicative-gerundive prescription may *connote* a corresponding imperative, syntactically, only a verb in the imperative mood "expresses" an imperative.[235]

In addition to *the* first practical principle, Aquinas refers to other *common* or first-order principles, chief of which are the precepts enjoining love of God and neighbor. Drawing on traditional terminology, Aquinas uses the term *"synderesis"* to designate the disposition or habit of practical intellect whereby it possesses these primary and universal principles.[236] Again, the principles of *synderesis* are expressed as indicative sentences with nominative gerundives that signify obligation or necessity. These gerundives convey that the basic ends of human action are rationally necessary or obligatory.[237]

234. Janice L. Schultz, "'Ought'-Judgments: A Descriptivist Analysis from a Thomistic Perspective," *New Scholasticism* 61 (1987): 400–426, states (407) that Aquinas "interprets" the gerundive as an indicative. But since the grammatical mood of the verb is in the indicative, no "interpretation" is required. Having thus conflated gerundives and imperatives (400), Schultz then erroneously asserts that (Thomistic) practical reason basically "derives its prescriptive aspect from the will" (ibid.). Cf. *III Sent.*, d. 33, q. 3, a. 1 (Moos, n. 281, p. 1075): "Ad rationem enim pertinet praecipere quod faciendum est. . . ."

235. Cf. Grisez, "The First Principle," 192: ". . . So far as grammar alone is concerned, the gerundive form can be employed to express an imperative."

236. See *II Sent.*, d. 24, q. 2, a. 4 (Mandonnet, 613): ". . . universalia principia juris ad synderesim pertinent. . . ."

For the doctrinal history of *"synderesis,"* see Lottin, "Syndérèse et conscience aux xiie et xiiie siècles," 101–349; and Vernon J. Bourke, "The Background of Aquinas' Synderesis Principle," in *Graceful Reason: Essays in Ancient and Medieval Philosophy Presented to Joseph Owens, CSsR,* ed. Lloyd P. Gerson (Toronto: Pontifical Institute of Mediaeval Studies, 1983), 345–60. Michael Bertram Crowe, "Synderesis and the Notion of Law in Saint Thomas," in *L' Homme et son destin d' après les penseurs du moyen âge,* Actes du Premier Congrès International de Philosophie Médiévale, 1958 (Louvain: Éditions Nauwelaerts; Paris: Béatrice-Naeuwelaerts, 1960), 601–9, thinks that the infrequency of the term in the *Summa theologiae* indicates "[Aquinas's] abandonment of a 'neo-Platonizing' moral philosophy." There is, however, no indication of any essential doctrinal change in Aquinas's treatment of the first principles.

237. See *ST,* I–II, q. 90, a. 1: "Et huiusmodi propositiones universales rationis

The natural law, in a strict sense, must be identified with these "first and common precepts" of practical reason; they are the ultimate principles governing moral reasoning and they constitute a kind of logical "ground" since from them practical reason "is led" *(deducitur)* to other precepts.[238] In contemporary philosophical parlance, this and other, even stronger, expressions of Aquinas suggest a kind of deductive "foundationalism."[239] But Aquinas, despite his metaphorical description of the first principles as "a sort of seed-bed of all the cognition that follows,"[240] does not hold that the large set of tertiary moral principles can be simply deduced from the immediate, "more certain and more stable"[241] primary practical principles. These tertiary precepts can only be known through rational inquiry or by religious belief, neither of which is a form of immediate knowledge.[242] We use, however, the first principles to judge what we learn from rational investigation.[243]

In the Thomistic theological framework, the natural law arises from an ontological feature of the created human intellect.[244] The human

---

practicae ordinatae ad actiones, habent rationem legis"; q. 97, a. 4, ad 3: ". . . lex naturalis inquantum continet praecepta communia, quae nunquam fallunt . . ."; q. 100, a. 5, ad 1: "Sicut enim prima praecepta communia legis naturae sunt per se nota habenti rationem naturalem, et promulgatione non indigent. . . ."

238. See *II Sent.*, d. 24, q. 2, a. 4 (Mandonnet, 613): ". . . lex naturalis nominat ipsa universalia principia juris; synderesis vero nominat habitum eorum . . ."; a. 3 (610): ". . . oportet quod ratio practica ab aliquibus principiis per se notis deducatur ut quod est malum non esse faciendum, praeceptis Dei obediendum fore, et sic de aliis. . . ."

239. See *De ver.*, q. 16, a. 1 (Spiazzi, 322): "Unde et in natura humana, in quantum attingit angelicam, oportet esse cognitionem veritatis sine inquisitione et in speculativis et in practicis; et hanc quidem cognitionem oportet esse principium totius cognitionis sequentis, sive speculativae sive practicae, cum principia oporteat esse stabiliora et certiora."

240. ". . . quasi quoddam seminarium totius cognitionis sequentis . . ." (*De ver.*, q. 16, a. 1 [Spiazzi, 322]).

241. Ibid.

242. See *II Sent.*, d. 39, q. 3, a. 2 (Mandonnet, 999): ". . . ex principiis communibus in conclusionem hujus operis determinati venit mediantibus quibusdam principiis propriis et determinatis. Haec autem propria principia non sunt per se nota naturaliter sicut principia communia; sed innotescunt vel per inquisitionem rationis, vel per assensum fidei."

243. See *ST*, I, q. 79, a. 12: ". . . iudicamus per principia per se naturaliter nota, de his quae ratiocinando invenimus."

244. See *De ver.*, q. 11, a. 3 (Spiazzi, 231): ". . . Deus hominis scientiae causa est excellentissimo modo; quia et ipsam animam intellectuali lumine insignivit, et notitiam primorum principiorum ei impressit, quae sunt quasi quaedam seminaria scientiarum . . ."; q. 16, a. 1 (322): "Sicut autem animae humanae est quidam habitus naturalis quo principia speculativarum scientiarum cognoscit, quem voca-

mind is created with both the agent intellect and the possible intellect. The former makes what is potentially intelligible actually intelligible: that is, it abstracts a sensible form from the individuating and unintelligible conditions of matter. As abstracted from the sensible phantasm, the form is actually intelligible, and exists immaterially in the possible intellect.[245] The possible intellect, however, naturally possesses certain natural habits, labeled *intellectus* and *synderesis*, comprising respectively the habitual knowledge of the first principles governing the speculative and practical uses of reason.[246] Universal knowledge of the first principles arises "quickly," "without inquiry" or "without inference"; in other words, the *truth* of these principles is immediately known *(per se nota)* "from the intelligible objects themselves."[247] Knowledge of the truth of these first principles is attributed immediately to the agent intellect itself;[248] they are like the instruments that the agent intellect uses to understand other things.[249] Nonetheless, knowledge of the first principles arises only in and through the operation of the agent intellect on sensible *phantasms*.[250] For this reason, Aquinas more precisely

mus intellectum principiorum; ita in ipsa est quidam habitus naturalis primorum principiorum operabilium, quae sunt naturalia principia iuris naturalis; qui quidem habitus ad synderesim pertinet."

245. See *II Sent.*, d. 24, q. 2, a. 2, ad 1 (Mandonnet, 606): ". . . oportet enim ut species phantasmatum, quae sunt objecta intellectus nostri, efficiantur in actu intelligibiles, quod ab agentem pertinet; et intellectui conjungantur in eo receptae, quod pertinet ad possibilem"; *De ver.*, q. 10, a. 6, ad 7 (Spiazzi, 202): "Et sic formae intelligibiles in actu non sunt per se existentes neque in phantasia neque in intellectu agente, sed solum in intellectu possibili."

246. See *De ver.*, q. 16, a. 1 (Spiazzi, 322): "Quod autem ipsa potentia rationis, prout naturaliter cognoscit, synderesis dicatur, absque omni habitu esse non potest; quia naturalis cognitio rationi convenit secundum aliquem habitum naturalem ut de intellectu principiorum patet"; *III Sent.*, d. 33, q. 2, a. 4, sol. 4 (Moos, n. 242, p. 1066): ". . . in ratione practica sunt innati fines connaturales homini; unde circa illa non est habitus acquisitus aut infusus, sed naturalis, sicut *synderesis*. . . ."

247. See *De ver.*, q. 14, a. 1 (Spiazzi, 280): ". . . intellectus possibilis determinatur. . . . Immediate, quando ex ipsis intelligibilibus statim veritas propositionum intelligibilium infallibiliter apparet. Et haec est dispositio intelligentis principia, quae statim cognoscuntur notis terminis. . . . Et sic ex ipso quod quid est, intellectus immediate determinatur ad huiusmodi propositiones."

248. See *De ver.*, q.16, a. 3 (Spiazzi, 325): ". . . impossibile est quod anima hominis privetur lumine intelletus agentis, per quod principia prima in speculativis et operativis nobis innotescunt. . . ."

249. See *De ver.*, q. 11, a. 3 (Spiazzi, 231): ". . . homo ignotorum cognitionem per duo accipit; scilicet per lumen intellectuale, et per primas conceptiones per se notas, quae comparantur ad istud lumen, quod est intellectus agentis, sicut instrumenta ad artificem."

250. *Q. de an.*, q. 5 (Robb, 102): ". . . ipsa principia indemonstrabilia cognoscimus abstrahendo a singularibus. . . . Unde oportet praeexistere intellectum agentem

describes *intellectus* and *synderesis* as natural but only "quasi-innate" *(quodammodo innatus)* cognitive habits.[251]

This latter qualification may reflect a certain tension in the historical sources of Aquinas's doctrine of *per se nota* principles, one that is latent in Boethius's identification of *"communes animi conceptiones"* with Aristotle's "first principles."[252] I shall not tarry over the latter issue since, in any case, it is the Aristotelian emphasis on the perceptual object which prevails in Aquinas's own account of self-evident propositions. The universal conceptions that function as the principles of practical as well as theoretical intellect are known immediately but not in a psychologically a priori fashion; we must first perceptually grasp a sensible instance of being and goodness.[253] Thus we first know the *ratio* of *"ens"* (= "being" taken concretely as a subject that exists) only by abstraction from determinate sensible beings.[254] Simi-

---

habitui principiorum sicut causam ipsius. Ipsa vero principia comparantur ad intellectum agentem ut instrumenta quaedam ejus, quia per ea facit alia intelligibilia actu."

251. Cf. *II Sent.*, d. 24, q. 2, a. 3 (Mandonnet, 610): "Unde dico quod synderesis a ratione practica distinguitur non quidem per substantiam potentiae, sed per habitum, qui est quodammodo innatus menti nostrae ex ipso lumine intellectus agentis, sicut et habitus principiorum speculativorum . . ."; *De ver.*, q. 10, a. 6, ad 6 (Spiazzi, p. 202): ". . . prima principia quorum cognitio est nobis innata. . . ."

252. See Tuninetti, *"Per Se Notum,"* 119: "Aristoteles bezieht sich damit aber auf die Erkennbarkeit von Gegenständen und nicht die Selbstverständlichkeit von Aussagen." Similarly, Bourke, "Aquinas' Synderesis Principle," 357. Cf. Boethius, *De hebdomadibus*, in *The Theological Tractates*, trans. H. F. Stewart, E. K. Rand, and S. J. Tester, Loeb Classical Library (Cambridge, Massachusetts: Harvard University Press, 1973) 74: 40; *In de Heb.*, lect. 1 (Calcaterra, nn. 13–18, pp. 393–394). For other relevant texts from Boethius, see Tuninetti, *"Per Se Notum,"* 48–58.

253. See *De ver.*, q. 10, a. 6 (Spiazzi, 202): ". . . verum est quod scientiam a sensibilibus mens nostra accipit; nihilominus tamen ipsa anima in se similitudines rerum format, inquantum per lumen intellectus agentis efficiuntur formae a sensibilibus abstractae intelligibiles actu, ut in intellectu possibili recipi possint. Et sic etiam in lumine intellectus agentis nobis est quodammodo omnis scientia originaliter indita, mediantibus universalibus conceptionibus, quae statim lumine intellectus agentis cognoscuntur, per quas sicut per universalia principia iudicamus de aliis, et ea praecognoscimus in ipsis."

254. See *II Sent.*, d. 34, q. 1, a. 1 (Mandonnet, 872): "Uno modo dicitur ens quod per decem genera dividitur: et sic ens significat aliquid in natura existens, sive sit substantia . . . Sive accidens . . ."; *Quod.* II, q. 2, a. 1 (Spiazzi, 24): ". . . ens, secundum quod importat rem cui competit huiusmodi esse, sic significat essentiam rei, et dividitur per decem genera . . ."; *In Metaph.*, X, lect. 3 (Cathala-Spiazzi, n. 1982, p. 472): "Sed ens quod dividitur per decem praedicamenta, significat ipsas naturas decem generum secundum quod sunt actu vel potentia"; VI, lect. 1 (n. 1146, p. 295): "De quolibet enim ente inquantum est ens, proprium est metaphysici considerare."

larly, we first know the *ratio* of *"bonum"* by abstraction from determinate goods.[255]

Neither the quasi-innate *per se nota* principles of theoretical reason nor the quasi-innate principles of *synderesis* should be regarded, in the fashion appropriate to either a Thomistic angel or to a Cartesian mind, as psychologically a priori intuitions whose intelligibility and truth is known independently of the sensible world.[256] Our habitual or natural knowledge of first principles must be actualized in and through a sensible phantasm.[257] In other words, we only actually cognize the *per se*

"Being," abstracted with precision from its subject (i.e., "being" taken abstractly), denotes the *actus essendi*: ". . . distinguitur actus essendi ab eo cui ille convenit. Ratio autem entis ab actu essendi sumitur, non ab eo cui convenit actus essendi . . ." *(De ver.,* q. 1, a. 2, ad 3 [Spiazzi, 4]). But the *actus essendi* is itself first grasped by judgment not by conceptualization: "Secunda vero operatio respicit ipsum esse rei . . ." *(Expos. de Trin.,* q. 5, a. 3 [Decker, 9–10, p. 182]).

On the problem of conceptualizing being, so as to preserve the priority of judgment whereby *"ens"* primarily signifies *actus essendi,* see Owens, *Elementary Christian Metaphysics,* 43–67, esp. 65–66, n. 17. For an interpretation critical of Gilson in particular and "Existential Thomism" in general, see Ralph McInerny, "Being and Predication," in *Being and Predication: Thomistic Interpreations,* Studies in Philosophy and the History of Philosophy, vol. 16, gen. ed. Jude P. Dougherty (Washington, D.C.: The Catholic University of America Press, 1986), 173–228, who, aligning himself with Cajetan and John of St. Thomas, argues that *"Being* signifies what-is, not 'something exists'" (186) . . . [and] "this *ratio* is the term of the operation called simple apprehension" (188). Cf. *ELPH,* I, 5, 16b23, 366–71 (Leonine ed., I, pt. 1, 31a): "Et si quidem hec dictio 'ens' significaret esse principaliter sicut significat rem que habet esse, procul dubio significaret aliquid esse; et ipsam compositionem, que importatur in hoc quod dico 'est', non principaliter significat, set consignificat eam in quantum significat rem habentem esse. . . ." The problem as to what *"ens"* principally signifies leads Joseph Owens, C.Ss.R., in "The Accidental and Essential Character of Being in the Doctrine of St. Thomas," *Mediaeval Studies* 20 (1958): 1–40 [reprinted in *St. Thomas Aquinas on the Existence of God: The Collected Papers of Joseph Owens,* 52–96], to conclude that "[t]he equivocity of the participle *ens* for St. Thomas consists then in the twofold usage of the term to denote on the one hand the very essence or nature of a created thing, and on the other hand to denote an actuality that lies outside the essence" (p. 8/60). Cf. *I Sent.,* d. 19, q. 2, a. 2, ad 3 (Mandonnet, 472): ". . . esse, secundum rationem intelligendi, consequitur principia ipsius entis quasi causas . . ."; d. 8, q. 4, a. 2 (223): "Ens autem non dicit quidditatem, sed solum actum essendi, cum sit principium ipsum. . . ."

255. Cf. Etienne Gilson, "Propos sur l' être et sa notion," in *San Tommaso e il pensiero moderno,* Studi tomistici 3, Pontificia accademia Romana di s. Tommaso d' Aquino (Rome: Città Nuova Editrice, 1974), 7–17: "On peut distinguer autant de degrés d'abstraction que l'on voudra, rien ne fera que notre appréhension de l'être ne soit pas une abstraction de l'intellect à partir du sensible" (11).

256. See Thomas S. Hibbs, "Against a Cartesian Reading of *Intellectus* in Aquinas," *Modern Schoolman* 66 (1988): 55–69.

257. See *De ver.,* q. 10, a. 6 (Spaizzi, 201): ". . . mens nostra non potest actu considerare etiam ea quae habitualiter scit, nisi formando aliqua phantasmata. . . ."

nota practical principles by first knowing and willing the determinate goods that correspond to our natural inclinations.[258]

Unlike an angel who possesses innate and actually intelligible universal species of things, Thomistic man can only grasp the universal concepts of *synderesis* in and through insight into a particular instantiation of the good in question.[259] Because of the innate habit, we are immediately able to recognize and pursue the goods that fall under the habit.[260] Yet actual knowledge of the principles of *synderesis* requires sensible experience of the instance; it arises through some combination of perception and imagination.[261] The sensible experience of the instance "triggers," as it were, the innate habit of the possible intellect, which is a passive power.[262] Inasmuch as certain experienced or imagined ends fulfill our natural inclinations, we necessarily apprehend them as goods and this "simple apprehension" is immediately accompanied by the intellectual judgment that they ought to be done or ought to be pursued.[263]

In explaining the indemonstrability of first-order practical principles, Aquinas distinguishes intellect from reason. Although they are acts of the same cognitive power,[264] understanding and reasoning are compared as perfect to imperfect, rest to motion. Whereas intellect

258. See *De ver.*, q. 16, a. 1 (Spiazzi, 321–22): "Unde anima humana . . . aliquid attingit de eo quod proprium est naturae angelicae; ut scilicet aliquorum cogitionem subito et sine inquisitione habeat, quamvis quantum ad hoc inveniatur angelo inferior, quod in his veritatem cognoscere non potest nisi a sensu accipiendo."

259. See *De malo*, q. 16, a. 2 (Bazzi-Pession, 664): "Sic ergo intellectus angeli habet quidem totalitatem in obiecto per comparationem ad nostrum intellectum, qui ex diversis singularibus colligit formam universalem."

260. See *De ver.*, q. 10, a. 8 (Spiazzi, 207): ". . . aliquis ex hoc quod habet alicuius scientiae habitum, ex ipsa praesentia habitus, est potens percipere illa quae subsunt illi habitui."

261. See *De malo*, q. 16, a. 8, ad 3 (Bazzi-Pession, 688): ". . . in usu cognoscendi quamdiu in hac vita sumus, semper est nobis phantasma necessarium, quantumcumque sit spiritualis cognitio. . . ." Cf. *II Sent.*, d. 39, q. 3, a. 1.

262. See *De ver.*, q. 16, a. 1, ad 14 (Spiazzi, 323): ". . . actus cognitionis non praeexigitur ad potentiam vel habitum synderesis, sed ad actum ipsius. Unde per hoc non excluditur quin habitus synderesis, sit innatus"; ad 13 (323): ". . . unde ipsa potentia quae habitui naturali subiicitur, magis videtur esse potentia passiva, quam activa."

263. See *SCG*, II, 54 (Pera, n. 1244, p. 169): "Forma apprehensa est principium movens secundum quod apprehenditur sub ratione boni vel convenientis; actio enim exterior in moventibus seipsa procedit ex iudicio quo iudicatur aliquid esse bonum vel conveniens per formam praedictam"; *I Sent.*, d. 4, q. 2, a. 2 (Mandonnet, 139): ". . . enutiatio sequitur apprehensionem. Unde secundum quod intelligimus aliqua, oportet quod enuntiemus illa."

264. See *ST*, I, q. 79, a. 8.

understands or intuits simple intelligible wholes, reason is discursive; it moves from one understood item to another.[265] Accordingly, it is understanding that cognizes the first principles of speculative as well as of practical reason.[266]

First principles are principles that intellect infallibly knows to be true because they are "immediate" principles in the epistemic sense of being "not mediate." They are, in a broadly contemporary sense, "basic propositions" not accepted on the basis of other propositions. Aquinas says that these immediate principles, because they are not derived from other propositions, are "known through themselves" *(per se nota)* once the meaning of their terms is known.[267] Hence, they are indemonstrable propositions. Now Aquinas's term *"per se nota"* is often translated as "self-evident" rather than as "immediate." But this can be a misleading translation since Aquinas regards some, but not all, immediate or *per se notae* propositions as self-evident. *Per se notae* propositions are true "in themselves" *(secundum se)*, but are not necessarily known to be true "to us" *(quoad nos)*. Only the *communes conceptiones*, the indemonstrable theoretical and practical principles that are known to be true by everyone (e.g., "The whole is greater than any one of its constituent parts"; "An innocent man is not to be harmed") can qualify as "self-evident" in the usual sense of the term. But other *per se notae* propositions (e.g., "An angel does not occupy space") are known to be true only by the philosophical experts who understand the definitions of the terms. Finally, Aquinas admits a class of *per se notae* propositions (e.g., "God exists") that cannot be known to be self-evidently true by anyone because no one can grasp the nature that instantiates the *ratio* of the definition.[268] In this life we cannot know the divine essence which necessarily exists because it is existence itself.

To return, however, to the main point: there are two sets of *per se nota* principles, a set of *per se nota* theoretical principles and a set of *per se nota* practical principles.

265. See *ST,* I, q. 59, a. 1: "Sed intellectus et ratio differunt quantum ad modum cognoscendi: quia scilicet intellectus cognoscit simplici intuitu, ratio vero discurrendo de uno in aliud."

266. See *III Sent.,* d. 35, q. 2, a. 2, sol. 1 (Moos, n. 139, p. 1198): "Unde si aliqua sunt quae statim sine discursu rationis apprehendantur, horum non dicitur esse ratio, sed intellectus; sicut principia prima quae quisque statim probat audita."

267. See *De ver.,* q. 14, a. 1 (Spiazzi, 280): "Quandoque vero intellectus possibilis determinatur ad hoc quod totaliter adhaereat uni parti. . . . Immediate, quando ex ipsis intelligibilibus statim veritas propositionum intelligibilium infallibiliter apparet. Et haec est dispositio intelligentis principia, quae statim cognoscuntur notis terminis. . . ."

268. See *ST,* I, q. 2, a. 1; I–II, q. 94, a. 2.

Just as in speculative matters there are certain things that are known naturally, such as indemonstrable principles and those [propositions] which are close to these, so too in practicable matters there are naturally known principles, principles which are quasi indemonstrable and [precepts] that are close to these. For example: "Evil is to be avoided"; "No one is to be harmed unjustly"; "Stealing is not to be done"; and similar [precepts]. . . . *(SLE,* V, 12, 1134b19, 49–56; *In Ethic.,* V, lect. 12 [Spiazzi, n. 1018, p. 280])[269]

The principles in both sets are "naturally known principles" *(principia naturaliter cognita),* that is, indemonstrable principles. These principles are expressed in the form of judgments.

For theoretical reason, the logically first judgment, which incorporates the logically most primitive concept, "being" *(ens),* is the self-evident first principle of demonstration, that is, the principle of contradiction: "The same thing at the same time and in the same respects cannot both be and not be." Although he nowhere provides a complete list of such theoretical *per se nota* principles, Aquinas mentions such propositions as: "The whole is greater than any of the parts comprising it"; "Two things equal to a third, are equal to each other"; and the like. For practical reason, the logically first judgment, which incorporates the logically most primitive practical concept, "good" *(bonum),* is the self-evident "Good is to be done and pursued; evil is to be avoided." Again, Aquinas does not catalogue all of the other primary practical principles.

Thomistic *per se nota* principles are naturally known or indemonstrably true subject-predicate judgments; they are the *necessary truths* of theoretical and practical reason.[270] For many contemporary philosophers, such necessary truths are (in opposition to factual truths) exclusively logical or semantic truths, that are tagged, in the modern philosophical vocabulary popularized by Kant and subsequently developed by modern empiricism, as "analytic propositions."[271] For Kant, an ana-

---

269. "Sicut enim in speculativis sunt quaedam naturaliter cognita, ut principia indemonstrabilia et quae sunt proprinqua . . . ita etiam in operativis sunt quaedam principia naturaliter cognita quasi indemonstrabilia principia et propinqua his, ut malum esse vitandum, nulli esse iniuste nocendum, non esse furandum et similia . . ." *(SLE,* V, 12, 1134b19, 49–56; *In Ethic.,* V, lect. 12 [Spiazzi, n. 1018, p. 280]).

270. See *De ver.,* q. 16, a. 1, ad 9 (Spiazzi, 322): "Dicitur etiam aliquid incommutabile propter necessitatem veritatis, quamvis sit circa res secundum naturam commutabiles, sicut ista veritas: *Omne totum est maius sua parte,* incommutabilis est etiam in commutabilibus rebus. Et hoc modo synderesis incommutabilibus intendere dicitur."

271. See Willard Van Orman Quine, "Two Dogmas of Empiricism," in *From a*

lytic judgment is an a priori or necessary truth because the concept of its predicate term is covertly "contained" in the concept of its subject term: "All bodies are extended."[272]

In the idiom of contemporary philosophers, who have attempted to refine Kant's ambiguous and rudimentary conception of analyticity, it is generally agreed that analytic propositions are necessarily true either (1) in virtue of their logical forms (tautologies), or (2) in virtue of the synonymous meanings of their terms (i.e., in virtue of semantic rules).[273] But since it is difficult to produce a satisfactory definition either of "synonymity" or "meaning," it is controverted whether type (2) analytic propositions are logically reducible to type (1) analytic propositions.

Some contemporary philosophers, notably Quine, deny that words have identical "meanings"; consequently, they recognize only type (1) analytic propositions, that is, logical tautologies. But if we allow that words have meanings, then an analytic proposition of the second type is usually said to be true "by definition." In the hackneyed example of this type of an analytic proposition, "Every bachelor is an adult, unmarried male," "adult, unmarried male" is a synonymous expression for—one that has the same *meaning* as—"bachelor."

On the presumption that the distinction between analytic and synthetic propositions is itself sound,[274] Aquinas's *per se nota* theoretical principles logically resemble, at least in some rough and preliminary fashion, type (2) analytic propositions. Thomistic *per se nota* theoretical principles are not logical tautologies; they are propositions that are immediately known to be (necessarily) true as soon as the (synonymous) meaning of their terms is known.

The truth and knowledge of indemonstrable principles depends on the meaning of [their] terms. By knowing what is a whole and what is a part, it

---

Logical Point of View: Nine Logico-Philosophical Essays, 2d ed., rev. (Cambridge, Mass.: Harvard University Press, 1953), 20–46.

272. See *Critique of Pure Reason,* B10–11.

273. See Samuel Gorovitz, Merrill Hintikka, Donald Provence, and Ron G. Williams, *Philosophical Analysis: An Introduction to Its Language and Techniques,* 3d ed. (New York: Random House, 1979), 121–23. On the many different definitions of "analyticity," see R. G. Swinburne, "Analyticity, Necessity, and Apriority," in *A Priori Knowledge,* ed. Paul K. Moser (Oxford: Oxford University Press, 1987), 170–89.

274. Quine argues, however, that the boundary between analytic and synthetic propositions is "the boundary that has seemed at length to waver and dissolve" (*Philosophy of Logic,* 2d ed. [Cambridge, Mass.: Harvard University Press, 1986], 101). For a survey of the controversy instigated by Quine, see Ilham Dilman, "Are There Logical Truths?" in *Quine on Ontology, Necessity, and Experience* (Albany: State University of New York Press, 1984), 72–105.

is immediately known that every whole is greater than its part. *(ST,* I–II, q. 66, a. 5, ad 4)[275]

In fact, the resemblance between a Thomistic *per se notum* principle and an "analytic proposition" is less close than one might initially suppose. How close they are depends on one's theory of "meaning." Granted that there are meanings, do only words have meanings or do things, as well as words, have meanings? Often modern and contemporary theories of meaning are nominalistic: only words have meanings. But for Aquinas, a "meaning" *(ratio)* is what the intellect conceives about the essence of the extralinguistic *thing;* subsequently, the same meaning, the *ratio* that is instantiated in the intellectual concept and the thing, is signified through a word.[276] In the framework of either Aristotelian or Thomistic metaphysics, a *per se nota* proposition has a meaning *(ratio)* but this meaning is certainly not restricted to words.[277] On the contrary, *per se nota* principles have a necessary meaning that is dependent on and derived from the meaning that is inherent in being.[278]

To know the meaning of being and nonbeing, and of the whole and of the part, and other things which follow from being, from which the indemonstrable principles are constituted as from terms, pertains to wisdom. *(ST,* I–II, q. 66, a. 5, ad 4)[279]

275. ". . . veritas et cognitio principiorum indemonstrabilium dependet ex ratione terminorum: cognito enim quid est totum et quid est pars, statim cognoscitur quod omne totus est majus sua parte" *(ST,* I–II, q. 66, a. 5, ad 4).

276. "Ratio enim significata per nomen, est id quo concipit intellectus de re, et significat illud per vocem . . ." *(ST,* I, q. 5, a. 2).

277. For an extended discussion of this topic, see Henry B. Veatch, *Two Logics: The Conflict between Classical and Neo-Analytic Philosophy* (Evanston, Ill.: Northwestern University Press, 1969).

278. See *ST,* I, q. 3, 4: ". . . non enim bonitas vel humanitas significatur in actu, nisi prout significamus eam esse"; q. 50, a. 2, ad 1: ". . . differentia est quae constituit speciem. Unumquodque autem constituitur in specie, secundum quod determinatur ad aliquem specialem gradum in entibus . . . ."

Quine, who rejects the notion of *de re* or "metaphysical necessity", observes that Aristotelian essentialism "is abruptly at variance with the idea . . . of explaining necessity by analyticity. For the appeal to analyticity can pretend to distinguish essential and accidental traits of an object only relative to how the object is specified, not absolutely" ("Reference and Modality," in *Logical Point of View,* 155). Quine argues that we specify objects pragmatically: according to our interests, attributes are "important" or "unimportant." And unless we have some "special bias toward a background grouping" which separates one set of objects against another, "there is no semblance of sense in rating some of [one object's] attributes as necessary and others as contingent" *(Word and Object* [Cambridge, Mass.: M.I.T. Press, 1960], 199.)

279. "Cognoscere autem rationem entis et non entis, et totius et partis, et ali-

In Thomistic doctrine, the intellect, in both its theoretical and practical operations,[280] begins to act from a natural habit of *per se nota*, first principles that are ontologically and logically prior to all conventional definitions and pragmatic interests.[281] The *per se nota* principles, as immediate, immutable, and infallibly true, reflect the nature of the agent intellect that immediately causes the known to be an actually intelligible universal;[282] but the actually intelligible is abstracted from the singular sensible species, which is a *similitudo* of the form of the singular sensible thing.[283] Of course, the tenets that support Aquinas's notion of *per se nota* principles, that the essences of sensible things can be rendered actually intelligible by being abstracted from their instantiation in material singulars, are repudiated by those who think that "essence has been left behind with Aristotelian science."[284]

Contemporary essentialism, however, has its defenders as well as its opponents.[285] And whether or not the defense is judged successful, it remains true that Aristotle and Aquinas grounded the meaning of words in the meaning that they took to be inherent in the natures of things.[286] The meaning of a "real definition" is the meaning of the essence of the thing defined.

Because the definition signifies the form and essence of a thing, the first mode of it which is *per se* is when the definition is predicated about

---

orum quae consequuntur ad ens, ex quibus sicut ex terminis constituuntur principia indemonstrabilia, pertinet ad sapientiam . . ." *(ST,* I–II, q. 66, a. 5, ad 4).

280. See *ST,* I–II, q. 63, a. 1: ". . . in ratione homini insunt naturaliter quaedam principia naturaliter cognita tam scibilium quam agendorum. . . ."

281. See *ST,* I–II, q. 51, a. 1: "Sunt ergo in hominibus aliqui habitus naturales, tanquam partim a natura existentes et partim ab exteriori principio. . . . Secundum quidem naturam speciei, ex parte ipsius animae: sicut intellectus principiorum dicitur esse habitus naturalis."

282. See *ST,* I–II, q. 53, a. 1: "Unde si aliquis habitus sit in intellectu possibili immediate ab intellectu agente causatus, talis habitus est incorruptibilis et per se et per accidens. Huiusmodi autem sunt habitus primorum principiorum, tam speculabilium quam practicorum, qui nulla oblivione vel deceptione corrumpi possunt. . . ."

283. See *De ver.*, q. 10, a. 6, ad 7 (Spiazzi, 202): ". . . intellectus possibilis recipit formas ut intelligibiles actu, ex virtute intellectus agentis, sed ut similitudines determinatarum rerum ex cognitione phantasmatum."

284. Christopher Hookway, *Quine: Language, Experience, and Reality* (Standford, Calif.: Stanford University Press, 1988), 121.

285. For some objections to Kripke's essentialism, see Raymond Bradley and Norman Swartz, *Possible Worlds: An Introduction to Logic and Its Philosophy* (Indianapolis, Ind.: Hacket, 1979), 158–67.

286. See Quine, "Two Dogmas," 22: "Things had essences, for Aristotle, but only linguistic forms have meanings. Meaning is what essence becomes when it is divorced from the object of reference and wedded to the word."

something or when something has been posited in the definition. *(ELP,* I, 10, 73a34, 27–30 [Leonine ed., I, pt. 2, 39a])[287]

A *per se notum* principle is an immediate or indemonstrable proposition the predicate of which is *per se* or necessarily affirmed of a subject. It is what Aristotle and Aquinas label a *per se* predication in the first mode. In the first mode of *per se* predication, the predicate defines or is part of the definition of the subject.[288] The definition pertains to the form of the subject; it determines the species of the subject or signifies its essence.[289] Hence, the essence cannot be understood apart from these predicates.[290]

In the second mode of *per se* predication, the definition of the predicate refers to the subject as the matter in which this accident inheres.[291] Thus "multiple" and "divisible" are predicated of "number" in the first mode of *per se* predication; "odd" is predicated of "number," and "straight" and "curved" are predicated of "line," in the second mode of *per se* predication. According to the second mode of *per se* predication, proper accidents are predicated of their subject.[292]

---

287. ". . . quia diffinitio significat formam et essenciam rei, primus modus eius quod est 'per se' est quando predicatur de aliquo diffinitio uel aliquid in diffinitione positum" *(ELP,* I, 10, 73a34, 27–30 [Leonine ed., I, pt. 2, 39a]).

288. See *ELP,* I, 35, 84a12, 47–50 [Leonine ed., I, pt. 2, 130a]: ". . . primo [modi predicandi] quidem predicantur per se quecunque insunt subiectis in eo quod quid est, scilicet cum predicata ponuntur in diffinitione subiecti. . . ."

289. See *ST,* I, q. 3, a. 3: ". . . essentia vel natura comprehendit in se illa tantum quae cadunt in definitione speciei . . ."; q. 29, a. 2, ad 3: ". . . essentia proprie est id quod significatur per definitionem. Definitio autem complectitur principia speciei. . . ."

290. See *De ver.,* q. 5, a. 3 [Decker, 3–6, p. 183]: "Quando ergo secundum hoc, per quod constituitur ratio naturae et per quod ipsa natura intelligitur, natura ipsa habet ordinem et dependentiam ad aliquid aliud, tunc constat quod natura illa sine illo alio intelligi non potest. . . ."

291. See *ELP,* I, 35, 84a12, 50–53 [Leonine ed., I, pt. 2, 130a]: ". . . Secundo [modo predicandi] quando ipsa subiecta insunt predicatis in eo quod quid est, id est quando subiecta ponuntur in diffinitione predicatorum."

292. The predicates that signify the principles of an essence must be distinguished from predicates that signify the the proper accidents *(propriae passiones)* of an essence: see *De spirit. creat.,* q. 1, a. 11, ad 7. Proper accidents or properties do not constitute but are educed from the principles of the species of the subject: "Quaedam autem sunt accidentia naturalia quae creantur ex principiis subiecti . . . vel causantur ex principiis speciei, et sic sunt propriae passiones, quae consequuntur totam speciem . . ." *(I Sent.,* d. 17, q. 1, a. 2 ad 2 [Mandonnet, 398]). Therefore, in simple apprehension, an essence can be understood, without falsity, apart from its properties, as, for example, the essence of the soul can be understood apart from its powers; see *Q. de an.,* q. 7, ad 15 [Robb, 184]: ". . . potentiae animae non sunt partes essentiales animae, quasi constituentes essentiam ejus, sed partes potentiales. . . ."

Although the other modes of *per se* predication can be reduced to these two,[293] it is worth noting that in the fourth mode of *per se* predication, a *per se nota* proposition expresses that the subject is the efficient cause of the predicate.[294]

The necessities expressed in the first, second, and fourth modes of *per se* predication are conceived along the lines of formal, material, and efficient causality. Yet none of the modes of *per se* predication can be understood apart from formal causality: proper accidents flow from the specific form of their subject; and the agent's form is the principle of its efficient causality.[295] Aquinas calls formal necessity *"necessitas naturalis et absoluta"* *(ST,* I, q. 82, a. 1). Today this kind of ontological necessity is commonly called a *de re* necessity in distinction to necessary propositions or *de dictu* necessity. For Aquinas, *per se* predication, especially in the first mode, is clearly a linguistic expression of the necessity inherent in the specific form or essence of a being.

One cannot, however, make a true *judgment* about a species that leaves out its proper accidents: "Sed species non potest intelligi esse sine accidentibus quae consequuntur principium speciei" *(Q. de an.,* q. 12, ad 7 [Robb, 183]). Cf. *De spirit. creat.,* q. 1, a. 11, ad 7 (Calcaterra-Centi, 414): "Hac vero operatione intellectus [componentis et dividentis] non potest intelligi substantia sine proprio: non enim potest intelligi quod homo non sit risibilis, vel triangulus non habeat tres angulos aequales duobus rectis: hic enim est repugnantia intellectuum, quia oppositum praedicati dependet ex natura subiecti." When a proper accident is unconditionally *(simpliciter)* predicated in a judgment, e.g., "A triangle is a figure having three angles equal to two right angles," it is said to be "convertible" with its subject; see *SLP,* I, 10, 73b18, 155–60 (41a).

293. See *ELP,* I, 35, 84a12, 59–60 (Leonine ed., I, pt. 2, 130a). The third mode of the *per se,* a singular that is not predicted of any subject, is not a mode of predication but a mode of existence *(modus existendi):* see *ELP,* I, 10, 73b5, 117–120 (Leonine ed., I, pt. 2, 40a–b).

294. See *ELP,* I, 10, 73b10, 122–24 (Leonine ed., I, pt. 2, 40b): ". . . quartum modum [dicendi per se], secundum quod hec prepositio 'per' designat habitudinem cause efficientis uel cuiuscunque alterius extrinsice . Et ideo dicit quod quicquid inest unicuique propter se ipsum, per se dicitur de eo. . . ."

The editorial interpolation, *"extrinsice,"* is problematic. Proper accidents are intrinsically caused by their subject: "Similiter etiam non potest esse ex causa intrinseca, sicut est per se in accidentibus, quae habent causam in subiecto" *(De pot.,* q. 7, a. 5 [Pession, 196]). They naturally result by way of emanation from their subject: ". . . emanatio propriorum accidentium a subiecto non est per aliquam transmutationem; sed per aliquam naturalem resultationem . . ." *(ST,* I, q. 77, a. 6, ad 3). Cf. John F. Wippel, "Thomas Aquinas on Substance as a Cause of Proper Accidents," in *Philosophie im Mittelalter* (Hamburg: Felix Meiner Verlag, 1987), 201–12: "Proper accidents which follow upon a thing's species are caused efficiently by that thing's essential and intrinsic principles."

295. See *ST,* I, q. 85, a. 4: "Nam modum cuiusque actionis consequitur formam quae est actionis principium."

Principles of this type [i.e., indemonstrable principles] are known immediately in knowing [their] terms. By knowing what is a whole and what is a part, it is at once known that every whole is greater than its part. The "understanding" is so called because it reads within by seeing the essence of a thing. . . . Thus it is appropriate that the knowledge of principles, which are immediately known by knowing what something is, is named "understanding." *(SLE, VI, 5, 1040b31, 54–63; In Ethic., VI, lect. 5 [Spiazzi, n. 1179, p. 322])*[296]

How do these considerations apply to Thomistic *per se nota* practical principles? Although Aquinas refers to the two great commandments ("Love God!"; "Love your neighbor!") as indemonstrable and "known through themselves,"[297] should we also characterize them as "analytic propositions"? The primary indemonstrable theoretical principles and the primary indemonstrable practical principles have similar functions within syllogistic reasoning,[298] but Aquinas notes that the first-order practical principles are only *"quasi* indemonstrable principles."[299] This suggests that *"per se notum,"* as applied to a practical principle, has an analogical meaning. Unlike what might be initially claimed about *per se nota* theoretical principles (if they are erroneously assimilated to a *nominalistic* version of the second type of analytic propositions), it is not even plausible to think that the first-

296. ". . . huiusmodi enim principia statim cognoscuntur cognitis terminis, cognito enim quid est totum et quid pars, statim scitur quod omne totus est maius sua parte; dicitur autem intellectus ex eo quod intus legit intuendo essentiam rei . . . et sic convenienter cognitio principiorum quae statim innotescunt cognito quod quid est circa terminos intellectus nominatur" *(SLE, VI, 5, 1040b31, 54–63; In Ethic., VI, lect. 5 [Spiazzi, n. 1179, p. 322]).*

297. *ST,* I–II, q. 100, a. 3, ad 1 states that the two precepts are *"per se nota rationi humanae"* either through nature or through faith. In this case, nature and faith are not the logical criteria for being "known through themselves" but they are the epistemic circumstances or conditions within which men grasp the immediate character of these propositions. Although "God exists" is not a *per se nota* proposition, to one who believes that God exists, "God ought to be loved" is a *per se nota* proposition. Cf. *ST,* I–II, q. 100, a. 4, ad 1: ". . . ita etiam et hoc quod est credere in Deum est primum et per se notum ei qui habet fidem. . . ."

298. See *III Sent.,* d. 33, q. 1, a. 1 (Moos, n. 22, p. 1019): "Sicut enim in speculativis est principium demonstrationis et medium, ita fines sunt in operationibus . . ."; *ST,* I–II, q. 90. a. 1, ad 2: ". . . ideo est invenire aliquid in ratione practica quod ita se habeat ad operationes, sicut se habet propositio in ratione speculativa ad conclusiones."

299. See *SLE,* V, 12, 1134b19, 49–54 *(In Ethic.,* V, lect. 12 [Spiazzi, n. 1018, p. 280]): "Sicut enim in speculativis sunt quaedam naturaliter cognita, ut principia indemonstrabilia et quae sunt propinqua his . . . ita etiam in operativis sunt quaedam principia naturaliter cognita, quasi indemonstrabilia principia et propinqua his. . . ."

order practical principles are known to be true solely in virtue of the meaning of their words.

The primary practical principles are indemonstrably true not because they are semantic truths but because they prescribe the "quasi-innate" ends that fulfill basic human inclinations. As correlates of natural human inclinations, these ends are practical goods that do not need any theoretical demonstration for their goodness to be grasped.[300]

> In reason there is something naturally known as if it were *[quasi]* an indemonstrable principle in matters of action, which [principle] is in the mode of an end. *(II Sent.,* d. 39, q. 2, a. 2, ad 2 [Mandonnet, 994])[301]

Without any kind of logical derivation from some more basic goal of human agents, these ends are immediately seen to be required in the practical order: given human nature and its needs or inclinations, they are the ends toward which human agents are necessarily *(de re)* oriented. Only by pursuing these ends will human nature be fulfilled. Practical reason, which necessarily or naturally pursues human fulfillment, is immediately directed toward them.

> The ends of human life, which relate to matters of action as naturally known principles relate to speculative matters, especially pertain to the prescriptions of natural reason. *(ST,* II–II, q. 56, a. 1)[302]

It might be argued, however, that *the* first principle of practical reason is certainly an "analytic proposition." Aquinas states *(ST,* I–II, q. 94, a. 2) that the first principle of practical reason ("Good is to be done . . .") is indemonstrable or *per se notum.* Now this principle does seem to be true solely in virtue of the meaning of its terms. Let us look at only the terms in the first half of the principle: the prescriptive meaning of "good" is "that which is to be done and to be pursued." Does this definition not fit the criteria for an "analytic definition"? Its contrary proposition, "Good is that which is not to be pursued," is a self-contradiction given the synonymy of the Thomistic definitions of

300. See *ST,* II–II, q. 47, a. 6: ". . . in ratione practica praeexistunt quaedam ut principia naturaliter nota, et huiusmodi sunt fines virtutum moralium, quia finis se habet in operabilibus sicut principium in speculativis. . . ."

301. ". . . in ratione est aliquid natualiter cognitum quasi principium indemonstrabile in operabilibus, quod se habet per modum finis" *(II Sent.,* d. 39, q. 2, a. 2, ad 2 [Mandonnet, 994]).

302. "Praecipue autem sunt de dictamine rationis naturalis fines humanae vitae, qui se habent in agendis sicut principia naturaliter cognita in speculativis . . ." *(ST,* II–II, q. 56, a. 1).

"good" and "end": "All who rightly define 'good' place in its definition something about it being an 'end.'"[303]

As Aquinas defines them, "good" and "end" have synonymous *rationes:* "'End' has the meaning [*ratio*] of 'good'; 'good' has the meaning [*ratio*] of 'end.'"[304] By substitution of these synonyms,[305] the precept "The good is to be done and pursued" has the same meaning as the precept "The end is to be done and pursued."[306] The latter precept, if any proposition can be so counted, is certainly a semantic truth; hence, the former proposition, "The good is to be done and to be pursued," is analytic by virtue of synonymy.

Notice, however, that this substitution of one synonym for another, of interchanging the meanings of "good" and "end"[307] is not a deduction of the precept to do good from the descriptive meanings of "good" but a reduction of the precept to another analytically true precept: "The end is to be done and pursued." Therefore, the indemonstrability of the first practical principle (i.e., the first precept) is *not* "founded on something theoretical"[308] if by "founded" we are referring to the deduction of a prescriptive conclusion from strictly descriptive premises.

Now the "analytic" character of the first practical principle, "Good is to be done . . . ," has led one scholar to wonder whether it is a "useless tautology."[309] But just this worry should signal that we need to

303. ". . . omnes recte definientes bonum ponunt in ratione eius aliquid quod pertineat ad habitudinem finis . . ." *(De ver.,* q. 21, a. 1 [Spiazzi, 376–77]).

304. ". . . finem, qui habet rationem boni"; ". . . bonum habet rationem finis . . ." (*ST,* I–II, q. 94, a. 2).

305. See *De ver.,* q. 21, a. 2 (Spiazzi, 378): ". . . omne id quod invenitur habere rationem finis, habet rationem boni."

306. See *II Sent.,* d. 27, q. 1, a. 2, ad 2 (Mandonnet, 699): ". . . bonum dicitur ex ratione finis. . . ."

307. See *De ver.,* q. 21, a. 1, ad 9 (Spiazzi, 377): ". . . bonum dicat aliquam specialem habitudinem, scilicet finis. . . ."

308. See Peter Simpson, "Practical Knowing: Some Comments on Finnis and Aquinas," *Modern Schoolman* 67 (1990): 120. Elsewhere, Simpson, "St. Thomas on the Naturalistic Fallacy," *Thomist,* 51 (1987): 67, grants that "for St. Thomas practical thinking begins not with an Is but with an Ought." Schultz, in "Thomistic Metaethics and a Present Controversy," 40–62, develops a complex argument to show that "[Thomistic] value-judgments about human goods are basically descriptive rather than prescriptive or normative" (42). Schultz, however, defines the good as the object of *possible* desire, while allowing (I think) that Aquinas emphasizes *actual* desire (see 54–55). Schultz's contention that the actually desirable *(appetible)* can be "descriptive through and through" without being "inherently prescriptive" (46) cannot be squared with Aquinas. Cf. *II Sent.,* d. 21, q. 1, a. 3 (Mandonnet, 530): ". . . bonum est objectum voluntatis et desiderii, eo modo aliquid est *adamandum* quo est bonum."

309. Simpson, "Practical Knowing," 113. Cf. R. A. Armstrong, *Primary and*

return to the Thomistic metaphysical doctrine of essences with essential properties, in this case, human nature with its powers and necessary inclinations, as the explanation (though, again, *not* the epistemic justification) of the cognitive immediacy of Thomistic *per se nota* practical principles.[310] Granted that "good" and "end" are synonymously defined; yet our practical knowledge that certain basic goods are ends to be pursued does not rest on merely semantic truths. We have immediate epistemic awareness of certain basic human goods because they are de facto the objects that correspond to the inclinations of human nature.[311] The prescriptions of the natural law enjoin pursuing those basic goods that, as ends to be achieved through acting, we immediately know will fulfill our desires.[312]

9. The Generic Character of the First Practical Principle

In developing his moral science in the *Secunda pars* of the *Summa theologiae*, Aquinas does not begin by first discussing the moral goodness or badness of actions. He begins *(ST,* I–II, q. 6) more radically by elaborating the conditions that make moral evaluation possible. The first such condition is that moral evaluation applies only to a voluntary or "human act" *(actus humanus)* as opposed to a nonvoluntary bodily process or "act of man" *(actus hominis)*.[313] A "human act" is equivalent to a rational and voluntary act, that is, an act *(actus voluntarius)* that arises from rational deliberation and choice.[314] Furthermore, it

Secondary Precepts in Thomistic Natural Law Teaching (The Hague: Martinus Nijhoff, 1966), 39, who questions the *analytic* character of the first practical principle, lest the truth of this principle seem "merely a question of arbitrary definition."

310. The return can be defended within a contemporary context: for an explanation of natural law principles as "analytic a posteriori propositions" (= necessary propositions whose truth is nonetheless known experientially), see Alfonso Gómez-Lobo, "Derecho natural: Un analisis contemporaneo de sus fundamentos," *Revista latino-americana de filosofia* 12 (1986): 143–60. Gómez-Lobo draws on Saul Kripke, "Identity and Necessity," in *Naming, Necessity, and Natural Kinds,* ed. Stephen P. Schwartz (Ithaca, N.Y.: Cornell University Press, 1977), 66–101.

311. See *De malo,* q. 6, a. 1 (Bazzi-Pession, 560): "Si ergo dispositio, per quam alicui videtur aliquid bonum et conveniens, fuerit naturalis et non subiacens voluntati, ex necessitate naturali voluntas praeeligit illud, sicut omnes homines naturaliter desiderant esse, vivere, et intelligere."

312. See *II Sent.,* d. 35, q, 1, a. 1 (Mandonnet, 645): "Determinatio autem agentis ad aliquam actionem, oportet quod sit ab aliqua cognitione praestituente finem illi actioni."

313. See *ST,* I–II, q. 6, prologus.

314. See *II Sent.,* d. 25, q. 1, a. 3 (Mandonnet, 652): ". . . omnes actus humani sunt liberi arbitrii, quia ab ipso imperati . . ."; *ST,* I–II, q. 1, a. 1: ". . . actiones proprie

should be noted that Aquinas equates "human acts" and "moral acts." Reason is the source of human morals.[315]

Since it is rationally motivated, a human act is, by definition, a moral act.[316] But this, too, is a generic use of the term "moral': "The genus of morality begins where the command of the will is first discovered."[317] A rational or generically moral act is one that can be further determined as specifically either a morally *good* or a morally *bad* act. The moral goodness or badness of actions is determined by rationally evaluating what the agent wills, that is, his proximate and remote volitional *ends* which, morally speaking, are the matter and form of external actions.[318] If both these ends (and any relevant circumstances surrounding the action) are in accordance with practical reason, then the action is morally good; if either end is contrary to right reason, the action itself is inordinate and morally bad.[319]

In *ST,* I–II, q. 18, Aquinas first considers the goodness and badness of human acts *"in generali."* This consideration is general because it abstracts from the specific psychological differentiation of acts into interior (elicited) acts of the will and exterior or bodily (commanded) actions. But when human acts are considered according to their species, then interior acts (q. 19) must be explicitly distinguished from exterior acts or actions (q. 20). Given the equation of voluntary acts and moral acts, this psychological distinction has moral significance. The interior act of willing an end is what is primordially voluntary. Thus what must be first judged to be morally good or bad is willing the (proximate) end that is the "matter" or "object" of the external action.

Aquinas's carefully ordered discussion gradually brings into focus how voluntary acts are the focus of moral judgments: "First of all, mo-

---

humanae dicuntur, quae ex voluntate deliberata procedunt"; prologus, q. 6: "Cum autem actus humani proprie dicantur qui sunt voluntarii. . . ."

315. See *ST,* I–II, 104, a. 1: ". . . a ratione dicuntur mores humani."

316. See *ST,* I–II, q. 18, a. 5: "Dicuntur autem aliqui actus humani, vel morales, secundum quod sunt a ratione"; q. 19, a. 1, ad 3: "Ratio enim principium et humanorum et moralium actuum. . . ."

317. ". . . incipit genus moris ubi primo dominium voluntatis invenitur" *(II Sent.,* d. 24, q. 3, a. 2 [Mandonnet, 620]).

318. *ST,* II–II, q. 11, a. 1, ad 2: ". . . vitia habent speciem ex fine proximo, sed ex fine remoto habent genus et causam"; q. 23, a. 8: ". . . in moralibus forma actus attenditur princpaliter ex parte finis: cuius ratio est quia principium moralium actuum est voluntas, cuius obiectum et quasi forma est finis. Semper autem forma actus consequitur formam agentis. Unde oportet quod in moralibus id quod dat actui ordinem ad finem, det ei et formam."

319. See *II Sent.,* d. 24, q. 3, a. 2 (Mandonnet, 620): "Peccatum enim . . . non est aliud quam inordinatus actus ad genus moris pertinens."

ral vice is found solely in the act of the will; and from this fact, it is reasonable to call an [external] act "moral" because it is voluntary" *(SCG,* III, 10 [Pera, n. 1946, p. 13]).[320] No bodily motion can count as a moral act unless it is voluntary; but an action is voluntary in the relevant sense only because (1) it is internally motivated and (2) it embodies the agent's intelligent pursuit of some end through the choice of some means.[321] But these are also the criteria for identifying a "moral act." Hence, the first principle of practical reason, "Good is to be done and to be pursued and evil is to be avoided," is logically extensional with the principle that equates *voluntary acts* (both elicited and commanded) with *human acts* and human acts with *moral acts.*[322]

If we are to preserve the sense of Aquinas's equation (voluntary act = human act = moral act), the first principle of practical reason must be counted as a "moral principle": it prescribes solely the good that is to be realized through volition, that is, through human or moral acts. The first principle of practical reason prescribes doing and pursuing what is generically but really morally good. As an action guiding principle, it enjoins the ends of human action that reason recognizes to be morally good to pursue.[323] Nonetheless, the principle does not itself provide any criteria for discriminating between really and apparently morally good ends. In that sense, the first principle of practical reason is not a specifically determinate, normative moral principle; nonetheless, it should not be classified as a "metaethical principle."

In contemporary parlance, metaethical principles are the logical, or semantic, or epistemological principles that explain, govern, or justify moral discourse; they are not themselves normative moral princi-

---

320. ". . . morale vitium in solo actu voluntatis primo et principaliter inveniatur: et rationabiliter etiam ex hoc actus moralis dicatur, quia voluntarius" *(SCG,* III, 10 [Pera, n. 1946, p. 13]).

321. See *ST,* I–II, q. 6, a. 2: ". . . ad rationem voluntarii requiritur quod principium actus sit intra, cum aliqua cognitione finis."

322. See *ST,* I–II, q. 74, a. 2: ". . . omne quod est principium voluntarii actus, est subiectum peccati. Actus autem voluntarii dicuntur non solum illi qui eliciuntur a voluntate, sed etiam illi qui a voluntate imperantur. . . ."

323. My interpretation concurs with what Vernon J. Bourke, in "The Synderesis Rule and Right Reason," *Monist* 66 (1983): 71–82, concludes: that "it is not the case that 'good' in the [Synderesis Rule] is non-moral" (73). Bourke, however, argues that "a context of surrounding conditions . . . places the [concrete] act in the moral area" (ibid.) whereas Aquinas seems to maintain that it is, generically, a moral act because it is a human act. Moreover, Bourke infuses into the first practical principle a metaphysical corollary about the nature of the good being prescribed: he interprets it as prescribing any ends "that are good for you *as a human being*" (ibid.; italics mine). The latter, put explicitly, is a theoretical inference about the nature of the perfective good that practical reason prescribes.

ples.[324] Metaethical principles, evidently, are theoretical principles. Aquinas, however, never treats the principle "Good is to be done and to be pursued, and evil is to be avoided" as a theoretical principle. Aquinas always refers to it as the first principle of practical reason, and looks at its function only in the sphere of practical reason, where it is the logical ground of the other universal normative principles. They are the more determinate principles that specify the basic instances of the good that is to be done and pursued.

Practical reason, however, does not rest with the universal consideration of good and evil ends; on the contrary, it typically moves to the moral evaluation of action-types and action-tokens.[325] Described at the specific level, some action-types—for example, taking a walk—are morally neutral since their object or matter, lacking any fixed relationship to the norms of practical reason, is neither morally good nor bad in itself. But Aquinas firmly denies that individual or singular actions can be morally neutral. A singular action, due to the circumstances under which it is accomplished or to the agent's intention in accomplishing it, will always be either morally good or morally bad: here and now, taking a walk to get exercise or taking a walk to avoid a responsibility. But even immoral actions must remain intelligible as actions. Given Aquinas's notion of acting (that one only desires an end because it *seems* good), an agent cannot aim at a morally bad end because it is bad. The agent can aim at a morally bad end but only insofar as the end appears, because the agent is ignorant or under the sway of passion, to be an apparent moral good, that is, something that, for some reason or other, can be intelligently chosen. The "reason" in question, however, is defective; it is not a product of "right reason," that is, it is not in accord with the intellectual virtue of prudence.[326]

Defective moral reasoning leads to what is apparently good. The apparent good, most often, is what is sensibly but not intellectually desirable by an agent operating in accordance with prudential reasoning.[327] In referring to "apparent goods," Aquinas usually does not dis-

324. See A. W. Sparks, *Talking Philosophy: A Wordbook* (New York: Routledge, 1991), 208; William K. Frankena, *Ethics*, 2d ed. (Englewood Cliffs, N.J.: Prentice-Hall, 1973), 5.

325. See *SCG*, III, 6 (Pera, n. 1905, p. 8): "In agentibus autem voluntariis intentio est ad bonum aliquod particulare, si debet sequi actio: nam universalia non movent, sed particulari, in quibus est actus."

326. See *ST*, I–II, q. 58, a. 2, ad 4: ". . . recta ratio, quae est secundum prudentiam, ponitur in definitione virtutis moralis. . . ."

327. See *ST*, I–II, q. 75, a. 2: ". . . causa peccati est aliquod bonum apparens

tinguish between ontological and moral goodness.[328] But, once again, it is necessary to advert explicitly to that distinction in order to comprehend, for example, an intemperate person's deliberate pursuit of immoral pleasure. Aquinas, perhaps to the confusion of the reader, sometimes describes the pursuit of immoral pleasure as though the agent were directly pursuing only a sensible (i.e., ontological) good.[329] The sinner is said to will directly the pleasure but *not* the moral evil that accompanies the pleasure.[330] But such descriptions do not adequately convey everything that Aquinas says about the appearance of moral good that colors the intemperate person's pursuit of pleasure.

I have already drawn attention to the distinction, which Aristotle and Aquinas make, between the "weak-willed" incontinent man (ἀκρατής = *incontinens*), who overcome by passion is said to lack any choice, and the *intemperatus* (ἀκόλαστος) who coolly chooses to pursue pleasure. The latter kind of man clearly does not *choose* to pursue pleasure solely because it is an ontological (sensible) good; he chooses it because it appears to be (even though it is not) a moral good.[331] So, *choosing* an "apparent good" is not just being a victim of ignorance or incontinently succumbing to passion; it is sometimes a case of what we call "rationalizing" our choices.

For Aquinas, calling an end an "apparent good" is to raise the question not of the ontological goodness but of the real *moral* goodness of our actions and their ends.[332] It is not the ontological goodness of an immoral action that is "apparent"; an immoral action aims at an apparent moral good, that is, an end that necessarily has an irreducible ontological goodness but no real moral goodness.[333] When all is said and

---

motivum cum defectu debiti motivi, scilicet regulae rationis vel legis divinae; ipsum motivum quod est apparens bonum, pertinet ad apprehensionem sensus et appetitum."

328. Cf. *ST*, I–II, q. 75, a. 4, ad 1: ". . . peccatum, inquantum est inordinatum, habet rationem mali; sed inquantum est actu quidam, habet aliquod bonum, saltem apparens, pro fine."

329. See *ST*, I–II, q. 73, a. 1: "Sed intentio peccantis non est ad hoc quod recedat ab eo quod est secundum rationem: sed potius ut tendat in aliquod bonum appetibile. . . ."

330. See *SCG*, III, 6 (Pera, n. 1907, p. 8): "Similiter propter aliquod bonum sensibile consequendum aliquis vult facere inordinatam actionem, non intendens inordinationem, neque volens eam simpliciter, sed propter hoc."

331. *ST*, I–II, q. 77, a. 2: "Quia cum voluntas sit boni vel apparentis boni, numquam voluntas in malum moveretur, nisi id quod non est bonum, aliqualiter rationi bonum appareret. . . ."

332. See *De malo*, q. 2, a. 6, ad 3 (Bazzi-Pession, 481): ". . . Species peccati non est species actus secundum suam naturam . . . Sed secundum esse morale. . . ."

333. See *ST*, I–II, q. 74, a. 1, ad 1: ". . . malum dicitur esse praeter voluntatem,

done, choosing to act in this fashion cannot be rationally justified according to the canons of right reason. "Apparent goods" must therefore be understood precisely: they are ontological goods (human actions or the effects of human actions) that are chosen because they appear to be but are not real moral goods.[334] Right practical reason judges these ontological goods, however sensibly attractive, to be inordinate or in some way irrational, and therefore morally bad.

Of course, a strong passion can indeed block, or distract, or even make it physically impossible for a moral agent to consider his habitual moral principles. But Aquinas also seems to recognize, albeit without the post-Freudian emphasis of a contemporary moralist, that the moral agent can "rationalize": passion makes it easy for the agent to "judge" that a particular pleasurable action, for example, this act of adulterous sexual intercourse, is morally good or morally indifferent here and now *for him*, even when this judgment goes against the universal rational principles that he or she holds.[335] In so judging and presumably choosing, the agent, once again, is pursuing apparent moral goods, and not just sensible or ontological goods.[336]

Immoral actions remain intelligible because they too fit under the aegis of the first principle of practical reason. Immoral actions, such as adultery and theft, are volitional and (in a restricted sense) rational because they are done in pursuit of some ontological good that also appears to be a moral good—in these cases, pleasure and utility.[337] But whether pleasure or utility is a real moral good, here and now, depends upon whether the agent's intention in pursuing them, and the object and circumstances of the acts that promote them, can be rationally justified. These are the criteria that distinguish apparent from real moral goodness, and these are the criteria that must always be taken into account when morally evaluating singular actions.

---

quia voluntas non tendit in ipsum sub ratione mali. Sed quia aliquod malum est apparens bonum, ideo voluntas aliquando appetit aliquod malum."

334. See *De malo*, q. 3, ad 2 (Bazzi-Pession, 498): ". . . deformitas peccati non consequitur speciem actus secundum quod est in genere naturae; sic autem a Deo causatur; sed consequitur speciem actus secundum quod est moralis, prout causatur ex libero arbitrio. . . ."

335. See *ST*, I–II, q. 77, a. 2, ad 2: ". . . hoc ipsum quod rationi videatur in particulari aliquid bonum, quod non est bonum, contingit ex aliqua passione. Et tamen hoc particulare iudicium est contra universalem rationis."

336. See *De ver.*, q. 24, a. 10, ad 11 (Spiazzi, 454): ". . . peccatum per liberum arbitrium non committitur nisi per electionem apparentis boni. . . ."

337. See *ST*, II–II, q. 122, a. 6, ad 4: "Sed adulterium habet aliquam rationem boni, scilicet delectabilis. Furtum etiam habet rationem alicuius boni, scilicet utilis."

10. The Basic Ends of Practical Reason

Aquinas does not attempt to specify the precise number of indemonstrable, first-order practical principles. He thinks, however, that there are only two basic ends of human action. Accordingly, he reduces the multiplicity of *per se nota* principles to these two fundamental precepts. The reduction introduces a biblical economy into Aquinas's natural law ethics.

In *ST,* I–II, q. 100, a. 3, ad 1, Aquinas states that the two great commandments mentioned in sacred scripture, "Thou shalt love the Lord thy God" and "Thou shalt love thy neighbor," are the first and general principles of the natural law. These two commandments do not need to be promulgated in the divinely revealed Decalogue because they are the *per se nota* precepts that specify the ultimate ends of practical reason.[338] These two ends, loving God and neighbor, are the fundamental moral goods that all other good ends instantiate in some fashion or other. For this reason, the other moral precepts of the divinely revealed law (and the natural law precepts that correspond to the Ten Commandments) can be reduced to these two first-order precepts.[339] Indeed, the love of neighbor may be called the "primary origin of observing the precepts"[340] since it includes the love of God.

Practical reason generates the "active life"—the life that is centered on the obligations that we owe to, or on the benefits that we confer on, our neighbor.[341] Action, if one chooses to act at all, is necessarily about doing the good that is due God and neighbor. Loving them is the ultimate end of human action. Other common or general *per se nota* precepts of practical reason[342] correspond to the basic ends or goods to

338. See *ST,* I–II, q. 100, a. 11: "Nam quaedam sunt certissima, et ideo manifesta quod editione non indigent; sicut mandata de dilectione Dei et proximi, et alia hujusmodi . . . quae sunt quasi fines praeceptorum. . . ."

339. See *III Sent.,* d. 37, a. 3 (Moos, n. 53, p. 1243): "Omnia praecepta legis ad dilectionem Dei et proximi aliqualiter reducuntur. . . ."

340. ". . . dilectio proximi est sicut prima radix observandi praecepta, prout in dilectione proximi etiam dilectio Dei includitur: est enim finis praecepti . . ." (*III Sent.,* d. 37, a. 2, sol. 2, ad 2 [Moos, n. 45, p. 1241]).

341. See *ST,* I–II, q. 69, a. 3: "Activa vero vita in his consistit praecipue quae proximis exhibemus, vel sub ratione debiti, vel sub ratione spontanei beneficii."

342. For example: "One ought to shun ignorance"; "One ought to obey divine precepts" (*II Sent.,* d. 24, q. 2, a. 3 [Mandonnet, 610]); "One ought to avoid offending one's neighbors" (*ST,* I–II, q. 94, a. 2); "One should do no evil to any man" (q. 100, a. 3); "One should love oneself" (a. 5, ad 1); "One should love one's children" (ad 4); "One ought to return benefits to those from whom one has received benefits" (a. 7); "Injury is not to be done" (ibid.).

which we are by nature inclined, and hence they too do not need to be specifically promulgated by divine law.[343] They are first-order principles inasmuch as they are immediate specifications of what it is to love God and neighbor.

The Ten Commandments are, to be sure, about loving God and loving neighbor;[344] and therefore they reflect the structure of practical reason itself.[345] But Aquinas does not consider the commandments of the Decalogue to be among the first-order or immediate principles of practical reason; he calls them "*quasi* primary and general principles of the law."[346] In effect, the Ten Commandments are second-order principles. They are, as Aquinas puts it, like conclusions that can be easily derived from the first-order indemonstrable principles that enjoin the love of God and neighbor.[347] In turn, the Ten Commandments are the principles of the third-order or derivative moral precepts of the law.[348]

Why, then, are the Ten Commandments revealed if they are so obvious and so easily derived from the primary precepts of the natural law? By reference to loving God and neighbor, the ordinary man, with but a little intellectual effort, should be able to assess the justice or injustice of certain actions.[349] God, it is "self-evident" to anyone who believes in His existence, is alone to be adored, reverenced, and worshiped. And it should be equally apparent that killing, committing adultery, bearing false witness, and stealing are not beneficent acts to one's neighbor.

343. See *ST,* I–II, q. 100, a. 4, ad 1: ". . . prima precepta communia legis naturae sunt per se nota habenti rationem naturalem, et promulgatione non indigent. . . ."

344. See *ST,* II–II, q. 122, a. 5: ". . . praecepta decalogi ordinantur ad dilectionem Dei et proximi."

345. See *ST,* I–II, q. 98, a. 5: ". . . lex vetus manifestabat praecepta legis naturae . . ."; II–II, q. 57, a. 1: ". . . praecepta decalogi, sicut data sunt omni populo, ita etiam cadunt in aestimatione omnium, quasi ad naturalem rationem pertinentia."

346. See *ST,* II–II, q. 122, a. 4: "Et quia praecepta decalogi sunt quasi quaedam prima et communia legis principia. . . ."

347. See *ST,* I–II, q. 100, a. 1: "Quaedam enim sunt in humanis actibus adeo explicita quod statim, cum modica consideratione, possunt approbari vel reprobari per illa communia et prima principia"; a. 3: "Illa ergo praecepta ad decalogum pertinent, quorum notitiam homo habet per seipsum a Deo. Huiusmodi vero sunt illa quae statim ex principiis communibus primis congnosci possunt modica consideratione"; a. 6: ". . . praecepta decalogi dantur de his quae statim in promptu mens hominis suscipit."

348. See *ST,* II–II, q. 122, a. 4: ". . . praecepta decalogi sunt quasi quaedam prima et communia legis principia. . . ."

349. See *ST,* II–II, q. 122, a. 1: ". . . praecepta decalogi oportuit ad iustitiam pertinere"; q. 140, a. 1, ad 3: ". . . Praecepta decalogi debuerunt esse principaliter de actibus iustitiae, in quibus manifeste invenitur ratio debiti. . . ."

These acts clearly violate the first-order principle that one should not harm or do evil to any person.[350]

Yet ordinary men, because of passions and evil habits, can ignore what is obviously just and what is obviously unjust.[351] The main purpose of the revealed or divine law is to lead men to eternal beatitude.[352] As a corrective to human sinfulness, God reveals in the Decalogue what I have called the "second-order principles"; the latter are the easy but easily derailed inferences drawn from the indemonstrable or first-order principles which themselves reduce to the two biblical precepts enjoining the love of God and neighbor.

Aquinas, however, recognizes that rational morality must provide more guidance than the easily grasped, second-order, natural law precepts embodied in the revealed Ten Commandments. There are numerous questions that have no obvious answers even if one's passions are well ordered. To guide their choices, men require more specific precepts, which promote the ends specified in the Decalogue,[353] but which are not rules that can be attained by simple logical deductions from the Decalogue. Like the immediate first-order principles, these third-order precepts have not been divinely revealed.[354] But their elaboration is required: life is complex; so too, at times, is love of neighbor.[355] Who is my neighbor and exactly what do I owe him? Of course, any adequate formulation of moral precepts presupposes that the moralist has the logical capacity to reason carefully from the primary and secondary moral principles. But complicated cases demand more than skill in logic; they demand experience, insight, and the accumulated wisdom

350. See *ST*, I–II, q. 95, a. 2: ". . . 'non esse occidendum' , ut conclusio quaedam derivari potest ab eo quod est 'nulli esse malum faciendum.'"

351. Irwin, in "The Scope of Deliberation," argues that Aquinas "must appeal to [synderesis] to explain the crucial difference between virtue and vice" (27). But Thomistic *synderesis*, like biblical rain, falls on the good and the bad alike. The virtuous person aims at the correct ends not because he (unlike the vicious man) has some privileged (nondeliberative) grasp of those ends, but because the virtuous man is not swayed by passions in drawing immediate conclusions from *per se nota* practical principles or in making judgments about the particular actions that fall under those principles; see *II Sent.*, d. 24, q. 3, a. 3; *ST.*, I–II, q. 94, a. 4; q. 99, a. 2; q. 100, a. 1; II–II, q. 47, a. 15.

352. See *ST*, I–II, q. 98, a. 1; q. 99, a. 4.

353. See *ST*, II–II, q. 57, a. 1, ad 3: ". . . alia doctrina veteris Testamenti ordinatur ad praecepta decalogi ut ad finem. . . ."

354. See *ST*, I–II, q. 100, a. 3.

355. See *ST*, I–II, q. 100, a. 11, ad 1: ". . . ad dilectionem Dei et proximi ordinantur quidem praecepta decalogi secundum manifestam rationem debiti; alia vero secundum rationem magis occultam."

of a moral tradition.[356] These are the real sources of our tertiary moral precepts. Capacity for this kind of deep consideration of our moral experience distinguishes the wise man from the ordinary man;[357] it pertains to the "perfection of the virtuous life."[358] Aware, then, of moral complexity, Aquinas draws an inegalitarian conclusion: wise men, presuming that there is a Moses or an Aaron, should instruct their more ordinary brethren about complex moral issues.[359]

Thomistic ethics thus begins with the indemonstrable principles of practical reason, but this is a beginning that it quickly surpasses. The logical adequacy of Aquinas's own account of the derivation of the secondary and tertiary moral precepts from the most common first-order principles has been questioned. It is charged that he provides no clearly specified rules to guide moral reasoning from the primary principles, instantiating the love of God and neighbor, to these further "conclusions."[360] But I shall not investigate this charge; true or not, it does not alter the indemonstrable status of the primary or *per se nota* precepts.

356. See *Quod.* VIII, q. 2, a. 2; *ST,* II–II, q. 47, a. 15: "Sed alia principia universalia posteriora, sive sint rationis specuativae sive praticae, non habentur per naturam, sed per inventionem secundum viam experimenti, vel per disciplinam."

357. See *SLE,* IV, 7, 1142a16, 209–13 *(In Ethic.,* VI, lect. 7 [Spiazzi, n. 1211, p. 331]).

358. ". . . ad perfectionem virtuosae vitae pertinet . . ." *(III Sent.,* d. 37, a. 2, sol. 2, ad 6 [Moos, n. 49, p. 1242]).

359. See *ST,* I–II, q. 100, a. 2; a. 11.

360. For a recent attempt to bridge Aquinas's logical gaps, see J. M. Finnis, "Natural Inclinations and Natural Rights: Deriving 'Ought' from 'Is' According to Aquinas," in *Lex et Libertas: Freedom and Law According to St. Thomas Aquinas,* ed. L. J. Elders, S.V.D., and K. Hedwig (Vatican City: Libreria Editrice Vaticana: 1987), 43–55.

VII

The Will: The Secondary Source of Natural Law

1. Natural Desire

As Aquinas identifies them, the precepts of the natural law are precepts of *practical reason*. Nonetheless, we cannot understand why some action is the end of practical reason, much less why agents pursue the goals that practical reason prescribes, unless we understand how practical reason operates in conjunction with desire or appetite. Desires, however, can be natural, sensible, or volitional (i.e., intellectual).[1] We shall begin with natural desire since it antecedes any sensible or intellectual apprehension of the object desired; ontologically, it is the first or fundamental type of desire. To have a natural desire or appetite is "to have a natural inclination to an end."[2] Every being and

---

1. Animals, in addition to natural tendencies, have an appetitive power whose object (the apprehended sensible good) actually moves them: "Similiter appetere, quod quodammodo commune est omnibus, fit quodammodo speciale animatis, scilicet animalibus, in quantum in eis invenitur appetitus, et movens appetitum. Ipsum enim bonum apprehensum est movens appetitum . . ." (De ver., q. 22, a. 3 [Spiazzi, 393]). In nonrational animals, the acts of the appetitive power are preceeded solely by sense apprehension of the desired goods: "[appetitus] animalis autem sequitur apprehensionem . . ." (ad 5 [394]). But in human animals, the acts of will, the intellectual appetite, are preceeded by intellectual apprehension of the desired sensible and intelligible goods to which rational agents may freely incline or not incline: "Appetitus autem sensitivus est qui ex praecedenti imaginatione vel sensu consequitur. . . . Appetitus autem rationalis est qui consequitur apprehensionem rationis, et hic dicitur motus rationis, qui est actus voluntatis" (II Sent., d. 24, q. 3, a. 1 [Mandonnet, 617]); De virt., q. 1, a. 6 (Odetto, 722): "Oportet autem ut appetitus animalis vel rationalis inclinetur in suum appetibile ex aliqua apprehensione praeexistente; inclinatio enim in finem absque praeexistente cognitione ad appetitum pertinet naturalem. . . ."

2. ". . . hoc est naturam appetere finem, scilicet habere aptitudinem naturalem ad finem" (In Phys., II, lect 13 [Maggiòlo, n. 257, p. 127]).

every potency, as a nature, necessarily tends to some end.[3] Natural desire is the principle of the other types of desire.[4] In man, the natural desire of the ultimate end is the cause of everything else that he wills.[5]

In regard to the attainment of any end, Aquinas distinguishes: (1) the nature or form that is proportioned to the end in question; (2) the natural inclination of the form; and (3) the motions or operations that may or may not actually follow upon the natural inclination.[6] According to these Thomistic metaphysical tenets, the human will is a nature *(voluntas ut natura)* with inherent inclinations.[7] Yet, it may seem contradictory, since the will is often distinguished from natural inclination, to attribute both natural and intellectual desires to the will.[8] Indeed, if the definition of "intellectual appetite" is understood as prescinding from or explicitly excluding natural appetite, then the two appetites are opposites.[9] Taken without precision, however, "intellec-

---

3. See *De ver.*, q. 22, a. 1 (Spiazzi, 390): ". . . omnia naturalia, in ea quae eis conveniunt, sunt inclinata, habentia in seipsis aliquod inclinationis principium, ratione cuius eorum inclinatio naturalis est . . ."; a. 3, ad 5 (394)". . . unaquaeque potentia appeti suum obiectum appetitu naturali."

4. See *ST,* I, q. 60, a. 2: ". . . cum natura sit primum quod est in unoquoque, oportet quod id quod ad naturam pertinet, sit principium in quolibet."

5. See *ST,* I, q. 60. a. 2: "Et ex hac naturali voluntate causantur omnes aliae voluntates: cum quidquid homo vult, velit propter finem."

6. See *De ver.*, q. 27, a. 2 (Spiazzi, 514): ". . . ad consecutionem alicuius finis in rebus naturalibus tria praeexiguntur: scilicet natura proportionata ad finem illum; et inclinatio ad finem illum, quae est naturalis appetitus finis; et motus in finem."

7. The will has natural as well as intellectual appetites: "Unde oportet in omnibus creaturis habentibus aliquem finem inveniri appetitum naturalem etiam in ipsa voluntate respectu finis ultimi *(III Sent.*, d. 27, q. 1, a. 2 (Moos, n. 43, p. 861); *ST,* I, q. 60, a. 1: "Unde in natura intellectuali invenitur inclinatio naturalis secundum voluntatem . . . ." The "natural" tendencies or appetites of the will are antecedent to any sensible or intellectual apprehension of the ends of these tendencies: "Appetitus autem naturalis non consequitur aliquam apprehensionem, sicut sequitur appetitus animalis et intellectualis" *(ST,* I–II, q. 17, a. 8). The natural tendencies of the human will reveal God's antecedent will for men: ". . . volitum divinum, quantum ad voluntatem antecedentem, est nobis notum ex ipsa naturali inclinatione . . ." *(I Sent.*, d. 48, a. 4, ad 1 [Mandonnet, 1090]); *De ver.*, q. 22, a. 5 (Spiazzi, 397): "Hoc autem est cuiuslibet naturae creatae, ut a Deo sit ordinata in bonum naturaliter appetens illud. Unde et voluntati ipsi inest naturalis quidam appetitus sibi convenientis boni." Hence, the natural inclinations of the will remain even in the damned: *II Sent.*, d. 39, q. 3, a. 1, ad 5 [Mandonnet, 998): ". . . in damnato manet naturalis inclinatio qua homo naturaliter vult bonum; sed haec inclinatio non dicit actum aliquem, sed solem ordinem naturae ad actum. Hic autem ordo et habilitas nunquam in actum exit, ut bonum actualiter velit. . . ."

8. Cf. *SCG*, III, 143 (Pera, n. 3171, p. 216): "Sicut est voluntas in hominibus, ita est inclinatio naturalis in rebus naturalibus"; *ST,* I, q. 60, a. 1: "Unde in natura intellectuali invenitur inclinatio naturalis secundum voluntatem. . . ."

9. See *De malo,* q. 16, a. 4 (Bazzi-Pession, 662): ". . . appetitus nihil est aliud

tual appetite" abstracts from without excluding "natural appetite" in the way that "man" is abstracted from but does not exclude "animal."[10] This is, of course, a semantic solution to a metaphysical problem, but it allows us to apply the Thomistic metaphysical doctrine of natural desire to the will without falling into an initial contradiction.[11]

Aquinas regards the *voluntas ut natura* as the "first principle" of the simple act of will *(velle)* that follows upon the simple intellectual apprehension of the good.[12] This tenet is important for a correct understanding of the Thomistic doctrine of natural law. For Aquinas, the natural law has an intellectual and an appetitive source, and although the latter is secondary and subordinate, both sources must be kept clearly in view. In regard to the will, then, we must distinguish: (1) the human will as a nature *(voluntas ut natura)*; (2) the innate natural tendencies of the will that bring certain goods under man's immediate practical cognition and (subsequent) intellectual appetite;[13] and (3) the natural acts of the will that follow (a) the simple intellectual conception of the good *(velle)*, and (b) the immediate or nondiscursive judgments about the apprehended good *(intendere)*.

---

quam inclinatio quaedam in appetibile; et sicut appetitus naturalis consequitur formam naturalem, ita et appetitus sensitivus, vel rationalis, sive intellectivus sequitur formam apprehensam: non enim est nisi boni apprehensi per sensum vel intellectum"; *In Metaph.*, V, lect. 6 (Cathala-Spiazzi, n. 829, p. 226): "In naturalibus quidem est impetus, sive inclinatio ad aliquem finem, cui respondet voluntas in natura rationali; unde et ipsa naturalis inclinatio appetitus dicitur"; *SLA*, II, c. 5, 414a29, 107–9; 113–17 *(In de An.*, II, lect. 5 [Pirotta, n. 286, p. 75]): ". . . ex unaquaque autem forma sequitur aliqua inclinatio et ex inclinatione operatio . . . ad formam igitur tam sensibilem quam intelligibilem sequitur inclinatio quedam que dicitur appetitus sensibilis uel intellectualis, sicut inclinatio consequens formam naturalem dicitur appetitus naturalis, ex appetitu autem sequitur operatio. . . ."

10. See *De ver.*, q. 22, a. 5, ad 6 (Spiazzi, 398): ". . . voluntas dividitur contra appetitum naturalem cum praecisione sumptum, id est qui naturalis tantum, sicut homo contra id quod est animal tantum; non autem dividitur contra appetitum naturalem absolute, sed includit ipsum, sicut homo includit animal."

11. Cf. *ST*, I, q. 60, a. 5: ". . . inclinatio enim naturalis in his quae sunt sine ratione, demonstrat inclinationem naturalem in voluntate intellectualis naturae."

12. See *ST*, I–II, q. 41, a. 3: ". . . motus cognitivae et appetitivae virtutis reducuntur in naturam, sicut in principium primum"; III, q. 18, a. 4: "Et sic simplex voluntas est idem quod voluntas ut natura: electio autem est idem quod voluntas est ratio. . . ." Cf. *ST*, I, q. 59, a. 4, ad 2: ". . . amor et gaudium . . . Secundum quod nominant simplicem voluntatis actum, sic sunt in intellectiva parte: prout amare est velle bonum alicui . . ."; I–II, q. 22, a. 3, ad 3: ". . . amor et gaudium et alia huiusmodi . . . Significant simplicem actum voluntatis. . . ."

13. See *De ver.*, q. 22, a. 12, ad 2 (Spiazzi, 409): ". . . non est procedere in infinitum; statur enim in appetitu naturali, quo inclinatur intellectus in suum actum."

In speaking of the "acts of intellect" and the "acts of will," we are in danger of reifying the powers of a specific kind of being. But the will, in fact, is only a power of an intellectual being; it is the appetite of a being that also has the power of intellect. But the usual definition of "will" as "intellectual appetite" does not mean that intellectual appetite is an act of the intellectual power, but of the being (i.e., the *suppositum*) possessing both powers.[14] It is in this sense that we must interpret the well-known tenet of Thomistic psychology that all of the *acts* of the will are always consequent upon the acts of the intellect.[15] We need, moreover, to balance this tenet with Aquinas's other observation that acts of intellect and will "bend back on" or "include" each other.[16] This *reflexio* does not negate the absolute or natural primacy of the intellect as the interior mover of the will,[17] but it does show the impossibility of divorcing intellect and will in their Thomistic context.[18] Here I will examine only the acts of practical intellect and will that bear on the *end* of human actions.

2. The Twofold Operation of the Intellect

In delineating the "twofold operation of the intellect,"[19] Aquinas contrasts the first operation, specified under various titles ("*intelligen-*

14. See *De ver.*, q. 22, a. 13 (Spiazzi, 411): ". . . intentio praesupponat aliquam cognitionem. Si loquamur de intentione animali, sic non est nisi cognoscentis, sicut nec velle. Non tamen oportet quod intendere et velle sint actus eiusdem potentiae, cuius est cognoscere, sed eiusdem suppositi: non enim proprie dicitur cognoscere vel intendere potentia aliqua, sed suppositum per potentiam."

15. See *ST*, I, q. 82, a. 4, ad 3: "Omnem enim voluntatis motus necesse est quod praecedat apprehensio: sed non omnem apprehensionem praecedit motus voluntatis."

16. See *ST*, I–II, q. 17, a. 3, ad 3: ". . . actus harum potentiarum supra seipsos invicem reflectuntur"; I, q. 82, a. 4, ad 1: ". . . ratio quare hae potentiae suis actibus invicem se includunt: quia intellectus intelligit voluntatem velle, et voluntas vult intellectum intelligere."

This *reflexio* also characterizes the objects as well as the acts of the two powers: ". . . intellectus intelligit voluntatem velle, et voluntas vult intellectum intelligere. Et simili ratione bonum continetur sub vero, inquantum est quoddam verum intellectum; et verum continetur sub bono, inquantum est quoddam bonum desideratum" (*ST*, I, q. 82., a. 4, ad 1).

17. On the exterior mover of the will, viz. God as the prime mover, see *ST*, I–II, q. 9, a. 4; a. 5; *De ver.*, q. 22, a. 9; *De malo*, q. 6. Cf. Mark D. Jordan, "The Transcendentality of Goodness and the Human Will," in *Being and Goodness*, ed. MacDonald, 129–50.

18. See *De ver.*, q. 22, a. 13: "Ratio autem et voluntas sunt quaedam potentiae operativae ad invicem ordinatae. . . ."

19. Among Aquinas's approximately sixty references to "*duplex operatio intellectus*," see *SLA*, III, c. 5, 430a26, 1–17; 430b26, 214–16 (*In de An.*, III, lect. 11 [Pirot-

tia indivisibilium," "simplex intelligentia," "informatio," "formatio quidditatis simplicis," "conceptio simplex," etc.), with the second operation, composing and dividing, or affirming and denying.[20] The intellect "judges" when it composes and divides the intelligibiles that fall under the first operation;[21] hence, the second operation of the intellect

---

ta, nn. 746–47, p. 178; n. 760, p. 180)); *ELPH*, I, 5, 16b20, 276–88 (Leonine ed., I, pt. 1, 29b); *I Sent.*, d. 19, q. 5, a. 1, ad 7; d. 38, q. 1, a. 3; *De ver.*, q. 14, a. 1; *Expos. de Trin.*, q. 5, a. 3.

For the Aristotelian background to this distinction, see *de An.*, III, 6, 430a26–28 (rev. Oxford trans.): "The thinking of indivisibles [τῶν ἀδιαιρέτων νόησις] is found in those cases where falsehood is impossible: where the alternative of true or false applies, there we always find a sort of combining of objects of thought in a quasi-unity [σύνθεσίς τις ἤδη νοημάτων ὥσπερ ἓν ὄντων]." Cf. *Metaph.*, VI, 4, 1027b18–28; XI, 8, 1065a21–23; IX, 10, 1051b2–27. The latter text refers to having "contact" (θιγγάνειν) with simples or incomposites (ἀσύνθετα) without further specifying the operation or the beings so contacted: cf. Owens, *Doctrine of Being*, 414; Pierre Aubenque, *Le Problème de l'être chez Aristote* (Paris: Presses Universitaires de France, 1972), 373–74.

For references to the third operation of the intellect, "reasoning" *(ratio)*, see *De ver.*, q. 15, a. 1, ad 5 (Spiazzi, 309): "Unde eadem potentia in nobis est quae cognoscit simplices rerum quidditates, et quae format propositiones, et quae ratiocinatur; quorum unum proprium est rationis in quantum est ratio; alia duo possunt esse intellectus, in quantum est intellectus." Cf. *ELP*, I, prooemium, 33–48 (Leonine ed., I, pt. 2, 4a–b); *ST*, II–II, q. 83, a. 1, ad 3.

20. See *In Metaph.*, VI, lect. 4 (Cathala-Spiazza, n. 1232, p. 310): "Intellectus autem habet duas operationes, quarum una vocatur indivisibilium intelligentia, per quam intellectus format simplices conceptiones rerum intelligendo quod quid est uniuscuiusque rei. Alia eius operatio est per quam componit et dividit"; *Super Ioannem*, c. I, lect. 1 (Cai, n. 26, p. 8): "Intellectus autem duo format, secundum duas ejus operationes; nam secundum operationem suam, quae dicitur indivisibilium intelligentia, format definitionem; secundum vero operationem suam, qua componit et dividit, format enunciationem, vel aliquid hujusmodi"; *De ver.*, q. 14, a. 1 (Spiazzi, 280): "Intellectus enim nostri . . . duplex est operatio. Una qua format simplices rerum quidditates; ut quid est homo. . . . Alia operatio intellectus est secundum quam componit et dividit, affirmando et negando . . ."; q. 1, a. 3, ad 1 (Spiazzi, 6): ". . . quamvis formatio quidditatis sit prima operatio intellectus. . . ."

In conformity with medieval Arabic philosophical usage, the second operation can be labeled "faith" *(fides)* or "credulity" *(credulitas)*: see *I Sent.*, d. 8, q. 1, a. 3; d. 19, q. 5, a. 1, ad 7; *De spirit. creat.*, q. 1, a. 9, ad 6.

21. On the coalescence of many intelligibles into one, whereby through the unity of what it understands, one act of understanding can grasp *multa*, see *III Sent.*, d. 14, q. 1, a. 2, sol. 4, ad 1 (Moos, n. 107, p. 451): ". . . quando plura intelliguuntur in uno, omnia illa sunt ut unum intelligibile . . ."; *Quod.* VII, q. 1, a. 2 (Spiazzi, 135): ". . . totum enim unum est primo intellectum, et illa plura sunt intellecta ex consequenti in illo . . . "; *SCG*, I, 55 (Pera, n. 457, p. 67): ". . . plura una specie cognoscuntur, simul possunt intelligi"; *ST*, I, q. 85, a. 4: "Quaeumque ergo intellectus potest intelligere sub una specie, simul intelligere potest. . . ." Cf. Bernard J. Lonergan, S.J., *Verbum: Word and Idea in Aquinas*, ed. David B. Burrell, C.S.C. (Notre Dame, Ind.: University of Notre Dame, 1967), 51–53.

is to judge.[22] Sometimes Aquinas contrasts "apprehension" *(apprehensio)*, which he identifies with the first operation of the intellect, with the second operation, "judgment" *(judicium)*.[23] But "to apprehend," without any qualification, can also be applied to judgments.[24] It is especially noteworthy that Aquinas, unlike the later Thomists, never uses the term *"simplex apprehensio"* to designate exclusively the first operation of the intellect; the term properly applies to any immediate or non-discursive apprehension whether of sense, imagination, or intellect.[25] Thus Aquinas allows a *simplex apprehensio* of the immediate or nondiscursive judgments that result from the second operation of the intellect.[26] The third operation is precisely the process of reaching a

22. See *In Metaph.*, VI, lect. 4 (Cathala-Spiazzi, n. 1236, p. 311): "Intellectus autem habet apud se similitudinem rei intellectae, secundum quod rationes incomplexorum concipit; non tamen propter hoc ipsam similitudinem diiudicat, sed solum cum componit vel dividit . . . et ideo in hac sola secunda operatione intellectus est veritas et falsitas . . ."; *ST*, I, q. 16, a. 2: "Intellectus autem conformitatem sui ad rem intelligibilem cognoscere potest: sed tamen non apprehendit eam secundum quod cognoscit de aliquo quod quid est, sed quando judicat rem ita se habere sicut est forma quam de re apprehendit . . . ." Cf. *De ver.*, q. 1, a. 11; *ELPH*, I, 3, 16a12, 39–50 (Leonine ed., I, pt. 1, 14b); *SCG*, I, 58–59; II, 76 (Pera, n. 1568, p. 223); *De malo*, q. 16, a. 1, ad 1.

23. See *De ver.*, q. 1, a. 3 (Spiazzi, 6): "Tunc autem iudicat intellectus de re apprehensa quando dicit quod aliquid est vel non est, quod est intellectus componentis et dividentis . . ."; a. 11 (Spiazzi, 22): ". . . ex apprehensione tali natum est sequi tale iudicium."

24. See *I Sent.*, d. 38, q. 1, a. 2, ad 2 (Mandonnet, 904): "Sed intellectus noster . . . non apprehendit illud esse nisi componendo et dividendo . . ."; *SLA*, II, c. 28, 427b6, 186–89 *(In de An.*, III, lect. 4 [Pirotta, n. 629, p. 155]): "Hec autem duo intellectiue cognicioni attribuuntur: intellectus enim habet iudicare, quod hic dicitur sapere, et apprehendere, quod hic dicitur intelligere." For other texts, see Owens, *Elementary Christian Metaphysics*, 54, n. 22.

25. See *De ver.*, q. 24, a. 5, ad 4; *SLA*, II, c. 28, 427b21, 273–84 *(In de An.*, III, lect. 4 [Pirotta, n. 635, p. 156]); *In Metaph.*, I, lect. 2 (Cathala-Spiazzi, n. 46, p. 13).

26. *I Sent.*, d. 19, q. 5, a. 1, ad 7 ranks the first principles *(dignitates)* with the propositions that result from the second operation of the intellect, but with the notation that the naturally known *primae affirmationes* cannot be false. The first principles are immediate judgments whose truth is known by *simplex acceptio*, and therefore *"simpliciter et absolute absque discursu" (De ver.*, q. 15, a. 1 [Spiazzi, 308]): ". . . non posset mens humana ex uno in aliud discurrere, nisi eius discursus ab aliqua simplici acceptione veritatis inciperet, quae quidem acceptio est intellectus principiorum" (Spiazzi, 307). Cf. *II Sent.*, d. 24, q. 3, a. 1 (Mandonnet, 617): "Sed rationis apprehensio dupliciter esse potest. Una simplex et absoluta, quando scilicet statim sine discussione apprehensum dijudicat, et talem apprehensionem sequitur voluntas quae dicitur non deliberata . . ."; *SLA*, II, c. 29, 428a1, 48–51 *(In de An.*, III, lect. 5 [Pirotta, n. 639, p. 158]): ". . . intellectus accipitur pro certa apprehensione eorum que absque inquisitione nobis innotescunt, sicut sunt prima principia . . ."; *Super Ioannem*, c. I, lect. 1 (Cai, n. 26, p. 8): ". . . in primis principiis, quae cum sint simpliciter nota, absque discursu rationis statim sciuntur."

judgment by way of a reasoned conclusion, that is, through a discursive process of reasoning, where one thing is known through another.[27]

For our present purposes, we may put aside any further consideration of the shifting terminology and contexts in which Aquinas elaborates his many-sided doctrine of judgment.[28] Here we only need to reiterate that in regard to both speculative and practical intellect, "simple apprehension" *(simplex apprehensio)* covers both (1) the first operation or the simple conception *(simplex conceptio)* of "being" and "good" as quiddities; (2) and the second operation or the immediate

---

To summarize: the first operation of the intellect is a *simplex apprehensio* that includes (a) the conception of absolutely simple natures; and (b) the immediately known definitions that express the essential parts of these natures. The second operation, judgment, includes (c) the *simplex apprehensio* of first principles which are immediate or nondiscursive judgments whose "essential predicates" are contained in the *rationes* of their respective subjects; and (d) the composing or dividing of "enunciations" or mediate judgments which add or subtract "accidental predicates" that are not contained in the *ratio* of the subject, see *ELPH*, I, 5, 16b10, 121–25 (Leonine ed., I, pt. 1, 27a); *ST*, I, q. 16, a. 2. Although "it is not possible to dissent from [first] principles" *(Quod.* VIII, q. 2, a. 2 [Spiazzi, p. 162]) because "they are naturally in us" *(Ibid.),* a mediate judgment that composes and divides "is not a work of nature, but is a work of reason and intellect" *(SLA,* III, c. 5, 430a26, 81–83; *In de An.,* III, lect. 11 [Pirotta, n. 751, p. 179]. Cf. *De ver.,* q. 15, a. 1, ad 5 (Spiazzi, 309), quoted in n. 19 above; *SLA,* II, c. 29, 428a16, 148 *(In de An.,* III, lect. 5 [Pirotta, n. 648, p. 159]).

For a distinction between judgment as the *act* of composing and dividing, and judgment as an *object* that can reflexively fall under the first operation of the intellect, see Joseph Owens, C.Ss.R., "Judgment and Truth in Aquinas," *Mediaeval Studies* 32 (1970): 138–58 [reprinted in Catan, *Aquinas on the Existence of God,* 34–51]. Truth is the *"adequatio"* of a judgment (= proposition) about a thing to the thing judged; it arises when the judgment (proposition) about the thing is compared to and seen to correspond with the thing. The comparison involves knowing the thing through a present act of judging: see Owens, "Judgment and Truth," 49. Cf. *SCG,* I, 59 (Pera, n. 495, p. 70): "Cum enim veritas intellectus sit adaequatio intellectus et rei, secundum quod intellectus dicit esse quod est vel non esse quod non est, ad illud in intellectu veritas pertinet quod intellectus dicit, non ad operationem qua illud dicit."

27. See *ELP,* prooemium, I, 1, 33–49 (Leonine ed., I, pt. 2, 4–5): "Sunt autem rationis tres actus. Quorum primi duo sunt rationis secundum quod est intellectus quidam: una enim actio intellectus est intelligencia indiuisibilium, siue incomplexorum, secundum quam concipit quid est res, et hec operatio a quibusdam dicitur informatio intellectus siue ymaginatio per intellectum . . . Secundo uero operatio intellectus est compositio uel diuisio intellectuum, in qua est iam uerum et falsum. . . . Tercius uero actus rationis est secundum id quod est proprium rationis, scilicet discurrere ab uno in aliud, ut per id quod est notum deueniat in cognitionem ignoti. . . ."

28. See Benoit Garceau, O.M.I., *Judicium: Vocabulaire, sources, doctrine de saint Thomas d'Aquin* (Montreal and Paris: Institut d'Études Médiévales and J. Vrin, 1968).

judgments *(iudicia)*, which are the first principles of theoretical and
practical reason, about "being" and "good." In the *duplex operatio
intellectus,* the first operation is to be understood as naturally (logically) not temporally prior to the second operation.[29] Thus in the many
ways that "being" *(ens)* and "good" *(bonum)* are said,[30] they are first
grasped as natures or quiddities[31] which fall *"in apprehensione quidditatis simplicis,"* that is, under the first operation, respectively, of

29. The priority of *simplex conceptio* to *iudicium* corresponds to the priority of
words to propositions, since the former are the grammatical elements of the latter.
But are the first *per se nota* propositions constructed from atomic insights? The
question was a bone of contestation between Thomists and Scotists: see P. Hoenen,
S.I., "De origine primorum principiorum scientiae," *Gregorianum* 14 (1933): 153–
84, who argues, with ample quotation from Aquinas, that "the first judgments do
not arise from the analysis or bringing together of notions, but are immediately
abstracted from sensible apprehension" (174). Hoenen convincingly establishes that
simple concepts and their nexus as expressed in immediate *propositions* can be
grasped by the same psychological act, i.e., abstraction: "Si igitur notum sit omnibus de praedicato et de subjecto quid sit, propositio illa erit omnibus per se nota:
sicut patet in primis demonstrationum principiis, quorum termini sunt quaedam
communia quae nullus ignorat, et ens et non ens, totum et pars, et similia" *(ST,* I, q.
2, a. 1). Yet, in "the order of nature" (cf. *ELPH,* I, 3, 16a9, 10 [Leonine ed., I, pt. 1,
14a]), the priority of the intelligibilities that are composed and divided in any given
judgment can hardly be challenged: "Harum autem operationum prima ordinatur ad
secundam, quia non potest esse compositio et diuisio nisi simplicem apprehen-
sorum . . ." *(ELPH,* I, 1, 16a1, 8–11 (Leonine ed., I, pt. 1, 6a].

Joseph Bobik, *Aquinas on Being and Essence: A Translation and Interpretation*
(Notre Dame, Ind.: University of Notre Dame Press, 1965), 5, refers to the "analytic
priority" of simple apprehension to judgment, i.e., of concepts to propositions. Cf.
M.D. Philippe, "Analyse de l'être chez saint Thomas," in *Tommaso d'Aquino nel
suo vii centenario,* 255–79: "Le première operation, qui est le lieu du concept ab-
strait, ne peut plus correspondre qu'au niveau de la logique et systématisation" (p.
264). Owens ("Judgment and Truth," 44) locates the problem at the metaphysical
level: "Because there are the two factors, quiddity and existence, in the thing itself,
there are the two corresponding activities in the intellect. . . ." Cf. Philippe, *op.
cit.,* 274: "l'*ens,* qui est au delà de la distinction quiddité-*esse,* est au delà de la
distinction des deux opérations et que, par le fait même, il fonde et justifie cette
distinction."

30. See *In Metaph.,* VI, lect. 2 (Cathala-Spiazzi, n. 1171, p. 301): ". . . ens simpliciter, idest universaliter dictum, dicitur multipliciter . . ."; *SLE,* I, 7, 1096b26,
199–200; 206–7 [*In Ethic.,* I, lect. 7 [Spiazzi, n. 96, p. 25]): ". . . bonum dicitur de
multis non secundum rationes penitus differentes . . . dicuntur omnia bona magis
secundum analogiam, id est proportionem eandem . . ."; *ST,* I, q. 5, a. 6, ad 1: ". . .
bonum, inquantum est idem subiecto cum ente, dividitur per decem praedicamenta . . ."; *I Sent.,* d. 19, q. 5, a. 2 (Mandonnet, 493): ". . . bonitas qua unumquodque
formaliter est bonum, diversa est in diversis."

31. See *II Sent.,* d. 1, q. 1, a. 1 (Mandonnet, 12–13): "Invenitur enim in omnibus
rebus natura entitatis, in quibusdam magis nobilis, et in quibusdam minus . . .
natura entitatis sit unius rationis in omnibus secundum analogiam. . . ."

speculative and practical intellect.[32] But the immediate judgments of speculative and practical reason, which are founded respectively on the *ratio* of "being" and the *ratio* of "good," only result from the second operation of the intellect. As adding to the *ratio* of *"ens"* a relationship to appetite, the *ratio* of *"bonum"* ("that which everything seeks"[33]) is applied analogously to (a) the objects of the antecedent natural inclinations of the will, and (b) the objects of the proper acts of the will taken as acts of intellectual appetite. Applied precisely to the objects of the *acts* of the will, the meaning or *ratio* of "good" contains both the notes of being intellectually "desirable" and of being intellectually pursued as an "end." The first note, *"bonum"* as having the *ratio* of *"appetible,"* characterizes the *simplex conceptio* that practical intellect has of any being that de facto corresponds to (i.e., is the object of) a natural inclination;[34] the latter note, *"bonum"* as having

32. See *In Metaph.*, I, lect. 2 (Cathala-Spiazzi, n. 46, p. 13): "Sed dicendum, quod magis universalia secundum simplicem apprehensionem sunt primo nota, nam primo in intellectu cadit ens . . ."; *De ver.*, q. 21, a. 4 ad 4 (Spiazzi, 383): ". . . primo cadit in apprehensione intellectus, est ens . . ."; *ST,* I–II, q. 94, a. 2: "Sicut enim ens est primum quod cadit in apprehensione simpliciter, ita bonum est primum quod in apprehensione practicae rationis, quae ordinatur ad opus. . . ."

33. See *ST,* I–II, q. 94, a. 2: ". . . [ratio] boni, quae est, *Bonum est quod omnia appetunt."*

34. Ramirez *(De actibus humanis,* 4: 105–7) denies that "simple apprehension" (which he equates with the first operation of practical intellect) is prior to the first judgments of *practical* reason; he argues that as the *ratio* of "truth" does not fall under the "simple apprehension of the [theoretical] intellect," a fortiori, the *ratio* of "good," which is a transcendental that is subsequent to "truth," does not fall under the simple apprehension of the pracical intellect: ". . . ratio formalis boni nequit haberi in simplici apprehensione practica, sed in solo iudicio practico" (106).

Aquinas, however, allows that "truth" falls, *secundum quid,* under the *simplex conceptio* of the practical as well as the speculative intellect. The object of the practical intellect is the truth related to action: see *De ver.*, q. 22, a. 10, ad 4 (Spiazzi, 405); quoted in n. 59 below. Both "truth" and "good" "are founded on the intention of being": ". . . verum et bonum, secundum proprias intentiones, fundantur supra intentionem entis" (*I Sent.*, d. 19, q. 5, a. 1, ad 8 [Mandonnet, 490]). "Truth" adds to the *ratio* of *"ens"* a relationship to the intellect; "good" a relationship to appetite: ". . . bonitas dicit rationem per quam essentia ordinatur ad appetitum, ita veritas dicit rationem per quam essentia ordinatur ad intellectum" (*I Sent.*, d. 19, q. 5, a. 1, ad 2 [Mandonnet, 488]). A being *(ens)*, however, is comprised of its quiddity and its act of being *(esse)*; but *"ens"* is "imposed from *esse"* (Ibid., a. 5 [p. 486]). Because *"verum"* adds the notion of the intellect being commensurate to the *esse* of the thing, "truth" can only be properly discovered through the second operation of the intellect which bears on *esse.* But since a quiddity is an *esse rationis,* truth may be said, *secundum quid,* to also fall under the intellect's first operation: ". . . etiam quidditatis esse est quoddam esse rationis, et secundum istud esse dicitur veritas in prima operatione intellectus . . ." (Ibid., ad 7 [489]).

the *ratio* of *"finis,"* is precisely grasped when practical intellect immediately judges that the good that is naturally desired but not yet possessed is, accordingly, a "good that is to be done."[35]

3. The Cognitive and Appetitive Sources of the Natural Law

With these distinctions in place, we can more precisely locate, from what Aquinas says in a variety of contexts, the cognitive and appetitive sources of the natural law. In regard to both its speculative and practical *ends*, intellect has a *duplex operatio*.[36] In the order of nature, practical intellect through simple apprehension cognitively grasps the basic human goods in a twofold way: (1) by its first operation, the simple conception (or what we might call "insight"[37]) into the human good as

---

Ramirez's second argument is based on the premise that "differentia practici [intellectus] et speculativi [intellectus] non est differentia potentiae, sed actus" (106). There can be no act of simple apprehension (= *simplex conceptio*) attributed to practical intellect, which "is naturally posterior to speculative intellect" (ibid.), because its act would then be subsequent to speculative reason's act of simple apprehension. But the act of simple apprehension (= *simplex conceptio*), since it is the first act of intellect, cannot be posterior to any other act. The simple rejoinder to this argument is to distinguish what is absolutely first, the *simplex conceptio* of *"ens"* in the order of speculative reason, from what is relatively first, the *simplex conceptio* of *"bonum"* in the order of practical intellect. So distinguished, the *simplex conceptio* of "good" does not follow upon any previous act in its own order. The argument is misdirected, however, because of its premise. Practical reason differs from speculative reason not because of its acts but *"secundum finem"*: see *SLA*, III, c. 9, 433a14, 46 (*In de An.*, III, lect. 15 [Pirotta, n. 820, p. 194]). A difference in its end does not require that we negate the *"duplex operatio intellectus"* in regard to practical reason.

35. Cf. *III Sent.*, d. 27, q. 1, a. 4, ad 11 (Moos, n. 90, p. 871): ". . . finis ratio proprie respicit motus et operationem et ordinem rei ad rem, et non esse rei absolute."

36. Cf. Ramirez, *De actibus humanis*, 4: pars 1, q. 9, a. 1, §1, n. 144, p. 107: ". . . videtur quod simplex apprehensio sit ante bifurcationem intellectus in speculativum et practicum, et pertinet ad intellectum simpliciter ut primus motus vel actus eius." But it is not the intellect that is "bifurcated"; its ends are: ". . . intellectus practicus differt a speculativo fine; finis enim speculativi est veritas absolute, sed practici est operatio . . ." (*De ver.*, q. 3, a. 1 [Spiazzi, 68]). Granted, the end of the speculative intellect (grasping the truth about *ens*) has a certain logical/ontological priority. But Aquinas describes the *simplex conceptio* of *"bonum,"* by which practical intellect *"ordinatur ad opus,"* as exactly parallel to speculative intellect's *simplex conceptio* of *"ens"*: "Sicut autem ens est primum quod cadit in apprehensione simpliciter, ita bonum est primum quod cadit in apprehensione practicae rationis, quae ordinatur ad opus." (*ST*, I–II, q. 94, a. 2).

37. In its basic sense, conceptual "insight" is "the simple intuition of the intellect into the intelligible that is present to it": "Intelligere autem dicit nihil aliud quam simplicem intuitum intellectus in id quod sibi est praesens intelligibile" (*I*

"desirable";[38] and (2) by its second operation, the immediate or nondiscursive judgments that prescribe the pursuing or the doing of the human good as an "end."[39] Consequent to these two acts of practical intellect, there are two elicited acts of the will that bear on the good that practical intellect first grasps:[40] (1a) the absolute willing of the good (= *simplex actus voluntatis* = *voluntas* = *velle*); (2a) the act of willing the good, grasped as an end desired but not yet possessed, and hence as an end to be attained by some means (= *intentio voluntatis* = *intendere*).[41]

This schema indicates that the naturally desired goods that are judgmentally prescribed in the *per se nota* practical principles are the goods that, in a metaphysical or natural order of priority, are first the object of simple intellectual insight and then *simplex actus voluntatis*.[42] The fact that these goods are prescribed connotes intellectual awareness of

---

Sent., d. 3, q. 5, a. 4 [Mandonnet, 122]). "Insight" is first attained when the intelligibility latent in the sensible phantasm is actually grasped through the abstractive power of the agent intellect: see *ST*, I, q. 84, a. 7. But *"intelligentia indivisibilium"* and its Thomistic synonyms connote both the reception of a simple intelligible into the possible intellect (*I Sent.*, d. 35, q. 1, a. 1, ad 4) and the consequent mental expression of the intellectual insight into that simple intelligible (*I Sent.*, d. 27, q. 2, a. 1): "Intellectus enim simplicem et absolutam apprehensionem designare videtur: ex hoc enim aliquis intelligere dicitur quod interius in ipsa rei essentia veritatem quodammodo legit" (*De ver.*, q. 15, a. 1 [Spiazzi, 307]). As can be discerned from the various redactions of *SCG*, I, 53, these aspects, reception and expression, become ever more sharply distinguished in the doctrine of the *verbum interius*, see *SCG*, IV, 11; *ST*, I, q. 27, a. 1; *Super Joannem*, I, lect. 1. For a famous discussion of this topic, see Lonergan, *Verbum: Word and Idea in Aquinas*.

38. See *ST*, II–II, q. 153, a. 5: "Sunt autem rationes quatuor actus in agendis. Primo quidem, simplex intelligentia quae apprehendit aliquem finem ut bonum."

39. See *De ver.*, q. 22, a. 13, ad 4 (Spiazzi, 411): ". . . relatio in finem activa est rationis; eius enim est referre in finem. . . ."

40. In regard to the necessity of coupling (a) *intellectus-velle*, and (b) *iudicium synderesis-intendere*: see *ST*, I–II, q. 8, a. 2; *De ver.*, q. 17, a. 1, ad 4; q. 22, a. 14, ad 3. Cf. esp. *De ver.*, q. 23, a. 3 (Spiazzi, 420): "Quantum ad prosecutionem boni, est duplex signum voluntatis: nam respectu boni necessarii, sine quo non potest voluntas finem suum consequi, est signum voluntatis praeceptum; respectu autem boni utilis, quo faciliori modo et convenientiori acquiritur finis, est signum voluntatis consilium."

41. See *De ver.*, q. 22, a. 13 (Spiazzi, 411): ". . . obiectum huius actus qui est intentio, sit bonum, quod est finis. . . . Non tamen est [intentio] actus voluntatis absolute, sed in ordine ad rationem."

42. See *De ver.*, q. 22, a. 13 (Spiazzi, 411): "Unde voluntas potest habere duplicem actum. Unum, qui competit ei secundum suam naturam, in quantum tendit in proprium obiectum absolute; et hic actus attribuitur voluntati simpliciter, ut velle et amare. . . . Alium vero actum habet, qui competit ei secundum id quod ex impressione rationis relinquitur in voluntate . . . et modo intendere est actus voluntatis. . . ."

a certain distance between the will and its object: they are ends to be pursued by some or other means because they are not yet actually possessed.[43] Mediating this distance characterizes the act of intention *(intendere)* as distinguished from the immediate or absolute or simple willing *(velle)* of these goods.[44] Thus the practical intellect's immediate "judgments of synderesis" *(iudicia synderesis)* are followed by the volitional act of intending the ends prescribed. From the good that is cognitively prescribed and volitionally intended emerge all the subsequent acts of intellect and will that bear on the determinate means that will allow this good to be realized or pursued through deliberating about and choosing a particular action.[45]

This way of coupling the initial acts of practical intellect and will bearing on the ends of human action *(simplex conceptio-velle, iudicium synderesis-intendere)* preserves the parallelism that Aquinas draws between speculative and practical intellects in regard to their respective apprehension of *ens* and *bonum*.[46] As the first principle of theoretical reason is based on the *simplex conceptio* of *"ens,"* so too the first principle of practical reason is based on the *simplex conceptio* of *"bonum."*[47] This parallelism grounds the schema for the complete human

43. See *ST*, I–II, q. 11, a. 4: "Habetur autem finis dupliciter: uno modo, perfecte; et alio modo, imperfecte. Perfecte quidem, quando habetur non solum in intentione, sed etiam in re. . . ."

44. See *II Sent.*, d. 38, q. 1, a. 3 (Mandonnet, 974): "Per hoc quod dicitur in aliquid tendere, importatur quaedam distantia illius in quod aliquid tendit; et ideo quando appetitus fertur immediate in aliquid, non dicitur esse intentio illius, sive hoc sit finis ultimus, sive sit aliquid ad finem ultimum: sed quando per unum quod vult, in aliud pervenire nititur, illius in quod pervenire nititur, dicitur esse intentio. Hoc autem est finis: propter quod intentio dicitur esse de fine, non secundum quod voluntas in finem absolute fertur, sed secundum quod ex eo quod est ad finem, in finem tendit"; *De ver.*, q. 22, a. 15 (Spiazzi, 414): "Sic ergo patet quod voluntatis actus est velle et intendere. Sed velle prout ratio proponit voluntati aliquid bonum absolute. . . . Intendere vero, secundum quod ratio proponit ei bonum ut finem consequendum ex eo quod est ad finem."

45. See *De ver.*, q. 22, a. 13; a. 15.

46. See *Quod.* VIII, q. 2, a. 2 (Spiazzi, 162): "Et similiter in intellectu insunt nobis etiam naturaliter quaedam conceptiones omnibus notae, ut entis, boni, et huiusmodi, a quibus eodem modo procedit intellectus et cognoscendum quidditatem uniuscuiusque rei, per quem procedit a principiis per se notis ad cognoscendas conclusiones. . . ."

47. See *In Metaph.*, IV, lect. 6 (Cathala-Spiazzi, n. 605, pp. 167–68): ". . . duplex sit operatio intellectus . . . in utroque est aliquod primum: in prima quidem operatione est aliquod primum, quod cadit in conceptione intellectus, scilicet hoc quod dico ens . . . hoc principium, impossibile est esse et non esse simul, dependet ex intellectu entis . . . ideo hoc etiam principium est naturaliter primum in secunda operatione intellectus, scilicet componentis et dividentis." Cf. Étienne Gilson, "Les Principes et les causes," in *Constantes philosophique de l'être*, 53–84

act found in many of the traditional Thomist commentators.[48] The traditional schema, which Pinckaers has brilliantly exploited,[49] provides a complete foundation, in the *duplex operatio* of the practical intellect and in the two corresponding acts of the will, for *per se nota* prescriptions of natural law that bear on the basic goods or natural ends of human action.[50] This dual foundation, first in intellect and second in will, though it is presently somewhat neglected and perhaps controversial,[51] better explains why practical reason *necessarily* prescribes certain goods. Given human nature and its innate inclinations, certain goods, although men remain free to choose whether or not to think about them or whether or not to pursue them through appropriate means, are (*de re*) necessary for nature's fulfillment. These goods are not merely objects of man's contingent desires; they are the proper objects of various human powers, and hence they are the objects of the will's natural or necessary inclinations.[52]

[revised version of an article published in *Revue thomiste* 52 (1952): 39–63]: ". . . il existe deux principes premiers de la connaisance, en raison de la double nature des opérations de l'intellect . . . quelque chose est premier dan chacune de ces deux sortes opérations" (58).

48. See F. C.-R. Billuart, *Summa sancti Thomae*, dissert. 3, prologus (Palmé ed., 2: 264).

49. See Pinckaers, *Les Actes humains*, I: 414–37.

50. Cf. *De ver.*, q. 1, a. 1 (Spiazzi, 3): "In anima autem est vis cognitiva et appetitiva. Convenientiam ergo entis ad appetitum exprimit hoc nomen bonum . . ."; *ST*, I–II, q. 19, a. 3, ad 1: ". . . bonum sub ratione boni, idest appetibilis, per prius pertinet ad voluntatem quam ad rationem. Sed tamen per prius pertinet ad rationem sub ratione veri, quam ad voluntatem sub ratione appetibilis . . ."; q. 94, a. 2 (my italics): ". . . omnia illa ad quae homo habet naturalem inclinationem, ratio naturaliter apprehendit ut bona, et *per consequens* ut opere prosequenda . . ."; *SCG*, II, 48 (Pera, n. 1243, p. 169): "Forma apprehensa est principium movens secundum quod apprehenditur sub ratione boni vel convenientis. . . . Si igitur iudicans ad iudicandum seipsum moveat, oportet quod per aliquam altiorem formam apprehensam se moveat ad iudicandum. Quae quidem esse non potest nisi ipsa ratio boni vel convenientis . . ."; *SLA*, II, c. 28, 427b21, 274–81 (*In de An.*, III, lect. 4 [Pirotta, n. 635, p. 156]): ". . . appetitus non patitur neque mouetur ad simplicem apprehensionem rei qualem proponit fantasia, set oportet quod apprehendatur sub ratione boni uel mali, conuenientis uel nociui, et hoc facit opinio in hominibus, componendo uel diuidendo, cum opinamur hoc esse terribile vel malum, illud autem esse sperabile uel bonum. . . ."

51. Cf. Germain G. Grisez, "The First Principle," 193: "Nor is any operation of our own will presupposed by the first principles of practical reason"; "Natural Law and Natural Inclinations: Some Comments and Clarifications," *New Scholasticism* 61 (1987): 307: ". . . according to St. Thomas no operation of our will is presupposed by the first principles of practical reason."

52. See *De ver.*, q. 22, a. 5 (Spiazzi, 397): "Unde et voluntati ipsi inest naturalis quidam appetitus sibi convenientis boni."

As Aquinas describes them, the initial acts of practical reasoning begin from the fact of the will's natural inclinations and those objects that necessarily *(de re)* satisfy them.[53] In accordance with this given relationship, practical intellect has an *immediate* or noninferential cognitive grasp of certain objects as perfective goods. As an elicited appetite following upon the simple intellectual conception of these goods, the will necessarily desires them *(= velle)*. Knowing them both as good and as necessarily desired, practical intellect immediately judges (i.e., prescribes) that these perfective goods are ends that ought to be pursued since they are not yet possessed. These judgments are "objective" in that they prescribe pursuing the intellectually grasped, necessary objects of human desire.

The basic or most common precepts of the natural law are nondiscursive *dictamina* of practical reason enjoining the pursuit of certain volitional objects that are self-evidently good to all practically rational human agents.[54] These are the goods that are necessary *(de re)* for fulfilling our natural desires. The immediate or *per se nota* precepts enjoin *ends* toward which we are already naturally inclined, and hence which we immediately recognize as good when we begin to reason in order to act.[55] Practical knowledge of the good amounts to an intelli-

---

53. See *III Sent.*, d. 27, q. 1, a. 2, ad 4 (Moos, n. 50, p. 863): ". . . ratio procedit de appetitu naturali . . . ."

54. See *ST*, I–II, q. 94, a. 6: ". . . ad legem naturalem pertinent primo quidem quaedam pracepta communissima, quae sunt omnibus nota. . . ." John I. Jenkins, in "Good and the Object of Natural Inclination in St. Thomas Aquinas," in *Medieval Philosophy and Theology* 3 (1993): 74, contends that ". . . we cannot suppose that the principles of practical reason—or any other science for that matter—are, at least initially, espistemically basic for a subject." Jenkins attempts to reach this remarkable conclusion by assimilating (69–76) the first principles of practical reason to the first premises of certain *particular* theoretical sciences. In some of the natural sciences, those which are not subalternated to the mathematical sciences, no one grasps the naturally immediate or *per se nota in se* principles of the science; such principles are not *per se nota quoad nos*. Hence, in these sciences, there can be only *quia* demonstrations, i.e., demonstrations that proceed from mediate premises that do not embody knowledge of the cause of the conclusion: see *Apo.*, I, 13; *ELP*, I, 23–25. However, Aquinas's claim about the *per se nota* character of the primary precepts of the natural law is exactly pitched at the level of the most general principles of both theoretical and practical reason; clearly, Aquinas takes both sets of these principles to be immediate *in se*, and—more pertinently here—*quoad nos*: "Sic igitur patet quod, quantum ad communia principia rationis sive speculativae sive practicae, est eadem veritas seu rectitudo apud omnes, et aequaliter nota" (*ST*, I–II, q. 94, a. 4).

55. See *SCG*, III, 136 (Pera, n. 3114, p. 208): "Praeceptum *[Crescite et multiplicamini]* enim illud respicit inclinationem naturalem quae est in hominibus ad conservandum speciem per actum generationis. . . ."

gent apprehension (insight) and rational prescription of the *(de re)* necessary objects of our natural inclinations.[56] As our natural inclinations or desires are both sensible (concupiscible and irascible) and rational (volitional),[57] so too practical intellect immediately apprehends and prescribes that some sensible and intelligible goods are ends that are to be done and to be pursued.

Although prescription is an act of practical reason, desire or willing plays an irreducible role in the Thomistic psychological account of the natural law.[58] The *simplex conceptio* of the basic goods, by which practical intellect grasps them as good but "under the aspect of truth" *(sub ratione veri)*,[59] is an immediate cognitive grasp of what satisfies the will's natural inclinations. But only inasmuch as we actually desire *(= velle)* these basic goods can practical intellect actually prescribe them as ends *"sub ratione boni."*[60] Here the differences between the ends of speculative and practical intellect,[61] as well as the reciprocity between practical intellect and will, are of the utmost importance in clarifying certain features of Thomistic natural law doctrine. However

---

Let us note that the precept "looks back to" *(respicit)* the inclination, not that the inclination "looks forward" to the precept. Cf. Jenkins, in "Good and the Object of Natural Inclination," 86, who maintains that ". . . Aquinas's view was that we infer what is good for us by considering that to which we are inclined (i.e., that which we genuinely factually desire)." But throughout his article, Jenkins conflates (a) giving a theoretical/metaphysical explanation of why practical reason grasps X as a *per se notum* good, and (b) the fact that for practical reason X is a *per se notum* good. However, according to everything that Aquinas explicitly says, knowing the latter "basic proposition" does not epistemically depend upon the former.

56. See *ST*, I–II, q. 41, a. 3: ". . . amor et odium, desiderium et fuga, important inclinationem quandam ad prosequendum bonum et fugiendum malum; quae quidem inclinatio pertinet etiam ad appetitum naturalem."

57. See *SLA*, III, c. 8, 432b3, 111–18 *(In de An.*, III, lect. 14 [Pirotta, n. 802, p. 190]): ". . . Si quis distinguat partes anime in tres subiecto distinctas, scilicet rationale, irascibile et concupiscibile, sequetur quod in unoquoque eorum erit appetitus: in rationatiua enim uoluntas, ut dictum est, irascibilis autem est appetitus et similiter concupiscibilis; erunt igitur tres appetitus in anima. . . ."

58. As there are "principia naturaliter cognita tam scibilium quam agendorum," so too ". . . in voluntate inest quidam naturalis appetitus boni quod est secundum rationem" *(ST*, I–II, q. 63, a. 1). Thus "voluntas naturaliter aliquid vult" (q. 10, a. 1, ad 1).

59. See *De ver.*, q. 22, a. 10, ad 4 (Spiazzi, 405): ". . . obiectum intellectus practici non est bonum, sed verum relatum ad opus"; *ST*, I–II, q. 19, a. 3: "Nam bonum intellectus est obiectum voluntatis proportionatum ei. . . ."

60. See *De ver.*, q. 22, a. 13 (Spiazzi, 411): "Unde, cum ratio proponit sibi aliquid ut absolute bonum, voluntas movetur in illud absolute; et hoc est velle"; *ST*, I–II, q. 11, a. 1: "Finis autem et bonum est obiectum appetitivae potentiae."

61. See *De ver.*, q. 3, a. 1; quoted in n. 36 *supra*.

many truths the agent possesses about the world and man, the speculative intellect as such does not grasp the ends of human action under the peculiar *ratio boni* that is relevant to action, that is, as rationally desired goods that ought to be pursued.[62] Thus, it is not merely practical insight into what is rationally desirable for us to do, but practical insight in conjunction with actually desiring these necessary goods, that leads to practical intellect immediately prescribing these as ends that we must pursue.[63]

4. Practical Judgments

Aquinas distinguishes a theoretical from a practical judgment by characterizing the latter as a judgment that is ordered to action. Ethics is a practical science because it makes universal judgments about what is to be done or not done.[64] Prudence tailors these universal judgments to singular actions that here and now are to be done or not done.[65] Yet the prudent man or woman can know what he or she is required to do and not actually do it. Practical judgments, therefore, can be merely habitual or virtually practical rather than actually practical.[66] But even actually practical judgments enjoining what is to be done need not be acted upon;[67] they prompt an action only when practical reason com-

---

62. See *De ver.*, q. 3, a. 3, ad 6 (Spiazzi, p. 69): ". . . idea practica et speculativa in Deo non distinguuntur quasi duae ideae; sed quia secundum rationem intelligendi, practica addit super speculativam ordinem ad actum . . ."; *ST,* I–II, q. 9, a. 1, ad 2: ". . . Sicut imaginatio formae sine aestimatione convenientis vel nocivi, non movet appetitum sensitivum; ita nec apprehensio veri sine ratione boni et appetibilis. Unde intellectus speculativus non movet, sed intellectus practicus. . . ." Cf. Grisez, "Natural Law and Natural Inclinations," 310.

63. See *SLA*, III, c. 9, 433a14, 65–71 (*In de An.*, III, lect. 15 [Pirotta, n. 821, p. 195]): "Vnde rationabiliter dictum est quod hec duo sunt mouencia, appetitus et intellectus practicus; quia enim ipsum appetibile mouet, quod est primum consideratum ab intellectu practico, propter hoc dicitur intellectus practicus mouere, quia scilicet eius principium, quod est appetibile, mouet"; *De pot.*, q. 1, a. 5 (Pession, 19): "Sed intellectus non movet nisi in quantum proponit voluntati suum appetibile; unde totum movere intellectum est in voluntate."

64. See *De virt.*, q. 1, a. 6 (Odetto, 723): ". . . nam ad scientiam practicam pertinet universale iudicium de agendis; sicut fornicationem esse malam, furtum non esse faciendum, et huiusmodi." Cf. *SLE,* VI, 9, 1143a7, 43–65 (*In Ethic.*, VI, lect. 9 [Spiazzi, nn. 1239–30, p. 337]).

65. See *De virt.*, q. 1, a. 6 (Odetto, 723): "Sed ad prudentiam pertinet recte iudicare de singulis agibilibus, prout sint nunc agenda: quod quidem iudicium corrumpitur per quodlibet peccatum."

66. See *De ver.*, q. 3, a. 3.

67. See *ST,* II–II, q. 51, a. 3, ad 3.

plements the judgment by a prescription (= command) that enacts what has been judged and chosen.[68]

Judgment about things to be done is ordered to something further. For it sometimes happens that someone judges well about doing something, but he does not rightly carry it out. But the ultimate conclusion is when reason rightly prescribes about what is to be done. (*ST,* I–II, q. 57, a. 6, ad 2)[69]

Aquinas, as in the above text, sometimes neatly separates practical judgments from precepts (which we can more precisely identify as "commands") that actually carry out or enact the judgment. It would be a mistake, however, to infer that practical judgments do not bear directly on actions, or are not in themselves prescriptive.[70] In the practical sphere, Aquinas retains an Augustinian notion of judgment: a judgment is the application of a rule.[71] Unlike a theoretical judgment that states what is or is not the case, a practical judgment states what ought to be or ought not to be the case.[72] A practical judgment

68. See *SLE,* VI, 9, 1143a7, 44–55 *(In Ethic.,* VI, lect. 9 [Spiazzi, n. 1239, p. 337]): ". . . in speculativis, in quibus non est actio, est solum duplex opus rationis, scilicet invenire inquirendo et de inventis iudicare; et haec quidem duo opera sunt etiam rationis practicae, cuius inquisitio est consilium, quod pertinet ad eubuliam, iudicium autem de consiliatis pertinet ad synesim . . . non autem stat hic ratio practica, sed ulterius procedit ad agendum et ideo necessarium est tertium opus quasi finale et completivum, scilicet praecipere quod procedatur ad actum, et hoc proprie pertinet ad prudentiam"; *ST,* I–II, q. 57, a. 6: ". . . iudicium in agendis ad aliquid ulterius ordinatur. . . . Sed ultimum complementum est quando ratio iam bene praecipit de agendis"; II–II, q. 47, a. 8: "Secundus actus [prudentiae] est iudicare de inventis: et hic sistit speculativa ratio. Sed practica ratio, quae ordinatur ad opus, procedit ulterius, et est tertius actus eius praecipere: qui quidem actus consistit in applicatione consiliatorum et iudicatorum ad operandum"; *De virt. card.,* q. 1, a. 1 (Odetto, 815): "Ex parte cognitionis practicae tria requiruntur. Quorum primum est consilium; secundum est iudicium de consiliatis; sicut etiam in ratione speculativa invenitur inventio vel inquisitio, et iudicium. Sed quia intellectus practicus praecipit fugere vel prosequi, quod non facit speculativus intellectus . . . ideo tertio ad rationem practicam pertinet praemeditari de agendis; et hoc est praecipuum ad quod alia duo ordinantur."

69. ". . . iudicium in agendis ad aliquid ulterius ordinatur; contingit enim aliquem bene iudicare de aliquo agendo, et tamen non recte exequi. Sed ultimum complementum est, quando ratio iam bene praecipit de agendis" *(ST,* I–II, q. 57, a. 6, ad 2).

70. See *ST,* I–II, q. 74, a. 7: "Cum autem de pluribus occurrit judicandum, finale judicium est de eo quod ultimo occurrit. In actibus autem humanis ultimo occurrit ipse actus. . . ."

71. See Garceau, *Judicium,* 162: "Le jugement pratique . . . consiste à déterminer d'après une norme ce qui devrait être fait. . . ." For the Augustinian background, see ibid., 62–69.

72. See *ST,* I–II, q. 93, a. 3, ad 3: ". . . iudicare de aliquo potest intelligi dupliciter.

(iudicium/sententia) is the conclusion of a practical syllogism. The conclusion states what action the agent ought to do or not to do,[73] and it is immediately linked with choice and the action that, once commanded, follows: "In conferring about what is to be done, [practical reason] uses a syllogism, whose conclusion is a judgment or a choice or an operation" *(ST,* I–II, q. 76, a. 1).[74] Although practical reason may have judged what is to be done, prescribing something is not the same as actually pursuing it.[75] Pursuit involves the will.

> Practical knowledge taken unconditionally relates commonly to knowledge of the end and of the means. But it does not presuppose willing the end, as though knowledge in some way includes the will. *(De ver.,* q. 5, a. 1, ad 2 [Spiazzi, 90])[76]

Aquinas, accordingly, distinguishes *(ST,* I–II, q. 17, a. 1) between prescriptions that appear in indicative judgments (gerundives) but which lack the determinate volitional impetus to move the agent to act here and now, and prescriptions put in imperative form (commands) that do effectively move the agent.[77] Practical reason, when it follows upon the volitional act of choice, is the source of the prudential *command* that moves the agent to attain practical reason's ends through some determinate means.[78]

5. The Intellectual and Volitional Elements
of the Complete Human Act

The distinction between practical judgment and command falls within Aquinas's account of the psychological complex of partial intel-

---

Uno modo sicut vis cognitiva diiudicat de proprio obiecto . . . an sit verum quod proponitur. Alio modo, secundum superior iudicat de inferiori quodam practico iudicio, an scilicet ita debeat esse vel non ita."

73. See *ST,* I–II, q. 13, a. 1, ad 2; II–II, q. 51, a. 2, ad 2; a. 3.

74. "Conferans enim de agendis, utitur quodam syllogismo, cuius conclusio est iudicium seu electio vel operatio" *(ST,* I–II, q. 76, a. 1).

75. See *ST,* I–II, q. 57, a. 6, ad 2: ". . . iudicium in agendis ad aliquid ulterius ordinatur: contingit enim aliquem bene iudicare de aliquo agendo, et tamen non recte exequi."

76. ". . . Scientia enim practica absolute communiter se habet ad cognitionem finis et eorum quae sunt ad finem; unde non praesupponit voluntatem finis, ut sic aliquo modo voluntas scientia includatur . . ." *(De ver.,* q. 5, a. 1, ad 2 [Spiazzi, 90]).

77. See *II Sent.,* d. 38, q. 1, a. 3 (Mandonnet, 975): ". . . intellectus practicus dicit aliquid de fugiendo vel prosequendo . . . unde judicium fugae et prosecutionis ad intellectum practicum pertinet, non autem ipsa prosecutio et fuga."

78. See *ST,* II–II, q. 83, a. 1: ". . . ad rationem practicam pertinet causare aliquid per modum imperii. . . ."

lectual and volitional acts that together comprise the complete human act. Traditionally, these acts are divided into two groups, those bearing on (a) the end, and (b) the means: (1a) the simple practical insight into the end *(simplex conceptio)*; (2a) the unconditional or simple act of willing the end *(velle)*; (3a) the immediate prescriptive judgment of synderesis about the ends known and willed *(iudicium universale synderesis)*; (4a) the willing of the end thus prescribed *(intendere)*; (5b) deliberation about which means will allow one to attain the end *(consilium)*; (6b) volitional consent *(consensus)* to the various means discovered; (7b) judgment about which of the possible means is best *(iudicium practicum)*; (8b) the volitional choice *(electio)* of what has been judged best; (9b) practical reason's command *(imperium)* to do what has been chosen; (10b the volitional use *(usus)* of the human faculties that allow one to effect the command; (11a) the will's enjoyment *(fruitio)* of the end attained. These partial acts can be schematized as follows:[79]

Table I

Intellect	*Will*
(a) End	
1a. Simple practical insight into the end = *simplex conceptio*	2a. Simple or unconditional act of willing the end = *velle*
3a. Immediate prescriptive judgment about the ends known and willed = *iudicium universale synderesis*	4a. Willing the prescribed end = *intendere*
	11a. Enjoyment of the end attained = *fruitio*
(b) Means	
5b. Deliberation about which means will allow one to attain the end = *consilium*	6b. Consent to the various means discovered = *consensus*
7b. Judgment about which of the possible means is best = *iudicium practicum* = *iudicium electionis*	8b. Choice of what has been judged best = *electio*
9b. Practical reason's command to do what has been chosen = *imperium*	10b. Use of the human faculties that allow one to effect command = *usus*

79. See *ST,* I–II, q. 12, a. 1, ad 3: "Unde hoc nomen *intentio* nominat actum voluntatis, praesupposita ordinatione rationis ordinantis aliquid in finem"; *SLE,* III, 9, 1113a4, 19–25 *(In Ethic.,* III, lect. 9 [Spiazzi, n. 484, p. 136]): ". . . determinatio consilii praecedit electionem, quia oportet quod post inquisitionem consilii sequa-

If this schema is viewed as a sequential account of the temporal or phenomenological genesis of the complete human act, these distinct acts can seem redundantly convoluted and psychologically fragmented.[80] Hence, it is important to note that, except for the final volitional act (enjoying the end), Aquinas *pairs off* all the sequential acts of intellect and will. In each pair, the volitional act follows upon and is thus subordinate to the intellectual act. Yet Aquinas clearly emphasizes, from the beginning of his analysis, the enveloping volitional character of the complete human act.[81] In comparison, the traditional schema, even if it is rigorously understood to be a logical sequence, blunts the import of Aquinas's own order of analysis.[82] In the *Prima secundae*, Aquinas's analysis of these partial acts runs as follows: (q. 8) *voluntas*; (q. 11) *fruitio*; (q. 12) *intentio*; (q. 13) *electio*; (q. 14) *consilio*; (q. 15) *consensus*; (q. 16) *usus*; (q. 17) *imperium*. Thus Aquinas analyzes *electio* and *usus* before the proper moment of their logical genesis: genetically, *electio* follows *consilio* and *usus* follows *imperium*. For Aquinas, evidently, adhering exactly to the correct logical sequence of partial acts is less significant, at least in moral science, than showing how the complete human act is essentially an act of willing *(velle)* the end.[83]

---

tur iudicium de inventis per consilium et tunc primo eligitur id quod prius est iudicatum.

80. Cf. Donagan, "Thomas Aquinas on Human Action," 642–54; McInerny, "Donagan on Thomas on Action," in *Aquinas on Human Action*, 178–83.

R.-A. Gauthier, O.P., in a review of *Psychologie et morale aux xiie et xiiie siècles*, vol. 3, and *Principes de morale*, by D. Odon Lottin, in *Bulletin thomiste* 8, no. 1 (1947–51): 68, argues that *imperium* should properly precede the act of choice *(electio)* but opines that Aquinas, out of misplaced loyalty to John Damascene, explicitly placed it afterward. For convincing doctrinal refutations of Gauthier, see Th. Deman, O.P., "Le "Précepte" de la prudence chez saint Thomas d'Aquin," *Recherches de théologie ancienne et médiévale* 20 (1953): 40–59; Servais Pinckaers, O.P., review of "Le "Précepte" de la prudence chez saint Thomas d'Aquin," by Th. Deman, O.P., and of "Saint Maxime le Confesseur et la psychologie de l'acte humain," by R.-A. Gauthier, O.P., in *Bulletin thomiste* 9 (1954–56): 345–62.

81. See *ST*, I–II, q. 6, prologus: "Cum autem actus humani proprie dicantur qui sunt voluntarii . . . oportet considerare de actibus, inquantum sunt voluntarii."

82. See Ramirez, *De actibus humanis*, 4: pars 1, q. 13, §1, nn. 446–51, pp. 319–27.

83. Daniel Westberg, *Right Practical Reason: Aristotle, Action, and Prudence in Aquinas* (Oxford: Clarendon Press, 1994) argues that it is "more sensible, and more faithful to Thomas to combine *[simplex] apprehensio* with *iudicium circa finem*, and *velle* with *intentio*" (133). But how faithful is this suggested recombination which, in effect, eliminates the Thomistic "duplex operatio intellectus"? Westberg regards *ST*, I–II, q. 8 as "still part of the general account of the relation between desire and action" and that "only with q. 12 . . . begins . . . [Thomas's] special discussion of the actual process of human action." Cf. *ST*, I–II, q. 8,

Aquinas attempts, by halting the completion of the human act at various logically distinct or separable points, to show how the first unconditional act, the simple act of willing an end, is internally determined or specified rather than merely followed by these subsequent acts. *"Velle"* is the essential and causally prior act that englobes all the subsequent intellectual and volitional acts.[84] It is the primordial whole of which they are the dynamic parts.[85]

Willing is properly of the end itself. Those things that are for an end are not good or willed for their own sake but in relation to the end. Hence the will is not led to them except insofar as it is led to the end. Consequently, the very thing that it wills in them is the end. *(ST,* I–II, q. 8, a. 2)[86]

---

prologus: "Deinde considerandum est de ipsis actibus voluntariis *in speciali.* . . . Actus autem voluntatis in finem videntur esse tres: scilicet velle, frui et intendere" (Italics mine). Westberg is concerned to shows that, since "one cannot intend an end that is impossible . . . there can be speculative thought about *impossibilia* but certainly no practical reasoning" (138). But practical reasoning and intention *tout court* are not confined to what is possible: Aquinas allows *(ST,* I–II, q. 14, a. 5, ad 3) that we can deliberate whether some means is conducive to some intended end before figuring out whether such a means is possible. Only choice *(electio)* is confined to what is possible for me *(ST,* I–II, q. 13, a. 5); yet Aquinas precisely distinguishes choice from the first acts of practical intellect and will *(velle)* ". . . voluntas non semper est impossibilium, sed aliquando; et hoc sufficit, secundum intentionem Philosophi, ad ostendum differentiam inter voluntatem et electionem, quae semper est possibilium, ut scilicet eligere non sit omnino idem quod velle; et similiter nec intendere est omnino idem quod velle . . ." *(De ver.,* q. 22, a. 13, ad 12 [Spiazzi, 412]). Since the *iudicium universale synderesis* is about prescribing the pursuit of natural or necessary ends, it is not only sensible but requisite to distinguish it from any prescriptive judgment about a secondary end (which was, at some point, a matter for deliberation) or from any deliberative judgment about the *means* by which such secondary ends may be attained. At bottom, Westberg's "new interpretation" (134) obscures the fact that, for Aquinas, the primordial act of willing is *velle* not *intendere:* "Simplex autem actus potentiae est in id quod est secundum se obiectum potentiae. Id autem quod est propter se bonum et volitum, est finis. Unde voluntas proprie est ipsius finis" *(ST,* I–II, q. 8, a. 2). *Velle* bears on the end "absolute secundum se" (a. 3) since the end "habet per se rationem boni" *(II Sent.,* d. 24, q. 1, a. 3, ad 3 [Mandonnet, 598]). Consequently, Westberg overstates (in opposition to the alleged "voluntarism" of Thomist commentators) the identity between Aristotle's and Aquinas's account of practical reason as the source of human action.

84. See *ST,* I–II, q. 90, a. 1, ad 3: ". . . ex hoc enim quod aliquis vult finem, ratio imperat de his quae sunt ad finem."

85. See Servais Pinckaers, O.P., "La Structure de l'acte humaine suivant saint Thomas," *Revue thomiste* 55 (1955): 393–412.

86. "Unde voluntas proprie est ipsius finis. Ea vero quae sunt ad finem, non sunt bona vel volita propter seipsa, sed ex ordine ad finem. Unde voluntas in ea non fertur, nisi quatenus fertur in finem: unde hoc ipsum quod in eis vult, est finis" *(ST,* I–II, q. 8, a. 2).

The order in which Aquinas examines these partial acts reflects their relative importance within the dynamic process of willing *(velle)*. Thus *electio* and *usus,* which are essentially volitional acts, are discussed before the intellectual acts of *consilium* and *imperium,* even though genetically and logically they follow the latter acts.

Since the object of the will is the good taken unconditionally, Aquinas concedes, deferring to Aristotle, that one may desire and will, in an incomplete way *(= "voluntas incompleta"* or *"velleitas"),* even goods that are impossible for men or for an individual to attain.[87] The "impossibility" in question is real, not logical, that is, willing or "wishing" something that the agent cannot bring about through his own or his friends" actions: for example, to have an immortal body, or that someone else win a race or contest.[88] However, the primordial act of *velle* is not to be standardly assimilated to this kind of *velleitas* for the impossible. Standardly, *velle* is what gives rise to the agent's intention actually to attain something really attainable, that is, to will something as actually attainable through some chosen means *(= "voluntas completa").*

Still, not everything that is really possible for the agent to attain is willed as it is may be actually attained through some chosen means.[89] Hence, the distinction, which can be easily seen in those cases where the first act is temporally prior to the second, between absolutely willing an end *(velle)* and conditionally intending an end through some range of means *(intendere).* Consider the medical scientist searching for a cure for a hithertofore incurable disease; he wills an end that, given the history of successful medical invention, may be responsibly thought to be really attainable. The scientist, although he has yet no idea how to cure the disease, is not indulging a wish for something "impossible." Now, compare the medical scientist to an ordinary physician who intends to cure his patient of pneumonia by using some or other drug known to be efficacious. Even in the latter case, as Aquinas observes, an agent can intend an actually attainable end without having deliberated about or chosen the determinate means by which it is to be attained.[90] *Intention,* then, is the volitional act whereby an agent

---

87. See *SLE,* III, 5, 1111b20, 160–62 *(In Ethic.,* III, lect. 5 [Spiazzi, n. 444, p. 126]): "Sed voluntas, quia respicit bonum absolute, potest esse cuiuscumque boni, licet sit impossibile . . ."; *ST,* I–II, q. 13, a. 5: ". . . voluntas completa non est nisi de possibili, quod est bonum volenti. Sed voluntas incompleta est de impossibili: quae secundum quosdam velleitas dicitur, quia scilicet aliquis vellet illud, si esset possibile."

88. See *EN,* III, 2, 1111b20–25.

89. See *ST,* I–II, q. 8, a. 3, ad 3: ". . . voluntas aliquando vult finem, et tamen non procedit ad volendum id quod est ad finem."

90. See *ST,* I–II, q. 12, a. 4 ad 3: ". . . inquantum motus voluntatis fertur in id

wills an end that he knows himself to be really capable of attaining, in a way yet to be deliberated about and chosen, through one or another of the possible means.[91]

Practical reason is prudential when it deliberates in order to determine which means are available that will enable the agent to attain the desired end.[92] The act of *consent* is a volitional act; it is the application of the actual desire or inclination of the will to the various possible means that deliberation discovers.[93] Which of the several efficacious drugs known and available to him shall the physician use to cure his patient of pneumonia? *Deliberation* ends in a particular *judgment* about what is the best thing to do in order to attain the intended end.[94] *Judgment* is followed by *choice*[95] which is the volitional act of accepting[96] the means that have been judged to be prefer-

---

quod est ad finem, prout ordinatur ad finem, est electio. Motus autem voluntatis qui fertur in finem, secundum quod acquiritur per ea quae sunt ad finem, vocatur intentio. Cuius signum est quod intentio finis esse potest, etiam nondum determinatis his quae sunt ad finem, quorum est electio."

91. See *II Sent.*, d. 38, q. 1, a. 3 (Mandonnet, 974–75): ". . . intentio dicitur esse de fine non secundum quod voluntas in finem absolute fertur, sed secundum quod ex eo quod est ad finem, in finem tendit. Unde intentio in ratione sua ordinem quemdam unius ad alterum importat." If ends and means are considered as two separate goods, they then fall under two different acts of simple volition. But considered together, they constitute one object of the will; the end is like the form, the means like the matter: ". . . finis et id quod est ad finem, inquantum hujusmodi consideratum, non sunt diversa objecta, sed unum objectum in quo finis sicut formale est, quasi ratio quaedam volendi; sed id quod est ad finem est sicut materiale . . ." (*II Sent.*, d. 38, q. 1, a. 4 [Mandonnet, 977]). Thus the one act of will in regard to the end, *intentio*, covers both the end and the means that are willed for the sake of that end.

92. See *ST,* I–II, q. 58, a. 5, ad 1: ". . . ratio, secundum quod est apprehensiva finis, praecedit appetitum finis: sed appetitus finis praededit rationem ratiocinantem ad eligendum ea quae sunt ad finem, quod pertinet ad prudentiam."

93. See *ST,* I–II, q. 15, a. 3: ". . . applicatio appetitivi motus ad determinationem consilii, proprie est consensus"; a. 4: "Finalis autem sententia de agendis est consensus in actum." If deliberation finds only one such means, then there is no real difference to be placed between consent and choice: ". . . non differunt re consensus et electio, sed ratione tantum" (ibid., ad 3).

94. See *ST,* I–II, q. 83, a. 3 ad 2: ". . . iudicium est quasi conclusio et determinatio consilii"; *De ver.*, q. 23, a. 8, ad 4: ". . . electio habet in se et rationis iudicium, et appetitum. Si ergo aliquis iudicio praeferat id quod est minus bonum magis bono, erit perversitas electionis; non autem in appetendo. . . ."

95. See *De ver.*, q. 22, a. 15, ad 2 (Spiazzi, 414): ". . . quod practicae inquisitionis est duplex conclusio: una quae est in ratione, scilicet sententia, quae est iudicium de consiliatis; alia vero quae est in voluntate, et huiusmodi est electio: et dicitur conclusio per quamdam similitudinem, quia sicut in speculativis ultimo statur in conclusione, ita in operativis ultimo statur in operatione."

96. See *De ver.*, q. 22, a. 15 (Spiazzi, 413): "Electio enim est ultima acceptio qua aliquid accipitur ad prosequendum. . . ."

able or best.[97] *Intention* and *choice* differ inasmuch as the former focuses on the end as indeterminately attainable through one or another means, and the latter on the rationally preferred or determinate means.[98]

In actually making a choice, the agent always follows the *particular* judgment of reason as to what seems best to do here and now. Of course, the practical judgment about the particular act does not always lead to doing what is really best. Accordingly, Aquinas distinguishes two judgments about particular acts: (1) the judgment of free choice *(iudicium liberi arbitrii)*; (2) the judgment of conscience *(iudicium conscientiae)*. The latter is a purely cognitive judgment about what is best here and now; the former applies what is known to what is desired. Hence, if one acquiesces in one's bad desires, the judgment of free choice can be perverted and in contradiction to the judgment of one's conscience.[99] In either case, however, our choices remain free.

A free choice, considered as a volitional act, is one that follows upon a free practical judgment. As long as the agent's practical judgment is free, his or her choice is free. A judgment is free if no rational necessity compels us to make it. A free judgment is one that can be subsequently undone when made. Our choices remain free because we can reflexively judge or undo our previous judgments about what it is good for us to do.[100] We undo our initial judgment by changing our ranking of the goodness of the various possible means to an end; the ranking changes as we compare these means from one or another angle.[101] Since the proper object of the will is the universal or infinite good, no judgment about a finite good can ever rationally compel the will. But once a means has been chosen, then, if nothing intervenes,

97. See *ST,* I, q. 83, a. 3: "Ad electionem autem concurrit aliquid ex parte cognitivae virtutis . . . requiritur consilium, per quod diiudicatur quid sit alteri praeferendum . . ."; I–II, q. 13, a. 1, ad 1: ". . . electio importat collationem quandam praecedentem . . ."; ad 3: ". . . collatio quae importat in nomine electionis, pertinet ad consilium praecedens, quod est rationis"; I–II, q. 15, a. 3, ad 3: ". . . electio addit supra consensum quandam relationem respectu eius cui aliquid praeeligitur."

98. See *De ver.,* q. 22, a. 13, ad 16 (Spiazzi, 412): ". . . intentio est actus voluntatis in ordine ad rationem ordinantem ea quae sunt ad finem, in finem ipsum; sed electio est actus voluntatis in ordine ad rationem comparantem ea quae sunt in finem ad invicem; et propter hoc intentio et electio differunt."

99. See *II Sent.,* d. 24, q. 2, a. 4, ad 2; *De ver.,* q. 17, a. 1; q. 24, a. 2. That there are, in fact, two distinct judgments has been recently controverted: cf. McInerny, "The Right Deed for the Wrong Reason: Comments on Theo Belmans," in *Aquinas on Human Action,* 220–39; Théo G. Belmans, O. Praem., "Le 'Jugement prudentiel' chez saint Thomas," *Revue thomiste* 91 (1991): 414–20.

100. See *De ver.,* q. 24, a. 1, ad 1; ad 17; a. 2; a. 4.

101. See *II Sent.,* d. 25, q. 1, a. 2; *ST,* I–II, q. 13, a. 6.

reason *commands* that it be done. Finally, the volitional execution of what is commanded, the application of the powers and habits of the soul to activity, is *use*.[102]

6. Prescription

The logical schematization of the inner moments or determinants of the complete human act allows Aquinas to identify (*ST*, II–II, q. 47, a. 8) practical reason with its chief virtue, prudence, and prudence with its principal act, prescription.[103] Thomistic practical reason or prudence generates, but always in conjunction with the will, a human action by deliberating, judging, and prescribing.[104] All of these acts bear on the means to some intended end, and it is this means-end relationship that defines the sphere of prudence. Prudence bears on the means to the end.[105]

The will, although its acts follow upon the acts of the intellect, plays an essential role in Aquinas's account of prudence. Prudence is described as the virtue of practical reason that deals precisely with the means.

> Prudence is in the practical intellect or practical reason . . . the object of prudence is not determined from the will, but only the end. For prudence

102. See *ST*, I–II, q. 17, a. 3, ad 1: ". . . post determinationem consilii, quae est iudicium rationis, voluntas eligit; et post electionem, ratio imperat ei per quod agendum est quod eligitur; et tunc demum voluntas alicuius incipit uti, exequendo imperium rationis. . . ."

103. See *III Sent.*, d. 33, q. 3, a. 1, sol. 3 (Moos, n. 285, p. 1076): "Sed quia in operabilibus cognitio ordinatur ad opus, ideo et consilium et iudicium de consiliatis ad praeceptum de opere reducitur ad finem . . ."; *ST*, I, q. 22, a. 1, ad 1: ". . . prudentia proprie est praeceptiva eorum, de quibus eubulia recte consiliatur, et synesis recte iudicat"; I–II, q. 48, a. 1: "Prudentia vero est circa principalem actum, qui est praecipere"; q. 51, a. 3, ad 3: ". . . virtus principalis quae sit bene praeceptiva, scilicet prudentia"; q. 51, a. 2: "Et sicut consiliari ordinatur ad praecipere tanquam ad principalius, ita etiam eubulia ordinatur ad prudentia tanquam ad principaliorem virtutem"; q. 61, a. 3: ". . . prudentia dicatur quae praeceptiva est . . ."; II–II, q. 47, a. 2: "Ratio autem quae sunt agenda propter finem est ratio practica. Unde manifestum est quod prudentia non consistit nisi ratione practica"; q. 48, a. 1: "Prudentia vero est circa principalem actum, qui est praecipere."

104. See *ST*, I–II, q. 57, a. 6: "Circa agibilia autem humana tres actus rationis inveniuntur: quorum primus est consiliari, secundus iudicare, tertius est praecipere"; II–II, q. 47, a. 10: ". . . ad prudentiam pertinet recte consiliari, iudicare, et praecipere . . ."; q. 48, a. 1, obj. 4: ". . . consiliari et iudicare et praecipere sunt actus rationis practicae. . . ."

105. See *ST*, I–II, q. 47, a. 6: ". . . ad prudentiam non pertinet praestituere finem virtutibus moralibus, sed solum disponere de his quae sunt ad finem."

seeks after the object: on the presupposition that the will has a good end, prudence seeks after the ways through which this good is perfected and preserved. *(De virt.,* q. 1, a. 7 [Odetto, 724])[106]

The acts of deliberating, judging, and prescribing/commanding the means to an end are attributed to prudence. But deliberating, judging, and prescribing means presuppose that the agent intends the end toward which these deliberations, judgments, and prescriptions are directed.[107] Prudential or providential reason actively commands how to realize or achieve an end through a chosen means only if that end is already *intended* as a good.[108] Prudence includes or presupposes the intentional act of the will in regard to the end.[109] Because one wills the end, one can deliberate about, judge, and prescribe the means.[110]

Providence is [rooted] in the intellect, but it presupposes the act of willing the end. For no one prescribes about things to be done on account of an end unless he wills [that] end. *(ST,* I, q. 29, a. 1, ad 3)[111]

An action is prescribed, according to the general sense of prescription, when reason judges that it *ought* to be done or *ought not* to be done to achieve a good or to avoid an evil.[112] Particular prescriptive practical

106. "Prudentia vero est in intellectu sive ratione practica . . . non quidem ita quod ex voluntate determinetur obiectum prudentiae, sed solum finis; obiectum autem ipsa perquirit: praesupposito enim a voluntate fine boni, prudentia perquirit vias per quas hoc bonum et perficiatur est conservetur." *(De virt.,* q. 1, a. 7 [Odetto, 724])

107. See *De ver.,* q. 6, a. 1 (Spiazzi, 113): ". . . Solius rationis est dirigere vel ordinare. . . . Sed ad directionem in finem praeexigitur voluntas finis: nullus enim aliquid in finem ordinat quod non vult . . ."; *ST,* I, q. 22, a. 1, ad 3: ". . . nullus enim praecipit de agendis propter finem, nisi velit finem"; q. 23, a. 4: "Non autem praecipitur aliquid ordinatum in finem, nisi praeexistente voluntate finis."

108. See *De ver.,* q. 5, a. 1 (Spiazzi, 90); "In omnibus autem virtutibus et actibus animae ordinatis hoc est commune, quod virtus primi salvatur in omnibus sequentibus; et ideo in prudentia quodammodo includitur et voluntas, quae est de fine, et cognitio finis."

109. *De ver.,* q, 5, a. 1, ad 8 (Spiazzi, 90–91): ". . . ratio illa in summo principe constituta non dicitur providentia nisi adiuncto ordine ad finem, ad quem praesupponitur voluntas finis, unde licet essentialiter ad cognitionem pertineat, tamen voluntatem aliquo modo includit."

110. See *ST,* I–II, q. 15, a. 3: ". . . consilium praesupponit appetitum finis"; *ST,* I–II, q. 90, a. 1, ad 3: ". . . ratio habet vim movendi a voluntate . . . ex hoc enim quod aliquis vult finem, ratio imperat de his quae sunt ad finem."

111. ". . . providentia est in intellectu, sed praesupponit voluntatem finis: nullus enim praecipit de agendis propter finem, nisi velit finem" *(ST,* I, q. 29, a. 1, ad 3).

112. See *ST,* II–II, q. 44, a. 1: ". . . praeceptum importat rationem debiti"; q. 47, a. 8, ad 1: ". . . actus praecipiendi se extendit et ad bona prosequenda et ad mala cavenda . . ."; *In psalmos,* 18 (Vivès, 5, p. 331): ". . . dicitur enim praeceptum quasi praecise ceptum, scilicet ad agendum; quasi quod praecise teneamur illud agere."

judgments (= *iudicia electionis*), as I have mentioned, are a prelude to prescriptions taken in a stronger sense, that is, prudential commands.[113] To prescribe, in the stronger sense that incorporates volition, is to bring it about that someone actually does some particular thing (or, by extension, does not do some particular thing).[114] Aquinas identifies the act of prescribing that follows deliberation, consent, judgment, and choice as the principal act of prudence.[115] Prudence prescribes in the strong sense when it issues a *command* that follows upon the will's intending the end.[116]

To urge someone [to attain] his end, which pertains to command, presupposes the appetite of the end and some pursuit of it. . . . And according to this, the will which has the end for [its] object is said to command, insofar as command, which is an act of reason, begins in the will, to which pertains the desire of the end. *(IV Sent.*, d. 15, q. 4, a. 1 [Moos, n. 527, p. 730])[117]

The distinction between (1) universal indicative-gerundive precepts and (2) particular indicative-gerundive precepts/commands reflects the distinction between the *ends* and *means* of practical reason. Aquinas identifies the natural law with practical reason's immediate indicative-gerundive judgments (= *iudicia synderesis*) that prescribe actions that bear on the universal or necessary *ends* of human life.[118] These ends are not set by deliberative reasoning but by natural inclination.[119]

113. See *ST*, II–II, q. 47, a. 9: "Hoc autem pertinet ad prudentiam, cuius praecipuus actus est circa agenda praecipere de praeconsiliatis et iudicatis."

114. See *In II Sent.*, d. 28, q. 1, a. 3 (Mandonnet, 725): ". . . hoc enim directe alicui praecipitur quod statim in ipso est ut faciat illud"; *ST*, II–II, q. 47, a. 8: ". . . praecipere: qui quidem actus consistit in applicatione consiliatorum et iudicatorum ad operandum"; q. 104, a. 1: "Movere autem per rationem et voluntatem est praecipere."

115. See *ST*, I–II, q. 57, a. 6; II–II, q. 47, a. 8.

116. See *ST*, I–II, q. 51, a. 1, ad 1: ". . . ad prudentiam pertinet bene consiliari imperative; ad eubuliam autem elicitive"; *II Sent.*, d. 24, q. 3, a. 2 (Mandonnet, 620): "Completum dominium habet in illis actibus qui ex imperio voluntatis procedunt; et hi sunt actus deliberationem sequentes, qui rationi adscribuntur."

117. "Advocare enim aliquem ad finem suum: quod est ad imperium pertinet, praesupponit appetitutum finis et est quaedam prosecutio illius. . . . Et secundum hoc voluntas quae habet finem pro objecto, dicitur imperare, inquantum imperium, quod est actus rationis, in voluntate incipit, ad quam pertinet desiderium finis." *(IV Sent.*, d. 15, q. 4, a. 1 [Moos, n. 527, p. 730])

118. "Et huiusmodi propositiones universales rationis practicae ordinatae ad actiones, habent rationem legis." *(ST*, I–II, q. 90, a. 1)

119. See *SLE*, III, 5, 1111b29, 193–97 (*In Ethic.*, III, lect. 5 [Spiazzi, n. 447, p. 126]: ". . . electio videtur esse circa ea quae sunt in potestate nostra. Et haec est causa quare nec est impossibilium neque eorum quae per alios fiunt neque finis qui

The ends of human life, which in regard to actions have the same relationship as naturally known principles have in speculative matters, are foremost in the prescription of natural reason. (*ST,* II–II, q. 56, a. 1)[120]

In contrast, prudential commands, since they follow deliberation, (particular) judgment, and choice, are said to bear precisely on *means* not ends.[121] Still, identification of an end and a means is contextual.[122] Only the ultimate end, happiness, is never a means to some further end; other ends are also basic but if considered in relationship to happiness, they are, in this context, "penultimate" ends. The primary precepts of the natural law *(iudicia synderesis)* bear on those basic ends of human life that Aquinas also identifies as being the ends of the virtues. They do not properly fall into the sphere of deliberation. But Aquinas allows that even these ends can be considered to be the means to the ultimate end, the good in general or happiness. So considered, the basic ends seem to be more like the constituents than the instrumental means to the ultimate end. But in either case, they can be objects of choice.[123]

Practical reason originally expresses the common or immediate precepts of the natural law in the form of universal indicative-gerundive *judgments,* not imperatives. Since all of the basic human goods are included in the proper object of the will, universal good, the will naturally and originally tends to these goods (and not only to happiness) as *ends* to be realized.[124] Once they are intellectually grasped, they are necessarily willed.[125] The secondary and tertiary precepts of

---

ut plurimum praestituitur nobis a natura"; SLE, VII, 8, 1151a11, 126–29 *(In Ethic.,* VII, lect. 8 [Spiazzi, n. 1431, p. 383]): "Sicut enim in mathematicis principia non docentur per rationem, sed statim intellecta creduntur, ita etiam in agilibus fines non docentur per rationem."

120. "Praecipue autem sunt de dictamine rationis naturalis fines humanae vitae, qui se habent in agendis sicut principia naturaliter cognita in speculativis . . ." *(ST,* II–II, q. 56, a. 1).

121. See *ST,* I–II, q. 17, a. 3, ad 1.

122. See *ST,* I–II, q. 13, a. 2; q. 14, a. 2.

123. See *ST,* I–II, q. 13, a. 3, ad 1: ". . . fines proprii virtutum ordinantur ad beatitudinem sicut ad ultimum finem. Et hoc modo potest esse eorum electio."

124. See *ST,* I–II, q. 10, a. 1: "Unde naturaliter homo vult non solum obiectum voluntatis, sed etiam alia quae conveniunt aliis potentiis: Ut cognitionem veri, quae convenit intellectui; et esse et vivere et alia huiusmodi, quae respiciunt consistentiam naturalem; quae omnia comprehenduntur sub obiecto voluntatis, sicut quadam particularia bona."

125. See *ST,* I–II, q. 10, a. 2, ad 3: ". . . finis ultimus ex necessitate movet voluntatem, quia est bonum perfectum. Et similiter illa quae ordinantur ad hunc finem, sine quibus finis haberi non potest, sicut esse et vivere et huiusmodi"; *De ver.,* q. 22, a. 6 (Spiazzi, 397): ". . . voluntas de necessitate vult quasi naturali

the natural law, however, are like proximate and remote "conclusions" drawn from the primary and common precepts;[126] they can be readily expressed in *imperative* form because, as inferences, they presuppose willing the ends immediately enjoined in the most common precepts.[127] The imperative prescribes the chosen "means," whether this is taken in an instrumental or a constitutive sense or even an instantiating sense, that allows one to pursue or realize the more basic ends.[128]

Thus practical reason makes an inference from the *end*, which is prescribed in an immediate indicative-gerundive judgment of practical intellect, to a *means* that instantiates that end, and the later can be specified in a command. For example, practical reason can easily infer from the universal prescriptive principle "Some benefit is to be done for another from whom one has received but not yet returned a benefit" the quasi-conclusion "One's father and mother are to be honored."[129] Put in imperative form, "Honor your father and mother," the derived precepts of the natural law incorporate, as commands, the moving force or intentionality of the human will.[130]

This way of characterizing the moving force of command, by tying it to volition, remains the same from Aquinas's early to late works.[131]

---

inclinatione in ipsum determinata, est finis ultimus, ut beatitudo, et ea quae in ipso includuntur, ut cognitio veritatis, et alia huiusmodi. . . ."

126. See *ST,* I–II, q. 94, a. 4.

127. See *ST,* I–II, q. 94, a. 6; q. 99, a. 2; q. 100, a. 11.

128. See *ST,* I–II, q. 99, a. 1: ". . . praeceptum legis, cum sit obligatorium est de aliquo quod fieri debet. Quod autem aliquid debeat fieri, hoc provenit ex necessitate alicuius finis. Unde manifestum est quod de ratione praecepti est quod importet ordinem ad finem, inquantum scilicet illud praecipitur quod est necessarium vel expediens ad finem."

129. See *ST,* I–II, q. 100, a. 1: ". . . necesse est quod omnia praecepta moralia pertineant ad legem naturae, sed diversimode. Quaedam enim sunt quae statim per se ratio naturalis cuiuslibet hominis diiudicat esse facienda vel non facienda: sicut, *Honora patrem tuum et matrem tuam, et Non occides, Non furtum facies.* Et huiusmodi sunt absolute de lege naturae"; a. 5, ad 4: "Sed ratio naturalis non statim dictat quod aliquid sit pro alio faciendum, nisi cui homo aliquid debet. Debitum autem filii ad patrem adeo est manifestum quod nulla tergiversatione potest negari . . ."; a. 7: "Inest autem primo dictamen rationis quod homo debitor est beneficii vel obsequii exhibendi illis a quibus beneficia accepit, si nondum recompensavit."

130. See *De ver.,* q. 4, a. 3, ad 4: ". . . imperium quamvis sit signum voluntatis. . . ."

131. See *III Sent.,* d. 33, q. 2, a. 4, sol. 4, ad 1 (Moos, n. 245, p. 1067): ". . . ratio etiam praecipit mediante voluntate, inquantum sententiat aliquid esse faciendum"; *De ver.,* q. 6, a. 1, ad 8 (Spiazzi, 114): "Ordinationis autem principium proximum est ratio, sed remotus est voluntas . . ."; q. 22, a. 12, ad 4 (Spiazzi, 409): ". . . imperium est et voluntas et rationis quantum ad diversa; voluntatis quidem secundum quod imperium inclinationem quamdam importat; rationis vero, secundum quod haec inclinatio distribuitur et ordinatur ut exequenda per hunc vel per illum"; *Quod.* IX, q. 5, a. 2 (Spiazzi, 191): "Et sic imperium erit immediate actus rationis, sed volunta-

And in this way the will which has the end for [its] object is said to command, insofar as command, which is an act of reason, begins in the will to which pertains the desire of the end. *(IV Sent.,* d. 15, q. 4, a. 1, ad 3 [Moos, n. 527, p. 730])[132]

A command pertains both to the will and reason [but] in regard to diverse things. It pertains to will inasmuch as "command" signifies some inclination; it pertains to reason inasmuch as this inclination is apportioned and ordered so that things are to be accomplished in this or that way. *(De ver.,* q. 22, a. 12, ad 4 [Spiazzi, 409])[133]

It should be stressed, however, that prudential commands are acts of reason.

Both command and petition or intercession signify some order: namely, that a man disposes that something be done through another. Hence it pertains to reason, whose [task] it is to order. . . . *(ST,* II–II, q. 83, a. 1)[134]

In fact, Aquinas emphasizes that both types of prescriptions, indicative-gerundive precepts and imperatives, are forms of reason "by intimating or declaring."[135] To command, although it is an act that follows the volitional acts of consent and choice, is to order one thing to another rationally, that is, to do something so as to achieve an end. But since a choice presupposes the rational acts of deliberation *(consilium)* and judgment *(iudicium),* Aquinas considers a command, notwithstanding its volitional impetus, to be essentially an act of reason. Aquinas expresses the logical and metaphysical priority of the rational over the volitional dimension of command by attributing the psychological act of command immediately to reason and mediately to the will.[136]

---

tis quasi primo moventis"; *ST,* II–II, q. 47, a. 8, ad 3: ". . . movere absolute pertinet ad voluntatem. Sed praecipere importat motionem cum quadam ordinatione. Et ideo est actus rationis. . . ."

132. "Et secundum hoc voluntas quae habet finem pro objecto, dicitur imperare, inquantum imperium, quod est actus rationis, in voluntate incipit, ad quam pertinet desiderium finis" *(IV Sent.,* d. 15, q. 4, a. 1, ad 3 [Moos, n. 527, p. 730]).

133. ". . . imperium est et voluntatis et rationis quantum ad diversa; voluntatis quidem secundum quod imperium inclinationem quamdam importat; rationis vero, secundum quod haec inclinatio distribuitur et ordinatur ut exequenda per hunc vel per illum." *(De ver.,* q. 22, a. 12, ad 4 [Spiazzi, 409])

134. "Utrumque autem horum, scilicet imperare et petere sive deprecari, ordinationem quandam important: prout scilicet homo disponit aliquid per aliud esse faciendum. Unde pertinet ad rationem, cuius est ordinare . . ." *(ST,* II–II, q. 83, a. 1).

135. See *ST,* I–II, q. 17, a. 1: " Sed ratio potest aliquid intimare vel denuntiare dupliciter."

136. See *Quod.* IX, q. 5, a. 2 [Spiazzi, 191]: "Et sic imperium erit immediate actus rationis, sed voluntatis quasi primo moventis."

7. *"Commands"*

I have been distinguishing between a weak and a strong sense of prescription. An imperative or *command* is a strong prescription because of the volitional force it embodies; a command follows the volitional act of choosing what practical reason has concluded should be done. To be sure, Aquinas does not always observe the precise terminological distinction that marks these two senses of prescription. He interchanges *"praecipere"* and *"imperare,"*[137] thus mixing the terminology of Aristotle and John Damascene,[138] and perhaps obscuring the distinction between a strictly psychological term *"imperium"* and a moral term *"praeceptum."*[139] But in *ST*, I–II, q. 17, a. 1, Aquinas does clearly distinguish two types of *precepts*: indicative-gerundive judgments and imperatives.[140] He identifies a *command (imperium)* only with the second type of precept.

---

137. See *IV Sent.*, d. 15, q. 4, a. 1a, co. (Busa, p. 515a): ". . . et ideo applicatio praedicta eorum qui extra nos sunt, ad consecutionem desiderati, quandoque dicitur imperium vel praeceptum, quando scilicet illi sunt in potestate nostra . . ."; *ST*, I–II, q. 92, a. 2: ". . . ponitur legis actus praecipere vel imperare . . ."; II–II, q. 47, a. 8, ad 3: "Sed praecipere importat motionem cum quadam ordinatione."

138. See R.-A. Gauthier, O.P., "Saint Maxime le Confesseur et la psychologie de l'acte humain," *Recherches de théologie ancienne et médiévale* 21 (1954): 51–100.

139. Thomists usually identify *imperium* with the prescriptive act of prudence; Aquinas, however, leaves the identification implicit: "Et ideo ubi invenitur specialis ratio regiminis et praecepti in humanis actibus, ibi etiam invenitur specialis ratio prudentiae" *(ST*, II–II, q. 50, a. 1). Cf. *ST*, I–II, q. 61, a. 3; q. 57, a. 6. Pinckaers, review of "Le 'Précepte' de la prudence," 360, while defending the propriety of this identification, notes that the term *"imperium"* originally belongs to a premoral or strictly psychological analysis of human acts. In a psychological context, an *imperium* can be about either a morally good or bad act, whereas a *praeceptum*, which results from an act of prudence, only commands a morally good act.

140. Cf. Grisez, "The First Principle of Practical Reason," 192: "Aquinas explicitly distinguishes between an imperative and a precept expressed in a gerundive form." Schultz, in "Is-Ought," 11, finds Grisez's interpretation of *ST*, I–II, q. 17, a. 1 "odd," but Schultz's textual counterexample does not support her pejorative characterization. She correctly notes that *ST*, II–II, q. 47, a. 8, obj. 3 equates *"praecipere'* and *"imperare'* and attributes both to the will. But Schultz concludes that since Aquinas does not explicitly distinguish *"praecipere'* and *"imperare'* in his response to this objection, they should not or cannot be distinguished in any way. In ad 3, however, Aquinas is only concerned to answer the main point of the objection: *"praecipere,"* because it is an act of ordering of one thing to another, must be essentially attributed to the intellect and not to the will. And Aquinas's response is congruent with the distinction drawn in I–II, q. 17, a. 1: an *imperium* derives *essentially* from reason and not from will, but because commands have a determinate volitional impetus (i.e., what has been chosen), they are to be distinguished (as a subset of prescriptions) from indicative-gerundive prescriptions. See Ramirez, *De actibus humanis*, 4: pars 1, q. 17, §1, nn. 556–57, pp. 408–9.

Whether put universally *(iudicium synderesis)* or particularly *(iudicium electionis)*,[141] an indicative-gerundive judgment is genuinely prescriptive since it states that some type or some token of an action ought to be done or ought to be avoided.[142] Nonetheless, the grammatical distinction between a particular indicative-gerundive judgment and an imperative allows Aquinas to draw attention to the difference between (1) merely judging that something ought to be done; and (2) effectively moving someone by commanding some determinate means (i.e., some particular action) that will enable the agent to attain what has been prescribed. The grammatical distinction is significant because it helps clarify the complex of rational and volitional acts that generate a command.[143] Gerundives express practical reason's intimations or declarations "in the absolute mode"—in the mode that expresses that their primary or absolute origin is in reason.[144] Imperatives or commands express reason's intimations or declarations not only as they are rooted in reason, but also as they are consequent upon the intentional acts of the will.[145] It is this volitional impetus that makes them "stronger" prescriptions.

Aquinas relies on the notion of the *reciprocal* causality of reason and will to explain how the precepts of practical reason effectively move *agents*. The particular practical *judgment* of which determinate means is rationally due or required to attain an intended end, although prescriptive as indicated by its gerundive form, does not by itself move the agent to pursue it. In other words, the practical intellect is not by itself the efficient cause of human action. In order to move an agent, a prescription must incorporate a particularized volitional impetus. A prescription about a particular action that incorporates the particularized impetus of the will is expressed in the imperative form: a "command" effectively moves the agent to do something.[146]

---

141. See *De ver.* q. 16, a. 1, ad 15 (Spiazzi, 323): ". . . iudicium est duplex: in universali, et hoc pertinet ad synderisem; et in particulari operabili, et hoc est iudicium electionis, et hoc pertinet ad liberum arbitrium."

142. See *ST*, I–II, q. 104, a. 1: ". . . praeceptorum cuiuscumque legis quaedam habent vim obligandi ex ispo dictamine rationis, quia naturalis ratio dictat hoc esse debitum fieri vel vitari."

143. See *ST*, II–II, q. 47, a. 9: ". . . motus pertinet quidem ad vim appetitivam sicut ad principium movens; tamen secundum directionem et praeceptum rationis. . . . "

144. See *III Sent.*, d. 33, q. 2, a. 1 sol. 3 (Moos, n. 281, p. 1075): "Ad rationem enim pertinet praecipere quod faciendum est. . . . "

145. See Gauthier, review of *Psychologie et morale*, 68: "L'*imperium* sera donc une ordination de la raison imprégnée d'un influx voluntaire et tenant de cet influx la force de mouvoir efficacement."

146. See *ST*, I–II, q. 12, a. 1: ". . . dicimus architectorem, et omnem praecipi-

The commander moves through his command. Therefore, the act of the soul to which motion immediately follows is called "command." (*IV Sent.*, d. 15, q. 4, a. 1, resp. ad 1, ad 3 [Moos, n. 526, p. 730])[147]

A command effectively moves the agent because it incorporates the volitional act of choice *(electio)* which is "the final acceptance by which something is received for the purpose of carrying it out."[148] A command prescribes the determinate means that ought to be done, inasmuch as this means has been judged and chosen as the one among other possible means that is necessary or most useful to an intended end.[149]

8. *"Voluntarism"*

Aquinas identifies the natural law with the *per se nota* precepts known through the intellectual habit of *synderesis*, which is a habit of the *practical intellect*. But in accordance with Aquinas's conception of the reciprocal causality of intellect and will, the natural law must be described as having a primary source, the practical intellect, and a secondary source, the will:

There is a twofold way to order [something] to an end: either by declaring the end or by inclining to the end. To declare the end is the work of reason, but to incline to the end is the work of the will. (*II Sent.*, d. 41, q. 1, a. 1 [Mandonnet, 1035])[150]

To understand why practical reason makes prescriptive judgments we must refer to Aquinas's doctrine that the complete human action is a *complexum* of reciprocal acts of intellect and will.[151] The precepts of

---

entem, movere suo imperio alios ad id quod ipse intendit"; q. 17, a. 1, ad 3: ". . . imperium non sit actus rationis absolute, sed cum quaedam motione . . ."; II–II, q. 83, a. 1: ". . . ad rationem practicam pertinet causare aliquid per modum imperii. . . ."

147. ". . . imperans per imperium suum movet, ideo actus animae ad quem motus statim sequitur, *imperium* dicitur" *(IV Sent.*, d. 15, q. 4, a. 1, resp. ad 1, ad 3 [Moos, n. 526, p. 730]).

148. See *De ver.*, q. 22, a. 15 (Spiazzi, 413): "Electio enim est ultima acceptio qua aliquid accipitur ad prosequendum; quod quidem non est rationis, sed voluntatis."

149. See *ST*, I–II, q. 13, a. 2: ". . . electio sit praeacceptio unius respectu alterius, necesse est quod electio sit respectu plurium quae eligi possunt."

150. "Sed ordinare in finem contingit dupliciter: vel ostendo finem vel inclinando in finem. Ostendere autem finem rationis est, sed inclinare in finem est voluntatis . . ." *(II Sent.*, d. 41, q. 1, a. 1 [Mandonnet, 1035]).

151. See *IV Sent.*, d. 33, q. 1, a. 1 (Vivès, 11, p. 140): "Sicut autem in rebus agentibus ex necessitate naturae sunt principia actionum ipsae formae, a quibus

the natural law cannot be identified as issuing from any act of the will alone.[152] However, the judgments of synderesis presuppose prior acts of intellect and will. The prescriptive judgments of *synderesis* enjoin the doing or the pursuing of the basic human goods that are the objects of the natural inclinations of the will. Practical intellect, in an act of *simplex conceptio*, first apprehends these perfective goods and it is this intellectual apprehension that is prior to any elicited act of the will (i.e., prior to the acts of *velle* or *intendere*). But once conceived, the primary goods of practical reason are the immediate object of the simple act of willing *(velle)* that necessarily accompanies the *simplex conceptio* of these natural goods. As goods that are known and necessarily desired, practical intellect immediately prescribes them as ends to be pursued. In turn, the immediate or noninferential judgmental prescription of these goods as ends to be done or pursued is followed by the volitional act of intending them.[153]

That Aquinas allows that the natural law has an irreducible source in the human will does not mean, however, that his conception of natural law is "voluntaristic." The natural *inclinations* of the will are antecedent to the simple intellectual conception of the goods to which these inclinations are directed. But the natural *acts* of willing *(velle)* and intending *(intendere)* these ends are subsequent to knowing them.[154] And within the complex of reciprocal human intellectual and volitional acts that give rise to particular prudential judgments about the means that will allow the agent to attain the end, Aquinas again clearly subordinates will to intellect. The volitional act of consent, for example, follows rational deliberation:

> In the order of things that are able to be done, it is first necessary to have the apprehension of the end, then the appetite of the end. Afterward, there is deliberation about the means, and then appetite of those means. *(ST, I–II, q. 15, a. 3)*[155]

---

operationes propriae prodeunt convenientes fini; ita in his quae cognitionem participant, principia agendi sunt cognitio et appetitus; unde opportet quod in vi cognoscitiva sit naturalis conceptio, et in vi appetitiva naturalis inclinatio, quibus operatio conveniens generi sive specie reddatur competens fini."

152. See *ST*, I–II, q. 56, a. 3.

153. See *III Sent.*, d. 33, q. 2, a. 5, sol. 4 (Moos, n. 243, p. 1066): "Unde cum negotiatio de his quae sunt ad finem, praesupponat naturalem cognitionem finis, quae sequitur naturalem inclinationem voluntatis in finem. . . ."

154. See *I Sent.*, d. 48, q. 1, a. 4 (Mandonnet, 1088–89): ". . . nullus appetitus tenetur tendere in illud bonum cujus rationem non apprehendit"; *ST*, I, q. 16, a. 4: ". . . cognitio naturaliter praecedit appetitum."

155. "In ordine autem agibilium, primo quidem oportet sumere apprehensionem

In regard, then, to the primary ends of human action, there is no elicited act of the will that is prior to the *simplex conceptio* of the practical intellect whereby it apprehends these goods. In regard to the means, "commands," while imbued with a volitional force, are described as essentially acts of reason. A command derives its impetus from the volitional act of choice, but choice follows the intellectual acts of deliberation and judgment that rationally order means and ends. Aquinas says, significantly, that commands fall under the natural law because they are rational:[156]

> Reason has the power of moving from the will . . . for from the fact that someone wills the end, reason commands those things that are [means] to the end. But for this willing of those things commanded to have the nature of a law, it is necessary that it be regulated by some reason. *(ST,* I–II, q. 90, a. 1, ad 3)[157]

Aquinas's conception of the virtues incorporates the volitional side of moral action. The virtues make men good, but, as acquired habits, they arise only from those repeated volitional acts, that is, *choices,* whereby men move to enact what they naturally know to be good. For this reason, Aquinas thinks that prudential commands, which bear on the means chosen, rather than *synderesis,* which bears on intellectually understood ends, more fully instantiate the meaning of "virtue': *synderesis* enables man to know the good that is to be done; prudential commands enable man to enact what is really good here and now.

> Habits that are in the speculative or practical intellect insofar as the intellect follows the will, more fully instantiate the meaning of "virtue" inasmuch as through [such habits] it is brought about that a man not only knows or is able to act rightly, but effectively wills [to do so]. This is seen in [the habits] of faith and prudence. . . . *(De virt.,* q. 1, a. 7 [Odetto, 724])[158]

---

finis; deinde appetitum finis; deinde consilium de his quae sunt ad finem; deinde appetitum eorum quae sunt ad finem" *(ST,* I–II, q. 15, a. 3).

156. *ST,* I, q. 21, a. 2, ad 1: ". . . iustitia, quantum ad legem regulantem, est in ratione vel intellectu: sed quantum ad imperium, quo opera regulantur secundum legem, estin voluntate."

157. ". . . ratio habet vim movendi a voluntate . . . ex hoc enim quod aliquis vult finem, ratio imperat de his quae sunt ad finem. Sed voluntas de his quae imperantur, ad hoc quod legis rationem habeat, oportet quod sit aliqua ratione regulata" *(ST,* I–II, q. 90, a. 1, ad 3).

158. "Habitus vero qui sunt in intellectu speculativo vel practico secundum quod intellectus sequitur voluntatem, habent verius rationem virtutis; in quantum per eos homo efficitur non solum potens vel sciens recte agere, sed volens. Quod quidem ostenditur in fide et prudentia . . ." *(De virt.,* q. 1, a. 7 [Odetto, 724]).

Whereas some contemporary interpreters, in reaction to what they regard as the Suarezian voluntarism distorting many modern Thomist accounts of the natural law, emphasize, rather one-sidedly, that the basic precepts of the natural law are grounded in practical reason,[159] it is noteworthy that Aquinas himself incorporates both the rational and the volitional moments of the complete human act into his doctrine of prescription.[160] He describes, without any hesitation, the natural law precepts as signs of the will inasmuch as the will itself *proposes* the pursuit of good and flight from evil.[161] Such descriptions, which might seem to blur the basic tenet that prescription is an act of the practical intellect, should be interpreted, however, in terms of the Thomistic *reflexio* which preserves the absolute priority of intellect over will.[162] Nonetheless, the primary precepts of the natural law, while absolutely grounded in *synderesis*, are a sign not only that we immediately know that certain basic ends are to be pursued but that we necessarily will to pursue them (= *intendere*).[163]

A complete account of Aquinas's natural law doctrine must incorporate, then, the details of how, in Thomistic psychology, the intellect and will interact. The intellect and will are reciprocal causes;[164] the acts of the two powers, to use Aquinas's phrase, "bend back on" each other.[165] Although motion is primarily attributed to the will, practical reason must first move the will.[166] The intellect and the will immedi-

---

159. See John Finnis, *Natural Law and Natural Rights* (Oxford: Clarendon Press, 1980), 45–49, 337–43.

160. See *De ver.*, q. 23, a. 7 (Spiazzi, 426): "Voluntas autem non habet rationem primae regulae, sed est regula recta: dirigitur enim per rationem et intellectum. . . ."

161. See *De ver.*, q. 23, a. 3 (Spiazzi, 420): "Cum autem voluntas possit designari et secundum quod proponit de agendis, et secundum quod impetum facit ad opus, utroque modo voluntati aliqua signa attribuuntur. Secundum enim quod proponit de agendis quantum ad fugam mali, est signum eius prohibitio. Quantum autem ad prosecutionem boni est duplex signum voluntatis: nam respectu boni necessarii, sine quo non potest voluntas finem suum consequi, est signum voluntatis praeceptum; respectu autem boni utilis, quo faciliori modo et convenientiori acquiritur finis, est signum voluntatis consilium."

162. See *SCG*, III, 26 (Pera, n. 2092, p. 37): "Nam primo et per se intellectus movet voluntatem . . . Voluntas autem movet intellectum quasi per accidens. . . ."

163. See *De ver.*, q. 23, a. 3, ad 2 (Spiazzi, p. 420): "Quamvis ergo praecipere in nobis sit signum volendi illud. . . ."

164. See *ST*, I–II, q. 17, a. 1: ". . . actus voluntatis et rationis supra se invicem possunt ferri, prout scilicet ratio ratiocinatur de volendo, et voluntas vult ratiocinari; contingit actum voluntatis praeveniri ab actu rationis, et e converso."

165. See *ST*, I–II, q. 17, a. 3, ad 3: ". . . eo quod actus harum potentiarum supra seipsos invicem reflectuntur."

166. See *II Sent.*, d. 24, q. 3, a. 3, ad 1 (Mandonnet, 624): ". . . ratio quamvis sit cognitiva potentia, tamen est directiva voluntatis. . . ."

ately move each other but in different orders of causality. The will moves the intellect *efficiently* by causing the intellect to exercise the act of understanding or reasoning.[167] The intellect moves the will in the order of *formal* and *final* causality by specifying the object of the will, the intellectually apprehended good, which is the end of the will. In the order of causality, the absolute priority of the intellect to the will follows from the priority of the final cause to the efficient cause. Agents move only because of an end:[168]

The first principle of motion in regard to the exercise of the [human] act is from the end. If, however, we consider the object of the will and the intellect, we discover that the object of the intellect is the first principle in the genus of formal causality, since its object is being and truth; but the object of the will is the first principle in the genus of final causality, since its object is the good, under which are comprehended all ends. . . . *(De malo*, q. 6, a. 1 [Bazzi-Pession, 559])[169]

The intellect is absolutely or in the order of nature prior to the will.[170] Practical intellect must first apprehend the basic human goods before the will moves to pursue them.[171] Practical reason, however, is a cognitive power; it apprehends the primary goods under the proper or formal object of the cognitive power, namely, under the essential notion *(ratio)* of truth.[172] Under the *ratio* of truth, practical reason is able

167. See *De malo*, q. 6, a. 1 (Bazzi-Pession, 559): "Intelligo enim quia volo; et similiter utor omnibus potentiis et habitibus quia volo. . . ." Cf. *ST*, I–II, q. 9, a. 1; q. 19, a. 3, ad 3.

168. See *SCG*, III, 26 (Pera, n. 2092, p. 37): ". . . voluntas movet intellectum ad operandum in actu per modum quo agens movere dicitur; intellectus autem voluntatem per modum quo finis movet, nam bonum intellectum est finis voluntatis; agens autem est posterior in movendo quam finis, nam agens non movet nisi propter finem."

169. ". . . primum principium motionis quantum ad exercitium actus, sit ex fine. Si autem consideremus obiecta voluntatis et intellectus, inveniemus quod obiectum intellectus est primum principium in genere causae formalis, est enim eius obiectum ens et verum; sed obiectum voluntatis est primum principium in genere causae finalis, nam eius obiectum est bonum, sub quo comprehenduntur omnes fines . . ." *(De malo*, q. 6, a.1 [Bazzi-Pession, 559]).

170. See *II Sent.*, d. 25, q. 1, a. 2, ad 4 (Mandonnet, 650): ". . . intellectus sit superior virtus quam voluntas ratione ordinis, quia prior est et a voluntate praesupponitur. . . ."

171. See *ST*, I, q. 82, a. 3, ad 2: ". . . bonum enim intellectum movet voluntatem."

172. See *De ver.*, q. 22, a. 10, ad 4 (Spiazzi, 405): ". . . obiectum intellectus practici non est bonum, sed verum relatum ad opus"; *De malo*, q. 6, a. 1 (Bazzi-Pession, 559): "Unde et ipsum bonum, in quantum est quaedam forma apprehensibilis, continetur sub vero quasi quoddam verum. . . ."

to know the *ratio* of the good.[173] "Good" falls under the intellect's understanding of "truth" because the *ratio* of one is included in the *ratio* of the other: truth is the good of the intellect and the good as understood is something true.[174] Because the practical intellect is able to grasp the *ratio* of the good, it is able to grasp the ends of human action.[175] But the good that is merely understood under the *ratio* of truth to be good and desirable and an end is not yet "good" in the full sense of the term; it is not yet grasped as *"bonum sub ratione boni,"* which is the good that is the actual object of the will, that is, the intelligible good that is actually desired.[176]

Against the background of Aquinas's psychological doctrine about the ordered, reciprocal causality of intellect and will,[177] we can readily understand why the Thomistic agent actually pursues the basic ends that practical reason prescribes. The agent desires and pursues these ends because the will, which is rational appetite or desire of the good, comes into play.[178] The act of intellectually desiring something originates in the *simplex actus voluntatis*, that is, in the absolute willing of the end.[179] In this primary act of willing *(velle)*, the will is unconditionally inclined to or desires the good that practical intellect apprehends

173. See *ST,* I, q. 79, a. 11, ad 2: ". . . obiectum intellectus practici est bonum ordinabile ad opus, sub ratione veri."

174. See *De ver.,* q. 22, a. 11, ad 3 (Spiazzi, 408): ". . . verum sit quoddam bonum: est enim bonum intellectus; *III Sent.,* d. 33, q. 1, a. 3, sol. 3 (Moos, n. 105, p. 1037): ". . . bonum virtutum intellectualium consistit in hoc quod verum dicatur"; *De virt.,* q. 1, a. 6, ad 5 (Odetto, 723): "Et ideo haec duo, bonum et verum, se invicem includunt: nam bonum est quoddam verum, in quantum est ab intellectu apprehensum . . . Similiter etiam et ipsum verum est quoddam bonum intellectus . . ."; a. 7 (Odetto, 724): ". . . ad cognoscendum verum; quod quidem est bonum intellectus."

175. See *SCG,* III, 26 (Pera, n. 2072, p. 34): ". . . verum autem, quod est obiectum intellectus, non habet rationem finis nisi inquantum et ipsum est bonum"; *ST,* I, q. 83, a. 3: ". . . obiectum intellectus est ipsa ratio boni appetibilis . . ."; I–II, q. 94, a. 2: "Quia vero bonum habet rationem finis. . . ."

176. See *De virt.,* q, 1, a. 6, ad 5 (Odetto, 723): ". . . bonum et verum sunt obiecta duarum partium animae, scilicet intellectivae et appetitivae . . ."; a. 7 (Odetto, 724): "Bonum autem sub ratione boni obiectum solius appetitivae partis; nam bonum est quod appetunt"; *ST,* I, q. 82, a. 3: ". . . bonum appetibile, cuius ratio est in intellectu, est obiectum voluntatis."

177. See *De malo,* q. 6, a. 1 (Bazzi-Pession, 558): "Hoc autem activum sive motivum principium in hominbius proprie est intellectus et voluntas. . . ."

178. See *Quod.* VI, q. 2, a. 1 (Spiazzi, 118): ". . . intellectus autem non agit nisi per voluntatem"; *SLA,* III, c. 9, 433a14, 87–89 *(In de An.,* III, lect. 15 [Pirotta, n. 824, p. 195]): ". . . intellectus non inuenitur mouens sine appetitu, quia uoluntas, secundum quam mouet intellectus, est quidam appetitus."

179. *ST,* I, q. 84, a.4: ". . . velle importat simplicem appetitum alicuius rei: unde voluntas dicitur esse de fine, qui propter se appetitur. . . ."

in the act of simple insight. The *simplex actus voluntatis* is further determined and internally specified as a consequence of practical intellect judgmentally prescribing the apprehended and simply willed good. In this second moment of willing, the will intends *(intendere)* these natural goods as necessary ends that can be achieved through some means:

"Intend" means, so to speak, "tend to another." To intend something belongs to that power to which pertains the pursuit or flight of something. This [power] is the appetite or the will, not the intellect. But it is true that the practical intellect says something about fleeing or pursuing . . . hence the judgment about what is to be fled and pursued pertains to the practical intellect, but not the [actual] pursuit and flight. *(In II Sent.,* d. 38, q. 1, a. 3 [Mandonnet, 974])[180]

What, though, explains the necessity of the volitional acts, *"velle"* and *"intendere"* in regard to the basic ends that practical intellect conceives and prescribes? Aquinas's explanation is that nature is the source of this necessity.[181]

9. Necessity and Freedom

The will, like any nature, is necessarily inclined to its proper end, which is variously designated as the ultimate end in general, or the good in general, or the universal and perfect good, or a complete and perfect good, or beatitude.[182] Included in this ultimate end are the "means" necessary for attaining it, that is, the necessary constituents of beatitude, such as knowledge of the truth.[183] But also included under

---

180. "Intendere enim dicitur quasi in aliud tendere. Intendere autem in aliquid est illius potentiae ad quam pertinet prosequi vel fugere aliquid. Haec autem est appetitus vel voluntas, non autem intellectus. Sed verum est quod intellectus practicus dicit aliquid de fugiendo vel prosequendo . . . unde judicium fugae et prosecutionis ad intellectum practicum pertinet, non autem prosecutio et fuga" (*In II Sent.,* d. 38, q. 1, a. 3 [Mandonnet, 974]).

181. See *De ver.,* q. 22, a. 5, ad 11 (Spiazzi, 398): "Et sic voluntas de necessitate vult bonum, in quantum naturaliter vult bonum"; a. 6 (Spiazzi, 399): ". . . cum voluntas indeterminate se habeat respectu multorum, non habeat respectu omnium necessitatem, sed respectu eorum tantum ad quae naturali inclinatione determinatur. . . ."

182. See *De ver.,* q. 22, a. 7; *ST,* I, q. 82, a. 2; I–II, q. 10, aa. 1–2; *II Sent.,* d. 25, q. 1, a. 2.

183. See *De ver.,* q. 22, a. 5 (Spiazzi, 397): ". . . voluntas de necessitate vult quasi naturali inclinatione in ipsum determinata, est finis ultimus, ut beatitudo, et ea quae in ipso includuntur, ut est cognitio veritatis, et alia huiusmodi . . ."; q. 23, a. 4 (Spiazza, 422): ". . . humana voluntas naturaliter appetit beatitudinem, et respectu

the proper object of the will are the proper or natural objects of the other human powers, which as particular goods fall under the good in general.[184] Once the practical intellect grasps these goods that are necessary for the well-being of the whole man, then the corresponding acts of the will are necessarily elicited in regard to these ends.[185] Hence, Aquinas refers to the *acts* of willing these basic human ends *(velle and intendere)*, which follow upon intellect naturally apprehending them, as acts of the *voluntas ut natura*[186] or *voluntas naturalis*. The latter designation perhaps has a certain advantage in that it more clearly refers to the natural *acts* of the will, which are subsequent to simple intellectual apprehension, from the antecedent or precognitive natural *inclinations* of the will.[187]

Other cases of willing, where inquiry has been required to determine which ends to pursue, are attributed to *voluntas ut deliberata*. But even in these cases, it can also be said that the will naturally wills as goods the contingent ends that practical reason (fallibly) prescribes because the formal object of intellectual appetite is the *bonum intellectum*, that is, the intelligible good or the good that is in accordance with reason.[188] Similarly, Aquinas attributes the same role to natural willing when explaining why the agent effectively utilizes the means that prudence commands. Since practical reason has judged these to be good means, the will naturally inclines to them.[189]

huius voliti voluntas necessitatem habet, cum in ipsum tendat per modum naturae; non enim potest homo velle non esse beatus. . . ."

184. See *ST,* I–II, q. 10, a. 1: "Unde naturaliter homo vult non solum obiectum voluntatis, sed etiam alia quae conveniunt aliis potentiis. . . ."

185. See *II Sent.,* d. 39, q. 2, a. 2 (Mandonnet, 993): ". . . voluntas autem rationalis, prout est natura hominis, sive prout consequitur naturalem apprehensionem universalium principiorum juris, est quae in bonum inclinat."

186. Cf. *II Sent.,* d. 39, q. 2, a. 2, ad 2 (Mandonnet, 994): ". . . in ratione est aliquid naturaliter cognitum quasi principium indemonstrabile in operabilibus, quod se habet per modum finis, quia in operabilibus finis habet locum principii. . . . Unde illud quod finis est hominis est naturaliter in ratione cognitum esse bonum et appetendum, et voluntas consequens istam cognitionem dicitur voluntas ut natura."

187. See *I Sent.,* d. 48, q. 1, a. 4 (Mandonnet, 1089): "Est et quaedam voluntas in nobis naturalis qua appetimus id quod secundum se bonum est homini, inquantum est homo; et hoc sequitur apprehensionem rationis, prout est aliquid absolute considerans: sicut vult homo scientiam, virtutem, sanitatem et hujusmodi."

188. See *De virt.,* q. 1, a. 5, ad 1 (Odetto, 721): ". . . voluntas appetit naturaliter quod est bonum secundum rationem . . ."; ad 7: "Nam bonum intellectus est obiectum voluntatis, ad quod naturaliter ordinatur voluntas. . . ."

189. See *De virt.,* q. 1, a. 5, ad 1 (Odetto, 721): " . . . ab imperandum sufficit voluntati iudicium rationis; nam voluntas appetit naturaliter quod est secundum rationem. . . ."

Because the will is defined as intellectual appetite, the question arises how the necessary inclinations of the *voluntas ut natura* are to be aligned with the acts of willing *(velle* and *intendere)* that are subsequent to the intellectual apprehension of these natural ends. Does the doctrine of natural ends limit the freedom of the will? Aquinas's answer is to find freedom within the sphere of necessity. He considers the freedom of the will in relationship to the object of the will and to the exercise of the act of the will. Since we can will or not will to think of any object, including the necessary *object* of the will (beatitude), the will is always free in regard to the *exercise* of its acts. But as a nature (i.e., as a power with a proper object), the will is necessarily inclined to its proper object, the *bonum commune* or *beatitudo* and its necessary constituents, and what falls under *bonum commune*, the particular goods that are the proper objects of the other powers.[190] If beatitude and the other necessary objects of the will are once thought about, then they are necessarily willed.[191] The freedom of the will in relation to other objects is found in the fact that many particular goods fall under the will's proper object.[192] These particular goods are contingent goods because none of them, nor all of them together, possess "the complete notion of the good" *(II Sent.,* d. 25, q. 1, a. 2 [Mandonnet, 649]) and hence they are not objects that necessitate the will. They can be freely chosen or rejected.

Nonrational animals, however, are necessitated by their natural inclinations in regard to both the ends that they seek and the means by which they seek them. Human freedom of choice, however, transcends man's "natural" inclinations. Here the internal determinations of the primordial act of *willing* are of paramount moral significance. Men necessarily will *(intendere)* as objects beatitude and those natural goods that are constituents of beatitude, but even in these cases they are free *to choose* or *not choose* different means whereby these necessary goods may be intended.[193]

190. See *ST,* I–II, q. 10, a. 1; *De malo,* q. 6, a. 1.

191. If they are considered apart from their intrinsic connection with happiness, or if they are viewed as subordinated to a good regarded as more necessary to happiness, then even these natural or necessary goods can be freely rejected. Thus one can choose to kill oneself in order to escape pain or to avoid idolatry; see *De ver.,* q. 22, a. 1, ad 7; *ST,* III, q. 18, a. 5.

192. See *ST,* I–II, q. 10, a. 1, ad 3: "Sub bono autem communi multa particularia bona continentur, ad quorum nullum voluntas determinatur."

193. See *II Sent.,* d. 7, q. 1, a. 1, ad 1 (Mandonnet, 181): ". . . rationalis potestas dicitur esse oppositorum, quae sub electione cadunt, quorum proprie est liberum arbitrium . . . de fine non potest voluntas contrarie se habere. Voluntas . . . semper

Accordingly, Aquinas distinguishes the immediate rational necessity inherent in the *per se nota* primary principles, which express the immediate intellectual apprehension of the objects of the *voluntas ut natura*, from the rational necessity of the conclusions or secondary precepts that can be easily inferred from the primary principles, and from the contingent tertiary precepts of the natural law. Doubtless many of our difficult moral choices fall into this last category. It is at this tertiary level in the Thomistic hierarchy of moral precepts that the Aristotelian notion of practical reason "making" the moral order seems directly relevant;[194] here our particular choices are not immediately directed by natural or innate precepts that correspond to the precognitive, necessary objects of the will. Tertiary moral precepts arise from fallible deliberations and judgments about the contingent ends or means that enable men to intend the basic or natural goods. Natural inclinations, and the first or natural prescriptive judgments based upon them, are universally invariant in what they seek and in what they prescribe as good.[195] But human agents must determine how these natural or necessary goods are good for them here and now, in this or that situation. In fact, the invariant and universal prescriptive principles, and the easily inferred secondary precepts, and the tertiary precepts that derive from inquiry, must all be further determined by the singular prudential judgments of practical reason. But only then, when prudence commands particular actions, can it be said that the natural law adequately prescribes what is to be done.[196]

10. The Divine Intellect and Will

In Aquinas's account, the natural law encompasses doing as well as knowing the good for man. Indeed, since doing the good is more im-

---

est de bono et de beatitudine: ad quam tamen consequendam possunt homines diversas vias eligere . . . unde potest esse error in electione eorum quae sunt ad finem ipsum"; d.39, q. 2, a. 2, ad 5 (Mandonnet, 994): ". . . voluntas est secundum hoc determinata et in unum natualiter tendens, ita quod in alterum naturaliter non tendit; non tamen in illud in quod naturaliter tendit de necessitate, sed voluntarie tendit; unde et potest illud non eligere."

194. See Chap. 2, 88–90, nn. 140–42.

195. See *II Sent.*, d. 7, q. 1, a. 2, ad 3 (Mandonnet, 185): "In synderesi autem sunt universalia principia juris naturalis; unde oportet quod remurmuret omni ei quod contra jus naturale fit"; d. 39, q. 3, a. 1 (997): ". . . Synderesis . . . extingui non potest, sed semper repugnat omni ei quod contra principia naturaliter sibi indita est."

196. See *De virt.*, q. 1, a. 6 (Odetto, 722): "Et ideo non sufficeret homini naturalis appetitus boni, nec naturale iudicium ad recte agendum, nisi amplius determinetur et perficiatur . . . ita oportet quod ratio practica perficiatur aliquo habitu ad

portant than merely knowing what good is to be done, the volitional dimension of the natural law must be kept in focus. Aquinas, however, considers not only the proximate volitional source of the natural law, the human will, but also its ultimate volitional source, the divine will.

From Aquinas's theological perspective, the natural law is seen to be causally dependent on the eternal law. The eternal law is the exemplar in the divine intellect of the order that divine providence effects in creation. This divinely created order, insofar as it is reflected in the innate principles of practical intellect, is called the "natural law." In accordance with basic Thomistic metaphysical doctrine, the natural law, as a created effect, is said to participate the eternal law. Accordingly, Aquinas *absolutely* grounds natural law not in the quasi-innate precepts of the practical intellect but in the eternal law that is the order of creation as known in the divine intellect. But since we can understand how the divine mind works only by analogy with the human mind, Aquinas also regards the acts of divine intellect as reciprocally involving acts of the divine will. In short, the reciprocity between intellectual and volitional acts that marks the Thomistic notion of human prudence now appears in Aquinas's explanation of divine providence.[197]

By analogy with human prudence, divine providence is understood to be essentially an act of (divine) intellect ordering means to ends: God's foresees the end of creation which is set forth in the eternal law; subsequently, by His providence, God orders the means for creation to attain that end. Through creation, divine providence instills the natural law within human understanding.[198] Natural law, in the human mind, is the immanent human similitude of eternal law in the divine mind. The eternal law, as the exemplar of the created order, is the principle of divine providence;[199] as the eternal law functions in the divine mind, the natural law in the human mind contains the quasi-

hoc quod recte diiudicet de bono humano secundum singula agenda. Et haec virtus dicitur prudentia, cuius subiectum est ratio practica. . . ."

197. See *I Sent.*, d. 39, q. 1, a. 1 (Mandonnet, 928): "Ista ergo excogitatio nominatur nomine scientiae, ratione solius cognitionis et non ratione alicujus operationis. Unde est et finis, et eorum quae sunt ad finem"; *De ver.*, q. 5, a. 1 (Spiazzi, 90): ". . . per scientiam enim Deus scit se et creaturas. Sed providentia pertinet tantum ad cognitionem eorum quae sunt ad finem, secundum quod ordinantur in finem; et ideo providentia includit et scientiam et voluntatem; sed tamen essentialiter in cognitione manet, non quidem speculativa, sed practica."

198. See *De ver.*, q. 5, a. 1, ad 7 (Spiazzi, 90): ". . . a providentia sit lex naturalis intellectus nostri . . . ."

199. The eternal law is to divine providence as the principles of a syllogism are to its conclusion; see *De ver.*, q. 5, a. 1, ad 6.

innate principles that govern human deliberations and decisions, and the latter are like remote conclusions drawn from these principles.[200]

Because it so clearly shows the theological character of the natural law in Thomistic ethics, I have been repeating Aquinas's tenet that the natural law participates the eternal law.[201] And, as I have also reiterated, this is a metaphysical proposition about the nature of the human intellect as divinely caused. God creates and structures creation in general and the human mind in particular in accordance with the ends of creation which are inscribed in the eternal law.[202] Since the eternal law is the exemplar of the natural law, the natural law may be said to instantiate in the human mind what is first in God's mind. But in delineating how the eternal law functions as the exemplar of the natural law, we must refer to the divine will as well as to the divine intellect. Within the divine economy of creation and salvation, God not only intellectually envisions an order of ends and means for creation, He *wills* to create men so that through the activity of their own intellects and wills men may realize that divine order.[203] Providence includes, then, *an act of the divine will*.[204] Indeed, Aquinas states that the act of creation, though regulated by the divine mind, is more immediately attributable to the divine will:

> The divine will is the immediate principle of creatures, ordering the divine attributes through the mode of understanding according to which [these attributes] are applied to operation. For a power does not go forth into an operation unless regulated by knowledge and determined by the will to do something. And, therefore, the order of things is more [immediately] referred to the divine will than to the [divine] power or knowledge. *(De ver.,* q. 23, a. 2, ad 3 [Spiazzi, 418])[205]

200. See *De ver.,* q. 5, a. 1, ad. 6: "Lex enim aeterna est consideranda in Deo, sicut accipiuntur in nobis principia operabilium naturaliter nota, ex quibus procedimus in consiliando et eligendo. . . ."

201. See *ST,* I–II, q. 91, a. 2: "Unde cum omnia quae divinae providentiae subduntur, a lege aeterna regulentur et mensurentur. . . . Et talis participatio legis aeternae in rationali creatura lex naturalis dicitur."

202. See *De ver.,* q. 5, a. 2, ad 10 (Spiazzi, 94): ". . . ordo ille qui est in natura, non est ei a se, sed ab alio; et ideo natura providentia indiget, a qua talis ordo instituatur in ea."

203. See *De ver.,* q. 23, a. 2 (Spiazzi, 418): "Illud ergo ad quod Deus creaturam ordinavit quantum est de se, dicitur esse volitum ab eo quasi prima intentione, sive voluntate antecedente."

204. See *De ver.,* q. 5, a. 1 (Spiazzi, 90): ". . . licet [providentia] essentialiter ad cognitionem pertineat, tamen voluntatem aliquo modo includit."

205. ". . . voluntas divina est immediatum creaturarum principium, ordinando attributa divina per modum intelligendi, secundum quod ad opus applicantur. Po-

Thus the precepts of the natural law, though first grounded in the divine intellect, must also be referred to the divine will. The natural law, whereby rational creatures are directed to their end, is a created effect of the divine will.[206] Since common human nature itself is the object of God's salvific will, all men and women are included in the divine plan of salvation.[207] Inasmuch as God wills to create rational human nature, the divine will, as included in divine providence, is the ultimate efficient cause of the natural law.[208]

Although the natural law derives from the will of the divine lawgiver,[209] the "divine command theory," as this theory is usually understood, is incompatible with the Thomistic conception of natural law: some actions are intrinsically right not only because they are commanded by the divine law but because they are in accordance with natural reason.[210] In ordinary usage, a "precept" connotes some promulgated command of a superior who wills what his subject should do.[211] But the natural law is explained in terms of human nature's participation of the eternal law. The natural law does *not* derive its immediate force from being a divinely revealed "command."[212] Rather, God, while remaining the first efficient cause of the natural law, works immanently through the exigencies of human nature. For this reason, natural law can properly fall under a philosophical as well as a theological consideration.

----

tentia enim non exit in opus nisi recta per scientiam, et determinata per voluntatem ad aliquid agendum; et ideo magis ordo rerum refertur in voluntatem divinam quam in potentiam vel scientiam" (*De ver.*, q. 23, a. 2, ad 3 [Spiazzi, 418]).

206. See *I Sent.*, d. 46, a. 1 (Mandonnet, 1051): "Et hujus voluntatis effectus est ipse ordo naturae in finem salutis, et promoventia in finem omnibus communiter proposita, tam naturalia quam gratuita, sicut potentiae naturales et praecepta legis, et hujusmodi."

207. See *I Sent.*, d. 46, q. 1, a. 1 (Mandonnet, 1051): "Si ergo in homine tantum natura ipsius consideretur, aequaliter bonum est omnem hominem salvari: quia omnes conveniunt in natura humana."

208. See *Comp. theol.*, I, c. 143: "Praeceptum nihil alius est quam dispositio divinae providentiae movens res naturales ad proprias. . . ."

209. See *ST*, I-II, q. 90, aa. 1-2; q. 98, a. 5.

210. See *SCG*, III, 128 (Pera, n. 3011, p. 191): "Homines ex divina providentia sortiuntur naturale iudicatorium rationis ut principium propriarum operationum. Naturalia autem principia ad ea ordinantur quae sunt naturaliter. Sunt igitur aliquae operationes naturaliter homini convenientes, quae sunt secundum se rectae, et non solum quasi lege positae."

211. See *In psalmos*, 18 (Vivès, 5, p. 331): "Praeceptum dicitur ad quod attenditur secundum imperium superioris; et est de agendis, et importat debitum faciendi in eo cui praecipitur. . . ."

212. See *ST*, I-II, q. 90, a. 4, ad 1: ". . . promulgatio legis naturae est ex hoc ipso quod Deus eam mentibus hominum inseruit naturaliter cognoscendam."

[God] now works in the things which he first created, guiding them in accordance with the nature that he first gave them *(De ver.,* q. 23, a. 2 [Spiazzi, 418]).[213]

Consequently, the divine will as the ultimate efficient cause that accounts for the motive force of the natural law, is to be clearly distinguished from the divine will as the immediate efficient cause that accounts for the motive force of the divine or revealed law (i.e., the Decalogue). The proximate efficient cause that accounts for the motive force of the basic natural law precepts is the human will intending the ends set forth by practical reason. But the Ten Commandments, although Aquinas thinks that they can be easily inferred from the common and immediate precepts of practical reason, are not innate; rather, they are divinely revealed imperatives, accepted on supernatural faith, that move recalcitrant men precisely because they are signs of the divine and not the human will.[214]

213. ". . . nunc tamen operatur in rebus quas primo creavit, eis administrans, praesupposita natura quam prius eis dedit . . ." *(De ver.,* q. 23, a. 2 [Spiazzi, 418]).

214. See *I Sent.,* d. 47, q. 1, a. 4 (Mandonnet, 1072): ". . . praeceptum est signum voluntatis divinae . . ."; *III Sent.,* d. 37, q. 1, a. 1 (Moos, n. 17, p. 1235): "Sed Dei voluntas nobis per legis praecepta innotescit, inquantum est signum divinae voluntatis."

VIII

Imperfect and Perfect Happiness

1. The Pertinence of Metaphysics

For Aristotle and Aquinas, metaphysics is a theoretical science and ethics is a practical science.[1] But the moral philosopher is not indifferent to the theoretical truths of metaphysics. Moral science, when considering human actions and their ends, must take into account and incorporate, where pertinent, the doctrinal conclusions of metaphysics about the most noble objects of knowledge (EN, VI, 7, 1141a20). The universe of the philosophically educated Aristotelian moral agent is the universe as known in the Aristotelian metaphysical treatises. Accordingly, the ultimate end of Aristotelian man can only be adequately specified within the framework of a metaphysical conception of being. In his metaphysical treatises, Aristotle demonstrates the existence of the highest beings, the immaterial, unmoved movers;[2] in the Nicomachean Ethics, he demonstrates that ultimate human happiness consists in contemplating. By implication, it consists in contemplating the highest beings.[3] Metaphysics knows the highest beings. Metaphysical knowledge, therefore, is the eudaimonic or quasi-divine form of human knowing.[4]

1. See In Metaph., II, lect. 2 (Cathala-Spiazzi, n. 290, p. 84): ". . . Sapientia sive philosophia prima non est practica, sed speculativa . . ."; Expos. de Trin., q. 5, a. 1, ad 4 (Decker, 16–18, p. 169): ". . . duas partes philosophiae distinxerunt, moralem dicentes practicam, naturalem et rationalem dicentes theoricam."

2. See Metaph., XII, 8.

3. See EN, X, 7, 1177a19–21 (rev. Oxford trans.): "For this [contemplative] activity is the best (since not only is intellect the best thing in us, but the objects of intellect are the best of knowable objects). . . ."

4. See Metaph., I, 2, 982a23–b10; 983a5–11.

Aristotelian metaphysical science culminates in demonstrating that the highest intelligible causes of the universe are the separate or immaterial substances which are, depending on variant calculations of the astral movements,[5] either the fifty-five or the forty-nine unmoved, self-contemplating movers of the heavenly spheres.[6] In the *Nicomachean Ethics*, Aristotle argues that the highest form of human fulfillment, the highest *eudaimonia* that is proper to man, consists in the exercise of man's highest capacity, the power to know. The philosophical life is focused on theoretical knowledge. We can infer from what Aristotle says that the highest form of theoretical knowing constitutes man's highest happiness.[7] Knowing reaches its acme when the highest or most noble beings are known.[8] Aristotle's life of philosophical contemplation, then, has as its end the theoretical knowledge of the most noble and knowable beings,[9] which Aquinas straightforwardly identifies as the contemplation of the separate substances or unmoved movers.[10]

As a commentator, Aquinas carefully exposes the Aristotelian framework wherein ethics draws upon metaphysics for a knowledge of how man fits into the universe. Aristotle states, with a tranquil conviction, that man is not the most noble being, and deliberative knowledge of human things, which is the proper sphere of *phronesis*,[11] is not the highest form of knowledge.[12] The doctrine of human happiness must be geared, therefore, to the highest act of contemplation (θεωρία), the act

---

5. Cf. *Expos. de Trin.*, q. 5, a. 1, ad 9 (Decker, 8–10, p. 172): "Indiget enim haec scientia ad cognitonem substantiarum separatarum cognoscere numerum et ordines orbius caelestium, quod non est possibile sine astrologia. . . ."

6. For discussions of the controverted relationship between Aristotle's different accounts identifying the prime mover in the *Physics* (apparently the soul of the besouled first heavenly sphere) and in the *Metaphysics* (the first unmoved final cause, i.e., the beloved separate mover), cf. Joseph Owens, "The Reality of the Aristotelian Separate Movers," *Review of Metaphysics* 3 (1949–50): 319–37, "Aquinas and the Proof from the 'Physics,'" *Mediaeval Studies* 28 (1966): 119–50; Anton C. Pegis, "St. Thomas and the Coherence of the Aristotelian Physics," *Mediaeval Studies* 35 (1973): 67–117.

7. See *EN*, X, 8; *Metaph.*, XII, 6–8.

8. See *EN*, VI, 7, 1141a19–20; 1141b3. Cf. *II Sent.*, d. 4, q. 1, a. 1; *III Sent.*, d. 35, q. 1, a. 2, sol. 3; *ST*, II–II, q. 182, a. 1.

9. See *EN*, VI, 7, 1141b2: ἡ σοφία ἐστὶ καὶ ἐπιστήμη καὶ νοῦς τῶν τιμιωτάτων τῇ φύσει; *Metaph.*, I, 2, 982b2: μάλιστα δ' ἐπιστητὰ τὰ πρῶτα καὶ τὰ αἴτια.

10. See *ST*, I, q. 88, a. 1: "Unde patet quod Aristoteles posuit ultimam felicitatem hominis in cognitione substantiarum separatarum, qualis potest haberi per scientias speculativas. . . ."

11. See *EN*, VI, 7, 1141b8–9.

12. See *EN*, VI, 7, 1141a20–22; 1141a33–b3.

of contemplating the highest beings, the most eminent of which is the first unmoved mover.[13]

The highest and most perfect act of understanding is of the highest and best [being]; and, thus, the greatest delight follows upon it. Therefore, it is evident that in that act of understanding, by which the first mover is understood, there is the greatest delight because [the first mover] is also the first intelligible. *(In Metaph.,* XII, lect. 8 [Cathala-Spiazzi, n. 2538, p. 594])[14]

Ultimate human happiness consists in what Aristotle himself accomplishes in the "divine science": knowing those rather sparse conclusions that *metaphysics* reaches about the existence and the nature of the first unmoved movers.[15] Aquinas stresses the limitation of this metaphysical knowledge: we lack knowledge of the essences of the separate substances.[16] Since we cannot abstract from material things the essences of the separate substances,[17] "we know about them more what they are not than what they are."[18] Nonetheless, Aristotelian *eudaimonia* is found in the knowledge, whatever its limitations, that physics and metaphysics afford of the separate substances. What, then, is the relevance and role of practical wisdom for the Aristotelian philosopher happily engaged in theoretical contemplation?

2. *Ethics and Politics*

Aristotle states that the scope of *phronesis* includes knowledge of: (1) the affairs of the individual himself (περὶ αὐτον καὶ ἕνα); (2) the science of household management (ἡ οἰκονομία); (3) the architectonic

---

13. See *EN*, VI, 7, 1141b2–3; *Metaph.,* XII, 7, 1073a3–5; 8, 1073b1–3. On *theoria* as knowledge of the divine, see ch. 8, n. 187. Cf. Kraut, *Aristotle on the Human Good*, 73–74; Michael W. Wedin, *Mind and Imagination in Aristotle* (New Haven: Yale University Press, 1988), 209–10.

14. ". . . maxima et perfectissima intelligentia sit maxime optimi; et ita sequitur maxima delectatio. Sic igitur manifestum est, quod in illa intelligentia, qua intelligitur primum movens, quod etiam est primum intelligibile, est maxima delectatio" *(In Metaph.,* XII, lect. 8 [Cathala-Spiazzi, n. 2538, p. 594]).

15. See *Metaph.,* I, 2, 982a30–b10; 983a5–11.

16. See *De ver.,* q. 18, a. 5 (Spiazzi, 347): "Per huiusmodi autem species [a phantasmatibus abstractae] impossibile est pervenire ad intuendam essentiam substantiae separatae."

17. Nor, for that matter, does Aquinas think that we know the essences of sensible things. We know only their proper accidents; see *De spirit. creat.,* q. 1, a. 11, ad 3 (Calceterra-Centi, 414): ". . . formae substantiales per seipsas sunt ignotae; sed innotescunt nobis per accidentia propria."

18. ". . . magis cognoscentis de eis quid non sunt quam quid sunt . . ." *(IV Sent.,* d. 49, q. 2, a. 7, ad 12 [Vivès, 11, p. 505]).

science of legislation (ἡ νομοθεσία); and (4) in the ordinary sense, the science of politics (ἡ πολιτική), which is subdivided into (a) deliberative (ἡ βουλευτική) and (b) judicial (ἡ δικαστική) sciences.[19] Aquinas defines the subject of moral philosophy as man's voluntary actions inasmuch as they are ordered to the pursuit of diverse ends.[20] Such ends can be personal, domestic, or civic. Corresponding to this classification of human ends, which replicates the distinctions made in regard to *phronesis*, moral philosophy *(philosophia moralis)* is divided into three parts that deal respectively with (1) the individual *(monastica)*; (2) the household *(oeconomica)*; and (3) the city *(politica)*.[21]

For Aristotle, it is the business of ethics to provide the arguments that show how good actions require virtue (ἀρετή) and practical wisdom (φρόνησις).[22] But courage, justice, and wisdom have the same efficacy (δύναμις) and form (μορφή) whether they belong to the city or the individual.[23] Both ethics and politics deal with virtuous actions that aim at human happiness.[24] Since the good for the individual and for the city are the same (i.e., happiness), ethics may be identified with politics.[25] Politics, however, is the architectonic science because the

---

19. See *EN*, VI, 8, 1141b29–33. Although φρόνησις and πολιτική exercise the same intellectual habit (ἕξις), common usage distinguishes their objects: see *EN*, VI, 8, 1141b23–24. Aquinas notes that this is a matter of nominal definitions entailing a distinction of their material but not their formal objects: "Dicit ergo primo quod politica et prudentia sunt idem habitus secundum substantiam, quia utraque est recta ratio rerum agibilium circa humana bona vel mala, sed differunt secundum rationem; nam prudentia est recta ratio agibilium circa unius hominis bona vel mala, id est sui ipsius, politica autem circa bona vel mala totius multitudinis civilis . . ." *(SLE*, VI, 7, 1141b23, 23–30; *In Ethic.*, VI, lect. 7 [Spiazzi, n. 1196, p. 329]).

20. See *SLE*, I, 1, *ante* 1094a1, 51–53 *(In Ethic.*, I, lect. 1 [Spiazzi, n. 3, p. 3]): ". . . Subiectum moralis philosphiae est operatio humana ordinata in finem"; *SLE*, I, 2, 1094a28, 138–40 *(In Ethic.*, I, lect. 2 [Spiazzi, n. 27, pp. 7–8]): ". . . actus inquantum sunt voluntarii pertinent ad materiam moralis, et sunt ordinabiles ad finem humanae vitae"; *SLE*, I, 3, 1094b11, 61–62 *(In Ethic.*, I, lect. 3 [Spiazzi, n. 35, p. 10]): "Nam scientia moralis est de actibus voluntariis . . ."; *SLE*, I, 3, 1095a2, 122–24 *(In Ethic.*, I, lect. 3 [Spiazzi, n. 38, p. 10]): ". . . rationes moralis scientiae procedunt ex his quae pertinent ad actus humanae vitae et etiam sunt de his. . . ."

21. See *SLE*, I, 1 *ante* 1094a1, 99–106 *(In Ethic.*, I, lect. 1 [Spiazzi, n. 6, p. 4]). "Moralis philosophia in tres partes dividitur": there is no indication, then, that Aquinas is guilty of "betraying the thought of Aristotle" by mistakenly identifying moral philosophy with "la sagesse individuelle": cf. Gauthier-Jolif, II, 2:500, nn. 1141b32–33.

22. See *Pol.*, VII, 1, 1323b39–40.

23. See ibid., 1323b33–36.

24. See *EN*, I, 13, 1102a5–12.

25. See *EN*, I, 4, 1095a15–17; 9, 1099b29–30; *Rh.*, I, 2, 1356a26–27. Cf. *SLE*, I, 14, 1099b28, 156–59 *(In Ethic.*, I, lect. 14 [Spiazzi, n. 174, p. 46]): "Posuimus enim

good of the city is a greater and more noble good than the good of the individual.[26] It is often observed, sometimes with hesitation or disapproval,[27] that Aristotle subordinates the good of the individual to the good of the city,[28] and thereby appears to subordinate, illegitimately, "ethics" to politics.[29] True, πολιτική is the supreme or architectonic moral science for Aristotle,[30] but his use of the term carries no Thrasymachian overtones. The realm of politics is certainly not beyond moral good and evil, and much less should politics promote evil. On the contrary, Aristotle identifies ethics only with the political science (more precisely, with legislation)[31] that pursues virtue—justice and moral goodness (τὸ καλόν)—rather than honor.[32] It is not even the virtuous politician but the political philosopher who can properly be called "the architect of the end" by reference to which things may be truly judged to be good or bad.[33] Nor does Aristotle simply equate ethics and politics.

Aristotle recognizes, albeit in an understated way, that politics and ethics, while both are forms of *phrone*sis dealing with human happiness, constitute two different "courses of study."[34] The distinction between ethics and politics is implied by what Aristotle says in the *Politics*. Politics pursues what constitution and form of life is best for the city; by inference, ethics is concerned with individuals.[35] Laws, as instruments to inculcate virtue, apply efficaciously to both individuals and the citizenry as a whole. In either case, the lawgiver would do well to acquire the science of legislation.[36] Indeed, good laws are what make

---

ibi quod optimum humanorum bonorum, scilicet felicitas, sit finis politicae, cuius finis manifeste est operatio secundum virtutem."

26. See *EN*, I, 2, 1094b7–10; *Pol.*, I, 2, 1253a18–19; VII, 2, 1324a5; 3, 1325b31–33. Cf. *SLE*, I, 2, 1094b7, 174–75 (*In Ethic.*, I, lect. 2 [Spiazzi, n. 30, p. 8]): "Et ideo, si idem bonum est uni homini et toti civitati. . . ."

27. See Donagan, *Theory of Morality*, 4: "[Aristotle] did not succeed in distinguishing moral virtue as such, the virtue of a man as a man, from political virtue. . . ."

28. See *EN*, I, 1, 1094a26–b7; VII, 11, 1152b1–3.

29. In fact, there is no strict Aristotelian equivalent to our term "ethics": Aristotle refers several times (*Metaph.*, I, 1, 981b25; *Pol.* II, 1, 1261a31; VII, 13, 1332a8; etc.) to "τοῖς Ἠθικοῖς" (= "τοῖς ἠθικοῖς λόγοις" or "moral discourses"), once to ἠθικὴ θεωρία (*Apo.*, I, 33, 89b9), but never to "ἡ ἠθική" (= "moral science"): see Gauthier-Jolif, II, 1:1–2.

30. See *EN*, I, 1, 1094a26–27.

31. See *EN*, X, 9, 1180b23–25.

32. See *EN*, I, 2, 1094b10–11.

33. See *EN*, VII, 11, 1152b1–3.

34. See *Pol.*, VII, 1, 1323b39–40.

35. See *Pol.*, VII, 2, 1324a19–23.

36. See *EN*, X, 9, 1180b1–2; b23–25.

good individuals, since only laws can guarantee that men are properly educated.[37] But while a father is concerned with legislating the happiness of individuals in his household, the legislator elevates to first importance the happiness or well-being of the city, or of a race of men and women, or of a community, not the happiness of the individual.[38]

Nonetheless, it is a basic and well-known tenet of Aristotle's political philosophy that right political order is in accordance with human nature. But in what Aristotle regards as the right political order, human nature is understood not to be homogeneous in all people. According to the Aristotelian conception of human nature, the good of the adult male citizens, since they alone can be fully rational, takes precedence over the good of the noncitizens: slaves, children, and women.[39] Yet Aristotle argues, too glibly for contemporary egalitarianism, that since the science of politics consists in maintaining right order, the best constitution would effectively promote the happiness of everyone living within the city, citizen and noncitizen alike.[40]

Is there ever a conflict between the good of the adult male citizens and the good of the city? No doubt, Aristotle admits that there will be conflicts in corrupt regimes between the real good of the citizen and what is regarded as good for him by the regime: in such corrupt regimes, a good man will not be counted as a good citizen.[41] But in well-governed cities, the city exists to promote the good of the citizens, and every citizen can live happily.[42] And in the best city, the best of the citizens would have leisure for the best of activities: philosophizing.[43]

Since Aristotelian *phronesis* overarches the division of the human good into personal and civic happiness, Aristotle has a strong reason not to distinguish sharply the respective spheres of "ethics" and "politics." But what the *Nicomachean Ethics* investigates is only "in a certain sense politics."[44] "Politics" taken with this qualification is not "politics" in the ordinary sense: it is a politics that assumes the overall identification of the moral and civic virtues in the good city.[45] It is these isomorphic personal and civic virtues that the wise legislator attempts to promote by rewards and punishments.

37. See *EN*, X, 9, 1180a14–18.
38. See *Pol.*, VII, 3, 1325b8–10; *EN*, I, 2, 1094b5–12.
39. See *Pol.*, I, 2; VII, 3, 1325b3–10.
40. See *Pol.*, VII, 2, 1324a23–25.
41. See *Pol.*, III, 2, 1276b33–35.
42. See *Pol.*, III, 11, 1280b30–1281a5; VII, 2, 13243a23–25.
43. See *Pol.*, VII, 15, 1334a22–25.
44. πολιτική τις οὐσία (*EN*, I, 2, 1094b11).
45. See *Pol.*, VII, 1, 1323b30–35.

For politics brings to this particular attention by framing laws and rewards and by applying punishments so that it makes good citizens and agents of good deeds, which is to act according to virtue. *(SLE, I, 14, 1099b28, 159–62; In Ethic., I, lect. 14 [Spiazzi, n. 174, p. 46])*[46]

Peter of Auvergne (d. 1304), whose commentary on Books III–VIII of the *Politics* was appended to Aquinas's commentary (which ends at III, 6, 1280a6),[47] explains the Aristotelian isomorphism between personal and civic happiness by grounding the pursuit of happiness in the human nature which is common to men qua individuals and qua citizens. Men desire happiness both as individuals and as citizens. If the city is happy, so too are the individual citizens.

For all agree that there is one happiness *[felicitas]* for each individual man and for the city since things that have the same nature have the same end. The individual man and all the citizens of a city are of one species; therefore there is one ultimate end for every individual and all citizens. *(*In Pol., VII, lect. 2 [Spiazzi, n. 1060, p. 344])*[48]

Aquinas, for his part, is eager, more eager than Aristotle anyway, to show the dependency of political science on ethics: the science of ethics provides the principles governing politics.[49] Aquinas distinguishes, with evident attention, the good of the city from the good of the individual: the good of the part is not the same as the good of the whole.[50] Politics, although concerned with human happiness, cannot subsume ethics. The two sciences remain irreducibly distinct according to the different kinds of unity that can be exemplified in the relationship of parts and wholes.[51]

---

46. "Politica enim ad hoc praecipuum [studium] adhibet ferendo leges et praemia, et poenas adhibendo, ut faciat cives bonos et operatores bonorum, quod est operari secundum virtutem" *(SLE, I, 14, 1099b28, 159–62; In Ethic. I, lect. 14 [Spiazzi, n. 174, p. 46])*.

47. See H.-F. Dondaine and L.-J. Bataillon, Preface, *SLP*, Leonine ed., 48, A5–A6. I have marked texts from Peter's commentary with an asterisk.

48. "Omnes igitur confitentur unam esse felicitatem uniuscuiusque hominis seorsum et civitatis . . . quoniam quorum est una natura, eorum est unus ultimus finis. Unus autem homo et omnes cives civitatis sunt unius speciei: ergo unius et omnium civium est unus ultimus finis" *(*In Pol., VII, lect. 2 [Spiazzi, n. 1060, p. 344])*.

49. See *SLE, I, 19, 1102a7, 31–33 (In Ethic., I, lect. 19 [Spiazzi, n. 225, p. 61])*: "Sed consideratio praesentis scientiae ad politicam pertinet, quia in hac scientia traduntur principia politicae."

50. See *ST, II–II, q. 58, a. 7, ad 2*: ". . . alia enim est ratio boni communis et boni singularis, sicut et alia est ratio totius et partis."

51. See *SLE, I, 1, ante 1094a1, 97–99 (In Ethic., I, lect. 1 [Spiazzi, n. 5, p. 4])*:

Aquinas explains that, in some compounds, the action of the part is indistinguishable from that of the whole. But the human community does not constitute this kind of compound; human beings are not "parts" that are completely subsumable to social wholes. The family and city have only a "unity of order" that exists conditionally. The order exists only so long as the members of these communities act together in pursuing the same ends. By contrast, an individual man in a city has an absolute unity apart from the city; the individual man or woman can act autonomously or independently of the city.[52] This Thomistic distinction, which singles out the individual from the city, is hardly Aristotelian, since it entails that men have ends that transcend the whole political order. This conclusion is congenial, to be sure, with what Aquinas's Christian faith affirms about man's otherworldly destiny.

Aquinas, however, acknowledges that, for Aristotle, it is precisely political science that sets forth the ultimate end of human life.[53] Since only the city has a perfect or self-sufficient form of good, the city is the natural end and goal of individuals, families, and villages.[54] Now it is at this point in his exegesis that Aquinas steps away from Aristotle's text. Aquinas demurs: theology, not politics, deals with the ultimate end of both man and the universe. Politics deals solely with the end of man in this life.[55]

Aquinas, however, does make one important concession to Aristotle, a concession that has proven difficult to place correctly in the context of Aquinas's own moral science: Aquinas concedes that there is a *good* in this world that is proportioned to human nature's ability to attain. Aquinas identifies this good with what Aristotle claims about contemplation: the preeminent form of this-worldly happiness is contemplation, what can be known of God and the separate substances

---

"Non autem ad eamdem scientiam pertinet considerare totum quod habet solam ordinis unitatem, et partes ipsius."

52. See *SLE*, I, 1, ante 1094a1, 78–99 (*In Ethic.*, I, lect. 1 [Spiazzi, n. 5, p.4]).

53. See *SLP*, I, prologus, 102–5 (*In Pol.*, prooemium [Spiazzi, n. 7, p. 2]): ". . . necesse est politicam inter omnes scientias practicas esse principaliorem et architectonicam omnium aliarum, utpote considerans ultimum et perfectum bonum in rebus humanis"; *SLE*, I, 2, 1094a26, 100–2, 109–11 (*In Ethic.*, I, lect. 2 [Spiazzi, n. 25, p. 7]): ". . . optimus finis pertinet ad principalissimam scientiam et maxime architectonicam . . . Sed civilis scientia videtur esse talis, scilicet principalissima et maxime architectonica . . ."; *SLE*, I, 19, 1102a7, 35–37 (*In Ethic.*, I, lect. 19 [Spiazzi, n. 225 p. 61]): ". . . in prooemio elegimus politicam prae omnibus aliis disciplinis, inquirentem ultimum finem humanorum."

54. See *Pol.*, I, 1, 1252b28–1253a2.

55. See *SLE*, I, 2, 1094b7, 193–202 (*In Ethic.*, I, lect. 2 [Spiazzi, n. 31, p. 8]).

through philosophy. Since the philosophical contemplation of God is the preeminent natural good, Aquinas stresses that the Aristotelian political order cannot be self-enclosed in political activity; *"the whole of political life"* is ordained to the theoretical activity that is the end of the contemplative life. Political activity is ultimately justified inasmuch as it provides the peace and security necessary for philosophical contemplation.

> For through the political life, we seek [happiness] as being something other than the political life itself. This is speculative happiness, to which the whole of political life is seen to be ordained, as long as through peace, which through the ordination of political life is instituted and preserved, the capacity of contemplating the truth is given to men. *(SLE,* X, 11, 1177b4, 46–49; *In Ethic.,* X, lect. 11 [Spiazzi, n. 2101, p. 546])[56]

3. *Aristotelian* Eudaimonia: *Inclusivist or Exclusivist?*

Aquinas's commentary subordinates, in straightforward fashion, politics to contemplation. But the ultimate status of Aristotelian political life, since it is the proper sphere within which to exercise the moral virtues, remains, for many contemporary interpreters, problematic. The most thorny question—whether the contemplative philosopher must be morally virtuous—revolves around the implications of what Aristotle says about *eudaimonia.* This question, although the relevant Aristotelian texts are few enough, has been a rich source of scholarly controversy.[57]

In *EN,* I, 5, 1095b17–19, Aristotle distinguishes three types of lives organized respectively around (1) enjoyment (ὁ ἀπολαυστικὸς βίος), (2) politics (ὁ πολιτικὸς βίος), and (3) contemplation (ὁ θεωρητικὸς βίος). Each of these three lives pursues an end or good that is loved for its own sake (1096a7–9; b16–19): pleasure, honor, and—as will be established—virtuous activity. In the first book of the *Nicomachean Ethics,* three themes pertinent to our present consideration emerge in Aristotle's discussion: (1) *eudaimonia* is not a life devoted to pleasure, at least

---

56. ". . . Sic enim per vitam politicam quaerimus eam quasi alteram existentem ab ipsa, haec est enim felicitas speculativa ad quam tota vita politica videtur ordinata, dum per pacem, quae per ordinationem vitae politicae statuitur et conservatur, datur hominibus facultas contemplandi veritatem" *(SLE,* X, 11, 1177b4, 46–49; *In Ethic.* X, lect. 11 [Spiazzi, n. 2101, p. 546]).

57. For a recent survey of the literature, see Lawrence Nannery, "The Problem of the Two Lives in Aristotle's Ethics: The Human Good and the Best Life for a Man," *International Philosophical Quarterly* 21, no. 3 (1981): 277–93.

as pleasure is vulgarly understood (1098a11–16); (2) *eudaimonia* is associated with rational activity (1098a12–14); and (3) the moral or ethical virtues (ἠθικαὶ ἀρεταί) are virtues of the rational part of the soul but they are rational only in a derivative or secondary sense (1103a1–5). Practical wisdom, or *phronesis*, however, is one of the intellectual virtues (ἀρεταὶ κιανοητικαί [1103a5]) but, as we will learn in the sixth book, exercising the virtues of speculative thought (θεωρητικὴ διάνοια), especially the virtue of wisdom (σοφία), is the highest form of rational activity (VI, 7, 1141a16–17). The significance of this latter claim is developed in the perplexing tenth and final book of the *Nicomachean Ethics*.

In *EN*, X, 8, 1178a9–10, Aristotle specifies that the life of moral virtue, referring to the paradigmatic political or practical life that is permanently and clearly distinct from the life of contemplation,[58] only produces a secondary, merely human kind of happiness in comparison with the quasi-divine happiness of the life of contemplation. This conclusion about the inferior status of the life of practical wisdom[59] is congruent with the definition of the human good given in *EN*, I, 7, 1098a16–18 (rev. Oxford trans.): "[The] human good turns out to be the activity of soul in conformity with excellence [ἀρετή], and if there are more than one excellence, in conformity with the best and most complete."[60] Although this text does not specify whether there is "one best and most complete virtue," it would appear that, in line with this initial definition of the human good, Aristotle first establishes that *sophia* (theoretical wisdom) and not *phronesis* (practical wisdom) is the best and most perfect of the virtues,[61] and then concludes that *eudaimonia* is to be identified with the exercise of *sophia*.[62] In turn, this has

58. See *EN*, X, 8, 1178a20–25, which counters Gauthier-Jolif's assertion (II, 2:891) about *EN*, X, 8, 1178a9 that the two types of life, although hierarchically subordinated, are led simultaneously by the one man who is both philosopher and politician. In his earlier study, Gauthier puts the issue differently and, I think, more illuminatingly: "Pourtant ce intellectualisme résolu de l'*Ethique* aristotélicienne reste contenu en certain limites. Le philosophe . . . reste homme et il lui faut vivre en homme . . . et surtout qu'il lui faudra rester un 'animal politique'. . ." (R. A. Gauthier, O.P., "Trois commentaires 'averroistes' sur l'*Ethique à Nicomaque*," *Archives d'histoire littéraire et doctinale du moyen âge* 16 [1948]: 244).

59. Cf. *SLE*, VI, 10, 1144a3, 133–38 (*In Ethic.*, VI, lect. 10 [Spiazzi, n. 1267, p. 343]): "Unde, cum sapientia sit quaedam species virtutis communis, ex hoc ipso quod aliquis habet sapientiam et operatur secundum eam, est felix. Et eadem ratio est de prudentia, sed specialiter expressit sapientiam, quia in operatione eius consistit potior felicitas. . . ."

60. Cf. *EN*, I, 8, 1099a24–31.

61. See *EN*, VI, 7, 1141a16–b6.

62. See *EN*, X, 7, 1177a12–21.

led some interpreters to deny that the moral virtues are to be included as components of the highest form of *eudaimonia;* they are at best means to the possession of the intellectual virtues.[63]

Part of Aristotle's doctrine is incontrovertible: a virtuous political life is second in value and happiness to the life of contemplation.[64] Debate, however, has centered on whether the highest form of *eudaimonic* life is, after all, a "mixed life" that deliberately seeks to combine politics and contemplation. Many interpreters contend that the highest form of *eudaimonia* must be, to use Hardie's terms, an "inclusivist" end (since it contains more than one good) and not merely a "dominant" or "exclusivist" end that contains but a single good.[65] They argue that to exclude moral virtue from the highest form of *eudaimonia* is an indefensible truncation: theoretical wisdom or *sophia* is but "a part of the whole of virtue."[66]

EN, I, 7, 1097b14–20 is the main, albeit obscure, text supporting the conclusion that *eudaimonia* must include all (compossible) intrinsic goods.[67] If *eudaimonia* were not inclusive, it could be improved on by some additional good. But since *eudaimonia* cannot, *ex definitione,* be improved, it must be therefore an inclusive good. So runs the reductio ad absurdum argument.[68]

In interpreting 1097b14–20, Aquinas does not explicitly state that happiness is a composite of all intrinsic goods, but he does argue that happiness is more choiceworthy if other goods are added to it.

---

63. See Greenwood, *Nicomachean Ethics, Book Six,* 58–59: "Now the final end *theoria kata sophian* is something quite different from good moral action and good moral actions are therefore not component but external and independent means to the end."

64. See *EN,* X, 8, 1178a9.

65. See W. F. R. Hardie, "The Final Good in Aristotle's Ethics," *Philosophy* 40 (1965): 277–95 [reprinted in *Aristotle: A Collection of Critical Essays,* ed. J. M. E. Moravcsik (Garden City, N.Y.: Doubleday & Co., 1967), 297–322]. J. L. Ackrill, "Aristotle on Eudaimonia," in *Essays on Aristotle's Ethics,* 17, notes the ambiguity of the term "dominant": in a weak sense, a dominant end might include several subordinate or lesser goods. But an end is dominant in the strong or exclusivist sense only if it contains a single or monolithic good.

66. *EN,* VI, 12, 1144a5.

67. See Ackrill, op. cit., for an interpretation that incorporates into *eudaimonia* all compossible intrinsic goods such as health, wealth, friendship, and bodily pleasures.

68. See, among others, Gauthier-Jolif, II, 1:53, n. 1097b16–20. For a relentless and important counterargument against this interpretation, see Kraut, "Inclusivism," in *Aristotle on the Human Good,* 267–311, who argues that since theoretical activity alone is sufficient for *eudaimonia,* it cannot be improved by the addition of any other intrinsic good. *Eudaimonia,* therefore, is an exclusive good.

This happiness about which we now speak is in itself sufficient, since it contains in itself all that which is necessary for man, not however [that it contains] every [good] thing which is able to come to a man. Hence [this happiness] is able to become better by some other [good] addition. However, there remains no unquiet desire in [the happy] man, since desire regulated by reason, such as is necessary to be happy, does not have any inquietude about those things which are not necessary although they are possible to attain. Therefore, this is what he says pertains above all things to happiness, that it is choiceworthy even when it is not numbered with other [good] things. However, if it is numbered with anything else, however small a good, it is evident that it will be more choiceworthy. The reason for this is that through the addition [of some good] it acquires a surplus or an increase of goodness. To the extent, however, that something is a greater good, so much more is it choiceworthy. *(SLE, I, 9, 1097b16, 198–212; In Ethic., I, lect. 9 [Spiazzi, n. 116, p. 31])*[69]

Thus, human happiness, as Aquinas views it, is not a perfect good, meaning by that a good that cannot be added to. Now Aquinas's view is, arguably, incompatible with Aristotelian doctrine.[70] In any case, inclusivist notions of *eudaimonia* must be reconciled with such texts as *EN*, X, 7, 1177a12–18 and 1178b24–25 where Aristotle unflinchingly champions the superiority of a life exclusively devoted to the pursuit of one exclusivist end: the exercise of the theoretical virtue of *sophia*.

---

69. "Et sic felicitas de qua nunc loquitur habet per se sufficientem, quia scilicet in se continet omne illud quod est homini necessarium, non autem omne illud quod potest homini advenire, unde potest melior fieri aliquo alio addito; nec tamen remanet desiderium hominis inquietum, quia desiderium ratione regulatum quale oportet esse felicis non habet inquietudinem de his quae non sunt necessaria licet sunt possibilia adipisci. Hoc est ergo quod dicit maxime inter omnia convenire felicitati quod ipsa etiam non connumerata aliis sit eligibilis, sed tamen, si connumeratur alicui alteri etiam minimo bonorum, manifestum est quod erit eligibilior; cuius ratio est quia per appositionem fit superabundantia vel augmentum bonitatis, quanto autem aliquid est magis bonum, tanto est magis eligibile" *(SLE, I, 9, 1097b16, 198–212; In Ethic., I, lect. 9 [Spiazzi, n. 116, p. 31]).*

70. Kraut assimilates Aquinas's interpretation to the ones offered by Kenny and Clark which he regards as "absurd" *(Aristotle on the Human Good, 272)* because he thinks that they commit Aristotle to (a) "saying that we can achieve a good that is more desirable than happiness." Moreover, Kraut argues that (a) entails (b) "[denying] that all our actions should be undertaken for the sake of happiness" (271). In regard to (a): Aquinas thinks that only God is the perfect good that cannot be improved by addition of finite goods which are indeed good but only by participation in infinite divine goodness. In the Thomistic metaphysical context, one is required to say that finite human happiness, especially if it is identifed [with Kraut] as a single exclusive good (contemplation), is a good that can be improved on. But even for Aristotle, contemplation is not, as Clark points out *(Aristotle's Man, 153, n. 2)*, "the good." As for Kraut's proposition (b): if (b) does follow from (a), this is,

Contemporary scholarship is ripe with incompatible explanations of why Aristotle's account even in the tenth book of the *Nicomachean Ethics* contains both "dominant/exclusivist" and "inclusivist" notions of *eudaimonia*.[71] Let me cite a few of the more ingenious, recent attempts to settle the texts of Aristotle.

Nannery approaches the problem by first concluding that there is a contradiction in Aristotle's doctrine about *eudaimonia:* "[Aristotle's] ideal is *both* exclusivist *and* inclusivist."[72] But the contradiction, he contends, is more apparent than real because the inclusivist ideal applies only to the species man and the exclusivist ideal only to the individual man. Individual men are either philosophers or politicians; they are devoted either to *theoria* or to *phronesis*. Nannery, however, attempts to merge the alternatives. He incorporates the inclusivist ideal into the individual contemplative life by affirming a form of "theoretical *phronesis*" by which the philosopher, who need not hold an actual political office, "inspires lawmakers, rulers, and citizens"[73] by his life and writings. Whatever else one can say about this interpretation, however, one must observe that "theoretical *phronesis*," by Aristotelian usage, is an oxymoron.

Engberg-Pedersen, like Nannery, assimilates parts of the *Nicomachean Ethics* to what could be called a "theoretical anthropology": he contends that Aristotle is not considering, at least in Book X of the

---

indeed, a troublesome entailment. But Aquinas does not hold *simpliciter* Kraut's proposition (a). Aquinas distinguishes not "the desirable" *(appetibilis)* from "the more desirable" but "the choiceworthy" *(eligibilis)* from "the more choiceworthy" *(eligibilior)*. Aquinas argues that what is "more choiceworthy" is not *simpliciter* always "more desirable." If one were presented with choice (1), happiness without any additional good, or choice (2), happiness with the addition of a superfluous good, there would be a reason to choose (2) as being the greater good. But it would not be reasonable to desire (2) since the only *necessary* good is happiness itself. Accordingly, Aquinas claims that the happy man, since *ex definitione* his desires are regulated by reason, will not desire the attainable but superfluous goods: a happy man already possesses the one necessary good that suffices in itself to satisfy his desires.

71. See *EN*, X, 8, 1179a1–17, where Aristotle refers to and apparently approves of the opinions of "the wise," that the exercise of the moral virtues is somehow "part" of the highest form of contemplative *eudaimonia*. Cf. David Keyt, "Intellectualism in Aristotle," in *Essays in Ancient Greek Philosophy*, ed. John P. Anton and Anthony Preuss (Albany: State University of New York Press, 1983), 2:364–87.

72. Lawrence Nannery, "The Problem of Two Lives in Aristotle's Ethics": 282. Cf. *Pol.*, VII, 3, 1325b31–32 (rev. Oxford trans.): ". . . Happiness is assumed to be acting well, the active life will be the best . . . Hence it is evident that the same life is best for each individual, and for states and for mankind collectively."

73. Nannery, "Problem of Two Lives," 284.

Nicomachean Ethics, man as he actually is but only "two abstract types of life and two abstract types of person."[74] But Engberg-Pedersen finds things in exactly the reverse order to Nannery: the exclusivist ideal applies to the human species, the inclusivist ideal to the individual. Abstractly or typologically, the life of contemplation is best; but an individual man cannot, of course, live abstractly. Actual human happiness for an actual human being, even allowing for Aristotle's rhapsodic divination of the human intellect, can only be embodied, and therefore happiness for "humans as they are" is inclusivist; it "consists in the exercise of *sophia* and *phronesis* (plus a certain amount of natural goods)."[75]

White, who rejects Hardie's dominant-inclusivist model, prefers to sacrifice the scientific unity of the *Nicomachean Ethics* by denying that it has a consistent or unitary end; he maintains that Aristotle looks at *eudaimonia* from both a theoretical and a practical point of view.[76] Thus the conflict, which is said to be already present in the first book of the *Nicomachean Ethics*, is between a metaethical theory of the formal features of goodness (stressing its self-sufficiency) and a quasi-naturalistic description of the ends actually sought by the human species.[77]

Devereux, however, finds his hermeneutical clue in Aristotelian logical doctrine; he thinks that Aristotle's definition of *eudaimonia* merely singles out its essence, contemplation, and not all the other properties entailed by this essence.[78] Consequently, the moral virtues may be thought to be presupposed by this definition, not as parts of happiness but as its necessary conditions or efficient causes.[79]

These explanations, though they finally go in different directions, first take a common turn: all of them appeal to some theoretical doctrine (whether Aristotelian or quasi-Aristotelian) in order to resolve what is supposed to be a conflict in the doctrines of Aristotle's practical

---

74. See Engberg-Pedersen, *Aristotle's Theory*, 119.

75. Ibid. Cf. *SLE*, X, 12, 1178a10, 52–69 (*In Ethic.*, X, lect. 12 [Spiazzi, nn. 2115–16, p. 550]).

76. Cf. *EN*, VI, 12, 1143b19–21 (Rackham trans.): "*Sophia* does not consider the means to human happiness at all, for it does not ask how anything comes into existence. *Phronesis*, it must be granted, does do this. . . ."

77. See Nicholas P. White, "Goodness and Human Aims in Aristotle's Ethics," in *Studies in Aristotle*, 225–46.

78. See Daniel T. Devereux, "Aristotle on the Essence of Happpiness," in *Studies in Aristotle*, 247–60.

79. See *EE*, I, 2, 1214b11–27; *EN*, I, 8; *Pol.*, VII, 7, 1328a21–35. Cf. Gauthier-Jolif, II, 2:546–47.

science. These authors take a theoretical turn because they begin with a theoretical problem: the logical dichotomy posed between the concepts of an "inclusivist" and an "exclusivist" end. It is this dichotomy that makes it so difficult to show that Aristotle has a consistent doctrine of *eudaimonia* since all of what he says in the *Nicomachean Ethics* about *eudaimonia* can hardly be put on the one or the other of its logical sides.[80] The difficulty is compounded by confusion when the inclusivist-exclusivist model is indifferently posed in reference to (a) *eudaimonia*, (b) the paradigm of "the philosophical/theoretical life," and (c) the life of the philosopher. But distinguishing among these three possible referents is crucial for making sense both of Aristotle and Aquinas's exegesis of Aristotle.

If we do not extravagantly expand the issue, Aristotle's apparently neat subordination of the political to the philosophical life provokes three basic questions: (1) Must the philosophical contemplative be a morally virtuous man? (2) If so, must he be in some sense a political man? (3) Finally, if we answer these two questions affirmatively, are we then to consider the highest form of Aristotelian *eudaimonia* to be an "inclusive good" because the *life* of the philosopher embraces at least two goods, contemplation and moral virtue? I shall answer the first and second questions affirmatively; the third I shall answer negatively, in the way suggested, by redefining the question.

Put in terms of the inclusivist-exclusivist dichotomy, I shall argue that, in the *Nicomachean Ethics*, the highest form of Aristotelian *eudaimonia* is exclusive—it is to be strictly and solely identified with the activity of contemplation—but that the *life of the Aristotelian philosopher* necessarily includes the moral virtues. That is, the actual life of the philosopher, which is to be distinguished from the exclusivist *paradigm* of "the philosophical/theoretical life," is inclusive even if the highest *eudaimonic* activity proper to the Aristotelian philosopher is not.

4. The Instrumental Value of Moral Virtue

Let us start with the most radical possibility. The philosopher, that is, the philosophical contemplative, leads a life that is more than human, a life that is divine.[81] Can the Aristotelian contemplative, like the

---

80. By contrast, the *Eudemean Ethics* is thought to be consistently inclusivist. Cf. *EE*, II, 1, 1219a38–39 (rev. Oxford trans.): "Happiness would be the activity of a complete life in accordance with complete excellence" (ἡ εὐδαιμονία ζωῆς τελείας ἐνέργεια κατ᾽ ἀρετὴν τελείαν).

81. See *EN*, X, 7, 1177b26–28.

gods, avoid the moral dimension of life altogether?[82] The very humanity of the contemplative shows that this is not an existential possibility; notwithstanding his encomium of the philosophical life, Aristotle does not think that the philosopher is a god.[83] The philosophical contemplative has a composite human nature; he, like all other humans, has bodily passions that need to be controlled by the moral virtues.[84]

Although Aristotle is vexingly obscure in Book X of the *Nicomachean Ethics* about the exact role of moral virtue in the life of the philosopher, it cannot be doubted that the moral virtues are at least *instrumentally* valuable for the Aristotelian contemplative. If the philosopher is to be able to contemplate, he must also be a morally virtuous man. The Aristotelian contemplative faces those necessities of life that are inextricably tied to the moral virtues.[85] Possessing or being deprived of life's necessities generates the pleasures and pains that must be regulated by the moral virtues, for pleasures and pains prompt good and bad actions.[86] Although the paradigm of the philosophical life and the *eudaimonia* proper to the philosophical life are focused on the intellectual virtues, the contemplative himself cannot be the plaything of his own passions.[87] The pursuit of contemplation itself dictates that the philosopher's actual life be ordered according to an irreducible minimum of practical wisdom which is itself tied to the moral virtues.[88]

Moral virtue thus plays an indispensable role in the life of the philosopher even if it is not described as part of the paradigm of the philosophical life. Although the act of theoretical contemplation is not dependent on external things, the contemplative, if he truly wants to contemplate, or, for that matter, to do anything else, must look after his bodily needs. The contemplative, since he is not a god or a disembodied soul, needs, as do all other men, some external goods—the necessities of life, as they are called.[89]

Aquinas's commentary picks up Aristotle's point and repeats it pre-

---

82. See *EN*, X, 8, 1178b8–18.
83. See *EN*, X, 8, 1178b33: "[The philosopher] being a man. . . ."
84. See *EN*, X, 8, 1178a19–21.
85. See *EN*, VII, 13, 1153b16–19; X, 8, 1178b33–35.
86. See *EN*, II, 3, 1105a10.
87. See *EN*, X, 8, 1178b3–5.
88. See *EN*, X, 8, 1178a16–18. On the ordering function of *phronesis* so that men may lead the kind of lives that will allow them to attain *sophia*, see *EN*, VI, 13, 1145a7–9; *SLE*, VI, 11, 1145a6, 194–98 (*In Ethic.*, VI, lect. 11 [Spiazzi, n. 1290, p. 347]). Cf. Beatriz Bossi De Kirchner, "Aquinas as an Interpreter of Aristotle on the End of Human Life," *Review of Metaphysics* 40 (1986): 45.
89. See *EN*, X, 8, 1178a25.

cisely. Both the contemplative and the fully engaged political man stand in equal need of the necessities of life: health, food, and the other things (and perhaps persons) that nurture the body.

It is true that both the speculative life and the moral life need the necessities of life, namely, food, and drink, and other such things . . . on this point there is not a great difference, since each [of the lives] equally needs the necessities. *(SLE,* X, 12, 1178a23, 73–80; *In Ethic.,* X, lect. 12 [Spiazzi, n. 2117, p. 550])[90]

To secure those necessities, both types of men will have to oversee a household or, as is preferable, supervise the overseer of his household.[91]

The Aristotelian contemplative, however, is not obliged to be a hermit or a household recluse; more self-sufficient than other men, he nonetheless appreciates how friendship with other morally virtuous men can foster his own contemplation. The philosopher can receive help from his friends in understanding things.[92] This is reason enough for the contemplative man to choose to live in at least a community of like-minded friends.[93] But sometimes a larger circle of associates may be required and joining that circle often may not be a matter of choice. Only in a good political order can men be properly educated for virtue.[94] The pursuit of his own good may compel the contemplative to leave the household, to venture even beyond the circle of his philosophical friends, to enter civil society since only in the political associations of the city can one establish and preserve that virtuous civil order that allows for contemplation.[95]

For whatever reason he is in society, whether from choice and friendship or from "necessity," so that he may secure the social order that supports his own contemplation, social life commits the contemplative to doing morally virtuous acts.[96] Aquinas's commentary, nourished by a deeper evangelical charity, strikes the same note more

---

90. "Verum est enim quod ambobus, idest tam speculativae quam morali, opus est habere necessaria vitae, puta cibum et potum et alia huiusmodi . . . tamen quantum ad hoc non est magna differentia, quin aequaliter necessariis utraque indigeat" *(SLE,* X, 12, 1178a23, 73–80; *In Ethic.,* X, lect. 12 [Spiazzi, n. 2117, p. 550]).

91. See *Pol.,* I, 2, 1253b23–25; 7, 1255b30–37.

92. See *EN,* VIII, 1, 1155a15–16; IX, 9; X, 7, 1177a34.

93. See *EN,* X, 8, 1178b5–7.

94. See *EN,* X, 9, 1180a14–18.

95. See *EN,* VI, 8, 1142a9–10.

96. See *EN,* X, 8, 1178b5–6 (rev. Oxford trans.): "In so far as he [the contemplative] is a man and lives with a number of people, he chooses to do excellent acts. . . ."

forcefully. To the extent that the contemplative chooses to live in society, he may be said to choose the life of moral virtue. To live in society is to be morally required to help one's fellow men from time to time. This solicitude for his fellow citizens expresses as well as presupposes moral virtue.[97]

Aquinas explicitly states what Aristotle leaves obscure in Book X: that the moral virtues are habits or dispositions necessary for attaining intellectual virtue; the two kinds of virtue could not, therefore, come into conflict.[98] Aquinas's heightened appreciation of the instrumental value of the moral virtues is completely in line with certain anthropological facts well known to Aristotle but which portions of the *Nicomachean Ethics* seem to ignore. Although the soul is the preeminent element in man, Aristotelian man is assuredly a composite of soul and matter.[99] Aquinas observes that the dignity of the soul does not detract from the fact that men are composites. In fact, man the composite is a more complete and noble being than the human soul which, although more noble than the body, is but a part of a man.[100]

Aquinas allows that we can consider the embodied human intellect as if it existed apart from the composite—"in its purity."[101] But the rational soul in its own nature is the form of a living body. The intellect as a power of the embodied soul does not, while it is embodied, exist apart from the human composite. Because of its embodied state, human reason is practical as well as speculative, human as well as metaphorically divine. Contemplation lifts man to God, but if the hu-

97. See *SLE*, X, 12, 1178a23, 115–8 *(In Ethic.*, X, lect. 12 [Spiazzi, n. 2120, p. 551]): ". . . inquantum convivit pluribus, quod interdum oportet iuvare; et inquantum homo contemplativus eligit vivere secundum virtutem moralem."

98. See *SLE*, II, 1, 1103a14, 12–13 *(In Ethic.*, II, lect. 1 [Spiazzi, n. 245, p. 69]): "Et ratio ordinis est quia virtutes morales sunt magis notae, et per eas disponimur ad intellectuales."

99. Cf. *EN*, X, 8, 1178a2–3 (rev. Oxford trans.): "This [intellect] would seem, too, to be each man himself, since it is the authoritative and better part of him."

100. See *III Sent.*, d. 5, q. 3, a. 2, ad 5 (Moos, n. 116, p. 207): ". . . quamvis anima sit dignior corpore, tamen unitur ei ut pars totius hominis, quod quodammodo est dignius anima, inquantum est completius." But in being united to the body, the human soul is inferior and less noble than an angel: ". . . anima acquiritur esse inferioris et minus nobile, in quo corpus sibi unitur, ut unum sit animae esse et corporis, quod est esse conjuncti . . ." *(II Sent.*, d. 17, q. 2, a. 1 [Mandonnet, 433]).

101. See *SLE*, X, 11, 1177b26, 99–104 *(In Ethic.*, X, lect. 11 [Spiazzi, n. 2106, p. 546]): "Et ideo quantum intellectus in sua puritate consideratus differt a composito ex anima et corpore, tantum distat operatio speculativa ab operatione quae fit secundum virtutem moralem, quae proprie est circa humana." Cf. *SLA*, III, c. 4, 430a22, 212–13 *(In de An.*, III, lect. 10 [Pirotta, n. 743, p. 175]): ". . . concludit quod hec sola pars anime, scilicet intellectiua, est incorruptibilis et perpetua. . . ."

man contemplative is to flourish on this earth he must act rationally about human matters and feelings. Moral virtue, consequently, is an inescapable necessity of man's bodily condition and circumstances.

5. The Intrinsic Value of Moral Virtue

Notwithstanding his hylemorphic conception of man, does Aristotle actually defend the intrinsic (and not merely the instrumental) goodness of the moral virtues for the contemplative?[102] In answering this question, we should note precisely what Aristotle does *not* say in Book X of the *Nicomachean Ethics*. While he nowhere spells out how or to what degree the philosopher can or should embody the moral virtues, Aristotle also does *not* say that the philosopher is indifferent to moral virtue.[103] On the contrary, Aristotle states, in Book VI, that the proper function of man presupposes the exercise of practical wisdom and moral virtue.[104] Of course, this claim by itself is compatible with a strictly instrumentalist evaluation of the moral virtues. But other texts indicate that moral virtue is not simply an instrumental value: it is desirable for its own sake.[105] We are told that no man is good without the moral virtues.[106] Moreover, there are certain base actions that can never be done for whatever end or reason.[107] These strictures on certain base actions should apply, a fortiori, to the philosopher.

It is not Aristotle, then, but some contemporary interpreters who, by isolating Book X from the rest of the *Nicomachean Ethics*, conjure up the specter of an immoral philosopher happily pursuing contempla-

---

102. Gauthier-Jolif conclude that there is a "functional incoherence" in Aristotle's affirmation of the intrinsic goodness of the moral virtues because he also relies on the mistaken means-end model (drawn from productive activity) which instrumentalizes the contribution of moral virtue to *eudaimonia*: see II, 1:6–7, n. 1094a16–18; II, 1:198–99, n. 1112a31–33.

103. Ackrill, although he argues for an inclusivist notion of *eudaimonia*, also concludes that Aristotle cannot explain how moral virues have intrinsic and not merely instrumental value in a life centered on contemplation. The alleged fault lies in Aristotle's anthropology: Aristotle is not able to draw a coherent portrait of the philosopher since the philosopher is a compound of "'something divine' and much that is not divine" ("Aristotle on Eudaimonia," 33).

104. See *EN*, VI, 12, 1144a6–7 (rev. Oxford trans.): "Again, the function [ἔργον] of man is achieved only in accordance with practical wisdom and moral excellence...."

105. See *EN*, X, 6, 1176b8–9 (rev. Oxford trans.): "... to do noble and good deeds is a thing desirable for its own sake."

106. See *EN*, I, 8,1099a 16–17 (rev. Oxford trans.): "... the man who does not rejoice in noble actions is not even good...."

107. See *EN*, II, 6, 1107a14–15.

tion while either ignoring or violating what is morally required of him. But even in Book X Aristotle does not imply, despite his identification of contemplation as the highest form of *eudaimonia*, that the philosopher should maximize his own happiness, if necessary by ignoring his moral obligations to other people and by subordinating everything and everyone to the egoistic pursuit of theoretical contemplation.[108] On the contrary, what Aristotle says elsewhere about friendship is incompatible with any portrait of the Aristotelian philosopher as an unrelenting egoist:[109] sometimes the philosopher should place the well-being of his friend above his own self-interest.[110] If the person is not morally incurable, the philosopher should attempt to rescue a friend who has become wicked.[111] Such an effort, one can easily imagine, would take time and energy away from the philosopher's contemplative pursuits.

Aristotle, in fact, recognizes that some moral obligations override the pursuit of one's own untrammeled happiness including, since nothing is said to the contrary, the philosopher's contemplative activities. Filial obligations clearly do: one should feed one's parents before oneself. And if it were a question of ransoming himself or his father from a life of bondage, the son—Aristotle appears to agree with common opinion—should ransom his father. No exemption is made or implied for the philosopher. And what exemption could the philosopher legitimately claim? The benefits that any parents have bestowed on their child—life, nurture, and education—cannot, no matter what sacrifice is called for, be adequately repaid.[112]

Although Aristotle holds that *sophia*, because of the nobility of its objects, is a superior form of knowledge than *phronesis*, it is nonetheless a mistake to think that the exercise of theoretical wisdom is in no way subject to practical wisdom. According to the natures of things, the separate substances that are treated in metaphysics are, independent of any human choices, divine beings.[113] To pursue contemplation

---

108. See Kraut, "Self and Others," in *Aristotle on the Human Good*, 78–154.

109. There is a good and bad self-love. The "self-love" that Aristotle praises involves always striving for moral excellence rather than wealth, honor, or bodily pleasures: see *EN*, IX, 8, 1168b12–31. Such morally legitimate self-love engenders a mutually beneficial "moral competition" among friends: see Kraut, *Aristotle on the Human Good*, 115–19.

110. It "is more characteristic of a friend to do well by another than to be well done by . . ." (*EN*, IX, 9, 1169b10–11 [rev. Oxford trans.]).

111. See *EN*, IX, 3, 1165b13–22.

112. See *EN*, VIII, 11, 1161a15–17; IX, 1, 1164b3–6; 2, 1164b33–1165a2; 1165a21–25.

113. See *Metaph.*, XII, 8, 1074b9–10: ὅτι θεοὺς ᾤοντο τὰς πρώτας οὐσίας εἶναι, θείως ἂν εἰρῆσθαι νομίσειεν.

of "beings noble and divine,"[114] since they indeed are what is best in the cosmos,[115] is to make the best of human choices.[116] Still, all human choices are subject to moral (i.e., political) considerations.

For political science orders that some teach or learn geometry. Since acts of this kind, insofar as they are voluntary, pertain to the matter of morals; they are able to be ordered to the end of human life. The politician, however, does not dictate to the geometer what he should conclude about the triangle, since this conclusion is not subject to the human will nor is it something that can be ordered to the end of human life, but [the conclusion] depends on the very nature of the [triangle]. *(SLE, I, 2, 1094a28, 134–44; In Ethic., I, lect. 2 [Spiazzi, n. 27, pp. 7–8])*[117]

Political science dictates to speculative science not in regard to its specification but in regard to its exercise. Thus to know when to contemplate, or to know how much time to dedicate to contemplation, is a matter that falls under practical wisdom. The *phronimos*, the man whose political science enables him to know what is morally good and just for the city,[118] also knows how to correctly order his own life. Because he possesses *phronesis*, the philosopher will know when it is morally just and good for the city to promote philosophical activity and when also it is morally appropriate for him to pursue with single-minded devotion the best possible life, the life of philosophical contemplation.

Aquinas, however, does not wholeheartedly embrace the Aristotelian philosopher. He observes, in an unfavorable comparison, that while the Christian seeks to contemplate out of love for what is contemplated, Aristotelian beatitude arises out of the contemplative's

---

114. See *Metaph.*, XII, 8, 1074b15: καὶ ἔννοιαν ἔχειν περὶ καλῶν καὶ θείων.

115. See *EN*, VI, 7, 1141b21–22: τὸ ἄριστον τῶν ἐν τῷ κόσμῳ.

116. See *EE*, VII, 15, 1249b16–21 (rev. Oxford trans.): "What choice, then, or possession of the natural goods—whether bodily goods, wealth, friends, or other things—will most produce the contemplation of God, that choice or possession is best; this is the noblest standard [ὁ ὅρος κάλλιστος], but any that through deficiency or excess hinders one from the contemplation and service of god [τὸν θεὸν θεραπεύειν καὶ θεωρεῖν] is bad. . . ."

117. "Sed scientiae speculativae praecipit civilis solum quantum ad usum, non autem quantum ad determinationem operis; ordinat enim politica quod aliqui doceant vel addiscant geometriam, huiusmodi enim actus in quantum sunt voluntarii pertinent ad materiam moralem et sunt ordinabiles ad finem humanae vitae; non autem praecipit politicus geometrae quid de triangulo concludat, hoc enim non subiacet humanae voluntati nec est ordinabile humanae vitae, sed dependet ex ipsa rerum ratione" *(SLE, I, 2, 1094a28, 134–44; In Ethic., I, lect. 2 [Spiazzi, n. 27, pp. 7–8]).*

118. See *EN*, I, 2, 1094a18–1094b11; *Pol.*, VII, 2, 1325a7–10.

love of himself.[119] But if the Aristotelian philosopher is self-centered so are his gods. Aristotle's gods, being perfectly actualized by their own self-knowledge, do not think about or, despite what the myths say, love men.[120] They do not will, as noble friends do, what is good for mankind for mankind's sake.[121] And whether it is possible to love, even as much as one loves oneself, a god who does not love in return is a moot question. Friendship, which is built on equality and oneness of soul, does not exist between the gods and men. The gods neither know nor need our good will toward them.[122] Perhaps, then, Aristotle thinks that men can only honor rather than love the gods. The gods, in a way, are like one's parents. Men honor the gods and their parents because of the benefits they have received.[123] Still, this counts for Aristotle as a noble form of self-subordination to a higher good.[124]

6. Contemplation and Politics

Despite Aquinas's reservations, we can safely conclude, then, that the Aristotelian philosopher appreciates the intrinsic as well as the instrumental goodness of the moral virtues. Since the philosopher does seek to lead a morally good life, he must exercise *phronesis* so that he can direct his actions to the things that are genuinely good for man.[125] I have noted that practical wisdom can be exercised in three spheres: in one's individual affairs, in the household, and in the polis.[126] Although I have already argued that necessity may compel the philosopher to enter the city, we need to explore further whether it would even be

---

119. See *I Sent.*, d. 1, q. 2, a. 1, ad 2; *III Sent.*, d. 35, q. 1, a. 2, sol. 1; *ST,* I–II, q. 11, a. 3, ad 3.

120. See *Metaph.*, XII, 9; *EN*, X, 7.

121. See *EN*, IX, 8, 1168b2–3.

122. See *EN*, VIII, 2, 1155b27–1156a5.

123. See *EN*, VIII, 12, 1162a4–7 (rev. Oxford trans.): "The friendship of children to parents, and of men to gods, is a relation to them as to something good and superior; for they have conferred the greatest benefits since they are the causes of their being and of their nourishment, and of their education from birth . . ."; *SLE*, VIII, 12, 1162a4, 179–83 *(In Ethic.*, VIII, lect. 12 [Spiazzi, n. 1715, p. 451): ". . . filii habent amicitiam ad parentes sicut ad quoddam bonum superexcellens, quia ipsi sunt maxime benefactores in quantum ipsi sunt filiis causa essendi et nutriendi et disciplinae; et talis est etiam amicitia hominis ad Deum."

124. See *EN*, IX, 2, 1165a23–24 (rev. Oxford trans.): ". . . it is more noble to help in this respect [in the matter of food] the authors of our being even before ourselves; and honour too one should give to one's parents as one does to the gods. . . ."

125. See *EN*, VI, 5, 1140b20–21.

126. See *EN*, VIII, 8, 1141b23–1142a.

morally appropriate, for the fortunate philosopher living in a congenial regime, to remain radically apolitical by deliberately confining himself to his own household where he can pay attention only to his own affairs. This exploration is motivated by the assumption that the philosopher must strive, in any circumstances, not only for the highest but for the most complete form of virtue.

Aristotle says, rather tentatively, that "perhaps one's own good cannot exist without household management, nor without a form of government" *(EN, VI, 8, 1142a9–10 [rev. Oxford trans.]).*[127] We know, however, that the philosopher does not have to manage his own household; it is better if he acts as supervisor to his household manager. Should we infer, then, that the philosopher also does not have to be active in civic affairs or does not have to be a politician? Perhaps, in a good regime, it would be sufficient for the philosopher to receive the benefits that flow from the work of politicians, while being quite content, indeed finding it preferable, to leave that work to others.

It can be shown, I think, that this portrait of the radically apolitical philosopher is misdrawn. The need to mix contemplation and politics *in the life of the philosopher,* however the mixture is precisely weighted, is unavoidable because Aristotle requires the philosopher to be a morally virtuous man. And the chain linking Aristotelian morality to politics is unbreakable: moral virtue depends on *phronesis* whose highest instantiation is political science. The two are expressions of the same intellectual virtue: "Political wisdom and practical wisdom are the same state of mind."[128] *Phronesis,* however, can only be fully embodied in political science. So too moral greatness and nobility are preeminently exercised in political and military actions.[129]

"Life is action":[130] from an Aristotelian perspective, a man preoccupied with his private affairs or the affairs of his household is not fully active; he has not yet moved into the larger sphere of action, the city, where political actions call for the highest exercise of practical wisdom and moral virtue.[131] It is the ruler of a city, and not of a household, who

127. *EN*, VI, 8, 1142a10: either ἄνευ πολιτείας or ἄνευ πολιτικῆς. See Rackham trans., 348, n. 7.

128. Ἔστι δὲ ἡ πολιτικὴ καὶ ἡ φρόνησις ἡ αὐτὴ ἕξις *(EN, VI, 8, 1141b23–24 [rev. Oxford trans.]).*

129. See *EN*, X, 7, 1177b16–17 (rev. Oxford trans.): ". . . among excellent actions political and military actions are distinguished by nobility and greatness. . . ."

130. ὁ δὲ βίος πρᾶξις *(Pol., I, 4, 1254a7).*

131. For a philosophically nuanced statement of the cultural and historical background of the Greek conception of political life, see Hannah Arendt, *The Human Condition* (Chicago: University of Chicago Press, 1958), 22–37.

has the highest form of *phronesis,* for it is in the city and not in the household that living the good life is found.[132] Once one grants that it is necessary for the contemplative man to be a morally virtuous man, then the full realization of moral virtue requires that the Aristotelian philosopher be involved, to a degree not easy to specify, in politics.

Of course, there is an irreducible difference between the paradigmatic lives, the life devoted to contemplation and the life devoted to politics. Only the philosophical life attains the highest form of *eudaimonia.* And the highest form of *eudaimonic* activity is not a mixture of contemplation and politics. The activity of contemplation as such does not lead to or require political activity; political science (ἡ πολιτική) is not a species of theoretical wisdom (σοφία).[133] Nonetheless, "Man is political by nature":[134] this fact of human nature, which Aristotle states so baldly, can hardly be ignored in any interpretation of the philosopher's actual life.

The same fact, however, is the source of a potential conflict recognized by Aristotle himself[135] and emphasized by some contemporary interpreters: the actual or possible requirements of theoretical wisdom can conflict with the actual or possible requirements of moral (i.e., civic) virtue.[136] What accounts for the tension between contemplation and political activity? Aquinas, repeating Aristotle *(EN,* X, 7, 1177b12), explains that political activity is inherently unleisurely; it involves the pursuit of honor, power, and prestige, and these are pursuits that do not constitute or allow the leisure necessary for the highest form of *eudaimonic* activity. Contemplation requires leisure.

Leisure is [defined as] resting in the end to which an operation is ordained. And thus leisure maximally pertains to the happiness which is the ultimate end. This [happiness] is not found in the operations of the practical virtues, the chief of which are those that exist in political affairs, namely, putting into order the common good, which is most divine. . . . *(SLE,* X, 11, 1177b4, 20–26; *In Ethic.,* X, lect. 11 [Spiazzi, n. 2099, p. 546])[137]

---

132. See *Pol.,* III, 1, 1275 b20–21; 4, 1278b21–24.
133. See *EN,* VI, 7, 1141b3–5.
134. *EN,* I, 7, 1097b11.
135. See *Pol.,* VII, 2, 1324b1–2.
136. For an extended argument against the subordination of the intellectual to the moral virtues in the *Nicomachean Ethics,* see Cooper, *Reason and Human Good in Aristotle,* 144–80. Cf. Daniel Devereux, "Aristotle on the Active and Contemplative Lives," *Philosophy Research Archives* 3, no. 1138 (Bowling Green State University: Philosophy Documentation Center, 1977), microfiche.
137. ". . . vacatio autem est requies in fine ad quam operatio ordinatur, et sic felicitati quae est ultimus finis maxime competit vacatio. Quae quidem non invenitur

In advance of any particular conflict between political activity and contemplation, how much can we alleviate the general tension between them? As one might expect about so practical a question, Aristotle offers no precise formula. He is content to observe that there are various degrees of involvement in politics. The form of political activity most congruent with a life of contemplation is for the contemplative to be active as an architect is active, by directing the external actions of others through expressing his thoughts on matters political.[138] In the city, the philosopher should seek to direct the legislators, as in the household he directs his household manager.

By ordinary standards, the philosophical architect who gives advice about laws or frames constitutions stands outside the daily flow of political life. Nonetheless, he is exercising practical not theoretical wisdom. And at some time or another, the philosophical architect must gain practical experience if he is to acquire the science of legislation that will enable him to direct legislators wisely.[139] Wise legislation arises from knowledge of particular cases. To have learned how to deal with particular cases, the contemplative must have held a political office or at least have exercised the rights and have fulfilled the duties of a citizen. Such requirements can be fulfilled only if the philosopher does not lead the philosophical life all the time. But such requirements do not mean that the philosopher seeks his highest happiness in political activity. Unlike the amoral gods who are eternally occupied with contemplating themselves, the Aristotelian philosopher is morally virtuous enough to know when he should enter and when he should leave the political realm.

Aristotle's texts lead us to conclude, then, that the philosopher does possess the moral/political virtues, above all that preeminent virtue of practical reason, *phronesis*, which directs the moral virtues.[140] But the political involvement and moral virtues of the philosopher do not give us license to interpret *eudaimonia* as an inclusivist end: Aristotelian *eudaimonia* is not composed of contemplation and politics.

---

in operationibus virtutum practicarum, quarum praecipue sunt illae quae consistunt in rebus politicis, utpote ordinantes bonum commune quod est divinissimum . . ." *(SLE*, X, 11, 1177b4, 20–26; *In Ethic.*, X, lect. 11 [Spiazzi, n. 2099, p. 546]).

138. See *Pol.*, VII, 3, 1325b23–25 (Rackam trans.): "And even with actions done in relation to external objects we predicate action in the full sense chiefly of the master-craftsmen who direct the action by their thoughts."

139. See *EN*, X, 9, 1181a10–20.

140. See *EN*, I, 8, 1098b23–25; 10, 1100b19–20. Cf. *Pol.*, VII, 1, 1323b21–23: "Let it be agreed among us that to each there belongs as much *eudaimonia* as there belongs *arete* and *phronesis* and action in accordance with these."

The highest form of *eudaimonic* activity, as can be seen in regard to the counterexamples provided by the gods and nonrational animals, consists solely in contemplation. The gods only contemplate and are supremely blessed; nonrational animals cannot contemplate at all, and for that reason do not have even a share in *eudaimonia*.[141] In the tenth book of the *Nicomachean Ethics*, Aristotelian *eudaimonia*, and its corresponding paradigmatic life, the *bios theoretikos*, is exclusivist: contemplation just by itself is the highest form of *eudaimonia* and the more one contemplates the happier one is.[142]

Happiness extends, then, just so far as contemplation does, and those to whom contemplation more fully belongs are more truly happy, not accidentally, but in virtue of the contemplation. *(EN, X, 8, 1178b28–31 [rev. Oxford trans.])*

Aquinas's comment on this text softens its exclusivist connotations: "Happiness is primarily *[principaliter]* some kind of speculation."[143] The comment shows that Aquinas, here and elsewhere in his commentary, leans to an inclusivist view of *eudaimonia*:[144] "[Moral] virtue is the measure by which human affairs are judged and a man is good insofar as he is [morally] virtuous."[145] That men need to exercise the moral virtues no less than the theoretical virtues is part of what Aquinas means by *"beatitudo imperfecta."* Given the intrinsic imperfection of man's contemplative activity and all the other obstacles that prevent men from contemplating, a lifetime of morally good actions

141. See *EN*, X, 8, 1178b7–27.

142. The *Politics*, however, supports an inclusivist reading of *eudaimonia*. See *Pol.*, VII, 1, 1323a25–30 (rev. Oxford trans.): "For no one would maintain that he is happy who has not in him a particle of courage or temperance or justice or practical wisdom . . ."; 1323b20–21 (rev. Oxford trans.): ". . . each one has just so much of happiness as he has of excellence and practical wisdom *[phronesis]*, and of excellent and wise action."

143. See *SLE*, X, 12, 1178b24, 175–81 *(In Ethic, X, lect. 12 [Spiazzi, n. 2125, p. 551])*: "Et sic patet quod quantum se extendit speculatio, tantum se extendit felicitas, et quibus magis competit speculari, magis competit esse felices, non secundum accidens, sed secundum speculationem, quae est secundum se honorabilis. *Unde sequitur quod felicitas principaliter sit quaedam speculatio."*

144. See *SLE*, I, 10, 1097b33, 118–21 *(In Ethic., I, lect. 10 [Spiazzi, n. 126, p. 33])*: ". . . felicitas principalius consistit in vita contemplativa quam in activa et in actu rationis vel intellectus quam in actu appetitus ratione regulati."

145. ". . . virtus [moralis] sit mensura secundum quam iudicetur de omnibus rebus humanis et bonus in quantum est virtuosus . . ." *(SLE, X, 8, 1176a15, 142–44; In Ethic., X, lect. 8 [Spiazzi, n. 2062, p. 536])*. The context, a discussion of how men find, depending on their moral virtues, different things pleasurable and painful, indicates that moral virtue is the measure of things human.

and habits is a necessary if secondary constituent of the highest but incomplete human happiness possible in this world.[146] Aquinas's explanation is precisely hedged:

> Since happiness is the absolutely first good of man, it follows that it consists more in what pertains essentially to reason than in what [only] participates in reason. Thus we can accept that happiness primarily consists in the contemplative life more than in the active life, [that is,] more in the act of reason or intellect than in the act of an appetite ruled by reason. *(SLE,* I, 10, 1097b33, 114–21; *In Ethic.,* I, lect. 10 [Spiazzi, n. 126, p. 33])[147]

This-worldly happiness, *"beatitudo imperfecta,"* cannot be identified exclusively with the activity of contemplation: rather, it *principally* consists of contemplation and, secondarily, of moral virtue;[148] otherworldly beatitude, by contrast, consists entirely and exclusively in contemplation.[149] Once again, Aquinas adopts a different perspective than Aristotle. But what lies behind this change of perspective and what else is implied by the Thomistic doctrine of "imperfect happiness"?

7. *Aquinas on "Imperfect Happiness"*

Thomistic ethics, in line with its Aristotelian model, is teleological and *eudaimonistic*: men naturally pursue some ultimate end or good, which can be called happiness *(felicitas)* or beatitude *(beatitudo)* or

146. At the same time, Aquinas also reports Aristotle's exclusivist doctrine: "... perfecta felicitas consistit in operatione speculationis" *(SLE,* X, 10, 1177a17, 64–65; *In Ethic.,* X, lect. 10 [Spiazzi, n. 2086, p. 543]); "... non erit in operationibus virtutum moralium perfecta felicitas" *(SLE,* X, 11, 1177b4, 59–60; *In Ethic.,* X, lect. 11 [Spiazzi, n. 2102, p. 546]).

147. "Quia igitur felicitas est principalissimum bonum hominis, consequens est ut magis consistat in eo quod pertinet ad id quod est rationale per essentiam quam in eo quod pertinet ad id quod est rationale per participationem. Ex quo potest accipi quod felicitas principalius consistit in vita contemplativa quam in activa et in actu rationis vel intellectus quam in actu appetitus ratione regulati" *(SLE,* I, 10, 1097b33, 114–21; *In Ethic.,* I, lect. 10 [Spiazzi, n. 126, p. 33]).

148. In *SLE,* I, 16, 1100b19, 84–90 *(In Ethic.,* I, lect. 16 [Spiazzi, n. 192, p. 51]), Aquinas does *not* say that *"felicitas* consists in both the active and contemplative life" (Anthony J. Celano, "Boethius of Dacia: 'On the Highest Good,'" *Traditio* 43 [1987]: 203, n. 17); rather, Aquinas observes that the happy man *(felix),* because of his perfect habit of virtue, is able in the active life to do virtuous things and in the contemplative life to theorize *"semper vel maxime."*

149. See *ST,* I–II, q. 3, a. 5: "Et ideo ultima et perfecta beatitudo, quae expectatur in futura vita, tota consistit in contemplatione. Beatitudo autem imperfecta, qualis hic haberi potest, primo quidem et principaliter consistit in contemplatione: secundario vero in operatione practici intellectus ordinantis actiones et passiones humanas. ...."

peace *(pax)*.[150] But while incorporating many elements of Aristotelian "naturalism" into his own moral theory, Aquinas engages in a probing analysis of Aristotle's conception of *eudaimonia*. Guiding this analysis is Aquinas's conception of supernatural beatitude.

For Aquinas, it is not the philosophical contemplation of the first unmoved mover but the "vision of divinity" that constitutes the "entire substance of our beatitude."[151] This vision outstrips the resources of metaphysical knowledge. The "vision of divinity" is not demonstrated propositional knowledge about the first unmoved mover; it is immediate cognitive awareness of the God who, while being the first unmoved mover, transcends the entire natural order of the universe and its causes.

> The soul is in some way everything. This is the ultimate perfection to which the soul is able to attain according to the philosophers: that in it is represented the entire order and causes of the universe. They posited this to be the ultimate end of man, but which we claim will be in the vision of God. . . . *(De ver.*, q. 2, a. 2 [Spiazzi, 27])[152]

The vision of God, the vision that Aquinas describes as the "full participation in divinity,"[153] is the vision of the divine essence.

> For perfect happiness it is required that the intellect attain the essence of the first cause. It will have this perfection through union with God as its object, in whom alone the happiness of man consists. . . . *(ST,* I–II, q. 3, a. 8)[154]

But the vision of the divine essence, for reasons that I will postpone setting forth until the next chapter, cannot be attained naturally. It is an end that lies beyond the realm of human action.

The human agent, however, can attain this-worldly happiness through his own actions.[155] Consequently, moral philosophy must pre-

---

150. See *Comp. theol.*, II, c. 9 (Verardo, n. 575, p. 133).

151. See *I Sent.*, d. 1, q. 1, a. 1 (Mandonnet, 33): ". . . ipsa visio divinitatis ponitur tota substantia nostrae beatitudinis. . . ."

152. " . . . animam esse quodammodo omnia. . . . Unde haec est ultima perfectio ad quam anima potest pervenire, secundum philosophos, ut in ea describatur totus ordo universi, et causarum eius; in quo etiam finem ultimum hominis posuerunt, qui secundum nos, erit in visione Dei . . ." *(De ver.*, q. 2, a. 2 [Spiazzi, p. 27]).

153. ". . . ad plenam participationem divinitatis, quae vere est hominis beatitudo, et finis humanae vitae" *(ST,* III, q. 1, a. 2).

154. "Ad perfectam igitur beatitudinem requiritur quod intellectus pertingat ad ipsam essentiam primae causae. Et sic perfectionem suam habebit per unionem ad Deum sicut ad objectum, in quo solo beatitudo hominis consistit . . ." *(ST,* I–II, q. 3, a. 8).

155. See *ST,* I–II, q. 1, prologus; q. 6, prologus.

suppose some understanding of the human act *(actus humanus)*, the act that is intelligently intentional and freely chosen.

Since it is necessary to reach beatitude through some actions, it follows that it is necessary to consider human actions, so that we may know by which acts beatitude is attained or the way to beatitude impeded. *(ST,* I–II, q. 6, prologus)[156]

But since Aquinas thinks that man's ultimate happiness or beatitude is supernatural, Thomistic ethics must account for both the naturally acquired virtues that lead to an "imperfect happiness," which does not exceed the powers of human nature, and the divinely infused virtues that lead to perfect or supernatural happiness Only the theological virtues—divinely infused faith, hope, and charity—and the accompanying infused intellectual and moral virtues sufficiently enable men to order their actions to the perfect, otherworldly, supernatural happiness that is man's ultimate end.[157] In fact, eternal life, the full knowledge of God, begins with the infused theological virtues.[158]

Because a man or a woman can possess both humanly acquired and supernaturally infused virtues, he or she simultaneously belongs to the two Augustinian cities, the City of Man and the City of God.

Virtues which belong to a man insofar as he is a man or a participant in the earthly city, do not exceed the faculty of human nature; hence man is able to acquire them from his natural [faculties], from his proper acts. . . . *(De virt.,* q. 1, a. 9 [Odetto, 731])[159]

In characterizing the ends that distinguish the spheres of the natural and the supernatural virtues, Aquinas uses a variety of formulae: "the twofold good of man," or "the twofold happiness of man," or "the end that is proportionate human nature," or "the end that exceeds the

156. "Quia igitur ad beatitudinem per actus aliquos necesse est pervenire, oportet consequenter de humanis actibus considerare, ut sciamus quibus actibus perveniatur ad beatitudinem, vel impediatur beatitudinis via . . ." *(ST,* I–II, q. 6, prologus).

157. See *De virt.,* q. 1, a. 10 (Odetto, 736): ". . . per fidem intellectus illuminetur de aliquibus supernaturalibus cognoscendis . . . per spem autem et caritatem acquirit voluntas quamdam inclinationem in illud bonum supernaturale ad quod voluntas humana per naturalem inclinationem non sufficienter ordinatur."

158. See *De ver.,* q, 14, a. 2 (Spiazzi, 283): "Unde oportet etiam quod ad hoc quod homo ordinetur in bonum vitae aeternae, quaedam inchoatio ipsius fiat in eo qui repromittitur. Vita autem aeterna consistit in plena Dei cognitione. . . ."

159. "Virtutes autem quae sunt hominis in eo quod est homo, vel in eo quod est terrenae civitatis particeps, non excedunt facultatem humanae naturae; unde eas per sua naturalia homo potest acquirere, ex actibus propriis . . ." *(De virt.,* q. 1, a. 9 [Odetto, 731]).

proportion of our nature."[160] To say that man has a twofold end is equivalent to saying that man has a twofold good.[161] The latter formula, especially if we are to avoid certain modern Thomist distortions, best fits Aquinas's doctrine.

The good for man is twofold: there is imperfect, or this-worldly, or civil happiness *(felicitas)* as contrasted with perfect or otherworldly beatitude *(beatitudo)*.[162] Although Aquinas sometimes refers to both the imperfect and the perfect goods as last ends,[163] it is clear that Thomistic man has only one last or ultimate end, the *supernatural* end that is the vision of God Himself.[164] The ends that are encompassed by the naturally acquired virtues, when subsumed into the order of the infused moral and intellectual virtues, are as so many means to the ultimate, supernatural end.

The theological virtues, although they come together in the same subject as the moral and intellectual virtues, differ nonetheless in [their] object. For the object of the theological virtues is the ultimate end itself; the object of the other virtues are those things which are the means to the end. *(De ver.,* q. 14, a. 3, ad 9 [Spiazzi, 287])[165]

What Aquinas labels *"beatitudo imperfecta"* (i.e., the philosophical contemplation of God) is an analogue for perfect happiness (the vision of the divine essence).[166]

160. See *De virt.*, q. 1, a. 10 (Odettto, 735): "duplex hominis bonum"; *ST,* I–II, q. 62, a. 1: "duplex hominis beatitudo"; *ibid.*, a. 12 (Odetto, 745): ". . . finis qui est naturae humanae proportionatus . . . finis naturae nostrae excedens proportionem. . . ."

161. See *ST,* II–II, q. 23, a. 7: "Sicut ergo duplex est finis, unus ultimus et alius proximus, ita etiam est duplex bonum. . . ."

162. See *De virt. card.*, q. 1, a. 4 (Odetto, 827): "Manifestum est autem quod virtutes acquisitae, de quibus locuti sunt philosophi, ordinantur tantum ad perficiendum homines in vita civili, non secundum quod ordinantur ad caelestem gloriam consequendam."

163. See *De ver.*, q. 14, a. 2 (Spiazzi, 283): "Est autem duplex hominis bonum ultimum, quod primo voluntatem movet quasi ultimus finis."

164. See *III Sent.*, d. 23, q. 1, a. 4, sol. 3 (Moos, 714): "Finis autem ad quem divina largitas hominem ordinavit vel praedestinavit, scilicet fruitio sui ipsius, est omnino supra facultatem naturae creatae elevatus. . . ."

165. "Virtutes autem theologicae, quamvis conveniant in subiecto cum moralibus et intellectualibus, differunt tamen in obiecto. Obiectum enim virtutum theologicarum est ipse finis ultimum obiectum vero aliarum ea quae sunt ad finem" (*De ver.*, q. 14, a. 3, ad 9 [Spiazzi, 287]).

166. For a discussion of Henry of Ghent's criticism of the Thomistic analogy, see Anthony J. Celano, "Act of the Intellect or Act of the Will: The Crticial Reception of Aristotle's Ideal of Human Perfection in the 13th and Early 14th Centuries," *Archives d'histoire doctrinale et littéraire du moyen âge* 57 (1990): 93–119.

The contemplative life both begins here and is consummated in the future, since the acts which are perfect in heaven are begun in a certain way in this life, but they are imperfect. *(III Sent.,* d. 34, q. 1, a. 4 [Moos, n. 113, p. 1127])[167]

Nothing in Aristotle corresponds to this Thomistic analogy. Aristotle's sense of the imperfection of human *eudaimonia* is in comparison to God's happiness, not in comparison with any possible human happiness. Aristotle maintains that philosophic contemplation is akin to the contemplation enjoyed by the gods, but he acknowledges that only the gods live a life that is entirely blessed.[168] Human contemplation, although godlike, cannot escape the imperfections of bodily existence; as human, it is subject to change and impermanence.

Aquinas, however, neither simply repeats nor simply rejects Aristotle. Aquinas's claim that only the beatific vision will satisfy man's desire for happiness falls entirely outside of the ken of Aristotle's philosophy.

We unconditionally concede that the true beatitude of man is after this life. We do not deny, however, that there is able to be some participation of beatitude in this life, insofar as a man is perfect, primarily, in the goods of speculative reason, and, secondarily, of practical reason. The philosopher discusses this happiness [the happiness in this life] in the books of the *Ethics;* the other happiness, which is after this life, [the Philosopher] neither asserts nor denies. *(IV Sent.,* d. 49, q. 1, a. 1, sol. 4 [Vivès, 11, p. 464])[169]

Evidently, the Thomistic notion of "imperfect happiness" does not rest on Aristotle's admissions about the imperfect character of human contemplative *eudaimonia*.[170] Yet Aquinas thinks that his own doc-

167. "Vita enim contemplativa et hic incipit, et in futuro consummatur, unde actus qui erunt perfecti in patria, quodammodo in hac vita inchoantur, sed imperfecti sunt" *(III Sent.,* d. 34, q. 1, a. 4 [Moos, p. 1127, n. 113]).

168. See *EN,* X, 7, 1177a10–20; 1177b25–30; X, 8, 1178b25–28; *Metaph.,* XII, 7, 1072b15–30.

169. "Et ideo simpliciter concedimus veram hominis beatitudinem esse post hanc vitam. Non negamus tamen quin aliqua beatitudinis participatio in hac vita esse possit, secundum quod homo est perfectus in bonis rationis speculativae principaliter, et practicae secundario; et de hac felicitate Philosophus in lib. *Ethic.* determinat; aliam, quae est post hanc vitam, nec asserens nec negans" *(IV Sent.,* d. 49, q. 1, a. 1, sol. 4 [Vivès, 464]).

170. See Anton C. Pegis, "Nature and Spirit: Some Reflections on the Problem of the End of Man," *American Catholic Philosophical Association* 23 (1949): 62–79; "St. Thomas and the *Nicomachean Ethics:* Some Reflections on *Summa Contra Gentiles* III, 44, #5," *Mediaeval Studies* 25 (1963): 1–25; Owens, "Aquinas as Aristotelian Commentator," 213–38.

trine, that men naturally desire a perfect happiness, is plausible precisely on Aristotelian grounds.[171] The Latin translation (if not the original Greek text) of *EN*, I, 10, 1101a21 puts in Aristotle's mouth the pregnant phrase *"beatos autem ut homines"*: *"Si ita autem, beatos dicemus viventium quibus existunt et existent quae dicta sunt, beatos autem ut homines."*[172] In translation: "Thus we call 'blessed' those among the living in whom exist and will exist [the conditions] that we have mentioned, but blessed as men." The last phrase states, however Aristotle meant it, that men can be blessed but "only blessed as men." The same phrase, as Aquinas read it, suggests to Aquinas that Aristotle himself recognized that this-worldly happiness is imperfect.

Now it is true that Aristotle acknowledges, in both the *Nicomachean Ethics* and the *Politics*, that it is necessary for the blessed man (ὁ μακάριος) to possess, in the right degree, all three types of good.[173] Aristotle also readily admits *(Pol., VII, 12, 1332a31)* that, in regard to the goods of fortune, men cannot escape the vicissitudes of life.

The happiness and well-being which all men manifestly desire, some have the power of attaining, but to others, from some accident or defect of nature, the attainment of them is not granted; for a good life requires a supply of external goods, in a less degree when men are in a good state, in a greater degree when they are in a lower state. *(Pol., VII, 12, 1331b35–1332a2 [rev. Oxford trans.])*

But the goods of fortune, external goods, and bodily goods are not constituents of *eudaimonia*; rather, they are the necessary conditions for virtuous activity[174] Aristotle, moreover, tries to soften the moral significance of such misfortunes. To be morally virtuous a man does not have "to rule land and sea"; moderate riches are sufficient. The good man's happiness lies in virtuous activity; he can nobly sustain the loss of fortune's goods—health, power, wealth, fame, and friends—since they are merely instrumental to the exercise of the moral virtues.[175] Furthermore, the highest form of happiness, the activity of contemplation which springs from the highest intellectual virtue (i.e.,

---

171. See Anthony J. Celano, "The Concept of Wordly Beatitude in the Writings of Thomas Aquinas," *Journal of the History of Philosophy* 25 (1987): 215–26.

172. SLE, *Textus Aristotelis*, I, 16, 1101a19–21 *(In Ethic.*, I, lect. 16, *Textus Aristotelis*, n. 123, 20–23). Probably, the original Greek text (containing the phrase μακαρίους δ' ἀνθρώπους) is a gloss but, even so, the thought squares with *EN*, III, 7, 1115b11; X, 7, 1177b22: see Gauthier-Jolif, II, 1, 1101a 16–21:84–85.

173. See *EN*, X, 8, 1179a1–3; *Pol.*, VII, 1, 1323a27.

174. See *Pol.*, VII, 1, 1324a1–2. Cf. *EN*, I, 8, 1099a31–1099b2.

175. See *Pol.*, VII, 13, 1332a19–21.

from *sophia*), needs even fewer external aids.[176] External goods are merely the conditions that promote or hinder contemplation; they are not the instruments of contemplation.[177]

Aquinas fastens on Aristotle's admission that the mundane happiness of the good man can never completely escape fortune's whims: to be truly blessed a happy man must be both virtuous and lucky enough to have a modest measure of external and bodily goods.[178] Aristotle acknowledges that life, too often, brings changes for the worse. For that reason, Aquinas unhesitatingly attributes to Aristotle the recognition that this-worldly happiness is imperfect or merely human.[179]

Whatever else needs to be said about his interpretation of this text, Aquinas puts his finger on a neuralgic point in the Aristotelian theory of happiness. First, Aristotle himself is forced to distinguish *(EN, I, 9, 1099b1–5)* the happiness *(eudaimonia)* that is concomitant with the exercise of the intellectual and moral virtues from the blessedness (ἡ μαχαρία) that crowns happiness with good fortune. Aquinas, correspondingly, distinguishes, although he does not always adhere to the terminological distinction, *"felicitas"* and *"beatitudo."* "Blessed" *(beatus)* is the man who, while virtuous, is also well-born, and who has wealth, friends, political influence, social status, health, physical beauty, and good children. Grave misfortunes—ugliness, untimely deaths, being childless—do not make virtuous activity impossible but they surely do take the bloom off life's rose.[180]

Indeed, the stakes are higher. Aristotle recognizes, secondly, that good fortune is more than a lucky addendum to virtue and *eudaimonia*.[181] Good fortune is necessary, as a sort of instrument, in order to accomplish

---

176. To the extent that the contemplative chooses to contemplate human character and action, the contemplative appears to need friends "if we can contemplate our neighbours better than ourselves and their actions better than own" *(EN, IX, 9, 1169b33–35)*. But these, of course, are not the highest of contemplative objects.

177. See *EN, X, 8, 1178b1–5.*

178. According to Aquinas, the Aristotelian *beatus* possesses *felicitas* "*secundum optimus quod esse potest*"(*SLE*, I, 16, 1101a14, 205–6; *In Ethic.,* I, lect. 16 [Spiazzi, n. 201, p. 53]).

179. See *SLE*, I, 10, 1098a18, 153–74 *(In Ethic.,* I, lect. 10 [Spiazzi, n. 129, p. 34]); X, 13, 1179a22, 141–44 (X, lect. 13 [Spiazzi, n. 2136, p. 554]); *Expos. de Trin.,* q. 6, a. 4, ad 3; *ST,* I–II, q. 3, a. 2, ad 4; a. 6, ad 1; *SCG,* III, 48.

180. Aquinas adds a final misfortune to Aristotle's list of woes: madness could prevent the good man from acting virtuously. But this misfortune cannot be put on the scale along with other woes. Madness is a condition equivalent to death which terminates rather than deprives the good man of his happiness; see *SLE,* I, 16, 1100b22, 152–59 *(In Ethic.,* I, lect. 16 [Spiazzi, n. 197, p. 52]).

181. See *Pol.,* VII, 13, 1332a20.

certain virtuous acts: without wealth, one cannot be liberal or be able to repay one's just obligations; without power or strength, one cannot be brave; without health and food, one is distracted and unsettled by bodily pain.[182] Nonetheless, fortune smiles on whom she will; happiness appears, then, to require something more than virtuous activity. It is conditioned by good fortune. Should one conclude, then, that *eudaimonia* is the plaything of chance?

To do so, claims Aristotle, would be pernicious; it would be equivalent to overturning the determinate causal order of nature in favor of the accidental, indeterminate, and obscure causes to which we attribute the workings of chance.[183] Perhaps the gods alone can bestow happiness on men—the idea is not implausible—but Aristotle does not pursue the idea since it involves attributing to the gods some interest in human affairs. In any case, happiness is still divine or godlike even if men win it solely by their own efforts. Since happiness is what men *naturally* desire, the most likely supposition is that happiness is attained, whatever be the obstacles, by human actions. Aquinas, however, adds his own observation: God is the cause of every nature. This remark has the effect of bridging Aristotle's disjunction between divine and human efforts. It allows Aquinas to project the Aristotelian notion of natural *eudaimonia* against the background of the Christian belief that God is not only the ultimate cause of natural happiness in this world but will also be the cause of supernatural happiness in the world to come.[184]

Because of that belief in otherworldly happiness, Aquinas adopts a different tone than Aristotle in assessing the probability of perfect this-worldly happiness. Men are happy when they achieve what is good for them. Aristotle, while accepting the current, threefold division of human goods (external goods, goods of the body, and goods of the soul),[185] makes external and bodily goods instrumental goods: they are limited goods, that is, good only to the extent that they promote the good of the soul which is found in the moral and intellectual virtues.[186]

It is worth noting that Peter of Auvergne adopts a strongly inclusivist view of happiness: he stresses that perfect human happiness not only includes the moral virtues but includes the goods of the body and

---

182. See *EN*, X, 8, 1178a29–33; 1178b33–35; *Pol.*, I, 8, 1256b31–37.

183. See *Pol.*, VII, 1, 1323b25; *Metaph.*, XI, 8, 1065a26–32.

184. See *EN*, I, 9, 1099b15–25; *SLE*, I, 14, 1099b20, 96–115 (*In Ethic.*, I, lect. 14 [Spiazzi, n. 171, p. 46]).

185. See *EE*, II, 1, 1218b32–34; *EN*, I, 8, 1098b12–14; *Pol.*, VII, 1, 1323a21–27.

186. See *EN*, I, 8, 1098b14–15; 1098b19–20; *Pol.*, VII, 1, 1323b18–21.

external goods. Perfect human happiness is an aggregate of the three types of goods.[187]

The good for man is threefold: namely, the good for the soul, the good for the body, and exterior goods. Since happiness is the most perfect good of man, it combines all these [goods]. (*In Pol.*, VII, lect. 1 [Spiazzi, n. 1049, p. 339])[188]

Although happiness "principally consists in the goods of the soul,"[189] human happiness, since man is a composition of soul and body, must include external goods and the goods of the soul and the body.[190] To lack the appropriate share of any of the bodily or external goods (health, riches, and friends) is to diminish one's own beatitude.[191] Although all three types of goods are necessary for the perfect good for man, it seems improbable that a man can always, at least in this world, possess the appropriate amount of bodily or external goods.

Even where Peter follows Aristotle more closely, and treats the goods of fortune not as constituents but as prerequisites (*praenecessaria*) for happiness, his cautionary note is unmistakable: as much as a man falls short of the required measure of external goods, by so much is his happiness decreased.[192] Peter, however, captures Aquinas's mood.

187. Aristotle, however, says only that the supremely happy man (ὁ μακάριος) must have all three types of goods: see *Pol.*, VII, 1, 1323a26–27. At 1325b16 the βίος πρακτικός is said to be the best for the city and the individual but this does not involve a product external to the activity itself since, in this context, Aristotle counts θεωρία and διάνοια as the superior activities of the "practical life."

188. "Et ideo est triplex bonum hominis: scilicet bonum secundum animam et secundum corpus, et exteriora bona. Felicitas autem cum sit bonum pefectissimum ipsius hominis, aggregat omnia ista" (*In Pol.*, VII, lect. 1 [Spiazzi, n. 1049, p. 339]).

189. "In bonis igitur animae principalius consistit feliciatas" (*In Pol.*, VII, lect. 1 [Spiazzi, n. 1055, p. 340]). Cf. *In Pol.*, VII, lect. 10 (Spiazzi, n. 1186, p. 385): "Similiter virtus seu ratio principium est felicitatis, sicut unde motus vel ratio; bona autem exteriora sicut materia vel organum motum ab illis."

190. See *In Pol.*, VII, lect. 1 (Spiazzi, n. 1049, p. 339): "Beatitudo enim est perfectissimum bonum hominis. Si ergo omnia ista sunt bona hominis, necesse est omnia ista in eo existere. Si enim aliquod istorum deficeret, ex illa parte contingeret imperfectio. Ex hoc est quod Boëtius dicit tertio *de Consolatione*, quod felicitas est status aggregatione omnium bonorum perfectum."

191. There is a close connection between moral virtue and bodily and external goods. The latter constitute the sphere in which the moral virtues are exercised. See *SLE*, X, 12, 1178a10, 37–39 (*In Ethic.*, X, lect. 12 [Spiazzi, n. 2113, p. 550]): "Sic igitur virtus moralis est circa humana bona inquantum est circa bona exteriora et circa bona corporis et circa animae passiones."

192. See *In Pol.*, VII, lect. 10 (Spiazzi, n. 1185, p. 385): "Verumtamen ipsae et usus earum qui non est sine ipsis, sunt praenecessaria ad ipsam [felicitatem] secundum quamdam mensuram et proportionem; a qua si deficiant secundum minus et parum, minus perfecta erit felicitas."

Aquinas observes that the darkest of tragedies can always strike: "Even the wisest and most perfect men are able to become insane through bodily infirmities."[193] In the face of tragedy, the moral virtues are seen not to be just instrumental goods. Due to the rigors of this life, the pursuit of theoretical knowledge is sporadic and the habits of science can evanesce, but just those rigors provide manifold opportunities to exercise the moral virtues.[194]

In formulating the doctrine of *beatitudo imperfecta*, Aquinas steps out of the Aristotelian framework: at this point, Aquinas ascends, in an explicitly theological way, from the likelihood of this-worldly unhappiness to the possibility of otherworldly happiness. But Aquinas attempts to ascend on the wings of sound Aristotelian doctrine: "Nature does nothing without reason or in vain."[195] Therefore, man's natural desire for perfect happiness, lest it be regarded as naturally "in vain," cannot be regarded as attainable in this life.

> But because [men] are seen not always to attain the conditions posited for happiness, [Aristotle] states that we call them happy [but] as men who, subject to change in this life, are not able to have perfect happiness. And because a natural desire is not vain, one is rightly able to consider that perfect happiness is reserved to a man after this life. (*SLE*, I, 16, 1101a14, 218–25; *In Ethic.*, I, lect 16 [Spiazzi, n. 202, p. 53])[196]

8. The Averroist Criticism of Aquinas

The Thomistic ascent to perfect otherworldly happiness troubled some thirteenth-century authors whom historians have labeled "Latin Averroists."[197] These anonymous commentators complain that Aqui-

---

193. ". . . cum etiam sapientissimi et perfectissime viri per infirmitates corporales possint in insaniam devenire . . ." (*IV Sent.*, d. 49, q. 1, a. 1, q. 4 [Vivès, 11, p. 459]).

194. See *SLE*, I, 14, 1100b11, 26–63 (*In Ethic.*, I, lect. 14 [Spiazzi, nn. 188–89, p. 51]).

195. ἡ δὲ φύσις οὐδὲν ἀλόγως οὐδὲ μάτην ποιεῖ (*De Cael.* II, 11, 291b13 [rev. Oxford trans.]).

196. "Sed qua ista videntur non usquequaque attingere ad conditiones supra de felicitate positas, subdit quod tales dicimus beatos sicut homines, qui in hac vita mutabilitati subiecti, non possunt perfectam beatitudinem habere. Et quia non est inane naturae desiderium, recte aestimari potest quod reservatur homini perfecta beatitudo post hanc vitam" *SLE*, I, 16, 1101a14, 218–25; *In Ethic.*, I, lect. 16 [Spiazzi, n. 202, p. 53]).

197. The term *"Averroista"* appears for the first time in Aquinas's *De unitate intellectus contra Averroistas*, written 1270. For a detailed study of the various historical and ideological senses of "averroist," see Van Steenberghen, "L'Averroisme latin," in *Introduction à l'étude la philosophie médiévale*, 531–54.

nas's reading of the *Nicomachean Ethics* distorts Aristotle.[198] For their part, these Averroist commentators seek to uphold—in Gauthier's words—"integral Aristotelianism."[199] They emphatically confirm what Aristotle asserts: that contemplation springs from something divine or, more precisely, quasi-divine in man—namely, intellect (νοῦς)—and that philosophical contemplation in this life can be perfect.[200]

There is, so the Averroists insist, an orthodox Aristotelian notion of "perfect human happiness" (τελεία εὐδαιμονία).[201] Aristotle identifies perfect or complete human happiness with the life of philosophical contemplation. Such a life is this-worldly and, in an important sense, focused on itself; it aims at no end beyond the activity of contemplating.[202] As the ultimate human activity, philosophical contemplation is complete. Contemplation, of all human activities, is the best, the most stable, the most desired for its own sake, the most self-sufficient, and the most leisurely.[203]

Aquinas looks in a different direction to find a standard; he uses angelic contemplation as the measure of what is lacking in human contemplation. Commenting on *EN*, X, 7, 1177b24–26, Aquinas once again dwells on the incomplete character of man's contemplative life. But on this occasion, human nature itself is said to be at fault: it is not a purely intellectual nature.

> To be busy solely with intellectual activity is seen to be proper to the superior substances, in which only an intellectual nature is discovered. . . . (*SLE*, X, 11, 1177b26, 90–93; *In Ethic.*, X, lect. 11 [Spiazzi, n. 2105, p. 546])[204]

The activity of contemplation brings happiness as Aristotle claims, but Aquinas unequivocally states that a philosopher, unlike a separate substance, is not solely an intellect but has a composite or bodily nature. And the philosopher, and not only his body, must continue to exist in this world. In this world, even though philosophers may contemplate,

---

198. See Gauthier, "Trois commentaires 'averroistes,'" 187–336.

199. Ibid., 281.

200. See *Vat. Lat.*, 2172, fol. 12va = 832, 9rb = 3173; *Paris Nat. Lat.* 15106, fol. 11ra (quoted Gauthier, ibid., 279, n. 1): "Sed dico quod in hac vita aliquis homo potest esse felix felicitate humana, perfecta etiam, secundum quod est possibile in hac vita."

201. See *EN*, X, 7, 1177b24.

202. See *EN*, X, 7, 1177b20–25.

203. See Gauthier-Jolif, II, 2:878–79, n. 1177a19.

204. "Sed vacare soli operatione intellectus videtur esse proprium superiorum substantiarum, in quibus invenitur sola natura intellectiva . . ." (*SLE*, X, 11, 1177b26, 90–93; *In Ethic.*, X, lect. 11 [Spiazzi, n. 2105, p. 546]).

it is not possible for the philosopher to attain complete self-sufficiency, perfect leisure, and perfect freedom from labor.[205]

For Aristotle, the active intellect is not only the superior element in man's composite nature; it is "something divine." As the active intellect is "separate" (κεχωρισμένη), so too the happiness that comes from the exercise of intellect may be considered apart from man's bodily state.[206] The Aristotelian gods are fully self-actualized intelligences; they are by nature supremely blessed. Men become blessed to the extent that they act wisely and spend time contemplating.[207] But Aristotle, it should be once again acknowledged, does remember that men are not gods; intellect is only what is most divine in man.

In *Metaph.*, XII, 7, 1072b15–30, Aristotle draws the comparison very precisely: humans, however long lived (and a long life is a necessary requirement for genuine happiness), enjoy but for a short time a life of intermittent contemplation; god is the actuality of eternal, contemplative life.[208] By comparison with any man, "god is in a better state" (*Metaph.*, XII, 7, 1072b26). Philosophical contemplation permits men to strive for immortality but not to achieve it.[209] Put starkly, men, whether or not they are philosophers, grow weary and die; the gods do not.[210]

Nonetheless, for Aristotle, the contemplative life, which provides the highest form of human happiness, is imperfect only by comparison with the superior state and happiness of the gods, not by comparison with any other possible state or form of human happiness.[211] This world is the only world in which men can live and die. Apart from suicide, one's death is not a voluntary human action but a natural process that is internal to the human organism (which is composed of

205. See *SLE*, X, 11,1177b, 60–73 (*In Ethic.*, X, lect. 11 [Spiazzi, n. 2103, p. 546]): "Et hoc dico quantum possibile est homini mortalem vitam agenti, in qua vita non possunt tales perfecte existere."

206. See *EN*, X, 7, 1177b28–29; 8, 1178a22; *de An.*, III, 5, 430a17. Cf. Gauthier-Jolif, II,2:893–96, n. 1178a22, who contend that Aristotle is speaking not about the active intellect but about "la partie rationelle" of the soul in "le composé platonicien."

207. See *Pol.*, VII, 1, 1323b20–25.

208. See *De Cael.*, II, 3, 286a9 (rev. Oxford trans.): "The activity of God is immortality, i.e., eternal life."

209. See *EN*, X, 7, 1177b31–34.

210. See *EN*, X, 7, 1178b8–9; b25–27.

211. Dante, imagining what only a Christian could believe, puts Aristotle, along with a host of other virtuous pagans, in Limbo where these immortals experience but one suffering, the desire to see God: see *Inferno*, Canto IV, ll.40–43, 130–33 (ed. Umberto Bosco and Giovanni Reggio [Florence: Le Monier, 1981]).

matter). The process, ultimately, is regulated by the solar cycles.[212] The perfection of human happiness, therefore, is to be had here or nowhere. Indeed, the more virtuous and happy one is here, the more death brings loss and pain.[213]

It is evident that Aristotle and Aquinas do not reach the same conclusions about the possibility of human happiness because their arguments do not share exactly the same premises. Aquinas agrees that the life of contemplation has a quasi-divine character but he continually contrasts the happiness possible in this world with the happiness of the world to come.[214] As Aquinas comments, relying on his own metaphysical doctrine, the human intellect is a similitude that *participates* in the divine intellect.[215]

Although Aquinas is eager to find in Aristotle an awareness of the imperfection of human happiness, he does not attribute to Aristotle any notion of otherworldly or perfect happiness. The Philosopher does not conceive, not even vaguely or indeterminately, that man's goal is the vision of God in the world to come.[216] And, consequently, Aristotle could not understand how this-worldly happiness, in the precise Thomistic sense, is "imperfect." But this is not a lacuna in Aristotle's philosophy. The concept of otherworldly happiness in every way exceeds the power of reason.

In this work, the Philosopher speaks about the happiness which is able to be attained in this life. For the happiness of the other life exceeds all rational investigation. *(SLE,* I, 9, 1097b6, 162–65; *In Ethic.,* I, lect. 9 [Spiazzi, n. 113, p. 31])[217]

---

212. See *EN,* V, 8, 1135a33–b1; *De Iuv.,* 23 [17], 478b26; *De Gen. Cor.,* II, 10, 336b17; *Meteor.,* I, 9, 346b22–33. For Aristotle's understanding of human death, that it represents "a victory of matter over form" (166), see Clark, *Aristotle's Man,* 164–73.

213. See *EN,* III, 9, 1117b9–11.

214. See *SLE,* I, 10, 1098a18, 164–76 *(In Ethic.,* I, lect. 10 [Spiazzi, n. 129, p. 34]); *SLE,* I, 16, 1101a14, 218–26 *(In Ethic.,* I, lect. 16 [Spiazzi, n. 202, p. 53]); *SLE,* IX, 11, 1170b17, 150–51 *(In Ethic.,* IX, lect. 11 [Spiazzi, n. 1912, p. 499]); *SLE,* X, 13, 1179a22, 141–44 *(In Ethic.,* X, lect. 13 [Spiazzi, n. 2136, p. 554]).

215. Cf. *EN,* X, 7, 1177a15–16 (rev. Oxford trans.): ". . . whether [νοῦς] be itself also divine or only the most divine element in us . . ."; 1177b28 (rev. Oxford trans.): ". . . Something divine is present in [man]"; *SLE,* X, 11, 1177b26, 98–99 *(In Ethic.,* X, lect. 11 [Spiazzi, n. 2106, p. 546]): ". . . Secundum intellectum divinam similitudinem participat."

216. See *ST,* I, q. 62, a. 1.

217. "Loquitur enim in hoc libro Philosophus de felicitate qualis in hac vita potest haberi, nam felicitas alterius vitae omnem investigationem rationis excedit" *(SLE,* I, 9, 1097b6, 162–65; *In Ethic.,* I, lect. 9 [Spiazzi, n. 113, p. 31]).

This last claim, which asserts the supernatural character of ultimate human beatitude, leads to a philosophical *aporia:* Aquinas is able to demonstrate, by a powerful philosophical argument based on the nature of the human intellect, only that men need to be given an otherworldly vision of God *if* they are ever to reach ultimate human happiness. From this conclusion, however, reason can find no "way of passage" (πόρος) to the knowledge of whether God grants men this supernatural vision of Himself. In the last chapter of this book, I shall explore the *aporetic* character of Aquinas's argument and its implications for Thomistic ethics.

Aristotelian happiness, as Aquinas consistently reiterates, is strictly and exclusively mundane. It is against this Aristotelian background that Aquinas refers to the twofold form of human happiness.

The happiness of man is twofold. One, which is imperfect, is found in this life. The Philosopher speaks about this and it consists in the contemplation of the separate substances through the habit of wisdom. . . . *(Expos. de Trin.,* q. 6, a. 4, ad 3 [Decker, 20–22, p. 228])[218]

But Aquinas's and Aristotle's respective doctrines about earthly happiness must be keep quite distinct. Aristotle's acknowledgment of the imperfection of this-worldly happiness does not mean that he anticipated, nor does Aquinas think that Aristotle anticipated, the Thomistic conception of *beatitudo imperfecta.*

9. Happiness and Immortality

The Averroist complaint about "perfect happiness" exposes if not Aquinas's view of human nature, then at least the theological context in which Aquinas read Aristotle. Christian faith professed from its inception that God has given eternal life to men; Christian theology connected, eventually, the biblical belief in eternal life to the Platonic conception of the immortal soul.[219] The Platonic soul, despite the ambiguity generated by Plato's more materialistic descriptions of it,[220] enjoys a radical noetic freedom (spelled out in the doctrine of recollec-

218. ". . . duplex est felicitas hominis. Una imperfecta quae est in via, de qua loquitur Philosophus, et haec consistit in contemplatione substantiarum separatum per habitum sapientiae . . ." *(Expos. de Trin.,* q. 6, a. 4, ad 3 [Decker, 20–22, p. 228]).
219. See Gilson, "Christian Anthropology," in *The Spirit of Mediaeval Philosophy,* 168–88.
220. See T. M. Robinson, "The *Phaedo,*" in *Plato's Psychology* (Toronto: University of Toronto Press, 1970), 21–33. For the materialist image of the soul as "permeated by the corporeal," see *Phaedo,* 67C7–8.

tion), and consequently ontological independence from the body. The Platonic soul is a distinct substance whose deathlessness is assured: such is the lesson of *Phaedo*, 72E–77A. Aristotle, by contrast, emphasizes *(de An.*, II, 1, 412b6–9) the unity of the living body and its soul. Because the soul is the form and actuality (ἐνέργεια) or perfection (ἐντελέχεια) of the living body, they are but one substance.[221] It is the individual man who thinks and learns, not his soul (I, 4, 408b13–15). Of course, human beings die, but a corpse is not the same body that once was alive; it is a substantially different body.[222] "It is only in name that the eye of a corpse is an 'eye.'"[223]

Nonetheless, Aristotle also holds that intellect (νοῦς), in good Platonic fashion, is "divine and impassible" *(de An.*, I, 4, 408b29–30): some part or parts of the soul, the part responsible for thought, may not be the perfection (ἐντελέχια) of the body (II, 1, 413a4–9). But is the human soul, Aristotle asks (III, 4, 429a10–11), a form that is "separable" (χωριστά) only notionally? Or can it actually exist separated from the body?[224] Aristotle's hesitation is entirely comprehensible. If the human soul survives death, it must be a separate substance capable of existing apart from the body.[225] How, then, can it be the form of matter, such that the ensouled body is truly one substance? In Aquinas's terminology, how can the soul be simultaneously "a form and a this something" *(forma et hoc aliquid)*?[226]

This dilemma "has caused unending difficulty in the Aristotelian tradition"[227] because there is no clear doctrinal basis for its resolution in Aristotle. Aristotle recognizes three kinds of substances—two of them "natural" and one "unmovable" or "separate."[228] Sensible or natural substances are composed of two principles: form, which is act,

---

221. For the distinction between ἐνέργεια and ἐντελέχεια, see *Metaph.*, IX, 8, 1050a23. On the English translations of ἐνέργεια (= "actuality") and ἐντελέχεια (= "perfection"), see Joseph Owens, "Arisotle's Definition of Soul," in *Aristotle: The Collected Papers of Joseph Owens*, 207, n. 4 (originally published in *Philomathes: Studies and Essays in the Humanities in Memory of Philip Merlan*, ed. Robert B. Palmer and Robert Hamerton-Kelly [The Hague: Martinus Nijhoff, 1971], 125–45 [126, n. 4]).

222. See *de An.*, II, 1, 413a4–10; *SLA*, II, c. 2, 412b17, 99–105 *(In de An.*, II, lect. 2 [Pirotta, n. 239, p. 64]).

223. "Dicitur enim oculus mortui aequivoce oculus . . ." (*Q. de an.*, q. 1 [Robb, 59]).

224. See *Metaph.*, XII, 3, 1070a24–26 (rev. Oxford trans.): "But we must examine whether any form also survives afterwards. For in some cases this may be so, e.g. the soul may be of this sort—not all soul but the reason (νοῦς)."

225. Cf. *de An.*, I, 4, 408b18–20.

226. *Q. de an.*, q. 1 (Robb, 59).

227. Owens, "Aristotle's Definition of Soul," 209, n. 19.

228. See *Metaph.*, XII, 1, 1069a30–33; 6, 1071b3–4.

and matter, which is potency. All natural substances are quantitative bodies or something "which cannot come into existence without body and magnitude" (De Cael., III, 1, 298b2 [rev. Oxford trans.]). Some natural substances, however, are imperishable: the heavenly bodies are composite but eternal; they are always active, being eternally in motion.[229] But most natural substances, and certainly human beings among other animals, are perishable.[230] All separate substances are nonsensible, unmoveable, and imperishable. These substances are pure forms—but form understood as pure actuality (ἐνέργεια)—that eternally exist apart or separate from matter.[231] In the Metaphysics, Aristotle argues that the "separate substances" are the immaterial prime movers (not, as Plato held, the separate species) of sensible substances.[232] These pure forms, which do not exist in matter, cannot be generated or corrupted in any way.[233]

Aristotle's definition of the soul (de An., II, 1, 412a27) as "the perfection [ἐντελέχεια] of a natural body potentially alive" appears to predestine the Aristotelian soul to the mortality of the human body. Human beings are obviously composite, perishable substances. But since the form of a perishable substance perishes when the composite perishes,[234] the human soul would seem to be likewise perishable. There seems, then, to be no ontological possibility for the Aristotelian soul to exist just "in itself," that is, as a substance apart from matter.[235] The human soul is the form of a material composite that is generated and corrupted, and it would seem therefore to be a form that perishes when the composite perishes. Certainly, there is no question of initially defining the Aristotelian soul apart from the matter it enlivens. Aquinas explains that since the Aristotelian soul is the form of a living composite, it is not a complete being and cannot even be defined apart from the matter to which it is joined.

229. See Part. An., I, 5, 644b23–24 (rev. Oxford trans.): "Of substances constituted by nature some are ungenerated, imperishable, and eternal, while others are subject to generation and decay"; De Cael., III, 1, 298a24–26 (rev. Oxford trans.): ". . . the first heaven and its parts, the moving stars within it, the matter of which these are composed and their nature . . . they are ungenerated and indestructible." Cf. Metaph., IX, 8, 1050b20–28.

230. The natural death of a sanguinous animal occurs when the heart runs out of heat, which has been "breathed away in the long period of life preceding" (De Iuv., 23[17], 479a17 [rev. Oxford trans.]).

231. See Metaph., XII, 6, 1071b20–22.

232. See Metaph., XI, 2; XII, 7.

233. See De Gen. Corr., I, 3, 318a9–10.

234. See Phys., I, 9, 192b1–2; Metaph., VII, 8; VIII, 3, 1043b15–20.

235. See Metaph., VIII, 3, 1043b18–21.

In every definition of a form something is posited which is outside the essence of the form, namely, its proper subject or matter. Hence, since the soul is a form, it is necessary that in its definition its matter or subject be posited. *(SLA,* II, c. 1, 412a6, 78–84; *In de An.,* II, lect. 1 [Pirotta, n. 213, p. 59])[236]

Nonetheless, Aristotle allows that one part of the rational soul, what Alexander of Aphrodisias labels the "productive intellect" (νοῦς ποιητικός),[237] is separable from matter and survives death.[238] Aquinas, quoting Averroes with approval, is quick to note the anomaly: the intellect, although the form of a composite, "is not said to be a form in the same way as the other material forms."[239]

There is, however, a reason for the ontologically anomalous character of the rational soul. Aristotle argues that part of the human soul, the *nous* or productive intellect, is not bodily because its act is not bodily.[240] Consequently, productive intellect is separable or separate (χωριστός)[241] from the body. Aquinas gives the principle underlying Aristotle's argument:

That which has an operation through itself, also has being and subsistence through itself; that which does not have an operation through itself, does not have being through itself. *(SLA,* I, c. 2, 403a5, 74–77; *In de An.,* I, lect. 2 [Pirotta, n. 20, p. 7])[242]

In more specific terms, Aristotle explains that intellectual understanding, although it has a bodily correlate (the phantasm in the imagination), is separable because it has a universal object, the essence or

236. ". . . in omni autem diffinitione form[a]e ponitur aliquid quod est extra essenciam form[a]e, scilicet proprium subiectum eius siue materia. Unde, cum anima sit forma, oportet quod in diffinitione ipsius ponatur materia siue subiectum eius" *(SLA,* II, c. 1, 412a6, 78–84; *In de An.,* II, lect. 1 [Pirotta, n. 213, p. 59]).

237. See Arthur Hyman, "Aristotle's Theory of the Intellect and Its Interpretation by Averroes," in *Studies in Aristotle,* ed. O'Meara, 172, n. 41.

238. See *de An.,* I, 4, 408b18 (rev. Oxford trans.): "But thought (νοῦς) seems to be an independent substance implanted within us and to be incapable of being destroyed."

239. ". . . intellectus non eodem modo dicitur forma cum aliis formis materialibus . . . " *(II Sent.,* d. 19, q. 1, a. 1 [Mandonnet, 383]).

240. Cf. *de An.,* I, 1, 403a10 (rev. Oxford trans.): "If there is any way of acting or being acted upon proper to soul, soul will be capable of separate existence; if there is none, its separate existence is impossible."

241. Χωριστός is ambiguous: it can mean either actually "separate" or potentially "separable": cf. *de An.,* III, 6, 430b6.

242. "Aliud est quod illud quod habet operationem per se, habet etiam esse et subsistenciam per se; et illud, quod non habet operationem per se, non habet esse per se . . . " *(SLA,* I, c. 2, 403a5, 74–77; *In de An.,* I, lect. 2 [Pirotta, n. 20, p. 7]).

nature, that is separable from individuated matter. Because the object of the productive intellect is immaterial, so too the power that grasps it must be immaterial.[243] To the chagrin of all of his commentators, Aristotle provides few details about this separable and immortal part of the soul.

No extant text definitively establishes whether the "*nous* that makes all things" (*de An.*, III, 5, 430a15), which the commentators refer to as the "productive intellect" (νοῦς ποιητικός), is a part of the human soul or whether is it something external to the human soul, coming from outside.[244] The question has been debated since the time of the ancient commentators when Alexander of Aphrodisias (fl. 200 A.D.) identified *nous* with the divine mind only to be countered by Themistius (fourth century A.D.) who contended that it is an integral part of the human mind.[245] It is well known that Aquinas, who devoted his *De unitate intellectus contra Averroistas* (written 1270) to the controversy, strongly opposed Siger of Brabant's interpretation of the agent intellect as one distinct substance existing in actual separation from all the human intellects upon which it acts.[246] This Averroist interpretation, Aquinas claims, "is not according to the conception of Aristotle who posited the agent intellect as something in the [human] soul."[247]

In any case, the separability of the Aristotelian productive intellect, whatever else it entails, does not guarantee what is usually called "personal immortality." As Aquinas acknowledges, personal immortality, especially as it relates to future rewards and punishments, entails the continuity of memory.[248] Aristotle, however, denies

243. See *de An.*, III, 4, 429b20–22.

244. Cf. *de An.*, III, 5, 430a17–18; *Gen. An.*, II, 3, 736b27–29.

245. For recent statements championing one or other of these alternatives, cf. W. K. C. Guthrie, *A History of Greek Philosophy*, Vol. 6: *Aristotle: An Encounter*, 315–30, who identifies the νοῦς τῷ πάντα ποιεῖν with the first unmoved mover; and Wedin, *Mind and Imagination in Aristotle*, 181–202, who identifies it as an activity of "the mind of an ordinary person" (182).

246. See *De unit. int.*, prooemium (Spiazzi, n. 173, p. 63). Cf. *SLA*, III, c. 7 (*In de An.*, III, lect. 7). For the textual difficulties surrounding Aquinas's interpretation of the crucial Aristotelian text, *de An.*, III, 5, 430a15–25, see Ivo Thomas, O.P., Introduction to *Aristotle's "De Anima" in the Version of William of Moerbeke with the Commentary of St. Thomas Aquinas*, trans. Kenelm Foster, O.P., and Sylvester Humphries, O.P. (New Haven, Conn.: Yale University Press, 1951), 34–37.

247. ". . . hoc non sit secundum intentionem Aristotelis, qui posuit intellectum agentem esse aliquid in anima . . ." (*De unit. int.*, c. 4 [Spiazzi, n. 236, p. 82]).

248. See *Q. de an.*, q. 20 (Robb, 256–57): "[Anima separata] cognoscit autem singularia quaedam, quorum prius cognitionem accepit dum corpori esset unita. Aliter enim non recordaretur eorum quae gessit in vita, et sic periret ab anima

that memory survives the productive intellect's separation from the body.[249] Death, therefore, is to be dreaded.

> Now death is the most terrible of all things; for it is the end, and nothing is thought to be any longer either good or bad for the dead. *(EN*, III, 6, 1115a26–27 [rev. Oxford trans.])

Aquinas states Aristotle's view tersely and starkly: "After the body is corrupted, [the intellectual part of the soul] neither remembers nor loves."[250]

What, then, are we to conclude about the immortality of the Aristotelian soul? It is clear that, in his mature works,[251] Aristotle's hylemorphism binds the soul to the body too intimately to allow for any separate existence of the totality of the human soul:[252]

> The soul is the actuality of a certain kind of body. Hence the rightness of the view that the soul cannot be without a body. . . . *(de An.*, II, 2, 414a19–21 [rev. Oxford trans.])

Aristotle is silent in the *de Anima:* unlike some of his interpreters, Aristotle makes no argument for the immortality of the soul of the individual human being. [253] In the *Nicomachean Ethics*, Aristotle is openly skeptical about the possibility of individual immortality; he assumes *(EN*, I, 10, 1100a11–14) that all human activity ceases with death. For a human being to wish for immortality is to wish for something impossible.[254]

For his part, Aquinas is well aware of the limitations of Aristotelian

---

separata conscientiae vermis." The memory that survives, however, is intellectual and not sensitive. Time is accidental to the object of intellectual understanding, but intellect can grasp that its own act is past, present, or future. See *ST*, I, q. 79, a. 6.

249. See *de An.*, I, 4, 408b24–29; III, 5, 430a25.

250. ". . . et quod corruptio corpore 'non reminiscitur neque amat'" *(SLA*, III, c. 4, 430a23, 228–30; *In de An.*, III, lect. 10 [Pirotta, n. 744, p. 175]).

251. For Aristotle's "Platonic" notion of immortality in his early work the *Eudemus*, see Werner Jaeger, "The *Eudemus*," in *Aristotle: Fundamentals of the History of His Development*, trans. Richard Robinson, 2d ed. (Oxford: Oxford University Press, 1948), 39–53.

252. See *Metaph.*, XII, 3, 1070a24–26; *de An.*, II, 1, 412b6–9.

253. Cf. Marcel De Corte, *La Doctrine de l'intelligence chez Aristote* (Paris: J. Vrin, 1934), 95, who argues that Aristotle has a theory of the soul's immortality that is "precisement la theorie thomiste de l'ame intellective." Gauthier dismisses this interpretation of Aristotle as "l'illusion propre aux scolastiques" (Gauthier-Jolif, I, 1:49, n. 121).

254. See *EN*, III, 2, 1111b20–23 (rev. Oxford trans.): ". . . for choice cannot relate to impossibles . . . but there may even be a wish for impossibles, e.g., for immortality." Grant, however, denies that this text bears on the question of immortality since

immortality: "[Aristotle] concludes that only this part of the soul, namely, the intellectual, is incorruptible and perpetual."[255] Yet Aquinas finds the doctrine of individual immortality consonant with the principles of Aristotle's psychology. But Aquinas uses his own metaphysical principles to enlarge the framework of Aristotle's psychology: since an individual man is a substantial unity, Aquinas attempts to prove that his substantial form, the individual human soul as a whole (and not just a "divine part"), is totally separable and immortal.[256] There results a psychology inspired by Aristotle and often sounding like Aristotle but uniquely Thomistic.[257]

To prove that the human soul is really and not only notionally "separable" from the body falls within the scope of metaphysics.[258] The separability of the soul is established by the fact that it operates independently of the body. The principle governing the proof is that "the being of a thing is proportioned to its operation."[259] What *operates* independently of matter *is* independent of matter.[260] The intellectual soul operates independently of matter, and therefore is independent of matter. Since the soul is really separable from the body, it is subsistent and immortal.

---

he translates *(Ethics of Aristotle,* II:16, n. 7) ἀθανασίας (1111b23) not as "immortal" but as "exemption from death."

255. ". . . [Aristoteles] concludit quod hec sola pars anime, scilicet intellectiua, est incorruptibilis et perpetua . . ." *(SLA,* III, c. 4, 430a22, 212–13; *In de An.,* III, lect. 10 [Pirotta, n. 743, p. 175]). Cf. *In Metaph.,* XII, lect. 3 (Cathala-Spiazzi, n. 2451, p. 575): "Forsitan enim impossibile est omnem animam esse talem, ut remaneat corrupto corpore. . . ."

256. For Aquinas's argument about why the whole human soul is immortal (since the rational soul includes the "substantia animae sensibilis" and the sense powers "sicut in radice"), see *Q. de an.,* qq. 11; 19.

257. See Anton C. Pegis, *St. Thomas and the Problem of the Soul in the Thirteenth Century* (Toronto: St. Michael's College, 1934), 180–87; "Some Reflections on *Summa Contra Gentiles* II, *56,*" in *An Etienne Gilson Tribute,* ed. Charles J. O'Neil (Milwaukee: Marquette University Press, 1959), 169–88; and *At the Origins of the Thomistic Notion of Man,* The Saint Augustine Lecture for 1962 (New York: Macmillan, 1963).

258. See *Phys.,* II, 2, 194b14–15 (rev. Oxford trans.): "The mode of existence and essence of the separable it is the business of first philosophy to define"; *In Phys.,* II, lect. 4 [Maggiòlo, n. 175, p. 88]: ". . . anima rationalis, secundum quod est separabilis et sine corpore existere potens, et quid sit secundum suam essentiam separabile, hoc determinare pertinet ad philosophium primum."

259. ". . . esse rei proportionatur eius operationi . . ." *(De spirit. creat.,* q. 1, a. 2 [Calcaterra-Centi, 377]).

260. See *II Sent.,* d. 19, q. 1, a. 1 (Mandonnet, 481): ". . . oportet illud quod per se habet operationem absolutam etiam esse absolutam per se habere. Operatio autem intellectus est ipsius absolute. . . ."

What has an operation through itself [per se] also has being and subsistence through itself; and that which does not have an operation through itself does not have being through itself. And therefore the intellect is a subsistent form; the other powers are forms [existing] in matter. *(SLA, I, 2, 403a5, 74–79; In de An., I, lect. 2 [Pirotta, n. 20, p. 7])*[261]

Many of the elements of Aquinas's proof for the immortality of the soul can be found in Aristotle: the Thomistic proof assumes the Aristotelian tenet that the act of intellectual knowing is intrinsically immaterial. But not everything in the Thomistic proof can be clearly and definitively found in Aristotle: Aquinas defends the crucial proposition that the act of intellectual knowing is proper to the human intellect and is not to be attributed to a separate agent intellect. Moreover, Aquinas recasts Aristotle's argument in terms of the Thomistic doctrine of the act of being *(actus essendi)* in order to explain how the soul can be the form of the body but yet be immortal.[262]

The Aristotelian soul, except for the "separable" part, is a form that actualizes the living body: as a "sensible form" it is destined to perish with the form-matter compound. Aquinas, however, presses the Aristotelian doctrine that form, more than matter, is "natural":[263] a material form *(forma materialis)* is imperfect as a form precisely because it perishes with the form-matter composite.[264] But every form, notwithstanding the fact that a sensible form perishes with the composite, is the principle of actuality. As Aquinas puts it, using a highly charged term, the being *(esse)* of the form is the being *(esse)* of the composite.[265]

In the nature of corporeal things, matter through itself does not participate its own being *(esse)*, but through form. For a form coming to matter

261. "Aliud est quod illud quod habet operationem per se, habet etiam esse et subsistenciam per se, et illud quod non habet operationem per se, non habet esse per se; et ideo intellectus est forma subsistens, alie potencie sunt forme in materia" *(SLA, I, c. 2, 403a5, 74–79; In de An., I, lect. 2 [Pirotta, n. 20, p. 7]).*

262. See Pegis, *St. Thomas and the Problem of the Soul,* 135–40.

263. See *In Phys.,* II, lect. 2 (Maggiòlo, n. 153, p. 80): "Unde forma, secundum quam aliquid est naturale in actu, est magis natura quam materia, secundum quam est aliquid naturale in potentia." Cf. *Phys.,* II, 1, 193b7–8.

264. *De sub. sep.,* c. 7 (Spiazzi, n. 80, p. 31): ". . . forma autem in suo esse non dependet a materia secundum propriam rationem actus. . . . Si igitur aliquae sint formae quae sine materia esse non possunt, hoc non convenit eis ex hoc quod sunt formae, sed ex hoc quod sunt *tales* formae, scilicet imperfectae, quae per se sustenari non possunt, sed indigent materiae fundamento."

265. See *I Sent.,* d. 8, q. 5, a. 2, ad 2 (Mandonnet, 230): ". . . anima sine dubio habet in se esse perfectum, quamvis hoc esse non resultet ex partibus componenti-

makes its to be in act, as the soul to the body. *(De spirit creat.*, q. 1, a. 1 [Calcaterra-Centi, 371])[266]

Now it is this notion of soul/form participating the act of being *(esse)*, the act by which form exists, that underlies Aquinas's proof for the immortality of the human soul. The rational soul, as form, is other than its *actus essendi*; it is a potency that participates being. Yet the rational soul, as its intellectual operation makes evident, is a subsistent form: it is not corrupted with the corruption of the material composite. As subsistent, the soul/form cannot lose its participated act of being since being naturally accompanies any form.[267] Although the being that is attendant upon subsistent form is caused by God,[268] a subsistent form naturally *has* its subsistent being.[269]

Aquinas's argument combines two distinct conceptions of "actuality": the Aristotelian conception of formal actuality and the Thomistic conception of existential act that underlies formal actuality. In relationship to the matter of the living body, Aristotle's notion of actuality pertains: the soul as form is the actuality of the composite body. But the soul can be considered, since it is distinct from its own existential act *(actus essendi)*, as an essence that, like matter *("sicut materiale")*, is in relationship to a further act, the act of being. Thus the soul/form not only gives formal actuality to the bodily composite, but the participated being of the human soul/form is also the *actus essendi* of the human composite.

Aquinas argues, however, that the being of the living human body is

---

bus quidditatem ipsius, nec per conjunctionem corporis efficitur ibi aliquod aliud esse; immo hoc ipsum esse quod est animae per se, fit esse conjuncti: esse enim conjuncti non est nisi esse ipsius formae."

266. "In natura igitur rerum corporearum materia non per se participat ipsum esse, sed per formam; forma enim adveniens materiae facit ipsam esse actu, sicut anima corpori" *(De spirit. creat.*, q. 1, a. 1 [Calcaterra-Centi, 371]).

267. See *ST*, I, q. 90, a. 2, ad 1: ". . . dicendum in anima est sicut materiale ipsa simplex essentia, formale autem in ipsa est esse participatum: quod quidem ex necessitate simul est cum essentia animae, quia esse per se consequitur ad formam."

268. See *De spirit. creat.*, q. 1, a. 1, ad 5 (Calcaterra-Centi, 371): "Sed forma non habet esse per aliam formam. Unde si sit aliqua forma subsistens, statim est ens et unum, nec habet causam formalem sui esse; habet tamen causam influentem ei esse. . . ."

269. God alone, however, *is* subsistent being itself: "Ipsum igitur esse per se subsistens est unum tantum. Impossibile est igitur quod praeter ipsum sit aliquid subsistens quod sit esse tantum" *(De sep. sub.*, c. 8 (Spiazzi, n. 87, p. 34). Cf. *Q. de an.*, q. 12, ad 16 (Robb, 184): "Anima autem est forma subsistens, et non est actus purus, loquendo de anima humana."

not strictly in proportion to the being of the soul.[270] Unlike other sensible forms, the being of the rational soul is not radically encompassed by the matter of the living compound that it perfects and actualizes. The being of the soul, as shown by its noetic acts,[271] transcends the being of the body, and hence the soul does not perish with the death of the body.

Aquinas attempts to defend both the substantial unity of man (i.e., the substantial unity of the soul-matter composite) and the subsistence of the soul by reference to the soul's *actus essendi*.

> The soul has subsistent being insofar as its being does not depend upon the body; indeed insofar as it is elevated above corporeal matter. Nonetheless, in order to communicate its being, the soul receives the body; so that it is one being comprised of soul and body, which is the being of man. *(De spirit. creat.,* q. 1, a. 2, ad 3 [Calcaterra-Centi, 376])[272]

Since a living human body constitutes one nature, the human soul receives its being (from God) only when it is united to matter as its form.[273] But the *esse* of the rational soul, a form unique among the forms united to matter,[274] is not exhausted insofar as the soul is the *actus essendi* of the composite soul-body composite.[275] As the rational soul has an operation that transcends matter (the intellectual understanding of universal natures),[276] so the being *(esse)* of the soul/form transcends matter. The human soul, to put the point in the vocabulary

270. See *Q. de an.,* q. 1, ad 5 (Robb, 61): ". . . corpus humanum est materia proportionata animae humanae; comparatur enim ad eam ut potentia ad actum. Non tamen oportet quod ei adaequetur in virtute essendi; quia anima humana non est forma a materia totaliter comprehensa, quod patet ex hoc quod aliqua ejus operatio est supra materiam."

271. See *II Sent.,* d. 17, q. 7, a. 1 (Mandonnet, 429): "Sed [anima] dicitur immaterialis respectu actus secundi, qui est operatio."

272. ". . . anima habet esse subsistem, in quantum esse suum non dependet a corpore, utpote supra materiam corporalem elevatum. Et tamen ad huius esse communionem recipit corpus, ut sic sit unum esse animae corporis, quod est esse hominis" *(De spirit. creat.,* q. 1, a. 2, ad 3 [Calcaterra-Centi, 376]).

273. See *De spirit. creat.,* q. 1, a. 9, ad 3 (Calcaterra-Centi, 403): "Esse autem animae acquiritur ei secundum quod unitur corpori, cum quo simul constituit naturam unam, cuius utrumque est pars."

274. See *I Sent.,* d. 8, q. 5, a. 2, ad 2 (Mandonnet, 230): "Sed verum est quod aliae formae materiales, propter earum imperfectionem, non subsistunt per illud esse, sed sunt tantum principia essendi."

275. See *SCG,* II, 51 (Pera, n. 1269, p. 172): "Formae enim secundum esse a materia dependentes non ipsae proprie habent esse, sed composita per ipsas."

276. See *De spirit. creat.,* q. 1, a. 1 (Calcaterra-Centi, 370): "Intelligit autem intellectus intelligibile praecipue secundum naturam communem et universalem; et sic forma intelligibilis in intellectu est secundum rationem suae communitatis."

of being, is a form that has an *"esse absolutum"*;[277] because it has an operation through itself, the soul has "being through itself" (*per se esse*),[278] and therefore it is able to survive the death of the human body.[279]

Since the Thomistic soul is a form that can exist separated from matter, it is a simple substance.[280] As a subsistent form, it cannot be separated from its own act of being except by being directly annihilated by God.[281] But the human soul, unlike God, is not pure being. Aristotle teaches that the living, human body is a composite: it is composed of soul/form and matter. But Aquinas holds, in a sense quite unknown to Aristotle, that no form can be identified with its own being.[282] The human soul, even when separated from its proper matter, remains composite: it is other than and in potency to its own act of being (*actus essendi*).[283] In Aquinas's Neoplatonic terminology, the soul *participates* its being, and therefore is not identical with its being; yet the soul, since it is not a form dependent upon matter, cannot be naturally separated from its being.[284]

The Thomistic position is paradoxical: the Thomistic soul is both a principle of a material substance and a substance in its own right when separated from the living body that it informs.[285] But how can a subsis-

277. See *II Sent.*, d. 18, q. 1, a. 1 (Mandonnet, 481): ". . . oportet illud quod per se habet operationem absolutam etiam esse absolutum per se habere."

278. See *Quod.* X, q. 3, a. 2 (Spiazzi, 201): "Nam quod non habet per se esse, impossibile est quod per se operetur. . . ."

279. See *SCG*, II, 55.

280. See *De spirit. creat.*, q. 1, a. 1, ad 5 (Calcaterra-Centi, 371): "Unde si sit aliqua forma subsistens, statim est ens et unum. . . ."

281. See *De pot.*, q. 5, a. 3 (Pession, 135): ". . . ubi ipsa forma in esse suo subsistit nullo modo poterit non esse; sicut nec esse potest a se ipso separari"; *Q. de an.*, q. 14 (Robb, 201): "Unde si id quod habet esse sit ipsa forma, impossibile est quod esse separetur forma ab eo."

282. See *De sub. sep.*, c. 8 (Spiazzi, n. 89, p. 34): "Invenitur igitur in substantia composita ex materia et forma duplex ordo: unus quidem ipsius materiae ad formam; alius autem ipsius rei iam compositae ad esse participatum. Non enim est esse rei neque forma eius neque materia ipsius, sed aliquid adveniens rei per formam."

283. See *De spirit. creat.*, q. 1, a. 1 (Calcaterra-Centi, 371): "Remotio igitur fundamento materiae, si remaneat aliqua forma determinatae naturae per se subsistens, non in materia, adhuc comparabitur ad suum esse ut potentia ad actum: non dico autem ut potentiam separabilem ab actu, sed quam semper suus actus comitetur."

284. For a discussion of how Aquinas attempts to preserve both (a) the essence-existence distinction in regards to the soul/form, and (b) the soul's inseparability from its own *esse*, see Joseph Owens, C.Ss.R., "The Inseparability of the Soul from Existence," *New Scholasticism* 61 (1987): 249–70.

285. See *II Sent.*, d.19, q. 1, a. 2 (Mandonnet, 484): ". . . anima potest dupliciter

tent substance be the form of a material substance? Although they seem contradictory in an Aristotelian context, Aquinas argues that the two propositions, when "diligently considered," can be shown not to be in opposition.[286] In the first place, the union of the soul/form with matter, contrary to any Platonic myth about the soul's "fall," is for the good of the soul. The soul is an intellectual substance with sense powers. Its power to know is intrinsically conditioned by those sensible species that result from perceptual contact with material objects.[287] Yet the intellectual soul is not circumscribed by matter. While the medium of human knowing is originally sensible and particular, the act of human knowing is not: the agent intellect can abstract an intelligible species from the particular sensible phantasm.[288] As the intelligible species is universal and therefore immaterial,[289] so too is the intellectual soul that knows the universal.

In Aquinas's metaphysics the human soul is the connecting link between living but perishable corporeal beings and living but imperishable separate intelligences.[290] Separate substances are subsistent forms that are never united to matter nor are they in any way dependent upon it as intelligences.[291] The human soul is an intellectual substance capable of existing apart from the body that it animates.[292] But the human soul, as the form animating a body, is created in order to exist in the corporeal world; it is a part of the human being and in the same genus as the human body.[293] And even when separated from matter, the hu-

---

considerari, scilicet secundum quod est substantia, et secundum quod est forma. . . ."

286. See *De spirit. creat.*, q. 1, a. 2 (Calcaterra-Centi, 375): "Sed tamen si quis diligenter consideret, evidenter apparet quod necesse est aliquam substantiam formam humani corporis esse."

287. See *De spirit. creat.*, q. 1, a. 5 (Calcaterra-Centi, 388): ". . . nostra cognitio a sensu incipit. . . ."

288. See *Q. de an.*, q. 2 (Robb, 70): ". . . phantasmata non est subjectum speciei intelligibilis secundum quod est intellecta in actu, sed magis per abstractionem a phantasmatibus fit intellecta in actu."

289. See *De spirit. creat.*, q. 1, a. 1 (Calcaterra-Centi, 370): ". . . nam materia prima recipit formam contrahendo ipsam ad esse individuale; forma vero intelligibilis est in intellectu absque huiusmodi contractione."

290. See *Q. de an.*, q. 1 (Robb, 60): ". . . manifestum quod ipsa [anima humana] est in confinio corporalium et separatarum substantiarum constituta."

291. See *De spirit. creat.*, q. 1, a. 8 (Calcaterra-Centi, 399): ". . . earum essentiae excedunt genus sensibilium naturarum et earum proportionem, ex quibus intellectus noster cognitionem capit."

292. See *II Sent.*, d. 29, q. 1, a. 1 (Mandonnet, 482): ". . . anima intellectiva sit substantia non dependens ex corpore. . . ."

293. See *De spirit. creat.*, q, 1, a. 2 (Calcaterra-Centi, 378): "Anima autem, licet

man soul retains its relationship to the body by which it was first individuated.[294]

Aristotle, if we do not read him with Christian spectacles, was not a proto-Christian; there is no basis for attributing to him any belief in personal or individual immortality or in the possibility of a direct vision of God. These beliefs color Aquinas's moral theory but not Aristotle's.[295] No less evidently, Aristotle did not hold the philosophical doctrine of being that grounds Aquinas's argument for the immortality of the human soul. Moreover, Aquinas himself was aware of how reticently Aristotle spoke, if he spoke at all, about the immortality of the intellect. In *de An.*, I, 4, 408b18, Aristotle refers to (and Aquinas thinks that he approves of) received philosophical opinion: that, among other souls, at least the human intellect is an incorruptible substance.[296] But in *Metaph.*, 12, 3, 1070a24, Aristotle inquires, without then answering the question, whether the soul is the kind of form that could survive the dissolution of the body. It is only Aquinas—albeit speaking on behalf of Aristotle—who draws the unambiguous conclusion.[297]

Whereas Aristotle is reticent and oblique or just skeptical, Aquinas is assertive and straightforward about the immortality of the soul. But for all that, Aquinas is not insensitive to the plight of Aristotelian man, who remains bound to a mortal and imperfect form of happiness. In fact, Aquinas recognizes that the concept of immortality, which he purports to find in Aristotle, is without consequence for the Aristotelian conception of human happiness. Aquinas's remarks are suffused with pathos. He admits that the brilliant Aristotle could see no further than this world, whatever the vague Aristotelian notion of the immortality of the *nous poietikos* implicitly entails. Aquinas,

---

sit incorruptibilis, non tamen est in alio genere quam corpus; quia cum sit pars humanae naturae. . . ."

294. See *De spirit. creat.*, q. 1, a. 9, ad 3 (Calcaterra-Centi, 403): "Sicut igitur de ratione animae est quod sit forma corporis, ita de ratione huius animae, in quantum haec anima, est quod habeat habitudinem ad hoc corpus."
For a useful discussion of Aquinas's texts dealing with the individuation of the separate human soul, see Allen H. Vigneron, "The Continued Ontological Limitation of the Separated Soul According to St. Thomas Aquinas" (M.A. thesis, The Catholic University of America, 1983).

295. Cf. Jean Vanier, *Le Bonheur: principe et fin de la moral Aristotélicienne* (Paris and Brughes: Desclée de Brouwer, 1965), 435: "Il n'y a donc aucune contradiction entre la morale d'Aristote et une morale toute inspirée d'un désir d'obtenir une récompense éternelle."

296. See *SLA*, I, c. 10, 408b18, 232–36 (*In de An.*, I, lect. 10 [Pirotta, n. 163, p. 42]).

297. See *SCG*, II, 79 (Pera, n. 1608, p. 231): "Hoc etiam apparet per auctoritatem Aristotelis . . ."; ibid., (Pera, n. 1610, p. 232): "Patet autem ex praemissis Aristotelis verbis. . . ."

however, takes it upon himself to free Aristotelian man from his self-imposed mortal straits.

> From these difficulties we will be freed if we grant, according to the proofs already set forth, that man is able to come to true felicity after this life, when the human soul exists immortally. . . . *(SCG,* III, 48 [Pera, n. 2261, pp. 65-66])[298]

The proof of the immortality of the human soul thus plays a central role in Aquinas's theological ethics. Since the soul is immortal, men are open to a beatitude that goes beyond what can be attained in this life. Inasmuch as the soul's immortality can be established philosophically, what faith affirms about the beatific vision, a doctrine that presupposes the immorality of the soul, is at least plausible on philosophical grounds.

10. Aristotelian Philosophy and the End of Man

The Latin Averroist criticism of Aquinas, perhaps because it attempts to stick to the letter of Aristotle's text, misses the spirit of Aquinas's exegesis of Aristotle. Aquinas, more than his Averroist contemporaries, takes care not to implicate Aristotle in Christian theological doctrine.[299] Whereas the Averroist commentators dwell on the alleged limitations that Aristotle's naturalism places on a philosophical as opposed to a theological conception of man's ultimate end, Aquinas does not find in Aristotle any implicit comparison between the earthly happiness of philosophy and the eternal joy of the beatific vision. The Christian contrast between this-worldly happiness and otherworldly happiness, as though the latter possibility revealed the philosophical limits of human nature, is not a problem for Aristotle but for the Averroist commentators.

When commenting on Aristotle, Aquinas (by comparison with what he says elsewhere in his own voice) states that supernatural happiness is not something that reason can in any way investigate—at least not in the context of Aristotelian philosophy. Aquinas is certainly correct: nowhere does Aristotle attempt to do so. But, more

---

298. "A quibus angustiis liberabimur si ponamus, secundum pobationes praemissas, hominem ad veram felicitatem post hanc vitam pervenire posse, anima hominis immortali existente . . ." *(SCG,* III, 48 [Pera, n. 2261, pp. 65–66]).

299. See *SLE,* I, 15, 1100a11, 52–55 *(In Ethic.,* I, lect. 15 [Spiazzi, n. 179, p. 49]): "Est notandum quod Philosophus non loquitur hic de felicitate futurae vitae, sed de felicitate praesentis vitae. . . ."

importantly, nowhere does Aquinas argue that Aristotle could have, much less should have spoken about, supernatural beatitude.[300] In a properly Aristotelian context, human nature is neither open nor, more importantly, closed to a supernatural vision of God.[301] Aquinas realizes that this is a theological problem unknown and unknowable in Aristotle's philosophy.[302]

To ask whether Aristotelian human nature is open to a supernatural end is to import a Christian problem into Aristotle for which there is no Aristotelian answer. Aristotle studies that end which does not transcend human nature only in the sense that he knows of no other end.[303]

The ultimate perfection of a rational or intellectual nature is two-fold. One can be attained by the power of its nature: and this is called beatitude or felicity after a fashion. Hence Aristotle says that man's ultimate felicity consists in the most perfect human contemplation [by] which the highest intelligible, God, can be contemplated in this life. But above this felicity is another felicity, which we await in the future, whereby we shall see God as He is. This [latter felicity] is above the nature of any created intellect. . . . (ST, I, q. 62, a 1)[304]

Without faith, men cannot know or attain their supernatural end.

In order to reach [our] supernatural end, we need faith in this life, by which we know this end that natural cognition does not attain. (De ver., q. 14, a. 10, ad 3 [Spiazzi, 300])[305]

300. See SLE, I, 9, 1097b6, 162–65 (In Ethic., I, lect. 9 [Spiazzi, n. 113, p. 31]), quoted at n. 84 supra.

301. For a profound discussion of this point, see Pegis, "Nature and Spirit," 62–79.

302. See SLE, I, 8, 1096b30, 31–34 (In Ethic., I, lect. 8 [Spiazzi, n. 98, p. 26]): "Unde manifestum est quod illud bonum commune vel separatum non est bonum humanum quod nunc quaerimus."

303. See De ver., q. 14, a. 3, ad 9 (Spiazzi, 287): "Ideo autem a theologis quaedam virtutes proponuntur circa finem ipsum, non autem a philosophis, quia finis humanae vitae quem philosophi considerant, non excedit facultatem naturae: unde ex naturali inclinatione homo tendit in ipsum; et sic non oportet quod habitu elevetur in illum finem, sicut oportet quod elevetur in finem qui facultatem naturae excedit, quem theologi considerant."

304. "Ultima autem perfectio rationalis seu intellectualis naturae est duplex. Uno quidem, quam potest assequi virtute suae naturae: et haec quodammodo beatitudo vel felicitas dicitur. Unde et Aristoteles perfectissimam hominis contemplationem, quae optimum intelligibile, quod est Deus, contemplari potest in hac vita, dicit esse ultimam hominis felicitatem. Sed super hanc felicitatem est alia felicitas, quam in futuro expectamus, qua videbimus Deum sicuti est. Quod quidem est supra cujuslibet intellectus creati naturam . . ." (ST, I, q. 62, a. 2).

305. "Et ideo ad perveniendum in finem supernaturalem in statu viae indigemus

Aquinas never eschews this position, but, especially in *SCG*, III, 48, he takes a highly nuanced stand about what reason can establish in regard to the only ultimate end that would beatify man. There, as the culmination of a long argument, he demonstrates that the vision of God is the only end that would satisfy man, whether or not one knows that this end is a possibility for man. An other-worldly vision of God is an end that is not natural, but nonetheless it is the only satisfying end of an intellectual nature.[306] In making this paradoxical claim, Aquinas parts company with Aristotle and advances philosophical reasons for doing so. The Aristotelian understanding of human nature and the this-worldly happiness that is its natural end, is—contrary to what the Latin Averroists assume—only one philosophical conception of human nature, and one that Aquinas thinks is not philosophically definitive. Motivated by his own belief in a generous God, Aquinas proposes a rational demonstration of man's orientation or openness to the other-worldly vision of the divine essence. Such is the dynamism of human nature as rationally grasped by Aquinas the theologian if not even imagined by the philosopher upon whom Aquinas comments.

---

fide, qua ipsum finem cognoscamus, ad quem cognitio naturalis non attingit" *(De ver.*, q. 14, a. 10, ad 3 [Spiazzi, 300]).

306. See *ST*, I, q. 64, a. 1: ". . . haec beatitudo non est aliquid naturae, sed naturae finis."

IX

A Paradoxical Ethic

1. "Seeing God"

In probing Aristotle's characterization of happiness, Aquinas reached a remarkable and, to some of his contemporaries in the Faculty of Arts at Paris,[1] a disturbing *philosophical* conclusion: since perfect human happiness must be uninterrupted and unchanging,[2] it cannot be found in this world. But, Aquinas, since he could provide a strictly rational demonstration of the soul's immortality, could also accept, far more comfortably than the so-called Averroist or heterodox or radical Aristotelians, that perfect human happiness could be found, since it must be considered possible, only in the world to come.[3] For a thirteenth-century Latin theologian, however, the philosophical question of immortality was not the only issue affecting the theological discussion of ultimate human happiness. In what does otherworldly or supernatural beatitude consist?

On 13 January 1241, the archbishop of Paris, William of Auvergne (1180 ca.–1249), condemned the thesis that *"Neither man nor angel is able to see the divine essence in itself."* The provenance of this forbid-

---

1. Celano, "Boethius of Dacia: 'On the Highest Good,'" 199–214, argues that historians should no longer enroll Boethius of Dacia (Master of Arts ca. 1270) among the heterodox Parisian Aristotelians: his *De summo bono* is *not* "a characteristic product of the Arts Faculty at Paris" (199) because it incorporates a theological, indeed "Thomistic," understanding of otherworldly beatitude.

2. See *IV Sent.*, d. 49, q. 1, a. 1, sol. 4 (Vivès, 11, p. 463): ". . . beatitudo, secundum suam perfectam rationem, perpetuitatem et immobilitatem. . . ."

3. See *SLE*, I, 16, 1101A14, 222–25; *In Ethic.*, I, lect. 16 (Spiazzi, n. 202, p. 53); quoted in ch. 8, 404, n. 196.

den thesis is uncertain: perhaps Alexander of Hales (1186–1245), Hugh of Saint-Cher (d. 1263), and Étienne de Venizy (1240–42, bachelor at Paris) were among the Latin theologians who held it.[4] In any case, William's condemnation ran counter to a venerable tradition, the *theologia negativa* of John Chrysostom (344–407), Dionysius the Pseudo-Areopagite (fl. mid-fifth century), Maximus the Confessor (ca. 580–662), and John Damascene (fl. mid-eighth century), which John Scotus Erigena (ca. 810–77) had introduced into the West.

Aquinas, who is well aware of this tradition, quotes John Chrysostom's fundamental question: "*How can the created see the uncreated?*"[5] The proposition that the created intellect can see God seems to collapse the infinite distance, which Aquinas himself carefully maintains, between the human mind and God.[6] Yet Aquinas also teaches from his earliest to his last works that ultimate human beatitude consists in the vision of God.[7] Evidently, Aquinas does allow that, somehow, the infinite gulf between the human intellect and the divine essence can be traversed since men must be able to achieve beatitude. The contrary position, that men are forever unable to attain the beatific vision, leads to an absurdity for the Christian believer: it is tantamount to denying that men attain beatitude or to denying that beatitude is found in God.[8]

If in the most perfect operation of [his] intellect man does not come to see the divine essence, but something else, then it would be necessary to say that something other than God beatifies man . . . which is absurd according to us [Christian believers]. . . . (*IV Sent.*, d. 49, q. 2, a. 1 [Vivès, 11, p. 482])[9]

4. See A. Callebaut, "Alexandre de Hales, O.F.M., et ses confrères en face de condemnations parisiennes de 1241 et 1244," *La France franciscaine* 10 (1927): 257–72.

5. "Quomodo, enim creabile videt increabile?" (*IV Sent.*, d. 49, q. 2, a. 1 [Vivès, 11, p. 482]); quoting John Chrysostom, *Homily XV*, in *MP*, vol. 59, col. 98. Cf. *De ver.*, q. 8, a. 1.

6. See *SCG*, III, 57 (Pera, n. 2333, p. 77): "Distantia intellectus secundum ordinem naturae supremi ad Deum est infinita in perfectione et bonitate."

7. See *II Sent.*, d. 29, q. 1, a. 5 (Mandonnet, 753): ". . . ad felicitatem seu ad beatitudinem aliquid pertinet quod est de substantia ejus, sicut visio Dei . . ."; *Comp. theol.*, I, c. 106 (Verardo, n. 214, p. 53): ". . . in hoc consistit hominis felicitas, sive beatitudo, quod Deum videat per essentiam. . . ."

8. See *SCG*, III, 54 (Pera, n. 2311, p. 73): "Quae quidem positio [quod divina substantia nunquam ab aliquo intellectu creato videtur] et veram creaturae rationalis beatitudinem tollit, quae non potest esse nisi in visione divinae substantiae . . . et auctoritati Sacrae Scripturae contradicit. . . ."

9. ". . . Si in perfectissima operatione intellectus homo non perveniat ad videndam essentiam divinam, sed aliquid aliud, oportebit dicere quod aliquid aliud sit beatificans ipsum hominem quam Deus . . . quod est absurdum secundum nos . . ." (*IV Sent.*, d. 49, q. 2, a. 1 [Vivès, 11, p. 482]).

Aquinas, however, preserves what he understands to be the central point of the *theologia negativa:* the finite human intellect can never perfectly *comprehend* the infinite God, even though men are enabled by grace to *see* (i.e., immediately know) the divine essence in the world to come.[10] Aquinas upholds the possibility of men seeing God because, first of all, this doctrine is an article of faith taught by sacred scripture. But, second, he is convinced that there are rational arguments, appealing to the universal or infinite scope of the human intellect and will, to support or to show the appropriateness of this revealed doctrine: only a universal truth and a universal good will satisfy the intellect and will.[11]

The object of the will, which is the human appetite, is universal good, just as the object of the intellect is universal truth. From this it is evident that nothing is able to quiet the will except the universal good. *(ST,* I–II, q. 2, a. 8)[12]

But since God is the source of all truth and goodness, one can easily reason to the conclusion that only God will satisfy the innate tendency of the human intellect and will.

Universal good is what man desires, since he apprehends universal good through the intellect . . . [but] the highest good is found in God, who is good through His essence, and [who] is the principle of all goodness: consequently, the ultimate perfection of man and his final good is in this, that he adhere to God. . . . *(Comp. theol.,* II, c. 9 [Verardo, n. 579, p. 134])[13]

10. For the distinction between "seeing" *(videre)* and "comprehending" *(comprendere)* the divine essence, see *ST,* I, q. 12, a. 7. What is known comprehensively is included in the knower. To *comprehend* the divine essence, which under all conditions is impossible for a finite intelligence, is to know God as God knows Himself—infinitely, perfectly, and exhaustively. See *III Sent.,* d. 14, a. 2, q. 1 (Moos, 442): "Sed capacitas finita non comprehendit infinitum."

11. See *SCG,* III, 25 (Pera, n. 2066, p. 33): "Intellectus autem humanus cognoscit ens universale. Desiderat igitur naturaliter cognoscere causam eius, quae solum Deus est . . ." Cf. *SCG,* II, 15 (Pera, nn. 925–26, pp. 123–24): "Omnibus autem commune est esse. Oportet igitur quod supra omnes causas sit aliqua causa cuius sit dare esse. . . . Deus autem est ens per essentiam suam: quia est ipsum esse."

Although the connatural object of the intellect is "being concreted in some nature" *(esse concretum in aliqua natura),* the intellect is naturally able to separate the *being* of the form from the form, and to know both "in abstraction" *(in abstractione)* from the other. Grace enables the created intellect to know "separate and subsistent being" *(esse separatum subsistens):* see *ST,* I, q. 12, a. 4, ad 3.

12. "Obiectum autem voluntatis, quae est appetitus humanus, est universale bonum; sicut obiectum intellectus est universale verum. Ex quo patet quod nihil potest quietare voluntatem hominis, nisi bonum universale" *(ST,* I–II, q. 2, a. 8).

13. ". . . universale bonum est quod homo desiderat, cum per intellectum universale bonum apprehendat. . . . Bonum autem summe invenitur in Deo, qui per

To know the universal or perfect good, however, is to attain the beatitude proper to an intellectual creature.[14] Since only God is the perfect or essential or universal good,[15] to know the divine essence, "the fountain of all goodness,"[16] is to attain beatitude. Aquinas argues *(ST,* I–II, q. 5, a. 1) that men are able to attain beatitude because they are "capable of the vision of the divine essence" *(capax visionis divinae essentiae).* This, evidently, is not a natural capacity to see a naturally intelligible but finite form.[17] Men are capable, in the absolute sense, of seeing the infinite God only because God, in the case of the blessed, supernaturally enables their intellects to be informed by the divine essence itself.[18]

Nonetheless, just what Aquinas's philosophical arguments about the *natural desire* for seeing God (especially as presented in *ST,* I, q. 12, a. 1; I–II, q. 3, a. 8; and *SCG,* III, 50 51) allow us to conclude about the *natural possibility* of seeing God is not evident; the issue has been a staple of commentary and debate for centuries.[19] In these provocative

essentiam suam bonus est, et omnia bonitatis principium: unde consequens est ut ultima hominis perfectio et finale bonum ipsius sit in hoc quod Deo inhaeret . . ." *(Comp. theol.,* II, c. 9 [Verardo, n. 579, p. 134]).

14. See *ST,* I–II, q. 5, a. 1.

15. See *SCG,* I, 41 (Pera, n. 330, p. 49): "Sed divina bonitas comparatur ad omnia alia sicut universale bonum ad particulare: cum sit omnis boni bonum. . . . Est igitur ipse summum bonum."

16. See *ST,* I–II, q. 5, a. 4: "Visio autem divinae essentiae replet animam omnibus bonis, cum coniungat fonti totius bonitatis. . . ."

17. See *De ver.,* q. 8, a. 3 (Spiazzi, 143): "Unde oportet etiam in intellectu esse aliquam dispositionem per quam efficitur perfectibile tali forma quae est essentia divina, quod est aliquod intelligibile lumen . . . Sed quod sit naturale est impossibile. . . . Essentia autem divina non est naturalis forma intelligibilis intellectus creati. . . ."

18. See *IV Sent.,* d. 49, q. 2, a. 1 (Vivès, 11, p. 485): ". . . in visione qua Deus per essentiam videbitur, ipsa divina essentia erit quasi forma intellectus quae intelligit . . ."; *ST,* I, q. 12, a. 5: "Cum autem aliquis intellectus creatus videt Deum per essentiam, ipsa essentia Dei sit forma intelligibilis intellectus"; *SCG,* III, 51 (Pera, n. 2285, p. 70): ". . . in tali visione divina essentia et quod videtur, et quo videtur."

19. In the contemporary period, the traditional controversy was vehemently renewed by the appearance of Henri de Lubac, *Surnaturel: Études historiques* (Paris: Aubier, 1946), which immediately provoked a spate of rejoinders; for initial bibliography, see *Bulletin thomiste* 7 (1943–1946): 465–72. As summarized by a friendly reviewer, M.[aurice] C.[uppens], *Bulletin de théologie ancienne et médiévale* 5 (1947): 251–54, de Lubac's thesis is: Aquinas's doctrine of the *"desiderium naturale"* establishes that "la nature humaine tend, de soi, nécessairement vers Dieu, c'est-à-dire vers la fin surnaturelle" (252).

For an important and textually detailed but highly polemical critique of de Lubac's interpretation of Aquinas, see M.-R. Gagnebet, O.P., "L'Amour naturel de Dieu chez saint Thomas et ses contemporains," *Revue thomiste* 48 (1948): 394–46,

texts, Aquinas attempts to prove: (1) that man's ultimate beatitude can only consist in seeing God[20] and (2) that it is possible for the created intellect, whether angelic or human, to see God.[21] It is the philosophical argument that Aquinas gives for affirming the latter possibility that has engaged the commentators. Aquinas appeals to the natural desire, implanted in all intellectual substances, to know "the substance of the cause" once the "substances of the effects" of that cause are known.[22]

The argument, demonstrating that it is possible to see God, assumes that we know that God is the First Cause of all created effects and that we know the substance of at least some of these effects.

Natural desire is not able to be vain. Therefore every created intellect is not impeded by the inferiority of [its] nature and is able to attain the vision of the divine substance . . . . (SCG, III, 57 [Pera, n. 2334, p. 77][23]

This text presents Aquinas's basic argument in summary form. Filled in, the argument has the following steps: (1) the desire to know the

---

and 49 (1949): 31–102. For de Lubac's response to his critics, see Henri de Lubac, S.J., *Le Mystère du surnaturel* (Paris: F. Aubier, 1965) [= *The Mystery of the Supernatural*, trans. Rosemary Sheed (New York: Herder and Herder, 1967)]; *Augustinisme et théologie moderne* (Paris: F. Aubier, 1965) [= *Augustinianism and Modern Theology*, trans. Lancelot Sheppard (London: Geoffrey Chapman, 1969)]; *Lettres de M. Étienne Gilson adressées au P. Henri de Lubac et commentées par celui-ci* (Paris: Les Éditions du Cerf, 1986) [= *Letters of Etienne Gilson to Henri de Lubac*, trans. Mary Emily Hamilton (San Francisco: Ignatius Press, 1988)].

20. See *ST*, I, q. 12, a. 1: ". . . Si nunquam essentiam Dei videre potest intellectus creatus, vel nunquam beatitudinem obtinebit . . ."; I–II, q. 3, a. 8: "Ad perfectam igitur beatitudinem requiritur quod intellectus pertingat ad ipsam essentiam primae causae." Cf. *De reg.*, I, 9 (Spiazzi, n. 784, p. 267): ". . . mens humana universalis boni cognoscitiva est per intellectum, et desiderativa per voluntatem; bonum autem universale non invenitur nisi in Deo. Nihil ergo est quod possit hominem beatum facere, eius implendo desiderium, nisi Deus. . . ."

21. See *SCG*, III, 51 (Pera, n. 2284, p. 69): ". . . necesse est dicere quod possibile sit substantiam Dei videri per intellectum, et a substantiis intellectualibus separatis, et ab animabus nostris."

22. See *SCG*, III, 51 (Pera, n. 2277, p. 68): "Non quiescit igitur sciendi desiderium, naturaliter omnibus substantiis intellectualibus inditum, nisi, cognitis substantiis effectuum, etiam substantiam causae cognoscant." Cf. *Comp. theol.*, I, c. 104 (Verardo, n. 209, p. 52): "Tale est autem in nobis sciendi desiderium, ut cognoscentes effectum, desideremus cognoscere causam, et in quacumque re cognita quibuscumque eius circumstantiis, non quiescit nostrum desiderium, quousque eius essentiam cognoscamus."

23. ". . . omnis intellectus naturaliter desiderat divinae substantiae visionem. Naturale autem desiderium non potest esse inane. Quilibet igitur intellectus creatus potest pervenire ad divinae substantiae visionem non impediente inferioritate naturae" (SCG, III, 57 [Pera, n. 2334, p. 77].

essence of the First Cause is a natural desire;[24] (2) a natural desire that is impossible to realize is "vain" *(vanum)* or futile, that is, absurd or unintelligible, if it is not able to attain the end that it desires;[25] (3) but a natural desire cannot, since it is natural, be "vain" or unfulfilled;[26] (4) therefore, it must be possible for men to see the essence of God.

Each one of these propositions has been minutely examined, usually with modern theological preoccupations in mind about the infinite inferiority of the human intellect vis-à-vis the divine nature. But the philosophical purport of Aquinas's argument can only be grasped if one first understands what it is not intended to prove. Aquinas does *not* intend to demonstrate what he shows *(ST,* I, q. 12, a. 4; *SCG,* III, 52) to be metaphysically impossible—that either the angelic or the human intellect can *naturally* see the divine essence.[27] Nor does he intend to demonstrate the philosophical necessity of what theology teaches to be *supernaturally* possible: that God, through the "light of glory," can dispose the intellects of the blessed to see the divine essence.[28] Aquinas states, very clearly, that the gift of the beatific vision is not a necessary concomitant of the creation of human nature, but rather it is something supernatural that God freely and gratuitously gives to those who love Him.[29] Hence,

24. See *ST,* I, q. 12, a. 1: "Si igitur intellectus rationalis creaturae pertingere non possit ad primam causam rerum, remanebit inane desiderium naturae"; I–II, q. 3, a. 8: "... nondum perfectio eius attingit simpliciter ad causam primam, sed remanet ei adhuc naturale desiderium inquirendi causam"; *SCG,* III, 25 (Pera, n. 2066, p. 33): "Desiderat igitur homo naturaliter cognoscere primam causam quasi ultimum finem"; *Comp. theol.,* I, c. 104 (Verardo, n. 209, p. 52): "Non igitur naturale desiderium sciendi potest quietari in nobis, quousque primam causam cognoscamus, non quocumque modo, sed per eius essentiam."

25. See *SCG,* III, 41 (Pera, n. 2213, p. 56): "Vanum enim est quod est ad finem quem non potest consequi."

26. See *SCG,* III, 48 (Pera, n. 2257, p. 65): "Impossibile est naturale desiderium esse inane: *natura enim nihil facit frustra" [De Cael.,* II, 11, 291b13–14]; 51 (Pera, n. 2284, p. 69): "Cum autem impossibile sit naturale desiderium esse inane. ..."

27. See *De ver.,* q. 8, a. 3 (Spiazzi, 8): "Cognitio autem Dei quae est per formam creatam, non est visio eius per essentiam: et ideo neque homo neque angelus potest pervenire ad Deum per essentiam videndum, ex naturalibus puris."

28. See *IV Sent.,* d. 59, q. 2, a. 6 (Vivès, 11, p. 498): "... essentia divina, quae est extra omne genus, excedit naturalem facultatem cujuslibet intellectus creati; et ideo dispositio ultima quae est ad unionem intellectus cum tali essentia, excedit omnem facultatem naturae; unde non potest esse naturalis, sed supra naturam; et ista dispositio est lumen gloriae. ..."

29. That men are given the beatific vision is neither necessary *"absolute"* nor *"ex suppositione":* see *ST,* I, q. 19, a. 3; *De ver.,* q. 23, a. 4. Apart from His own being and goodness, God wills nothing absolutely. Thus there is no absolute necessity for God to create man, since the divine goodness is perfect and complete without creation. Supposing, however, that God wills to create man, it necessarily follows that He wills to create the rational soul since human nature necessarily requires it:

the actuality (i.e., factuality) of this gift (and a fortiori the necessity of man's attaining the vision of the divine essence) cannot be proven philosophically. Men, indeed, could have been created and left to remain in a "state of pure nature" without benefit of the supernatural gift of the beatific vision.[30] The question remains, however, whether men would have had, in this state of pure nature, an *ultimate natural end*? For the moment, we shall leave this vexing question open.

Aquinas's philosophical argument based on the natural desire to see God must be read in the light of his two fundamental tenets: not only is it impossible to see God naturally, but it is also impossible to know philosophically whether men are actually given the supernatural vision of God. The Thomistic arguments, accordingly, reach two carefully restricted conclusions about the *natural possibility* of seeing God: they conclude that (1) *if* men are to attain perfect beatitude, they must attain the vision of the divine essence; and (2) since the desire for beatitude is a "natural desire," one must conclude that it is somehow possible for men to see God. Of course, it is the second conclusion that poses all the difficulties for the Thomist commentators. Here we are not drawing a conclusion about *how* men may be supernaturally enabled to see God, but a conclusion about *whether* men can attain beatitude by seeing God. Does Aquinas's argument from the "natural desire" of seeing the essence of the First Cause elide the *possibility* of seeing God into the *natural necessity* of seeing God?[31]

For the moment, though, let us look at the first conclusion: it rests on the proposition that nothing short of the vision of the divine essence, whether in this or the other world, will bring human beatitude. While this seems the less controversial of Aquinas's two conclusions, it directly leads to the same problematic view of human destiny and happiness.

---

see *SCG*, I, 83 (Pera, n. 705, p. 96). But on the supposition that God freely wills to create man, it does not follow that human nature necessitates the gift of the beatific vision; since the beatific vision is supernatural, human nature could have been created and left to remain *"in solis naturalibus"*: see *De malo*, q. 5, a. 1, ad 15. On the entire subject of the "necessity" of the beatific vision, see Vitus de Broglie, S.J., *De fine ultimo humanae vitae* (Paris: Beauchesne, 1948), 245–64.

30. See *SCG*, III, 53 (Pera, n. 2300, p. 72): "Nam si talis visio facultatem naturae creatae excedit. . . potest intelligi quivis intellectus creatus in specie suae naturae consistere absque hoc quod Dei substantiam videat"; *Quod.* I, q. 4, a. 3 (Spiazzi, 9): "Sed quia possibile fuit Deo ut hominem facerent in puris naturalibus, utile est considerare ad quantum se dilectio naturalis extendere possit."

31. Cf. *SCG*, III, 25 (Pera, n. 2066, p. 33): "Non sufficit igitur ad felicitatem humanam, quae est ultimus finis, qualiscumque intelligibilis cognitio, nisi divina cognitio adsit, quae terminat naturale desiderium sicut ultimus finis. Est igitur ultimus finis homina ipsa Dei cognitio."

Since God cannot be seen in this life, ultimate human happiness cannot be found here.

If, therefore, ultimate human happiness does not consist in the knowledge of God according to the confused estimation by which He is known generally by all or by most men, nor in the demonstrative knowledge of God [attained] in the speculative sciences, nor in the knowledge of God by which He is known in faith . . . [and since] it is not possible in this life to attain that higher knowledge of God by which He is known through [His] essence . . . [then] it is impossible that the ultimate happiness of man be in this life. *(SCG,* III, 48 [Pera, n. 2246, p. 63])[32]

The desire for beatitude, however, is a natural desire; it cannot be forever unfulfilled. Since ultimate happiness cannot be found in this life, it must be found in the world to come.[33] But even on the assumption that the human soul is immortal, the natural knowledge of God in the world to come falls far short of that vision of God that is perfect beatitude. If men are to see God, they must be divinely enabled to do so in the world to come. Without this divine gift, men can never attain beatitude. But are they given this vision? The philosopher can only argue that *if* men do not attain the vision of God, then men, lacking any possibility of attaining beatitude, are ultimately creatures made "in vain." In that case, human nature—indeed, perhaps all of nature—is unintelligible, at least by any standards of intelligibility that can be drawn from Aristotle. But human nature cannot be unintelligible. With this last consideration, we have reached the essential premise of Aquinas's philosophical argument about the natural desire to see God.

2. *Ultimate Beatitude*

Aquinas's many arguments demonstrating that man's ultimate beatitude is found in seeing God can be grouped into three patterns or

32. "Si ergo humana felicitas ultima non consistit in cognitione Dei quam communiter ab omnibus vel pluribus cognoscitur secundum quandam aestimationem confusam, neque iterum in cognitione Dei qua cognoscitur per viam demonstrationis in scientiis speculativis, neque in cognitione Dei qua cognoscitur per fidem . . . non est autem possibile in hac vita ad altiorem Dei cognitionem pervenire ut per essentiam cognoscatur . . . impossibile est quod in hac vita sit ultima hominis felicitas" *(SCG,* III, 48 [Pera, n. 2246, p. 63]).

33. See *SCG,* III, 48 (Pera, n. 2257, p. 65): "Esset autem inane desiderium naturae si nunquam posset impleri. Est igitur implebile desiderium naturale hominis. Non autem in hac vita. . . . Oportet igitur impleatur post hanc vitam."

families.[34] The arguments appeal to: (1) the coincidence of efficient and final causality; (2) the nature of exemplar causality; and (3) the ultimate fulfillment of the human desire to know. Since the argument from knowing plays a central role in Thomistic ethics, I shall concentrate on it, but to confirm the importance of their common conclusion I shall summarize all three types of argument.

(1) An early version of the first type of argument can be found in *IV Sent.*, d. 49, q. 2, a. 1. The argument presupposes that knowing is the proper activity of an intelligence and that human beatitude is a concomitant of this proper activity. More precisely, the argument develops the idea that human beatitude is attained when a man perfectly knows. To know perfectly is to know what is perfectly knowable.

Since the supreme, proper operation of man is to know, it is necessary to assign human beatitude to this operation when it will be perfect. However, the perfection of this kind of understanding is the perfectly intelligible. *(IV Sent.*, d. 49, q. 2, a. 1 [Vivès, 11, p. 482])[35]

Aquinas reiterates the same argument and the same conclusion in later works. Since there is no doubt that God is the supremely intelligible, then beatitude must lie in knowing God.[36]

Hence, it is necessary that the ultimate completion of human perfection is in understanding the most perfect intelligible, which is the divine essence. *(De ver.*, q. 18, a. 1 [Spiazzi, 338])[37]

This conclusion can be supported by entertaining the contrary thesis. If it is assumed that men cannot know the divine essence, then human beatitude is either impossible or it must lie in knowing some being that is less intelligible than God. This latter hypothesis, however, contradicts the metaphysical principle that every being achieves its perfection when it is joined to or attains its source or efficient cause.[38]

---

34. See Gilles Langevin, S.J., *"Capax dei": la créature intellectuelle et l'intimité de Dieu* (Brughes and Paris: Desclée de Brouwer, 1966), 33.

35. ". . . intelligere sit maxime propria operatio hominis, oportet quod secundum eam assignetur sibi sua beatitudo, cum haec operatio in ipso perfecta fuerit. Cum autem perfectio intelligentis inquantum hujusmodi, sit ipsum intelligibile. . ." *(IV Sent.*, d. 49, q. 2, a. 1 [Vivès, 11, p. 482]).

36. See *II Sent.*, d. 4, q. 1, a. 1 (Mandonnet, 133): "Intellectus autem perfectissima operatio est in contemplatione altissimi intelligibilis, quod Deus est."

37. "Unde oportet quod ultimus terminus humanae perfectionis sit in intelligendo aliquod perfectissimum intelligibile, quod est essentia divina" *(De ver.*, q. 18, a. 1 [Spiazzi, 338]).

38. See *IV Sent.*, d. 49, q. 2, a. 1 (Vivès, 11, p. 482): ". . . cum ultima perfectio cujuslibet sit in conjunctione ad suum principium . . ."; *De ver.*, q. 8, a. 1 (Spiazzi, p.

The human intellect, if it is to attain perfection, must also must be joined to its source. It is manifest that the ultimate beatitude or felicity of man consists in his most noble operation, which is to understand. The ultimate perfection [of understanding] is attained when our intellect is joined to its active source. *(Q. de an.,* q. 5 [Robb, 100])[39]

Since God is the efficient cause of the human intellect, the human intellect can only attain its perfection by being joined to God. An intellect, however, can only be joined to God by immediately knowing God. To know a created similitude of God is not to know God immediately. Therefore, if the human intellect fails to attain God by knowing the divine essence, it cannot attain its proper perfection.

De ver., q. 8, a. 1 and *Quod.* X, q. 8, a. 1 present more nuanced versions of the same argument.[40] To reach its own perfection, the human intellect must know God; otherwise not God but some inferior being would be man's beatitude, which is a supposition contrary to the Christian faith. Aquinas notes, however, that an objector might grant all of this and still ask why the human intellect must know the divine essence. Perhaps the optimum intelligible being *for man* is something less, either a less perfect knowledge of God or a less perfect being than God.[41] In answering this further query, Aquinas reformulates more precisely the metaphysical principle that supports his argument: "Nothing is finally perfect unless, according to its own mode, it attains its source."[42]

According to this reformulation, it is not sufficient for the perfection of a being that it merely be united to its source; it must be united "according to its own mode" *(secundum modum suum).* What, then,

---

138]: ". . . ultima perfectio cujuslibet rei est quando pertingit ad suum principium"; *ST,* I, q. 12, a. 1: ". . . intantum enim unumquodque perfectum est, inquantum ad suum principium attingit."

39. "Manifestum est enim quod ultima beatitudo sive felicitas hominis consistit in sua nobilissima operatione, quae est intelligere, cujus ultimam perfectione, oportet esse per hoc quod intellectus noster suo activo principio conjungitur" *(Q. de an.,* q. 5 [Robb, 100]).

40. Approximate dates: *Scripta super libros Sententiarum,* 1253–55; *De Veritate,* 1256–59; *Quaestiones quodlibetales* VII–XI, 1256–59; *Quaestiones de anima* (1268–69): see Raymundus Spiazzi, O.P., Introduction to *Quaestiones quodlibetales,* ed. Raymundus Spiazzi, O.P. (Turin: Marietti, 1956), vii–xii; I. T. Eschmann, O.P., "A Catalogue of St. Thomas's Works," in Gilson, *The Christian Philosophy of St. Thomas Aquinas,* 384, 392; and James H. Robb, Introduction to *St. Thomas Aquinas: Quaestiones de Anima,* ed. James H. Robb (Toronto: Pontifical Institute of Mediaeval Studies, 1968), 27–37.

41. See *SCG,* III, 25 (Pera, n. 2058, p. 32).

42. "Nihil autem est finaliter perfectum, nisi attingat ad suum principium secundum modum suum" *(Quod.* X, q. 8, a. 1 [Spiazzi, 210]).

is the mode of being that is proper to the rational soul? It is a subsistent and not a material form.[43] As a subsistent form, the rational soul is not generated by a secondary agent from the potency of matter but is a form that is immediately created by God.[44] Since God is the immediate efficient cause of the human soul,[45] any knowledge of God that stops short of knowing the divine essence fails to rejoin the rational soul to its principle according to the soul's own mode of being, which is as a subsistent form that is immediately created by God.[46] A created similitude of God is a medium that unites the created intelligence to God. In such a mediate union with God, the rational soul would not attain its ultimate perfection as an intelligence. It would not, in these terms, be immediately joined to its cause.

(2) The second family of arguments, based on exemplar causality, is grounded on the resemblance that an effect has to its cause. Again, Aquinas stresses the immediacy of the causal relationship between the human mind and God.

The human mind is immediately created by God, and immediately formed by Him as from an exemplar. From this it is immediately beatified in Him as its end. (De ver., q. 18, a. 1, ad 7 [Spiazzi, 339])[47]

The argument is developed in reference to the traditional analogy that specifies the likeness between creatures and God. Every creature, since it is an effect of the divine cause, variously represents God. Some creatures represent only the divine causality itself; they are called "traces" or "vestiges" (vestigia). But an intellectual creature represents the fact that God acts by intellect and will; it is, therefore, appropriately called an "image" (imago) of God.[48]

Nonetheless, the term "image," as its is ordinarily used, is problematic. Ordinarily an image represents its exemplar by sharing in its

43. See *II Sent.*, d. 18, q. 2, a. 1 (Mandonnet, 460): ". . . anima rationalis non est quid ex materia . . . nec est forma materialis, quae possit educi de potentia materiae, sicut aliae formae materiales. . . ."

44. See *Quod.* I, q. 3, a. 1 (Spiazzi, 44): ". . . anima rationalis educitur in esse per creationem. Sed creare, cum sit potentiae infinitae, est solius Dei."

45. See *Quod.* X, q. 8, a. 1 (Spiazzi, p. 210): "Et quia anima [rationalis] immediate facta est a Deo. . . ."

46. See *ST*, I, q. 90, a. 3.

47. "Ipsa enim humana mens immediate a Deo creatur, et immediate ab ipso sicut exemplari formatur; et per hoc immediate in ipso sicut in fine beatificatur" (*De ver.*, q. 18, a. 1, ad 7 [Spiazzi, 339]).

48. See *ST*, I, q. 93, a. 9, ad 2: ". . . essentia animae pertinet ad imaginem, prout repraesentat divinam essentiam secundum ea quae sunt propria intellectualis naturae. . . ."

species or essence. But God and creatures do not share a common nature or species. Intellectual creatures are called "images" of God only by analogy. By knowing and loving, they share in an imperfect likeness to the divine intellect and will.[49] But because man is an image of God, it can be said, on the strength of this analogy, that human beatitude resembles divine beatitude.

Man, the image of God, finds beatitude in intellectual contemplation. We place the ultimate felicity of an intellectual creature in the same operation in which consists God's felicity, namely, in intellectual contemplation. And hence only the intellectual creature is said to be in the image of God rationally. *(II Sent.,* d. 16, q. 1, a. 1 [Mandonnet, 400])[50]

Divine beatitude is God's own perfect intellectual possession of Himself.[51] By His nature, God is beatitude.[52] The human intellect merely tends toward this perfect knowledge of God but does so by an inclination that expresses its very nature. Moreover, as the image of God, man has the capacity for receiving grace and God Himself; thus man is *"capax gratiae"* and *"capax Dei."*[53] In receiving divine grace, and thereby meriting the "light of glory," man is enabled to attain beatitude by knowing and loving God Himself.

Between our mind and God, nothing is a medium as though it were the object of beatitude, but our mind immediately tends toward God, from whom it is immediately vivified by grace. . . . *(II Sent.,* d. 16, q. 1, a. 3, ad 3 [Mandonnet, 403])[54]

(3) In the *Summa contra gentiles,* the *Summa theologiae,* and the *Compendium theologiae,*[55] Aquinas emphasizes that men have a

49. See *II Sent.,* d. 16, q. 1, a. 1; a. 3, ad 5.
50. ". . . et inde est quod in eadem operatione ponimus ultimam felicitatem intellectualis creaturae, in qua est felicitas Dei, scilicet in contemplatione intellectiva; et ideo sola intellectualis creatura rationabiliter ad imaginem Dei dicitur esse" *(II Sent.,* d. 16, q. 1, a. 1 [Mandonnet, 400]).
51. See *ST,* I, q. 12, a. 4: ". . . cognoscere ipsum esse subsistens, sit connaturale soli intellectui divino. . . ."
52. See *Comp. theol.,* I, c. 106 (Verardo, n. 214, p. 53): ". . . cum hanc beatitudinis [quod Deum videat per essentiam] Deus per suam naturam habeat. . . ."
53. See *ST,* I–II, q. 113, a. 10: "Naturaliter anima est gratiae capax; eo enim ipso quod facta est ad imaginem Dei, capax est Dei per gratiam"; III, q. 4, a. 1, ad 2: "Similitudo imaginis attenditur in natura humana secundum quod est capax Dei; scilicet ipsum attingendo propria operatione cognitionis et amoris."
54. ". . . inter mentem nostram et Deum nihil est medium quasi objectum beatitudinis, sed immediate in Deum nostra mens tendit, a quo etiam immediate per gratiam vivificatur . . ." *(II Sent.,* d. 16, q. 1, a. 3, ad 3 [Mandonnet, 403]).
55. See *ST,* I, q. 12, a. 1; I–II, q. 3. a. 8; *SCG,* III, 50–54; *Comp. theol.* I, cc. 104–6.

natural desire to know God inasmuch as they have a natural desire
for ultimate beatitude. Beatitude consists in man's highest activity:
knowing the essence of the most intelligible of beings.[56] Since God is
supremely intelligible, man's beatitude can lie only in knowing
God.[57]

Again, any other supposition—say, that man's ultimate beatitude
lies in knowing the separate substances—is contrary not only to Sacred
Doctrine but to reason. Since even noncognitive beings seek God, who
is the highest good, it is hardly reasonable to posit a less noble end for
man, who is an intellectual being. Indeed, no other end is possible for
an intellectual being. The human intellect knows universal being from
which arises the desire for a universal good.[58]

The argument from nature that Aquinas uses to demonstrate that
men must be able to know the divine essence has an elegant simplicity. Men have a natural desire to attain perfect beatitude. Perfect beatitude comes from knowing the divine essence. Since a natural desire
cannot be "in vain," the conclusion follows that it is possible for men to
see God.

> Since it is impossible that a natural desire be in vain, which would be
> the case if it were not possible to come to understanding the divine sub-
> stance, which all minds naturally desire, it is necessary to say that it be
> possible that the substance of God be seen through the intellect, both by
> the separate intellectual substances and by our souls. (SCG, III, 51 [Pera, n.
> 2284, p. 69)][59]

The argument rests squarely on the principle "*It is impossible that a
natural desire be in vain.*"[60] A desire that can never be satisfied is "in
vain." Aquinas, however, does not say that the vision of God is necessary; rather, he concludes that it is necessary *to say* that the vision of

56. See *ST,* I, q. 12, a. 1: "Cum enim ultima hominis beatitudo in altissima eius
operatione consistat, quae est operatio intellectus. . . ."

57. See *SCG,* III, 25 (Pera, n. 2057, p. 32): "Et sic intelligere perfectissimum
intelligibile, quod Deus est, est perfectissimum in genere huius operationis quae est
intelligere."

58. See *Comp. theol.,* II, c. 9 (Verardo, n. 579, p. 134): ". . . universale bonum est
quod homo desiderat, cum per intellectum universale bonum apprehendat. . . ."

59. "Cum autem impossibile sit naturale desiderium esse inane, quod quidem
esset si non esset possibile pervenire ad divinam substantiam intelligendam, quod
naturaliter omnes mentes desiderant; necesse est dicere quod possibile sit substantiam Dei videri per intellectum, et a substantiis intellectualibus separatis, et ab
animabus nostris" *(SCG,* III, 51 [Pera, n. 2284, p. 69]).

60. "Impossibile est autem naturale desiderium esse vanum" *(Comp. theol.,* I, c.
104 [Verardo, n. 208, p. 52]).

God is *possible*. But why is Aquinas so convinced that a natural desire can never be universally frustrated?

His conviction reflects, to be sure, a profoundly Aristotelian point of view, that all *natures* are teleologically ordered: "Action for an end is present in things which come to be and are by nature."[61] An individual of a given nature may, of course, be prevented by misfortune or defect from attaining its proper end. But an allegedly "natural desire" of an universally unattainable end is not, in fact, a natural desire. The contrary proposition, that a vain natural desire is possible, repudiates the universal teleology of nature; it is equivalent to the assertion that nature is fundamentally unintelligible or is ruled by chance and not intelligence.[62] But such a view of nature is not only impossible for an Aristotelian; for a Christian, God's providence extends to all beings, particulars as well as universals. A vain natural desire is impossible because such an alleged desire would fall outside the order of God's providential governance of creation.[63]

Aquinas's conviction that a natural desire must be realizable finally rests on the demonstrable theological proposition that God does act intelligently.[64] The intelligent author of nature does not instill unintelligible or vain natural desires.[65] Still, even the theological assertion that natural desire is not in vain does not immediately support the conclusion that it is possible for men to see God. One must first ascertain in what sense men naturally desire to see God.

That men desire beatitude, that is, the possession and enjoyment of perfect good, is a psychological datum that can hardly be challenged; but that men, in naturally desiring beatitude, *explicitly* desire to know the divine essence, as the object in which beatitude is achieved, is far from obvious. Aquinas, in fact, denies that the latter necessarily follows upon the former.[66] One does not necessarily and explicitly desire

61. *Phys.*, II, 8, 199a7–8 (rev. Oxford trans.).

62. See *I Sent.*, d. 35, a. 1, a. 1 (Mandonnet, 809): "Omne autem desiderium finis praecedit aliqua cognitio praestituens finem, et dirigens in finem ea quae sunt ad finem. Sed in quibusdam ista cognitio non est conjuncta ipsi tendenti in finem; unde oportet quod dirigatur per aliquod prius agens . . ."; *SCG*, I, 44 (Pera, n. 378, p. 57): "Naturalia autem tendunt in fines determinatos. . . . Cum ergo ipsa non praestituant sibi finem, quia rationem finis non cognoscunt; oportet quod eis praestituatur finis ab alio, qui sit naturae institutor."

63. See *ST*, I, q. 103, a. 5; a. 7.

64. See *I Sent.*, d. 35, q. 1; *ST*, I, q. 14; q. 19.

65. See *I Sent.*, d. 39, q. 2, a. 2 (Mandonnet, 932): "Cum igitur providentiae non sit destruere ordinem rerum, expletur effectus providentiae in rebus secundum convenientiam rei prout nata est consequi finem."

66. See *ST*, I–II, q. 5, a. 8.

to see God because one necessarily and explicitly desires to be perfectly happy. This point, as we shall see, becomes central in Thomist commentaries.

Although the divine vision is beatitude itself, it does not follow that anyone who desires beatitude desires the divine vision, since beatitude, insofar as it is such, signifies the essential object of the will, not, however, the divine vision. For example, someone might desire something sweet, who does not, however, desire an apple. *(IV Sent.,* d. 49, q. 1, a. 3, sol. 1, ad 2 [Vivès, 11, p. 473]) [67]

In short, men need to determine, whether through Christian faith or philosophy, in what thing or object beatitude is to be found. The philosophical judgment that beatitude is found in "seeing God" follows, so Aquinas explains, only upon the developed desire to know philosophically. Men explicitly pursue philosophical knowledge of God when they seek to know the first cause of sensible beings. But only to know that there is a First Cause and not to know its nature is to leave actual knowledge incomplete, the desire to know unfulfilled, and the knower unhappy:[68] "While something remains to be desired, man has not yet reached his ultimate perfection" *(Comp. theol.,* II, c. 9 [Verardo, n. 575, p. 133]).[69] The mind, once it attempts to know the First Cause, cannot rest until it knows the essence of the First Cause.

The desire to know God is at first only implicit, submerged in the desire and knowledge of particular goods, but it arises from the nature of the will that has universal good as its object and the intellect that has universal being as its object.[70] Men seek to know the cause of universal being that is the object of the human intellect.[71] In knowing

67. ". . . quamvis divina visio sit ipsa beatitudo, non tamen sequitur quod quicumque appetit beatitudinem, appetat divinam visionem: quia beatitudo, inquantum hujusmodi importat per se objectum voluntatis, non autem ipsa divina visio; sicut aliquis appetit dulce, qui tamen non appetit mel" *(IV Sent.,* d. 49, q. 1, a. 3, sol. 1, ad 2 [Vivès, 11, p. 473]).

68. See *SCG,* III, 50 [Pera, n. 2281, pp. 68–69]: "Nos autem, quantumcumque sciamus Deum esse, et alia . . . non quiescimus desiderio, sed adhuc desideramus eum per essentiam suam cognoscere."

69. ". . . quamdiu aliquid desiderandum restat, nondum pervenit homo ad ultimam perfectionem suam" *(Comp. theol.,* II, c. 9 [Verardo, n. 575, p. 133]).

70. See *De ver.,* q. 22, a. 2, ad 1 (Spiazzi, 392); ". . . omnia cognoscentia cognoscunt implicite Deum in quolibet cognitio. Sicut enim nihil habet rationem appetibilis nisi per similitudinem primae bonitatis, ita nihil est cognoscibile nisi per similitudinem primae veritatis."

71. See *SCG,* III, 25 [Pera, n. 2066, p. 33]: "Intellectus autem humanus cognoscit ens universale. Desiderat igitur naturaliter cognoscere causam eius. . . ."

that cause, they attain the "perfection of intelligible being."[72] Paradoxically, the way to this perfection is blocked by what man is; the human intellect is at once open and closed to its own perfection. The range of the passive intellect, which has universal being as its object, extends beyond the capacity of the active intellect, which can only render intelligible the forms of sensible beings.[73] The perfection of intelligible being, the infinite God, cannot be known through any species abstracted from a finite being. If men are to attain knowledge of the divine essence, then God Himself must somehow inform or immediately actualize the human intellect.

God, however, acts freely and not from any necessity that creatures impose on Him. Yet a natural desire that is forever unfilled is precisely a natural desire that is in vain. Holding to these principles, the Thomistic argument seems to founder on an antinomy. The divinely established order of nature, wherein men are naturally desirous of the vision of God, must be subordinated to God's freedom to give or not to give man the supernatural vision of Himself. But if men do not attain knowledge of God, have they not been made in vain?

Everyone acknowledges that Aquinas states the problem clearly:

Since man was made for this, that he know the divine substance, if he is not able to obtain it, it seems that he would be made in vain. *(Comp. theol.*, II, c. 7 [Verardo, n. 568, p. 131])[74]

But hardly anyone agrees as to how Aquinas solves it. The exact significance of Aquinas's metaphysical argument that the natural desire for human beatitude can be satisfied only in the vision of the divine essence has vexed even the most authoritative of the Thomist theologians.[75] Although often underplayed by Thomist philosophers, it should be no less a troubling issue for anyone who wishes to construct a Thomistic philosophical ethics. The latter, especially if it holds to its Aristotelian prototype, must be grounded in human nature and what naturally fulfills it. What other ground could philosophy discern? But how can "seeing God" fall within the scope of human nature or be counted a natural achievement?

---

72. See *SCG*, III, 59 (Pera, n. 2348, p. 79): "Perfectio autem esse intelligibilis est cum intellectus ad suum ultimum finem pervenerit. . . ."

73. See *Q. de an.*, q. 5, ad 9.

74. "Cum enim ad hoc factus sit homo, ut magnitudinem divinam cognoscat, si ad eam percipiendam pervenire non possit, videtur in vanum constitutus esse . . ." *(Comp. theol.*, II, c. 7 [Verardo, n. 568, p. 131]).

75. See A.-R. Motte, O.P., "Désir naturel et béatitude surnaturelle," *Bulletin thomiste* 3 (1932): 651–75.

3. A Theological Contradiction?

Historically, Aquinas's doctrine about the natural desire for seeing God has posed an untenable contradiction for either the theologian or the philosopher who insists that reason cannot transcend its Aristotelian boundaries.[76] Such a philosopher and his theological counterpart identify philosophy and reason with Aristotle, one to protect the autonomy of reason from religious authority, the other to preserve the gratuity of supernatural happiness. For each, philosophy does not know about, and much less is it able to guarantee that men can attain, what is certainly a supernatural end—the vision of the divine essence. But especially for the theologian, Aquinas's conclusions about human beatitude, even when they were read as part of his theology, have been perplexing. For centuries Thomist theologians have pedantically rehearsed whether the desire to see the divine essence may be legitimately called a *natural* desire without thereby jeopardizing the supernatural character of that end.[77] I shall look briefly at the three Dominicans who are the most eminent of the classic Thomist commentators: Thomas de Vio, O.P. (1468–1534), known as Cajetan; Francis Sylvester of Ferrara, O.P. (1474–ca.1528), known as Ferrariensis; and Domingo Báñes, O.P. (1528–1604).[78]

Cajetan, whose commentary on the *Summa theologiae* (first published at Lyons in 1540–41) was uniquely authoritative for subsequent Thomist theologians, precisely formulates the standard and often repeated objection: *"Nature does not bestow an inclination to something, to which the total power of nature is unable to lead."*[79] The principle, in various formulations, is well known to Aquinas.[80] But

76. For an attack on Aquinas's doctrine that is both theological and philosophical, see Pedro Descoqs, S.J., *Praelectiones theologiae naturalis: de dei cognoscibilitate, II* (Paris: Gabriel Beauchesne, 1935), 214–53.

77. For the history of the question, see Juan Alfaro, S.J., *Lo natural y lo sobrenatural: Estudio historico desede Santo Tomas hasta Cayetan (1274–1534)* (Burgos: Matriti, 1952); Remigius Ritzler, O.F.M. Conv., *De naturali beatitudinis supernaturalis ad mentem s. Thomae* (Rome: Pontificia Facultas Theologica O.F.M. Conv., 1938).

78. For discussion and criticism of other commentators, see de Lubac, *Le Mystère* and *Augustinisme.*

79. ". . . natura non largitur inclinationem ad aliquid, ad quod tota vis naturae perducere nequit" *(ST,* I, q. 12, a. 1; *Commentari Card. Caietani,* n. IX [Leonine ed., IV, 116]).

80. See *III Sent.,* d. 27, q. 2, a. 2 ad 4 (Moos, n. 129, p. 879): "Desiderium autem naturale non potest esse nisi rei quae naturaliter haberi potest"; *De virt.,* q. 1, a. 10 (Odetto, p. 735): ". . . potentiae enim passivae naturali proportionatur virtus activa naturalis."

Cajetan concludes, unlike Aquinas, that since unaided human nature cannot attain the vision of God's essence, men cannot by nature innately desire it. And it is true that no other conclusion follows from Cajetan's *Aristotelian* consideration of nature.[81]

Yet Cajetan's conclusion, left without nuances, flies only too obviously in the face of Aquinas's repeated statements about men naturally desiring to see God.[82] To avoid literally contradicting Aquinas, Cajetan adds nuances. Cajetan explains that in addition to the *absolute* or philosophical consideration of nature, there is the Christian theological understanding of nature which presupposes the revelation of man's present grace and future glory. The theologian knows by faith that man is actually ordained to the supernatural vision of God. Since Aquinas is a theologian, Cajetan contends that Aquinas must be viewing nature from this theological perspective, since it is only from this perspective that Cajetan is prepared to admit a "natural desire" to see God.[83] Only the believer, who has first been informed of man's supernatural destiny, can then "naturally" desire to achieve what has been promised.[84] As Cajetan explains it, the desire to see God is not, in fact, a natural or innate desire but a desire *elicited* by a supernatural theological faith. The elicited desire, therefore, is conscious and explicit; it is an effect of grace. It is "natural" only for the believer.

Therefore, the desire of the divine vision, although it is not absolutely natural to the intellectual creature, is nonetheless natural to it having supposed the revelation of such effects. *(ST,* I, q. 12, a. 1; *Commentaria Card. Caietani,* n. IX [Leonine ed., IV, 116])[85]

Ferrariensis, whose parallel commentary on the *Summa contra gentiles* (Paris, 1552) enjoyed a similar prestige among Thomists, demurs:

81. Cf. *ST,* I, q. 12, a. 1; *Commentaria Card. Caietani,* n. IX (Leonine ed., IV, 116): ". . . organa natura dedit cuilibet potentiae quam intus in anima posuit."

82. Almost one hundred years ago, Joachim Sestili, *In Summa theologicam s. Thomae Aquinatis, I^aP^e q. xii a. 1: De naturali intelligentis animae capacitate atque appetitu intuendi divinam disquisitio* (Naples-Rome: Salvatoris Festa, 1896), 30–31, cautiously observes that "Cardinalis Cajetanus in Schola S. Thomae Theologus . . . a communiori via recedere videtur."

83. See *ST,* I–II, q. 3, a. 8; *Commentaria Card. Caietani,* n. I (Leonine ed., VI, 36): "Et sic licet homini absolute non insit naturale hujusmodi desiderium, est tamen naturale homini ordinato a divina Providentia in illam patriam."

84. Cf. *Expos. de Trin.,* q. 1, a. 3, ad 4 (Decker, 18–20, p. 73): ". . . quamvis deus sit ultimus finis inconsecutus et primus in intentione appetitus naturalis, non tamen oportet quod sit primus in cognitione mentis humanae quae ordinatur in finem. . . ."

85. "Et propterea desiderium visionis divinae, etsi non sit naturale intellectui

Cajetan's explanation of *ST,* I, q. 12, a. 1 "does not seem to be according to the mind of Saint Thomas."[86] Ferrariensis contends that apart from the *elicited* and strictly supernatural desire to see the divine essence, which as the object of supernatural beatitude is desired solely because of faith, there is also a strictly natural desire to see the essence of the First Cause, which is *elicited* by the metaphysical knowledge that there is a First Cause.[87] This consideration applies with greater force to angels than to men. The angels or separate substances, although they can know God in more perfect fashion than men, continue to desire to know the essence of the First Cause because they are not fulfilled by the natural knowledge of God that they attain through knowing their own essences. But this desire, contrary to what Cajetan claims, does not arise from knowing the supernatural effects of grace and glory. It remains, even with the angels, strictly a case of the natural desire to know the first cause of a given natural effect.

Nonetheless, Ferrariensis remains no less than Cajetan in the orbit of Aristotelian natures. Despite what Aquinas says,[88] he, like Cajetan, denies that there is an *innate* or *natural* desire to see the essence of the First Cause. Ferrariensis uses a distinction that Cajetan himself draws between two ways of understanding *"naturalis appetitus."*[89] There is: (1) an *innate natural appetite* that necessarily follows upon the natural form of a being; (2) an *elicited natural appetite* of the will that follows only upon some prior intellectual apprehension.[90] By calling them both "appetites," Cajetan and Ferrariensis conflate what Aquinas distin-

---

creato absolute, est tamen naturali ei, supposita revelatione talium effectuum" *(ST,* I, q. 12, a. 1; *Commentaria Card. Caietani,* n. IX [Leonine ed., IV, 116]).

86. ". . . non videtur esse ad mentem Sancti Thomae . . ." (*SCG,* III, 51; *Commentaria Ferrariensis,* n. III [Leonine ed., XIV, 141a]).

87. See *SCG,* III, 51; *Commentaria Ferrariensis,* IV, 1 (Leonine ed., XIV, 141b: ". . . dupliciter potest visio divinae essentiae et naturae considerari. Uno modo, inquantum est visio essentiae primae causae absolute. Alio modo, inquantum est visio obiecti supernaturalis beatitudinis"

88. Cf. *De virt.,* q. 1, a. 10 (Odetto, p. 735): ". . . patet quod naturale hominis desiderium in nullo alio quietari potest, nisi in solo Deo."

89. See *ST,* I, q. 78, a. 1; *Commentaria Card. Caietani,* n. V (Leonine ed., V, 252): "Appetitus naturalis dupliciter sumi consuevit. Primo, pro inclinatione a natura indita. Et sic non est actus aliquis elicitus. . . . Secundo, sumitur pro actu secundo, quo tenditur in praecognitum sic quod non potest in oppositum tendi. Et haec est operatio appetitus animalis, sive intellectualis sive sensitivi"; q. 82, a. 1; n. XII (Leonine ed., V, 295): "Unde nos appelamus naturalem appetitum, non solum inclinationem voluntatis in obiectum etc., sed illum actum elicitum determinatum quoad specificationem. . . ."

90. See Robert P. Sullivan, O.P., *Man's Thirst for Good* (Westminster, Maryland:

guishes:[91] the unalterable, precognitive finality or tendency or *appetite* of the will, which expresses the very nature that God gives to the will,[92] and the intellectual, free, natural, and elicited *act* of the will:[93] "The will, inasmuch as it is a certain nature, wills something naturally" *(ST,* I, q. 41, a. 2, ad 3).[94] Nonetheless, Ferrariensis claims that, in the first sense of the term, there is no natural appetite to see God

---

Newman Press, 1952) for a recent defense of Cajetan, Sylvester, and John of St. Thomas's "division [of *"appetitus naturalis"*] into a twofold natural appetite" (52).

91. See *De malo,* q. 6, a. 1 (Calcaterra-Centi, 558): ". . . in rebus naturalibus invenitur forma, quae est principium actionis, et inclinatio consequens formam, quae dicitur appetitus naturalis, ex quibus sequitur actio . . ."; *III Sent.,* d. 27, q. 1, a. 2 (Moos, n. 39, p. 861): ". . . appetitum naturalem qui nihil aliud est quam inclinatio rei in finem suum naturalem qui est ex directione instituentis naturam, et iterum appetitum voluntarium qui est inclinatio cognoscentis finem et ordinem ad finem illum"; *ST,* I-II, q. 35, a. 1: "Omnis autem motus appetitivus, seu inclinatio, consequens apprehensionem, pertinet ad appetitum intellectivum vel sensitivum; nam inclinatio appetitus naturalis non consequitur apprehensionem ipsius appetentis, sed alterius. . . ."

On the commentators replacing *"actus elicitus"* with *"appetitus elicitus,"* see William R. O'Connor, *The Eternal Quest: The Teaching of St. Thomas Aquinas on the Natural Desire for God* (New York: Longmans, Green and Co., 1947), 112, 249–50, nn. 32–33.

92. See *De ver.,* q. 22, a. 8 (Spiazzi, 402): ". . . ex ipsa natura, quam Deus voluntati dedit, inclinatur voluntas in aliquid volendum. . . ."

93. Aquinas distinguishes the natural appetite of the will from the *naturally elicited acts* of the will: "Sed quia voluntas in aliqua natura fundatur, necesse est quod motus proprius naturae, quantum ad aliquid, participetur in voluntate: sicut quod est prioris causae, participatur a posteriori. Est enim prius in unaquaque re ipsum esse, quod est per naturam, quam velle, quod est per voluntatem. Et inde est quod voluntas naturaliter aliquid vult" *(ST,* I-II, q. 10, a. 1, ad 1). See *Comp. theol.,* I, c. 122, for the distinction between *voluntas actualis, voluntas habitualis,* and *appetitus naturalis voluntatis.* The natural appetite of the will is prior to any of the acts of the will; it is the innate tendency, which is determined by the proportion between the will (as a power) and its end "the good in general" *(De ver.,* q. 27, a. 2): "Hoc autem est bonum in communi, in quod voluntas naturaliter tendit, sicut etiam quaelibet potentia in suum obiectum . . ." *(ST,* I-II, q. 10, a. 1). The natural appetite of the will (which corresponds to its precognitive finality or determinate tendency) is revealed in the simple act of willing which is intellectual: "Et sic simplex voluntas [= *velle]* est idem quod voluntas ut natura" *(ST,* III, q. 18, a. 4). Thus, by nature, the will is directed to willing *(velle)* certain necessary ends, i.e., beatitude and that which is necessarily contained in beatitude: ". . . quod voluntas de necessitate vult quasi naturali inclinatione in ipsum determinata, est finis ultimus, ut beatitudo, et ea quae in ipso includuntur, ut cognitio veritatis, et alia huiusmodi; ad alia vero non de necessitate determinatur naturali inclinatione, sed propria dispositione absque necessitate" *(De ver.,* q. 22, a. 5 [Spiazzi, 397]).

94. ". . . etiam voluntas, inquantum est natura quaedam, aliquid naturaliter vult . . ." *(ST,* I, q. 41, a. 2, ad 3).

because, once again, it is impossible for nature to innately desire what nature cannot attain.

It is impossible that something naturally desire what by its own power is not able to be obtained: because a natural form does not incline to something that exceeds the faculty of nature. *(SCG, III, 51, Commentaria Ferrariensis, n. IV, 2 [Leonine ed., XIV, 141b])*[95]

There is, however, a "natural desire" to see God in the second sense of the term. In an intellectual creature, there is an intellectual desire to see God. And this desire is consciously *elicited* from the will; it follows upon the prior metaphysical knowledge that a given being is an "effect," that it is causally dependent on God.[96]

Ferrariensis, however, evidently shares Cajetan's anxiety to protect the gratuity of the supernatural vision of God. The *naturally* elicited desire to see the essence of the First Cause must be sharply distinguished from the *supernaturally* elicited desire for supernatural beatitude.

For we are able to be know naturally what is the cause of other [beings]: we do not naturally know what is the object of supernatural beatitude, the vision of which is the highest good. *(SCG, III, 51; Commentaria Ferrariensis, n., IV, 1 [Leonine ed., XIV, 141b])*[97]

Men cannot desire, by any naturally elicited desire of the will, what is de facto the supreme good for an intellectual nature, the vision of God, because to know that the vision of God is man's supreme good is strictly supernatural knowledge, and so too the elicited desire for it is strictly supernatural.[98]

Domingo Báñez rehearses, refines, and gives canonical shape to the interpretations of the other sixteenth-century Thomist commentators. With Cajetan and Ferrariensis, he too repudiates the idea that there can be an innate natural inclination or desire (what Báñez calls the *"inclinatio naturae"* or *"propensio"* or *"pondus naturale"*) to see God. A stone has a *pondus naturale* (instilled by the Author of Nature) to

---

95. ". . . inconveniens est aliquid appeti naturaliter in quod virtute naturae non possit perveniri: quia forma naturalis non inclinat ad id quod naturae facultatem excedit" *(SCG, III, 51; Commentaria Ferrariensis, n. IV, 2 [Leonine ed., XIV, 141b])*.
96. See *SCG, III, 51; Commentaria Ferrariensis, n. IV, 2 (Leonine ed., XIV, 141b)*.
97. "Naturaliter enim cognosci potest quod sit aliorum causa: non autem naturaliter scimus quod sit obiectum supernaturalis beatitudinis, et quod eius visio sit summa bonum" *(SCG, III, 51; Commentaria Ferrariensis, n. IV, 1 [Leonine ed., XIV, 141b])*.
98. See *SCG, III, 51; Commentaria Ferrariensis, n. IV, 1 (Leonine ed., XIV, 141b)*: ". . . naturaliter desideramus visionem Dei inquantum est visio primae causae: non autem inquantum est summum bonum."

move downward. But man has no *pondus naturale* to see God: man cannot have that natural tendency because "man is not able to reach that end through the total powers of nature."[99] Using Cajetan's principle, Báñez is no more able than Cajetan to view *human nature* outside the confines of the Aristotelian conception of "nature." Accordingly, the "natural desire" to see God is regarded *solely* as a conscious or elicited desire of the will,[100] and one that is, so Báñez takes pains to characterize it, *inefficacious* and *conditional*. The desire is conditional "because from the powers of nature, man is not able to be certain that such a good is possible."[101]

Báñez's hesitant formula neutralizes the force of the natural desire that impels Thomistic philosophical reason: Báñez says that *if* it is possible to do so, the philosopher *would like to see* the essence of the First Cause. This formula, clearly enough, cannot carry the weight of Aquinas's conclusion: only the vision of God can satisfy man's desire to know the First Cause.[102]

In denying that there is an innate natural desire to see God, these sixteenth-century Dominican commentators significantly diverged from Aquinas's own doctrine. Cajetan, Ferrariensis, and Báñez did not adequately attend to Aquinas's distinction, which, of course, they knew, between "*voluntas ut natura*" (will as nature) and "*voluntas ut ratio*" (will as reason):[103] "Any potency of the soul is a form or nature, and has a natural inclination to something."[104] Aquinas says with unequivocal clarity that the will *as a nature* does have a natural appetite or an innate desire for good in general or happiness.[105] This

---

99. "... Sed homo non potest pervenire ad illud finem per totas vires naturae ..." *(Bañes Scholastica commentaria,* I, q. 12, a. 1 [ed. Urbino, 250]).

100. Cf. *ST,* I–II, q. 41, a. 3: "Alio modo dicitur motus naturalis, ad quem natura inclinat, licet non perficiatur nisi per apprehensionem: quia ... motus cognitivae et appetitivae virtutis reducuntur in naturam, sicut in principium primum."

101. "[Dixi *conditionale,*] quia ex viribus naturae non potest homini certum esse, tale bonum esse possibile ..." *(Bañes Scholastica commentaria,* I, q. 12, a. 1 [ed. Urbino, 249]).

102. See P. Labourdette, O.P., review of *La Destinée de la nature humaine selon saint Thomas d'Aquin,* by Jorge Laporta, *Revue thomiste* 66 (1966): 283.

103. See *III Sent.,* d. 17, a. 1, sol. 3, ad 1 (Moos, n. 27, p. 532); d. 27, q. 1, a. 2; *ST,* I, q. 41, s. 2, ad 3; q. 60, aa. 1–2; III, q. 18, a. 3; q. 21, a. 4; *De ver.,* q. 22, a. 3, ad 5.

104. "... unaquaeque potentia animae est quaedam forma seu natura, et habet naturalem inclinationem in aliquid" *(ST,* I, q. 80, a. 1, ad 3).

105. See *ST,* I, q. 41, a. 2, ad 3: "...voluntas, inquantum est natura quaedam, aliquid naturaliter vult; sicut voluntas hominis naturaliter tendit ad beatitudinem"; *De ver.,* q. 22, a. 9 (Spiazzi, 403): "... Sic invenitur voluntatis duplex obiectum. Unum, ad quod de necessitate naturalis inclinatio determinatur. Et hoc quidem

innate desire for happiness, which is not an elicited desire[106] since it is antecedent to any intellectual act,[107] is certainly an *inclinatio naturae*.[108] The natural desire to see God is *implicitly* contained in the necessary desire for the perfect good or happiness that structures the will, or in the necessary desire, which follows upon the nature of the intellect, to know in general the cause of any known effect.[109] God is the source of the goodness that is the necessary object of the will, and is therefore implicitly desired inasmuch as the will necessarily seeks universal good.[110] With the necessary qualification that the term refers to an *implicit* desire, "the desire to see God" can be acknowledged as an *inclinatio naturae* in Aquinas.[111] Precisely because it is a natural desire, this inclination must be carefully distinguished from the explicit or elicited desire to know God that only follows upon anteced-

---

obiectum est voluntati inditum et propositum a creatore, qui ei naturalem inclinationem dedit in illud."

106. Contra Labourdette, review of *La Destinée de la nature humaine*, 283. All men *naturally* desire beatitude, and do so implicitly and preconsciously under the common formality *(ratio communis)* of "the perfect good" *(bonum perfectum)*, but only the philosopher is able to discern the *ratio communis* under which they desire it. What men consciously and explicitly pursue is not the *ratio communis* of beatitude, but some particular end or ends (riches, power, pleasure, philosophical contemplation, etc.) that they *think* is beatitude. The conscious desire for such specific ends is, of course, an "elicited desire": see *ST*, I–II, q. 5, a. 8.

107. See *ST*, I–II, q. 4, a. 4, ad 2: ". . . omnis actus voluntatis praeceditur ab aliquo actu intellectus: aliquis tamen actus voluntatis est prior quam aliquis actus intellectus. Voluntas enim tendit in finalem actum intellectus, qui est beatitudo."

108. See *III Sent.*, d. 27, q. 1, a. 2, resp. (Moos, n. 43, pp. 861–62): "Unde oportet in omnibus creaturis habentibus aliquem finem inveniri appetitum naturalem etiam in ipsa voluntate respectu finis ultimi. Unde naturali appetitu vult homo beatitudinem et ea quae ad naturam voluntatis spectant"; *ST*, I, q. 12, a. 1: "Inest enim homini naturale desiderium cognoscendi causam, cum intuetur effectum"; q. 41, a. 2 ad 3: ". . . voluntas, inquantum est natura quaedam, aliquid naturaliter vult; sicut voluntas hominis naturaliter tendit ad beatitudinem"; I–II, q. 10, a. 1: "Sed quia voluntas in aliqua natura fundatur, necesse est quod motus proprius naturae, quantum ad aliquid, participetur in voluntate . . ."; *De ver.*, q. 22, a. 5 (Spiazzi, 397): "Et ideo, quod voluntas de necessitate vult quasi naturali inclinatione in ipsum determinata, est finis ultimus, ut beatitudo, et ea quae in ipso includuntur, ut est cognitio veritatis. . . ."

109. To know the particular cause (A) of any particular effect (B) is an elicited desire.

110. See *De ver.*, q. 22, a. 2 (Spiazzi, 392): ". . . omnia naturaliter appetunt Deum implicite, non autem explicite . . . Sicut Deus, propter quod est primum efficiens, agit in omni agente, ita propter hoc quod est ultimus finis, appetitur in omni fine. Sed hoc est appetere ipsum Deum implicite."

111. See *SCG*, I, 11 (Pera, n. 70, pp. 14–15): "Sic enim homo naturaliter Deum cognoscit sicut naturaliter ipsum desiderat. Desiderat autem ipsum homo naturaliter inquantum desiderat naturaliter beatitudinem. . . ."

ent metaphysical knowledge that there is a First Cause of all sensible beings.[112] Although the two desires, implicit and explicit, are directed to the same object (God), the explicit (i.e., "elicited") metaphysical desire to see God cannot, despite what Ferrariensis and Báñez suggest, be called, in the precise Thomistic sense, a "natural desire."[113]

Still, the Thomist commentators, whose exegesis seems as much ruled by their theological anxieties as by the texts of Aquinas,[114] must be given their due. In their attenuated explanations of Aquinas, more than Aristotle's authority or the Aristotelian conception of "nature" is at stake.[115] Something far more fundamental to Christian faith is at question. Does the concept of a natural desire to see God compromise the supernatural character of man's ultimate end?[116] Fearing that it does, Cajetan, Ferrariensis, and Báñez blunt Aquinas's striking affirmations of what men actually desire by nature. These eminent Thomist commentators argue that there can be no innate or natural desire for the beatific vision because there is no such active potency whereby man can attain such a vision. The desire to see God corresponds only to an "obediential potency" activated by grace.[117] The commentators,

---

112. See *ST,* I–II, q. 30, a. 1, ad 3: ". . . unicuique potentiae animae competit appetere proprium bonum appetitu naturali, qui non sequitur apprehensionem."

113. See *ST,* I–II, q. 30, a. 3, ad 1; ". . . illud idem quod appetitur appetitu naturali, potest appeti appetitu animali cum fuerit apprehensum."

For other texts distinguishing the natural appetite of the will from its elicited acts, see Jorge Laporta, "Pour trouver le sens exact des termes *appetitus naturalis, desiderium naturale, amor naturalis, etc.* chez Thomas d'Aquin," *Archives d'histoire doctrinale et littéraire du moyen âge* 40 (1973): 37–95.

114. For example, Ferrariensis (*SCG,* III, 51; *Commentaria Ferrariensis,* n. IV, 2 [Leonine ed., XIV, 141b]) quotes *Expos. de Trin.,* q. 6, a. 4, ad 5 with the bracketed interpolation: "Quamvis enim homo natualiter inclinetur *[scilicet sub communi ratione beatitudinis]* in finem ultimum, non tamen potest naturaliter illum consequi, sed solum per gratiam, et hoc est propter eminentiam illius finis".

Báñez cautions about Durandus's interpretation: "Sed certe Durandus solum ait, esse homini naturalem et necessarium appetitum velut inclinationem sine actu elicito ad beatitudinem in communi: nusquam tamen ait esse talem appetitum naturalem homini, respectu beatitudinis, quae est visio Dei in speciali" *(Bañes Scholastica commentaria,* I, q. 12, a. 1 [ed. Urbano., 248]).

115. For a rehearsal by a "devil's advocate" of the philosophical difficulties raised by Aquinas's alleged rejection of Aristotelian natures, see Gerard Smith, S.J., "The Natural End of Man," *Proceedings of the American Catholic Philosophical Association* 23 (1949): 47–61.

116. Cf. Ritzler, *De naturali beatitudinis supernaturalis,* 86: ". . . non tantummodo ad possibilitatem metaphysicam Dei visionis et ad potentiam atque capacitatem hominis; sed ad necessarium actuationem, seu impletionem concludere licet, uti Aquinas de facto facit. . . ."

117. See *ST,* I, q. 12, a. 1; *Commentaria Card. Caietani,* n. X (Leonine ed., IV, 116).

however, anxiously focus on the *explicit* or elicited desire to see God; in doing so, they obfuscate and ignore the emphasis that Aquinas places on the naturalness of the desire to see God that is *implicitly* contained in the desire for happiness.

4. Obediential Potency

Cajetan, Ferrariensis, and Báñez appeal to obediential potency to explain how it may be said that men may desire the vision of God.[118] "*Potentia obedientialis*" is, admittedly, a doctrine found in Aquinas.

> In every creature there is some obediential potency, inasmuch as every creature obeys God in receiving in itself what God shall will. *(De virt.*, q. 1, a. 10 [Odetto, 737])[119]

Creatures are said to have a "potency of obedience" *(potentia obedientiae)* in that they are able to be changed or used supernaturally by God. Such "potencies," however, are not passive potencies inherent in the nature of the creature so used. The term signifies what God can do supernaturally with creatures. In contrast, a being has strictly natural (passive) potencies in regard to its own proper operations and motions.[120] But Aquinas does not push the contrast between obediential and natural potencies too far. God creates and orders nature and whatever he does to creatures is, in the ultimate sense, "natural."[121]

An event is "miraculous," however, because it is above nature, or occurs without nature, or occurs contrary to the fixed or at least the usual order of particular created causes (including the highest natural

118. See *ST*, I, q. 1, a. 1; *Commentaria Card. Caietani*, n. IX (Leonine ed., IV, 116): ". . . vocatur autem potentia obedientialis, aptitudo rei ad hoc ut in ea fiat quidquid faciendum ordinaverit Deus. Et secundum talem potentiam, anima nostra dicitur in potentia ad beatitudinem pollicitam, et finem supernaturalem . . ."; *SCG*, III, 156; *Commentaria Ferrariensis*, n. III, 2 (Leonine ed., XIV, 461b): ". . . cum duplex sit potentia animae ad bonum, scilicet ad bonum naturale et ad bonum supernaturale . . . Et quia potentia ad supernaturalia proprie potentia obedientalis est, non autem naturalis"; *Bañes Scholastica commentari*, I, q. 12, a. 1 (ed. Urbano, 250): "In homine est capacitas naturae et aptitudo secundum potentiam obedientialem ut possit elevari ad videndum Deum."

119. ". . . in tota creatura est quaedam obedientialis potentia, prout tota creatura obedit Deo ad suscipiendum in se quidquid Deus voluerit" *(De virt.*, q. 1, a. 10 [Odetto, 737]).

120. See *De pot.*, q. 1, a. 3 (Pession, 15): ". . . distinguitur potentia duplex: una naturalis ad proprias operationes vel motus; alia quae obedientiae dicitur, ad ea quae a Deo recipiunt."

121. See *De pot.*, q. 1, a. 3, ad 1 (Pession, 15): ". . . [Deus] frequenter faciat contra consuetum cursum naturae; sed quia quidquid in rebus facit, non est contra natu-

cause, the heavens). A miraculous event derives immediately from the First Cause and not from created, intermediate causes.[122] Yet a miracle does not turn the whole universe topsy-turvy: God never violates the moral order nor the *universal* natural order of the universe. Even a miracle falls under divine providence whereby God orders the universe to its supreme end, Himself.[123]

By the power of God something is able to occur that is contrary to universal nature, which derives from the power of the heavens; however, it will not be absolutely contrary to nature, because it will be according to the most universal nature, which is considered from the order of God in regards to all creatures. *(De pot.,* q. 6, a. 1, ad 1 [Pession, 160])[124]

Creatures have neither the active nor, strictly speaking, the passive capacity for miracles; yet, they are naturally subject to God and can be used by Him miraculously.

Those things that take place in things by divine influence are above nature but not contrary to nature, because there is in every created thing a natural subjection to the Creator. . . . *(De malo,* q. 5, a. 5, ad 4 [Bazzi-Pession, 554])[125]

The "obediential potency" of the creature corresponds to nothing other than God's infinite power to work supernaturally in and through a creature.[126]

This potency of obedience corresponds to the divine potency, according to which it is said that what is able to happen from a creature is what God is able to do with it. *(III Sent.,* d. 2, q. 1, a. 1 [Moos, n. 16, p. 54])[127]

Miracles, then, serve as the Thomistic prototype for understanding the obediential potency of a creature.[128] Aquinas, however, never calls

---

ram, sed eis natura, eo quod ipse est conditor et ordinator naturae . . . et hoc modo omnes creaturae quasi pro naturali habent quod a Deo in eis fit."

122. See *De pot.,* q. 6, a. 2, ad 3; *De ver.,* q. 12, a. 3.

123. See *De pot.,* q. 6, a. 1, ad 6; ad 21.

124. ". . . virtute Dei potest aliquid fieri contra naturam universalem, quae est virtute caeli; non tamen erit secundum naturam universalissimam, quae consideratur ex ordine Dei ad omnes creaturas" *(De pot.,* q. 6, a. 1, ad 1 [Pession, 160]).

125. ". . . ea quae divinitus fiunt in rebus, supra naturam quidem sunt, non autem contra naturam; quia inest cuilibet rei creatae naturalis subiectio ad Creatorem . . ." *(De malo,* q. 5, a. 5, ad 4 [Bazzi-Pession, 554]).

126. See *De ver.,* q. 8, a. 12, ad 4.

127. "Haec autem potentiae obedientiae correspondet divinae potentiae, secundum quod dicitur, quod ex creatura potest fieri quod Deus ex ea facere potest" *(III Sent.,* d. 2, q. 1, a. 1 [Moos, n. 16, p. 54]).

128. See *ST,* III, q. 1, a. 3, ad 3.

the beatific vision, as he does the Incarnation, a "miracle." He does not do so for a good reason:[129] a miracle precisely does not realize or perfect the natural tendency of a being but goes contrary to it.[130] But while the beatific vision is supernaturally attained, it is, according to Aquinas, profoundly in accordance with the intellect's natural tendency: *Every intellect naturally desires the vision of the divine substance.*"[131]

Furthermore, Aquinas specifically contrasts the beatific vision with miraculous forms of knowledge; only the latter are said to involve the obediential potency of a creature. God can infuse knowledge into the human soul that transcends the natural capacities of the soul.

In the human soul, as in every creature, the passive power is considered to be twofold: one in comparison to a natural agent; the other in comparison to the first agent, who is able to bring any creature to an higher actuality to which it is not able to be brought by a natural agent. And this latter is usually called the "obediential potency" of the creature. (*ST,* IIIa, q. 11, a. 1)[132]

In this same text, Aquinas outlines Christ's infused knowledge, which enabled Christ to know, in a way that was conformed to His human nature, all things natural and supernatural. Aquinas's Chalcedonian Christology, in conjunction with his "Aristotelian" metaphysics, dictates the terms of the problem and its exceedingly complex solution: Christ was the incarnation of the one divine person or *hypostasis* (the eternal Son or Word), who as incarnate had two distinct natures, divine and human.[133] In His divine nature, which He shares with the other persons of the Trinity (Father and Spirit), Christ enjoyed the knowledge of the divine essence and all created beings through the

---

129. After being resurrected, the human body will have a form of glory which is miraculous, i.e., above nature. In the same sense, the Incarnation, the assumption of human nature by the Divine Word, is the greatest of all miracles; see *De pot.,* q. 6, a. 2, ad 3; ad 9.

130. See *De pot.,* q. 6, a. 2 (Pession, 162): ". . . et ideo illa quae sola virtute divina fiunt in rebus illis in quibus est naturalis ordo ad contrarium effectum vel ad contrarium modum faciendi, dicuntur proprie miracula. . . ."

131. ". . . omnis intellectus naturaliter desiderat divinae substantiae visionem" (*SCG,* III, 57 [Pera, n. 2334, p. 77]).

132. ". . . in anima humana, sicut in qualibet creatura, consideratur duplex potentia passiva: una quidem per comparationem ad agens naturale; alia vero per comparationem ad agens primum, qui potest quamlibet creaturam reducere in actum aliquem altiorem, in quem non reducitur per agens naturale—et haec consuevit vocari potentia obedientiae in creatura" (*ST,* III, q. 11, a. 1).

133. See *ST,* III, q. 9, a. 2, ad 1: ". . . divinitas unita est humanitati Christi secundum personam, et non secundum naturam vel essentiam; sed cum unitate personae remanet distinctio naturarum."

divine essence itself.[134] This uncreated knowledge is proper to God alone; it is not an act of Christ's human soul but it is a consequent of His divine nature. What is important here, however, is Christ's perfect *human* knowledge. The perfect, according to Aristotelian metaphysics, is what is fully actual.[135] In His human nature, Christ was fully and perfectly man, and therefore Christ must have possessed the perfection of fully actualized human knowledge.

Christ possessed perfect human knowledge throughout the course of His human life, because of the unity of His person. The one divine person or *hypostasis*, the eternal Word, sustains both the human and divine natures of Christ.[136] As the divine Word, Christ divinely infused intelligible species into His own human soul. Aquinas, however, changed his mind on one issue: by the time that he wrote the *Summa theologiae*, Aquinas allowed that a fully human Christ must also have had "experientially acquired knowledge" *(scientia experimentalis acquisita)* that came to perfection in normal fashion, that is, only in Christ's human adulthood.[137] Christ acquired experiential knowledge, as does any man, by the exercise of His agent intellect on the abstracted species of sensible things. Consequently, Christ's perfect experientially acquired human knowledge was attained gradually as Christ passed in his human nature from youth to maturity.[138] Christ's divinely infused human knowledge, by contrast, was instantaneously perfect.[139]

In Aquinas's mature schema, Christ in his human nature enjoyed three different kinds of perfect human knowledge: (1) *experientially acquired knowledge* that only reached perfection when Christ was an adult; (2) *divinely infused knowledge* (natural and supernatural) that Christ possessed throughout his life; and (3) the *beatific vision*, the "created beatitude" *(ST, III, q. 9, a. 2, ad 2)* or information of Christ's human intellect by the divine essence. Although in His human enjoyment of the beatific vision, Christ knew all things "through the Word,"

134. See *ST*, III, q. 9, a. 1, ad 1: ". . . Christus cognovit omnia per scientiam divinam operatione increata, quod est ipsa Dei essentia."

135. See *ST*, III, q. 9, a. 3: "Omne autem quod est in potentia est imperfectum nisi reducatur ad actum."

136. See *ST*, III, q. 9, a. 1, ad 3: ". . . est eadem hypostasis Dei et hominis. . . ."

137. Cf. *ST*, III, q. 9, a. 4; *III Sent.*, d. 14, a. 3, q. 5.

138. But Christ knew through his humanly acquired knowledge, once it reached perfection, "all those things that are able to be known through the action of the agent intellect" *(omnia illa quae possunt sciri per actionem intellectus agentis)*: see *ST*, III, q. 12, a. 1.

139. See *ST*, III, q. 12, a. 2, ad 1.

Aquinas notes that only His divinely *infused* knowledge allowed Christ to know things in their proper natures.[140] These divinely infused intelligible species, which actualized both the natural and the obediential powers of Christ's human soul,[141] brought the possible intellect of Christ to its perfection.[142] Divinely infused knowledge enabled Christ to comprehend perfectly and instantaneously everything that men could possibly know through natural experience, or men and angels could know through supernatural revelation.[143] Infused knowledge, however, is created knowledge; consequently, these infused intelligible species cannot effect knowledge of the divine essence.

In regard to infused knowledge of *sensible things*, Aquinas explains that God directly actualized Christ's possible intellect by infusing into it the totality of intelligible species that men could ever grasp through the natural power of their agent intellects.[144] Although all infused intelligible species are proportioned to human nature,[145] infused knowledge of sensible things, of everything that falls under the human sciences, is strictly natural in content since these intelligible species could have been abstracted from sensible things.[146] (Aquinas, however, grants that Christ could supernaturally *use* his infused knowledge of

---

140. See *ST*, III, q. 9, a. 3: ". . . praeter scientiam divinam increatam, est in Christo, secundum ejus animam, scientia beata, qua cognoscit Verbum et res in Verbo: et scientia indita sive infusa, per quam cognoscit res in propria natura per species intelligibiles humanae menti proportionatas"; *III Sent.*, d. 14, a. 3, sol. 1 (Moos, n. 131, p. 456): ". . . cognitio quae est rerum in Verbo, habet medium cognoscendi ipsum Verbum; cognitio autem rerum in proprio genere, habet medium cognoscendi similitudinem rerum quae sunt in intellectu."

141. See *ST*, III, q. 11, a. 1. Christ had infused supernatural knowledge of all existent singular things–past, present, and future; see *ST*, III, q. 11, a. 1, ad 3.

142. See *ST*, III, q. 12, a. 1: ". . . per scientiam inditam scivit anima Christi omnia illa ad quae intellectus possibilis est quocumque modo in potentia. . . ."

143. See *III Sent.*, d. 14, a. 3, sol. 1 (Moos, n. 132, pp. 456–57).

144. See *III Sent.*, III, d. 14, a. 3, sol. 1, ad 1 (Moos, n. 134, p. 457); *De ver.*, q. 20, a. 6; *ST*, III, q. 11, a. 1. Cf. *III Sent.*, d. 14, a. 3, sol. 1 (Moos, n. 132, p. 457); *De ver.*, q. 20, a. 6 (Spiazzi, 374); *ST*, III, q. 10, a. 2: "*gesta particularium hominum et hujusmodi*" and "*futura contingentia*" cannot be known by infused knowledge but only "*in Verbo*." But even in His finite or human knowledge of the Word (i.e., in the created beatific vision), Christ is not able to know all the infinity of possible things that God, in His infinite power, is able to do in the past, present, or future; see *III Sent.*, d. 14, a. 2, sol 2 (Moos, n. 92, p. 448). Such knowledge comprehends the divine infinity and is proper to God (i.e., to Christ in His divine nature) alone: see *De ver.*, q. 20, a. 5; *Comp. theol.*, I, c. 216 (Verardo, nn. 436–37, pp. 103–4).

145. See *ST*, III, q. 11, a. 5: "Alia autem cognitio fuit in Christo secundum modum proportionatum humanae naturae, prout scilicet cognovit res per species sibi divinitus inditas . . ."; a. 6: ". . . Scientia indita animae Christi habuit modum connaturalem animae humanae. . . ."

146. See *ST*, III, q. 11, a. 1.

sensible things without adverting to the sensible phantasms from which intelligible species are ordinarily abstracted. Nonetheless, the intelligible forms of sensible things remain natural to the human intellect.[147]) In the case of infused knowledge of sensible things, what Christ knows and the manner in which these intelligible species are received in the human subject are natural;[148] only the agent infusing (God) and the act of infusion is supernatural.[149] Accordingly, such infused sensible knowledge corresponds to a natural not an obediential potency in Christ:[150]

Our intellect is in natural potency in respect of those intelligibles which are able to be reduced to act through the agent intellect. . . . (*Comp. theol.*, I, c. 104 [Verardo, n. 207, p. 51])[151]

Christ, however, possessed a second kind of infused knowledge which, since it transcends what can be known from sensible beings, is properly a case of God actualizing an obediential potency in Christ.[152] In this case, what Christ knows is supernatural in origin, content, and sometimes even in mode of reception. Christ has perfect understanding of what can be known through revelation and prophecy and the other gifts of the Holy Spirit. Prophecy is miraculous; not even the human intellect of Christ has a natural capacity for infallible knowledge of the future.[153] So too it is impossible for any man in the present life to know the essences of the separate substances or to understand without recourse to sensible images. Christ, because He has divinely infused intelligible species and, more importantly, because His human intellect is joined to the divine essence in the beatific vision, is able to do both.[154]

---

147. See *ST*, III, q. 9, a. 3, ad 3; q. 11, a. 2.

148. See *De ver.*, q. 12, a. 7: "Cum autem intellectus humanus sit in potentia naturali ad omnes formas intelligibiles sensibilium rerum, non erit supernaturalis acceptio, quaecumque species intelligibiles in intellectu fiant. . . ."

149. See *ST*, III, q. 9, a. 4.

150. See *De ver.*, q. 8, a. 4, ad 4 [Spiazzi, 148]: ". . . anima secundum potentiam naturalem non se extendit ad plura intelligibilia quam ad ea quae possunt manifestari per lumen intellectus agentis; quae formae sunt abstractae a sensibilibus."

151. "Est enim intellectus noster in potentia naturali respectu quorumdam intelligibilium, quae scilicet reduci possunt in actum per intellectum agentem . . . " (*Comp. theol.*, I, c. 104 [Verardo, n. 207, p. 51]).

152. See *ST*, III, q. 9, a. 3; q. 11, a. 1.

153. See *De ver.*, q. 12, a. 3, ad 18.

154. See *ST*, III, q. 11, a. 2. Cf. *De ver.*, q. 12, a. 7 [Spiazzi, 251]: "Sed tunc solum intellectus supernaturaliter accipit, quando videt ipsas substantias intelligibiles per essentiam suam, utpote Deum et angelos, ad quod pertingere non potest secundum virtutem naturae suae."

In His divine nature, Christ possesses a different and incomparably higher form of knowledge than either the perfect acquired or the perfect infused knowledge that He possesses in His human nature. Both as man and God, Christ enjoyed in this life the immediate vision of the divine essence but in diverse fashions corresponding to the diversity of His human and divine natures: in His divine nature, the beatific vision is connatural, uncreated, and fully comprehensive of the divine infinity; in His human nature, the beatific vision is created, not fully comprehensive, and only participatory in the divine essence.[155] Christ's divine enjoyment of the divine essence is not a form of infused knowledge; it entirely exceeds human nature and is identical with the divine essence itself. But neither is Christ's human enjoyment of the beatific vision a form of infused knowledge which knowledge pertains only to things that are proportioned to human nature.[156]

Thus, outside [His] divine, uncreated knowledge, there is in Christ—in relation to His [human] soul—the beatifying knowledge by which He knows the Word and things in the Word, and an infused or implanted knowledge, through which He knows things in their proper natures through intelligible species proportioned to the human mind. (ST, III, q. 9, a. 3)[157]

Infused knowledge is knowledge of particular things through their intelligible species, which are "similitudes" (similitudines) of the things that are directly known through these species.[158] But no finite

155. See ST, III, q. 9, a. 2, ad 1; ad 2; q. 10, a. 1, ad 2.

156. See ST, III, q. 11, a. 5, ad 1.

157. ". . . ita, praeter scientiam divinam increatam, est in Christo, secundum ejus animam, scientia beata, qua cognoscit Verbum et res in Verbo: et scientia indita sive infusa, per quam cognoscit res in propria natura per species intelligibles humanae menti proportionatas" (ST, III, q. 9, a. 3).

158. The infused knowledge of a sensible thing occurs through an infused species or similitudo of the thing. The similitudo is formally identical with the form of the sensible thing, but numerically and existentially distinct. Thus the similitudo can be said to "represent" the thing but without compromising the direct knowledge of the thing, i.e., the immediate unity of the knower and of the thing known.

See De ver., q. 8, a. 8 (Spiazzi, 157): ". . . omnis cognitio est per assimilationem; similitudo autem inter aliqua duo est secundum convenientiam in forma"; a. 7 (Spiazzi, 156): "Et sic similitudo rei quae est in intellectu, est similitudo directe essentiae eius . . ."; a. 9 (Spiazzi, 160): "Non enim potest aliquid alteri conformari nisi secundum quod forma eius apud ipse fit"; a. 9 (Spiazzi, 161): ". . . Sicut in intellectu non est ipsa forma qua res existit, sed similitudo eius . . ."; a. 11, ad 3 (Spiazzi, 164): ". . . inter cognoscens et cognitum non exigitur similitudo quae est secundum convenientiam in natura, sed secundum repraesentationem tantum . . . Sed inquantum repraesentat eam, sic est principium ducens in cognitionem eius"; a. 6, ad 11 (Spiazzi, 153): ". . . operatio intelligibilis non est media secundum rem inter intelligens et intellectum, sed procedit ex utroque, secundum quod sunt unita"; a.

similitude can represent the infinite.[159] Consequently, Aquinas explicitly denies that the beatific vision is a form of infused knowledge. The blessed see God because the human intellect is informed by the divine essence itself. It is important to note, however, that Aquinas makes no reference whatsoever to obediential potency when speaking of Christ enjoying the beatific vision in His human soul. The term is *not* mentioned at the very juncture where it could be used if Aquinas had thought it should be used.

It is evident, however, that Aquinas does not want to assimilate the beatific vision and infused miraculous or prophetic knowledge.[160] Aquinas maintains the distinction between them even in regard to the angels who, while enjoying the beatific vision, do not *comprehend* God, and therefore do not know all things that God knows. Such things, however, could be revealed and such a revelation would then be a case of God activating the *potentia obedientiae* of the angelic intellect, but the latter term does not apply to the angel's enjoyment of the beatific vision. The reason for not applying the term is the same for angels as for men: no created intelligence has a natural capacity for supernatural prophecy, but there is a sense in which men and angels, as intellectual substances, have a natural capacity for the vision of the divine essence since this vision alone fulfills their natural desire to know God.[161]

5. The Thomistic Concept of "Natural Desire"

In support of their interpretation, that only an obediential potency corresponds to the "natural desire" for seeing God, Cajetan, Ferrariensis, and Báñez appeal to various Thomistic texts, but their point of view owes more to Aristotle than to Aquinas. Cajetan uses a strictly Aristotelian conception of nature to cast into relief the Christian concept of the supernatural. He refers,[162] as do a host of other commentators, to Aristotle's argument *(De Cael.,* II, 8, 290a29–35) that if the stars had a natural potency for progressive self-motion, then nature

16, ad 11 (Spiazzi, 177): "Cognitio autem sequitur formae repraesentationem; unde res, cum non sit in anima nisi secundum quid, per suam similitudinem, simpliciter tamen cognoscitur."

159. See *III Sent.*, d. 14, a. 1, sol. 3 (Moos, n. 49, p. 438): ". . . essentiae divinae similitudo non potest in aliqua creatura recipi, quae perfecte repraesentet ipsam, propter infinitam distantiam creaturae ad Deum."

160. See *De ver.*, q. 8, a. 4, ad 13.

161. See *ST,* III, q. 9, a. 2, ad 3.

162. See *ST,* I, q. 12, a. 1; *Commentaria Card. Caietani*, n. IX (Leonine ed., IV, 116).

would have provided them with the organs to do so. The inference, which Cajetan draws against Scotus, is that there is no natural desire to the beatific vision since nature has not provided the means whereby it can be attained. But Cajetan's Aristotelianism, which holds to a univocal conception of "nature,"[163] misses Aquinas's point. To equate the natural potencies of the stars with the natural potencies of intellectual substances is to negate the uniqueness of human nature: human nature is *"capax Dei."* "Natural desire," for Aquinas, is clearly an analogical concept when applied to human nature and its desire to know God.

By interjecting the concept of obediential potency into Aquinas's discussion of the natural desire to see God, Thomist commentators not only say something that Aquinas does not say, but, more importantly, they say something that attenuates Aquinas's repeated affirmations of the naturalness of the desire.

Because man is capable of this [beatific] vision, it does not follow that it is natural to him or that he had a natural potency for it. More is required for something to be unconditionally natural or for a natural potency: namely, some natural inclination to that act. It only follows that [man] has a nature which is able to be elevated to that act. *(ST,* III, q. 9, a. 2, ad 3; *Commentaria Card. Caietani,* n. IV [Leonine ed., XI, 141–42])[164]

That Cajetan felt constrained to interject the notion of obediential potency indicates his profound awareness of how the natural knowledge of God differs from what the Christian faith promises and, conversely, a certain lack of awareness of how profoundly Aquinas's conception of human nature differs from Aristotle's.

Aquinas, however, acknowledges that the term *"natura"* is irreducibly ambivalent, especially when it is used in the present context. Aquinas flatly states that the desire for the vision of God is both natural and not natural:

Vision or beatifying knowledge is in some way above the nature of the rational soul, insofar as it is not able to attain it by its own proper power. In another way it is in accord with [the rational soul's] nature, insofar as it

163. See Caietanus, *De potentia neutra,* q. 2, ad 4, tertio (1496); quoted in de Lubac, *Augustinianism,* 185: ". . . in materia vel anima vel quacumque alia re est naturalis potentia ad actum supernaturalem. . . ."

164. "Non enim quia homo est capax illius visionis, sequitur. Ergo est illi naturalis, aut habet ad illam potentiam naturalem: quia plus requiritur ad naturalitatem simpliciter et ad potentiam naturalem, scilicet naturalis inclinatio ad illum actum. Sed solum sequitur quod habet naturam quae potest elevari in illum actum" *(ST,* III, q. 9, a. 2, ad 3; *Commentaria Card. Caietani,* n. IV [Leonine ed., 141–42]).

is capable of [the vision] through its nature, because it is made in the image of God. . . . *(ST,* III, q. 9, a. 3, ad 3)[165]

From this fundamental ambivalence arises all the difficulties in interpreting the Thomistic notion of a natural desire to see God.

As everyone who has studied the issue notes, there are two series of Thomistic texts, which verbally contradict each other and which Aquinas himself does not conciliate.[166] In the first series, Aquinas regards the desire to know the essence of the First Cause as a natural desire and says so without any of the hesitations or qualifications that so characterize the interpretations of the classic Thomist commentators.[167]

When a man knows an effect and knows that it has a cause, there remains in man a natural desire to know about the cause what it is. . . . Consequently, for perfect happiness, the intellect must reach the very essence of the First Cause. *(ST,* I–II, q. 3, a. 8)[168]

But in the second series, which also runs from the early to the later works, Aquinas emphatically states that the desire to know the divine essence is supernatural.[169] In regard to its object and cause [God Himself], the desire arises not from nature but from the infused theological virtues. Indeed, we know about this desire or tendency only from revelation.[170]

There is another good of man that exceeds the proportion of human nature because the natural powers are not sufficient for attaining, or thinking, or desiring it. *(De ver.,* q. 14, a. 2 [Spiazzi, 283])[171]

165. ". . . visio seu scientia beata est quodammodo supra naturam animae rationalis, inquantum scilicet propria virtute ad eam pervenire non potest. Alio vero modo est secundum naturam ipsius, inquantum scilicet per naturam suam est capax ejus, prout scilicet ad imaginem Dei facta est . . ." (*ST,* III, q. 9, a. 3, ad 3).

166. See Ritzler, *De naturali beatitudinis supernaturalis,* 59–60; Descoqs, *Praelectiones,* II: 239.

167. This is the ineluctable conclusion of the lengthy argument of *SCG,* III, 25–51.

168. "Et ideo remanent naturaliter homini desiderium, cum cognoscit effectum, et scit eum habere causam, ut etiam sciat de causa quid est. . . . Ad perfectam igitur beatitudinem requiritur quod intellectus pertingat ad ipsam essentiam primae causae" (*ST,* I–II, q. 3, a. 8).

169. For a complete list of all the texts, see Jorge Laporta, *La Destinée de la nature humaine selon Thomas d'Aquin* (Paris: J. Vrin, 1965), 147–61.

170. For an important statement of this position, see *III Sent.,* d. 23, q. 1, a. 4, sol. 3 (Moos, nn. 95–100, pp. 714–16).

171. "Alius est bonum hominis naturae humanae proportionem excedens, quia ad ipsum obtinendum vires naturales non sufficiunt, nec ad cogitandum vel desiderandum; sed ex sola divina liberalitate homini repromittitur . . ." (*De ver.,* q. 14, a. 2 [Spiazzi, 283]).

Aquinas himself does not attempt to harmonize these texts, which suggests that he did not find them contradictory. The traditional commentators, however, strongly felt the need to reconcile these two sets of texts. But can one series of texts be harmonized with the other, or are the two series irreducible, thus providing strong evidence that Aquinas's doctrine, as some think, is incoherent?

Certainly the alleged contradiction between these two series of texts is generated by what, at first glance, appears to be Aquinas's orthodox Aristotelian conception of "nature." Frequently enough, Aquinas reiterates without any caveat the Aristotelian equation of a passive potency with its corresponding active potency. In nature the two orders are strictly coordinated:

> For a passive potency is in potency only to those things in which there is able to be a proper active principle. For, in nature, to every passive potency there corresponds an active potency. Otherwise the passive potency would be frustrated, since it is not able to be reduced to act except through an active potency. (SCG, III, 45 [Pera, n. 2222, p. 58)][172]

Yet Aquinas remains remarkably free with Aristotle. When it suits his purposes, he reverses the Aristotelian formula: a being can have active potencies for which it has no passive potencies. The reversal comes because, in the Christian universe, there is a unique supernatural agent. In the natural order, there is a strict coordination of passive and active powers in a being. God, however, can cause a being to have active powers that transcend that being's passive potencies. For example, intellectual knowledge transcends the potency of the human body, but God infuses the rational soul into matter. Thus, there can be intelligent bodies.

Aquinas draws an interesting parallelism between man's first perfection, the rational soul, and man's last perfection, supernatural beatitude. Both perfections transcend natural human potencies and therefore both must be immediately received from God.[173] The two cases, however, are importantly different: there is no active power for attaining the beatific vision in man. Yet Aquinas argues that the human intellect can be supernaturally elevated to God only because it already transcends matter. The human intellect is able to consider sensible

---

172. "Potentia enim passiva ad illa solum est in potentia in quae potest proprium eius activum: omni enim potentiae passivae respondet potentia activa in natura; alias potentia passiva esset frustra, cum non possit reduci in actum nisi per activam . . ." (SCG, III, 45 [Pera, n. 2222, p. 58]).

173. See De virt., q. 1, a. 10.

forms in abstraction from matter; it can even intellectually separate a form from its act of being. By nature, the intellect can know being; by grace, it can come to know the essence of subsistent being.[174]

For Aquinas, the desire to attain perfect happiness is a natural desire, even though perfect happiness cannot be naturally attained either in this life or in the life to come. Perfect happiness results from seeing God. The desire to see God is natural not in the sense that all men explicitly know that God is their final end, but natural in the sense that knowing God is the only way to satisfy the necessary desire for happiness.[175]

Although God is the ultimate end in attainment and the first in the intention of the natural appetite, it is not the case that [God] is first in the cognition of the human mind which is ordained to the end but in the cognition of the one who ordains, as is the case in other things that tend to the end by natural appetite. In a general way, [God] is known and intended from the beginning, since the mind seeks to be well and to live well, which only happens for it when [the mind] has God. *(Expos. de Trin.,* q. 1, a. 3, ad 4 [Decker, 18–24, p. 73])[176]

The desire to see God, then, is *implicit* in the desire for perfect beatitude: in making this claim, Aquinas is certainly not repeating what Aristotle said about happiness, nor is he pushing Aristotelian man to the doorstep of the baptistery. Aristotelian man could never articulate the desire—since he does not have it—for an eternal vision of the First Cause who brings the universe into existence. According to Aristotle, man—or at least the philosopher—can strive only for the sporadic, earthly contemplation of the unmoved movers that eternally move the cosmos. Thomistic man is more mysterious: he is created by an utterly transcendent God who plants in human nature an innate orientation to Himself.

In claiming that men desire to see a God who transcends their

---

174. See *ST,* I, q. 12, a. 4, ad 3.

175. See *De malo,* q. 3, a. 3 (Bazzi-Pession, 501): "Bonum autem perfectum, quod est Deus, necessariam quidem connexionem habet cum beatitudine hominis, quia sine eo non potest homo esse beatus; verumtamen necessitas huius connexionis non manifeste apparet homini in hac vita, quia Deum per essentiam non videt. . . ."

176. ". . . quamvis deus sit ultimus finis in consecutione et primus in intentione appetitus naturalis, non tamen oportet quod sit primus in cognitione mentis humanae quae ordinatur in finem, sed in cognitione ordinantis, sicut et in aliis quae naturali appetitu tendunt in finem suum. Cognoscitur tamen a principio et intenditur in quadam generalitate, prout mens appetit se bene esse et bene vivere, quod tunc solum est ei, cum deum habet" *(Expos. de Trin.,* q. 1, a. 3, ad 4 [Decker, 18–24, p. 73]).

power of vision, Aquinas is not thinking within an Aristotelian world or about an Aristotelian human nature.[177] But the desire, so Aquinas reiterates time and again, is "natural." The claim certainly flies in the face of Aristotle. How could Aristotelian man naturally desire what he cannot naturally achieve? Such a man is a paradox. At the same time, the claim, as the anxious explanations of the traditional Thomist commentators reveal, appears to offend orthodox Christian doctrine. If the vision of God is naturally desired, how then is it supernatural in character? This is the question that Cajetan resolutely posed and, as posed, answered negatively. According to Cajetan's Aristotelian understanding of natural desire, there is no natural desire to see God's essence since the desire cannot be naturally realized.

The Thomistic problem, however, has no genuinely Aristotelian counterpart. Thomistic man, who by nature implicitly desires a supernatural end that he cannot naturally achieve, cannot be found in the historical Aristotle, and for that reason Thomistic man is all but repudiated by the Thomist commentators and other readers of Aquinas who continue to juxtapose Aristotle and the Christian faith.[178] Yet the Aristotelian anxieties of Cajetan and subsequent Thomist commentators deserve sympathetic consideration; their anxious efforts to rescue Aquinas from the quasi-Aristotelian heterodoxy, that they themselves formulated and feared, confirm that Aquinas's own philosophical conception of nature is novel. Cajetan's dichotomy—either a "natural" (as that term is understood by Aristotle) or an "obediential" potency—should not be superimposed on Aquinas. This dichotomy, whether or not Thomistic doctrine is judged to be theologically orthodox by the standards of modern ecclesiastical doctrine, does not encompass what Aquinas thought to be human nature's unique openness to God.

Nonetheless, even if one prescinds from the standards of modern theological orthodoxy, it may be wondered whether there is a fatal contradiction in Aquinas's position. Is Aquinas's whole theology "tainted" by a nature-grace dualism that cannot be reconciled with the

---

177. See De ver., q. 13, a. 3, obj. 6/ad 6: "Sed naturale est intellectui humano quod Deum per essentiam videat, cum ad hoc creatus sit. . . . Ad sextum dicendum, quod quamvis naturale sit intellectui humano quod quandoque ad visionem divinae essentiae perveniat: non tamen est sibi naturale quod ad hoc perveniat secundum statum viae huius. . . ."

178. See H. Ligeard, La Théologie scolastique et la transcendance du surnaturel (Paris: Beauchesne, 1908), 39–50 [quoted in Descoqs, Praelectiones, 2: 222]: ". . . la distinction entre la fin naturelle quant au désir et surnaturelle quant à la réalisation, est purement arbitraire. Si, en effet, la nature a réellement pour fin le surnaturel, elle doit pouvoir l'atteindre et il y en elle une exigence stricte du surnaturel."

natural desire for seeing God? Once again, the author of this charge, which is too global to be fully evaluated here, argues that Aquinas illegitimately superimposes a patristic doctrine (man's "natural" desire for God) on a classical Greek philosophical conception of human nature.[179] Such a superimposition, if one looks to the example of the medieval Averroists, does indeed lead to a theological dualism in which grace is an unintelligible *superadditum*. But the fact that Aquinas constantly reiterates the complimentarity of nature and grace suggests not only that Aquinas himself was unaware of any such dualism, but that the Thomistic conception of human nature cannot be reduced to the conception of nature found in Aristotle. In fact, it is this putative reduction, both as a historical presupposition and as a systematic framework for reading Aquinas, that must be decisively rejected.

For the reader of Aquinas, Thomistic man can only be found by transcending Aristotle and the quasi-Aristotelian perspectives of the Thomist commentators. Once seen in his own context, Thomistic man is certainly a philosophical mystery, but he need not fall victim to Aquinas's allegedly contradictory formulations about human nature.

Interpretation of the apparently variant Thomistic texts should begin, as Aquinas did, by noting the ambiguity of the (Thomistic) term *"natura."* Especially as it applies to man's way of knowing God, *"natural"* has analogical meanings. What is natural knowledge for man depends upon his condition. In the present life, it is natural for man to know God through reasoning from sensible effects. In heaven but not in this life, it will be natural for men to know God through His essence.[180]

Still, the alleged contradiction between Aquinas's texts arises not from comparing the various states in which men know God but from comparing the way that Aquinas speaks about man's desire for the vision of God *in this life.* Is the desire to see God natural or supernatural in this life? Aquinas, we should admit straightaway, says both. The temptation of the interpreter, however, is to say one or the other, and in doing so to dissolve the paradox that Aquinas saw as inherent in human nature. To his credit, Ferrariensis notices the paradox despite viewing Aquinas through the prism of *potentia obedientialis:*

> It is said that the order of something receptive of some form is able to be called "natural" in two ways. In one way, because it follows after the nature of the recipient through comparison to some created agent, which

179. See A. Vanneste, "Saint Thomas et le problème du surnaturel," *Ephemerides theologicae Lovanienses* 64 (1988): 348–70, esp. 357, 361, 362.

180. See *De ver.*, q. 13, a. 1, ad 1; ad 2; ad 9; a. 3, ad 6.

in this place is called a natural agent. And in this way, the order of the soul to grace is not natural. In another way, because the recipient nature is capable of that form; and is instituted and ordained by God to this [form] even though [considered] in itself alone, it has some repugnance to that form. Such a potency is said to be an obediential potency in some way, insofar as its capacity to receive that form is from God alone: nonetheless, it is able to called in some way a natural [potency], inasmuch as the nature of the subject according to divine institution is ordered by God to that form, and was made in itself capable of that form. And in this way there is natural order in the soul to grace. For God from the beginning instituted man so that he was in regard [to his] soul capable of grace and beatitude, and, unless it was impeded by himself, it would be received from God. . . . However, such a natural order is not found in miraculous works which occur only from God alone. (SCG, III, 101; Commentaria Ferrariensis, n. IV, 3 [Leonine ed., XIV, 314b])[181]

Man naturally desires a beatitude that he cannot naturally acquire. Now it is just this paradox that must be preserved: it is central to Aquinas's understanding of the natural desire to see God. But it is also central, I shall maintain, to Aquinas's understanding of the limitations of Aristotle's ethics.

Aquinas's texts about the natural desire to see God appear contradictory because they encompass two quite different *philosophical* notions of human nature that are not always clearly juxtaposed nor kept neatly isolated from his *theological* beliefs about human nature. Aquinas recognizes that both theologians and philosophers speak about human nature and human beatitude, and Aquinas's own doctrine takes into account both points of view.[182] The Thomist commen-

---

181. "Dicitur quod dupliciter potest ordo alicuius susceptivi ad aliquam formam dici naturalis. Uno modo, quia consequitur naturam susceptivi per comparationem ad aliquod agens creatum, quod hoc loco vocatur agens naturale. Et sic non intelligitur ordinem animae ad gratiam esse naturalem. Alio modo, quia natura susceptivi est capax illius formae; et ad hoc est instituta a Deo et ordinata ut ab ipso solo talem formam suscipiat, et non ab alio; nec talis natura in se habet aliquid illi formae repugnans. Talis enim potentia dici obedientalis aliquo modo, inquantum est ad formam a solo Deo suscipiendam: potest etiam dici aliquo modo naturalis, inquantum natura subiecti est a Deo ad illam formam secundum institutionem divinam ordinata, et facta est illius formae secundum se capax. Et hoc modo in anima est ordo naturalis ad gratiam. Hominem enim Deus a principio instituit ut esset secundum animam gratiae et beatitudinis capax, eamque, nisi sibi ipsi impedimento esset, nancisceretur a Deo. . . . Talis autem ordo naturalis non invenitur in operibus miraculosis quae a solo Deo fiunt" (SCG, III, 101; Commentaria Ferrariensis, n. IV, 3 [Leonine ed., XIV, 314b]).

182. See IV Sent., d. 49, q. 2, a. 1 (Vivès, 11, p. 481): ". . . ideo circa hanc

tators attempt to keep Aristotelian philosophy and Christian theology neatly separated, so as not to confuse the natural with the supernatural. Aquinas, however, does not divide the issue so neatly. He adopts his own philosophical point of view on human nature which is always held in implicit contrast not only to Aristotle's conception of human nature but to what Christian theology specifically teaches about the supernatural destiny of man.[183] There are, then, three dimensions to Aquinas's doctrine that need to be kept in view: (1) Aristotle's conception of human nature; (2) Aquinas's conception of human nature; and (3) the theological doctrine of man's supernatural end.

First, Aquinas distinguishes the philosophers from Christian theologians. The two groups have different conceptions of how men are able to attain their ultimate end. The philosophers strictly coordinate man's end with the resources of human nature; the theologians posit an end that goes beyond the capacity for human nature to achieve unless nature is divinely "elevated."

> The end of human life which the philosophers consider does not exceed the faculty of nature. Man tends toward it from natural inclination; and thus it is not necessary that he be elevated to that end by some habit, as it is necessary that he be elevated to the end that the theologians consider, which exceeds the faculty of nature. (*De ver.*, q. 14, a. 3, ad 9 [Spiazzi, 287])[184]

Aquinas, however, affirms a supernatural end that is above not contrary to human nature.[185] Aquinas pointedly observes that the vision of the divine essence is *not* "altogether extraneous" to human nature inasmuch as human nature is rational and intellectual.[186] But this observation, certainly, is a point made not to Aristotle but to Christian theologians. Aquinas argues—and this seems to be a preeminent ex-

---

quaestionem eadem [circa finem ultimum humanae vitae] difficultas et diversitas invenitur apud philosophos et apud theologos."

183. See *III Sent.*, d. 17, a. 1, sol. 1, resp. (Moos, n. 16, p. 530): ". . . homo secundum naturam suam ad imaginem Dei factus est: consistit autem imago in memoria, intelligentia et voluntate."

184. ". . . finis humanae vitae quem philosophi considerant, non excedit facultatem naturae: unde ex naturali inclinatione homo tendit in ipsum; et sic non oportet quod habitu elevetur in illum finem, sicut oportet quod elevetur in finem qui facultatem excedit, quem theologi considerant" (*De ver.*, q. 14, a. 3, ad 9 [Spiazzi, 287]).

185. See *ST*, I, q. 62, a. 7, ad 1: "Imperfectio autem naturae non opponitur perfectioni beatitudinis, sed substernitur ei. . . ."

186. See *SCG*, III, 54 (Pera, n. 2312, p. 73): "Divina enim substantia non sic est extra facultatem creati intellectus quasi aliquid omnino extraneum ab ipso. . . ."

ample of Aquinas arguing as a "Christian philosopher" within his own theology—that the range of the human intellect encompasses universal being *(ens universale)*.[187] In an Aristotelian sense of "natural," it is natural for men to seek to know the first cause of universal being. Since God is the cause of universal being,[188] it is natural for men to seek knowledge of God.

The desire of knowing, which is naturally implanted in all intellectual substances, does not rest until, after they know the substances of the effects, they also know the substance of the cause. . . . No matter how much we know that God is, and other such matters that have been previously mentioned, we do not stop desiring but we [continue] desiring to know Him through His essence. *(SCG,* III, 50 [Pera, n. 2277; n. 2281, pp. 68–69])[189]

Yet the Thomistic argument also establishes that the First Cause, or the universal principle of being, is the infinite God whose essence cannot be naturally known by any finite intelligence.[190] God is "seen" when the divine essence is the intelligible form of the human intellect,[191] and such information can only result from divine and not human action.[192] Left to its own resources, the human intellect is radically incapable of seeing God. Nonetheless,—and this conclusion generates Aquinas's philosophical dilemma—Aquinas proves that knowledge of God's essence, although naturally unknowable, is the only ultimately satisfying object for human intelligence which naturally seeks

---

187. See *SCG,* III, 25 (Pera, n. 2066, p. 33): "Intellectus autem humanus cognoscit ens universale. Desiderat igitur naturaliter cognoscere causam eius, quae solunt Deus est. . . ." Cf. *ST,* I–II, q. 5, a. 1: ". . . [hominis] intellectus apprehendere potest universale et perfectum bonum, et eius voluntas appetere illud."

188. See *ST,* I–II, q. 65, a. 5, ad 4: ". . . quia ens commune est proprius effectus causae altissimae, scilicet Dei."

189. "Non quiescit igitur sciendi desiderium, naturaliter omnibus substantiis intellectualibus inditum, nisi, cognitis substantiis effectuum, etiam substantiam causae cognoscant. . . . Nos autem, quantumcumque sciamus Deum esse, et alia quae supra dicta sunt, non quiescimus desiderio, sed adhuc desideramus eum per essentiam suam cognoscere *(SCG,* III, 50 [Pera, nn. 2277–81, pp. 68–69]).

190. See *SCG,* III, 52; *In de Div. Nom.,* I, lect. 3 (Pera, n. 82, p. 28): "Visio enim Dei per essentiam est super naturam cuiuslibet intellectus creati, non solum humani, sed etiam angelici."

191. See *De ver.,* q. 8, a. 3 (Spiazzi, 143): ". . . Deus per essentiam videatur, oportet quod essentia divina uniatur intellectui quodammodo ut forma intelligibilis."

192. See *II Sent.,* d. 23, q. 2, a. 1 (Mandonnet, 573): "Ad primum ergo modum visionis [qui est per essentiam], qui soli Deo ex conditione naturae debetur, elevatur angelus et homo per gloriam. . . ."

to know not only that God is but to see what He is. The divine essence is not included in Aristotle's list of the objects of philosophical contemplation.[193] Indeed, Aquinas's paradoxical conclusion about man's ultimate beatitude, that it is naturally desired but supernaturally attained, overturns Aristotelian naturalism.[194]

This conclusion provokes the genuinely philosophical question of whether this natural desire to see the divine essence is "in vain." A vain natural desire, if there were such, would certainly contradict the Aristotelian conception of nature. But this question, as Aquinas precisely raises it, cannot be considered an Aristotelian question: a vain natural desire, if there were such, would also contradict the Christian conception of the freedom and intelligence of the transcendent creator of nature.[195] More importantly, it would contradict the Christian doctrine that God actually does create man for the vision of Himself.

If the created intellect is never able to see the essence of God, either it would not obtain beatitude or its beatitude would consists of something other than in God. [Both of] which are contrary to the faith. *(ST,* I, q. 12, a. 1)[196]

Man exists, according to Christian theology, in a supernatural state that Aristotle did not and could not have envisioned. Nevertheless, there is only one way to understand human nature: by reference to what one understands to be the actual human condition. What is natural to man corresponds to the state that he is in.[197] Man is in the state,

---

193. In *Metaph.,* IV, 3, 1005a35, Aristotle notes that metaphysics deals with "primary substance," i.e., the unmoved movers who are themselves in a state of perfect self-contemplation: see *Metaph.,* XII, 7. But, more vaguely, *EN,* X, 7, 1177a18 states that contemplation is aimed at "things noble and divine" (rev. Oxford trans.): these include the stars and other beings more noble than man (*EN,* VI, 7, 1141b1–2). In *SLE,* X, 10, 1177a19, 90–91 (*In Ethic.,* X, lect. 10 [Spiazzi, n. 2087]), Aquinas notes that the objects of contemplation are supersensible and divine, but he specifies that "God is the most noble, knowable being" ("nobilissimum scibile, quod Deus est": *SCG,* III, 25 [Pera, n. 2067, p. 34]). For Aristotle's changing opinions about the objects of contemplation, see Gauthier-Jolif, II, 2:851–55.

194. See *SCG,* III, 52 (Pera, n. 2295, p. 71): "Videre autem Dei substantiam transcendit limites omnis naturae creatae . . ."; ibid., (Pera, n. 2296, p. 71): "In ipsa enim divina visione ostendimus esse hominis beatitudinem. . . ."

195. See *ST,* I, q. 60, a. 1, ad 3: ". . . cum amor naturalis nihil aliud sit quam inclinatio naturae indita ab auctore naturae. Dicere ergo quod inclinatio naturalis non sit recta, est derogare auctori naturae."

196. ". . . Si nunquam essentiam Dei videre potest intellectus creatus, vel nunquam beatitudinem obtinebit, vel in alio eius beatitudo consistet quam in Deo. Quod est alienum a fide" *(ST,* I, q. 12, a. 1).

197. See *De ver.,* q. 13, a. 1: "Uni enim et eidem rei est aliquid contra naturam et secundum naturam, secundum eius status diversos. . . ."

and the believer knows that he is in the state, of being supernaturally ordained to the vision of God in the world to come. Men were created to achieve this end.[198] But Aquinas does not simply confront Aristotle with what Christian faith believes about human destiny. Rather, he first instructs Aristotle—that is, *Aristotle's Christian readers*—philosophically. Aristotle knows that men desire beatitude and that the metaphysical knowledge of the first causes is beatifying; Aquinas leads the Christian philosopher—if not the Aristotelian philosopher—to acknowledge that when men explicitly desire beatitude, they implicitly desire to know the essence of the First Cause.

Aquinas argues that despite the delights of paradise, prelapsarian Adam *naturally* desired to see the essence of God.[199] He did so because this desire essentially constitutes man as an intellectual creature.

For every nature something is assigned, in which its ultimate perfection consists. The perfection of man, insofar as he is man, consists only in an act of the intellect, from which he is constituted as a man. . . . It is the case that the final term of human perfection is in understanding something perfectly intelligible, which is the divine essence. *(De ver.,* q. 18, a. 1 [Spiazzi, 338])[200]

Men, as intellectual creatures, were created with the desire to see the divine essence, a desire that no natural happiness could assuage. Creation would be a vain thing if that desire were left unfulfilled.

Against the background of Christian faith, which prompted Aquinas to develop his own metaphysical conception of human nature, and throw a bright light on what Aristotle dimly grasped about the range of human intelligence, the desire for the beatific vision seems and is eminently "natural." In an intellectual creature, the desire to know the essence of the First Cause is as natural as the tendency of every nonintellectual creature to attain some likeness of God, who is the supreme end of every being.

Since all creatures, even those lacking intelligence, are ordered to God as to [their] ultimate end, all achieve this end insofar as they share in

198. See *De malo,* q. 5, a. 5 (Bazzi-Pession, 553): ". . . homo factus est propter finem perpetuae beatitudinis."

199. See *II Sent.,* d. 23, q. 2, a. 1, obj. 4/ad 4 (Mandonnet, 572, 574); *De ver.,* q. 18, a. 1, obj. 6/ad 6 (Spiazzi, 337, 339).

200. "Cuiuslibet enim naturae est aliquod ultimum assignare, in quo eius ultima perfectio consistit. Hominis autem, in quantum homo, perfectio non consistit nisi in actu intellectus, ex quo habet quod homo sit. . . . Unde oportet quod ultimus terminus humanae perfectionis sit in intelligendo aliquod perfectissimum intelligibile, quod est essentia divina" *(De ver.,* q. 18, a. 1 [Spiazzi, 338]).

some likeness of Him. Intellectual creatures attain it in a more special way by understanding Him through their [own] operations . . . and this happens when one knows something of the divine substance rather than when one reaches some similitude of Him. *(SCG,* III, 25 [Pera, nn. 2055–56, pp. 31–32])[201]

The desire to see God that arises from man's intellectual nature is, *ex definitione,* not supernatural.[202] The natural love of God, that is, the inclination toward God built into all natures, unites all creatures whether intellectual or not.[203] It must therefore be distinguished from the explicit desire for the vision of the triune God that only arises because God has revealed that He will indeed "show" Himself to the blessed.[204] Since knowledge of the Trinity exceeds the grasp of reason, this latter desire is certainly supernatural and can only be *"elicited"* by supernatural acts of faith, hope, and charity.

No potency according to its own nature is determined to those things which are above the nature of our reason. Faith is about those things. *(III Sent.,* d. 23, q. 3, a. 2. [Moos, n. 254, p. 747][205]

Aquinas, as a theologian, views man's natural desire to know God (which can be established by philosophical argument) from the standpoint of man's actual supernatural end (which can only be known by faith). According to Aquinas's philosophical argument, human nature *needs or requires* a supernatural vision of God *if* it is to achieve beatitude. Aquinas's argument can be misinterpreted, and is bound to be

---

201. "Cum autem omnes creaturae, etiam intellectu carentes, ordinentur in Deum sicut in finem ultimum; ad hunc autem finem pertingunt omnia inquantum de similitudine eius aliquid participant . . . quod fit dum aliquid quis cognoscit de divina substantia, quam dum consequitur eius aliquam similitudinem" *(SCG,* III, 25 [Pera, nn. 2055–56, pp. 31–32]).

202. See *ST,* I, q. 60, a. 5: ". . . inclinatio enim naturalis in his quae sunt sine ratione, demonstrat inclinationem naturalem in voluntate intellectualis naturae."

203. See *De malo,* q. 16, a. 4, ad 15 [Bazzi-Pession, 672]: ". . . diligere se propter Deum, in quantum est obiectum supernaturalis beatitudinis et auctor gratiae, est actus caritatis. Sed diligere Deum super omnia, et se propter Deum, in quantum in eo consistit naturale bonum omnia creaturae, competit naturaliter non solum creaturae rationali, sed etiam brutis animalibus, et corporibus inanimatis, in quantum participant naturali amore summi boni. . . ."

204. See *ST,* I, q. 60, a. 5, ad 4: ". . . Deus, secundum quod est universale bonum, a quo dependet omne bonum naturale, diligitur naturali dilectione ab unoquoque. Inquantum vero est bonum beatificans naturaliter omnes supernaturali beatitudine, sic diligitur dilectione caritatis."

205. "Nulla autem potentia secundum naturam suam determinatur ad illa quae sunt supra naturam rationis nostrae, quorum est fides" *(III Sent.,* d. 23, q. 3, a. 2 [Moos, n. 254, p. 747]).

misinterpreted, if one looks at human nature in isolation, as though nature apart from God could fulfill its own desire. Aquinas would un-hesitatingly deny any such notion.[206]

Still, the need or requirement for supernatural fulfillment seems to imply a certain metaphysical necessity latent in human nature.[207] Na-ture, as Aristotle teaches,[208] does nothing in vain. It must be possible for men to see God because their desire to do so is natural. Aquinas admits that nature is not able to fulfill this desire. But does the desire somehow necessitate God to fulfill it?

The Thomist commentators, fearful of any such inference, felt obliged to deny that the desire to see God is natural. But, for Aquinas, this unique natural desire is fulfilled not because human nature neces-sitates God not to frustrate it, but because God, as the Christian faith teaches, freely and lovingly chooses to fulfill the nature He has cre-ated. This conviction—that God has actually ordained man to a super-natural end—and it alone, sustains Aquinas's unhesitating affirmation that the natural desire to see God is not in vain.

Thus [nature] is not deficient for man in necessary things, although it does not give to him some principle by which he is able to attain beati-tude; for this was impossible. But it gave to him free choice, by which he is able to be converted to God, who will make him blessed. (ST, I–II, q. 5, a. 6, ad 1)[209]

The vision of God, since the human desire for it is not in vain, is somehow possible. The possibility in question is not just logical; the possibility is existential. It expresses the dynamism of human nature. But this latter possibility has seemed obscure. It has two radically different grounds, depending on whether one is talking about the hu-man subject or the divine agent. In one sense, the possibility of seeing God is simply grounded in an intellectual nature's openness to univer-sal being and goodness. But in the other sense, the possibility of seeing God is not grounded in human nature at all since man is utterly impo-

206. See *ST,* III, q. 10, a. 4, obj. 2: ". . . perfectio visionis non excedit potentiam visivam . . ."; ibid., ad 2: "Ad secundum dicendum quod visio divinae essentiae excedit naturalem potentiam cujuslibet creaturae. . . ."

207. Cf. *Quod.* I, q. 4, a. 3 (Spiazzi, 9): "Nihil autem naturale est perversum. Impossibile est ergo quod aliqua naturalis inclinatio vel dilectio sit perversa. . . ."

208. See *De Caelo,* II, 11, 291b13.

209. ". . . ita [natura] nec deficit homini in necessariis, quamvis non daret sibi aliquod principium quo posset beatitudinem consequi; hoc enim erat impossi-bile. Sed dedit ei liberum arbitrium, quo possit converti, ad Deum, qui eum faceret beatum" (*ST,* I–II, q. 5, a. 6, ad 1).

tent to fulfill this desire. The possibility of fulfilling the desire is solely due to the grace of God. And God, Aquinas is convinced, has made man for this grace.[210]

Medieval Aristotelians, who although they knew what Christian faith teaches about man's actual ordination to a supernatural end, tended to ignore just this point:

> *First Objection:* For the salvation and perfection of anything those things are seen to suffice which pertain to the thing according to its nature. . . . *Response:* Since the nature of man depends upon a superior nature, natural cognition does not suffice to its perfection but some supernatural [knowledge] is required. . . . *(ST,* II–II, q. 2, a. 3, ad 1)[211]

This response indicates that Aquinas's understanding of human nature is not limited by what anyone could plausibly attribute to Aristotle. By placing man within the Christian economy of grace, Aquinas reformulates both the Aristotelian conception of human nature and the Aristotelian notion of beatitude as the end of nature.[212]

> For perfect beatitude, it is required that the intellect reach the essence of the first cause. And it will have its perfection through union with God as [its] object, in which consists the only beatitude of man. . . . *(ST,* I–II, q. 3, a. 8)[213]

From Aristotle, Aquinas borrows the notion of beatitude: perfect happiness results from knowing the most noble being there is. But the Thomistic corollary to this thesis goes far beyond what Aristotle could imagine. Perfect happiness, Aquinas repeats what every believer accepts, is only found in seeing God. Christian theology insists that actually attaining the divine essence is a supernatural act and a supernatural end. On this crucial theological point, Aquinas never wavers. But he asserts, no less forcefully, that a natural desire is not in vain and that the desire to see God is natural because the vision of God is the implicit terminus of the natural desire for beatitude.

---

210. See *ST,* I, q. 12, a. 4; I–II, q. 5, a. 2; *De malo,* q. 5, a. 5.

211. "1. Ad salutem enim et perfectionem cuiuslibet rei ea sufficere videntur quae conveniunt ei secundum suam naturam. . . . Ad primum . . . quia natura hominis dependent a superiori natura, ad eius perfectionem non sufficit cognitio naturalis, sed requiritur quaedam supernaturalis . . ." *(ST,* II–II, q. 2, a. 3, ad 1).

212. See *ST,* I, q. 62, a. 4: "Cuiuslibet autem creaturae esse beatum non est naturae, sed ultimus finis."

213. "Ad perfectam igitur beatitudinem requiritur quod intellectus pertinget ad ipsam essentiam primae causae. Et sic perfectionem suam habebit per unionem ad Deum sicut ad obiectum, in quo solo beatitudo hominis consistit . . ." *(ST,* I–II, q. 3, a. 8).

Before this mysterious Thomistic conception of a human nature naturally open and supernaturally elevated to God which therefore does not vainly desire to see Him, and a God who freely shows Himself to man and thereby fulfills a natural human desire, Cajetan, Ferrariensis, and Báñez, and a host of other commentators, hesitate. Báñez says it is "no solution" to claim that the supernatural vision of God falls under the "adequate object of the created intellect," namely, "being qua being" *(ens inquantum ens)*. What is so wrong, though, about this solution? It leads, Báñez thinks, to an untenable doctrine.

> This, however, is no solution. For from this [solution] it follows that the created intellect has a natural inclination to knowing God intuitively, which is a supernatural object, although the attainment [of this object] is supernatural because of the defect in the [intellectual] potency. *(ST,* I, q. 12, a. 1; *Bañes Scholastica commentaria* [ed. Urbano, 246])[214]

Although this statement is arguably a very accurate summary of what Aquinas often enough says, Báñez rejects it, doubtless fearing that if this is Aquinas's doctrine, it is beset by philosophical contradiction and theological heterodoxy. On behalf of Báñez and the other Thomist commentators, one can only agree that Aquinas's doctrine is unintelligible from the point of view of a theology that would try to impose a modern theological orthodoxy on a strictly Aristotelian conception of human nature. The commentators rightly judge that the combination is impossible; but Aquinas, especially in the extended argument of *SCG,* III, 25–51, transcends the Aristotelian conception of human nature. In this argument, Aquinas develops the philosophical analogue to the theological doctrine that human nature is *"imago Dei"*:[215] "The image [of God] is discovered in the [human] soul according as it is led or has been born to be led to God."[216]

The commentators, unlike Aquinas, attempt to protect the generosity of God by circumscribing man; they put reins on human nature by confining it to what Aristotle said about human nature. Accordingly, they transform what Aquinas took to be the universal, spontaneous, implicit, pre-cognitive desire to see God, the desire that determines the intrinsic finality of an intellectual nature, into the particular, ex-

---

214. "Haec tamen solutio nulla est. Nam ex ea sequitur, quod intellectus creatus naturalem habeat inclinationem ad cognoscendum Deum intuitive, ut est objectum supernaturale, quamvis assequutio sit supernaturalis propter defectum potentiae" *(Bañes Scholastica commentaria,* I, q. 12, a. 1 [ed. Urbano, 246]).

215. See *ST,* III, q. 9, a. 3, ad. 3.

216. "Imago attenditur in anima secundum quod fertur, vel nata est ferri in Deum" *(ST,* I, q. 93, a. 8).

plicit, cognitively elicited desire either of a believer (Cajetan) or of a metaphysician (Ferrariensis and Báñez). In the process, the commentators resolve the paradox built into Thomistic human nature by denying that a strictly natural desire to see God exists. Aquinas, however, cannot be accurately viewed through the Thomist commentators' Aristotelian spectacles. Modern theological controversies introduce even greater distortions into the interpretation of Aquinas's doctrine [217]

6. Modern Theological Controversies

By the mid-seventeenth century, theological anxiety to preserve the irreducibly supernatural character of man's ultimate end was full blown. On 1 October 1567 Pope Pius V promulgated the bull *"Ex Omnibus Afflictionibus,"* which condemns although it does not specifically name the Louvain theologian Michel de Bay, commonly known as Baius (1513–89). Among the seventy-nine condemned propositions, Proposition Twenty-One denies that prelapsarian man had a supernatural end. On the contrary, this proposition asserts that man's destiny, union with God, was to be attributed to the resources of sinless human nature.

The elevation and exaltation of human nature into communion with the divine nature was due to the integrity of the first condition, and hence should be called natural and not supernatural.[218]

In response to the condemnation of Baius, theologians attempted to clarify the gratuitous and supernatural character of man's elevation by means of a hypothesis that became for modern theologians the standard orthodoxy: man—considered entirely apart from anything known through revelation and given through grace—could have been created in a state of pure nature, in which state man would have had a solely natural end. Moreover, it was agreed that man retains this natural end even in the present supernatural economy. To know God is the natural end of man; but this knowledge, according to the anti-Baianist hypothesis, does *not* arise from any natural desire to see nor does it in any way entail the natural possibility of seeing the divine essence. In origination and termination, the latter desire is exclusively supernatural.

217. Descoqs, *Praelectiones*, I: 105, argues that these later controversies establish that the Thomistic theory—if Aquinas himself actually held it—is now no longer tenable according to the norms of modern theological orthodoxy.

218. Quotation found in X. Le Bachelot, "Baius," in the *Dictionnaire de Théologie Catholique*, 2/1, cols. 38–111.

The modern theological hypothesis of a strictly natural end for man, which has been radically devalued by some contemporary theologians,[219] goes far beyond what Aquinas said and thought necessary to say about *civil* or *imperfect beatitude*. The theological climate and purport of the two doctrines are entirely different. After the condemnation of Pius V, modern theologians vigorously asserted the doctrine of a strictly natural end against Baius's alleged negation of the gratuity of supernatural happiness. According to his critics, Baius obliges God, as a matter of justice, to grant prelapsarian man the vision of Himself.[220] This gift is owed to human nature. The modern theologians insist, to the contrary, that prelapsarian Adam had his own strictly natural end and that God was under no obligation to provide him with another, supernatural end.

In tracing this modern hypothesis to its historical origins, Vanneste[221] argues that Augustine's interpretation of original sin as a "privation of original justice" *(privatio originalis justitiae)* implicitly contains the idea of "pure nature" *(natura pura)*. If so, Aquinas was unaware of this implication. On the contrary, the state of pure nature must be distinguished from the state of original sin. Original sin infects nature; it does not return nature to a purely natural state.[222] Men "created solely in the conditions of nature" would lack the vision of the divine essence, but this deprivation should be considered merely a

219. Among others, Vanneste, "Le Problème du surnaturel," regards the theological retention of man's natural end, alongside of his supernatural end, as a "dualisme très dangereux" (352) that leads to naturalism, atheism, and secularism. De Broglie, *De fine ultimo*, 184–86, distinguishes a positive and a negative sense of *"natura pura."* The positive sense of the term presupposes a philosophical theory about human nature (that nature has its own proper powers and end) but one that is not entailed by any doctrine of faith regarding the supernatural character of the beatific vision. In a negative but improper sense of the term, "pure nature" refers to "any economy in which man is *not* called to the end of the divine vision" (186); the negative sense is thus obviously entailed by the doctrine of man's supernatural end.

220. Baius, however, does not mention the elevation of human nature, only the integrity of man's nature. In the state of innocence, the Holy Spirit dwelled within man and man naturally possessed the gifts of the Spirit. In response to Proposition Twenty-One Baius complains: "I have not said (what has been calumniously attributed to me) that the elevation of human nature is to be called natural and not supernatural. But I have said that it is natural [in the state of innocence] what in us [in our present state] is called supernatural, just as sight is called supernatural in those who are restored [to sight] by divine power through a miracle" (*Baiana*, "Ex libro primo de prima hominis justitia," in *Opera omnia*, ed. Gerberon [Cologne: 1696], 92).

221. See Vanneste, "Le Problème du surnaturel," 358–59.

222. See *II Sent.*, d. 33, q. 1, a. 2.

defect, a *lack* of grace;[223] whereas it is by way of punishment that men through original sin are *deprived* of the beatific vision.[224]

Aquinas shows none of the compulsion, so characteristic of modern theologians, to sever even sinful man's natural orientation from its supernatural fulfillment. The doctrine of original sin, the fact that man is deprived of original justice, does not entail that man ever was or even could have been in a state of nature called "pure" because it has been evacuated of everything supernatural. Instead, Aquinas serenely affirms that God intended to provide sinful men, from the moment of their creation, with the restorative grace of Christ. Men were not created in order to be frustrated; they can attain their most profound desire, the vision of God, despite the punishment consequent upon original sin.

Man would have been created frustrated and in vain if he were not able to attain beatitude, as is the case with anything that is not able to attain its ultimate end. Lest man be created frustrated and inane, because he is born with original sin, God proposed from the beginning a remedy for the human race, through which man could be liberated from this inanity—the mediator, himself God and man, Jesus Christ. Through faith in Him the impediment of original sin is able to be taken away. *(De malo*, q. 5, a. 1, ad 1 [Bazzi-Pession, p. 546])[225]

The controversy between Baius and his orthodox counterparts should not be superimposed on Aquinas.[226] The historical and doctrinal differences between Aquinas and Baius are too marked.[227] Baius speaks

223. See *De ver.*, q. 26, a. a, ad 11 (Spiazzi, 484): " . . . in pueris propter defectum gratiae est sola carentia divinae visionis sine aliquo contrario impediente active. . . ."

224. See *De malo*, q. 5, a. 1, ad 15 (Bazzi-Pession, 547): ". . . homo in solis naturalibus constitutus careret quidem visione divina, si sic decederet; sed tamen non competeret ei debitum non habendi. Aliud est enim non debere habere, quod non habet rationem poenae, sed defectus tantum; et aliud debere non habere, quod habet rationem poenae."

225. ". . . homo frustra et vane factus esset, si beatitudinem consequi non posset, sicut quaelibet res quae non potest consequi ultimum finem. Unde ne homo frustra et vane factus esset, cum peccato originali nascens, a principio humani generis proposuit Deus homini remedium, per quod ab hac vanitate liberaretur, sicut ipsum mediatorem Deum et hominem Iesum Christum per cuius fidem impedimentum peccati originalis subtrahi posset" *(De malo*, q. 5, a. 1, ad 1 [Bazzi-Pession, 546]).

226. See de Lubac, *Augustinisme*.

227. See Labourdette, review of *La Destinée de la nature humaine*, 282: "Or, depuis le XVIe siècle, ce que nous appellerions la "problematique," en tout cas la perspective, a complètement changé. . . ."

of a divine justice *owed* to innocent human nature; Aquinas speaks of the divine liberality and the radical natural desire to see God that not even sin can extinguish. The fact that man's ultimate natural desire is satisfied only by a supernatural end does not oblige God. Even though nature is ordered to grace, grace is never a matter of justice but of divine generosity.[228]

From its first institution, human nature was ordained to the end of beatitude, not as an end due man according to his nature, but solely from the divine liberality. *(De ver.*, q. 14, a. 10, ad 2 [Spiazzi, 300])[229]

Creation is itself an act of divine generosity but even the creation of human nature places no necessity on God: men could have been created without a supernatural destiny. Lacking that destiny, human nature, nevertheless, would be human nature.

Suppose that God wishes to makes something. On the supposition of His liberality, it follows as something due that He [also] make those things which necessarily accompany the things that He has [first] willed. For example, if he wishes to make a man that He give him reason. But wherever God is able to will something without willing something else, this other thing does not proceed from God as something that is required but as something [reflecting God's] sheer generosity. The perfection of grace and glory are goods of this kind because [human] nature is able to be without them; they surpass the limits of natural powers. Hence that God wishes to give grace and glory to anyone follows from His sheer generosity. *(De ver.*, q. 6, a. 2 [Spiazzi, 117])[230]

Grace and glory are gratuitously given by God over and above what He gives when creating human nature. From the point of view of nature itself, then, the actual elevation of man to the vision of God cannot be presupposed. The perfection of the universe, considered ab-

---

228. See *De malo*, q. 2, a. 11, ad 14 (Bazzi-Pession, 492): "... habilitas ad gratiam non est idem quod iustitia naturalis, sed est ordo boni naturalis ad gratiam."

229. "... ab ipsa prima institutione natura humana est ordinata in finem beatitudinis, non quasi in finem debitum homini secundum naturam eius, sed ex sola divina liberalitate" *(De ver.*, q. 14, a. 10, ad 2 [Spiazzi, 300]).

230. "Sed ex quo supponitur quod Deus aliquid facere velit; ex suppositione liberalitatis ipsius per modum debiti cuiusdam sequitur quod faciat ea sine quibus res ipsa vult hominem, quod det ei rationem. Ubicumque autem occurrit aliquid sine quo aliud a Deo volitum esse possit, hoc non procedit ab eo secundum rationem alicuius debiti, sed secundum meram liberalitatem. Perfectio autem gratiae et gloriae sunt huiusmodi bona quod sine eis natura esse potest, excedunt enim naturalis virtutis limites; unde quod Deus velit alicui dare gratiam et gloriam, hoc ex mera liberalitate procedit" *(De ver.*, q. 6, a. 2 [Spiazzi, 117]).

stractly, entails only man's natural ordination to God; it does not require that men necessarily have a supernatural end.[231]

For if such a vision exceeds the power of a created nature, as has been proven, any intellectual creature is able to be understood to exist in the species of its nature without this condition, that it should see the substance of God. *(SCG,* III, 53 [Pera, n. 2300, p. 72])[232]

Men, of course, have natures; and since they have natures, they can be considered to have an end proportioned to their natures—"some contemplation of divine things."[233] But is this natural end, the end that men can naturally reach, *the* end of man? Certainly it is only the philosophers, and not Aquinas, who take this natural contemplation of God to be man's ultimate felicity.[234] Aquinas constantly reiterates that man's ultimate beatitude is found only in "seeing God."

Aquinas, however, acknowledges that in a state of pure nature, men cannot attain the beatific vision.[235] He also occasionally remarks that it is possible that God could have created and, presumably, have left man in a state of pure nature.[236] This conceptual possibility is a corollary of the supernatural character of the beatific vision.[237] Now this corollary is the "hypothesis" that looms so large among the modern theologians reacting negatively to Baius. But the hypothesis enjoys no such importance for Aquinas. Aquinas, assuredly, affirms the gratuity of man's supernatural elevation. Yet he never puts into abeyance the divine generosity; he never argues that men de facto have or ever have had a strictly natural ultimate end.[238] Although he admits that the proposition cannot be rationally demonstrated, since "the beginning of creatures depends solely on the will of the Creator,"[239] Aquinas holds that

231. See *ST,* III, q. 1, a. 3, ad 3: "Ad perfectionem etiam universi sufficit quod naturali modo creature ordinetur sic in Deum sicut in finem."

232. "Nam si talis visio facultatem naturae creatae excedit, ut probatum *est,* potest intelligi quivis intellectus creatus in specie suae naturae consistere absque hoc quod Dei substantiam videat" *(SCG,* III, 53 [Pera, n. 2300, p. 72]).

233. ". . . aliqua contemplatio divinorum" *(De ver.,* q. 27, a. 2 [Spiazzi, 514]).

234. See *ST,* I, q. 62, a. 1.

235. See *II Sent.,* d. 28, q. 1, a. 1; d. 29, q. 1, a. 1; *De ver.,* q. 24, a. 14; *ST,* I–II, q. 109, a. 4.

236. See *Quod.* I, q. 4, a. 3 [Spiazzi, 9]: "Sed quia possibile fuit Deo ut hominem facere in puris naturalibus, utile est considerare ad quantum se dilectio naturalis extendere possit."

237. See *SCG,* III, 53 [Pera, n. 2300, p. 72]: quoted in n. 28 above.

238. See *De malo,* q, 4, a. 2, ad 1 [n. 22] (Bazzi-Pession, 531); ". . . nec credo verum esse, quod homo sit creatus in naturalibus puris."

239. See *II Sent.,* d. 4, q. 1, a. 3 [Mandonnet, 138]: ". . . eo quod creaturarum principium ex simplici Creatoris voluntate dependet, quam ratione investigare im-

both angels and men were created in the state of sanctifying grace.[240]
This, rather than its contrary, that men were created in the state of
pure nature, is the more probable proposition.[241]

Christian faith affirms, then, that in the actual order of creation
and redemption, man has only one, actual, ultimate, and supernatural
end: the vision of the divine essence. Indeed, it is not nature but
original sin that is the obstacle between man and his actual supernatural destiny. Christ, however, has overcome that obstacle.[242]
Through Christ, human nature is healed by divine grace. And sanctifying grace is like a seed that will come to its full growth in the beatific
vision.

Yet the Thomistic sphere of grace is certainly circumscribed by the
Augustinian doctrine of original sin and Aquinas's consequent understanding of the necessity of baptism. Without baptism, no one can be
saved.[243] But what kind of ultimate end can be postulated for those
infants who die innocent of personal sin but without the sanctifying,
supernatural grace of baptism? Augustine confines to hell those infants
who die unbaptized; Aquinas relies on the notion of a strictly natural
beatitude in order to guarantee some repose and tranquillity to the
souls of unbaptized infants. In developing his own position (II Sent., d.
33, q. 2, a. 2), Aquinas first explores the possibility whether infants,
who died before the cognitive powers of their souls were actually exercised, would remain in a kind of ignorance and thus not experience any
longing to know God. Such a condition, Aquinas thinks, is improbable
because, presumably even in the case of infants, knowledge and not
ignorance is natural to the separated soul.[244] Aquinas therefore regards

---

possibile est. . . ." In this text, Aquinas allows only an argument "secundum convenientiam": the proposition "Angels were created in the state of grace," which
here is held "without prejudice to its contradictory," is nonetheless more congruent
than its contradictory with the doctrine that everything, from the beginning, was
created in distinct species.

ST, I, q. 95, a. 1 takes a stronger line: the argument for the proposition that "Men
were created in the state of grace" "seems to be required by the very rectitude of
the first state" (videtur requirere ipsa rectitudo primi status): i.e, the proposition is
required in order to explain how, in the first state, human reason was subordinated
to God, the sense powers to reason, and the body to the soul.

240. See ST, I, q. 62, a. 3; q. 95, a. 1; II–II, q. 5, a. 1.
241. See ST, I, q. 62, a. 3. Elsewhere Aquinas hints that creation in the state of
pure nature is a dubious notion. Cf. ST, II–II, q. 5, a. 1 : "Et si homo et angelus
fuerunt creati in puris naturalibus, qui quidam dicunt. . . ."
242. See De malo, q. 5, a. 1, ad 1.
243. See ST, III, q. 1, a. 1.
244. See De malo, q. 5, a. 3 (Bazzi-Pession, 549): "Est autem naturale animae
separatae, ut non minus, sed magis in cognitione vigeat quam animae quae sunt hic;

it as probable that the souls of unbaptized infants know and participate in natural goods and that by such means they are joined to God.[245] But this knowledge of natural goods, which includes knowledge of God as the cause of those goods, is not equivalent to "seeing God." In *II Sent.*, d. 33, q. 2, a. 2, Aquinas allows that the souls of the unbaptized infants know *about* the beatific vision. But he claims that they feel no sorrow at their lack of the beatific vision because they also know that such a good is not naturally proportioned to their soul. Aquinas, however, takes a different tack in the later text from *De malo*, q. 5, a. 3: here he claims that the souls of unbaptized infants could be in a state of supernatural ignorance about "the glory that the saints possess," that is, the beatific vision.[246] Thus they feel no sorrow because they do not have the *supernatural* knowledge about the good that they lack.

Now there is some ambiguity in Aquinas's position about what the separated souls of unbaptized infants can naturally know. These souls, which possess neither innate nor naturally acquired intelligible forms, know because of infused intelligible forms which are received "from the influence of the divine light [through] the cooperating ministry of the angels."[247] According to *II Sent.*, d. 33, q. 2, a. 2 (especially ad 1), the souls of unbaptized infants know that they lack the beatific vision, but this text does not specify whether this is a case of either natural or supernatural knowledge, or of both. In *De malo*, q. 5, a. 3, ad 1, any knowledge of the beatific vision is supernatural: naturally, the souls of the unbaptized infants know only the general conception of beatitude, that is, that beatitude is the possession of a perfect good, not that beatitude is, in particular, the beatific vision. Nonetheless, the earlier text unsettles Aquinas's later assertion.

The text from the *Sentences* argues that it is probable that the souls of the unbaptized infants are able to know "those things that are at least able to be investigated by reason and many more things."[248] Is it not probable, then, that souls of unbaptized infants would know, by

---

et ideo non est probabile quod tantam ignorantiam patiantur [qui cum solo originali decedunt]."

245. See *II Sent.*, d. 33, q. 2, a. 2, ad 5; *De malo*, q. 5, a. 3, ad 4.

246. See *De malo*, q. 5, a. 3 (Bazzi-Pession, 549): ". . . animae puerorum . . . carent supernaturali cognitione, quae hic in nobis per fidem plantatur, eo quod nec hic fidem habuerunt in actu, nec sacramentum fidei susceperunt . . . illa gloria quam sancti possident, est supra cognitionem naturalem."

247. See *IV Sent.*, d. 50, q. 1, ad 6 (Vivès, 11, p. 536): ". . . ex influentia divini luminis, cooperante ministerio Angelorum."

248. See *II Sent.*, d. 33, q. 2, a. 2 (Bazzi-Pession, 862): " . . . probabile non videtur, ut anima ab onere corporis absoluta ea non cognoscat quae saltem ratione investigari possint, et etiam multo plura."

natural means, that only the beatific vision *could* fully satisfy the intellectual desire for a universal and perfect good?[249] Of course, Aquinas developed this conclusion fully and definitively in *SCG*, III, 25–51, and this was written (1259–64), according to Weisheipl's chronology, before the *De malo* (1266–67). But the same argument is repeated in *Comp. theol.*, I, cc. 104–5, which was written (1269–73) after the *De malo*. From the systematic point of view, the conclusion remains one of those "things that are able to be investigated by reason" especially, one would suppose, by the separated soul.

Nonetheless, Aquinas's teaching on the natural happiness of the souls of those infants who died unbaptized has been taken to be the definitive refutation of any interpretation of Aquinas that allows for an innate natural desire for the beatific vision.[250] But, properly nuanced, this interpretation, as even its critics admit, is as strong as the arguments that Aquinas provides in *SCG*, III, 49–50. Given the strength of those arguments, how can the separate souls of these unbaptized infants, granted that they actually know, attain satisfaction if their natural knowledge of God does not fully correspond to the dynamism of an intellectual nature?[251] Doubtless, texts can be found to show that human nature, before it is supernaturally elevated, suffers no loss because it *lacks* what by nature it has no "right" to have, the beatific vision.[252] But the question remains, however one balances Aquinas's texts, how any intellectual substance, including the separate soul of an unbaptized infant, can be fully satisfied until it "sees God"? The point of the question is that the will of an intellectual creature reaches its natural end only in possessing the universal good.[253] Yet Aquinas's answer *(II Sent.*, d. 33, q. 2, a. 2, ad 2), which must be squared with what he says about willing beatitude,[254] is that souls of the unbaptized infants only

249. See *ST*, I, q. 82, a. 2, ad 2: "Cum autem possibilitas voluntatis sit respectu boni universalis et perfecti, non subiicitur eius possibilitas tota alicui particulari bono."

250. See Gagnebet, "L'Amour naturel," 67–69, esp. 67, n. 3.

251. In denying that the lack of the beatific vision is a punishment *(poena)* for the soul of the unbaptized infant, Aquinas himself grants that such a lack would be a punishment if it were to go against "natural inclination": see *De malo*, q. 5, a. 4, ad 3.

252. Cf. *ST*, III, q. 52, a. 5: although the souls of the saints detained in hell, awaiting the redemption of Christ, did not suffer, they were deprived of the beatific vision. Christ's descent to hell precisely allows them to attain this vision which is "man's perfect beatitude."

253. See *ST*, I, q. 105, a. 4: "Velle enim nihil aliud est quam inclinatio quaedam in obiectum voluntatis, quod est bonum universale. Inclinare autem in bonum universale est primi moventis, cui proportionatur ultimus finis. . . ."

254. Cf. *ST*, II–II, q. 30, a. 1: "Tripliciter autem aliquis vult aliquid. Uno quidem

have a "wish" *(velleitas)* and not an "ordered and complete will" *(voluntas ordinata et completa)* to see God.[255] Since they are *wishing* for what is naturally impossible for them to attain, they do not feel suffering at lacking the beatific vision. Nevertheless, the thrust of the argument from *SCG*, III, 49–50, which presupposes that the universal truth is the intellect's formal object, is that intellectual substances do will *(velle)* what is naturally impossible for them to attain.[256] The natural desire of an intellectual substance only comes to rest when it knows the divine essence.[257]

In any case, the separated souls of unbaptized infants constitute a restricted category of intellectual substances. And Aquinas shows no eagerness to expand the category. He focuses on those who, morally speaking, are "adults." Anyone who attains the use of reason, who is capable of moral good and evil, is by his moral choices incorporated into the order of grace, and is either moving toward or away from his supernatural end.[258]

> After they have the use of reason, [men] are obliged to take care for their salvation, because if they have done so, they are already without original sin [since] grace has supervened; however, if they have not done so, such omission is for them a mortal sin. *(De malo,* q. 5, a. 2, ad 8 [Bazzi-Pession, 548])[259]

---

modo, appetitu naturali: sicut omnes homines volunt esse et vivere"; I, q. 41, a. 2, ad 3: ". . . voluntas, inquantum est natura quaedam, aliquid naturaliter vultus; sicut voluntas hominis naturaliter tendit ad beatitudinem."

255. See *ST,* I, q. 62, a. 2: "Unde nulla creatura rationalis potest habere motum voluntatis ordinatum ad illam beatitudinem [videre Deum per essentiam], nisi mota a supernaturali agente." Cf. *ST,* I–II, q. 62, a. 1, ad 3: "Sed ad ipsum [Deum] secundum quod est obiectum beatitudinis supernaturalis, ratio et voluntas secundum suam naturam non ordinantur *sufficienter.*" In regard to this last text, Laporta, *La destinée,* 155, exclaims: "Notons: *non ordinantur sufficienter.* Donc: *ordinantur!*"

256. See *Expos. de Trin.,* q. 1, a. 3, ad 4 (Decker, 18–19, p. 73): ". . . quamvis deus sit ultimus finis in consecutione et primus in intentione appetitus naturalis . . ."; q. 6, a. 4, ad 5 (Decker, 9–12, p. 229): "Quamvis enim homo naturaliter inclinetur in finem ultimum, non tamen potest naturaliter illum consequi, sed solum per gratiam, et hoc est propter eminentiam illius finis"; *ST,* II–II, q. 2, a. 3: ". . . natura autem rationali, inquantum cognoscit universalem boni et entis rationem, habet immediatum ordinem ad universale essendi principium."

257. See *SCG,* III, 50 (Pera, n. 2277, p. 68): "Per hoc igitur quod substantiae separatae cognoscunt omnium rerum quarum substantias vident, esse Deum causam, non quiescit desiderium naturale in ipsis, nisi etiam ipsius Dei substantiam videant."

258. See *II Sent.,* d. 33, q. 2, a. 2 (Mandonnet, p. 863): ". . . omnis homo usum liberi habens proportionatus est ad vitam aeternam consequendam, quia potest se ad gratiam praeparare . . . ."

259. "Postquam vero usum rationis habent, tenentur salutis suae curam agere:

Once again, it should be noted that Aquinas, unlike the later Scholastic theologians, does not sharply separate the good proportioned to man's nature from man's actual supernatural end in the world to come.

We are endowed with principles by which we can prepare for that perfect knowledge of separate substances but not with principles by which to reach it. For even though by nature man is inclined to his ultimate end, he cannot reach it by nature but only by grace, and this owing to the loftiness of that end. *(Expos. de Trin.,* q. 6, a. 4, ad 5 [Decker, 7–12, p. 229])[260]

Modern theologians, however, were eager to prove that not only unbaptized infants but even adults, if God had left them to their own devices, would have been satisfied by a strictly natural end. We can only look to the context to explain the differences between the moderns and Aquinas. The Baianist controversy about the necessity of supernatural happiness turned on Augustine. Aquinas's account of perfect happiness looks to Aristotle. Aquinas reiterated that man *while in this world* naturally desires perfect happiness which can only be found in the otherworldly vision of God.

In commenting on Aristotle, Aquinas contrasts imperfect and perfect beatitude. Perfect beatitude is the vision of God in the world to come. As men naturally and explicitly seek perfect beatitude, they implicitly but necessarily desire to see God while yet in this world. These propositions Aquinas attempts to demonstrate. But the Thomistic argument concludes that the vision of God is not a naturally attainable end. Only God, in a gratuitous act of love that infinitely transcends the capacity of human nature, can give the vision of Himself. God must elevate the human mind so that the human mind may be informed by the divine essence.

At this point in his argument, Aquinas undoubtedly speaks as a theologian who believes but who cannot, in the strict sense, prove what he believes. The immortality of the soul lends plausibility to the idea of an otherworldly, perfect beatitude. But only the Christian faith can affirm that God gives the vision of Himself in the world to come.

---

quod si fecerint, iam absque peccato originali erunt, gratia superveniente: si autem non fecerint, talis omissio est eis peccatum mortale" *(De malo,* q. 5, a. 2, ad 8 [Bazzi-Pession, p. 548]).

260. ". . . nobis sunt indita principia, quibus nos possimus praepare ad illam cognitionem perfectam substantiarum separatarum, non autem quibus ad eam possimus pertingere. Quamvis enim homo naturaliter inclinetur in finem ultimum, non tamen potest naturaliter illum consequi, sed solum per gratiam, et hoc est propter eminentiam illius finis *(Expos. de Trin.,* q. 6, a. 4, ad 5 [Decker, 7-12, p. 229]).

Subsequently, the theologian can explain that men and women, in this life, can begin to participate in that transcendent end through the divinely infused supernatural virtues.[261]

Nonetheless, it remains necessary for the theologian—even if the human soul is immortal—to have a cogent conception of this-worldly happiness.[262] Thomistic theology embodies what Aquinas considered to be two unimpeachable truths. First, the concept of a strictly natural beatitude is an unsurpassable boundary for philosophical thought; consequently, the theologian will always mark this boundary in his own delineation of man's ultimate beatitude. Second, the *concept* of the same boundary is indispensable, for properly theological reasons, as an aid to understanding the *fact* that God freely destines man to a supernatural end.[263]

Since this-worldly beatitude is imperfect, Aristotle's conception of *eudaimonia* must be reassessed. This reassessment, rather than the commentators hypothesis of a strictly natural end, is an explicit theme in Thomistic theology. The commentators' hypothesis, if it can be found in that form at all, is merely a minor motif in Aquinas. Aquinas, however, leaves an important issue unresolved. Does the conclusion reached in *SCG*, III, 25–51 (that only the vision of God can satisfy man's natural desire to know God) leave the philosopher *"wishing"* for the impossible?[264]

261. See *ST*, I–II, q. 62, a. 1.

262. See *SLE*, I, 10, 1098a18, 154–174 (*In Ethic.*, I, lect. 10 [Spiazzi, n. 129, p. 34]); *ST*, I, q. 64, a. 1.

263. See *ST*, I, q. 62, a. 1: ". . . haec beatitudo non est aliquid naturae, sed naturae finis . . . ."

264. See *II Sent.*, d. 23, q. 2, a. 2, ad 2.

X

A Thomistic Philosophical Ethics?

1. The Dilemma

Although Aquinas certainly allowed for a natural morality, that is, a sphere in which practical reason is competent to make moral judgments in the light of its naturally known principles, he did not ever develop an autonomous philosophical ethics. Yet, numerous modern and contemporary Thomists have attempted to construct one from his theological writings, by gathering a *florilegium* of texts picked mostly from the *Secunda pars* of the *Summa theologiae*. These various Thomist ethics commonly assume that reason's natural capacity to make moral judgments unambiguously reveals or is equivalent to or necessarily entails reason's capacity to construct a systematic moral philosophy modeled, with some improvements, after Aristotle.[1] But this is too

1. Cf. María C. Donadío Maggi de Gandolfi, "El papel de la Filosofía moral e la moral teológica de Santo Tomás," in *S. Tommaso filosofo: Ricerche in occasione dei due centenari accademici,*" ed. Antonio Piolanti, Studi tomistici, vol. 60 (Vatican City State: Libreria Editrice Vaticana, 1995), 113–28 who states that "la ética filosófica tomasiana posee: 1) principios racionales; 2) objecto racional y 3) certeza racional" (121). From these elements can be constructed a scientific moral philosophy, one which is universal and necessary (122), that is, systematic. This view, however, is juxtaposed to a more correctly nuanced characterization of Thomistic moral science: "La moral tomasiana es propiamente una *moral de la fe,* por lo tanto, es teologogía moral" (120) that "asume sin anular la naturaleza propia del orden moral" (120). But in support of the latter claim, the author oddly appeals to a truncated text from *ST,* I–II, q. 69, a. 2. There, Aquinas notes that "spes futurae beatitudinis potest esse in nobis propter duo . . ."; Maggi de Gandolfi's translated quotation omits *"spes,"* and begins "La beatitud futura se puede realizar en nosotros de dos modos . . ." (120). The precise point of this article, however, neither bears on nor can be sustained by consideration of the properly natural moral order: *"in viris*

facile an assumption: the line between the first principles of practical reason, which do bear on the ends of our natural inclinations, and the putative ultimate natural end of man, which the classical Thomist philosophers use to ground and close their moral teleology, is by no means direct or obvious in Aquinas. On the contrary, Aquinas insists that God generously endowed human nature from its "first institution" with its ordination to the supernatural vision of God.[2] Therefore, any construction of a systematic Thomistic philosophical ethics, that is to be centered on the ultimate natural end of man, necessarily involves, first of all, a deconstruction of Aquinas's *theological* moral science.[3] What results from such a procedure?

The elements of Aquinas's moral science (the humanly acquired moral and intellectual virtues, their divinely infused counterparts, and, above them all and grounding them all, the theological virtues that direct and enable men to move by their free acts toward God) are originally united in a theology that focuses, not as the *Nicomachean Ethics* does, on the human exercise of the virtues but on God as the ultimate objective end and beatitude of man.[4] Aquinas structures his

---

sanctis" or *"in viris perfectis,"* one may have the supernatural hope that there is a kind of imperfect beginning, through the gifts of the Holy Spirit (ad 3), of future or otherworldly beatitude.

2. Cf. *De ver.*, q. 14, a. 10, ad 2 (Spiazzi, 300): ". . . ab ipsa prima institutione natura humana est ordinata in finem beatitudinis, non quasi in finem debitum homini secundum naturam eius, sed ex sola divina liberalitate."

3. In his translation of the *Prima secundae* of the *Summa theologiae*, Joseph Rickaby, S.J., *Aquinas Ethicus: The Moral Teaching of St. Thomas* (New York: Benziger Brothers, 1892), deliberately omits "Phrases, Articles, and whole Questions . . . because they deal with Theology rather than with Ethics . . ." (6).

4. See *ST*, I, q. 2, prologus; I–II, prologus. Aquinas's moral science incorporates a *theological* "virtue ethics" that brings the nonrational "matter" of the passions under the rule of practical reason. Such matter is the proper object of the virtues: "tota materia morali ad considerationem virtutum reducta" (*ST*, II–II, prologus). The moral virtues or dispositions, whether infused or acquired, reduce to the corresponding four "cardinal" virtues (infused or acquired justice, fortitude, temperance, and prudence). But only the infused cardinal virtues lead, like a door swinging on hinges, to eternal life: "Ille autem virtutes quibus ad aeternam vitam pervenitur et super eas aliarum virtutum motus fundantur, dicitur proprie cardinales" (*III Sent.*, d. 33, q. 2, a. 1, sol. 1 (Moos, n. 142, p. 1046). Because their object is man's ultimate end, which is the principle of human actions, Thomistic ethics commences by considering the theological virtues: "Cum enim in agibilibus finis sit principium . . . necesse est virtutes theologicas, quarum obiectum est ultimus finis, esse priores ceteris virtutibus" (*ST*, II–II, q. 4, a. 7). From this perspective, the *acquired* cardinal virtues are not "true virtues unless faith is presupposed" (*ST*, II–II, q. 4, a. 7, ad 1). But when considered insofar as "they have some relationship to God" or as they are by divine help "directed to enjoying God," the acquired cardinal virtues fall under the formal object of theology: see *ST*, II–II, q. 1, a. 1.

discussion of human acts, and analyzes their intrinsic and extrinsic principles, in reference to that supernatural end.[5] Once extracted, these elements of Thomistic moral science need to be reunited. But in reference to what *philosophical conception* of the ultimate natural end should they be reunited? Here we should not hastily answer *"beatitudo imperfecta,"* thus substituting the only end that—according to the theologian—we can naturally attain, for the only ultimate end that we naturally desire but cannot attain, *"beatitudo perfecta."*[6] The answer is misguided because *"beatitudo imperfecta"* is one of two correlates that properly frame a theological conception of human happiness. Nor, then, should we simply mistake a contemporary version of Aristotle for Aquinas.[7] Aquinas clearly states that the ultimate end of man is not the exercise of the intellectual and moral virtues.[8]

There remains, then, the fundamental question—What is man's ulti-

---

On the various contemporary types of "virtue ethics," and on the priority of practical reason's precepts enjoining basic human goods to the acquired virtues in Aquinas, see Kevin M. Staley, "Thomas Aquinas and Contemporary Ethics of Virtue," *Modern Schoolman* 66 (1989): 285–300.

5. See *ST,* I–II, q. 6, prologus.

6. From a theological point of view, *beatitudo imperfecta* is evidently *the* end that men naturally attain: ". . . beatitudo imperfecta quae in hac vita haberi potest potest ab homine acquiri per sua naturalia, eo modo quo et virtus, in cuius operatione consistit . . . ." *(ST,* I–II, q. 5, a. 5) *Beatitudo perfecta,* of course, is not naturally attainable: ". . . homo per sua naturalia non potest beatitudinem consequi" (ibid.). Yet it is the only *ultimate* end that men naturally seek ". . . nihil enim satiat naturalem hominis appetitum, nisi bonum perfectum, quod est beatitudo" (ibid., a. 8, ad 3).

7. In providing a modern reinterpreation of *Aristotle* (or perhaps application of Aristotle to a modern world bereft of the most noble objects of contemplation), Henry B. Veatch, *Rational Man: A Modern Interpretation of Aristotelian Ethics* (Bloomington: Indiana University Press, 1962), 117, recommends that "[Man's natural end] consists in living intelligently and leading an examined life." McInerny, *Aquinas on Human Action,* 170, appears to attribute this doctrine to *Aquinas:* "If there is no one activity whose end is identical with the good for man, there is none the less a set of such ends, which variously realize the *ratio boni* and which together can be seen as fully perfective of the kind of agent man is."

8. See *ST,* I–II, q. 3, a. 5, ad 3: ". . . si ipsemet homo esset ultimus finis suus: tunc enim consideratio et ordinatio actuum et passionum eius esset eius beatitudo. Sed quia ultimus hominis finis est aliquod bonum extrinsecum . . ."; a. 7: ". . . ultima hominis beatitudo non possit esse in consideratione speculativarum scientiarum"; *SCG,* III, 35 (Pera, n. 2145, p. 42): "Non est autem in actibus moralium virtutum ultima hominis felicitas"; *SCG,* III, 25 (Pera, n. 2064, p. 33): "Est igitur ultimus finis totius hominis, et omnium operationum et desideriorum eius, cognoscere primum verum, quod est Deus." Cf. John M. Finnis, "Practical Reasoning, Human Goods, and the End of Man," *Proceedings of the American Catholic Philosophical Association* 58 (1984): 30: ". . . man's true last end is *integral human fulfillment."*

mate natural end?—which any attempted philosophical reconstruction of Aquinas's theological ethics must answer. The answer that the classical Thomist philosophers and the legion of scholastic manualists give is that man's ultimate natural end consists in knowing from created effects the God Who is their First Cause. In short, man's natural end is the analogical knowledge of God attained by the whole man reasoning in this world, or through the species infused into the separate immortal soul in the world to come. But this answer, which *mutatis mutandis* replicates in the natural order the end of man in the supernatural order, leads to many antinomies, since the unfrustrable natural desire "to see" the divine essence can neither be eliminated from nor fulfilled in the strictly natural order of human desires and ends.[9]

Aquinas himself, although he pursued many themes in parallel with Aristotle, provides no precedent for solving these antinomies; he did not attempt to construct, by extracting it from his theology, a systematic philosophical version of his moral science. There is at least one overriding reason for him not to have done so: a *systematic* philosophical ethics (unlike the particular rational arguments that are its bits and pieces) cannot be simply extracted from a theological one. In regard to the arts, sciences, and the whole sphere of human actions in general, those instruments, concepts, or actions that are "for an end" are determined in their use and meaning by the end pursued. Conversely, pursuing a different end entails finding different means:[10] "In regard to everything that is ordained to an end, it is necessary that [its] rule of governance and order be taken from the end. . . ." *(SCG*, I, 1 [Pera, n. 2, p. 2])[11]

The Aristotelian principle, to which Aquinas adheres in developing

9. P. N. Zammit, *Introductio in philosophiam moralem Thomisticam* (Rome: Institutum Pontificium Internationale "Angelicum," 1934), 145, is forced to postulate, in order to save men from a vain natural desire for seeing God, that philosophers, who know nothing of the supernatural order, would in such circumstances conclude that God is able to give men *natural powers* sufficient for seeing the essence of the First Cause: see n. 162 *infra*. E. Elter, S.I., "De natuali hominis beatitudine ad mentem scholae antiquioris," *Gregorianum* 9 (1928): 269–306, propounds an even more radical solution, one that he admits goes against "multa S. Thomae dicta" (286); Elter eliminates the natural (i.e., precognitive) desire for "seeing God" by eliminating the natural (precognitive) desire for attaining a perfect good: "Bonum perfectum appetitur quidem naturaliter, sed non appetitu innato, sed appetitu elicito . . ." (285).

10. See *SLE*, I, 2, 1094a6, 223–25 *(In Ethic.*, I, lect. 1 [Spiazzi, n. 15, p. 5]): ". . . cum multae sint operationes et artes et doctrinae, necesse est quod earum sint diversi fines, quia fines, et ea quae sunt ad finem sunt proportionalia."

11. "Omnium autem ordinatum ad finem, gubernationis et ordinis regulam ex fine sumi necesse est . . ." *(SCG*, I, 1 [Pera, n. 2, p. 2]).

his own moral science,[12] is that the end determines the order, character, and significance of the means: "[F]rom the end is taken the *ratio* of those things which are for the end."[13] The principle, as Aristotle and Aquinas use it, applies both to the practical ordering of actions to particular ends and to the construction of a systematic moral science that would attempt to give an overall direction to human actions by locating man's ultimate end. Aquinas states that the proper task of moral philosophy is "to consider human actions insofar as they are ordered to each other and to [their] end."[14] Thomistic moral science begins, even more radically, with an examination of the nature of an ultimate end in general.[15]

For precisely this Aristotelian reason, Thomistic theological moral science, although it does have many obvious parallels to the *Nicomachean Ethics*, is not merely a reflection of, nor without further ado can its extracted elements be reconstructed according to, the Aristotelian philosophical model.[16] Aquinas notes that Aristotle's ethics reflects what Aristotle thinks to be the supreme *telos* of human life itself.

It is necessary that the entirety of human life be ordered to the final and best end of human life. For the right ordering of human life, therefore, it is necessary to have knowledge of the final and best end of human life. The reason is that the order of those things that are for the end is always taken

12. See *ST,* II–II, q. 141, a. 6: "Praecipuus autem ordo rationis consistit ex hoc quod aliqua in finem ordinat, et in hoc ordine maxime consistit bonum rationis: nam bonum habet rationem finis, et ipse finis est regula eorum quae sunt ad finem."

13. ". . . ex fine sumitur ratio eorum quae sunt ad finem" *(SLE,* III, 15, 1115b20, 114–15; *In Ethic.,* III, lect. 15 [Spiazzi, n. 550, p. 156]). Cf. *EN,* III, 7, 1115b22: τοιοῦτον δὴ καὶ τὸ τέλος.

14. "Sic ergo moralis philosophiae . . . proprium est considerare operationes humanas, secundum quod sunt ordinatae ad invicem et ad finem" *(SLE,* I, 1, ante 1094a1, 40–43; *In Ethic.,* I, lect. 1 [Spiazzi, n. 2, p. 3]).

15. See *ST,* I–II, q. 1, a. 1, prologus: "Et quia ultimus finis humanae vitae ponitur esse beatitudo, oportet primo considerare de ultimo fine in communi deinde de beatitudine."

16. For example, Aquinas's account of how man acts for an ultimate end does imitate Aristotle's: cf. *EN,* I, 1–2; *ST,* I–II, q. 1, aa. 1; 4. But the rest of the articles in q. 1, which elaborate how God uniquely is the ultimate end for all men, are more directly inspired by Aquinas's own theology: see Ramirez, *De hominis beatitudine,* 3: 1, proloquium, n. 229, pp. 219–20. Cf. S. Pinckaers, O.P., "La Béatitude dans l'éthique de saint Thomas," in *The Ethics of St. Thomas Aquinas,* ed. Elders and Hedwig, 80–94: "Si la question du bonheur est première pour saint Thomas, en morale, c'est finalement à cause de sa dimension objective, parce qu'elle ordonne l'homme et l'œuvre à l'Oject divin" (86).

from the end itself. . . . *(SLE,* I, 2, 1094a22, 67–73; *In Ethic.,* I, lect. 2 [Spiazzi, n. 23, p. 7])[17]

Thomistic moral science, however, is grounded on what Christian faith takes as the ultimate end of human life, the vision of God *"in patria."* But while a systematic Aristotelian moral philosophy must order human action in terms of the ultimate end of human action, no strictly philosophical ethics can incorporate the supernatural end that specifies Thomistic moral science. Aquinas bluntly states, moreover, that a moral philosophy that lacks knowledge of the true end of man is radically deficient as a science of morals. Indeed, it cannot be considered to be a truly scientific moral philosophy.

Since the end relates to actions as a principle does to speculative [truths], there is not able to be, in the strict sense, a true science if it lacks the right estimation of the first indemonstrable principle. . . . *(ST,* II–II, q. 23, a. 8)[18]

In his *Commentary on Matthew,* Aquinas states that all philosophical opinions about ultimate beatitude, including Aristotle's, "are false, although not in the same way."[19] Why are they all false? From the point of view of Thomistic theology, every philosophical ethics lacks knowledge of man's true final end: the supernatural vision of God's essence in the world to come.[20] No philosophy is capable of grasping this end; it is known with certitude to faith alone and can be attained only through the divinely infused theological virtues of faith, hope, and charity.

Aquinas's animadversion about philosophical conceptions of human beatitude surely applies to Thomist philosophical ethics. A Thomist philosophical ethics, no less than Aristotle's ethics, is unable to incorporate the true end of human actions: "Natural knowledge is not able

17. ". . . sed tota humana vita oportet quod ordinetur in ultimum et optimum finem humanae vitae; ergo ad rectitudinem humanae vitae necesse est habere cognitionem de ultimo et optimo fine humanae vitae. Et huius ratio est quia semper ratio eorum quae sunt ad finem sumenda est ab ipso fine . . ." *(SLE,* I, 2, 1094a22, 67–73; *In Ethic.,* I, lect. 2 [Spiazzi, n. 23, p. 7]).

18. ". . . cum finis se habeat in agibilibus sicut principium in speculativis, sicut non potest esse simpliciter vera scientia si desit recta aestimatio de primo indemonstrabili principio. . . ." *(ST,* II–II, q. 23, a. 8).

19. *Super Matth.,* c. 5, 2 (Marieti 1925 ed., p. 70b): "Omnes autem istae opiniones falsae sunt; quamvis non eodem modo. Unde Dominus omnes reprobat."

20. See *Super Matth.,* c. 5, 2 (Marieti 1925 ed., p. 71a): "Illorum autem opinio qui dicunt beatitudo consistit in contemplatione divinorum, reprobat Dominus quantum ad tempus, quia alias vera est: quia ultima felicitas consistit in visione optimi intelligibilis, scilicet Dei."

to attain God insofar as He is the object of beatitude, which is how hope and charity tend toward Him" *(ST,* II-II, q. 4, a. 7).[21] Is philosophical ethics, then, of any value? According to Aquinas, the moral agent can reach, through philosophical moral science in conjunction with the virtue of prudence, the second grade of virtue.

Those virtues which reach the level of right reason attain the second grade. They do not, however, attain God Himself through charity. In one sense, these virtues are perfect by comparison to the human good, but they are not perfect in any unconditional sense, since they do not reach the primary rule [of human acts], which is the ultimate end [God]. . . . Hence they are deficient in regard to the true meaning of virtue. . . . *(De virt.,* q. 1, a. 2 [Odetto, 818])[22]

Traditional Thomists, however, usually insist that philosophical ethics can be adequately structured around the ultimate *natural* end of man, which, they claim, is the natural knowledge of God. There are, to be sure, many well-known texts of Aquinas that baldly state that ultimate human beatitude, and the virtues that allow us to attain it, is twofold, the perfect and the imperfect or, equivalently, the supernaturally infused and the humanly acquired.[23] But in Aquinas's own doctrine, the assertion that men can achieve imperfect or civil beatitude is subject to profound restrictions and transformations of meaning that are largely ignored by Thomist philosophical ethics.

Aquinas appends to the notion of natural beatitude an important caveat. While not denying the capacity of moral philosophy to pursue the happiness that is naturally proportionate to human nature,[24] Aquinas contends that philosophy is not *morally* sufficient to guide men, philosophers included, to what traditional Thomists consider to be man's ultimate natural end, the philosophical knowledge of God.

If philosophical knowledge of God is the ultimate natural end of man, it must be acknowledged that most men are unable to reach this

---

21. ". . . naturalis cognitio non potest attingere ad Deum secundum quod est obiectum beatitudinis, prout tendit in ipsum spes et caritas" *(ST,* II–II, q. 4, a. 7).

22. "Secundus autem gradus virtutum est illarum quae attingunt rationem rectam, non tamen attingut ad ipsum Deum per caritatem. Hae quidem aliqualiter sunt perfectae per comparationem ad bonum humanum, non tamen sunt simpliciter perfectae, quia non attingunt ad primam regulam, quae est ultimus finis . . . Unde et deficiunt a vera ratione virtutis. . . ." *(De virt.,* q. 1, a. 2 [Odetto, 818])

23. See *ST,* I–II, q. 5, a. 5.

24. See *De virt.,* q. 1, a. 12, ad 6 (Odetto, 745): ". . . quod respectu finis qui est naturae humanae proportionatus, sufficit homini ad bene se habendum naturalis inclinatio; et ideo philosophi posuerunt aliquas virtutes, quarum obiectum esset felicitas, de qua ipsi tractabant."

ultimate end through philosophical reasoning. Metaphysical contemplation of God is not an activity that engages the young, or the stupid, or those preoccupied with daily toil, or those engaged in worldly affairs; it comes, if it comes at all, to an intelligent man usually at the end of a leisurely life devoted to philosophy. But not even the philosopher can circumvent the roadblock that Aquinas spies. A philosopher must make, along the entirety of life's way, moral decisions. To make correct moral decisions, one must have—at the beginning of one's moral life—an adequate understanding of man's natural end and the way to attain that end.

It is impossible to intend the end unless the end is known precisely under the aspect of [it] being the end and [also] the proportion of the means to the end itself [must be known]. *(III Sent.*, d. 27, q. 1, a. 2 [Moos, n. 38, p. 860])[25]

This knowledge of the end *first* derives, for the philosopher no less than the ordinary man, from virtuous habits, whether innate or acquired.[26] Moral virtue inclines men to the right understanding of their proper end. We have already seen how many problems are latent in this Aristotelian doctrine. But both Aristotle and Aquinas agree, despite other doctrinal differences, that speculative knowledge of man's natural end is remarkably inefficacious in promoting moral virtue. Theoretical wisdom comes too late, morally speaking, to do much good. The usual philosophical time table, which involves preliminary but lengthy study of the speculative sciences, reserves contemplation of God until the end of life.[27] But this timetable does not coincide with what the

25. "Intendere autem finem impossibile est, nisi cognoscatur finis sub ratione finis, et proportio eorum quae sunt ad finem in finem ipsum." *(III Sent.*, d. 27, q. 1, a. 2 [Moos, n. 38, p. 860])

26. See *SLE*, VI, 11, 1144a28, 239–42 *(In Ethic.*, VI, lect. 11 [Spiazzi, n. 1273, p. 344]): "Sed quod hoc sit optimum, non apparet nisi bono, id est virtuoso, qui habet rectam existimationem de fine, cum virtus moralis faciat rectam intentionem finis . . ."; VII, 8, 1151a11, 129–32 (VII, lect. 8 [Spiazzi, n. 1431, p. 383]): ". . . sed per habitum virtutis sive naturaliter sive per assuetudinem acquisitae consequitur rectam aestimationem circa principium agibilium quod est finis."

27. See *III Sent.*, d. 35, q. 1, a. 2, sol. 3 (Moos, n. 44, pp. 1179–80): ". . . felicitas contemplativa, de qua Philosophi tractaverunt, in contemplatione Dei consistit. . . . Unde etiam Philosophi ultimum tempus vitae suae reservabant, ut dicitur, ad contemplandum divina, praecedens tempus in aliis scientiis expendentes, ut ex illis habiliores fierent ad considerandum divina"; *In de Causis*, I, lect. 1 (Pera, n. 7, p. 4): "Et inde est quod Philosophorum intentio ad hoc principaliter erat ut per omnia quae in rebus considerabant, ad cognitionem primarum causarum pervenirent. Unde scientiam de primis causis ultimo ordinabant, cuius considerationi ultimum tempus suae vitae deputarent."

philosopher naturally desires to know and needs to know from the *beginning* of his moral life: God and how to attain Him.[28]

The end of human life is to know God, even according to the philosophers who place ultimate felicity in an act of wisdom in accordance with knowledge of the most noble intelligibles.

One [type of] knowledge of God exceeds our nature, namely, the vision which is through [His] essence. Through our natural abilities we are not sufficiently enabled to foresee this end. And, therefore, it was necessary to have faith about those things that essentially pertain to faith.

Another [type of] knowledge of God, namely, through natural reason, is commensurate to our nature. But because this [knowledge of God] is had in the last stages of human life, although it is the end [of human life] and it is necessary that human life be regulated from [our] knowledge of God, just as those things relating to the end are [regulated] from knowledge of the end, human nature, therefore, does not sufficiently provide even in regard to this [type of] knowledge of God. Hence, it was necessary that those things, which reason was not able to attain, became known through faith from the beginning [of man's life]. And this is the case in regard to those things that are required for [attaining the end of human life]. *(III Sent.*, d. 24, q. 1, a. 3 [Moos, nn. 88–89, p. 774])[29]

Moral philosophy, then, cannot comprehend, in a fashion timely enough to meet the exigencies of man's moral life, what Aquinas calls the end *commensurate to our nature* and what Thomists usually identify as *the ultimate natural end of man*. The major difficulty, however, is not just that philosophical contemplation comes too late but, more

---

28. Cf. *SLE*, VI, 7, 1142a16, 189–92 *(In Ethic.*, VI, lect. 7 [Spiazzi, n. 1210, p. 330]): "Quantum autem ad sapientiam, subiungit quod iuvenes sapientialia quidem, scilicet metaphysicalia, non credunt, id est non attingunt mente, licet ea dicant ore. . . ."

29. ". . . dicendum quod finis humanae vitae est cognitio Dei etiam secundum philosophos qui ponunt felicitatem ultimam in actu sapientiae secundum cognitionem nobilissimi intelligibilis.

Cognitio autem Dei quaedam excedit nostram naturam, sicut visio quae est per essentiam. Et ad istum finem non potuit sufficienter nobis provideri per nostra naturalia. Et ideo necessaria fuit fides eorum quae essentialiter ad fidem pertinent.

Alia autem cognitio Dei est commensurata nostrae naturae, scilicet per rationem naturalem. Sed quia haec habetur in ultimo humanae vitae, cum sit finis, et oportet humanam vitam regulari ex cognitione Dei, sicut ea quae sunt ad finem ex cognitione finis, ideo etiam per naturam hominis non potuit sufficienter provideri quantum etiam ad hanc cognitionem Dei. Unde oportuit quod per fidem a principio cognita fierent, ad quae ratio nondum poterat pervenire; et hoc quantum ad ea quae ad [finem] praeexiguntur" *(III Sent.*, d. 24, q. 1, a. 3 [Moos, nn. 88–89, p. 774]).

importantly, that it provides too little. Although it may correctly understand that contemplation of God is the end that is commensurate with human nature, moral philosophy when evaluating human actions uses arguments that are difficult or controvertible, reaches only general principles, and expresses itself in figurative or symbolic language.[30] In short, the philosophical pursuit of divine contemplation does not readily translate into detailed instructions enabling men to order their actions toward God.

What is needed are more specific principles that will enable the moral agent to make correct moral judgments about particular actions that lead to or impede attaining man's end.[31] Nothing that Aquinas says suggests that the task is easy to accomplish,[32] or that once accomplished the principles reached are sufficient for judging particular cases. Indeed, in making particular moral choices, where passion and stupidity often befog the moral agent, "prudence is more important than practical science."[33] But humanly acquired prudence is insufficient to guide choices that bear on the ultimate supernatural end. Divinely infused charity is required. It alone marks the highest moral standpoint, that of perfect moral goodness, and it is the connecting link in Aquinas's schema between all the humanly acquired virtues and the supernaturally infused virtues. Prudence, the prime virtue in Aristotle's schema, is also to be maintained as a connecting link, but only if we are talking about the secondary grade of virtue.

If we are talking about absolutely perfect virtues, they are connected because of charity, because no such virtue is able to be had without charity, and [where] charity is possessed, they are all had. If we are talking about the second grade of perfect virtue, in regard to the human good, they are connected through prudence. No moral virtue is able to exist without prudence, [but] neither is prudence able to be had if moral virtue is lacking [to prudence]. *(De virt. card.,* q. 1, a. 2 [Odetto, 819])[34]

30. See *SLE,* I, 2, 1094a24, 74–93 *(In Ethic.,* I, lect. 2 [Spiazzi, n. 24, p. 7]); I, 11, 1098a20, 1–54 (I, lect. 11 [nn. 131–33, pp. 35–36]).

31. See *De virt.,* q. 1, a. 8 (Odetto, 728): "Nam ex universiis principiis in specialia pervenitur per inquisitionem rationis. Rationis etiam officio ex appetitu ultimi finis homo deducitur in ea quae sunt convenientia illi fini."

32. See *ST,* I–II, q. 94, a. 3: "Multa enim secundum virtutem fiunt, ad quae natura non primo inclinat; sed per rationis inquisitionem ea homines adinvenerunt, quasi utilia ad bene vivendum."

33. ". . . prudentia plus importat quam scientia practica." *(De virt.,* q. 1, a. 7, ad 1 [Odetto, 723])

34. "Sic ergo, si accipiamus virtutes simipliciter perfectas, connectuntur propter caritatem; quia nulla virtus talis sine caritate haberi potest, et caritate habita

Aquinas, then, preserves a role for natural virtues, and consequently for moral philosophy, but he secures this role only by relativizing their value. The province of moral philosophy is the humanly acquired virtues, but they are only virtues of the "second rank." Still, Aquinas's reservations about the relative inadequacies of moral philosophy have not deterred numerous Thomists from believing that a systematic philosophical ethics, constructed from the extracted elements of Thomistic theological moral science, is not only philosophically possible but morally salutary. Aquinas's caveat, however, remains for us to consider, although in doing so we shall undoubtedly be using a theological criterion to judge the sufficiency of any philosophical ethics.

To suppose that any historical philosophical ethics, Aristotle's included, has provided a morally adequate knowledge of how to attain "the end commensurate with human nature" appears to be an optimism not shared by Aquinas. The fundamental problem, however, is more radical than any deficiency that can be attributed to Aristotle's ethics. No autonomous philosophical ethics, even one that is allegedly constructed solely out of the rational elements of Aquinas's theological moral science, can guide men to their ultimate *supernatural* end, and consequently not one of them can adequately clarify their natural or "penultimate ends" which can only be rightly understood in subordination to the ultimate end. In practice, Thomist philosophical ethicians have regarded *the* ultimate natural end of man as obvious, self-enclosed, and readily attainable by philosophical reason. These Thomist certitudes, which seem to have had remarkably little influence on other moral philosophers, may indeed flow from a "dead theology" presenting itself as philosophy. Let us suppose, however, that Thomist moral philosophy, because it, if no other modern philosophy, correctly grasps the natural end of man, adequately enables men and women to attain at least a "second level" of moral goodness. What, nevertheless, is the relationship between this philosophical ethics to Aquinas's theological ethics?

The proponent of an autonomous Thomistic philosophical ethic, if he or she wishes to remain a disciple of Aquinas, faces a grave dilemma. To incorporate a theological truth about the actual supernatural end of man into a philosophical ethics transgresses, everyone would

---

omnes habentur. Si autem accipiamus virtutes perfectas in secundo gradu, respectu boni humani, sic connectuntur per prudentiam; quia sine prudentia nulla virtus moralis esse potest, nec prudentia haberi potest, si cui deficiat moralis virtus" *(De virt. card.,* q. 1, a. 2 [Odetto, 819]).

agree, the proper boundaries of philosophy.[35] But to argue, contrariwise, that a Thomistic philosophical ethics can and should ignore man's supernatural end, suppresses the precise end-means relationship that structures Aquinas's own moral science.

Because God provides man with an end that is above the nature of man, namely, the full participation in His beatitude, it is necessary that he who tends to this end, if he acts from free choice, know the end from which consideration he is directed in regard to those things which are for the end.

35. Owens unequivocally maintains that philosophy has only naturally known starting points which allow for "reasoning [that] is based solely on the naturally evident premises" (Introduction to *Towards a Christian Philosophy*, 27). But Owens's formula describing the global *object* of "Christian philosophy," "the universe as known through both reason and revelation" (*Cognition*, 330), does not incorporate, nor does his explanation of the formula explicitly utilize, the standard Scholastic distinction between material and formal objects. But the explicit distinction between material and formal object is helpful, and perhaps necessary, for clarifying how "Christian philosophy faces an object that has both natural and supernatural facets" (Epilogue to *Towards a Christian Philosophy*, 317). The same universe as *material object* (= the universe taken in nonprecisive abstraction from the distinction of its natural and supernatural "facets") falls under the habits of both reason and faith. But the universe in both its natural and supernatural "facets," qua known through revelation, only falls under the *formal object* of theology.

Although "Christian philosophy" is a "general philosophy" (*Towards a Christian Philosophy*, 18) and thus not to be confined to the philosophy of religion or any particular philosophical domain, Owens allows that a non-Christian as well as a Christian "philosophy of religion can deal with divinely revealed doctrines as objects" (*Cognition*, 330). Christian philosophy, however, is "a discipline radically and drastically different from sacred theology" because it strictly forbids "any recourse to divinely revealed premises" (*Towards a Christian Philosophy*, ix). But how can a philosophy take a "revealed doctrine" as an *object* for its consideration without thereby becoming a theology whose principles depend on supernatural faith? A phenomenology of religion could, of course, bracket any strictly rational effort to establish the truth of a revealed doctrine and concentrate solely on the "eidetic content" of the religious object enshrined in the doctrine. But precisely as a "general philosophy," Christian philosophy must have the rationally demonstrable truth of the revealed doctrine in view.

Within a Thomistic context, it would seem necessary for "Christian philosophy," however existentially, psychologically, morally, or historically indebted the Christian philosopher is to the Christian faith, to hold steadfastly and clearly to the distinction between (1) doctrines that are "divinitus revelata" but are *only* "divino lumine cognoscibilia"; and (2) doctrines that are "divinitus revelata" but can *also* be known "ex naturali lumine rationis humanae." The formal object of *theology* covers both (1) and (2) inasmuch as both kinds of revealed doctrines are precisely being considered as "divinitus revelabilia": ". . . omnia quaecumque sunt divinitus revelabilia, communicant in una ratione formali obiecti huius scientiae. Et ideo comprehenduntur sub sacra doctrina sicut sub scientia una" (*ST*, I, q. 1, a. 3). But philosophy, lest it be natural water changed covertly into the supernatural wine of

Hence it is necessary that man have knowledge of something that exceeds his natural reason, which knowledge is given to man through the grace of faith. *(III Sent.,* d. 24, q. 1, a. 3, q. 3, sol. 1 [Moos, n. 81, p. 773])[36]

The Thomist solution, however, is to return, or apparently to return, to Aristotle. In place of an avowedly supernatural end, Thomist moral philosophers unhesitatingly label a quasi-Aristotelian end, the intellectual contemplation of God in this life (and, they quickly add, in the immortal life to come) as "the ultimate natural end of man." But the notion of the ultimate natural end of human life, especially since this notion is allegedly lifted from Aquinas's theology, is itself highly problematic. Solely by its own natural powers, reason cannot attain what Thomist philosophers take to be the ultimate human good: that "reason be perfected in the knowledge of the truth."[37] Aquinas proves that the this-worldly life of philosophical contemplation, and any natural contemplation of God that can be allowed an immortal or separate intellectual substance, is not, in fact, "perfect," because it does not terminate in "seeing God" and hence does not bring ultimate beatitude.[38] This is not to deny that Aquinas allows that some men, though

---

theology (cf. Owens, *Towards a Christian Philosophy,* 45–47), may properly take as its "object" only doctrines whose propositions fall into the second category; in considering *these* revealed docrines, it is considering the same *material* object as theology. But in their precise philosophical consideration, these revealed doctrines are taken solely as "cognoscibilia lumine naturalis ratione," and thus they constitute a different *formal* object from the same doctrines considered theologically. Revealed doctrines can fall as formal objects under the purview of philosophy if and only if there is some "intrinsic evidence offered for their truth" (Owens, *Towards a Christian Philosophy,* 41).

36. "Quia enim homini Deus providit finem qui est supra naturam hominis, scilicet plenam participationem suae beatitudinis; oportet autem eum qui in finem tendit, si libero arbitrio agat, cognoscere finem ex cujus consideratione dirigitur in his quae sunt ad finem; ideo oportuit ut homo alicujus rei cognitionem haberet quae rationem naturalem ejus excedit: quae quidem cognitio homini per gratiam fidei datur" *(III Sent.,* d. 24, q. 1, a. 3, q. 3, sol. 1 [Moos, n. 81, p. 773]).

37. See *De virt.,* q. 1, a. 9 (Odetto, 731): "Nam bonum hominis in quantum est homo, est ut ratio sit perfecta in cognitione veritatis, et inferiores appetitus regulentur secundum regulam rationis: nam homo habet quod sit homo per hoc quod sit rationalis."

38. Cf. *Q. de an.,* q. 17, ad 8 (Robb, 231): ". . . felicitas ultima hominis non constitit in cognitione alicujus creaturae, sed solum in cognitione Dei"; ad 10 (232): ". . . animae separatae licet competat ille modus cognosendi quo ea quae sunt notiora simpliciter magis cognoscit, non tamen sequitur quod haec anima separata vel quaecumque alia substantia separata creata per sua naturalia divinam essentiam possit intueri"; *ST,* q. 64, a. 1, ad 1: ". . . perfecta eius felicitas sit in cognoscendo primam substantiam, scilicet Deum"; ad 2: "Unde nec ipse angelus secundum suam naturam, potest cognoscere Dei substantiam."

perhaps not many, are able to achieve the conditional or imperfect happiness that is proportionate to human nature.[39] But because man's attainable natural happiness is necessarily imperfect, it cannot fulfill man's desire for happiness; it is not, in the equivalent sense, "ultimate." Is it not, therefore, more in line with Aquinas's own argument, especially as developed in the third book of the *Summa contra gentiles*, to ask whether man has an ultimate natural end? In any case, traditional Thomists, inasmuch as they minimize the paradox of man's natural unfulfillment, neglect this question.[40]

Here, then, is the dilemma facing those who would advocate an autonomous "Thomistic philosophical ethics": one can have either a Thomist theology illegitimately calling itself a moral philosophy or one can have a Thomist moral philosophy, purportedly derived from Aquinas, that is no longer authentically Thomistic because it cannot incorporate the only ultimate end of human action recognized by Aquinas. Now, there are contemporary examples, easy enough to find, that show how an extracted and autonomously reconstructed "Thomistic philosophical ethics" inevitably gets impaled on one or the other of the horns of this dilemma. I shall consider only the two most important examples found among twentieth-century Thomists, Jacques Maritain and Santiago Ramírez, O.P.

2. *Jacques Maritain: "Moral Philosophy Adequately Considered"*

Among contemporary Thomists, Jacques Maritain devoted singular attention to what he called "moral philosophy adequately considered."[41] Moral philosophy is "adequate" when it is exists as a science *sub-*

---

39. See *De virt.*, q. 1, a. 10, ad 1 (Odetto, 736): ". . . ita ad quantum ad perfectionem finis, dupliciter homo potest esse perfectus: uno modo secundum capacitatem suae naturae, alio modo secundum quamdam supernaturalem perfectionem: et sic dicitur homo perfectus esse simpliciter; primo autem modo secundo quid."

40. Cf. Umberto Galeazzi, *L'etica filosofica in Tommas d'Aquino: dalla Summa contra gentiles alla Summa theologiae: Per una riscoperta dei fondamenti della morale* (Rome: Città Nuova Editrice, 1990), 144–48 who does recognize (contra Kluxen and Melina) that a "Thomistic philosophical ethics" cannot be legitimately confined to "l'ambito" of "la felicità imperfetta della vita presente" (147). But, this recognition leads to no further questions about the paradoxical consequences of explicitly incorporating into a philosophical ethics the Thomistic *desiderium naturale* for seeing God. Hence, Galeazzi again presents one more *florilegium* of texts which supposedly comprise Aquinas's philosophical ethics.

41. See Jacques Maritain, *Science and Wisdom*, trans. Bernard Wall (London: Geoffrey Bles, 1940); *An Essay on Christian Philosophy*, trans. Edward H. Flannery (New York: Philosophical Library, 1955).

alternated to theology,[42] that is, when it borrows from theology at least two revealed propositions that *complement* the indemonstrable principles of practical reason: (1) that man has a supernatural end; and (2) that man's existential state is fallen and sinful. Without utilizing these two additional theological principles, moral philosophy "could not validly judge"[43] human actions and their true orientation. Maritain acknowledges, however, that Aquinas himself never developed, as so defined, an adequate moral philosophy; Aquinas's own ethics is purely theological.[44] The task of developing an adequate moral philosophy has fallen to Maritain.

"Moral philosophy adequately considered" presupposes a moral reason "enlightened and completed by faith."[45] But Maritain contends that while this moral philosophy is "indispensably Christian,"[46] it remains a philosophical science distinct from revealed theology. Sciences are distinguished by reference to their proper formal objects. The formal object of "moral philosophy adequately considered," although it is a science subalternated to theology, is different from the formal object of theology. In explaining how they differ, Maritain uses the terminology of Cajetan and John of St. Thomas.

Accordingly, Maritain distinguishes two different senses of "formal object": (1) the "what" of the object = *ratio formalis quae* = *ratio formalis objecti ut res*; and (2) how the object is known = *ratio formalis sub qua* = *ratio formalis objecti ut objectum*.[47] Theology and "moral philosophy adequately considered," since they are both moral sciences, cover the same domain. Both are focused on (1) the same formal object considered merely as a thing: human actions as directed to the ultimate end of human life, the supernatural vision of God. But in considering human actions precisely as an object of knowledge, theology and "moral philosophy adequately considered" take different cognitive perspectives and thus each science has a different formal object (2). Theology knows

42. Maritain follows Cajetan's explanation of subalternation: "The conclusions of a subalternating science are evident in and through their principles immediately and without the intermediary of another habitus; those of the subalternated sciences are evident in and through principles mediately, or through the intermediary of the subalternating scientific habitus" *(ST,* I, q. 1, a. 2; *Commentaria Card. Caietani,* n. II [Leonine ed., IV, 9; as translated in *Essay in Christian Philosophy,* 83]).

43. Maritain, *Science and Wisdom,* 182.

44. See Jacques Maritain, *Moral Philosophy: An Historical and Critical Survey of the Great Systems* (London: Geoffrey Bles, 1964), ix–x, and *Science and Wisdom,* 160–61.

45. Maritain, *Science and Wisdom,* 203.

46. Ibid., 112.

47. See ibid., 178, n. 2. Cf. *Essay on Christian Philosophy,* 70–71, 79.

human action under the light and from the standpoint of revelation, that is, *sub ratione Dei.* "Moral philosophy adequately considered" knows "human conduct . . . *inasmuch as* even in its most supernatural character and moments it is human and created action"[48] capable of being regulated by reason.

Maritain frames his conception of "moral philosophy adequately considered" in terms of the Scholastic doctrine of the logical subalternation of sciences. The fact that "moral philosophy adequately considered" is subalternated to theology justifies its own supposedly *philosophical* use of two revealed principles. Let us recall that an inferior or subalternated science receives its principles from a superior or subalternating science which, in turn, demonstrates those propositions by deducing them from prior, indemonstrable or immediate *(per se nota)* principles. Thus a subalternated science assumes, as its principles, the *conclusions* of a superior science.

The inferior sciences, which are subalternated to the superior [sciences], are not derived from immediate principles, but suppose the conclusions proven in the superior sciences, and use them [these conclusions] for principles which in truth are not immediate principles, but [these conclusions] are proven in the superior sciences through immediate principles. *(I Sent.,* prologus, q. 1, a. 3, q. 3, sol. 2 [Mandonnet, 13])[49]

Using this model, Aquinas holds that theology is a human science subalternated to divine science. The principles of theology are the articles of faith from which the theologian reasons to further conclusions.[50] However, the articles of faith are themselves like revealed conclusions derived from divine science, that is, from the knowledge possessed by God and the blessed. Given its epistemic source (divine knowledge), there is an important difference between a hierarchy of subalternated theological sciences and a hierarchy of subalternated philosophical sciences. Theology, as a work of deductive reason, is a human science.[51] But theology is not "epistemically continuous" with the subalternating divine science that is both the peak and the ground

---

48. *Essay on Christian Philosophy,* 80.

49. "Inferiores autem scientiae, quae superioribus subalternantur, non sunt ex principiis per se notis, sed supponunt conclusiones probatas in superioribus scientiis, et eis utuntur pro principiis quae in veritate non sunt principia per se nota, sed in superioribus scientiis per principia per se nota probantur . . ." *(I Sent.,* prologus, q. 1, a. 3, q. 3, sol. 2 [Mandonnet, 13]).

50. See *ST,* I, q. 1, a. 7: ". . . ex principiis huius scientiae, quae sunt articuli fidei. . . ."

51. See *De ver.,* q. 14, a. 9, ad 3 (Spiazzi, 298): "Et sic fidelis potest dici habere scientiam de his quae concluduntur ex articulis fidei."

of the hierarchy.[52] Whereas the philosopher is able to reduce the principles (i.e., conclusions) taken from the subalternating science to immediate *(per se nota)* propositions, the theologian cannot reduce the revealed principles of his subalternated human science, the articles of faith, to the immediate principles of the higher or subalternating divine science.

> If there were some science which is not able to be reduced to naturally known principles, it would not be of the same species as the other sciences, nor would it be univocally called a science. *(III Sent.,* d. 33, q. 1, a. 2, sol. 4 [Moos, n. 74, p. 1031])[53]

As Aquinas signals, the notions of "science" and "subalternation" as applied to a theological hierarchy of sciences are analogous. Perhaps with less caution than is called for, Maritain further complicates the notion of a theological hierarchy of subalternated sciences by appending to it "moral philosophy adequately considered." But like the theology from which it receives its principles, "moral philosophy adequately considered" can only be a subalternate science in an analogous sense. Theology is subalternated to the divine science in which the theologian believes. Hence, a "moral philosophy adequately considered" that is subalternated to theology must also be subalternated, via the supernaturally revealed principles received from theology, to the divine science in which the theologian *believes.*

Maritain, however, resists and obfuscates what otherwise seems to be the clear logical requirement of resolving "moral philosophy adequately considered" into supernatural faith. He proposes that "moral philosophy adequately considered" should accept the two relevant principles from theology as "simply data offered to it in the same manner as the mathematical or empiriological truths it has occasion to use."[54] Put more stringently, these two borrowed theological truths must be received merely as *hypotheses;* otherwise nothing would stand logically in the way of resolving "moral philosophy adequately considered," via its subalternation to revealed theology, into the science of the blessed. But to make this resolution, Maritain admits, would be to identify "moral philosophy adequately considered" as

---

52. Cf. *De ver.,* q. 14, a. 9, ad 3 (Spiazzi, 298): ". . . ille qui habet scientiam subalternatam, non perfecte attingit ad rationem sciendi, nisi in quantum eius cognitio continuatur quodammodo cum cognitione eius qui habet scientiam subalternantem."

53. "Si autem esset aliqua scientia quae non posset reduci ad principia naturaliter cognita, non esset ejusdem specie cum aliis scientiis, nec univoce scientia dicitur" *(III Sent.,* d. 33, q. 1, a. 2, sol. 4 [Moos, n. 74, p. 1031]).

54. Maritain, *Essay on Christian Philosophy,* 87.

really a theology. Yet, what Maritain does not admit, *not* to make this resolution undermines the alleged logical subalternation of "moral philosophy adequately considered" to theology.[55] Instead, to avoid compromising the philosophical status of his subalternated moral science, Maritain "relinquishes" to the theologian the task of resolving the principles of "moral philosophy adequately considered" into divine science.[56] But this relinquishment seems merely an arbitrary rather than a logically necessitated division of labor since Maritain admits that the two principles that the moral philosopher takes from the theologian "can themselves be resolved in revealed principles."[57]

Maritain observes that, in the Thomist tradition, theology has a supernatural object but is considered to be a naturally acquired science. He argues, by analogy, that "moral philosophy adequately considered," though it accepts from theology a supernatural truth about man's ultimate end, also remains a natural science. But what is the logical relevance of this analogy? Whether in theology or in philosophy, deductive reasoning is certainly a natural activity; any science that results from such activity results from the exercise of a natural cognitive habit. But this does not remove the supernatural foundation of theology. Theology, whether or not it is considered a "natural science," remains grounded in supernatural beliefs.[58] Similarly, the natural scientific character of "moral philosophy adequately considered" does not alter its status as a science subalternated to theology. Hence, it too remains grounded, via theology, in certain supernatural beliefs.[59] Maritain, however, minimizes the epistemic significance of this ground; he acknowledges only that "moral philosophy adequately considered" is "mediately or indirectly attached to a supernatural root."[60]

55. Cf. Joannis a Sancto Thoma, *Cursus theologici, In primae partis,* disp. 2, a. 5 (Solesmes Edition, 1: § 4, p. 363): "[Subalternatio] ex parte principiorum, quando principia unius scientiae non possunt esse immediate per se nota, sed manifestantur per lumen superioris scientiae; et ita scientia inferior non resolvit immediate in principia per se nota, scientia vero superior sic. Et in hoc consistit essentialis et praecipua ratio subalternationis. . . ."

56. See Maritain, *Essay on Christian Philosophy,* 87–88.

57. Ibid., 89.

58. See *I Sent.,* prooemium, q. 1, a. 3c, ad 1 (Busa, 3b): "Habitus autem istorum principiorum, scilicet articulorum, dicitur fides et non intellectus, quia ista principia supra rationem sunt. . . ."

59. Cf. *III Sent.,* d. 24, q. 1, a. 2b, ad 3 (Busa, 348c): "Unde fides nostra ita se habet ad rationem divinam qua deus cognoscit, sicut se habet fides illius qui supponit principia subalternatae scientiae ad scientiam subalternantem, quae per propriam rationem illa probavit."

60. Maritain, *Essay on Christian Philosophy,* 90.

Nonetheless, the fact that "moral philosophy adequately considered" is a natural science rooted (even mediately) in supernatural faith, confirms that it is isomorphic with theology. Moreover, how *mediately* is this moral philosophy attached to its "supernatural root"? Like theology, the grounding principle of "moral philosophy adequately considered," that the actual end of man is the beatific vision, is a supernatural truth that can be originally received *only* from revelation and intellectually assented to *only* because there has been a divine infusion of faith in the intellect and charity in the will of the one receiving it.[61] Of course, nonbelievers as well as believers can reason using the *propositions* that enshrine the supernatural belief. This is just an exercise in "natural reasoning" from premises to conclusion. But only the believer can reason about the thing that is the *object* of these propositions.[62] Still, even in the reasoning of the believer the supernatural object can never become, as Maritain inadvertently but revealingly puts it, "an object of knowledge" in itself.[63]

Maritain, however, usually states his case very carefully: "[T]he theological truths received by moral philosophy "adequately considered" present themselves to the non-believing philosopher as superior hypotheses from which one starts to work."[64] But Maritain's assertion, although precisely nuanced, is utterly implausible as applied to the nonbelieving philosopher. If one happens to believe that theology is in possession of revealed truth, it is naturally reasonable for such a person "to trust theology" about the supernatural character of the actual human order.[65] Now nonbelievers can certainly concede, but only so that they can explicitly disavow for themselves, the role that theology has for believers. But what nonbelieving philosopher has ever granted that theological principles are "data" or "superior hypotheses"

---

61. See *ST*, II–II, q. 1, a. 6, ad 1: ". . . fides principaliter est de his quae videnda speramus in patria . . ."; q. 2, a. 3: ". . . ultima beatitudo hominis consistit in quadam supernaturali Dei visione. Ad quam quidem visionem homo pertingere non potest nisi per modum addiscentis a Deo doctore . . ."; ad 2: ". . . per lumen fidei divinitus infusum homini homo assentit his quae sunt fidei . . ."; a. 5: ". . . fidei obiectum per se est id per quod homo beatus efficitur . . ."; *De ver.*, q. 14, a. 6 (Spiazzi, 292): ". . . credere dependeat ex intellectu et voluntate . . . non potest esse talis actus perfectus, nisi et voluntas sit perfecta per caritatem, et intellectus per fidem."

62. Cf. *ST*, II–II, q. 1, a. 2: "Actus autem credentis non terminatur ad enuntiabile, sed ad rem: non enim formamus enuntiabilia nisi ut per ea de rebus cognitionem habeamus, sicut in scientia ita et in fide."

63. Cf. Maritain, *Science and Wisdom*, 234.

64. Ibid., 197.

65. See ibid., 196.

for philosophy? Lacking infused supernatural faith, the nonbelieving philosopher has no reason to think that theology can certify such hypotheses, much less a compelling reason to accept them as starting points for his own thinking.[66] Aquinas concludes that miracles and persuasive arguments on behalf of revealed truths are *never* of themselves sufficient to move people to believe; the Gospels recount that many saw and heard but did not believe.[67] What reason, then, does the nonbelieving philosopher have for thinking that any theological "hypothesis" will actually perfect his naturally known moral principles?

In fact, Maritain's notion of moral hypotheses, which the philosopher supposedly receives from the subalternating science of theology, is logically incoherent. It requires that the nonbelieving moral philosopher somehow has a strictly natural belief or intellectual confidence in certain revealed theological truths. Maritain benignly urges the nonbelieving philosopher to "put trust in the truths of theology."[68] But one may rationally take some information "on trust" if it is rational to believe that the information is truthful. A natural belief, however, is equivalent to a strongly held opinion.[69] But even strong opinions are "falsifiable" by human reason;[70] what is naturally believed (as distinguished from what is supernaturally believed) to be true could be otherwise.[71] A rational natural belief, in other words, rests on nondefinitive reasons leading one to assent conditionally to the contingent proposition enshrining the belief.[72] But Maritain's two theological

---

66. Cf. *De ver.*, q. 14, a. 8 (Spiazzi, 295): ". . . fides . . . faciat intellectum hominis adhaerere veritati quae in divina cognitione consistit, transcendendo proprii intellectus veritatem."

67. See *ST*, II–II, q. 6, a. 1: ". . . ad assensum hominis in ea quae sunt fidei, potest considerari duplex causa. Una quidem exterius inducens: sicut miraculum visum, vel persuasio hominis inducentis ad fidem. Quorum neutrum est sufficientis causa."

68. Maritain, *Science and Wisdom*, 187. Cf. ibid., 237: ". . . this object [the supernatural last end and the state of fallen redeemed nature] is received from theology by moral philosophy adequately considered–not as theologically *known* but as *taken on trust* by the subalternated science."

69. See *SLA*, II, c. 29, 428a22, 165–67 (*In de An.*, III, lect. 5 [Pirotta, n. 650, p. 159]): ". . . ad omnem opinionem consequitur fides, quia unusquisque credit illud quod opinatur . . ."; *III Sent.*, d. 23, q. 3, a. 4c (Busa, 347a): "Fides proprie dicitur ex hoc quod aliquis assentit eis quae non videt . . . Uno modo secundum quod homo inducitur per rationem humanam: et sic dicitur fides opinio vehemens."

70. See *ST*, I–II, q. 55, a. 4: ". . . opinio se habet ad verum et ad falsum. . . ."

71. See *ELP*, I, 44, 88b32, 35–38 (Leonine ed., I, pt. 2, 167a); *ST*, II–II, q. 4, a. 8.

72. See *SLA*, II, c. 29, 428a1, 53–54 (*In de An.*, III, lect. 5 [Pirotta, n. 639, p. 158]): ". . . opinio autem pro cognitione eorum de quibus certum iudicium non habemus . . ."; *I Sent.*, prooemium, q. 1, a. 3c, ad 1 (Busa, 3b): ". . . de fide acquisita, quae est opinio fortificata rationibus"; *III Sent.*, d. 23, q. 2, a. 2a, co. (Busa, 343a): "Opinans autem habet cognitionem sine assensu perfecto; sed habet aliquid assen-

"hypotheses" about man's supernatural end and sinful condition are revealed propositions whose truth, by definition, can never be proved or disproved by strictly rational arguments. Their status is such that they cannot be logically falsified by any evidence rationally available. Hence, it is logically illegitimate for even a believing philosopher to regard such propositions as appropriate objects of *natural* belief.

Maritain, however, claims that "moral philosophy adequately conceived" is a unique case among subalternated sciences because it receives its two theological principles only as *complements* to its own naturally known first principles. This claim, however, twists the traditional notion of subalternation: the subalternated science takes its proper principles from the subalternating science.[73] Moreover, it seems incomprehensible how the principle setting forth man's true supernatural end could be considered merely a "complement" when, as Maritain himself acknowledges, it is the *"first principle"* of the whole science of "moral philosophy adequately considered."[74]

Critics, notably the trenchant Santiago Ramírez, O.P.,[75] argued that Maritain's notion of "moral philosophy adequately considered" is "unintelligible . . . and unacceptable as philosophy."[76] The complaint is justified: the philosophical status of Maritain's moral philosophy cannot be established by appealing to the notion of subalternation as it applies to an epistemically continuous hierarchy of strictly rational sciences. For the nonbeliever, however, there is no theology that could function as a normatively superior or subalternating science in any *philosophical* hierarchy of the sciences. Only a believer, holding first to the truths of faith and then acknowledging theology's preeminent status in manifesting those truths, can construct a hierarchy of sciences in which a moral science borrows its principles from theology.

---

sus, inquantum adhaeret uni magis quam alii"; d. 33, q. 2, a. 4, sol. 1, ad 2 (Moos, n. 20, p. 737): ". . . ratio quae inclinat voluntatem ad credendum alia, est vel aliquod signum fallibile vel dictum alicujus scientis qui et falli et fallere potest."

73. See *ST,* I, q. 1, a. 1: the subalternated sciences "procedunt ex principiis notis lumine superioris scientiae: sicut perspectiva procedit ex principiis notificatis per geometriam, et musica ex principiis per arithmeticam notis." Cf. *Expos. de Trin.*, q. 2, a. 2, ad 5 (Decker, 7–9, 89): ". . . in scientiis subalternatis supponuntur et creduntur aliqua a scientiis superioribus. . . ."

74. Cf. Maritain, *Science and Wisdom*, 158: ". . . if philosophical ethics is a science . . . it must relate its conclusions to that which stabilises moral knowledge scientifically, as its first principle, that is, to the last end of man."

75. See J.-M. Ramírez, O.P., review of *Distinguer pour unir ou Les degrés du savoir*, by Jacques Maritain, *Bulletin thomiste* 4 (1934–36): 423–32; "De philosophia morali Christiani," *Divus Thomas* 14 (1936): 87–204.

76. Ramírez, review of *Distinguer pour unir*, 432.

Only a believer holds that man has a supernatural end and is wounded by sin.[77] Maritain admits as much: "The philosopher who believes knows by faith that the proper object of moral philosophy involves conditions known to theology but not known to philosophy in its own right."[78]

One can defend, of course, the legitimacy of a philosophy inspired by religious faith. But by what right can one label a moral science "philosophy" if its principles can be held only on faith? The doctrine of man's supernatural end is one of the articles of faith that grounds theology.[79] Despite Maritain's disclaimers, the same doctrine also functions as the proper grounding principle and not as a mere complement of "moral philosophy adequately considered." A moral science that is grounded on a theological principle about man's supernatural end is no less theological.[80]

There is, however, a reason, internal to theology itself, for rejecting Maritain's conception of "moral philosophy adequately considered." Maritain's two points of view, by which he means to distinguish the formal object *(ratio formalis sub qua)* of his subalternated moral philosophy from the formal object of theology, actually merge. Supposedly theology considers man's supernatural end "from the standpoint of the sharing of intimate life with God"; "moral philosophy adequately considered" regards the same end "from the point of view of the completion it brings to human nature."[81] But, remarkably enough, Maritain acknowledges that Thomistic theology also regards man's supernatural end from this latter—allegedly philosophical—point of view.[82] What

77. Cf. *ST*, II–II, q. 2, a. 5: ". . . fidei obiectum per se est id per quod homo beatus efficitur. . . ."
78. Maritain, *Science and Wisdom*, 196–97.
79. By Thomistic criteria, a subordinated or subalternated science only takes the conclusions not the principles of the superior or subalternating science. But "moral philosophy adequately considered" actually borrows two articles of faith (i.e., two principles) from theology. Maritain, who knows that theological demonstrations sometimes reason to "conclusions" that are actually articles of faith, admits that he is extending the usual notion of subalternation. But this admission is besides the point. A science that depends on theological conclusions derived from the articles of faith (whether or not these "conclusions" are also principles or articles of faith) is no less theological.
80. Cf. *De ver.*, q. 14, a. 3 (Spiazzi, 287): "Sed theologus considerat quasi bonum ultimum id quod est naturae facultatem excedens, scilicet vitam aeternam. . . ."
81. Maritain, *Science and Wisdom*, 118. The *ratio formalis sub qua* of "moral philosophy adequately considered" is variously described: man's elevation to the supernatural order "from the point of view of our temporal existence . . . [or] civil life . . . [or] the order of culture." (Ibid., 185)
82. See Maritain, *Essay on Christian Philosophy*, 96–97, 107–8, n. 54, 108.

need, then, does Thomistic moral science have of "moral philosophy adequately considered"?

Maritain allows the theologian (specifically Aquinas) to gather anew "the most essential findings on human nature which moral philosophy itself had reaped."[83] By "gathering anew," Maritain means, apparently, that theologians subsume what moral philosophers have already discovered. But this description, when applied to Thomistic theology, is historically and systematically untenable. The Thomistic theological conception of man's ultimate end incorporates a rational anthropology and "a metaphysics of action," but neither can be substantively attributed to any previous philosopher. In short, Thomistic theology from its own perspective already assumes what is supposed to be the distinctive standpoint of Maritain's "moral philosophy adequately considered," but there is no doubt that Thomistic moral science remains theology in doing so. So too a contemporary theology, more directly focused than Thomistic theology on the historical and sociological dimensions of man's existence, need not forfeit its theological status because it highlights these existential dimensions of human life and action.

The distinction between a subalternated "moral philosophy adequately considered" and moral theology, if it is proposed as in any way relevant for a contemporary philosophy, must be able to encompass the practices of contemporary theology. But several generations of contemporary theologians have erased the faint line that Maritain drew between the formal objects of theology and "moral philosophy adequately considered." What Maritain describes as a consequence of moral philosophy's distinct formal object, its orientation to "natural and terrestrial evidence,"[84] is, indeed, a point of view but one that now serves to distinguish Scholastic from contemporary *theology*. Scholastic theology looks at action metaphysically—not historically, or psychologically, or sociologically—whereas contemporary theology, without thereby ceasing to be a theology under the aegis of revealed doctrine, has eagerly incorporated the latter "terrestrial" dimensions into its supernatural perspective on human action.

What, finally, is the epistemic status of Maritain's "moral philosophy adequately considered"? To claim that we can know a formal object that is supernatural (human actions directed to the supernatural end of man) without thereby assuming "the formal viewpoint of revelation" is unsustainable not only for the nonbelieving philosopher but also for the believing theologian. For both, the distinction between the

83. Ibid., 97.
84. Ibid., 88.

formal objects of moral theology and "moral philosophy adequately considered" proves to be a distinction without a difference. Simply put, no philosophy can claim any knowledge of man's true supernatural end. And theology, if one follows Aquinas's example, is fully able to explore the strictly rational dimensions of action from its own viewpoint, as falling under its formal object, "omnia quaecumque sunt divinitus revelabilia" *(ST,* I, q. 1, a. 3).[85]

Despite his erudite and subtle responses, Maritain was never able to satisfy his original critics.[86] Indeed, those critics rightly denied that moral philosophy could be a science logically subalternated to theology and yet remain philosophy. Maritain's efforts to prove otherwise must be judged a failure. His arguments on behalf of a "moral philosophy adequately considered" fail for reasons that are both internal and external to Maritain's Scholasticism. There is no way to keep separate the formal objects of moral theology and "moral philosophy adequately considered." A moral science subalternated to theology only fits into a theological hierarchy of sciences that is ultimately grounded in divine science. And this hierarchy cannot be constructed from solely philosophical principles.[87]

How, then, should we label Maritain's "moral philosophy adequately considered"? Maritain admits that "moral philosophy adequately considered" is "no longer a work of pure philosophy."[88] But if it can in anywise be legitimately called a "philosophy," "moral philosophy adequately considered" should only be labeled a philosophy *within,* not

---

85. Human actions fall under the "una ratio formalis" *(ST,* I, q. 1, a. 3) of Thomistic theology because man, who is "suorum operum principium, quasi liberum arbitrium habens et suorum operum potestatem" (I–II, prologus), is the image of God. This exploration is rational but theological: it looks at human actions as constituting the "motu[s] rationalis creaturae in Deum" (I, q. 2, prologus). Human actions are viewed "sub ratione Dei" (q. 1, a. 7) precisely as God and human actions "sunt divino lumine cognoscibilia" (a. 5).

86. See German Marquinez Argote, *El "si" y el "no" de la filosofía moral christiana: Exposicion y critica de una teoria de Jacques Maritain* (Madrid: Ediciones Studium, 1964).

87. Cf. Maritian, *Science and Wisdom,* 191: ". . . faith brings the reason of the philosopher to acknowledge the value and necessity—so far as a given object the reason is considering is concerned—of the data of a transcendent science such as theology, to which henceforth the science of the philosopher will be subalternated." But to what *"necessity"* is Maritain referring: logical necessity? Presumably not, since reason can never grasp the logical necessity of what per se belongs to supernatural faith: ". . . rationes quae inducuntur ad auctoritatem fidei non sunt demonstrationes quae in visionem intelligibilem intellectum humanum reducere possunt. Et ideo non desinunt esse non apparentia" *(ST,* II–II, q. 2, a. 10, ad 2).

88. Maritain, *Science and Wisdom,* 191.

below, a theology, that is, a philosophy without a distinct or subalternated status. But, just for that reason, it would be more accurate to call Maritain's ambiguous subalternated moral science what it truly is: a moral theology, grounded in infused supernatural faith, that has been illegitimately separated, unlike its Thomistic antecedent, from its native theological whole.

3. Santiago M. Ramírez, O.P.

Ramírez, whose five-volume commentary on *ST,* I–II, qq. 1–5, *De hominis beatitudine,* is a monumental, twentieth-century addition to the genre of classic Thomist commentaries, rightly insists that Aquinas's moral doctrine is, from start to finish, a *theology* that focuses "only on supernatural beatitude."[89] Ramírez, moreover, accurately contrasts Aquinas's point of view with that of the seventeenth-century Thomist theologian Petrus de Godoy, O.P., who divides his *Disputationes* on the *Prima secundae* into two separate tracts, the first devoted to supernatural beatitude, the second to natural beatitude.[90] But, as Ramírez takes care to note,[91] *ST,* I–II, q. 1, which establishes that man acts for an ultimate end, does not explicitly distinguish man's natural and supernatural ends.

Petrus de Godoy, however, justifies his division of the *Disputationes* into two tracts by arguing that natural beatitude is both a possibility if one considers man in a hypothetical state of pure nature, and, more significantly, an actual end that remains even if one supposes the elevation of man to a supernatural end.[92] And Ramírez, despite his awareness that Petrus de Godoy deviates from Aquinas, follows suit; he too proceeds to impose the distinction between supernatural and natural beatitude on the whole Thomistic discussion of beatitude.[93] Ramírez does so advertently and for three reasons: (1) in order to enter into the philosophical discussion of the problem; (2) so as not to conflate *natu-*

89. See Ramirez, *De hominis beatitudine,* 3: 1, prolegomenum 2, c. 23, n. 198, p. 138: "Sed S. Thomas . . . noluit separatim agere in theologia Sacra de beatitudine hominis naturali et supernaturali, sed *de una beatitudine supernaturali tantum.* . . ."

90. See Petrus de Godoy, O.P., *Disputationes theologicae: In primam partem divi Thomae* (Venice: 1696): Vol. 1: Tractatus 1, *De beatitudine supernaturali;* Tractatus 2, *De beatitudine naturali.*

91. See Ramirez, *De hominis beatitudine,* 3: 1, prolegomenum 2, n. 201, p. 139.

92. Natural beatitude, or that beatitude which is possible solely through man's natural powers, is "the most perfect knowledge and love of God, as He is the Author of Nature" (*Disputationes theologicae,* Vol. 1, Tract. 2, n. 5, p. 55).

93. See Ramirez, *De hominis beatitudine,* 3: 2, introductio, c. 2, n. 50, pp. 63–64.

ral objective/material beatitude (God as prime mover) and *supernatural objective/material beatitude* (God as divine Trinity); and (3) to distinguish sharply, in regard to man's *subjective/formal* appropriation of objective beatitude: (a) possessing the natural knowledge of God (= *natural formal beatitude)* from (b) possessing the supernatural knowledge of God (= *supernatural formal beatitude).*[94]

Ramírez admits that the explicit and developed distinction between supernatural and natural beatitude is not, in fact, the axis of Aquinas's discussion of beatitude. But he regards this mainstay of modern theology as a scientific advance. Ramírez therefore proposes to develop what he takes to be the Thomistic conception of natural beatitude. But Ramírez acknowledges that Aquinas did not develop an autonomous moral philosophy and cautions that we cannot know how Aquinas himself might have structured such a philosophy; we know only that it would have an "essentially distinct structure"[95] from his theology.

Among contemporary Thomists, Ramírez's detailed knowledge of Aquinas's texts was extraordinary. Nonetheless, the pressing issue of modern theology overrode his cautionary observations about the development of a Thomistic moral philosophy. Ramírez elaborated a philosophical theory of beatitude that revolves around the distinction between natural and supernatural knowledge of God. On the strength of this distinction, which he used as the universal hermeneutical key to unlocking Thomistic moral science, Ramírez extracted the philosophical ethics that he thought to be *implicitly* contained in Aquinas's theology.[96]

According to Ramírez, *ST*, I–II, q. 1, which Aquinas says is a treatment of the ultimate end "in general,"[97] is an analysis of man's *natural end* because none of its arguments "transcend[s] the limits of natural reason."[98] Ramírez's argument is cogent only if theology can be exclu-

---

94. For the meaning of these terminological distinctions, see Ramirez, *De hominis beatitudine,* 3: 2, introductio, c. 1, n. 20, p. 27: "But the theologians, who properly speak of supernatural beatitude, explicitly distinguish *objective* or *material* beatitude, which is the thing or beatifying object, and *subjective* or *formal* beatitude, which is the attainment or possession of objective beatitude." Aquinas, however, does not use these tags; he refers to the *"res quae est finis."* See *IV Sent.,* d. 49, q. 1, a. 2, sol. 1; *ST,* I–II, q. 3, a. 1. Cf. Guindon, *Beatitude et théologie morale,* 259.

95. See Ramírez, "De philosophia morali Christiana," 86.

96. See Ramírez, *De hominis beatitudine,* 3: 1, proloquium, n. 236, pp. 222–23.

97. See *ST,* I–II, q. 1, prologus: ". . . oportet primo considerare de ultimo fine in communi. . . ."

98. Ramirez, *De hominis beatitudine,* 3: 1, proloquium, n. 224, p. 217. The other reason Ramírez gives to justify his interpretation is that if *ST,* I–II, q. 1 were

sively identified with faith and philosophy with reason.[99] But Aquinas, we have seen, does not make this identification. Nonetheless, if *ST*, I–II, q. 1 is viewed in this fashion, it then seems to look like Aquinas's quasi-philosophical[100] preamble to a strictly theological discussion of supernatural beatitude. But Ramírez, with a numbing capacity for repetitive arguments, goes far beyond Aquinas. He devotes hundreds of pages to spelling out the notion of man's ultimate, natural end. This extended consideration provides the ground for the autonomous moral philosophy that Ramírez regards as congruent with but distinguishable from Thomistic moral theology.

On what basis, however, can one rest the purported distinction between an autonomous Thomistic moral philosophy and Aquinas's "moral theology"? Ramírez appeals, like Maritain, to the standard Thomistic doctrine that sciences are diversified "according to the diverse orders that reason properly considers."[101] Yet it is not initially clear how, on this basis, moral theology and moral philosophy can be distinguished, since both sciences consider the same rational order: the order of human acts to their ultimate end.[102] In the Scholastic tradition, both moral philosophy and theology regard God as the ultimate end of human acts, and in both sciences God Himself is taken to be "objective beatitude." But in line with this tradition, Ramírez carefully explains that, while these two sciences take God to be the ultimate end of human acts, they assert this only in a material sense *(= ratio formal objecti ut res)*. Inasmuch as their concepts of God differ, philosophical ethics and theological ethics possess formally different conceptions of God and objective beatitude *(= ratio formalis objecti ut objectum)*.

Materially, the same objective thing—God alone—is man's true natural and supernatural beatitude. But formally, the thing is truly diverse, because the one and the same God, according to an essentially different

---

merely to abstract from the division between natural and supernatural ends, it might seem (falsely) that man's supernatural end is implicitly contained in his natural end.

99. See Ramirez, *De hominis beatitudine*, 3: 2, introductio, c. 2, n. 50, p. 63. Cf. my ch. 1, sec. 5.

100. "Quasi-philosophical" is my term. Ramirez, *De hominis beatitudine*, 3: 1, proloquium, n. 225, p. 218, says that *ST*, I–II, q. 1 "est elicitive philosophica, sed theologica imperative. . . . Haec ergo quaestio est praeambula ad articulum fidei. . . ."

101. *SLE*, I, 1, ante 1094a1, 26–27 *(In Ethic.*, I, lect. 1, [Spiazzi, n. 1, p. 3]): ". . . secundum hos diversos ordines quos proprie ratio considerat sunt diversae scientiae."

102. See *SLE*, I, 1, ante 1094a1, 40–43 *(In Ethic.*, I, lect. 1 [Spiazzi, n. 2, p. 3]); text quoted in n. 14 *supra*.

formal, objective concept, is the object of natural and supernatural human beatitude. *(De hominis beatitudine,* 3:2, introductio, n. 50, p. 63)[103]

Philosophical ethics orders human acts in terms of the strictly natural beatitude that comes from knowing God as the First Cause of nature. In a theological ethics, human acts are considered insofar as they are ordered to the supernatural beatitude that is consequent upon the gratuitously offered vision of the triune God Himself.

Because this beatitude is natural, namely, God as the author and end of nature, this order constitutes natural or philosophical morality; if, however, this beatitude is supernatural, that is God as He is God or as He is the author and end of grace, then such order formally constitutes supernatural or theological morality. *(De hominis beatitudine,* 3:1, prol. 1, c. 2, n. 76, p. 74)[104]

Supernatural beatitude, which results from the "light of glory" elevating the human mind, is the vision of the divine essence; natural beatitude—the metaphysical contemplation of the First Cause—is merely a *participation* in that vision by the natural light of the human intellect. The two beatitudes are objectively and formally diverse, and so too are the moral sciences that they respectively ground.

Ramírez grounds his moral philosophy on what he takes to be Aquinas's strictly rational consideration of man's natural beatitude; he attempts, in other words, to exploit the Thomistic doctrine of man's twofold end. How should one assess Ramírez's strategy? Certainly, the doctrine of man's twofold end is Thomistic; and, undoubtedly, Aquinas has a notion of man's (imperfect) natural beatitude. Nonetheless, Ramírez's interpretation of Aquinas, for all of its devoted erudition, has a questionable emphasis. It proceeds, admittedly under the influence of a modern theological preoccupation, by sharply and (it seems fair to say) rather mechanically distinguishing natural and supernatural beatitude, a distinction that does not structure Aquinas's extended analysis of human beatitude in either *Summa.*

Ramírez, however, first *presupposes* the notion of supernatural be-

---

103. "Est siquidem *materialiter* eadem res obiectiva verae beatitudinis humanae naturalis et supernaturalis, nempe solus Deus; at *formaliter* est valde diversa, cum sit essentialiter differens ratio formalis obiectiva secundum quam unus idemque Deus est obiectum beatitudinis naturalis et supernaturalis, hominis" (Ramirez, *De hominis beatitudine,* 3: 2, introductio, c. 2, n. 50, p. 63).

104. "Quod si haec beatitudo sit naturalis, nempe Deus ut est auctor et finis naturae, ordo iste constituit moralitatem naturalem seu philosophicam; sin auten beatitudo haec sit supernaturalis, id est Deus ut Deus est seu ut est auctor et finis gratiae, talis ordo constituit formaliter moralitatem supernaturalem seu theologicam" *(De hominis beatitudine,* 3:1, prol. 1, c. 2, n. 76, p. 74).

atitude; then he attempts to demonstrate, by distinct and redundant arguments, that riches, honors, fame, power, health, pleasure, and the like cannot constitute either natural or supernatural beatitude. But Aquinas's analysis of created goods is structured quite differently; his argument leads to the *conclusion* that no created good in this life or the life to come can beatify man fully. Only then does Aquinas take up what would constitute perfect beatitude for man which he shows to be, necessarily, a supernatural end.[105]

Ramírez gives, but oddly enough does not embrace, two good reasons—one historical, the other doctrinal—for rejecting the modern theological perspective when interpreting Aquinas. First of all, Aquinas worked within the historical tradition of Boethius and Augustine and that tradition does not make, and could be said to eschew, any explicit division between man's ultimate natural and ultimate supernatural ends.[106] To conform Aquinas to the modern theological model results in grave distortions of Thomistic doctrine. To avoid them, Aquinas must be viewed against the background of the pagan philosophies that preceded him and not the Christian heresies that followed him.[107] In the present instance, the Thomistic concept of natural beatitude plays a significant role only in Aquinas's doctrinal encounter with Aristotle. Aquinas shows little or none of the modern theological fascination with "pure nature," that is, with the hypothesis of a mankind never given its actual supernatural end.

The second—and I think overriding—reason that Ramírez mentions for not assimilating Aquinas to the modern theological problematic, concerns the doctrinal foundation of Thomistic moral science. Aquinas focuses only on supernatural beatitude. But this is not merely a

---

105. See *ST,* I–II, q. 2, a. 8; q. 3, a. 1; aa. 7–8.

106. Petrus de Godoy, aware that the modern theological perspective needs to be reconciled with the Augustinian tradition, solves the problem by merely asserting that the two points of view are compatible. "Augustine spoke theologically about true beatitude, which consists in the clear vision of God, but he did not deny that the Philosophers had philosophical knowledge about a certain kind of beatitude, namely, natural beatitude. [Speaking] theologically, [the latter], is not true beatitude, since it is not in every way perfect and does not satisfy every appetite of man, but [it] is, nonetheless, true beatitude. That is, it preserves the true essence of beatitude" *(Disputationes theologicae,* Vol. 1, Tract. 2, n. 19, p. 56).

107. See Pierre Rousselot, *L'Intellectualisme de saint Thomas* (Paris: Beauchesne, 1924), 181. Ramírez grants half the point: *ST,* I–II, qq. 1–5 imitate the Aristotelian treatment of beatitude by defining first the nature and then the efficient cause of beatitude. But the imitation allegedly depends on Aquinas drawing "a theological parallelism between supernatural beatitude and natural beatitude": see Ramirez, *De hominis beatitudine,* 3: 1, prol. 2, c. 3, n. 204, pp. 140–41.

matter of Aquinas's personal or professional interest as a theologian. Nor does it reflect an undeveloped state of theological science. To claim either is to miss the fundamental point. As Aquinas so thoroughly demonstrates, the only beatitude that will satisfy man is supernatural.

All of Aquinas's references to natural beatitude, or to twofold goods, or to twofold ends, should in no wise obscure for the interpreter the fact that Thomistic man is destined for and can only be satisfied by his one, actual, ultimate, and *supernatural* end. On that unambiguous fact rests Aquinas's whole systematic analysis of human beatitude. By contrast, what Aquinas mentions rarely—the possibility of a strictly natural end—is the possibility that structures Ramírez's whole interpretation. Ramírez continuously contrasts natural and supernatural beatitude, and the methodology of his argument keeps these two worlds neatly circumscribed. Consequently, Ramírez's argument seems to lead to the conclusion that there are two self-enclosed forms of beatitude, natural and supernatural. If so, "beatitude" is an equivocal notion.[108] Such a conclusion would, of course, deeply fragment the Thomistic doctrine of man's *implicit* but unitary existential quest for *supernatural* beatitude.

Ramírez, however, attempts to counterbalance the tendency of his own argument. He claims that the concepts of supernatural and natural beatitude are analogically related. They are related as perfect to imperfect, prior to posterior, essence to accident.[109] Yet Ramírez's appeal to the analogical similarities between natural and supernatural beatitude, even if we grant that Aquinas affirms them,[110] does not resolve the fundamental contradiction between the Thomist effort to

108. See Ramírez, *De hominis beatitudine,* 3: 2, introductio, c. 1, n. 22, p. 30: "Quin etiam vel in ipsamet beatitudine obiectiva vera non est idem omnino conceptus secundum quod agitur de beatitudine naturali et de beatitudine supernaturali."

109. See Ramírez, *De hominis beatitudine,* 3: 2, introductio, c. 1, n. 24, p. 34:"... omnes acceptiones beatitudinis obiectivae dicuntur analogice, secundum prius et posterius, per ordinem ad summam et perfectissimam beatitudinem obiectivam, quae est beatitudo supernaturalis, hoc est Deus, Deus quatenus, reduplicative ut Deus. . . ."

For various kinds of analogy recognized by Aquinas, see *SLE,* I, 7, 1096b26, 168–98 *(In Ethic.,* I, lect. 7 [Spiazzi, n. 95, p. 25]). This text mentions: (1) reference to one principle; (2) reference to one end; (3) diverse proportions to the same subject; and (4) one proportion to diverse subjects. Cf. *ST,* I–II, q. 61, a. 1, ad 1: "Sed quando est divisio alicujus analogi, quod dicitur de pluribus secundum prius est posterius. . . ."

110. See *IV Sent.,* d. 39, q. 1, a. 2, sol. 1, ad 1 (Vivès, 11, p. 467): ". . . beatitudo creata est quaedam participatio et similitudo beatitudinis increatae . . ."; *ST,* I–II, q. 66, a. 5, ad 2: ". . . actus sapientiae est quaedam inchoatio seu participatio futurae felicitatis."

ground moral philosophy on the concept of ultimate natural beatitude and Aquinas's claim that only supernatural beatitude can ultimately satisfy man.[111] The adequacy or, more radically, the possibility of any such ultimate natural beatitude is exactly what is called into question by the conclusion of Aquinas's extended argument.[112] According to Aristotle, our highest natural end is to contemplate the highest beings, an end that the Christian can equate with knowing the one God. But we desire to know more about God than nature, that is, philosophy, can ever provide.[113] It is this fact, so profoundly elaborated by Aquinas, that effectively blocks the construction of any systematic, quasi-Aristotelian philosophical ethics grounded on *the* natural end of man. Insofar as no natural end—including a life combining contemplation and action[114]—adequately satisfies man's desire for beatitude, man is *naturally* endless.[115]

The modern theological problematic, however, inserts a developed theory of natural beatitude into Aquinas. But the Thomistic doctrine of man's twofold end must be interpreted by reference to Aquinas's constant affirmation of man's de facto supernatural end. To claim, as Ramírez does, that this modern juxtaposition of natural and supernatural beatitude, although not in the letter, is in the spirit of Aquinas is effectively to repudiate Ramírez's own astute observations about the unitary theological and supernatural character of the Thomistic con-

---

111. The same criticism can be leveled at Kevin M. Staley, "Happiness: The Natural End of Man?" *Thomist* 53 (1989): 215–34, who claims that "imperfect as well as perfect beatitude both respond to man's desire for goodness as such, though in different degrees of completeness." Perfect beatitude, however, is complete, and therefore cannot be characterized as different in degree but as different in kind from imperfect beatitude. Only various forms of imperfect beatitude can differ in *degree* of completion.

112. See *SCG*, I, 102 (Pera, n. 847, p. 112): "Fatigatio, et occupationes variae quibus necesse est contemplationem nostram in hac vita interpolari, in qua consistit praecipue humana felicitas, si qua consistit praecipue humana felicitas, si qua est praesentis vitae; errores, dubitationes, et casus varii quibus subiacet praesens vita; ostendunt omnino incomparabilem esse humanam felicitatem, praecipue huius vitae, divinae beatitudini."

113. See *SCG*, III, 39 (Pera, n. 2172, p. 45): "Illa igitur cognitio Dei essentialiter est ipsa felicitas, qua habita non restabit alicuius scibilis desideranda cognitio. Talis autem non est cognitio quam philosophi per demonstrationes de Deo habere potuerunt. . . ."

114. See *Comp. theol.*, II, c. 9 (Verardo, n. 578, p. 134): "Et sic consequens fit quod nec in propria ipsa operatione intellectus speculativi vel practici quae corporalibus rebus intendi, ultima hominis felicitas, et perfectio possit poni."

115. See *ST*, I, q. 62, a. 4: "Cuiuslibet autem creaturae esse beatum non est natura, sed ultimus finis. . . . Beatitudo autem ultima excedit naturam angelicam et humanam. . . ."

ception of beatitude.[116] Why, nevertheless, did Ramírez regard this modern point of view, although it is alien to that of Aquinas, as a sound, not to say the required, framework for interpreting the Thomistic texts? The only plausible answer is that Ramírez also shared the anxieties of the classical Thomist commentators; he too desired to safeguard Aquinas from being implicated in later heresies.[117]

Ramírez constructs a parallel, autonomous, Thomist, philosophical ethics that rests on the notion of ultimate natural beatitude, but this project reorients—more strongly put, disorients—Aquinas's own moral science. Ramírez's Thomist moral philosophy solidifies the Thomistic concept of natural beatitude so that it is no longer a dialogical contrast, whose meaning must be continuously determined by Aquinas's conversation with Aristotle; it has become, instead, a fixed doctrinal point independent of that conversation. Here, once again, the Thomist commentator seems to depart significantly from his master, Aquinas. At the least, Ramírez alters the whole tone of the Thomistic discussion, and, more importantly, neglects the philosophical implications of Aquinas's argument about earthly happiness. Ramírez's quasi-Aristotelian notion of "ultimate natural beatitude" discards Aquinas's paradoxical conclusion: *Natural beatitude in any form does not satisfy man's natural desire for beatitude.* The Thomistic doctrine of man's twofold end does not mitigate this paradox; on the contrary, the doctrine enshrines it. What we find in any natural beatitude is neither the ultimate natural end of man nor a constituent of ultimate beatitude. All that Aquinas allows is that natural beatitude that can never "satisfy" is a participation or similitude of perfect or supernatural beatitude.[118]

Thomist moral philosophers readily subordinate man's natural beatitude to his supernatural beatitude. But this easy subordination again

116. Cf. Ramirez, *De hominis beatitudine*, 3: 1, proloquium, n. 236, pp. 222–23: ". . . distincte considerabimus tum existentiam tum naturam alicuius ultimi finis et naturalis et supernaturalis humanae vitae in communi." For criticism of Ramírez's procedure, see Jean Tonneau, O.P., Comptes rendus, *Bulletin thomiste* 7 (1943–46): 21–22. M.-Michel Labourdette, O.P., in "Theologie morale," *Revue thomiste* 50 (1950): 203–5, gently observes that Ramírez's lengthy commentary on *ST,* I–II, q. 3, a. 8 never explains "le seul argument de l'article, *le désir naturel de voir Dieu*" (205).

117. Cf. Ramirez, *De hominis beatitudine,* 3: 2, pars 2, sect. 4, §1, nn. 362–63, p. 385: ". . . distinctio humanae beatitudinis, nedum formalis est et obiectivae, in naturalem et supernaturalem. . . . In re ipsa conveniunt philosophi sane philosophantes et theologi, recta ratio et fides." Also see 385–419.

118. See *ST,* I–II, q. 3, a. 6: ". . . naturaliter desideratur non solum perfecta beatitudo, sed etiam qualiscumque similitudo vel participatio ipsius."

misses the upshot of Aquinas's argument. Natural beatitude is not a sort of "penultimate" end complete in its own order. Rather, any kind of natural beatitude leaves human nature radically unfulfilled. It is this Thomistic conclusion that cannot be put into the framework of Aristotelian eudaimonism and that obviates any autonomous Thomist moral philosophy appealing to *the* ultimate natural end of man.

In interpreting Aquinas, then, it is just as necessary to offset as to affirm the twofold end of man. Aquinas as much proves that any form of natural beatitude is *not* man's ultimate end as he proves that it is, in any qualified sense, man's end. Aquinas's philosophically novel insight is into the radical disparity between what human nature desires and what human nature can achieve. Yet this is the paradox that Ramírez, and all of the classical Thomist philosophical moralists, neglect. But how can one build a systematic Thomistic moral philosophy on the fact of human nature's endlessness? One aspect of the answer is clear. Certainly, we cannot look, as do the traditional Thomists, to Aristotle to provide us the model of that philosophy. A human nature that is naturally endless cannot be fitted into an Aristotelian universe.[119]

4. Thomistic Moral Science: A Philosophical Paradox

Aquinas's view of what reason can understand about human nature is remarkable. For Aquinas, reason can know: (1) that human nature is forever unsatisfied unless man attains the vision of God; but (2) attainment of this knowledge must be considered a supernatural achievement that is beyond any merely human ability.

> Although man is naturally inclined toward the ultimate end, he is not able to attain it naturally but only through grace. And this is because of the excellence of his end. *(Expos. de Trin.*, q. 6, a. 4, ad 5 [Decker, 9⁻12, p. 229])[120]

These, then, are the two carefully balanced conclusions that emerge from the various rehearsals of Aquinas's painstaking argument that runs some eleven articles in *IV Sent.*, d. 39, qq. 1–2; twenty-seven chapters in *SCG*, III, 25–52; sixteen articles in *ST*, I–II, qq. 2–3; and which is elegantly summarized in a lengthy chapter in *Comp. theol.*, II, c. 9.

---

119. See Anton C. Pegis, "Matter, Beatitude and Liberty," *Thomist* 5 (1943): 273: "If man [i.e, the Aristotelian metaphysician] looks to God, it is in and through this life: he approaches and imitates, in his self-enclosed way, the divine immobility."

120. "Quamvis enim homo naturaliter inclinetur in finem ultimum, non tamen potest naturaliter illum consequi, sed solum per gratiam, et hoc est propter eminentiam illius finis" *(Expos. de Trin.*, q. 6, a. 4, ad 5 [Decker, 9–12, 229]).

The two conclusions follow from an argument that is about a "truth that faith professes and reason investigates."[121] Both conclusions are important, but especially the first should command the interest of the philosopher. That human nature can only be fully satisfied by the vision of God is a conclusion that can be established by a metaphysical argument based on the nature of the human intellect; this conclusion coincides with but does not depend upon any premise held only on faith about the actual supernatural gift of such a divine vision.

Within its own context, Aquinas's argument is certainly prompted by and is in the service of a theology.[122] In this context, reason is first oriented by faith; faith enables man to believe something which hitherto no philosopher could have seen. The Christian believer accepts on faith that man actually has an otherworldly and supernatural end, but Aquinas gives a cogent metaphysical argument to support the conclusion that no other end could ultimately satisfy the human intellect. This argument too is theological in its original context. But could a philosopher, working in a purely philosophical context—a context devoid of any Christian beliefs guiding his philosophical investigations—reach at least some of the premises on which Aquinas's conclusion is based? The question is both historical and systematic. In order to ascertain what philosophy can say about ultimate human happiness, we need to determine whether philosophy can know about (1) the otherworldly character of human beatitude and (2) the supernatural character of human beatitude.

Aquinas, considering *some* of the Greek and Arabic philosophers known to him, finds that history sometimes answers the first of these two questions negatively. Many philosophers mistakenly think that ultimate happiness is to be found in this-worldly philosophical contemplation.

> The philosophers, who were not able to have a full notion of ultimate happiness, posited the ultimate happiness of man in the contemplation which is possible in this life. *(SCG, III, 63 [Pera, n. 2382, p. 84])*[123]

Yet Aquinas is characterizing only some figures in the history of philosophy. Other philosophers, he acknowledges, have reached a better understanding of human beatitude; they know that perfect beatitude

---

121. ". . . fides profitetur et ratio investigat . . ." *(SCG, I, 9 [Pera, n. 55, p. 12])*.

122. On the theological character of the *Summa contra gentiles*, see Pegis, "Qu'est-ce que la *SCG?*" 169–82.

123. "Et ideo philosophi, qui de illa felicitate ultima plenam notitiam habere non potuerunt, in contemplatione quae est possibilis in hac vita, ultimam felicitatem hominis posuerunt" *(SCG, III, 63 [Pera, n. 2383, p. 84])*.

must be possible but that it cannot be found in this life. These are the philosophers, however, who are also prepared to think that the soul is immortal.

Beatitude is not able to be placed in this life because of the various changes to which man is subject. Hence it is necessary that beatitude which is the end of human life be [found] after this life. And all the philosophers who posit that the soul, which is the form of the body, is essentially intellectual, concede this. For they posit that the soul is immortal. *(IV Sent.*, d. 39, q. 1, a. 1, sol. 4 [Vivès, 11, p. 464])[124]

Consequently, a philosophy that lacks the doctrine of immortality can never attain a concept of perfect beatitude, but "only of some [concept] of participated beatitude."[125]

Aquinas's observations about various philosophers show that he readily distinguishes between the past achievements of philosophers and the possibilities of philosophical thought as such. From the standpoint of Christian faith, there are some things about God and man that philosophy can never know: reason cannot demonstrate the triune nature of God or the fact of the incarnation of the second person of the Trinity. Aquinas, however, argues that it is a philosophical mistake for either a theologian or a philosopher to assert that men are unable to be cognitively joined with the first cause (or causes) of their being.

A being reaches its perfection only when it is "united to its principle." Rational beings are united to their first principle through cognition. Consequently, whether the First Cause be understood by the theologians as God, or as the separate substances by the philosophers, men must be able to reach knowledge of the divine essence or of the essences of the separate substances. To deny this possibility leads to the absurd conclusion that something other than God (or the separate substances) is the "effective principle of man."

Hence it is necessary for us [theologians] to posit that our intellect sometime attains to the vision of the divine essence and for the philosophers that it attains to the vision of the essence of the separate substances. *(IV Sent.*, d. 39, q. 2, a. 1 [Vivès, 11, p. 482])[126]

---

124. "Beatitudo autem vera non potest poni in hac vita propter mutabilitates varias quibus homo subjacet; unde necesse est beatitudinem quae est finis humanae vitae, esse post hanc vitam. Et hoc quidem concesserunt omnes philosophi qui posuerunt animam, quae est forma humani corporis, esse intellectum per essentiam: posuerunt enim animam immortalem" *(IV Sent.*, d. 39, q. 1, a. 1, sol. 4 [Vivès, 11, p. 464]).

125. Ibid.

126. "Unde oportet ponere secundum nos, quod intellectus noster quandoque

Joseph Owens, when exploring the question whether the endlessness of human nature is a properly *philosophical* insight, quotes approvingly a text from the *Ordinatio* of Duns Scotus.[127]

Philosophers hold to the perfection of nature and deny supernatural perfection; theologians truly know the defect of nature and the necessity of grace and supernatural perfection. *(Ord.,* prologus, 1.1.5; I, 4.14–17)[128]

Owens, like Scotus, denies that a philosopher, working outside the context of theology, could grasp the imperfection of human nature. Because "the incompleteness of nature escapes philosophic scrutiny,"[129] the philosopher is forever unable to know that human nature can be adequately fulfilled only by a supernatural end. Owens's historical claim is simple: no past philosopher, if he was not also a theologian, has ever propounded such a notion.[130] But Owens's systematic conclusions are more complex. He allows that poetry has an affective awareness of nature's deficiency but denies that either poetry or philosophy can ever precisely conceptualize that nature is incomplete. The incompletion of nature remains hidden from any autonomous philosophical investigation, because the philosopher "has no means of knowing about the elevation of nature through grace."[131]

Owens assumes that only knowledge of (i.e., belief in) the *fact* of man's supernatural end can ground any philosophical thematization and exploration of the *possibility* of such an elevation or of human nature's openness to God.[132] Accordingly, he interprets Aquinas's argument that no natural end will satisfy man as already *presupposing* "the incompleteness of nature,"[133] and he maintains that the Thomistic argument, although it generates "important philosophical reflec-

---

perveniat ad videndam essentiam divinam, et secundum philosophos quod perveniat ad videndam essentiam substantiarum separatarum" *(IV Sent.,* d. 39, q. 2, a. 1 [Vivès, 11, p. 482]).

127. See Joseph Owens, C.Ss.R., "Tenent Philosophi Perfectionem Naturae," in *Essays Honoring Allan B. Wolter,* ed. William A. Frank and Gerard J. Etzkorn (St. Bonaventure, N.Y.: Franciscan Institute Publications, 1985), 221–44, and *Human Destiny: Some Problems for Catholic Philosophy* (Washington, D.C.: The Catholic University of America Press, 1985).

128. "Et tenent philosophi perfectionem naturae, et negant perfectionem supernaturalem; theologi vero cognoscunt defectum naturae et necessitatem gratiae et perfectionem supernaturalem" *(Ord.,* prol., 1.1.5; I, 4.14–17; quoted in Owens, "Tenent Philosophi," 222, n. 5).

129. Owens, "Tenent Philosophi," 241. Cf. ibid., 240.

130. See ibid., 232.

131. Ibid., 243.

132. See Owens, *Human Destiny,* 51–52.

133. Owens, "Tenent Philosophi," 236.

tions,"[134] cannot in any way be separated from its original theological context. Consequently, the endlessness of human nature must remain hidden, on Owens's interpretation, for any philosophy.[135] But has Owens provided sound arguments for rejecting the alternative reading of Aquinas, that the Thomistic argument for the endlessness of human nature is *philosophically* cogent, and is therefore able to be maintained outside of its original theological setting?[136]

In their original settings, the argument for the endlessness of human nature found in the *Summa contra gentiles* and in the *Summa theologiae* are undoubtedly theological arguments given the overall purpose and design of those works, which essay to see things "*sub ratione Dei.*" Yet the arguments are rigorously metaphysical and are meant, as was the earlier version of the argument in *Scriptum super libros Sententiarum*, to be a rational correction of the Aristotelian doctrine of beatitude.[137]

> We do not deny, however, that some participation of beatitude in this life is possible, primarily, insofar as man is perfect in the goods of speculative reason and, secondarily, in [the goods of] of practical reason. And the Philosopher delimits this happiness in the books of the *Ethics*; he neither asserts nor denies the other happiness that is after this life. (*IV Sent.*, d. 49, q. 1, a. 1, sol. 4 [Vivès, 11, p. 464])[138]

This-worldly beatitude is but a "participation of beatitude" *(participatio beatitudinis)*. It is real but not ultimate. Against Aristotle,

---

134. Owens, *Human Destiny*, 40.

135. See ibid., 34.

136. Between the time he wrote his first commentary on the *Nicomachean Ethics* (1248–52) and his second commentary (Gauthier: 1263–67), it seems that Albert the Great had read Aquinas's arguments in *SCG*, II 79 and III, 48, and as a consequence became convinced that from the tenets of Aristotelian philosophy, it is clear that ". . . animae quae virtute et scientia hunc intellectum adeptae sunt, felicitatem habent post mortem" (lib. I, tract. 7, c. 17; ed. A. Borgnet: 7, 133ab). Accordingly, Jean Dunbabin, in "The Two Commentaries of Albertus Magnus on the *Nicomachean Ethics*," *Recherches de théologie ancienne et médiévale* 30 (1963): 248, observes: "So Albertus had incorporated into his second commentary one of the most recent controversial pieces of *philosophical speculation* which can have reached him in Cologne" [my italics].

137. See *SCG*, III, 48, (Pera, n. 2255, p. 64). Cf. Laporta, *La Destinée de la nature humaine*, 49–50.

138. "Non negamus tamen quin aliqua beatitudinis participatio in hac vita esse possit, secundum quod homo est perfectus in bonis rationis speculativae principaliter, et practicae secundario; et de hac felicitate Philosophus in lib. *Ethic.* determinat; aliam, quae est post hanc vitam, nec asserens nec negans" (*IV Sent.*, d. 49, q. 1, a. 1, sol. 4 [Vivès, 11: 464]).

Aquinas argues that philosophical contemplation cannot satisfy human nature. Not even the superior knowledge that the Christian believer derives from divinely infused faith ultimately satisfies man's intellectual desire.[139] Our desire to know God Himself, which knowledge is ultimate human beatitude, cannot be found in this life. Nor can beatitude, on the assumption that the human soul is naturally immortal, be found in a fully satisfying form in the next life *unless* God freely grants a *supernatural vision* of Himself. Philosophy, however, can say nothing about what God has chosen or might freely choose to do supernaturally for men.

When removed from their theological setting, Aquinas's arguments about human beatitude remain philosophically challenging. But can Aquinas's argument about the natural endlessness of human nature be cogently developed in a strictly philosophical context? Owens denies that it can. In arguing that nature's incompletion (i.e., its need to be fulfilled supernaturally) remains opaque to any philosophical investigation, Owens refers to the fact that the human mind cannot naturally grasp in positive fashion the infinite divine nature, and indeed would not even look there for satisfaction of its appetite to know: instead, "the unlimited range of the intellect's *concept* of being would be satisfied with the unendingly successive grasp of finite existents within its reach."[140] Owens's claim, however, is not relevant to the basis of Aquinas's argument: Aquinas argues that man's "infinite" *psychological desire* to know, not the infinite *logical extension* of the concept of being, can only be satisfied by a vision of the infinite divine essence.

The argument from "the concept of being," moreover, is ambivalent. Emerich Coreth appeals to the concept of being to support the position exactly contrary to Owens's.[141] Coreth grants that God cannot be positively grasped in the concept of being; yet, the concept of being, from the very way it is predicated, entails the concept of the uncaused cause of being. Coreth quotes Aquinas: "For being is not predicated of beings equivocally, but analogically, and thus a reduction to one must be made" *(SCG, II, 15)*. The intellect is dissatisfied just because the concept of being opens upon but cannot positively grasp the nature of

---

139. See *SCG*, III, 39–40.

140. Owens, "Tenent Philosophi," 237. To base an argument on the "concept of being" is uncharacteristic of Owens, who has repeatedly stressed that being is fundamentally existential act (*actus essendi*) that cannot be properly grasped in a concept: see Joseph Owens, C.Ss.R., "The Intelligibility of Being," *Gregorianum* 26 (1955): 169–93.

141. See Emerich Coreth, *Metaphysics*, ed. Joseph Donceel (New York: Herder and Herder, 1968), 170–96.

uncaused being. Coreth does not admit, then, that this natural dissatisfaction can be mitigated by knowing an infinite succession of finite
beings. On the contrary, it is this dissatisfaction that allows the Christian philosopher to discern the insufficiency of any natural end proposed for human nature.

Is Aquinas's argument for the endlessness of human nature philosophically cogent? The Thomistic argument is "dialectical": it begins
with an Aristotelian tenet about nature, that a nature must be able to
attain its proper end and satisfaction, but it demonstrates that, in fact,
human nature cannot reach its own ultimate perfection or completion
in any naturally attainable end. The conclusion of the Thomistic argument is not that man actually has a supernatural end but that human
nature has no ultimately satisfying natural end and that unless a supernatural end (the vision of God) is possible and can be achieved men are
creatures made "in vain."

Human nature, so Aquinas reasons, has no satisfying and, in that
sense, no ultimate natural end; it is, in other words, naturally "endless." Aquinas reaches this *conclusion* inductively: upon examination,
none of the proposed natural ends can actually satisfy man's intellectual appetite. Since this inductive argument for the endlessness of
human nature does not incorporate any premise that can only be
known through theological faith, why cannot it not be put in a purely
philosophical context? To say that it cannot is to nullify its rational
character. If it is countered that the argument is not exclusively
rational, which premise cannot be rationally sustained apart from
faith? It is hardly surprising, then, that certain authors champion the
autonomous philosophical value of Aquinas argument for the endlessness of human nature.[142] These authors acknowledge that Aquinas
himself first *believed* that man has a supernatural end. And, likewise,
they grant that orthodox ecclesiastical teaching undoubtedly posits
that no philosophy can demonstrate the fact of man's actual supernatural end. But Aquinas's *argument* for the endlessness of human
nature neither presupposes nor attempts to demonstrate this supernatural fact.

Reason can ask new questions born of faith and in the process
transform philosophy. Any proposed Thomistic moral philosophy
must inevitably appeal to this last consideration. Aquinas, the theologian, begins by affirming what only Christian faith can affirm, that

---

142. Among the most influential, see Joseph Maréchal, "De naturali perfectae
beatitudinis desiderio," in *Mélanges Joseph Maréchal*, Desclée de Brouwer (Paris:
Desclée de Brouwer, 1950), 1:323–37; de Broglie, *De fine ultimo*, 197.

human nature is not ultimately endless: human nature is not only open to but can actually receive, as a divine gift, the supernatural vision of God. But, as a moment in his theological consideration of human beatitude, Aquinas also demonstrates, in a philosophically rigorous argument, that human beatitude could not be attained in any natural end but only in the vision of God. These complementary insights, philosophical and theological, were first expressed in a theology. But despite the theological provenance of Aquinas's argument, the Thomistic philosopher claims that it provides a properly philosophical point of departure.

To be sure, no philosopher prior to Aquinas had reached using the resources of Aristotelian philosophy the Thomistic conclusion about the endlessness of human nature. But surely what is now at issue is not philosophy's past achievements but its future possibilities. And all would agree that if Aquinas teaches, by example, any lesson about philosophy, it is that philosophy need not be a prisoner of its own history. In Books I–III of the *Summa contra gentiles*, Aquinas effects a profound philosophical transformation of Aristotle's doctrines in regard to the nature of the first Unmoved Mover and its relationship to the world, the immortality of the soul, and the pursuit of human beatitude. Aquinas's new philosophy, which Pegis labels "the Christian Aristotelianism"[143] of the *Summa contra gentiles*, leads the Aristotelian philosopher to ask questions about the destiny of man that only Christian theology can fully answer. But the questions are genuinely philosophical questions in the context of thirteenth-century Aristotelianism.

What is the contemporary moral philosopher to make, if anything, of human nature's fundamental desire for and openness to the direct vision of God? Martin Rhonheimer, who rightly notes the theological character of *"beatitudo imperfecta,"* raises this question after explicitly acknowledging the *philosophical* paradox posed by the Thomistic argument on behalf of the *"desiderium naturale"* for seeing the divine essence.[144] But this acknowledgement, for Rhonheimer, does not affect the status of moral philosophy: its object remains the same for both believer and non-believer, *not* what the classical Thomists thought, the natural as distinguished from the supernatural end of man, but what Aristotle thought, "the happiness of earthly life" (67).

---

143. Pegis, "Qu'-est-ce que la *SCG?*" 180.
144. Martin Rhonheimer, *La prospettiva della morale: Fondamenti dell'etica filosofica* (Rome: Armado Editore, 1994), 65.

However, is Rhonheimer's conception of the object of moral philosophy, from a strictly philosophical point of view, coherent or theologically neutral? Supposedly, the object of moral philosophy must be defined solely by reference to what "pure reason" can know about earthly happiness; actually, Rhonheimer frames his conception of earthly happiness in oppostion to a theological view of both this-worldly and other-wordly happiness. His "philosophical" notion emerges from and can only be sustained by the contrast which he draws between moral theology and moral philosophy. On the one hand, Christian faith, although it directs us to hope for a future life, cannot ground "a practical science that refers itself to the state of perfect beatitude" (67). Accordingly, moral theology knows only "an earthly life" which is "under the condition of grace" (67). On the other hand, Rhonheimer argues, now surely from a theological perspective, that any moral philosophy, is necessarily incomplete, "a fragment or section of the whole" (67). Non-believers, inevitably mistaking a fragmentary for the whole view of man, are liable to fall into reductionism or ideology about the content and the possiblity of *earthly* human happiness. Consequently, a moral philosophy "circum-scribed by faith," which knows that naure cannot provide an ultimate answer to questions about human happiness, *precisely for this reason*, "will always be able to present itself as a critical instance in opposition to non-believing [moral] philosophies" (67).

The genesis and the basis of this critical oppostion is unclear. Does it arise from and can it be only sustained within the *"fides quaerens intellectum"* of the believing philosopher, or is it allegedly an intrinsic requirement of moral philosophy itself? The latter is implausible. No less in the latter than the former case, a theological doctrine of man's transcendence over nature dominates Rhonheimer's statement of the opposition between the moral philosophy of a believer and a non-be-liever. This is evident in the reason that Rhonheimer gives for rejecting philosophical speculation about the possibility of natural happiness after death: "The *philosophical* ethics of the believer is not able to concern itself with any 'natural happiness of the life hereafter' simply because the believer, even insofar as he is a philosopher, knows that such a thing does not really exist."[145] Apparently, Rhonheimer is eager to save the believing philosopher from futile pursuits.[146] But such de-

---

145. "L'etica *filosofica* del credente però non si può occupare di una 'felicità naturale della vita dell'aldilà', semplicemente perché il credente, anche in quanto filosofo, sa che una tale cosa non esiste affatto" (Rhonheimer, *La prospettiva*, 69).

146. Suarez, bk. 1, *De natura legis in communi, de eiusque causis, et effectibus,*

finitive knowledge of man's de facto supernatural end, as the classical Thomist philosophers would be quick to insist,[147] is exclusively theological; it indicates that Rhonheimer's "moral philosophy of the believer" is not so much circumscribed as underwritten by faith. It is, in other words, a moral theology not a philosophy, as Rhonheimer himself almost acknowledges.[148]

The question about the significance for moral philosophy of the Thomistic doctrine of the *"desiderium naturale"*—at least, in this precise form that we have been discussing it—can arise only for a philosopher who also accepts Aquinas's metaphysical principles. In practice, the question arises only for a Christian philosopher who would attempt to derive a Thomistic moral philosophy from Aquinas's theology. I shall argue that the question, although it is properly philosophical, sets paradoxical and unsurpassable limits to the project of an autonomous Thomistic philosophical ethics. Rhonheimer maintains—correctly I think—that there should be a critical confrontation between the moral philosophy of a believer and the moral philosophy of a non-believer. But the Thomistic model suggests that such a confrontation, which is a rational necessity solely for the believer, arises and can be coherently sustained only as a moment within a rationally developed theology.

Still, could not the Thomistic doctrine of the natural desire for seeing God, assuming that it can be defended solely on rational grounds, be incorporated into a theologically neutral moral philosophy? For the moment, therefore, let us grant that Aquinas's argument, most fully articulated in the third book of the *Summa contra gentiles*, does initially appear to warrant the development of an autonomous Thomistic philosophical ethics, but now one based on the natural *endlessness* of man. So based, this Thomistic moral philosophy would have a radically different starting point and outlook than the traditional Thomist ethics based on the doctrine of the twofold end of man. The latter is a quasi-Aristotelian ethics that stresses the ulti-

---

ch. 3, "De necessitate et varietate legum," n. 11 (Vivès, 5: 10a): "Est enim advertendum philosophos non agnovisse supernaturalem hominum finem, sed solum de hujus vitae aliquali felicitate. . . ."

147. Cf. Suarez, tract. 1, disp. 4, sect. 3, n. 6 (Vivès, 4: 45a): "Atque ita philosophi naturalem beatitudinem hominis possuerunt praecipe pro statu hujus vitae: supposita vero animi immortalitate, necesse est, ut etiam post hanc vitam possit esse beata, quae dicitur etiam beatitudo hominis ratione partis pracipuae. . . ."

148. Cf. Rhonheimer, *La prospettiva*, 69: "La prospettiva filosofica della beatitudine imperfetta è però . . . molto compromessa e, in ultima analisi, essa è veramente sostenibile solo con riferimento alla fede."

mate sufficiency, in the natural order, of a strictly natural end, the philosophical contemplation of God.

Suppose, then, a would-be Thomistic philosopher who finds that Aquinas has provided a cogent metaphysical argument for human nature's endlessness, and therefore for a cogent metaphysical argument for man's natural *openness* to a supernatural end. Certainly this reading of *SCG*, III, 25–52, as well as of Aquinas's other versions of the same argument, is plausible and defensible. First, there is no question of our Thomistic philosopher trying to prove the fact of man's actual supernatural elevation. Second, he or she grants that whether God does actually elevate man to this supernatural vision is a fact accepted only on faith and discussed only in theology.

Nonetheless, what can be philosophically proven, our Thomistic philosopher would maintain, is man's natural endlessness and the radical congruence of the theological belief in supernatural beatitude with the exigencies of human nature. To that purpose, does not Aquinas demonstrate, without relying on any premise drawn from revealed doctrine, that perfect happiness for an intellectual being is to know the essence of God? Any other end leaves man's natural desire unfilled. Unlike the traditional Thomist moral philosopher, our would-be Thomistic philosopher emphasizes that there is, in the natural order, no ultimately satisfying natural end for men.

If man falls short of attaining the supernatural vision of God, then he fails to attain ultimate beatitude since no strictly natural end can be ultimate for an intellectual nature. And if such failure is somehow inevitable, we should then be forced to conclude, contrary to everything that Aristotle thought, that human nature is something vain and futile. Aquinas, we know, does not draw the latter conclusion. He says instead that human nature *requires* that it attain the divine vision.[149]

How, though, is the Thomistic philosopher to explain this *requirement* that Aquinas places on human nature? A careful exposition of Aquinas's argument for the endlessness of human nature will acknowledge that it is surrounded with strictures. Aquinas, as I have reiterated, does not attempt to demonstrate that man is, as a matter of fact, ordained to the supernatural vision of God. Men cannot know that they are actually capable of attaining the vision of God except through faith based on divine teaching. That God actually does ordain men to Him-

---

149. See *ST*, I–II, q. 3, a. 8: "Ad perfectam igitur beatitudinem requiritur quod intellectus pertingat ad ipsam essentiam primae causae."

self is a revealed truth known only by faith. Only the believer can hope and pray for this divine gift.[150]

The ultimate beatitude of man consists in a supernatural vision of God. Man is not able to attain this vision except through the way of learning from God the teacher. *(ST,* II–II, q. 2, a. 3)[151]

At the core of Thomistic moral science, there is to be found— at least for the philosopher—a deeply puzzling paradox.[152] Aquinas makes the point with great force: man has a natural desire to know God's essence but lacks the ability to fulfill this natural desire. But without the possibility of that fulfillment, human beings are vain creatures whose natures promise only a restless pursuit of happiness.

Since man was made for this, that he know the divine substance, if he is not able to perceive it, it seems that he is made in vain. . . . *(Comp. theol.,* II, c. 7 [Verardo, n. 568, p. 131])[153]

How, then, is the philosopher to interpret this desire to see God, presuming, of course, that he has first been able to identify it? The philosopher cannot begin, as does the theologian, with what sacred doctrine teaches, that men are destined through grace to the supernatural vision of God.[154] The philosopher, nonetheless, is confronted by the fact that reason, albeit working first within a theological context, can demonstrate that natural happiness is insufficient and that only knowledge of the divine essence could fulfill man perfectly.[155]

The natural desire of knowing is not able to be quieted in us until we know the first cause, and not just in any fashion, but through its essence. *(Comp. theol.,* c. 104 [Verardo, n. 209, p. 52])[156]

150. See. *Comp. theol.,* II, c. 7.
151. ". . . ultima beatitudo hominis consistit in quadam supernaturali Dei visione. Ad quam quidem visionem homo pertingere non potest nisi per modum addiscentis a Deo doctore . . ." *(ST,* II–II, q. 2, a. 3).
152. See Étienne Gilson, "Sur le problematique thomiste de la vision béatifique," *Archives d'histoire doctrinale et litteraire du moyen âge* 31 (1964): 67–88, esp. 78, 80.
153. "Cum enim ad hoc factus sit homo, ut magnitudinem divinam cognoscat, si ad eam percipiendam pervenire non possit, videtur in vanum constitutus esse . . ." *(Comp. theol.,* II, c. 7 [Verardo, n. 568, p. 131]).
154. To be precise, the philosophers "know nothing" about the *theological* virtues: see *III Sent.,* d. 23, q. 1, a. 4, sol. 3 (Mandonnet, n. 96, p. 715).
155. See Pegis, "Nature and Spirit," 62–79. For the opposite claim, that reason can posit that man has an ultimate end, see Vanni Rovighi, "C'è un'etica filosofica in san Tommaso?" 144.
156. "Non igitur naturale desiderium sciendi potest quietari in nobis, quousque

Historically, this is an argument spawned by Christian theology. Yet, if the theologian's demonstration is correct, the philosopher is now confronted by a fact about the nature of man and not just a fact about what Christian faith believes about man's supernatural destiny.

The philosophical relevance and importance of Aquinas's conclusion is inescapable: for the would-be Thomistic philosopher, surely, Aristotelian naturalism is no longer the horizon or encompassing philosophical view of the human pursuit of beatitude. As Pegis remarked so sagely,[157] Aristotelian natures are neither "open" nor "closed" to the supernatural vision of God in the world to come. Much less, then, can Aristotelian natures be considered in any way naturally "endless" in this world.[158] Yet, for Aquinas, seeing the divine essence is the only form of beatitude that will satisfy the natural exigencies of human nature either in this world or in the world to come.

To take away from men the possibility of the vision of the divine essence, is to take away beatitude itself. Hence it is necessary to the beatitude of the created intellect that the divine essence be seen. (*Super Ioannem*, c. 1, lect. 11 [Cai, n. 212, p. 43])[159]

This "necessity," which irrevocably separates Aquinas from Aristotle, as well as from traditional Thomist moral philosophers, leads to a philosophical *aporia* or impasse. Reason, while it can demonstrate that man's natural inclination cannot be satisfied naturally, cannot demonstrate that men are destined to receive a supernatural form of beatitude. At best, the Thomistically inspired philosopher can show that men, as *intellectual* creatures, are open to the vision of God.

Man is in potency to the knowledge of the blessed, which consists in the vision of God, and to which [man] is ordained as to [his] end. For the rational creature is capable of this beatifying knowledge insofar as he exists in the image of God. (*ST*, III, q. 9, a. 2)[160]

---

primam causam cognoscamus, non quocumque modo, sed per eius essentiam" (*Comp. theol.*, I, c. 104 [Verardo, n. 209, p. 52]).

157. See Pegis, "Nature and Spirit," 68.

158. Cf. Pegis, "Matter, Beatitude, and Liberty," 273: "For how can there be any sort of other-worldliness in the *Ethics* of Aristotle if none is possible within the framework of the Aristotelian *Physics*?"

159. "Et ideo auferre possibilitatem visionis divinae essentiae ab hominibus, est auferre ipsam beatitudinem. Necesse est ergo ad beatitudinem intellectus creati, ut divina essentia videatur" (*Super Ioannem*, c. 1, lect. 11 [Cai, n. 212, p. 43]).

160. "Homo autem est in potentia ad scientiam beatorum, quae in visione Dei consistit, et ad eam ordinatur sicut ad finem; est enim creatura rationalis capax illius beatae cognitionis, inquantum est ad imaginem Dei" (*ST*, III, q. 9, a. 2).

From the theological point of view, the intrinsic orientation of the human intelligence toward the vision of God, the openness that constitutes human nature as intellectual, validates the description of man as being created in the "image of God." But philosophical reason cannot demonstrate that God gives man the vision of Himself. Human nature, however, is "in vain" if it cannot attain the only end that will satisfy its natural desire.

That which exists for an end that it cannot reach is vain. Therefore, since the end of man is happiness, to which his natural desire tends, the happiness of man is not able to be placed in that which man is not able to reach; otherwise it would follow that man is something in vain, and that his natural desire is in vain. [But] this is impossible. *(SCG, III, 44 [Pera, n. 2213, p. 56])*[161]

But are men divinely enabled to attain the vision of God Himself? The question is unanswerable philosophically. Just at this point, human destiny is utterly opaque to the philosopher. The philosopher cannot know whether human nature is able to attain the vision of God, since it cannot do so naturally.

This, then, is the deep paradox confronting the Thomistic philosopher. Philosophical reason, beginning with the natural desire for happiness, demonstrates that human nature cannot be satisfied by any end naturally attainable, and concludes that only a supernatural end, the vision of the divine essence, could satisfy man's natural desire. This conclusion is both a paradox and an *aporia*.[162] It marks an impasse beyond which reason can go no further. Once philosophical reason has reached its paradoxical conclusion, the natural endlessness of human nature, it must also acknowledge that it is impossible to know philo-

---

161. "Vanum enim est quod est ad finem non potest consequi. Cum igitur finis hominis sit felicitas, in quam tendit naturale ipsius desiderium, non potest poni felicitas hominis in eo ad quod homo pervenire non potest: alioquin sequeretur quod homo esset in vanum, et naturale eius desiderium esset inane, quod est impossibile" *(SCG, III, 44 [Pera, n. 2213, p. 56])*.

162. Zammit acknowledges *(Introductio in philosophiam moralem Thomisticam, 142)* the mystery: "Hic incipit mysterium pro philosopho. Homo enim naturaliter ordinatur ac tendit ad obiectum aliquod [primam causam . . . quidditative videndum (145)] sicut in suum ultimum finem quem tamen, . . . attingere numquam posset nisi gratuite ad alium ordinem naturam superexcedentem, a Deo elevetur." But he denies that the "mystery" consitutes either a philosophical paradox or an *aporia*: ". . . homo nesciret consecutionem talis finis requirere elevationem ad ordinem supernaturalem, quia exsistentiam talis ordinis ignoraret, et tale obiectum naturali illo desiderio desideraret ut mere naturale . . . . Et putans tale desiderium naturale non esse frustra, concluderet Deum vires proportionatas sibi dare posse." See n. 9 *supra*.

sophically whether man, whose intelligence is naturally oriented to the vision of God, is actually given such fulfillment. On the contrary, the philosopher must allow that it is entirely possible that human nature is vain or futile.

What, then, is the Thomistic philosopher to think of human nature? He cannot reject the conclusion that he has reached: human nature, whether or not it is supernaturally enabled to attain the vision of God, cannot be satisfied by any end that is naturally attainable. Indeed, the philosopher who has developed the Thomistic argument to this point can provide a systematic metaphysical demonstration of Augustine's acute psychological insight: human nature is indeed "restless" or, put more radically, "endless."[163] Now, it is as this point that the Thomistic philosopher should also reconsider the status of a putatively autonomous, Thomistic philosophical ethics. Initially, the development of this Thomistic philosophical ethics seemed congruent with the overall ideal of an autonomous Christian philosophy. Since "Christian philosophy," in keeping with de facto or de jure philosophical pluralism, is possible, why not develop a systematic, autonomous "Christian ethics" based solely on the philosophical principles of Thomas Aquinas? Nonetheless, it would now seem that the latter cannot be successfully constructed, at least not on the basis of Thomistic principles. The Thomist tradition relied on the doctrine of man's twofold end to ground a quasi-Aristotelian ethics. But the doctrine of *beatitudo imperfecta*, rightly understood, does not negate Aquinas's argument about the natural endlessness of human nature. This conclusion, moreover, not only radically distinguishes Aquinas from the quasi-Aristotelianism of the traditional Thomists, but it also obviates the project of an autonomous Thomistic philosophical ethics.

A philosophically autonomous Thomistic ethics, unlike, for example, an autonomous Thomistic metaphysics or epistemology, cannot be legitimately derived from Aquinas's theological ethics. Thomistic moral science is built on knowledge of the actual supernatural end of man, and that knowledge is strictly theological.[164] Especially here, one cannot conflate the formal object of Christian philosophy and the formal object of Christian theology: no intrinsic rational evidence, and especially not the Thomistic argument from "natural desire," allows us to demonstrate that men actually can attain the vision of the divine essence. Nonetheless, we must suppose that any systematic philoso-

163. See *SCG*, III, 59; *ST*, I, q. 62, a. 1. Cf. Joseph Buckley, *Man's Last End* (St. Louis: B. Herder, 1949), 164–210.

164. See *ST*, II–II, q. 4, a. 7; quoted in n. 21 *supra*.

phical ethics that can be identified as "Thomistic" will be a teleological and eudaimonistic ethics. But what attainable human end, one that can be known without a cloaked recourse to Christian faith, will ground an autonomous Thomistic philosophical ethics?[165] Thomistic philosophical reason reaches only the paradoxical conclusion that human nature has no naturally attainable end that can satisfy its desire for perfect happiness. If human nature is naturally endless, a *systematic teleological ethics* based on the ultimate natural end of man is manifestly impossible.

The projected development of an autonomous Thomistic philosophical ethics founders on the paradox latent in Aquinas's doctrine of man's natural endlessness. Reason could lead any philosopher who concurs with the Thomistic argument to affirm the endlessness of human nature. The Christian philosopher, as a Christian believer, understands human nature's endlessness as man's openness to the supernatural. Yet even the Christian philosopher qua philosopher can only remain poised, unable to utter a definitive "yea!" or "nay!" about hu-

---

165. Vernon J. Bourke, *Ethics: A Textbook in Moral Philosophy*, rev. ed. (New York: Macmillan, 1966), 41, acknowledges that "[i]t is necessary in [philosophical] moral science to know what the ultimate end of man is." Admitting that knowledge of our ultimate supernatural end is "beyond the limits of any kind of natural philosophy," Bourke nonetheless urges "the Christian moral philosopher . . . to consider this suggestion from theology. . . ." (ibid.). The consideration leads to the conclusion, "demonstrable from history," that "this concept of a supernatural end does bring reason and order into the lives of men who think and act in terms of it," especially into the lives of "the great Christian saints" (ibid.). Bourke has, with this conclusion, embraced a weaker version of Maritain's "moral philosophy adequately considered."

One cannot deny that belief in man's supernatural end has brought at least *order* into some human lives. But about the Christian martyrs, it has been remarked that their deaths do not prove the truths of Christianity, but instead only that the martyrs believed that Christianity was true. Cf. *ST*, II–II, q. 124, a. 5: ". . . unde et martyres Christi dicuntur, quasi testes ipsius. Huiusmodi autem est veritas fidei. Et ideo cuiuslibet martyrii causa est fidei veritas." And who, in this ecumenical age, would doubt that the most disparate and contradictory religious beliefs have brought "reason and order into the lives of men" and women? Cf. Emil L. Fackenheim, *God's Presence in History: Jewish Affirmations and Philosophical Reflections* (New York: New York University Press, 1970), 53: "The Messianic faith has been implicit in Judaism since its origins. . . . If, nevertheless, for nearly two thousand years they [i.e., believing Jews] have resisted the Christian Good News even at the price of continued exile, it has been because acceptance seemed a betrayal of the Jewish past so long as this world was unredeemed." What motivates the Christian philosopher "to accept the evidence of moral theology as to the real purpose of human life" (Bourke, *Ethics*, 42) is the divinely infused *theological virtue* of faith, not any "demonstration" from history: ". . . fides dirigit intentionem respectu finis ultimi supernaturalis" (*ST*, II–II, q. 10, a. 4, ad 2).

man destiny; the latter lies hidden within a God who may or may not choose to fulfill human nature. Such speechlessness or silence before what cannot be known rationally marks the end, not the beginning, of any autonomous philosophy.[166] This impasse can be escaped either by accepting what Christian faith teaches about man's actual supernatural destiny, but this is not an act of philosophy, or by proposing a naturalistic interpretation of the meaning of human nature's endlessness, and this is not an act of *Thomistic* philosophy.

The philosopher, especially a philosopher who could be described both as "post-Christian" and "postmodern," will surely take the latter alternative.[167] In a certain sense, Aquinas's doctrine of human endlessness is a remarkable anticipation of the postmodern notion of the contingency and open-endness of human pursuits. Of course, we should not exaggerate the similarity; Thomistic man has a nature, with various powers, and hence there remain the various natural *ends* to which

---

166. George P. Klubertanz, S.J., "Ethics and Theology," *Modern Schoolman* 27 (1949): 29–39, readily concedes that the Thomistic doctrine of man's natural endlessness leads to a philosophical "antinomy": the Thomistic philosopher can demonstrate that " seeing God" is the *finis qui* without being able to demonstrate the *finis quo*. The (presumably Thomistic) *philosophical science* of "Christian ethics may then be defined as that practical science of human action which even as a science recognizes . . . the antinomy of its argument . . ." (38). But can this antinomy really be maintained as the "operative principle" of a genuine philosophical ethics? Anguished incertitude about the possibility of ultimate human happiness hardly seems to provide an operative *practical* principle upon which to ground an autonomous and stable philosophical ethics. Although eager to deny any *theoretical* knowledge of God's existence and immortality, Kant argued that firm moral faith in "uninterrupted future happiness" is necessary in order to avoid an *absurdum practicum* that would otherwise undermine morality itself: see Immanuel Kant, *Lectures on Philosophical Theology*, trans. Allen W. Wood and Gertrude M. Clark (Ithaca, N.Y.: Cornell University Press, 1978), 122–23, 130. Klubertanz himself, however, destabilizes the foundation of his antinomous philosophical ethics by admitting that a Christian (Thomistic?) philosopher needs "Christian faith and theology . . . to maintain his hold on the first principle of ethics . . ." (38). If Klubertanz is correct, a return to Aristotle is both understandable and more philosophically coherent. Cf. Henry Veatch, "Natural Law: Dead or Alive?" in *Swimming against the Current*, 265: ". . . all human duties and human rights may be reasonably adjudged to be duties and rights only in so far as they can be justified, and thus shown to be duties or rights, in the light of man's natural end and perfection. Take away, then, this notion of a natural end or a natural perfection of human life, and there would no longer appear to be any ground on the basis of which rights or duties of any kind might be rationally justified."

167. Cf. Gerard Smith, S.J., "Philosophy and the Unity of Man's Ultimate End," in *Proceeding of the American Catholic Philosophical Association* 27 (1953): 81: "Philosophers can't quite see how the laws of spirit, which point to [the beatific] vision, can be fulfilled without vision. . . . Philosophers must come to the point of realizing that their thinking needs grace if it is to remain good thinking."

he is directed by the first principles of practical reason. But nothing ultimate comes from realizing these ends. Thomistic man, like postmodern man, has no natural orientation to some ultimate good or goods that can be realized either in time or eternity. As human nature is open-ended, so is human history and human fulfillment. This point of view, of course, is intolerable for anyone who holds for *the* natural end of man.[168]

Nonetheless, a return to the morally enclosed Aristotelian world, wherein the life of philosophical contemplation provides man with ultimate satisfaction, is impossible on both cosmological and metaphysical grounds. There are no "supremely noble beings," the unmoved movers, to populate our scientific cosmos. To be sure, the Thomistic philosopher likely will contend, against the current of modern and contemporary philosophical skepticism about such metaphysical proofs, that the existence of the supremely noble being, the infinite God, is demonstrable. Then one could argue that contemplating the God of metaphysics is morally salutary. But could one maintain, after Aquinas, that such philosophical contemplation "satisfies" human nature and thus, as Aristotle thought, ultimately delimits the meaning and end of human life and virtue on earth?

Aquinas's paradoxical insight about the vision of God, which nature demands but cannot provide, is Christian, but it is also part of the conceptual legacy of the so-called postmodern age. Of course, what

168. Cf. Grisez, "Man, Natural End of,"138, who simultaneously affirms that (1) "no single natural mode of human action has the perfection that Aristotle required of the end," and (2) "all goods truly perfective of man have a place in his natural end." Nonetheless, although Grisez does not relinquish the notion of *the* natural end of man, he does not argue in this early encyclopedia article that in naturally achieving the "ensemble of perfective goods" (ibid.), human nature is thereby ultimately fulfilled.

However, in *The Way of the Lord Jesus*, Vol. 1: *Christian Moral Principles*, 809–10, Grisez abandons the Augustinian notion of the *naturally* restless human heart, and the Thomistic notion that the natural endlessness of man is the mark of his supernatural calling. Instead Grisez now contends that "the human heart is not naturally oriented toward adoption as a child of God and the heavenly inheritance which goes with this status. It is naturally oriented toward human fulfillment, which is found in human goods. . . . [But] [t]his fulfillment is naturally only an ideal, not a determinate goal. . . ." In support of his present view, Grisez appeals to the traditional hypothesis that God could have created humanity in the state of pure nature without the addition of man's supernatural destiny. In the state of pure nature, the human heart is "restless," not for the vision of God, but solely (as Merleau-Ponty opined) "to keep mankind growing and progressing endlessly" (810). Grisez, however, admits (ibid.) that, de facto, man has a supernatural vocation and hence the human heart is now *supernaturally* restless for God.

was originally a theological paradox, the natural endlessness of human nature, is now seen as a neutral anthropological fact.[169] The paradox too has been neutralized since human endlessness is no longer viewed in reference to its original coordinates: the supernatural or transcendent Christian God and the order of Aristotelian nature. Nonetheless, the postmodern philosopher, if he or she is not content to rest with a neutral anthropological fact, will attempt to put to good philosophical use this now common insight into the endlessness of human nature. But what place can an originally theological insight have in philosophies that appeal neither to God nor to nature?[170]

At this juncture, many philosophical paths, which begin in the nineteenth-century reactions to Hegel's effort to ground human reason solely in itself,[171] could be explored, but I shall barely allude to a few that have been exceedingly well publicized in the middle and late twentieth century. Sartre recognized that human nature is, indeed, "vain," but he enjoined that authenticity in human choices brings value, although obviously not "ultimate value," to a human world that is otherwise meaningless.[172] In more sober terms, Merleau-Ponty meditated on the contingency of human history, which we interpret as the outcome of the endlessness of human nature, as the "condition of

169. Cf. Robert B. Pippin, *Modernism as a Philosophical Problem* (Cambridge, Mass.: Basil Blackwell, 1991), 165: ". . . modernity . . . is itself irresistibly provoked by the growing, ever more plausible possibility that what had been taken to be the absolute and transcendent was contingent and finite, since always "self-determined," a contingent product of a human positing."

170. Lucien Goldmann, *Immanuel Kant*, trans. Robert Black (London: NLB, 1971) asks why Kant postulated a "a superhuman and supernatural realization [of man] in eternity" (198). Goldman allows one "only serious answer" to his own question: "the social situation of Germany and particularly of Prussia at that time . . . made any hope in a *historical* future appear largely as illusion or utopia" (199).

171. Cf. Terry Pinkard, *Hegel's Phenomenology: The Sociality of Reason* (Cambridge: Cambridge University Press, 1994), 262: "[Hegelian] absolute *knowledge* is thus the way in which absolute *spirit* articulates itself in modern life; it is the practice through which the modern community thinks about itself without attempting to posit any metaphysical "other" or set of "natural constraints" that would underwrite those practices . . . [it] takes its authoritative standards to come only from within the structure of the practices it uses to legitimate and authenticate itself."

172. Cf. Jean-Paul Sartre, *Being and Nothingness: An Essay on Phenomenological Ontology*, trans. Hazel E. Barnes (NewYork: Philosophical Library, 1956), 627: ". . . ontology and existential psychoanalysis . . . must reveal to the moral agent that he is *the being by whom values exist*. It is then that his freedom will become conscious of itself and will reveal itself in anguish as the unique source of value and the nothingness by which the world exists."

possibility" for a more benign future.[173] A contingent future can be, but also may not be, morally and intellectually better than the human past or present. In this fashion, Merleau-Ponty turns "human endlessness" into the source of the good for man; it is properly and exclusively the human source of hope.[174] Still more recently, philosophers who celebrate the "deconstruction" of the modern era (with its allegedly "repressive" notion of an ahistorical or neutral rationality) have contended that the endlessness of contingent human pursuits permits an endless philosophical discourse which is the proper ideological matrix, so they claim, of the political freedoms and personal pleasures that we citizens of liberal democracies and consumer societies enjoy.[175]

There is, then, a changing variety of contemporaneous post-Christian, postmodern philosophical ethics, richly cognizant of the endlessness of man, but not at all oriented toward the Christian belief about the supernatural vision of God. Now a Christian philosopher would surely wish to confront these recent philosophical views that ignore and contradict, if not flatly reject, so fundamental a doctrine of the Christian faith. The Christian philosopher, if he or she does not wish to remain arcanely silent about the significance of the paradox of human endlessness, will doubtless respond by taking a route that differs from any of the above philosophies. However one proceeds, the contrary modern challenge, the Hegelian notion of a radically self-grounded human rationality, must also be fully articulated and somehow met. The Christian philosopher could argue, minimally, that the endlessness of human nature makes faith at least relevant to man's condition; this endlessness, *for the believer,* is the experienced opening

173. See Maurice Merleau-Ponty, "Man and Adversity," in *Signs,* trans. Richard C. McCleary ([Evanstan, Ill.: Northwestern University Press, 1964), 239: ". . . our times have experienced and are experiencing, more perhaps than any other, contingency. The contingency of evil to begin with: there is not a force at the beginning of human life which guides it towards its ruin or towards chaos. . . . But good is contingent too. . . . Progress is not necessary with a metaphysical necessity"; 241: "Today a humanism does not oppose religion with an explanation of the world. It begins by becoming aware of contingency."

174. See Maurice Merleau-Ponty, *In Praise of Philosophy,* trans. John Wild and James M. Edie (Evanstan, Ill.: Northwestern University Press, 1963), 43: "[The Philosopher] does not place his hope in any destiny, even a favorable one, but in something belonging to us which is precisely not a destiny—in the contingency of our history."

175. See Richard Rorty, *Contingency, Irony, and Solidarity* (Cambridge: Cambridge University Press, 1989), 61: "To see one's language, one's conscience, one's morality, and one's highest hopes as contingent products, as literalizations of what once were accidentally produced metaphors, is to adopt a self-identity which suits one for citizenship in such an ideally liberal state."

of human nature not to an endless secularity but to a supernatural destiny that precisely cannot be humanly self-grounded.[176] How much of this experience, though, can be exploited from a strictly philosophical angle? The answer can only be determined vis-à-vis one's own philosophical principles and method. Yet, in pondering this question, every Christian philosopher will inevitably be confronted with a much bigger step; he or she could attempt to develop Aquinas's metaphysical insight into human nature in a contemporary theological context. To take this step is to become, at least in this context and for this purpose, a theologian who views things *"sub ratione Dei."* But who would deny it is necessary, from the standpoint of a contemporary theological commitment to *sacra doctrina,* to enter into rational dialogue with post-Christian, postmodern philosophies?[177] To do so, would mark a return to the kind of "Christian philosophy" that Aquinas himself practiced.

176. Here I shall make but one observation about Grisez's view of human restlessness, a view that he acknowledges to be central to his whole moral theology: see *The Way of the Lord Jesus,* Vol. 1: *Christian Moral Principles,* 809. By confining human nature's restlessness for God as ultimate end *exclusively* to the supernatural level, it is doubtful that Grisez can overcome the split, as he aspires to do, between (secular) "humanism and fideistic supernaturalism" (811). On the contrary, it is the self-enclosed "naturalism" of secular humanism that created and maintains the split between it and Christian faith. If the *ideal* ensemble of perfective natural goods really orients man only to his historical future, Christian faith seems precisely an unwarranted fideistic leap into religious fantasy. In the modern period, Kant's conception of the *summum bonum* for man (happiness as a consequence of being morally virtuous), which is Kant's version of the naturally unattainable *ideal* of "integral human fulfillment," is exactly what led him to postulate the divine moral governor, whose *otherworldly realization* of the ideal makes it possible for the philosopher to believe in real human fulfillment and thus to act morally in this otherwise absurd life. Kant's act of philosophical faith, however incongruous it is with his other tenets about the absolute autonomy of the moral motive and however much it eviscerates Christian faith in a gratuitous redemption, rightly poses for his critics, then and now, the greatest threat to their self-enclosed humanism: "... Kant's resort to Providence was a betrayal of the heart of his moral philosophy, the principle of autonomy ... [which] requires that we make our own history, or take responsibility for our own fate" (Frederick C. Beiser, *Enlightenment, Revolution, and Romanticism: The Genesis of Modern German Political Thought, 1790–1800* [Cambridge, Mass.: Harvard University Press, 1992], 54–55). Cf. Lewis White Beck, *A Commentary on Kant's "Critique of Practical Reason"* (Chicago: University of Chicago Press, 1960), 244–45.

177. See Owens, *Human Destiny,* 43–44.

Bibliography and Indices

Works by Saint Thomas Aquinas

Sent.

Scriptum super libros Sententiarum magistri Petri Lombardi episcopi Parisiensis. Vols. 1–2. Edited by Pierre Mandonnet, O.P. Paris: P. Lethielleux, 1929. Vols. 3–4. Edited by Maria Fabianus Moos, O.P. Paris: P. Lethielleux, 1933–1947.

Commentum in quartum librum Sententiarum magistri Petri Lombardi. Vol. 11 of *Opera omnia Doctoris Angelici divi Thomae Aquinatis.* Edited by Stanislaus Eduardus Fretté. Paris: Ludovicus Vivès, 1874.

In quattuor libros Sententiarum. Vol. 1 of *Thomae Aquinatis opera omnia,* supplement to the *Index Thomisticus.* Supervised by Roberto Busa, S.J. Stuttgart-Bad Cannstatt: Frommann-Holzboog, 1980 [= First American Edition, vols. 6, 7/1, 7/2 (New York: 1948); reprinted Parma Edition, vols. 6 (1856), 7 (1858)].

SCG

Liber de veritate catholicae fidei contra errores infidelium seu "Summa contra gentiles." 4 vols. Edited by Ceslaus Pera, O.P., Petrus Marc, O.S.B., and Petrus Caramello. Turin and Rome: Marietti, 1963.

Summa contra gentiles. Vols. 13–15, *S. Thomae Aquinatis opera omnia.* Leonine Edition. With a commentary by Franciscus de Sylvester of Ferrara [Ferrariensis]. Rome: R. Garroni, 1918–1930.

ST

Summa theologiae. Ottawa Institute of Medieval Studies Edition. 5 vols. Ottawa: Dominican College of Ottawa, 1941–1945.

Summa theologiae. Vols. 4–12, *S. Thomae Aquinatis opera omnia*. Leonine Edition. With a commentary by Thomas de Vio, O.P. [Cajetan]. Rome: 1888–1906.

De ver.

De veritate. Vol. 1 of *Quaestiones disputatae*. Edited by Raymundus Spiazzi, O.P. Turin and Rome: Marietti, 1964.

De veritate. Vol. 22, pts. 1–3, *Sancti Thomae de Aquino opera omnia*. Leonine Edition. Rome: Editori di San Tommaso, 1975–1976.

De pot.

De potentia. Edited by Paulus M. Pession. In *Quaestiones disputatae*, ed. Raymundus Spiazzi, O.P. Vol. 2. Turin and Rome: Marietti, 1965.

De malo

De malo. Edited by P. Bazzi and P. M. Pession. In *Quaestiones disputatae*, ed. Raymundus Spiazzi, O.P. Vol. 2. Turin and Rome: Marietti, 1965.

De malo. Vol. 23, *Sancti Thomae de Aquino opera omnia*. Leonine Edition. Rome: Commissio Leonina; Paris: J. Vrin, 1982.

De spirit. creat.

De spiritualibus creaturis. Edited by M. Calcaterra and T. S. Centi. In *Quaestiones disputatae*, ed. Raymundus Spiazzi, O.P. Vol. 2. Turin and Rome: Marietti, 1965.

Q. de an.

Quaestiones de anima. Edited by James H. Robb. Toronto: Pontifical Institute of Mediaeval Studies, 1968.

De virt.

De virtutibus in communi. Edited by P. A. Odetto. In *Quaestiones disputatae*, ed. Raymundus Spiazzi, O.P. Vol. 2. Turin and Rome: Marietti, 1965.

De car.

De caritate. Edited by P. A. Odetto. In *Quaestiones disputatae*, ed. Raymundus Spiazzi, O.P. Vol. 2. Turin and Rome: Marietti, 1965.

De virt. card.

De virtutibus cardinalibus. Edited by P. A. Odetto. In *Quaestiones disputatae*, ed. Raymundus Spiazzi, O.P. Vol. 2. Turin and Rome: Marietti, 1965.

Quod.

Quaestiones quodlibetales. 9th ed. Edited by Raymundus Spiazzi, O.P. Turin and Rome: Marietti, 1956.

In psalmos

In psalmos Davidis expositio. Vol. 5, *Opera omnia Doctoris Angelici divi Thomae Aquinatis*. Edited by Stanislaus Eduardus Fretté. Paris: Vivès, 1874.

Super Ioannem	*Super evangelium s. Ioannis.* 5th ed. Edited by Raphaelis Cai, O.P. Turin: Marietti, 1952.
Super Matth.	*Super evangelium secundum Matthaeum.* Vol. 1 of *In evangelia s. Matthaei et s. Joannis.* 4th ed. Turin: Marietti, 1925.
Ad Ephes.	*Ad Ephesios.* Vol. 2 of *Super epostolas s. Pauli.* Edited by Raphael Cai, O.P. Turin and Rome: Marietti, 1953.
ELPH	*Expositio libri Peryermenias.* Vol. 1, pt. 1, *Sancti Thomae de Aquino opera omnia.* 2d rev. Leonine Edition. Rome: Commissio Leonina; Paris: J. Vrin, 1989.
ELP	*Expositio libri Posteriorum.* Vol. 1, pt. 2, *Sancti Thomae de Aquino opera omnia.* 2d rev. Leonine Edition. Rome: Commissio Leonina; Paris: J. Vrin, 1989.
In Phys.	*In octo libros Physicorum Aristotelis expositio.* Edited by P. M. Maggiòlo, O.P. Turin and Rome: Marietti, 1965.
SLA	*Sentencia libri de anima.* Vol. 22, pts. 1–3, *Sancti Thomae de Aquino opera omnia.* Leonine Edition. Rome: Commissio Leonina; Paris: J. Vrin, 1984.
In de An.	*In Aristotelis librum de anima commentarium.* 6th ed. Edited by Angelus M. Pirotta, O.P. Turin and Rome: Marietti, 1959.
In Metaph.	*In duodecim libros Metaphysicorum Aristotelis expositio.* 2d ed. Edited by M. R. Cathala, O.P., and Raymundus M. Spiazzi, O.P. Turin and Rome: Marietti, 1971.
SLE	*Sententia libri Ethicorum.* Vol. 47, pt. 1, bks 1–3; Vol. 47, pt. 2, bks 4–10, *Sancti Thomae de Aquino opera omnia.* Leonine Edition. Rome: 1969.
In Ethic.	*In decem libros Ethicorum Aristotelis ad Nicomachum expositio.* 3d ed. Edited by Raymundus M. Spiazzi, O.P. Turin and Rome: Marietti, 1964.
SLP	*Sententia libri Politicorum.* Vol. 48, *Sancti Thomae de Aquino opera omnia.* Leonine Edition. Rome: 1971.
In Pol.	*In octo libros Politicorum Aristotelis expositio.* Edited by Raymundus M. Spiazzi, O.P. Turin and Rome: Marietti, 1966.

Expos. de Trin.   *Expositio super librum Boethii de trinitate.* Rev.
                         ed. Edited by Bruno Decker. Leiden: J. Brill, 1959.

In de Heb.   *In librum Boethii de hebdomadibus expositio.* In
                         Opuscula theologica, ed. by Mannis Calcaterra, O.P.
                         Turin and Rome: Marietti, 1954.

In de Div. Nom.   *In librum beati Dionysii de divinis nominibus*
                         expositio. Edited by Ceslaus Pera, O.P. Turin and
                         Rome: Marietti, 1950.

In de Causis   *In librum de causis expositio.* Edited by Ceslaus
                         Pera, O.P. Turin and Rome: Marietti, 1955.
                         Super librum de causis expositio. Edited by H. D.
                         Saffrey, O.P. Fribourg: Société Philosophique;
                         Louvain: Éditions E. Nauwelaerts, 1954.

De unit. int.   *De unitate intellectus contra Averroistas.* In
                         Opuscula philosophica, ed. by Raymundus M.
                         Spiazzi, O.P. Turin and Rome: Marietti, 1954.
                         De unitate intellectus contra Averroistas. Vol. 43,
                         Sancti Thomae de Aquino opera omnia. Leonine
                         Edition. Rome: Editori di San Tommaso, 1976.

De ente   *De ente et essentia.* In *Opuscula philosophica,* ed.
                         by Raymundus M. Spiazzi, O.P. Turin and Rome:
                         Marietti , 1954.
                         De ente et essentia. Vol. 43, *Sancti Thomae de*
                         Aquino opera omnia. Leonine Edition. Rome: Editori
                         di San Tommaso, 1976.

Comp. theol.   *Compendium theologiae ad fratrem Reginaldum*
                         socium suum carissimum. In *Opuscula theologica,*
                         ed. by Raymundus A. Verardo, O.P. Turin and Rome:
                         Marietti, 1954.
                         Compendium theologiae. Vol. 42, *Sancti Thomae*
                         de Aquino opera omnia. Leonine Edition. Rome:
                         Editori di San Tommaso, 1979.

De sub. sep.   *De substantiis separatis seu de angelorum natura*
                         ad fratrem Reginaldum socium suum carissimum. In
                         Opuscula philosophica, ed. by Raymundus M.
                         Spiazzi, O.P. Turin and Rome: Marietti, 1954.
                         De substantiis separatiis. Vol. 40, *Sancti Thomae*
                         de Aquino opera omnia. Leonine Edition. Rome:
                         1969.

De reg.   *De regimine principium ad regem Cypri.* In
                         Opuscula philosophica, ed. by Raymundus M.
                         Spiazzi, O.P. Turin and Rome: Marietti, 1954.

Works by Ancient, Medieval, and Early Modern Authors

Albertus Magnus. *Super Ethica: commentum et quaestiones.* Edited by Wilhelmus Kübel. Vol. 14, pt. 1 of *Opera omnia.* Cologne Albertus Magnus Institute Edition. Munster: Aschendorff, 1968.

_____. *Ethica.* Vol. 7 of *Opera omnia.* Edited by Augustus Borgnet and Aemilius Borgnet. Paris: Vivès, 1890–1899.

Alighieri, Dante. *Inferno.* Edited by Umberto Bosco and Giovanni Reggio. Florence: Le Monier, 1981.

Aristotle. *Opera.* Revised Royal Prussian Academy Edition (1831). Edited by Olof Gignon. 2 vols. Berlin: Walter de Gruyter, 1960.

_____. *The Complete Works of Aristotle.* Rev. Oxford Trans. Edited by Jonathan Barnes. 2 vols. Princeton, New Jersey: Princeton University Press, 1984.

_____. *The Nicomachean Ethics.* Trans. by H. Rackham. Loeb Classical Library, vol. 19. Cambridge, Mass.: Harvard University Press, 1968.

Augustine, Saint. *De trinitate.* Edited by W. J. Mountain and Fr. Glorie. *Corpus Christianorum, Series Latina,* vols. 50–5a. Turnholti: Brepols, 1968.

Baius, Michael. "*Ex libro primo de prima hominis justitia.*" In *Opera omnia,* ed. Gerberon. Cologne: 1696.

Bañes, Dominico. *Scholastica commentaria in primam partem Summae theologicae s. Thomae Aquinatis.* [Salamanca: 1585] Edited with a general introduction by Luis Urbano. Madrid and Valencia: Biblioteca de Tomistas Españoles, 1934.

Billuart, Carolus Renatus, O.P. *Summa sancti Thomae hodiernis academiarum moribus accommodata.* [Liège, 1746–1751] 8 vols. Paris: Victor Palmé, 1872–1877.

Capreolus, Ioannes. *Defensiones theologiae divi Thomae Aquinatis.* [Venice: 1480–1484] 7 vols. Edited by C. Paban and T. Pègues. Turin: Cattier, 1900–1908.

de Godoy, Petrus, O.P. *Disputationes theologicae: In primam partem divi Tho-mae.* Vol. 1, tractatus 1, *De beatitudine supernaturali;* tractatus 2, *De beati-tudine naturali.* Venice: 1696.

Descartes, René. "Dedicatory Letter to the Sorbonne." In *Meditations on First Philosophy,* Vol. 2 of *The Philosophical Writings of Descartes,* translated by John Cottingham, Robert Stoothhoff, and Dugald Murdoch, 3–6. Cambridge: Cambridge University Press, 1984.

Joannis a Sancto Thoma, O.P. *Cursus theologici.* [Lyons: 1643] Solesmes Edi-tion. 5 vols. Paris: Desclée, 1931–1964.

Suarez, Franciscus, S.J., *Opera omnia.* Edited D. M. André. 2d ed. 30 vols. Paris: Vivès, 1886.

Works by Modern and Contemporary Authors

Abbà, Giuseppe. *Lex et virtus: studi sull'evoluzione della dottrina morale di san Tommaso d'Aquino.* Rome: Libreria Ateneo Salesiano, 1983.

Ackrill, J. L. "Aristotle on *Eudaimonia.*" *Proceedings of the British Academy* 60 (1974): 339–59. Reprinted in Richard Rorty, ed., *Essays on Aristotle's Ethics* (Berkeley and Los Angeles: University of California Press, 1980), 15–33; Christian Mueller-Goldingen, ed., *Schriften zur aristotelischen Ethik* (Hildesheim: Georg Olms Verlag, 1988), 335–55.

Aertsen, Jan. *Nature and Creature: Thomas Aquinas's Way of Thought.* Leiden: E. J. Brill, 1988.

Alfaro, Juan, S.J. *Lo natural y lo sobrenatural: Estudio historico desede Santo Tomas hasta Cayetan (1274–1534).* Burgos: Matriti, 1952.

Allan, D. J. "Aristotle's Account of the Origin of Moral Principles." In *Proceedings of the XIth International Congress of Philosophy,* Vol. 12: *History of Philosophy: Methodology, Antiquity and the Middle Ages,* 120–27. Amsterdam and Louvain: North Holland Publishing Co. and Editions E. Nauwelaerts, 1953.

———. *The Philosophy of Aristotle.* Rev. ed. London: Oxford University Press, 1963.

———. "The Practical Syllogism." In *Autour d'Aristote,* 325–40. Louvain: Publications Universitaires de Louvain, 1955.

Allard, G. H. "The Primacy of Existence in the Thought of Eriugena." In *Neoplatonism and Christian Thought,* ed. Dominic J. O'Meara, 89–96. Albany: State University of New York Press, 1982.

Anagnostopoulos, Georgios. *Aristotle on the Goals and Exactness of Ethics.* Berkeley and Los Angeles: University of California Press, 1994.

Ando, Takatura. *Aristotle's Theory of Practical Cognition.* The Hague: Martinus Nijhoff, 1971.

Anscombe, G. E. M. "Modern Moral Philosophy." *Philosophy* 33 (1958): 1–19. Reprinted in *The Is-Ought Question: A Collection of Papers on the Central Problem in Moral Philosophy,* ed. W. D. Hudson, 175–95. London: Macmillan Press, 1963.

Anton, John P., and Anthony Preuss, eds. *Aristotle's Ethics*. Albany: State University of New York Press, 1991.

Apostle, Hippocrates G. *Aristotle's Posterior Analytics*. Grinnell, Iowa: Peripatetic Press, 1981.

Arendt, Hannah. *The Human Condition*. Chicago: University of Chicago Press, 1958.

Argote, German Marquinez. *El "si" y el "no" de la filosofia moral christiana: Exposicion y critica de una teoria de Jacques Maritain*. Madrid: Ediciones Studium, 1964.

Armstrong, R. A. *Primary and Secondary Precepts in Thomistic Natural Law Teaching*. The Hague: Martinus Nijhoff, 1966.

Arniz, O., Fr. Candido. "Definicion Augustiniano—Tomista del acto de fey." *La Ciencia Tomista* 80 (1953): 25–74.

Arrington, Robert L. *Rationalism, Realism, and Relativism: Perspectivies in Contemporary Moral Epistemology*. Ithaca, N. Y.: Cornell University Press, 1989.

Aubenque, Pierre. *La Prudence chez Aristote*. Paris: Presses Universitaires de France, 1963.

———. "La Prudence Aristotélicienne portetelle sur la fin ou sur les moyens?" *Revue des études grecques* 78 (1965): 40–51.

———. *Le Problème de l'être chez Aristote*. Paris: Presses Universitaires de France, 1972.

———. "Gilson et la question de l'être." In *Étienne Gilson et nous: La philosophie de sa histoire*, ed. Monique Couratier, 79–92. Paris: J. Vrin, 1980.

Audi, Robert. *The Structure of Justification*. Cambridge: Cambridge University Press, 1993.

Aubert, Roger. "Le Traité de la foi de S. Thomas." In *Le Problème de l'acte de foi: données traditionnelles et résultats des controverses récentes*, 43–71. 3d ed. Louvain: E. Warny, 1958.

Barnes, Jonathan. "Aristotle's Theory of Demonstration." In *Articles on Aristotle*, Vol. 1: *Science*, ed. Jonathan Barnes, Malcolm Schofield, and Richard Sorabji, 65–87. London: Duckworth, 1975.

———. *Aristotle's Posterior Analytics*. Oxford: Clarendon Press, 1975.

Batalló, Ricardo Marimón. "Los fundamentos de la etica en Tomas de Aquino." In *Morale et diritto nella prospettiva tomistica*, 7–21. Atti dell'VIII congresso tomistico internazionale. Studi tomistici, vol. 15. Vatican City: Libreria Editrice Vaticana, 1982.

Beck, Lewis White. *A Commentary on Kant's "Critique of Practical Reason."* Chicago: University of Chicago Press, 1960.

Beiser, Frederick C. *The Genesis of Modern German Political Thought, 1790–1800*. Cambridge, Mass.: Harvard University Press, 1992.

Belmans, Théo G., O. Praem. "Le 'Volontarisme' de saint Thomas d'Aquin." *Revue thomiste* 85 (1985): 181–96.

———. "Au croisement des chemins en morale fondamentale." *Revue thomiste* 89 (1989): 254–55.

———. "Le 'Jugement prudentiel' chez saint Thomas." *Revue thomiste* 91 (1991): 414–20.

Bennett, Owen, O.M.C. *The Nature of Demonstrative Proof According to the Principles of Arisotle and St. Thomas Aquinas.* Philosophical Studies, Vol. 75. Washington, D.C.: The Catholic University of America Press, 1943.

Berti, Enrico. "The Intellection of 'Indivisibles' According to Aristotle, *De Anima* III 6." In *Aristotle on Mind and the Senses: Proceedings of the Seventh Symposium Aristotelicum,* ed. G. E. R. Lloyd and G. E. L. Owen, 141–63. Cambridge: Cambridge University Press, 1978.

Blackburn, Simon. "Supervenience Revisited." In *Essays in Moral Realism,* ed. Geoffrey Sayre-McCord, 59–75. Ithaca, N. Y.: Cornell University Press, 1988.

Boas, George. *Rationalism in Greek Philosophy.* Baltimore: Johns Hopkins University Press, 1961.

Bobik, Joseph. *Aquinas on Being and Essence: A Translation and Interpretation.* Notre Dame, Ind.: University of Notre Dame Press, 1965.

Bogliolo, Luigi. *La filosofia Christiania: Il problema, la storia, la struttura.* Studi tomistici, vol. 28. Vatican City: Libreria Editrice Vaticana, 1986.

Bolton, Robert. "Definition and Scientific Method in Aristotle's *Posterior Analytics* and *Generation of Animals.*" In *Philosophical Issues in Aristotle's Biology,* ed. Allan Gotthelf and James G. Lennox, 145–46. Cambridge: Cambridge University Press, 1987.

Bonnefoy, J.-F., O.F.M. "La Théologie comme science et l'explication de la foi selon saint Thomas d'Aquin." *Ephemerides theologicae Lovaniensis* 14 (1937): 421–46, 600–631; 15 (1938): 491–516. Reprinted as *La Nature de la théologie selon saint Thomas d'Aquin.* Paris and Bruges: J. Vrin and Ch. Beyaert, 1939.

Bossi De Kirchner, Beatriz. "Aquinas as an Interpreter of Aristotle on the End of Human Life." *Review of Metaphysics* 40 (1986): 41–54.

———. "On the Power of Practical Reason." *Review of Metaphysics* 43 (1989): 41–71.

Bourke, Vernon J. Review of *Philosophische Ethik bei Thomas von Aquin,* by Wolfgang Kluxen. *New Scholasticism* 39 (1965): 265–67.

———. *Ethics: A Textbook in Moral Philosophy.* Rev. ed. New York: Macmillan, 1966.

———. *St. Thomas and the Greek Moralists.* Aquinas Lecture 1974. Milwaukee: Marquette University Press, 1974.

———. "The Nicomachean Ethics and Thomas Aquinas." In *St. Thomas Aquinas, 1274–1974: Commemorative Studies,* editor-in-chief Armand A. Maurer, C.S.B., 2 vols., 2: 239–59. Toronto: Pontifical Institute of Mediaeval Studies, 1974.

———. "The Background of Aquinas' Synderesis Principle." In *Graceful Reason: Essays in Ancient and Medieval Philosophy Presented to Joseph Owens, CSsR.,* ed. Lloyd P. Gerson, 345–60. Toronto: Pontifical Institute of Mediaeval Studies, 1983.

———. "The Synderesis Rule and Right Reason." *Monist* 66 (1983): 71–82.

Boyle, Leonard, O.P. *The Setting of the "Summa Theologiae" of Saint Thomas.* Toronto: Pontifical Institute of Mediaeval Studies, 1982.

Bradley, Denis J. M. "Aristotelian Science and the Science of Thomistic Theology." *Heythrop Journal* 22 (1981): 162–72.

————. "Philosophy and Theology, Western: To Mid 12th Century." In *Dictionary of the Middle Ages*, 9: 582–90. New York: Charles Scribner's Sons, 1987.
————. "Philosophical Pluralism and 'The Internal Evolution of Thomism': Some Realist Animadversions." In *Thomistic Papers VI*, ed. John F. X. Knasas, 195–228. Houston, Texas: Center for Thomistic Studies, 1994.

Bradley, Raymond, and Norman Swartz. *Possible Worlds: An Introduction to Logic and Its Philosophy*. Indianapolis, Ind.: Hacket, 1979.

Bréhier, Emil. "La Notion de philosophie chrétienne." *Bulletin de la société française de philosophie* 31 (1931): 37–93, passim.

Broadie, Sarah Waterlow. "The Problems of Practical Intellect in Aristotle's *Ethics*." In *Proceedings of the Boston Area Colloquium in Ancient Philosophy*, ed. John J. Cleary, 3: 229–52. Lanham, Md.: University Press of America, 1988.
————. *Ethics with Aristotle*. Oxford: Oxford University Press, 1991.

Brown, Oscar J. *Natural Rectitude and Divine Law in Aquinas*. Toronto: Pontifical Institute of Mediaeval Studies, 1981.

Bruch, Jean-Louis. *La Philosophie religieuse de Kant*. Paris: Aubier, 1968.

Buckley, Joseph. *Man's Last End*. St. Louis: B. Herder Book Co., 1949.

Buckley, Michael J., S.J. *At the Origins of Modern Atheism*. New Haven, Conn.: Yale University Press, 1987.

Bullet, Gabriel. *Vertus morales infuses et vertus moral acquises selon saint Thomas D'Aquin*. Fribourg, Switzerland: Editions Universitaires, 1958.

Burnet, John, ed. *The Ethics of Aristotle*. London: Methuen, 1900. Reprint. New York: Arno Press, 1973.

Butchvarov, Panayot. *Skepticism in Ethics*. Bloomington: Indiana University Press, 1989.

Callebaut, A. "Alexandre de Hales, O.F.M., et ses confrères en face de condemnations parisiennes de 1241 et 1244." *La France franciscaine* 10 (1927): 257–72.

Callus, Daniel A., O.P. "Les Sources de saint Thomas." In *Aristote et saint Thomas d'Aquin*, by Paul Moraux et al., 95–174. Louvain: Publications Universitaires de Louvain; Paris: Éditions Béatrice-Nauwelaerts, 1957.

Catan, John R., ed. *St. Thomas Aquinas on the Existence of God: The Collected Papers of Joseph Owens*. Albany: State University of New York Press, 1980.
————. *Aristotle: The Collected Papers of Joseph Owens*. Albany: State University of New York Press, 1981.

Cauchy, Venant. *Désir naturel et béatitude chez saint Thomas*. Montreal: Fides, 1958.

Celano, Anthony J. "Boethius of Dacia: 'On the Highest Good.'" *Traditio* 43 (1987): 199–214.
————. "The Concept of Wordly Beatitude in the Writings of Thomas Aquinas." *Journal of the History of Philosophy* 25 (1987): 215–26.
————. "The 'Finis Hominis' in the Thirteenth-Century Commentaries on Aristotle's *Nicomachean Ethics*." *Archives d'histoire doctrinale et littéraire du moyen âge* 53 (1987): 23–53.
————. "Act of the Intellect or Act of the Will: The Crticial Reception of

Aristotle's Ideal of Human Perfection in the 13th and Early 14th Centuries." *Archives d'histoire doctrinale et littéraire du moyen âge* 57 (1990): 93–119.

Charles, David. *Aristotle's Philosophy of Action.* Ithaca, N. Y. : Cornell University Press, 1984.

Charlier, L., O.P. *Essai sur le problème théologique.* Thuillies, Belgium: Ramboux-Gallot, 1938.

Chenu, M.-D., O.P. *Toward Understanding St. Thomas.* Translated by A.-M Landry, O.P., and D. Hughes, O.P. Chicago: Henry Regnery, 1964.

Chenu, M.-D., O.P. *La Science théologique.* 3d ed. Paris: J. Vrin, 1957. An expanded version of "La Théologie comme science au xiiie siècle," published in *Archives d'histoire doctrinale et littéraire du moyen âge* 2 (1927): 31–71.

Clark, Stephen R. L. *Aristotle's Man: Speculations upon Aristotelian Anthropology.* Oxford: Clarendon Press, 1975.

Collins, James. "Christian Philosophers and the Modern Turn." In *The Impact of Belief: The New Dialogue of Philosophy and Theology,* ed. George F. McLean, 1–24. Lancaster, Pa.: Concorde, 1974.

———. *The Emergence of Philosophy of Religion.* New Haven, Conn.: Yale University Press, 1967.

Congar, M.-J., O.P. Comptes rendus. *Bulletin thomiste* 5 (1937–1939): 490–505.

Cooper, John. *Reason and Human Good in Aristotle.* Cambridge, Mass.: Harvard University Press, 1975.

Coreth, Emerich. *Metaphysics.* Edited by Joseph Donceel. New York: Herder and Herder, 1968.

Corvez, M. Review of *Philosophische Ethik bei Thomas von Aquin,* by Wolfgang Kluxen. *Revue thomiste* 69 (1969): 514.

Costa, Christina D'Ancona. Introduction to *Tommaso D'Aquino, Commento al Libro delle cause.* Translated and edited by Christina D'Ancona Costa. Milan: Rusconi, 1986.

Courtès, Pierre-Ceslas, O.P. "Coherence de l'être et premier principe selon saint Thomas d'Aquin." *Revue thomiste* 70 (1970): 387–423.

Crosignani, Giacomo, C.M. *La teoria del naturale e del soprannaturale secondo s. Tommaso d'Aquino.* Piacenza, Italy: Collegio Alberoni, 1974.

Crowe, Michael Bertram. "Synderesis and the Notion of Law in Saint Thomas." In *L'Homme et son destin d'après les penseurs du moyen âge,* 601–9. Actes du premier congrès international de philosophie médiévale, 1958. Louvain: Éditions Nauwelaerts; Paris: Béatrice-Naeuwelaerts, 1960.

C[uppens], M[aurice]. Review of *Surnaturel: études historiques,* by Henri de Lubac. *Bulletin de théologie ancienne et médiévale* 5 (1947): 251–54.

Dahl, Norman O. *Practical Reason, Aristotle, and Weakness of the Will.* Minneapolis: University of Minnesota Press, 1984.

Davidson, Donald. *Actions and Events.* Oxford: Clarendon Press, 1980.

de Broglie, Vitus, S.J. *De fine ultimo humanae vitae.* Paris: Beauchesne, 1948.

de Corte, Marcel. *La Doctrine de l'intelligence chez Aristote.* Paris: J. Vrin, 1934.

de Finance, J., S.J. Review of *Philosophische Ethik bei Thomas von Aquin,* by Wolfgang Kluxen. *Gregorianum* 46 (1965): 432–33.

de Lubac, Henri. *Surnaturel: études historiques.* Paris: F. Aubier, 1946.
———. *Le Mystère du surnaturel.* Paris: F. Aubier, 1965.
———. *Augustinisme et théologie moderne.* Paris: F. Aubier, 1965.
———. *The Mystery of the Supernatural.* Translated by Rosemary Sheed. New York: Herder and Herder, 1967.
———. *Augustinianism and Modern Theology.* Translated by Lancelot Sheppard. London: Geoffrey Chapman, 1969.
———. *Lettres de M. Étienne Gilson adressées au P. Henri de Lubac et commentées par celui-ci.* Paris: Les Éditions du Cerf, 1986.
———. *Letters of Etienne Gilson to Henri de Lubac.* Translated by Mary Emily Hamilton. San Francisco: Ignatius Press, 1988.
de Vogel, C. J. "On the Character of Aristotle Ethics." In *Philomathes: Studies and Essays in the Humanities in Memory of Philip Merlan,* ed. Robert B. Palmer and Robert Hamerton-Kelly, 116–24. The Hague: Martinus Niihjoff, 1971. Reprinted in Christian Mueller-Goldingen, ed., *Schriften zur aristotelischen Ethik* (Hildesheim: Georg Olms Verlag, 1988), 273–81.
de Vries, J., S.J. Review of *Philosophische Ethik bei Thomas von Aquin,* by Wolfgang Kluxen. *Scholastik* 40 (1965): 114–16.
Deely, John. "Editorial Afterword." Appendix to *Tractatus De Signis: The Semiotic of John Poinsot,* 391–514. Berkeley and Los Angeles: University of California Press, 1985.
Deman, Th., O.P. "Le 'Précepte' de la prudence chez saint Thomas d'Aquin." *Recherches de théologie ancienne et médiévale* 20 (1953): 40–59.
Descoqs, Pedro, S.J. *Praelectiones theologiae naturalis: cours de théodicée.* 2 vols. Paris: Beauchesne, 1935.
———. *Le Mystère de notre élévation surnaturelle.* Paris: Gabriel Beauchesne, 1938.
Devereux, Daniel T. "Aristotle on Essence of Happiness." In *Studies in Aristotle,* ed. Dominic O'Meara, 247–60. Washington, D.C.: The Catholic University of America Press, 1981.
———. "Aristotle on the Active and Contemplative Lives." *Philosophical Research Archives* (Bowling Green State University: Philosophy Documentation Center): 3, no. 1138 (1977), microfiche.
———. "Particular and Universal in Aristotle's Conception of Practical Knowledge." *Review of Metaphysics* 39 (1986): 483–504.
Dilman, Ilham. "Are There Logical Truths?" In *Quine on Ontology, Necessity, and Experience,* 72–105. Albany: State University of New York Press, 1984.
Donadío Maggi de Gandolfi, María C. "El papel de la Filosofía moral e la moral teologíca de Santo Tomás." In *S. Tommaso filosofo: Ricerche in occasione dei due centenari accademici,* 113–28. Edited Antonio Piolanti. Studi tomistici, vol. 60. Vatican City State: Libreria Editrice Vaticana, 1995.
Donagan, Alan. *The Theory of Morality.* Chicago: University of Chicago Press, 1977.
———. "Thomas Aquinas on Human Action." In *The Cambridge History of Later Medieval Philosophy,* ed. Norman Kretzman, Anthony Kenny, and Jan Pinborg, with Eleonore Stump, 642–54. Cambridge: Cambridge University Press, 1982.

————. *Human Ends and Human Actions: An Exploration in St. Thomas's Treatment*. The Aquinas Lecture for 1985. Milwaukee, Wis.: Marquette University Press, 1985.

Dondaine, H.-F., and L.-J. Bataillon. Preface to *Sententia libri Politicorum*. In *Sancti Thomae Aquinatis opera omnia*. Leonine Edition, Vol. 48. Rome, 1971.

Dumas, Marie-Noëlle. "La Definition de la prudence chez Thomas d'Aquin et ses relations avec la definition d'Aristote." *Bulletin du cercle thomiste, Caen*, no. 2 (1978): 19–30; no. 3, (1978): 3–14.

Dunbabin, Jean. "The Two Commentaries of Albertus Magnus on the *Nicomachean Ethics*." *Recherches de théologie ancienne et médiévale* 30 (1963): 232–50.

Dworkin, Gerald. "Autonomy, Science, and Morality." In *The Theory and Practice of Autonomy*, 48–61. Cambridge: Cambridge University Press, 1988.

Elders, Leon, S.V.D. *Faith and Science: An Introduction to St. Thomas' "Expositio in Boethii De Trinitate."* Rome: Herder, 1974.

————. "Saint Thomas d'Aquin et Aristote." *Revue thomiste* 88 (1988): 357–76.

Elders, Leon, S.V.D., and K. Hedwig, eds. *The Ethics of St. Thomas Aquinas*. Vatican City: Libreria Editrice Vaticana, 1984.

Elter, E., S.I. "De natuali hominis beatitudine ad mentem scholae antiquioris." *Gregorianum* 9 (1928): 269–306.

Engberg-Pedersen, Troels. *Aristotle's Theory of Moral Insight*. Oxford: Clarendon Press, 1983.

Eriksen, Trond Berg. *Bios Theoretikos*. Oslo: Universitets-forlaget, 1976.

Eschmann, I. T., O.P. "A Catalogue of St. Thomas's Works: Bibliographical Note." Appendix in Etienne Gilson, *The Christian Philosophy of St. Thomas Aquinas*, trans. L. K. Shook, C.S.B., 381–439. New York: Random House, 1956.

Ewbank, Michael B. "Remarks on Being in St. Thomas Aquinas' *Expositio De Divinis Nominibus*." *Archives d'histoire doctrinale et littéraire du moyen âge* 56 (1989): 123–49.

Fabro, Cornelio, C.P.S. *Participation et causalité selon s. Thomas d'Aquin*. Louvain and Paris: Publications Universitaires de Louvain and Éditions Béatrice-Nauwelaerts, 1961.

————. *God in Exile: Modern Atheism*. Translated by Arthur Gibson. New York: Newman Press, 1968.

————. "Platonism, Neo-Platonism, and Thomism: Convergencies and Divergencies." *New Scholasticism* 44 (1970): 69–100.

————. "The Intensive Hermeneutics of Thomistic Philosophy: The Notion of Participation." *Review of Metaphysics* 27 (1974): 449–91.

————. "La dialettica d'intelligenza e voluntà nella costituzione esistenziale dell'atto libero." In *Etica e società contemporanea*, Acts of the Third International Congress of the Società internazionale s. Tommaso d'Aquina, 3 vols., ed. L. Lobato, O.P., 1: 25–53. *Studi tomistici*, vol. 48. Vatican City: Libreria Editrice Vaticana, 1992.

Fackenheim, Emil L. *God's Presence in History: Jewish Affirmations and Philosophical Reflections*. New York: New York University Press, 1970.

————. *The Religious Dimension in Hegel's Thought.* Bloomington: Indiana University Press, 1971.

Falanga, Anthony J. *Charity the Form of the Virtues According to Saint Thomas.* Studies in Sacred Theology, Second Series, No. 18. Washington, D.C.: The Catholic University of America Press, 1948.

Ferejohn, Michael. *The Origins of Aristotelian Science.* New Haven, Conn.: Yale University Press, 1991.

Finnis, J. M. *Natural Law and Natural Rights.* Oxford: Clarendon Press, 1980.

————. "Practical Reasoning, Human Goods, and the End of Man." *Proceedings of the American Catholic Philosophical Association* 58 (1984): 23–36.

————. "Natural Inclinations and Natural Rights: Deriving 'Ought' from 'Is' According to Aquinas." In *Lex et Libertas: Freedom and Law According to St. Thomas Aquinas,* ed. L. J. Elders and K. Hedwig, 43–55. Vatican City: Pontificia Accademia di S. Thommaso, 1987.

Frankena, William K. *Ethics.* 2d ed. Englewood Cliffs, N. J.: Prentice-Hall, 1973.

————. "Love and Principles in Christian Ethics." In *Perspectives on Morality,* ed. Kenneth E. Goodpaster, 74–92. Notre Dame, Ind.: University of Notre Dame Press, 1976.

————. "'Ought' and 'Is' Once More." In *Perspectives on Morality,* ed. Kenneth E. Goodpaster, 133–47. Notre Dame, Ind.: University of Notre Dame Press, 1976.

Gagnebet, M. R., O.P. "La Nature de la théologie spéculative." *Revue thomiste* 44 (1938): 1–39, 235–55, 645–74.

————. "L'Amour naturel de Dieu chez saint Thomas et ses contemporains." *Revue thomiste* 48 (1948): 394–446; 49 (1949): 31–102.

Galeazzi, Umberto. *L'etica filosofica in Tommas d'Aquino: dalla Summa contra Gentiles alla Summa theologiae: Per una riscoperta dei fondamenti della morale.* Rome: Città Nuova Editrice, 1990.

Gallagher, David M. "Aquinas on Goodness and Moral Goodness." In *Thomas Aquinas and His Legacy,* ed. David M. Gallagher, 37–60. Studies in Philosophy and the History of Philosophy, vol. 28, general editor Jude P. Dougherty. Washington, D.C.: The Catholic University of America Press, 1994.

Garceau, Benoit, O.M.I. *Judicium: Vocabulaire, sources, doctrine de saint Thomas d'Aquin.* Montreal and Paris: Institut d'Etudes Médiévales and J. Vrin, 1968.

Garrigou-Lagrange, Reginald, O.P. *De revelatione per Ecclesiam Catholicam proposita.* 2 vols. Rome: Libreria Religiosa, 1945.

Gauthier, René Antoine, O.P., and Jean Yves Jolif. *"L'Éthique à Nicomaque": Introduction, traduction et commentaire.* 4 vols. Louvain: Publications Universitaires, 1970; Paris: Béatrice-Nauwelaerts, 1970.

Gauthier, R.-A., O.P. "Trois commentaires 'averroistes' sur l' *Ethique à Nicomaque.*" *Archives d'histoire littéraire et doctinale du moyen âge* 16 (1948): 187–336.

————. "Saint Maxime le Confesseur et la psychologie de l'acte humain." *Recherches de théologie ancienne et médiévale* 21 (1954): 51–100.

————. Review of *La Prudence chez Aristote*, by Pierre Aubenque. *Revue des études grecques* 76 (1963): 265–68.

————. Review of *Psychologie et morale aux xiie et xiiie siècles*, vol. 3; and *Principes de morale*, by D. Odon Lottin. *Bulletin thomiste* 8, no. 1 (1947–1951): 64–71 .

————. "Saint Thomas et *L'Éthique à Nicomaque*." Appendix to *Sententia libri Politicorum*, in *S. Thomae Aquinatis opera omnia*. Leonine Edition, Vol. 48. Rome: 1971.

Geiger, L. B., O.P. "Les Idées divines dans l'oeuvre de s. Thomas." In *St. Thomas Aquinas, 1274–1974: Commemorative Studies*, editor-in-chief, Armand A. Maurer, C.S.B.,2 vols., 1: 175–209. Toronto: Pontifical Institute of Mediaeval Studies, 1974.

Geraghty, Richard P. *The Object of Moral Philosophy According to St. Thomas Aquinas*. Washington, D.C.: University Press of America, 1982.

Gillon, L.-B. "Aux origines de la 'puissance obédientielle.'" *Revue thomiste* 47 (1947): 304–10.

Gilson, Étienne. "La Notion de philosophie chrétienne." *Bulletin de la société française de philosophie* 31 (1931): 37–93, passim.

————. *Le Réalisme méthodique*. 3d. ed. Paris: Chez Pierre Téqui, n.d.[1936].

————. *The Spirit of Mediaeval Philosophy*. Translated by A. H. C. Downes. New York: Charles Scribner's Sons, 1940.

————. "Historical Research and the Future of Scholasticism." In *A Gilson Reader*, ed. Anton C. Pegis, 156–67. Garden City, N.Y.: Doubleday & Company, 1957. Originally published in *Modern Schoolman* 29 (1951): 1–10.

————. *Being and Some Philosophers*. 2d ed., rev. Toronto: Pontifical Institute of Mediaeval Studies, 1952.

————. "Les Principes et les causes." In *Constantes philosophique de l'être*, 53–84. Paris: J. Vrin, 1983. Revised version of an article originally published in *Revue thomiste* 52 (1952): 39–63.

————. "Note sur le *Revelabile* selon Cajétan." *Mediaeval Studies* 15 (1953): 199–206.

————. *History of Christian Philosophy in the Middle Ages*. New York: Random House, 1955.

————. *The Christian Philosophy of St. Thomas Aquinas*. Translated by L. K. Shook, C.S.B. New York: Random House, 1956.

————. "What Is Christian Philosophy?" In *A Gilson Reader*, ed. Anton C. Pegis, 177–91. Garden City, N.Y.: Doubleday & Company, 1957.

————. "La Possibilité philosophique de la philosophie chrétienne." *Revue des sciences religieuses* 32 (1958): 168–96.

————. "Philosopher dans la foi." In *Introduction à la philosophie chrétienne*, 13–28. Paris: J. Vrin, 1960.

————. *Elements of Christian Philosophy*. Garden City, N.Y.: Doubleday & Company, 1960.

————. "De la Nature du principe." In *Constantes philosophiques de l'être*, 85–105. J. Vrin: Paris, 1983.

————. "Notes pour l'histoire de la cause efficiente." *Archives d'histoire doctrinale et littéraire du moyen âge* 29 (1962): 7–31.

———. "Sur le problematique thomiste de la vision béatifique." *Archives d'histoire doctrinale et littéraire du moyen âge* 31 (1964): 67–88.

———. *Les Tribulations de sophie.* Paris: J. Vrin, 1967.

———. *Linguistique et philosophie: essai sur les constantes philosophiques du langage.* Paris: J. Vrin, 1969.

———. *Saint Thomas moraliste.* 2d ed., rev. Paris: J. Vrin, 1972.

———. *Constantes philosophiques de l'être.* J. Vrin: Paris, 1983.

———. "Propos sur l'être et sa notion." In *San Tommaso e il pensiero moderno*, 7–17. Studi tomistici, vol. 3. Pontificia accademia Romana di s. Tommaso d'Aquino. Rome: Città Nuova Editrice, 1974.

———. *Thomist Realism and the Critique of Knowledge.* Translated by Mark A. Wauck. San Francisco: Ignatius Press, 1986. Translation of *Réalisme thomiste et critique de la connaissance* (Paris: J. Vrin, 1983); first published 1939.

Goldman, Alvin I. *A Theory of Human Action.* Princeton, N.J.: Princeton University Press, 1970.

Goldmann, Lucien. *Immanuel Kant.* Translated by Robert Black. London: NLB, 1971.

Gómez-Lobo, Alfonso. "Aristotle's Hypotheses and the Euclidean Postulates." *Review of Metaphysics* 30 (1977): 430–39.

———. "The So-Called Question of Existence in Aristotle, AN. POST., 2. 1–2." *Review of Metaphysics* 34 (1980): 71–89.

———. "Definitions in Aristotle." In *Studies in Aristotle*, ed. Dominic O'Meara, 25–46. Washington, D.C.: The Catholic University of America Press, 1981.

———. "Natural Law and Naturalism." *Proceedings of the American Catholic Philosophical Association* 59 (1984): 232–49.

———. "Derecho natural: Un analisis contemporaneo de sus fundamentos." *Revista latinoamericana de filosofia* 12 (1986): 143–60.

———. "The Ergon Inference." *Phronesis* 34 (1989): 170–84 .

Gorovitz, Samuel, Merrill Hintikka, Donald Provence, and Ron G. Williams. *Philosophical Analysis: An Introduction to Its Language and Techniques.* 3d ed. New York: Random House, 1979.

Grabmann, Martin. "Die Aristoteleskommentare des Heiligen Thomas von Aquin." In *Mittelalterliches Geistesleben: Abhandlungen zur Geschichte der Scholastik und Mystik*, 266–313. Munich: Max Hueber Verlag, 1926.

Graeser, Andreas. "On Aristotle's Framework of *Sensibilia*." In *Aristotle on Mind and the Senses: Proceedings of the Seventh Symposium Aristotelicum*, ed. G. E. R. Lloyd and G. E. L. Owen, 69–97. Cambridge: Cambridge University Press, 1978.

Grant, Alexander. *The Ethics of Aristotle.* 4th ed., rev. 2 vols. London: Longmans, Green, and Co., 1885. Reprint, New York: Arno Press, 1973.

Greenwood, L. H. G. *Aristotle: Nicomachean Ethics, Book Six.* With Essays, Notes, and Translation. Cambridge: University Press, 1909.

Grisez, Germain G. "The First Principle of Practical Reason: A Commentary on the *Summa theologiae*, 1-2, Question 94, Article 2." *Natural Law Forum* 10 (1965): 168–201. Reprinted in an abridged version in *Aquinas: A Collec-*

tion of *Critical Essays*, ed. Anthony Kenny (Notre Dame, Ind.: University of Notre Dame Press, 1969), 340–82.

———. "Man, Natural End Of." In *New Catholic Encyclopedia*, 9: 132b–138a. New York: MacGraw-Hill, 1967–1988.

———. *The Way of the Lord Jesus*, Vol. 1: *Christian Moral Principles*. Chicago: Franciscan Herald Press, 1983.

———. "Natural Law and Natural Inclinations: Some Comments and Clarifications." *New Scholasticism* 61 (1987): 307–20.

Guindon, Roger, O.M.I. *Béatitude et théologie morale chez saint Thomas d'Aquin*. Ottawa: Éditions de l'Université d'Ottawa, 1955.

Gustafson, James M. *Ethics from a Theocentric Perspective*, Vol. 1: *Theology and Ethics*. Chicago: University of Chicago Press, 1981.

Guthrie, W. K. C. *A History of Greek Philosophy*. 6 vols. Cambridge: Cambridge University Press, 1962–1981.

———. Vol. 4, *Plato: The Man and His Dialogues: Earlier Period*. Cambridge: Cambridge University Press, 1975.

———. Vol. 5, *The Later Plato and the Academy*. Cambridge: Cambridge University Press, 1978.

———. Vol. 6, *Aristotle: An Encounter*. Cambridge: Cambridge University Press, 1981.

Hadot, Pierre. *Porphyre et Victorinus*. 2 vols. Paris: Les Études Augustiniennes, 1968.

———. "L'Être et l'étant dans le néoplatonisme." In *Études néoplatoniciennes*, ed. Jean Trouillard et al., 27–39. Neuchatel: La Baconnière, 1973.

———. "Dieu comme acte d'être dans le néoplatonisme: A propos des théories d' É. Gilson sur la métaphysique de l'Exode." In *Dieu et l'être: exégèse d'Exode 3,14 et de Coran 20, 11–24*, 57–63. Centre d'études des religions du livre, CNRS. Paris: Études Augustiniennes, 1978.

Hampshire, Stuart. *Morality and Conflict*. Oxford: Basil Blackwell, 1983.

Hankey, W. J. *God in Himself: Aquinas' Doctrine of God as Expounded in the Summa theologiae*. Oxford: Oxford University Press, 1987.

Hardie, W. F. R. "The Final Good in Aristotle's Ethics." *Philosophy* 40 (1965): 277–95. Reprinted in *Aristotle: A Collection of Critical Essays*, ed. J. M. E. Moravcsik (Garden City, N.Y.: Doubleday & Company, 1967), 297–322.

———. "Note on the Practical Syllogism." In *Aristotle's Ethical Theory*, 240–57. Oxford: Clarendon Press, 1968.

Hare, R. M. "Descriptivism." In *The Is/Ought Question: A Collection of Papers on the Central Problem in Moral Philosophy*, ed. W. D. Hudson, 240–58. London: Macmillan Press, 1969.

Harris, Errol. "Natural Law and Naturalism." *International Philosophical Quarterly* 23 (1983): 115–24.

Hegel, Georg Wilhelm Friedrich. *Lectures on the Philosophy of Religion*, Vol. 1: *Introduction and the Concept of Religion*. Edited by Peter C. Hodgson. Berkeley and Los Angeles: University of California Press, 1984.

———. *The Logic of Hegel: Encyclopedia of the Philosophical Sciences*. 2d ed., rev. Translated by William Wallace. Oxford: Oxford University Press, 1892. Reprinted 1965.

Heidegger, Martin. *An Introduction to Metaphysics.* Translated by Ralph Manheim. New Haven, Conn.: Yale University Press, 1959.

Henle, R. J., S.J. *Saint Thomas and Platonism: A Study of Plato and Platonic Texts in the Writings of Saint Thomas.* The Hague: Martinus Nijhoff, 1956.

———. "A Note on Certain Textual Evidence in Fabro's *La Nozione Metafisica de Partecipazione.*" *Modern Schoolman* 34 (1957): 265–82.

Hibbs, Thomas S. "Principles and Prudence: The Aristotelianism of Thomas's Account of Moral Knowledge." *New Scholasticism* 61 (1987): 271–84.

———. "Against a Cartesian Reading of *Intellectus* in Aquinas." *Modern Schoolman* 66 (1988): 55–69.

Hintikka, Jaakko. "On the Ingredients of an Aristotelian Science." *Noûs* 6 (1972): 55–69.

Hoenen, P., S.I. "De origine primorum principiorum scientiae." *Gregorianum* 14 (1933): 153–84.

———. *Reality and Judgment According to St. Thomas.* Translated by Henry F. Tiblier, S.J. Chicago: Henry Regnery, 1952.

Hookway, Christopher. *Quine: Language, Experience, and Reality.* Stanford, Calif.: Stanford University Press, 1988.

Hudson, W. D., ed. *The Is/Ought Question: A Collection of Papers on the Central Problem in Moral Philosophy.* London: Macmillan Press, 1969.

———. *Modern Moral Philosophy.* 2d ed. New York: St. Martin's Press, 1983.

Hughes, Christopher. "Identity and the Trinity." In *On a Complex Theory of a Simple God: An Investigation in Aquinas' Philosophical Theology,* 186–240. Ithaca, N.Y.: Cornell University Press, 1989.

Hume, David. *A Treatise of Human Nature.* Garden City, N.Y.: Doubleday & Company, 1961.

Hyman, Arthur. "Aristotle's Theory of the Intellect and Its Interpretation by Averroes." In *Studies in Aristotle,* ed. Dominic O'Meara, 161–91. Washington, D.C.: The Catholic University of America Press, 1981.

Irwin, Terence H. "First Principles in Aristotle's Ethics." In *Midwest Studies in Philosophy,* Vol. 3: *Studies in Ethical Theory,* ed. Peter A. French, Theodore E. Uehling, Jr., and Howard K. Wettstein, 252–72. Minneapolis: University of Minnesota Press, 1980.

———. "Aristotle's Methods of Ethics." In *Studies in Aristotle,* ed. Dominic O'Meara, 193–223. Washington, D.C.: The Catholic University of America Press, 1981.

———. *Aristotle's First Principles.* Oxford: Clarendon Press, 1988.

———. "The Scope of Deliberation: A Conflict in Aquinas." *Review of Metaphysics* 44 (1990): 21–42.

Isaac, Ioannes, O.P. "Saint Thomas interprete des oeuvres d'Aristote." In *Scholastica ratione historico-critica instauranda,* 355–63. Acta congressus scholastici internationalis. Rome: Pontificium Athenaeum Antonianum, 1951.

Jacobi, Friedrich Heinrich. "Open Letter to Fichte." In *Philosophy of German Idealism,* ed. Ernst Bekler, 119–41. New York: Continuum, 1987.

Jaeger, Werner. *Aristotle: Fundamentals of the History of His Development.* 2d ed. Translated by Richard Robinson. Oxford: Oxford University Press, 1948.

Jaffa, H. W. *Thomism and Aristotelianism: A Study of the Commentary by Thomas Aquinas on the "Nicomachean Ethics."* Chicago: University of Chicago Press, 1952.

Jenkins, John I. "Good and the Object of Natural Inclinations in St. Thomas Aquinas." *Medieval Philosophy and Theology* 3 (1993): 62–96.

Joachim, H. H. *Aristotle, "The Nicomachean Ethics": A Commentary.* Edited by D. A. Rees. Oxford: Clarendon Press, 1951.

Johnson, Mark F. "Did St. Thomas Attribute a Doctrine of Creation to Aristotle?" *New Scholasticism* 63 (1989): 129–54.

Jordan, Mark D. "The Transcendentality of Goodness and the Human Will." In *Being and Goodness: The Concept of the Good in Metaphysics and Philosophical Theology,* ed. Scott MacDonald, 129–50. Ithaca, N.Y.: Cornell University Press, 1991.

Kant, Immanuel. *Groundwork of the Metaphysics of Morals.* Translated by H. J. Paton. New York: Harper and Row, 1964.

———. *Critique of Practical Reason.* Translated by Lewis White Beck. New York: Liberal Arts Press, 1956.

———. *Critique of Judgment.* Translated by Werner S. Pluhar. Indianapolis, Ind.: Hackett, 1987..

———. *Religion within the Limits of Reason Alone.* Translated by Theodore M. Greene and Hoyt H. Hudson. New York: Harper & Row, 1960.

———. *Lectures on Philosophical Theology.* Translated by Allen W. Wood and Gertrude M. Clark. Ithaca, N. Y.: Cornell University Press, 1978.

Kenny, Anthony. *Aristotle's Theory of the Will.* New Haven, Conn.: Yale University Press, 1979.

Keyt, David. "Intellectualism in Aristotle." In *Essays in Ancient Greek Philosophy,* ed. John P. Anton and Anthony Preuss, 2: 364–87. Albany: State University of New York Press, 1983.

Kiblansky, R., and H.-D. Saffrey. "*Le Corpus Platonicum medii aevi.*" In *Recherches sur la tradition platonicienne au moyen âge et à la renaissance,* ed. Henri D. Saffrey, 27–42. Paris: J. Vrin, 1987.

Kilwardby, Robert, O.P. *De ortu scientiarum.* Edited by Albert G. Judy, O.P. Toronto: British Academy and the Pontifical Institute of Mediaeval Studies, 1976.

Klubertanz, George, S.J. "Ethics and Theology." *Modern Schoolman* 27 (1949): 29–39.

———. "Une Théorie sur les vertus morales 'naturelles' et 'surnaturelles.'" *Revue thomiste* 59 (1959): 565–75.

———. "The Nature of Philosophical Inquiry: An Aristotelian View." *Proceedings of the American Catholic Philosophical Association* 41 (1967): 27–38.

Kluxen, Wolfgang. *Philosophische Ethik bei Thomas von Aquin.* 2d ed. Hamburg: Felix Meiner Verlag, 1980.

———. "Metaphysik und praktische Vernunft: Über ihre Zuordnung bei Thomas von Aquin." In *Thomas Von Aquin 1274/1974,* 73–96. Munich: Kösel-Verlag, 1974.

Kraut, Richard. *Aristotle on the Human Good.* Princeton, N. J.: Princeton University Press, 1989.

Kremer, Klaus. *Die neuplatonische Seinsphilosophie und ihre Wirkung auf Thomas von Aquin.* Leiden: E. J. Brill, 1966.

Kretzman, Norman, Anthony Kenny, and Jan Pinborg, eds., with Eleonore Stump, assoc. ed. *The Cambridge History of Later Medieval Philosophy.* Cambridge: Cambridge University Press, 1982.

Kripke, Saul. "Identity and Necessity." In *Naming, Necessity, and Natural Kinds,* ed. Stephen P. Schwartz, 66–101. Ithica, N. Y.: Cornell University Press, 1977.

Labourdette, P., O.P. Review of *De hominis beatitudinis,* by Jacobus M. Ramirez. *Bulletin thomiste* 50 (1950): 203–5.

———. Review of *La Destinée de la nature humaine selon saint Thomas d'Aquin,* by Jorge Laporta. *Revue thomiste* 66 (1966): 281–89.

Langan, John Patrick. "Desire, Beatitude, and the Basis of Morality in Thomas Aquinas." Ph.D. diss., University of Michigan, 1979.

Langevin, Gilles, S.J. *"Capax dei": la créature intellectuelle et l'intimité de Dieu.* Brussels and Paris: Desclée de Brouwer, 1966.

Laporta, Jorge. *La Destinée de la nature humaine selon Thomas d'Aquin.* Paris: J. Vrin, 1965.

———. "Pour trouver le sens exact des terms *appetitus naturalis, desiderium naturale, amor naturalis,* etc. chez Thomas d'Aquin." *Archives d'histoire doctrinale et littéraire du moyen âge* 40 (1973): 37–95.

Larcher, F. R., O.P., trans. *Commentary on the Posterior Analytics of Aristotle by St. Thomas Aquinas.* Albany, New York: Magi Books, 1970.

Lauer, Quentin, S.J. "Hegel on the Identity of Content in Religion and Philosophy." In *Essays in Hegelian Dialectic,* 153–68. New York: Fordham University Press, 1977.

Lear, Jonathan. *Aristotle and Logical Theory.* Cambridge: Cambridge University Press, 1980.

Le Bachelot, X. "Baius." In *Dictionnaire de Théologie Catholique,* ed. by A. Vacant, E. Mangenot, and E. Amann, vol. 2/1, cols. 38–111. Paris: Letouzey and Ane, 1909–1950

Le Blond, J. M. *Logique et méthode chez Aristote.* Paris: J. Vrin, 1939.

Leclercq, Jacques. *La Philosophie morale de saint Thomas devant la pensée contemporaine.* Louvain and Paris: Publications Universitaires de Louvain and J. Vrin, 1955.

Lee, Patrick. "Etienne Gilson: *Thomistic Realism and the Critique of Knowledge.*" *New Scholasticism* 63 (1989): 81–100.

Lehrer, Keith. *Theory of Knowledge.* San Francisco: Westview Press, 1990.

Lehu, Léonard. *La Raison, règle de moralité d'après Saint Thomas.* Paris: Librairie Lecoffre, 1930.

Lesher, James H. "The Meaning of *NOUS* in the *Posterior Analytics.*" *Phronesis* 18 (1973): 44–68.

Ligeard, H. *La Théologie scolastique et la transcendance du surnaturel.* Paris: Beauchesne, 1908.

Lindbeck, George. "Participation and Existence in the Interpretation of St. Thomas Aquinas." *Franciscan Studies* 17 (1957): 1–22, 107–25.

Little, Arthur, S.J. *The Platonic Heritage of Thomism.* Dublin: Golden Eagle Books Limited, 1950.

Lloyd, G. E. R., and G. E. L. Owen, eds. *Aristotle on Mind and the Senses.* Proceedings of the Seventh Symposium Aristotelicum. Cambridge: Cambridge University Press, 1978.

Loening, Richard. *Die Zurechnungslehre des Aristoteles.* Jena: 1903. Reprinted, Hildesheim: Georg Olms, 1967.

Lohr, C. H. "The Medieval Interpretation of Aristotle." In *The Cambridge History of Later Medieval Philosophy,* ed. Norman Kretzman, Anthony Kenny, and Jan Pinborg, with assoc.ed. Eleonore Stump, 80–98. Cambridge: Cambridge University Press, 1982.

Lonergan, Bernard J., S.J. *Verbum: Word and Idea in Aquinas.* Edited by David B. Burrell, C.S.C. Notre Dame, Ind.: University of Notre Dame Press, 1967.

Lottin, Odon D. "Syndérèse et conscience aux xii⁰ et xiii⁰ siècles." In *Psychologie et morale aux xiie et xiiie siècles,* Vol. 2, pt. 1: *Problèmes de morale,* 101–349. Louvain: Abbaye du Mont César, 1948.

———. "Pour un commentaire historique de la morale de saint Thomas d'Aquin." In *Psychologie et morale aux xiie et xiii siècle,* Vol. 3, pt. 2: *Problèmes de morale,* 576–601. Louvain: Abbaye de Mont Cesar; Gembloux: J. Duculot, 1949.

———. *Études de morale: histoire et doctrine.* Gembloux: J. Duculot, 1961.

Louden, Robert B. "What Do Antitheorists Mean by Theory?" In *Morality and Moral Theory: A Reappraisal and Reaffirmation,* 85–98. New York and Oxford: Oxford University Press, 1992.

Lowith, Karl. *From Hegel to Nietzsche: The Revolution in 19th Century Thought.* Translated by David E. Green. London: Constable, 1965.

MacDonald, Scott, ed. *Being and Goodness: The Concept of the Good in Metaphysics and Philosophical Theology.* Ithaca, N.Y.: Cornell University Press, 1991.

MacIntyre, Alasdair C. "Hume on 'is' and 'ought.'" *Philosophical Review* 68 (1959): 451–68. Reprinted in V. C. Chappell, ed., *Hume* (Notre Dame, Ind.: University of Notre Dame Press, 1968), 240–64; and in W. D. Hudson, ed., *The Is/Ought Question: A Collection of Papers on the Central Problem in Moral Philosophy* (London: Macmillan Press, 1969), 35–50.

———. *Whose Justice? Whose Rationality?* Notre Dame, Ind.: Notre Dame University Press, 1988.

———. *First Principles, Final Ends, and Contemporary Philosophical Issues.* The Aquinas Lecture for 1990. Milwaukee: Marquette University Press, 1990.

Mackie, J. L. *Ethics: Inventing Right and Wrong.* Middlesex, England: Penguin Books, 1977.

Mandonnet, Pierre, O.P., and A.-R.Motte, O.P. Remarks in "La philosophie chrétienne." *Journées d'études de la société thomiste.* Tournai, Belgium: Les Éditions du Cerf, 1933.

Maréchal, Joseph, S.J. "De naturali perfectae beatitudinis desiderio." In *Mélanges Joseph Maréchal,* 2 vols., 1: 323–37. Paris: Desclée de Brouwer, 1950.

Maritain, Jacques. "La Notion de philosophie chrétienne." *Bulletin de la société française de philosophie* 31 (1931): 37–93, passim.

————. "La Philosophie chrétienne." *Journées d'études de la société thomiste.* Tournai, Belgium: Les Éditions du Cerf, 1933.

————. *Science and Wisdom.* Translated by Bernard Wall. London: Geoffrey Bles, 1940.

————. *An Essay on Christian Philosophy.* Translated by Edward H. Flannery. New York: Philosophical Library, 1955.

————. *Degrees of Knowledge.* 4th French ed. Translation supervised by Gerald B. Phelan. New York: Charles Scribner's Sons, 1959.

————. *Moral Philosophy: An Historical and Critical Survey of the Great Systems.* Edited Joseph W. Evans. London: Geoffrey Bles, 1964.

————. *An Introduction to the Basic Problems of Moral Philosophy.* Translated by Cornelia N. Borgerhoff. Albany, N. Y.: Magi Books, 1990.

Maurer, Armand A., C.S.B. "James Ross on the Divine Ideas: A Reply." *American Catholic Philosophical Quarterly* 65, no. 2 (1991): 213–20.

————, trans. With Introduction and Notes to St. Thomas Aquinas, *On Being and Essence.* 2d ed., rev. Toronto: Pontifical Institute of Mediaeval Studies, 1968.

————, editor-in-chief. *St. Thomas Aquinas, 1274–1974: Commemorative Studies.* 2 vols. Toronto: Pontifical Institute of Mediaeval Studies, 1974.

McEvoy, James. "The Divine as the Measure of Being in Platonic and Scholastic Thought." In *Studies in Medieval Philosophy,* ed. John F. Wippel, 85–116. Washington, D.C.: The Catholic University of America Press, 1987.

McInerny, Ralph. "The Principles of Natural Law." *American Journal of Jurisprudence* 25 (1980): 1–15.

————. *Ethica Thomistica: The Moral Philosophy of Thomas Aquinas.* Washington, D.C.: The Catholic University of America Press, 1982.

————. "Being and Predication." In *Being and Predication: Thomistic Interpretations,* 173–228. Studies in Philosophy and the History of Philosophy, vol. 16, general editor Jude P. Doherty. Washington, D.C.: The Catholic University of America Press, 1986.

————. "The Right Deed for the Wrong Reason: Comments on Belman." *Doctor communis* 43 (1990): 234–49.

————. *Aquinas on Human Action: A Theory of Practice.* Washington, D.C.: The Catholic University of America Press, 1992.

————. *The Question of Christian Ethics.* Washington, D.C.: The Catholic University of America Press, 1993.

McKeon, Richard. "Truth and the History of Ideas." In *Thought, Action, and Passion,* 54–88. Chicago: University of Chicago Press, 1954.

————. "Discourse, Demonstration, Verification, and Justification." In *Démonstration, vérification, justification,* 37–92. Entretiens de l'Institut International de Philosophie, Liege, Septembre 1967. Louvain: Editions Nauwelaerts, 1968. Text without replies reprinted in *Rhetoric: Essays in Invention and Discovery,* ed. Mark Backman, 37–55. Woodbridge, Conn.: Ox Bow Press, 1987.

McKirahan, Richard D., Jr. *Principles and Proofs: Aristotle's Theory of Demonstrative Science.* Princeton, N. J.: Princeton University Press, 1992.

Melina, Livio. *La conoscenza morale: Linee di reflessione sul Commento di* san Tommaso all'Etica Nicomachea. Rome: Città Nuova Editrice, 1987.

Merken, Paul. "Transformation of the Ethics of Aristotle in the Moral Philosophy of Thomas Aquinas." In *Atti del congresso internazionale, Tommaso d'Aquino nel suo settimo centenario*, Vol. 5: *L'Agire morale*, 151–62. Naples: Edizioni Domenicane Italiane, 1977.

Merleau-Ponty, Maurice. *In Praise of Philosophy*. Translated by John Wild and James M. Edie. Evanston, Ill.: Northwestern University Press, 1963.

———. *Signs*. Translated by Richard C. McCleary. Evanston, Ill.: Northwestern University Press, 1964.

———. "Everywhere and Nowhere." In *Signs*, 126–58.

———. "Man and Adversity." In *Signs*, 224–43.

Michelakis, Emmanuel M. *Aristotle's Theory of Practical Principles*. Athens: Cleisiounis Press, 1961.

Mignucci, Mario. *La theoria Aristotelica della scienza*. Florence: G. C. Sansonie Editore, 1965.

———. *L'argomentazione dimostrativa in Aristotele: Commento agli Analitici Secondi*. Vol. 1. Padua: Editrice Antenore, 1975.

Miller, Fred D. "Aristotle on Rationality in Action." *Review of Metaphysics* 38 (1984): 499–520.

Monan, J. Donald. *Moral Knowledge and Its Methodology in Aristotle*. Oxford: Clarendon Press, 1968.

Mondin, Battista. "Ermeneutica, metafisica, e analogia in s. Tommaso d'Aquino." *Divus Thomas* 12 (1995): 11–227.

Motte, A.-R., O.P. "Désir naturel et béatitude surnaturelle." *Bulletin thomiste* 3 (1932): 651–75.

Moravscik, Julius M. E. "On What We Aim At and How We Live." In *The Greeks and the Good Life*, ed. David J. Depew, 198–235. Indianapolis, Ind.: Hackett., 1980.

Mueller-Goldingen, Christian, ed. *Schriften zur aristotelischen Ethik*. Hildesheim: Georg Olms Verlag, 1988.

Nagel, Ernest. *The Structure of Science: Problems in the Logic of Scientific Explanations*. New York: Harcourt, Brace, & World, 1961.

Nannery, Lawrence. "The Problem of the Two Lives in Aristotle's *Ethics*: The Human Good and the Best Life for a Man." *International Philosophical Quarterly* 21, no. 3 (1981): 277–93.

Naus, John E., S.J. *The Nature of the Practical Intellect According to Saint Thomas Aquinas*. Rome: Libreria Editrice dell'Università Gregoriana, 1959.

Nussbaum, Martha C. *The Frailty of Goodness: Luck and Ethics in Greek Tragedy and Philosophy*. Cambridge: Cambridge University Press, 1986.

O'Connor, William R. *The Eternal Quest: The Teaching of St. Thomas Aquinas on the Natural Desire for God*. New York: Longmans, Green, and Co., 1947.

———. *The Natural Desire for God*. The Aquinas Lecture for 1948. Milwaukee: Marquette University Press, 1948.

O'Meara, Dominic, ed. *Studies in Aristotle*. Washington, D.C.: The Catholic University of America Press, 1981.

Owens, Joseph, C.Ss.R. *The Doctrine of Being in the Aristotelian Metaphysics:*

A Study in the Greek Background of Mediaeval Thought. 3d ed., rev. Toronto: Pontifical Institute of Mediaeval Studies, 1978.

———. "The Reality of the Aristotelian Separate Movers." *Review of Metaphysics* 3 (1949–1950): 319–37.

———. "The Causal Proposition—Principle or Conclusion?" *Modern Schoolman* 32 (1955): 159–71, 257–70, 323–39.

———. "The Intelligibility of Being." *Gregorianum* 26 (1955): 169–93.

———. *St. Thomas and the Future of Metaphysics.* The Aquinas Lecture for 1957. Milwaukee: Marquette University Press, 1957.

———. "The Accidental and Essential Character of Being in the Doctrine of St. Thomas." *Mediaeval Studies* 20 (1958): 1–40. Reprinted in *St. Thomas Aquinas on the Existence of God: The Collected Papers of Joseph Owens*, 52–96.

———. *A History of Ancient Western Philosophy.* New York: Appleton-Century-Crofts, 1959.

———. "Diversity and Community of Being in St. Thomas Aquinas." *Mediaeval Studies* 22 (1960): 257–302. Reprinted in *St. Thomas Aquinas on the Existence of God: The Collected Papers of Joseph Owens*, 97–131.

———. *An Elementary Christian Metaphysics.* Milwaukee: Bruce Publishing Company, 1963.

———. "The Unity in a Thomistic Philosophy of Man." *Mediaeval Studies* 25 (1963): 54–82.

———. "The Aristotelian Conception of the Sciences." *International Philosophical Quarterly* 4 (1964): 200–216. Reprinted in *Aristotle: The Collected Papers of Joseph Owens*, 23–34.

———. "Quiddity and Real Distinction in St. Thomas Aquinas." *Mediaeval Studies* 27 (1965): 1–22.

———. "The Ethical Universal In Aristotle." *Studia moralia*, 3: 27–47. Accademia Alfonsiana. Rome: Desclée & Socii, 1965.

———. "Aquinas and the Proof from the *Physics.*" *Mediaeval Studies* 28 (1966): 119–50.

———. "The Grounds of Ethical Universality in Aristotle." In *Man and World* 2 (1969): 171–93. Reprinted in *Aristotle: The Collected Papers of Joseph Owens*, 148–64.

———. "Nature and Ethical Norm in Aristotle." *Proceedings of the XIVth International Congress of Philosophy*, 5: 442–47. Reprinted in *Aristotle: The Collected Papers of Joseph Owens*, 165–68.

———. "Judgment and Truth in Aquinas." *Mediaeval Studies* 32 (1970): 138–58.

———. "Aristotle's Definition of Soul." In *Philomathes: Studies and Essays in the Humanities in Memory of Philip Merlan*, ed. Robert B. Palmer and Robert Hamerton-Kelly, 125–45. The Hague: Martinus Nijhoff, 1971. Reprinted in *Aristotle: The Collected Papers of Joseph Owens*, 109–21.

———. "Reality and Metaphysics." *Review of Metaphysics* 25 (1971–1972): 638–58.

———. "Aquinas as Aristotelian Commentator." In *St. Thomas Aquinas, 1274–1974: Commemorative Studies*, editor-in-chief Armand A. Maurer, C.S.B., 2 vols., editor-in chief Armand A. Maurer, C.S.B, 1: 213–38. Toronto: Pontifical Institute of Mediaeval Studies, 1974. Reprinted in *St. Thomas Aquinas on the Existence of God: The Collected Papers of Joseph Owens*, 1–19.

———. "The Primacy of the External in Thomistic Noetics." *Église et Théologie* 5 (1974): 189–205.

———. "Aquinas and the Five Ways." *Monist* 58 (1974): 16–35. Reprinted in *St. Thomas Aquinas on the Existence of God: The Collected Papers of Joseph Owens*, 132–41.

———. "Aquinas on Knowing Existence." *Review of Metaphysics* 29 (1976): 670–90. Reprinted in *St Thomas Aquinas on the Existence of God: The Collected Papers of Joseph Owens*, 20–33.

———. "The Relation of God to World in the *Metaphysics*." In *Études sur la Métaphysique d'Aristote: Actes du VI Symposium Aristotelicum*, 207–28. Paris: J. Vrin, 1979.

———. *St. Thomas Aquinas on the Existence of God: The Collected Papers of Joseph Owens, C.Ss.R.* Edited by John R. Catan. Albany: State University of New York Press, 1980.

———. "Stages and Distinction in *De Ente*: A Rejoinder." *Thomist* 45 (1981): 99–123.

———. *Aristotle: The Collected Papers of Joseph Owens.* Edited by John R. Catan. Albany: State University of New York Press, 1981.

———. "The *Kalon* in Aristotelian Ethics." In *Studies in Aristotle*, ed. Dominic O'Meara, 261–77. Washington, D.C.: The Catholic University of America Press, 1981.

———. "The Acratic's 'Ultimate Premise' in Aristotle." In *Aristotle's Werk und Wirkung*, ed. Jürgen Wiesner, 376–92. Berlin and New York: Walter de Gruyter, 1985.

———. "*Tenent Philosophi Perfectionem Naturae*." In *Essays Honoring Allan B. Wolter*, ed. William A. Frank and Gerard J. Etzkorn, 221–44. St. Bonaventure, N. Y.: Franciscan Institute Publications, 1985.

———. *Human Destiny: Some Problems for Catholic Philosophy.* Washington, D.C.: The Catholic University of America Press, 1985.

———. "Aquinas and Philosophical Pluralism." In *Thomistic Papers, II*, ed. Leonard A. Kennedy, C.S.B., and Jack C. Marler, 133–58. Houston: Center for Thomistic Studies, 1986.

———. "Confronto fra la coscienza cristiana e la retta ragione aristotelica." In *La coscienza morale oggi: omaggio al prof. Domenico Capone*, 109–43. Editiones Academiae Alphonsianae Roma. Rome: Accademia Alfonsiana, 1987. Translated and reprinted as "Christian Conscience vs. Aristotelian Right Reason," in Joseph Owens, C.Ss.R., *Towards A Christian Philosophy*, Studies in Philosophy and the History of Philosophy, vol. 21, general editor Jude P. Doherty (Washington, D.C.: The Catholic University of America Press, 1990), 150–73.

———. "The Inseparability of the Soul from Existence." *New Scholasticism* 61 (1987): 249–70.

———. Review of *Lex et Libertas: Freedom and Law According to St. Thomas Aquinas*, ed. L. J. Elders and K. Hedwig. *Thomist* 52 (1988): 539–42.

———. *Towards A Christian Philosophy.* Studies in Philosophy and the History

of Philosophy, vol. 21, general editor Jude P. Doherty. Washington, D.C.:
The Catholic University of America Press, 1990.

———. "Value and Practical Knowledge in Aristotle." In *Aristotle's Ethics*, ed.
John P. Anton and Anthony Preuss, 143–57. Albany: State University of
New York Press, 1991.

———. "Human Reason and the Moral Order in Aquinas." In *Historia: Memoria Futuri. Mélanges Louis Vereecke*, ed. Réal Tremblay and Dennis J. Billy,
159–77. Editiones Academiae Alphonsianae Roma. Rome: Accademia Alfonsiana, 1991.

———. *Cognition: An Epistemological Inquiry.* Houston, Texas: Center for
Thomistic Studies Studies, 1992.

Papadis, Dimitrios. *Die Rezeption der Nikomachischen Ethik des Aristoteles
bei Thomas von Aquin: Eine vergleichende Untersuchung.* Frankfort: R. G.
Fischer, 1980.

Patzig, Günther. *Aristotle's Theory of the Syllogism.* Translated by Jonathan
Barnes. Dordrecht, Holland: D. Reidel, 1968.

Pegis, Anton C. *St. Thomas and the Problem of the Soul in the Thirteenth
Century.* Toronto: St. Michael's College, 1934.

———. "Matter, Beatitude and Liberty." *Thomist* 5 (1943): 265–80.

———. "Cosmogony and Knowledge." *Thought* 18 (1943): 642–64; 19 (1944):
269–90; 20 (1945): 473–98.

———. "The Dilemma of Being and Unity." In *Essays in Thomism*, ed. Robert
E. Brennan, O.P., 151–83. New York: Sheed and Ward, 1944.

———. *Basic Writings of Saint Thomas Aquinas.* Edited and annotated by
Anton C. Pegis. 2 vols. New York: Random House, 1945.

———. "The Middle Ages and Philosophy." *American Catholic Philosophical
Association* 21 (1946): 16–25.

———. "Gilson and Thomism." *Thought* 21 (1946): 435–54.

———. "Nature and Spirit: Some Reflections on the Problem of the End of
Man." *American Catholic Philosophical Association* 23 (1949): 62–79.

———. "Creation and Beatitude in the *Summa Contra Gentiles* of St. Thomas Aquinas." *American Catholic Philosophical Association* 29 (1955):
52–62.

———. "St. Thomas and the Unity of Man." In *Progress in Philosophy*, ed.
James A. McWilliams, S.J., 153–73. Milwaukee: Bruce, 1955.

———. General Introduction to *On the Truth of the Catholic Faith: "Summa
Contra Gentiles."* Book 1: *God*, 15–44. Translated by Anton C. Pegis. Garden City, N.Y.: Hanover House, 1955.

———. "Some Reflections on *Summa Contra Gentiles* II, 56." In *An Etienne
Gilson Tribute*, ed. Charles J. O'Neil, 169–88. Milwaukee: Marquette University Press, 1959.

———. "Thomism as a Philosophy." In *Saint Thomas Aquinas and Philosophy.*
The McAuley Lectures for 1960. West Hartford, Conn.: Saint Joseph College, 1961.

———. *At the Origins of the Thomistic Notion of Man.* The Saint Augustine
Lecture for 1962. New York: Macmillan, 1963.

———. "St. Thomas and the *Nicomachean Ethics*: Some Reflections on *Sum-*

ma Contra Gentiles III, 44, #5." *Mediaeval Studies* 25 (1963): 1–25.

———. *The Middle Ages and Philosophy: Some Reflections on the Ambivalence of Modern Scholasticism.* Chicago: Henry Regnery, 1963.

———. *St. Thomas and Philosophy.* The Aquinas Lecture for 1964. Milwaukee: Marquette University Press, 1964.

———. "Qu'est-ce que la *Summa Contra Gentiles*?" In *L'Homme devant Dieu": Mélanges offerts au Père Henri de Lubac,* 2 vols, 2: 169–82. Paris: Aubier, 1964.

———. "*Sub Ratione Dei*: A Reply to Professor Anderson." *New Scholasticism* 39 (1965): 141–57.

———. "Catholic Intellectualism at the Crossroad." In *In Search of Saint Thomas Aquinas,* the McAuley Lectures for 1966. West Hartford, Conn.: Saint Joseph College, 1966.

———. "Thomism 1966." In *In Search of Saint Thomas Aquinas,* the McAuley Lectures for 1966. West Hartford, Conn.: Saint Joseph College, 1966. Also published in *American Catholic Philosophical Association* 40–41 (1966): 55–67.

———. "Who Reads Aquinas?" *Thought* 42 (1967): 488–504.

———. "St. Thomas and the Coherence of the Aristotelian Physics." *Mediaeval Studies* 35 (1973): 67–117.

———. "After Seven Hundred Years: St. Thomas Aquinas in 1974." *Eglise et théologie* 5 (1974): 137–53.

Persson, Per Erik. *Sacra Doctrina: Reason and Revelation in Aquinas.* Translated by Ross Mackenzie. Oxford: Basil Blackwell, 1970.

Philippe, M.-D., O.P., "Αφαίρεσις, πρόθεσις, χωρίζειν dans la philosophie d'Aristote." *Revue thomiste* 48 (1948): 461–75.

———. "Analyse de l'être chez saint Thomas." In *Tommaso d'Aquino nel suo vii centenario,* 255–79. Congresso internazionale, Roma-Napoli, 17–24 April 1974. Rome and Naples: [1974?].

Pieper, Joseph. *Living the Truth: The Truth of All Things and Reality and the Good.* San Francisco: Ignatius Press, 1989.

Pinckaers, Servais, O.P. Notes and appendices to Saint Thomas d'Aquin, *Somme théologique: Les actes humains.* New edition. Vol. 1, 1^a–2^a, questions 6–17; Vol. 2, 1^a–2^a, questions 18–21. French trans. by H.-D. Gardeil, O.P. (Paris: Desclée & Cie; Rome: Tournai, 1962–66).

———. "La Structure de l'acte humaine suivant saint Thomas." *Revue thomiste* 55 (1955): 393–412.

———. Review of "Le 'Précepte' de la prudence chez saint Thomas d'Aquin," by Th. Deman, O.P.; and "Saint Maxime le Confesseur et la psychologie de l'acte humain," by R.-A. Gauthier, O.P. *Bulletin thomiste* 9 (1954–1956): 345–62.

———. "La Béatitude dans l'éthique de saint Thomas." In *The Ethics of St. Thomas Aquinas,* ed. Leon Elders, S.V.D., and K. Hedwig, 80–94. Vatican City: Libreria Editrice Vaticana, 1984.

Pinkard, Terry. *Hegel's Phenomenology: The Sociality of Reason.* Cambridge: Cambridge University Press, 1994.

Piper, Adrian M. "A Distinction without a Difference." In *Midwest Studies in*

Philosophy, Vol.7: *Social and Political Philosophy*, ed. Peter A. French, Theodore E. Uehling, Jr., and Howard K. Lettstein, 403–35. Minneapolis: University of Minnesota Press, 1982.

Pippin, Robert B. *Modernism as a Philosophical Problem*. Cambridge, Mass.: Basil Blackwell, 1991.

Pizzorni, Reginaldo M., O.P. *Il diritto naturale dalle origini a S. Tommaso d'Aquino*. 2d ed., rev. Rome: Pontificia Università Lateranense, Città Nuova Editrice, 1985.

Plantinga, Alvin. "Reason and Belief in God." In *Faith and Rationality*, ed. Alvin Plantinga and Nicholas Wolterstorff, 16–93. Notre Dame, Ind.: University of Notre Dame Press, 1983.

Platts, Mark. "Moral Reality." In *Essays in Moral Realism*, ed. Geoffrey Sayre-McCord, 282–300. Ithaca, N. Y.: Cornell University Press, 1988.

Porter, Jean. *The Recovery of Virtue: The Relevance of Aquinas for Christian Ethics*. Louisville, Ky.: Westminster Press, 1990.

Quine, Willard Van Orman. *From A Logical Point of View: Nine Logico-Philosophical Essays*. 2d ed., rev. Cambridge, Mass.: Harvard University Press, 1953.

———. *Word and Object*. Cambridge, Mass.: M.I.T. Press, 1960.

———. *Philosophy of Logic*. 2d ed. Cambridge, Mass.: Harvard University Press, 1986.

Quinn, John Francis. *The Historical Constitution of St. Bonaventure's Philosophy*. Toronto: Pontifical Institute of Mediaeval Studies, 1973.

Quinton, Anthony. *The Nature of Things*. London and Boston: Routledge & Kegan Paul, 1973.

Ramirez, Jacobus M. *De hominis beatitudine: In I–II Summae theologiae divi Thomae commentaria (qq. i–v)*. Vol. 3 of *Opera omnia*, ed. by Victorino Rodriguez, O.P. Madrid: Consejo Suerior de Investigaciones Cientificas, 1972.

———. *De actibus humanis: In I–II Summa Theologiae divi Thomae expositio (qq. vi–xxi)*. Vol. 4 of *Opera omnia*, ed. by Victorino Rodriguez, O.P. Madrid: Consejo Suerior de Investigaciones Cientificas, 1972.

———. Review of *Distinguer pour unir ou les degrés du savoir*, by Jacques Maritain. *Bulletin thomiste* 4 (1934–1936): 423–32.

———. "De philosophia morali Christiani." *Divus Thomas* 14 (1936): 87–204.

Rawls, John. *A Theory of Justice*. Oxford: Clarendon Press, 1972

Raz, Joseph, ed. *Practical Reasoning*. Oxford: Oxford University Press, 1978.

Reale, Giovanni. *A History of Ancient Philosophy*. 4 vols. Edited and translated by John R. Catan. Albany: State University of New York Press, 1985–1990.

———. Vol. 2, *Plato and Aristotle*. 5th Italian ed. Edited and translated by John R. Catan. Albany: State University of New York Press, 1990.

———. Vol. 4, *The Schools of the Imperial Age*. 5th Italian ed. Edited and translated by John R. Catan. Albany: State University of New York, 1990.

Reeve, C. D. C. *Practices of Reason: Aristotle's "Nicomachean Ethics."* Oxford: Clarendon Press, 1992.

Riesenhuber, Klaus. *Die Transzendenz der Freiheit zum Guten*. Munich: Berchmanskilleg Verlag, 1971.

Rescher, Nicholas. *The Strife of Systems: An Essay on the Grounds and Implications of Philosophical Diversity.* Pittsburgh: University of Pittsburgh Press, 1985.

Rhonheimer, Martin. *Natur als Grundlage der Moral: Die personale Struktur des Naturgesetzes bei Thomas von Aquin: Eine Auseinandersetzung mit autonomer und teleologischer Ethik.* Innsbruck: Tyrolia-Verlag, 1987.

——. *Praktische Vernunft und Vernünftigkeit der Praxis: Handlungstheorie bei Thomas von Aquin in ihrer Entstehung aus dem Problemkontext der aristotelischen Ethik.* Berlin: Akademie Verlag, 1994.

——. *La prospettiva della morale: Fondamenti dell'etica filosofica.* Rome: Armado Editore, 1994.

Richardson, Henry S. "Commentary on Broadie." In *Proceedings of the Boston Area Colloquium in Ancient Philosophy,* ed. John J. Cleary, 3: 253–61. Lanham, Md: University Press of America, 1988.

Rickaby, Joseph, S.J. *Aquinas Ethicus: The Moral Teaching of St. Thomas.* New York, Cincinnati, Chicago: Benziger Brothers, 1892.

Ritzler, Remigius, O.F.M. Conv. *De naturali beatitudinis supernaturalis ad mentem s. Thomae* Rome: Pontificia Facultas Theologica O.F.M. Conv., 1938.

Robb, James H. Introduction to *St. Thomas Aquinas: Quaestiones de Anima,* ed. James H. Robb, 1950. Toronto: Pontifical Institute of Mediaeval Studies, 1968.

Robinson, T. M. *Plato's Psychology.* Toronto: University of Toronto Press, 1970.

Roland-Gosselin, M.-D., O.P. *Le "De ente et essentia" de s. Thomas d'Aquin.* Paris: J. Vrin, 1948.

Rorty, Amélie Oksenberg, ed. *Essays on Aristotle's Ethics.* Berkeley and Los Angeles: University of California Press, 1980.

Rorty, Richard. *Contingency, Irony, and Solidarity.* Cambridge: Cambridge University Press, 1989.

Ross, J. F. "Aquinas on Belief and Knowledge." In *Essays Honoring Allan B. Wolter,* ed. William A. Rank and Girard J. Etzkorn, 245–69. St. Bonaventure, N.Y.: Franciscan Institute Publications, 1985.

——. "Aquinas's Exemplarism; Aquinas's Voluntarism." *American Catholic Philosophical Quarterly* 64 (1990): 171–98.

Ross, W. D. *Aristotle's Prior and Posterior Analytics.* Oxford: Clarendon Press, 1949.

——. *Plato's Theory of Ideas.* Oxford: Clarendon Press, 1951.

Rousselot, Pierre. *L'Intellectualisme de saint Thomas.* Paris: Beauchesne, 1924.

Sartre, Jean-Paul. *Being and Nothingness: An Essay on Phenomenological Ontology.* Translated Hazel E. Barnes. New York: Philosophical Library, 1956.

Schiffini, Sancto, S.J. *Disputationes philosophiae moralis.* 2 vols. Turin: J. Speirani, 1891.

Schuchman, Paul. *Aristotle and the Problem of Moral Discernment.* Frankfort: Peter D. Lang, 1980.

Schultz, Janice L.,"Is-Ought: Prescribing and a Present Controversy." *Thomist* 49 (1985): 1–23.

————. "'Ought'-Judgments: A Descriptivist Analysis from a Thomistic Perspective." *New Scholasticism* 61 (1987): 400–426.

————. "Thomistic Metaethics and a Present Controversy." *Thomist* 52 (1988): 40–62.

————. "St. Thomas Aquinas on Necessary Moral Principles." *New Scholasticism* 62 (1988): 150–78.

Schuster, Johann, S.J. "Von den ethischen Prinzipien: Eine Thomasstudie zu S. Th. Iᵃ·IIᵃᵉ, q. 94, a. 2." *Zeitschrift für katholische Theologie* 57 (1933): 44–65.

Seidl, Horst. "Natürliche Sittlichkeit und Metaphysische Voraussetzung in der Ethik des Aristoteles und Thomas von Aquin." In *The Ethics of St. Thomas Aquinas*, ed. L. J. Elders, S.V.D., and K. Hedwig, 95–117. Vatican City: Libreria Editrice Vaticana, 1984.

Sellars, Wilfrid, and John Hospers, eds. *Readings in Ethical Theory.* New York: Appleton-Century-Crofts, 1952.

Sertillanges, A. D., O.P. *La Philosophie morale de saint Thomas d'Aquin.* Rev. ed. Paris: Aubier, 1942.

Sestilli, Joachim. *In summam theologicam s. Thomae Aquinatis I.ᵃ p.ᵉ q. XII. a. 1.: De naturali intelligentis animae capacitate atque appetitu intuendi divinam essentiam.* Naples and Rome: Salvatoris Festa, 1896.

Sherman, Nancy. "Character, Planning, and Choice in Aristotle." *Review of Metaphysics* 39 (1985): 83–106.

————. *The Fabric of Character: Aristotle's Theory of Virtue.* Oxford: Clarendon Press, 1989.

Sidgwick, Henry. *The Methods of Ethics.* 7th ed. London: Macmillan and Company, 1907. Reprinted, Indianapolis, Ind.: Hackett, 1981.

Simmons, Edward D. "Demonstration and Self-Evidence." *Thomist* 24 (1961): 139–62.

Simpson, Peter. "St. Thomas on the Naturalistic Fallacy." *Thomist* 51 (1987): 51–69.

————. "Practical Knowing: Some Comments on Finnis and Aquinas." *Modern Schoolman* 67 (1990)): 111–22.

Smith, Gerard, S.J. "The Natural End of Man." *Proceedings of the American Catholic Philosophical Association* 23 (1949): 47–61.

————. "Philosophy and the Unity of Man's Ultimate End." *Proceeding of the American Catholic Philosophical Association* 27 (1953): 60–83.

Solignac, A., S.J. "La Doctrine de l'*esse* chez Saint Thomas, est-elle d'origine néo-Platonicienne?" *Archives de philosophie* 30 (1967): 439–52.

Sorabji, Richard. "Aristotle on the Role of Intellect in Virtue." *Proceedings of the Aristotelian Society* 74 (1973–1974): 107–29. Reprinted in Amélie Oksenberg Rorty, ed., *Essays on Aristotle's Ethics* (Berkeley and Los Angeles: University of California Press, 1980), 201–19.

Spanneut, Michel. *Permanence du stoïcisme: de Zeno à Malraux.* Gembloux, Belgium: Éditions J. Duculot, 1973.

Sparks, A. W. *Talking Philosophy: A Wordbook.* London and New York: Routledge, 1991.

Spiazzi, Raymundus, O.P. Introduction to *S. Thomae Aquinatis Quaestiones quodlibetales*, ed. Raymundus Spiazzi, O.P., vii–xxi. Turin: Marietti, 1956.

Staley, Kevin M. "Thomas Aquinas and Contemporary Ethics of Virtue." *Modern Schoolman* 66 (1989): 285–300.

———. "Happiness: The Natural End of Man?" *Thomist* 53 (1989): 215–34.

Stout, Jeffrey. *Ethics after Babel: The Language of Morals and Their Discontents.* Boston: Beacon Press, 1988.

Strauss, Leo. *Natural Right and History.* Chicago: University of Chicago Press, 1950.

———. "On Aristotle's Politics." In *The City and Man,* 13–49. Chicago: Rand McNally, 1964.

———. *The Argument and the Action of Plato's Laws.* Chicago: University of Chicago Press, 1975.

———. "The Mutual Influence of Theology and Philosophy." *Independent Journal of Philosophy* 3 (1979): 111–18.

Stump, Eleonore, and Norman Kretzman. "Being and Goodness." In *Being and Goodness: The Concept of the Good in Metaphysics and Philosophical Theology,* ed. Scott MacDonald, 98–128. Ithaca, N.Y.: Cornell University Press, 1991.

Sullivan, Robert P., O.P. *Man's Thirst for Good.* Westminster, Md.: Newman Press, 1952.

Sweeney, Leo, S.J. "Participation in Plato's Dialogues." *New Scholasticism* 62 (1988): 125–49.

Swinburne, Richard. *Faith and Reason.* Oxford: Clarendon Press, 1981.

———. "Analyticity, Necessity, and Apriority." In *A Priori Knowledg,* ed. Paul K. Moser, 170–89. Oxford: Oxford University Press, 1987.

Synave, P., O.P. "La Révélation des vérités divines naturelles d'après s. Thomas d'Aquin." In *Mélanges Mandonnet,* 2 vols., 2: 327–70. Paris: J. Vrin, 1930.

Taylor, C.C.W. "Aristotle's Epistemology." In *Companions to Ancient Thought,* Vol. 1: *Epistemology,* ed. Stephen Everson, 116–42. Cambridge: Cambridge University Press, 1990.

Thiry, André, S.J. "Saint Thomas et la moral d'Aristote." In *Aristote et saint Thomas d'Aquin,* 229–58. Louvain, Brussels: Publications Universitaires de Louvain; Paris: Éditions Béatrice-Nauwelaerts, 1957.

Thomas, Ivo, O.P. Introduction to *Aristotle's "De Anima" in the Version of William of Moerbeke and the Commentary of St. Thomas Aquinas.* Translated by Kenelm Foster, O.P., and Sylvester Humphries, O.P., 13–37. New Haven, Conn.: Yale University Press, 1951.

Tonneau, Jean, O.P. Review of *De hominis beatitudine,* vols. 1–3, by J. M. Ramirez. *Bulletin thomiste* 7 (1943–1946): 7–45.

Torrell, Jean-Pierre, O.P. *Saint Thomas Aquinas,* Vol. 1: The Person and His Work. Translated by Robert Royal. Washington, D.C.: The Catholic University of America Press, 1996.

Trendelenburg, Adolf. *Historische Beiträge zur Philosophie.* 3 vols. Berlin: G. Bethge, 1856–1867.

Tshibangu, Tharcisée. *Théologies positive et théologie spéculative: position traditionnelle et nouvelle problématique.* Louvain, Brussels, and Paris: Publications Université de Louvain and Beatrice-Nauwelaerts, 1965.

Tuninetti, Luca F. *"Per se Notum": Die logische Beschaffenheit des Selbstver-

568 Bibliography

ständlichen im Denken des Thomas von Aquin. Leiden: E. J. Brill, 1996.

Upton, Thomas V. "Psychological and Metaphysical Dimensions of Non-Contradiction in Aristotle." *Review of Metaphysics* 36 (1983): 591–606.

———. "Aristotle on Hypothesis and the Unhypothesized First Principle." *Review of Metaphysics* 39 (1985): 283–301.

Van Overbeke, Paul-M., O.P. "La Loi naturelle et le droit naturel selon s. Thomas." *Revue thomiste* 57 (1957): 52–78, 451–95.

Van Riet, Georges. "The Problem of God in Hegel." *Philosophy Today* 2, no. 1 (1967): 3–16; 2, no. 2 (1967): 75–102.

Van Steenberghen, Fernand. *Introduction à l'étude de la philosophie médiévale*. Louvain, Brussels, and Paris: Publication Universitaires and Beatrice-Nauwelaerts, 1974.

———. "The Problem of the Existence of God in Saint Thomas' *Commentary on the Metaphysics* of Aristotle." *Review of Metaphysics* 27 (1974).

———. "Étienne Gilson, historien de la pensée médiévale." *Revue philosophique de Louvain* 77 (1979): 487–507.

———. "Comment être thomiste aujourd'hui?" *Revue philosophique de Louvain* 85 (1987): 171–97.

———. "La Conception de la philosphie au moyen âge. Nouvel examen du problème." In *Philosophie im Mittelalter: Entwicklungslinien und Paradigmen.*, ed. Jan Beckmann, Ludger Honnefelder, Gangolf Schrimpf, and Georg Wieland, 187–99. Hamburg: Felix Meiner Verlag, 1987.

Vanier, Jean. *Le Bonheur: principe et fin de la moral aristotélicienne*. Paris and Brughes: Desclée de Brouwer, 1965.

Vanneste, A. "Saint Thomas et le problème du surnaturel." *Ephemerides theologicae Lovanienses* 64 (1988): 348–70.

Vanni Rovighi, Sofia. "C'è un'etica filosofica in san Tommaso d'Aquino?" In *Studi di filosofia medioevale*, vol. 2: *Secoli xiii e xiv*, 129–48. Milan: Catholic University of the Sacred Heart, 1978.

Veatch, Henry B. *Rational Man: A Modern Interpretation of Aristotelian Ethics*. Bloomington: Indiana University Press, 1962.

———. Two Logics: The Conflict between Classical and Neo-Analytic Philosophy. Evanston, Ill.: Northwestern University Press, 1969.

———. *For an Ontology of Morals: A Critique of Contemporary Ethical Theory*. Evanston, Ill.: Northwestern University Press, 1971.

———. "Kant and Aquinas: A Confrontation on the Contemporary Metaethical Field of Honor." *New Scholasticism* 48 (1974): 73–99.

———. "Natural Law and the 'Is'-'Ought' Question." *Catholic Lawyer* 26 (1981): 251–65.

———. "Variations, Good and Bad, on the Theme of Right Reason in Ethics." *Monist* 66 (1983): 49–68.

———. *Swimming against the Current in Contemporary Philosophy: Occasional Essays and Papers*. Studies in Philosophy and the History of Philosophy, vol. 20, general editor Jude P. Doherty. Washington, D.C.: The Catholic University of America Press, 1990.

———. "Natural Law and the 'Is'-'Ought' Question: Queries to Finnis and Grisez." In *Swimming against the Current in Contemporary Philosophy: Occasional Essays and Papers*, 293–311.

————. "Can John Finnis Bring Off a Revival of Natural Law?" In *Swimming against the Current in Contemporary Philosophy: Occasional Essays and Papers*, 279–92.

Vignaux, Paul. "Philosophie chrétienne et théologie de l'histoire." In *De saint Anselme à Luther*. Paris: J. Vrin, 1976.

Vigneron, Allen H. "The Continued Ontological Limitation of the Separated Soul According to St. Thomas Aquinas." Master's thesis, The Catholic University of America, 1983.

Voegelin, Erich. *Order and History*, Vol. 3: *Plato and Aristotle*. Baton Rouge: Louisiana State University Press, 1957.

Walgrave, J. H. "The Use of Philosophy in the Theology of Thomas Aquinas." In *Aquinas and Problems of His Time*, ed. G. Verbeke and D. Verhelst, 181–93. Leuven and The Hague: University Press and Martinus Nijhoff, 1976.

Wallace, William A., O.P. *The Role of Demonstration in Moral Theology: A Study of Methodology in St. Thomas Aquinas*. Washington, D.C.: Thomist Press, 1962.

Wallace, William, trans. *The Logic of Hegel: Encyclopedia of the Philosophical Sciences*. 2d ed., rev. Oxford: Oxford University Press, 1892.

Wallis, R. T. *Neoplatonism*. New York: Charles Scribner's Sons, 1972.

Walter, Julius. *Die Lehre von der praktischen Vernunft*. Jena: Mauke, 1874.

Warnock, Mary. *Ethics since 1900*. 2d ed. London: Oxford University Press, 1966.

Watson, Walter. *The Architectonics of Meaning: Foundations of the New Pluralism*. Albany: State University of New York Press, 1985.

Wedin, Michael V. *Mind and Imagination in Aristotle*. New Haven, Conn.: Yale University Press, 1988.

Weisheipl, James A., O.P. "Classification of the Sciences in Mediaeval Thought." *Mediaeval Studies* 27 (1965): 54–90.

————. *Friar Thomas D'Aquino: His Life, Thought, and Work*. New York: Doubleday & Company, 1974.

————. "The Meaning of *Sacra Doctrina* in *Summa Theologiae*, I, q. 1." *Thomist* 38 (1974): 49–80.

Weissman, David. *Intuition and Ideality*. Albany: State University of New York Press, 1987.

Westberg, Daniel. *Right Practical Reason: Aristotle, Action, and Prudence in Aquinas*. Oxford: Clarendon Press, 1994.

Wheeler, Mother Mary Cecelia, R.S.C.J. *Philosophy and the "Summa Theologica" of Saint Thomas Aquinas*. Philosophical Studies, Vol. 169. Washington, D.C.: The Catholic University of America Press, 1956.

White, Nicholas P. "Goodness and Human Aims in Aristotle's Ethics." In *Studies in Aristotle*, ed. Dominic O'Meara, 225–46. Washington, D.C.: The Catholic University of America Press, 1981.

Wieland, Georg. *Ethica—Scientia Practica: Die Anfänge der philosophischen Ethik im 13. Jahrhundert*. Munster: Aschendorff, 1981.

Wieland, W. "Aristotle's Physics and the Problem of Inquiry into Principles." In *Articles on Aristotle*, Vol. 1: *Science*, ed. Jonathan Barnes, Malcolm Schofield, and Richard Sorabji, 127–40. London: Duckwork, 1975.

Wiggins, David. "Deliberation and Practical Reason." In *Essays on Aristotle's Ethics*, ed. Amélie Oksenberg Rorty, 221–40. Berkeley and Los Angeles: University of California Press, 1980. For an earlier version of this paper, see *Proceedings of the Aristotelian Society* 76 (1975–1976): 29–51; an extract of pp. 43–51 is reprinted in Joseph Raz, ed., *Practical Reasoning* (Oxford: Oxford University Press, 1978), 144–52.

Williams, Bernard. "Foundations: Well-Being." In *Ethics and the Limits of Philosophy*, 30–53. Cambridge, Mass.: Harvard University Press, 1985.

Wippel, John F. "Aquinas's Route to the Real Distinction: A Note on *De ente et essentia*." *Thomist* 43 (1979): 279–95. Reprinted in Wippel, *Metaphysical Themes in Aquinas*, 107–32.

———. "Thomas Aquinas and the Problem of Christian Philosophy." In *Metaphysical Themes in Aquinas*, 1–33.

———. "Essence and Existence in Other Writings." In *Metaphysical Themes in Aquinas*, 133–61.

———. "The Reality of Nonexisting Possibles According to Thomas Aquinas, Henry of Ghent, and Godfrey of Fontaines." *Review of Metaphysics* 34 (1981): 729–58. Reprinted in Wippel, *Metaphysical Themes in Aquinas*, 163–89.

———. *Metaphysical Themes in Thomas Aquinas*. Studies in Philosophy and the History of Philosophy, vol. 10, general editor Jude P. Doherty. Washington, D.C.: The Catholic University of America Press, 1984.

———. "Thomas Aquinas and Participation." In *Studies in Medieval Philosophy*, ed. John F. Wippel, 117–58. Washington, D.C.: The Catholic University of America Press, 1987.

———. "Thomas Aquinas's Derivation of the Aristotelian Categories (Predicaments)." *Journal of the History of Philosophy* 25 (1987): 13–34.

———. "Thomas Aquinas on Substance as a Cause of Proper Accidents." In *Philosophie im Mittelalter*, 201–12. Hamburg: Felix Meiner Verlag, 1987.

———. "Essence and Existence." In *The Cambridge History of Later Medieval Philosophy*, ed. Norman Kretzman, Anthony Kenny, and Jan Pinborg, with assoc. ed. Eleonore Stump, 385–410. Cambridge: Cambridge University Press, 1982.

Wood, Ellen Meiksins, and Neal Wood. *Class Ideology and Ancient Political Theory: Socrates, Plato, and Aristotle in Social Context.* New York: Oxford University Press, 1978.

Wylleman, André. Review of *Philosophische Ethik bei Thomas von Aquin*, by Wolfgang Kluxen. *Revue philosophique de Louvain* 62 (1964): 673–77.

Zammit, P. N. *Introductio in philosophiam moralem thomisticam.* Rome: Institutum Pontificium Internationale Angelicum, 1934.

Name Index

Typeface of page reference: regular=name citation found only in the footnotes; *italics*=name citation found only in the text; **bold**=name citation found both in the footnotes and text.

Subject Index

Subject references: regular typeface page number followed by "n" refers to a subject appearing only in a note; **bold typeface** page number followed by "n" refers to a subject appearing in both text and note(s).

Aristotle: Texts Cited

Thomas Aquinas: Texts Cited

	n260, n261; 253n288	
ad3	246n255	
a4 sol1 ad2	501n72	
sol4	240n223; 247n264; 289n192; 295n223; 299n246	
sol4 ad1	351n131	
sol4 ad2	245n258	
a4d	246n252	
a5 ad6	246n254	
sol4	356n153	
q3 a1	297n234	
sol1	129n134; 242n235	
sol1-3	129n134	
sol3	129n133; 260n16; 347n103	

d34

| q1 a4 | 399n167 |

d35

q1 a2 sol3	489n27
a3 sol2	270n80
q2 a2 sol1	303n266

d37

a2 sol2 ad2	319n340
sol2 ad6	322n358
a3	319n339
q1 a1	368n214
a5 sol2	260n13

d39

| q3 a2 | 7n16 |
| a3 sol1 | 15n45 |

d41

| q1 a2 | 283n166 |

Book IV
d1

| q2 a5 ad3 | 260n13 |

d13

| q2 a1 ad6 | 99n199 |

d15

q4 a1	349n117
ad1	355n147
ad3	352n132; 355n147
a1a	353n137

d33

| q1 a1 | 136n171; 355n151 |

d39

q1 a1	516n126
sol4	516n124; n125
a2 sol 1 ad1	511n110
qq1-2	514

d49

q1 a1 sol1	
ad1	127n124
sol2	127n125
sol4	399n169; 424n2; 518n138

a2 sol1	507n94
a3 sol1 ad2	127n124; 438n67
a3 sol3	286n178
q2 a1	425n5, n9; 427n18; 432n35, n38; 462n182
a7 ad12	371n18
q3 a4 sol1	277n126
sol1 ad2	279n137; 281n148

d50

| q1 a1 ad6 | 477n247 |

d59

| q2 a6 | 429n28 |

SCG
Book I

1	n2	485n11
3		80n99
4		82n110
5	n9	54n211; 77n84
9		79n95
	n55	515n121
10-11		602n39
11	n70	446n111
23	n214	124n107
26	n241	114n51; 117n67
41	n330	427n15
44	n378	437n62
53		332n37
54	n452	131n142
55	n457	326n21
57		66n22
58-59		328n22
59	n495	328n26
67		133n156
83	n705	429n29; 102n847
102	n847	512n112

Book II

5		79n95
15	nn925-26	426n11; 519
48	n1243	335n50
52		117n68
54	n1244	302n263
55		418n279
76	n1568	328n22
79	n1608	420n297; 518n136
	n1610	420n297

Book III

1		79n95
2	n1868	273n97
	n1869	273n98
3	n1880	274n103
	n1884	280n142
4	n1893	280n142; 283n184
6	n1905	316n325
	n1907	317n330

Secunda secundae

q6	a1	76n83; 501n67	q104	a1	349n114	
q8	a3 ad3	135n168	q109	a1	295n228	
q10	a4 ad2	529n165	q110	a1	295n228	
q11	a1 ad2	72n53; 314n318	q112	a1 ad1	58n229	
	a2	88n141	q122	a1	320n349	
q17	a1	140n13		a4	320n346; 320n348	
q23	a2 ad1	126n117		a5	320n344	
	a4 ad2	16n52		a6	274n106	
	a7	18n62, n65; 19n69;		ad4	318n337	
		20n79; 21n81,	q124	a5	529n165	
		n83; 22n85;	q129	a7 ad3	126n118	
		278n136; 398n161	q140	a1 ad3	320n349	
	a8	18n67; 314n318;		a2	255n298	
		487n18		ad2	242–43n240	
q30	a1	478n254	q141	a6	486n12	
q35	a1	278n134		ad1	245n251	
q44	a1	289n192; 348n112	q153	a5	333n38	
q45	a1	73n61	q173	a1	135n170	
	a2	28n108				
q47	a1 ad2	246n256	*Tertia pars*			
	a2	347n103	q1	a1	476n243	
	a3 ad3	247n262		a2	396n153	
	a4	247n261		a3 ad3	449n128; 475n231	
	a6	260n19; 311n300;	q4	a1 ad2	435n53	
		207n34	q9	a1 ad1	451n134	
	ad1	246n253		ad3	451n136	
	ad3	246n254; 248n271		a2	526n160	
	a7	245n251		ad1	450n133; 454n155	
	a8	295n228; 339n68;		ad2	454n155	
		349n114; 349n115		ad3	455n161; 456n164	
	obj3	353n140		a3	451n135; 452n140;	
	ad1	348n112			453n152; 454n157	
	ad3	351n131; 353n137;		ad3	453n147; 457n165;	
		353n140			470n215	
	a9	349n113; 354n143		a4	451n137; 453n149	
	a10	347n104	q10	a1 ad2	454n155	
	a15	321n351; 212n59;		a2	452n144	
		247n263		a4 obj2	468n206	
q48	a1	347n103	q11	a1	450n132; 452n141;	
	obj4	347n104			452n144; 452n146;	
q49	a2	165			452n152	
	ad1	160n107; 166n141		ad3	452n141; 452n147	
	ad3	164n134		a2	453n154	
	a6 ad1	129n134		a5	452n145	
q50	a1	353n139		ad1	454n156	
q51	a2 ad2	340n73		a6	452n145	
	a3	340n73	q12	a1	451n138; 452n142	
	ad3	338n67		a2 ad1	451n139	
q56	a1	311n302; 350n120	q18	a3	445n103	
q57	a1	320n345		a4	325n12; 443n93	
	ad3	321n353		a5	363n191	
q58	a7 ad2	375n50	q21	a4	445n103	
q62	a3	134n166	q42		91n152	
q83	a1	139n8; 293n213;	q52	a5	478n252	
		340n78; 352n134;				
		354n146	*De ver.*			
	ad3	326n19	q1	a1	38n153; 276n118;	

c2	412b17	99–105	409n222
c5	414a29	107–9	325n9
c28		113–17	325n9
	427b6	186–89	328n25
	b21	273–84	328n25
		274–81	335n50
c29	428a1	48–51	328n26
		53–54	501n72
	a22	165–67	501n69

Book III

c4	430a22	212–13	386n101; 414n255
	a23	228–30	413n250
c5	430a26	1–17	326n19
		81–83	328n26
	430b26	214–16	326n19
c7			412n246
c8	432b3	111–18	337n57
	b26	273–276	292n208
c9	433a14	46	331n34
		53–57	295n225
		57–60	209n44
		65–71	338n63
		67–71	208n38
		87–89	360n178
	a26	104–109	251n279
		106–109	243n246
		109–10	240n224
	433b	191–94	274n109
c10	434a16	128–33	160n111

In Metaph.

prooemium		87n136; 114n51; 138n1

Book I

lect1	n11	271n89
	n18	172n179
lect2	n46	328n25; 331n32, 265n40
	n47	
lect10	n69	111n39
lect15	n225	109n31
	n231	111n37
	n232	120n80
	nn232–33	110n36

Book II

lect2	n290	271n87; 293n214; 369n1
lect5	n336	187n254

Book III

lect5		63n6
lect6	n396	265n40

Book IV

lect4	n1263	328n22
lect6	n605	334n47

Book V

lect6	n829	325n9
lect9	nn890–93	272n92

lect16	n1000	266n47, n51

Book VI

lect1	n1145	265n40
	n1146	300n254
	n1149	265n40
	n1154	196n305; 265n45; 266n49
	n1155	265n40; 267n54
	n1159	265n40
	n1161	187n252
	n1164	103n8
	n1167	92n161
lect2	n1171	330n30
lect3	n1222	133n154
lect4	n1232	327n20
	n1236	328n22

Book VII

lect9	n1468	187n252

Book X

lect3	n1982	300n254

Book XI

lect7	n2253	268n67
	n2264	187n253
lect9	n2313	272n93

Book XII

lect3	n2451	414n255
lect8	n2538	371n14
lect12	n2631	109n32

SLE

Book I

1 ante 1094			
	a1	1–4	266n47
		21–22	88n140; 139n8
		26–27	508n101
		35–37	139n5
		39–43	139n5
		40–43	486n14; 508n102
		51–53	270n81; 372n20
		51–54	133n159; 138n4
		78–99	376n52
		97–99	375n51
		99–106	372n21
		99–110	4n6
1094			
	a1	142–145	271n89
	a2	153–160	274n105
		165–75	104n11
		178–80	109n27
		180–81	127n123
	a6	223–25	485n10
2	a22	67–71	142n20
		67–73	487n17
24		74–93	491n30
26		100–102	376n53
		109–11	376n53
28		134–44	389n117

CPSIA information can be obtained
at www.ICGtesting.com
Printed in the USA
BVHW070007290519
549520BV00001B/2/P